ANCIENT INDIAN EDUCATION

(BRAHMANICAL AND BUDDHIST)

ANCIENT INDIAN EDUCATION

(BRAHMANICAL AND BUDDHIST)

BY

RADHA KUMUD MOOKERJI

GYAN

Published by

GYAN

Gyan Publishing House
5, Ansari Road
Daryaganj, New Delhi-110002
Phone: 011-47034999, 9811692060
E-mail: books@gyanbooks.com

Distribution Network
gyanbooks.com
India, USA, Canada, UK, Australia

ISBN: 978-93-6280-026-8 (HB)
First Published, 1947

2nd Impression 2024

Printed at: Gyan Press, Delhi.

ANCIENT INDIAN EDUCATION (BRAHMANICAL AND BUDDHIST)
Author: RADHA KUMUD MOOKERJI

ANCIENT INDIAN EDUCATION

PLATE I

NĀLANDA.
A Stone Image of Standing Bodhisattva.

[Frontispiece]

ANCIENT INDIAN EDUCATION

(BRAHMANICAL AND BUDDHIST)

BY

RADHA KUMUD MOOKERJI, M.A., PH.D.

Itihāsa-Śiromani (Baroda), Professor of Indian History, Lucknow University; Sayaji Rao Gaekwad Prizeman; Member of Bengal Legislative Council, and of Land Revenue Commission

MACMILLAN AND CO., LIMITED
ST. MARTIN'S STREET, LONDON
1947

To

My Wife

ANASŪYĀ DEVĪ

and

My Son

PRADYUMNA KUMUD MOOKERJI

PREFACE

The present work is intended to fill up a gap in the literature on the history of Education, which has not taken adequate account of the unique contributions made by Hindu Thought to both educational Theory and Practice.

The work has been long in the making. The bulk of it was written in 1918–1920, but its completion has been delayed by writings on other subjects in response to the needs of my teaching work and research at the University. Parts of the work have, however, been published from time to time as articles in various Periodicals since 1920, such as Asutosh and Malaviya Commemoration Volumes; the *Journals* of the Universities of Lucknow, Allahabad, and Benares; of the United Provinces Historical Society, Mythic Society of Bangalore, Viśvabhārati, Śāntiniketana; the *Indian Antiquary* and the *Aryan Path*; and Dr. B. C. Law's *Buddhistic Studies.* Some of these articles have been drawn upon in some recent publications on the subject, and this has stimulated completion of the work. It will now form a companion volume to my work on *Hindu Civilization* recently published.

The work brings together for the first time the representations of educational scenes and figures to be found in old Indian sculpture and painting. For purposes of Illustration, Line Drawings have been preferred to photographs as the only means of restoring as far as possible defaced or mutilated originals.

My special obligations are due to my learned colleague (and whilom pupil), Dr. Narendra Nath Sengupta, Professor of Philosophy at the University, for his valuable suggestions and notes on several philosophical points and problems, which it is alike my pleasure and duty to gratefully acknowledge. I am deeply grateful to my esteemed friend, Dr. Bimala Churn Law, for his kind subvention in aid of the publication of the work. I owe to Mr. O. C. Gangoly, the renowned art-critic, the suggestion to include the Illustrations shown in Plates III, VII, XIV. Plates I, IV, VI, VIII, XI–XIII, XVIII, XIX–XXII are based on photo-prints supplied by the Archæological Department of the Government of India to whom belongs their copyright. Plate XVI is based on the photo-print supplied by the Archæological Department of H.E.H. the Nizam's Government to whom belongs its copyright.

A simplified system of transliteration of Sanskrit and Prakrit words has been adopted in this work, and may be understood from the following examples: *Kṛishṇa*, *Śāṭyāyana*, *Lichchhavi*, *Aṅga*, *Pūrva-Mīmāṁsā*. The vast amount of transliteration involved may have left some mistakes, in spite of best efforts to correct them, which, I hope, will be overlooked.

THE UNIVERSITY,
LUCKNOW.
March, 1940.

RADHA KUMUD MOOKERJI.

The printing of the work was completed as far back as 1939, but its publication has been delayed so long by conditions created by the War.

I am grateful to my friend, Professor G. C. Raychaudhuri, M.A., for kindly helping to expedite the publication by passing for me the final proofs on the spot in London where I met him at the School of Oriental Studies of the London University, and thus obviating the delay of my doing it from India.

CONTENTS

[The numbers are those of pages]

PART II

BUDDHIST EDUCATION

PAGE

LIST OF ILLUSTRATIONS

I

Yastu vijñānavān bhavati
Yuktena manasā sadā |
Tasyendriyāṇi vaśyāni
Sadaśvā iva sāratheḥ ||

" He, who is possessed of supreme knowledge by concentration of mind, must have his senses under control, like spirited steeds controlled by a charioteer " (Kaṭha-Upanishad, iii, 6).

II

Manopubbaṅgamā dhammā
Manoseṭṭhā manomayā |

" Mental states always precede action of which they are the determining factors " (Dhammapada, i, 1).

III

Chittameva asya vaśaṁ gachchhati | Chittena asya vaśībhūtena sarvadharmā vaśībhavanti |

" The Mind has come into his power. When one has thus brought the Mind under his control, all principles of things are under his control " (Śāntideva's Śikshāsamuchchaya, chap. vi).

IV

Mana eva manushyāṇāṁ kāraṇaṁ bandha-mokshayoḥ |
Tasmāt tat abhyaset mantrī yat ichchhet mokshamavyayam |

" The mind of man is at once the cause of his bondage and salvation. Therefore, one should train his mind, if he desires abiding freedom, by the discipline of mantra " (Mālinīvijayottara-Tantra, xv, 38).

V

Rāgādidurvāramalāvaliptaṁ |
Chittaṁ hi saṁsāramuvācha Vajrī ||

" Says the teacher of Vajra-yāna : The Mind that is tainted by the indelible impurities of passions constitutes what is called the Saṁsāra or the world " (Prajñopāya-Viniśchaya-Siddhiḥ, iv, 22).

VI

" Brahmacharya *does not mean mere physical self-control. It means much more. It means complete control over all the senses. Thus an impure thought is a breach of* brahmacharya ; *so is anger. . . And since thought is the root of all speech and action, the quality of the latter corresponds to that of the former. Hence perfectly controlled thought is itself power of the highest potency, and can become self-acting. That seems to me to be the meaning of the silent prayer of the heart. If Man is after the image of God, he has but to will a thing in the limited sphere allotted to him, and it becomes* " (*Mahatma M. K. Gandhi in* Harijan *for 23rd July, 1938*).

PROLOGUE

I

BACKGROUND

A singular feature of ancient Indian or Hindu Civilization is that it has been moulded and shaped in the course of its history more by religious than by political, or economic, influences. Religion, as the ancient Hindus understood it, practically dominated every sphere of their national life. The fundamental principles of social, political, and economic life were welded into a comprehensive theory which is called Religion in Hindu thought. Practical attitudes thus followed theoretic orientations. The total configuration of ideals, practices, and conduct is called *Dharma* (Religion, Virtue, or Duty) in this ancient tradition. Thus it is Religion that gave its laws to the social life and organization of the ancient Hindus, and regulated even their economic activities and pursuits. In politics, its influence has been no less profound and pervasive, though not so apparent, and explains much of the political history of the ancient Hindus. From the very start, they came, under the influence of their religious ideas, to conceive of their country as less a geographical and material than a cultural or a spiritual possession, and to identify, broadly speaking, the country with their culture. The Country was their Culture and the Culture their Country, the true Country of the Spirit, the 'invisible church of culture' not confined within physical bounds. India thus was the first country to rise to the conception of an extra-territorial nationality and naturally became the happy home of different races, each with its own ethno-psychic endowment, and each carrying its particular racial traditions and institutions. The political and social reality for Hindus is not geographical, nor ethnic, but a culture-pattern. Country and patriotism expand, as ideals and ways of life receive acquiescence. Thus, from the very dawn of its history has this Country of the Spirit ever expanded in extending circles, Brahmarshideśa, Brahmāvarta, Āryāvarta, Bhāratavarsha, or Jambudvīpa, and even a Greater India beyond its geographical boundaries. In different ages of its history has it thus had different territorial embodiments, but never any territorial limits. This domination of politics by religion is also responsible for the initial and fundamental difficulty of its history. The problem of India has been the problem of the world, so to speak, the finding of a workable compromise between different nationalities and social systems, and is, therefore, yet to be solved. But the lines on which it may be solved are perhaps more clearly indicated in Hindu than in any other polity. In political organization, India has believed more in group-life which has received full scope throughout. It has had a most exuberant and luxuriant growth on the Indian soil, illustrating in the manifold forms of its organization all the vital and natural modes and forms of human association. India, indeed, thus offers the best study in group-types, and in group-organization in which is now being increasingly found in the West " the best solution of popular government ". [See Miss Follet's *The New State : Group Organization the Solution of Popular Government* (Longmans, London)].

The revolt against modern democracies is not mere party politics or expediency but Nature's own revenge against the violation of her laws by Man in his political arrangements. The Group has not been given its proper place in the organization of individuals into the State. The democracy of to-day stresses alternately the Group and the Individual. Hindu Thought effects a happy compromise by placing the worth of the real Personality above all things. The concept of Personality is the point of meeting of the social group and the biological individual. Emphasis on the personality-values then brings within the purview of politics biological facts, social traditions, and the pattern of inner culture. The Indian Polity, recognizing the claims of the Group as the necessary and inevitable intermediary formation between the individuals and the sovereign central authority of the State, points to that principle of comprehension by which a true, stable, and living League of Nations can be organized and the state of war between them abolished. Thus has India sought to spiritualize her politics by taking stand upon its broader and truer foundations.

Similarly, in the sphere of economic life and interests, the free choice of occupations, or the movement of labour, horizontal or vertical, was subordinated to the choice of the ideals and ends of life. Castes determined Crafts or vice versa. Some occupations were approved for certain castes and condemned for others. Thus economic life was controlled by religion as man's supreme interest and concern, and was not left to be moulded freely by the operation of natural laws. For religion or *Dharma* reflects the wider outlook of the group and its material needs.

The entire ancient Indian social organization, too, was planned on the principle that it should, in all its classes, ranks, and grades, offer the best scope for the development of the individual as its centre and chief concern, though it is possible to argue that the means adopted have not always shown themselves to be as sound as the ends. In a word, the entire Hindu view of life is characterized by its instinctive 'choice of realities' of a particular order, the ideal and the spiritual as distinguished from the physical and temporal. Indeed, contrary to the generally accepted view, the Hindu thinkers are always anxious to translate nebulous ideals into determinate concepts, vague social attitudes into specific rules of conduct, and to envisage the group-life not as an indefinite æsthetic or romantic reality but as a system of laws. In the same way, the process of adjustment to the group-life is not left to chance, to the raw impulses of the individual, or to the changing patterns of *mores* and fashions. The ideals of the group, its scheme of values, and the realities that the group-tradition conceives as supreme, must be clearly reflected in the mind of the individual. The end can only be achieved through a course of training that reshapes the psychic and bodily life of man.

Nowhere is this distinctive tendency of Hindu thought more manifest than in the sphere of learning and education. Learning in India through the ages had been prized and pursued not for its own sake, if we may so put it, but for the sake, and as a part, of religion. It was sought as the means of salvation or self-realization, as the means to the highest end of life, viz. *Mukti* or Emancipation. The result is that it is Religion that creates Literature in India and wields it as an instrument for its own purposes, a vehicle of its expression. It fixes its very body and form and determines the course of its evolution. As Macdonell puts it [*Sanskrit Literature*, p. 39], since the birth of the oldest Vedic poetry, we find Indian Literature, for a period of more than a thousand years, bearing "an exclusively religious stamp; even those latest productions of the Vedic age which cannot be called directly religious are yet meant to further religious ends. This is, indeed, implied by the term *Vedic*, for

Veda, primarily signifying *Knowledge* (from root *Vid*, to know), designates 'sacred lore' as a branch of literature. Besides this general sense, the word has also the restricted meaning of 'sacred book'".

II

THEORY

Ancient Indian Education is also to be understood as being ultimately the outcome of the Indian theory of knowledge and a part of the corresponding scheme of life and values. That scheme takes full account of the fact that Life includes Death and the two form the whole truth. This gives a particular angle of vision, a sense of perspective and proportion in which the material and the moral, the physical and spiritual, the perishable and permanent interests and values of life are clearly defined and strictly differentiated.

Of all the peoples of the world the Hindu is the most impressed and affected by the fact of death as the central fact of life. He cannot get away from the fact that while Man proposes, God disposes. Therefore, he feels he cannot take life seriously, and scheme for it, without a knowledge of the whole scheme of creation. He takes the biological vital process in the context of the total life-situation, comprising the inner self into the depths of which he can descend by means of contemplation (*svarūpānubhūti*), the ideal self that he can discover through intellection (*manana*), and the social self into the laws of which tradition initiates him. Thus he devotes himself to a study of the fundamental truths of life and does not care for half-truths and intermediate truths. His one aim in life is to solve the problem of death by achieving a knowledge of the whole truth of which Life and Death are parts and phases. He perceives that it is the individual that dies, and not the whole or the Absolute. Thus the Individual must merge himself in the Universal to escape from the sense of change, decay, and dissolution. The Absolute is not subject to change. Individuation is Death, a lapse from the Absolute. Individuation results from the pursuit of objective knowledge, and this has to be stopped. Thus the aim of Education is *Chitta-vṛitti-nirodha*, the inhibition of those activities of the mind by which it gets connected with the world of matter or objects.

Hindu Thought takes up the position that the individual as conceived in the context of social life, and the laws of the State, is essentially a psychological and biological fact. But the individual, in order that his ultimate datum of personality may be understood, must be viewed from other perspectives, those of his elemental nature, his potentiality for growth and transformation, his self-sufficiency, his capacity for effecting harmony between conflicting trends of impulses. Such a view of the self will necessarily take it out of its usual habitat. It means that the normal functions in terms of which the biological self ties itself to its material home must be checked so as to lay bare the core and kernel of one's being, the true self, the naked personality, stripped of the envelope with which it is shrouded by the accretions of passing impulses and emotions. When the personality is thus denuded of its material and social trappings, five planes of vital and psychic tendencies reveal themselves. These are called, in the writings of the Hindu thinkers, the five *Koshas* (sheaths). Normal worldly life sets up barriers between them so that they manifest themselves one at a time. The purpose of Hindu Culture seems to be (1) to disclose the personality as a continuum, rather than as a stratified structure, and (2) thus to make the human self the meeting point of Heaven and Earth. As the Upanishadic text says: "He drew out the lustre of the heavenly fire and filled the earth" (Agnerjyotir-nichāyya pṛithivyā adhyābharat). Thus the inhibitions that daily life necessitates, the processes of 'rationalization', symbolization, dramatization, and other kinds of distortions, must be righted in the course of spiritual culture.

The individual's supreme duty is thus to achieve his expansion into the Absolute, his self-fulfilment, for he is a potential God, a spark of the Divine.

Education must aid in this self-fulfilment, and not in the acquisition of mere objective knowledge. It is more concerned with the subject than the object, the inner than the outer world. But there is a method in this madness. The theory is that it is hopeless to get at the knowledge of the whole in and through its parts, through the individual objects making up the universe. The right way is directly to seek the source of all life and knowledge, and not to acquire knowledge piecemeal by the study of objects. The pursuit of objective knowledge is thus not the chief concern of this Education. When the mind is withdrawn from the world of matter, and does not indulge in individuation,

Omniscience, the Knowledge of the Whole, dawns on it. Individuation shuts out omniscience. Individuation is concretion of the Mind. The Mind takes the form of the object in knowing it. It limits itself to the object, like the water rained down from the clouds limiting itself in a tank. Thus Individuation is Bondage. It limits vision, knowledge, omniscience. Perception of Life in the perspective of the whole is Mukti, Emancipation. The individual must achieve his emancipation, his escape from bondage, *saṁsāra*, the ills which flesh is heir to, from disease, decline, death, desire, and its satisfaction, recurring in a vicious circle of birth and death, to use the Buddha's words.

In its indifference to objective knowledge, the system assumes that the Universe is not limited to what is revealed by the mere bodily senses which man shares with the lower animals ; that man's faculties of perception are not necessarily limited to the five senses ; and that mental life is not entirely bound up with or completely dependent upon what is called the cerebral mechanism or the brain. It is, therefore, considered as the main business of Education to open up other avenues of knowledge than the mere brain or the outer physical senses. It seeks to educate the mind itself as the creative principle in man, the creative principle of his culture and civilization. The Mind is its supreme concern and objective, the chief subject of its treatment. It seeks to train the Mind as the medium and instrument of knowledge, transform the entire psychic organism, overhaul the mental apparatus itself, rather than to fill the mind with a store of learned lumber, objective knowledge. It addresses itself more to the principle of knowing, the roots from which knowledge springs and grows, than to the objective content of knowledge. The chase counts more than the game.

Its method, therefore, is the method of *Yoga*, the science of sciences and the art of arts in the Hindu system, the science and art of the reconstruction of self by discipline and meditation. Yoga is defined as *Chitta-Vṛitti-Nirodha*. It is to stop the functioning of Mind as the avenue or vehicle of objective knowledge, the inhibition of individuation. The theory is that the Mind, seeking external knowledge, contacts, and is contaminated and transformed by Matter, and communicates this contamination to the Soul, Self, or Purusha, who thus enters into bondage. The question is, How to break this bondage and escape from the clutches of Matter. By simply cutting off the inflow of Matter upon Mind, checking the materialization of the Mind and Soul, for the Soul, too, in Milton's words of insight, "embodies and imbrutes." Thus Education is a process of control of Mind, to drive it down to its deeper layers, its subterranean depths, not ruffled by the ripples of the surface, the infinite distractions of the material world by which the Mind wears itself out in fatigue. When the Mind is thus led to rest in itself, and fall back upon its innate strength and resources, and does not lose itself in the pursuit of the knowledge of individual objects, there dawns and bursts forth on the Mind the totality of knowledge, Omniscience, as already stated.

Bergson also has stressed this point and insists on the withdrawal of the Mind from the world of Matter which "imposes upon it its spatial forms, and thus arrests the natural creativity, inwardness, and suppleness of conscious life". For, as he says, "Consciousness, in shaping itself into Intelligence, that is to say, in concentrating itself on Matter, seems to externalize itself." It is only when the Self "brackets" itself out from the realm of things that the psychic processes regain their normal ways. Such withdrawal, says Bergson, permits the fusion of the varied functions of life and mind into a unitary and concrete process—the Intuition. He further points out that "the individual's consciousness, delving downwards, reveals to him, the deeper he goes, his original personality, to which he may cling as something solid, as means of escape from a life of impulse, caprice, and regret. In our innermost selves, we may discover an equilibrium more desirable than the one on the surface. Certain aquatic plants, as they rise to the surface, are ceaselessly jostled by the current; their leaves, meeting above the water, interlace, thus imparting to them stability above. But still more stable are the roots which, firmly planted in the earth, support them from below" [*Morality and Religion*, p. 6]. The Upanishads also have a similar conception in which the Universe is likened to a peepul tree rooted in the universal consciousness (ūrddhamūlam), spreading its branches and leaves as the life and the phenomenal world (*guṇa-pravṛiddhā vishaya-pravālāḥ* . . . Karmānubandhīni manushya-loke).

III

PLAN

As the individual is the chief concern and centre of this Education, Education also is necessarily individual. It is an intimate relationship between the teacher and the pupil. The relationship is inaugurated by a religious ceremony called *Upanayana*. It is not like the admission of a pupil to the register of a school on his payment of the prescribed fee. The spiritual meaning of *Upanayana*, and its details inspired by that meaning, are elaborated in many texts and explained below in the proper place. By Upanayana, the teacher, " holding the pupil within him as in a womb, impregnates him with his spirit, and delivers him in a new birth." The pupil is then known as a *Dvija*, " born afresh " in a new existence, " twice-born " [*Śatapatha Brāhmaṇa*, xi, 5, 4]. The education that is thus begun is called by the significant term *Brahmacharya*, indicating that it is a mode of life, a system of practices.

This conception of education moulds its external forms. The pupil must find the teacher. He must live with him as a member of his family and is treated by him in every way as his son. The school is a natural formation, not artificially constituted. It is the home of the teacher. It is a hermitage, amid sylvan surroundings, beyond the distractions of urban life, functioning in solitude and silence. The constant and intimate association between teacher and taught is vital to education as conceived in this system. The pupil is to imbibe the inward method of the teacher, the secrets of his efficiency, the spirit of his life and work, and these things are too subtle to be taught. The same principle also holds in the sphere of industrial education. As will be seen below, the apprentice must elect to live with the master craftsman to learn the secrets of his work, assimilate his spirit and method, which are not revealed in any formal manner.

India has believed in the domestic system in both Industry and Education, and not in the mechanical methods of large production in institutions and factories turning out standardized articles. Artistic work is the product of human skill and not of machine. The making of man depends on the human factor. It depends on individual attention and treatment to be given by the teacher. Here the personal touch, the living relationship between the pupil and teacher make education. The pupil belongs to the teacher and not to an institution or the abstraction called the school. A modern school teaches pupils by " classes ", and not as individuals with their differences. Is it possible to think of a common treatment of patients each of whom has his own ailment ? While it cannot be applied to the diseases of the body that can be visualized, how can it be applied in handling invisible, intangible, and sometimes intractable material, different minds and moral conditions ?[1] Certainly, Education is the last subject to be " mechanized " even in a modern socialist State.

But there are deeper psychological reasons for this individual treatment in Education. The investigations of Psychologists like Jung, Jaensch, Spranger, and Kretschmer point out that individuals divide themselves into a number of personality-types in accordance with the trend of their usual behaviour-patterns and the ends they seek. These also determine their social and intellectual activities and their vocations, which will vary with the types to which they correspond. This, therefore, makes individual treatment of pupils essential in education. A common scheme may economize effort and expense, but it will not make for maturation of the self which depends on the uniqueness of personal equipment and freedom of choice, factors which are ignored in such a scheme.

Further, social psychology has proved that every individual has his own equipment of emotions, action-attitudes, and ways of thinking, which is the gift of the traditions and the social environment in which he is brought up. These can be disturbed only at the risk of severe derangement of the personality. Each scheme of training must, therefore, take into account the concrete individual, a product of biological gifts and social heritage. A neglect of this basic situation renders the process of education less fruitful, and sometimes even risky to the personality.

The investigations of Haggerty, Nash, and Goodenough show further that the educational status and vocation of the parents have a significant correlation with the level of capacity of the children, as indicated by the Intelligence Quotient. For instance, the children of professional parents or of those of a higher academic standing possess, on the whole, a higher value of *I.Q.* The implications of such facts cannot be ignored in schemes of national education.

There are a few other fundamental pedagogic principles

[1] That advanced educational thought in the West is seeking reform in this direction may be illustrated by a recent donation of the American philanthropist, Mr. Harkness, added to the millions of dollars with which he has endowed his old school, the Phillips Academy at Exeter, in the State of New Hampshire. The donation has been made on the condition that there should be on the staff of the school at least one teacher for every ten boys. A leading journal commenting on this singular gift states : " Mr. Harkness, like many thoughtful Americans, is apprehensive that in the large numbers flooding into the higher educational institutions of the U.S.A., there was a danger of mass-production, and a loss of all that was of the highest value in education. As Wordsworth said : ' Numbers swamp humanity.' "

involved in this educational condition of intimate relationship between the teacher and his pupil. The Guru takes the place of what Freud defines as the Super-Ego of the individual pupil, i.e. the embodiment of the ideals and traditions in which he is brought up. Every individual is subject to an innate conflict between a sense of what he *is* and what he *ought* to be. He imbibes the ideals and traditions of his society, which regulate his life from the outside, or from the plane of the unconscious. In both cases, he feels himself to be the passive instrument of social, or mysterious forces. The ideals, however, are sometimes assimilated as parts of his conscience or Super-Ego, when his actions come under the regulation of his own self, though not without a conflict between the different parts of his nature. This inner conflict is resolved by the Guru, to whom, a different personality, the pupil can project his Super-Ego. The ideals can now more easily enforce themselves, as there is no longer now any loophole for ignoring them, as one could in the matter of one's own thoughts suggesting them. Bergson also points out that man obeys a moral obligation against his will, yielding to the pressure or propulsive force of its social consequences. But he will obey it naturally when its appeal comes from "a Great personality incarnating morality" which is not relative but "complete or absolute", "as the multiplicity and generality of its maxims merge more completely into a man's unity and individuality" (*Morality and Religion*, p. 24).

There is another moral factor involved in this intimate relationship between two personalities. The process of sharing experiences with his Guru prevents the tendency to repression in the pupil. Thus the inner life can grow in a normal manner under this system.

Then, again, the pupil's membership of the family of his Guru constitutes a constant stimulus to the ideals to which he is dedicated, while it also operates as a protective sheath, shutting out unwholesome influences. It operates as a restraining force. Again, the novice feels that he is not lost in a crowd. He feels one of a family where he has a distinct place. Hence there grows in him a sense of personal worth and of placid individuality which a healthy social group always engenders.

Apart from the special educative value of the teacher's home as the school, there is the factor of its environment or setting as an integral part of the scheme. The school is set in sylvan surroundings. The pupil's first daily duty is to walk to the woods, cut and collect fuel, and fetch it home for tending the sacred Fire. The Upanishads frequently mention pupils approaching their teacher with fuel in hand, as a token that he is ready to serve the teacher and tend his household fire. The *Śatapatha Brāhmaṇa* explains (xi, 5, 4, 5) that the Brahmachārī " puts on fuel to enkindle the mind with fire, with holy lustre ". A profound spiritual and cultural significance attaches to this worship of Agni by the offering of *choice* objects and oblations. It is the visible image and reminder of the primordial cosmic sacrifice at which the Supreme Being whom the Veda calls the *Virāṭ-Purusha* (Rigveda, *Purusha-Sūkta*, x, 90), offered up His infinite body as the material and the foundation for the construction of the Universe. It was an act of supreme self-immolation by which the Universe is created and sustained. "Man is created after God's image " and is subject to the same law of being which governs creation. He, too, is the creator of his system which depends on his self-sacrifice. The ceremony of Agnihotra brings home to the pupil the reality of religion in the form of sacrifice.

The pupil's next duty was to tend the teacher's house and cattle. Tending the house was training the pupil in self-help, the dignity of labour, of menial service for his teacher and the student-brotherhood. Tending cattle was education through craft as a part of the highest liberal education. The craft selected is the primary industry of India. The school and the homestead centre round the cow whom the Indian counts as his second mother whose milk nourishes the child and is the best food even for the grown-up. Three acres and a cow has been India's economic plan through the ages. The pupils received a valuable training in the love of the cow and the industry of rearing up cattle and dairy-farming, with all the other advantages it gave of outdoor life and robust physical exercise, which was more fruitful in every way than the modern barren games of Football and Hockey. The Chhāndogya Upanishad tells of the great sage Satyakāma Jābāla who in his boyhood was apprenticed by his teacher to take charge of his cattle whose number grew under his guardianship from 400 to 1,000. And this training in industry was the foundation of the highest knowledge for which the Ṛishi was known. The Bṛihadāraṇyaka also tells of Ṛishi Yājñavalkya, the foremost philosopher of the times, good enough, with his band of pupils, to drive away home from the court of Janaka 1,000 cows the king bestowed on him as the reward of his learning.

That education was not exclusively theoretical and academic

but was related to a craft as a part of liberal education may also be seen in the following description of the home of a Rigvedic Ṛishi (*Rv.* ix, 112):

"We different men have different aptitudes and pursuits (dhiyo vi vratāni). The carpenter (Takshā) seeks something that is broken; the physician (Bhishag) a patient (rutam); the priest (Brahma) someone who will perform sacrifice (Sunvantam).

"I am a poet (Kāruḥ), my father is a physician, and my mother a grinder of corn (upala-prakshiṇī)."

Here we find the highest philosophy yoked to the humble craft of grinding corn in a Ṛishi and his mother, while his father was pursuing the useful art of healing as a physician. Therefore, the highest education was quite consistent with manual and vocational training to give a practical turn to human nature, and training to deal with objects and the physical environment.

Another duty of the Brahmachārī is to go out on a daily round of begging. It was not begging for himself but for the support of his school. Its educative value is explained in the *Śatapatha Brāhmaṇa* (xi, 3, 3, 5), which points out that it is meant to produce in the pupil a spirit of humanity and renunciation. But its moral effects may be examined more closely. First, the contrast between his own life and that of the world at large brings home to him the value of the scheme for which he stands, which he will now all the more try to consolidate. This makes for a more complete organization of the personality, a deeper loyalty to his system. Further, the daily duty of begging makes the Ego less and less assertive, and, with it, all unruly desires and passions, which do not shoot forth, as their roots wither. Thus there is reached a greater balance of the inner life. A sense of balance and harmony further brings out the contrast between the behaviour of his own group and that of the men of the world, and this further confirms his faith in his own group or order.

Again, an acquaintance through begging with worldly life and its trials makes him realize more vividly the security of his own life. Lastly, begging makes the pupil feel how unattached he is to any ties, and a sense of independence contributing to a sense of self-hood. It is like a ritual for the cultivation of impersonal relations in life. This contact of the recluse with the world is a valuable corrective to the exaggerated subjectivity of isolated meditative life in the hermitage. Isolation and intercourse thus lead to a higher synthesis of the inner and the outer, Purusha and Prakṛiti, Self and the World.

In such a scheme of Education, mere study as such occupies a very subsidiary place. The Upanishads mention three steps of education called (1) *Śravaṇa*, (2) *Manana*, and (3) *Nididhyāsana* [*Bṛi. Upa.*, ii, 4, 5]. *Śravaṇa* is listening to words or texts as they are uttered by the teacher. It is the system of oral tradition by which India has built up her whole culture through the ages; the system called *Gurupāramparya* or *Sampradāya* which Udyotakara (in his *Nyāya-Vārttika*) defines as 'the uninterrupted ideal succession of pupils and teachers, by which knowledge is conserved and transmitted' (Sampradāyo nāma Sishyopādhyāyasaṁbandhasya avichchhedena śāstraprāptiḥ). Thus the Book of Knowledge in those days was called *Śruti*, "what was heard." This character of Knowledge also fixed its form known as *Mantra* or *Sūtra* by which the maximum of meaning was compressed within the minimum of words, of which the crowning example is the letter *OM* containing within itself a world of meaning. Knowledge did not then exist in the form of MSS. which could be stored up in a library like household furniture, for knowledge was the furniture of the mind, while the teacher himself was the living and walking library of those days. For thousands of years, even up to the time of Kumārila (*c.* eighth century A.D.), it was considered sacrilege to reduce the Veda to writing, for learning was not reading but realization, and knowledge was to be in the blood, as an organic part of one's self. Another point to be noted in this connection is that *Śabda* or Sound by itself has its own potency and value, apart from its sense, and its intrinsic attributes, its rhythm, and vibrations should be captured. *Śabda* is Brahma. "The Word is God."

In accordance with the high aim of this Education, the achievement of the supreme, saving Knowledge, Śaṅkara in his *Viveka-Chūḍāmaṇi* defines *Śravaṇa* as listening to the instruction of the teacher and knowing from him the primary truth that the Self is to be differentiated fron Non-Self appearing in various forms. To identify Self with Non-Self is Ignorance, causing Bondage. Bondage is removed by Knowledge.

Hearing of texts and words uttered by the teacher is to be followed by the process of *Manana*, deliberation, reflection on the topic taught, but it results only in an intellectual apprehension of its meaning. Therefore, there is the stage of learning, called *Nididhyāsana* or Meditation, by which can be attained the realization of truth. As the *Muṇḍaka* points out (ii, 2, 24) "a mere intellectual apprehension of truth, a reasoned conviction, is not sufficient, though it is necessary as the first stage as a sort of mark at which to shoot". The distinction between the intellectual apprehension of truth and its realization may be well explained in the words of Gautama describing his own training for his attainment of Buddhahood or Enlightenment. His first teacher was Ālāra Kālāma who was so used to meditation that "he would not, sitting on the roadside, be conscious of a caravan of 500 carts rattling past him". He taught Gautama the doctrine of *Nirvāṇa*. "Very speedily," says Gautama, "I learned the doctrine, and so far as concerns uttering with mouth and lips the words, 'I know, I understand,' I, and others with me, knew the word of wisdom and the ancient lore. We speedily acquired this doctrine so far as concerns lip-profession. Then the thought occurred to me, 'when Ālāra Kālāma declares: Having myself realized, and known this doctrine, I abide in the attainment thereof, it cannot all be a mere profession of faith; surely, Ālāra Kālāma sees and knows this doctrine.'" Gautama states that very soon he achieved the stage at which he was able 'to abide in a realization and knowledge of the doctrine'.

This realization of truth is described as *Darśana* or 'perception' of Truth. *Ātmā vā are drashtavyaḥ* in the passage quoted above means that the Ātman or the Self must be "seen". The theory is that seeing is believing, and so the reality of the diversity of the material objective world, in which we believe, because we *see* it, is to be pitted against the other reality of unity, which must be equally *seen*. The *Ātman* must be as much the subject of immediate perception as the material world of diversity. Then alone will the one result of immediate perception be wiped off and replaced by the other. At the Congress of Philosophers that met at the court of King Janaka of Videha (the world's first Philosophical Congress), the philosopher Ushasta put to Yājñavalkya the question: "when any one says 'that is an ox, that is a horse', it is thereby pointed out. Point out to me the revealed, unveiled Brahma, the Ātman which dwells in everything. The Ātman which dwells in everything—What is that, O Yājñavalkya?" (*Bṛi. Upa.*)

Nididhyāsana represents the highest stage of meditation which, with reference to Brahma or the One Reality, has been defined as "Vijātīya-dehādipratyayavirahita advitīya-vastu-sajātīya-pravāhaḥ, as the steady stream (pravāha) of consciousness of the One, undisturbed by the slightest consciousness of the Many, or any material object, contradictory to the sense of the One or the Soul". The Upanishads prescribe certain preliminary exercises in meditation to lead up to its final stage. These are called *Upāsanās* giving training in contemplation.

The situation is best summed up in the words that Nārada addresses to Sanatkumāra (Chhāndogya, vii, 1), which throw light not merely on the methods of this education but also on the then subjects of study.

Nārada states that he had studied subjects like the Rigveda, the Yajurveda, the Sāmaveda, the Atharva-Veda as fourth, Itihāsa-Puraṇa as the fifth Veda, Grammar (called *Vedānāṁ Vedam*, 'the Veda of Vedas'), Biology (*Bhūta-Vidyā*), Arithmetic (*Rāśi*), Divination (*Daiva*), Chronology (*Nidhi*), Dialectics (*Vākovākyam* = *Tarkaśāstram*), Politics (*Ekāyana*), Theology (*Deva-Vidyā*) or Exegetics (= *Nirukta*, as explained by Śaṅkara), the Doctrine of Prayer (*Brahma-Vidyā*), which Śaṅkara, however, explains as the Vedāṅgas of *Śikshā* (Phonetics), *Kalpa* (Ceremonial) and *Chhandas* (Metrics, Prosody), Necromancy (*Pitrya*), Military Science (*Kshatra-Vidyā*), Astronomy (*Nakshatra-Vidyā*), study of Snake-Venoms (*Sarpa-vidyā*), and the Fine Arts (*Devajana-Vidyā*) explained by Śaṅkara to mean *Nṛitya* (Dancing), *Gīta*, *Vādya* (Music Vocal and Instrumental) and other Arts (Śilpādi); but Raṅga Rāmānuja takes it as *Deva*-Vidyā (Gandharva-Śāstram) or Music and *Jana*-Vidyā or Āyurveda (Medical Science). Said Nārada: "These subjects, sir, have I studied. Therefore am I learned in the scripture (*Mantra-vit*), but not yet learned in the *Ātmā* (Ātma-vit). Yet have I heard from such as are like you that he who knows the Ātman vanquishes sorrow. I am in sorrow. Lead me then over, I pray, to the farther shore that lies beyond sorrows."

Nārada here utters the prayer of all human beings carrying the common and universal burden of sorrow, the ills which flesh is heir to. It was given to India to find the knowledge which would achieve man's release from this fundamental burden and bondage of life.

The reply of Sanatkumāra to this appeal of Nārada is interesting: "Whatever you have studied is mere words." Similarly, Śvetaketu spending twelve years in a "thorough study of all the Vedas" is found by his father, Ṛishi Uddālaka Āruṇi, only "full of conceit and confidence in his study and wisdom, without the knowledge of the One through whom anything is known" (Chhāndogya, vi, 1).

Upakosala Kāmalāyana was another student who by his twelve years' study and austerities was not considered fit by his teacher for the highest knowledge (ib., iv, 10).

Therefore, the *Bṛihadāraṇyaka* states (iv, 4, 21): "The seeker after the highest knowledge should not seek after the knowledge of the books, for that is mere weariness of the tongue." Again: "Therefore, let a Brāhmaṇa, after he has done with learning, wish to stand by real strength (knowledge of the Self which enables us to dispense with all other knowledge)." The *Kaṭha* also points out: "Not by the Veda is the Ātman attained, nor by intellect, nor by much knowledge of books (i, 2, 23).

We may now have an idea of the working of the school as a whole. Its physical surroundings away from centres of population gives to its students opportunities for contact with Nature and for solitude. Urban life and human society wean away man's affections from the phenomena of Nature. The individual becomes in this way wholly dependent upon the social group; he feels himself gradually as a mere limb of the Great Society. One way of counteracting this sense of dependence, and of poverty of spirit, is to place Man in the world of Nature, and give scope to the growth of an emotive relation between Man and his milieu. He can break away from his social habits and reshape them. Alone in the woods or pastures, he gets emotive responses in the form of fear, wonder, or joy which reawaken in him the consciousness of self which he loses in the crowd of the city. For emotional tension brings in its wake the feeling of self-hood.

Then, again, solitude has its own effects on a man's inner development. In the normal course of life, each desire is directed to an object. The fulfilment that an impulse finds in its working obscures the phase of recoil that arises through the operation of a man's instinctive tendencies. Isolation from objects, material and social, permits man to observe both the aspects of his reaction, the urge and the recoil, elicited by an object-situation. Hence the life of conation can pursue a course of more complete growth when man is alone with himself, untrammelled by the external environment. Thus the system helps in the elimination of the disharmonies of inner life (Chitta-śuddhi) by giving scope for reflection and isolation, for self-possession, for the integration of different life-processes, and a complete awareness of one's individuality or self-hood, so that man's being may not be dissipated like "broken shreds of cloud" (Chhinnābhramiva naśyati).

It is these sylvan schools and hermitages that have built up the thought and civilization of India.

As has been pointed out in the graphic words of the poet Rabindra Nath Tagore :

" A most wonderful thing we notice in India is that here the forest, not the town, is the fountain-head of all its civilization.

" Wherever in India its earliest and most wonderful manifestations are noticed, we find that men have not come into such close contact as to be rolled or fused into a compact mass. There, trees and plants, rivers and lakes, had ample opportunity to live in close relationship with men.

" In these forests, though there was human society, there was enough of open space, of aloofness ; there was no jostling. Still this aloofness did not produce inertia in the Indian mind ; rather it rendered it all the brighter. It is the forest that has nurtured the two great ancient ages of India, the Vaidic and the Buddhist.

" As did the Vaidic Ṛishis, Lord Buddha also showered his teaching in the many woods of India.

" The current of civilization that flowed from its forests inundated the whole of India."

No doubt these ancient ideals of education have to be adapted to modern conditions. The principles on which the West is ordering life do not seem to make for stability. That can only come from the Indian view of life, which makes for universal peace by its toleration. The exaggerated nationalism of the West is defeating itself, a victim of its own system. In this world-situation, surely Indian thought has its own place to fill. India must carefully conserve and foster the particular type of personality or character she has been building up through the ages by a corresponding system of education. Modern Psychology conceives of the personality as built out of diverse planes of psycho-vital processes. Deep down in the recesses of the Self, as Jung points out, lies the racial unconscious representing the cues of the long forgotten storms and stresses through which the race has evolved. These supply the archetypes that create myths and fables and impart form to the yearnings and gropings of desires. There is then the plane of experience that the individual has passed through and has laid aside in the interest of imperative reactions which the immediate situation demands. Lastly, there are the configurations, impulses, and ideas of conscious life slowly and selectively built up by the forces of the society and the physical environment. A scheme of education introduced for the sake of transient interests and ideology often fails to encompass the total personality thus conceived. It violates the laws of self-development and leads the process of growth through tortuous alleys.

For the present, in India, various schemes of reform of education are in the air, but it is to be remembered that no reform can take root or bear fruit unless it conforms to national ideals and traditions. The course of growth of social and national life is regulated by certain basic ideals and norms. These define the structure that society and the trends of social activity assume in the course of historical evolution. They may be called, in Kantian terminology, the "categories" of national life. Divorced from them, social thoughts, activities, and institutions, to use the Kantian notion again, follow a "blind" course. The discovery of these concepts is essential for the formulation of schemes for any phase of national activity. Our educational thought, like every other strand of social life, must orient itself to these regulative principles which have validated themselves pragmatically, by "working", through the ages, and through tensions and crises.

One may not believe so much in national systems in economic life and organization in the larger interests of the collective welfare of mankind, but there can be no doubt about the national system in education, aiding in the evolution of each nation along its own lines, so that it may make its particular contribution to the culture of mankind. "God has written a line of His thought on the brow of every nation" [Mazzini]. It is the supreme duty of every nation to preserve and unfold its own genius and individuality. The culture of a nation, the civilization of a country, is the product of its system of education.

In several spheres of her national life, India is being swept off her traditional moorings, the anchor of her soul, to drift in the unfathomed waters of uncharted seas. It is, therefore, of the utmost concern and consequence to her future that she must not drift away from her national heritage and basic ideals in the sphére of culture and learning, where her achievements constitute to this day her only title to recognition in the comity of nations. India is still in request in the world for the treasures of her thought. These treasures are embedded in Sanskrit literature, together with its offshoots, Pāli and the Prākṛits, which is remarkable in the literature of the world for its vastness, volume, variety, quality, and longevity, and justifies the education of which it is the product.

PART I

BRAHMANICAL EDUCATION

CHAPTER I

SOME VEDIC CONCEPTS AND TERMS

'Key-words.' Vedic education is to be studied as an integral part of Vedic Thought and Life. It will be best understood in the light of certain concepts and technical terms in which are concealed and stored up the traditions governing the general philosophy and scheme of life of the Vedic age. These terms came to be established as the outcome of important movements and trends of thought which they reflect. In some cases, as will be seen below, they directly point to the educational principles and institutions which were typical of the culture of the age. They are the "key-words" of Vedic Culture, supplying the cue to much of Vedic Thought that appears to be somewhat mystical and mysterious, and strange to modern ways of thinking. A study of these is a necessary preliminary to an adequate appreciation of the system of Vedic Education, its ideals and institutions. These terms are, therefore, discussed at the outset.

'Veda.' The term *Veda* is from root *Vid*, to know, and indicates that by which is obtained the knowledge of the ways and means of achieving spiritual ends (Alaukikaṁ purushārthopāyaṁ vetti aneneti). Its meaning is also defined in the following text :—

Pratyaksheṇānumityā vā yastūpāyo na vudhyate |
Etaṁ vidanti Vedena tasmād Vedasya Vedatā ||

"The end which cannot be known by the evidence of direct perception, inference, and the like, can be known through Veda and, therefore, this determines the character of *Veda*."

Its Subject-matter: (1) 'Dharma' and (2) 'Brahma'. The subject-matter of Veda, therefore, is described as twofold: (1) *Dharma* and (2) *Brahma* which can be known only through the Veda and not through any other source [*Dharmabrahmaṇī Vedaikavedye* (Jaimini, Pūrva-Mīmāṁsā Sutra)]. *Dharma* is something which is not objective or within the ken of sense-perception. It is the fruit of the performance of prescribed rites and is something which is not visible (adṛishṭamiti sarvairabhidhīyate). Similarly, *Brahma*, too, has been explained as something which, as the Cause of Creation, can be known only through the evidence of Śāstras (Śāstrādeva pramāṇāt jagatojanmādi-kāraṇaṁ Brahmādhigamyate). There is also the Śruti text: NāVedavinmanute taṁ bṛihantam [*Tai. Br.*, iii, 12, 9, 7]; "He who does not know the Veda cannot comprehend *Brahma*," because, as further pointed out, *Brahma*, being formless and causeless, cannot be known except through the Veda.

The Veda imparts the knowledge of its aforesaid two subjects, *Dharma* and *Brahma*, in its three parts called (1) *Pūrva-* or *Karma-kāṇḍa*, (2) *Madhya-* or *Devatā* (*Upāsanā*)-*Kāṇḍa*, and (3) *Uttara-* or *Jñāna-kāṇḍa*.

The term *Veda* is also taken to denote the whole literature made up of two different portions called *Mantra* and *Brāhmaṇa*, as pointed out in the following texts: "*Mantra-Brāhmaṇāt-makaḥ Śabdarāśir Veda iti*," "The Veda is that mass of words which constitute Mantra and Brāhmaṇa works"; *Mantra-Brāhmaṇayor Vedanāmadheyam* [Āpastamba in *Yajña-pari-bhāshā*], "Mantra and Brāhmaṇa are both called *Veda*."[1]

'**Mantra.**' Yāska [*Nirukta*, vii, 3, 6] derives the word *Mantra* from *manana*, "thinking," so that it means an "instrument of thought", speech, sacred text addressed to a deity. Yāska [*Ib.*, vii, 1, 1] further defines *Mantra* to mean the words employed by Ṛishis in praise of the Gods for fulfilment of those desires (*artha*) which are in their gift (*arthāpatyam*). Thus the Mantras are meant to be recited for the performance of worship in the form of what is called a *Yajña* or sacrifice. The entire Mantra portion of the Veda derives its usefulness from its practical application at the performance of sacrifices (*prayogasama-vedārthasmārakā mantrāḥ*).

Jaimini, in his Pūrva-Mīmāṁsā Sūtras, has pointed out that the Mantras have a double significance. They convey a mystical meaning and produce unseen results, for which their mere recitation according to the prescribed order of their words (*pāṭha-kramaniyama*) is sufficient (*Mantrāṇāṁ adṛishṭārtha-*

[1] It is interesting to note that this orthodox Hindu view of the Veda being made up of *Mantra* and *Brāhmaṇa* has been practically accepted by Bloomfield who states [*JAOS.*, xv, 144] "that *Mantra* and *Brāhmaṇa* are for the least part chronological distinctions; that they represent two modes of literary activity, and two modes of literary speech, which are largely contemporaneous. . . . Both forms existed together, for aught we know, from the earliest times; only the redaction of the *Mantra* collections seems on the whole to have preceded the redaction of the *Brāhmaṇas*. . . . The hymns of the Rigveda, like those of the other three Vedas, were liturgical from the very start. This means that they form only a fragment . . . late texts and commentaries may contain the correct explanation."

muchchāraṇa-mātram ; *uchchāraṇāt adṛishṭārthāḥ*). But they also convey a meaning for the fact that the sense of a sentence (*vākyārtha*) can always be deduced from the relations of its constituent parts like verbs and cases, whether the sentence is in Vedic or secular speech (*kriyā-kāraka-sambandhena pratīya-māno vākyārtho lokaVedayoraviśishṭaḥ*) [Jaimini, i, 2, 40]. Therefore, while the Mantras must be properly pronounced to secure their spiritual effects, their meanings also must be properly mastered with the aid of the six Vedāṅgas.

The Mantras have a threefold meaning, (1) Spiritual (adhyātma), concerning Knowledge and Liberation (*jñāna* and *mukti*), (2) Etymological (Nairukta), concerning objective truths, and (3) Ritualistic (Yājñika), concerning Sacrifices. The *Yājñika* interpretation of Mantras is the subject of Pūrva-Mīmāṁsā, and the other two interpretations, of Uttara-Mīmāṁsā.

'Āhāva.' The Vedic Mantras had been growing from time immemorial. Their earliest forms are known as *Āhāva*, a "call" to worship or *śaṁsana* in the words: "Śaṁsāva Om," "Let us invoke the formless Parabrahma." The priest called Hotā makes this call which is answered by the Adhvaryu priest by the words: Śaṁsāmo Daivom, "Yes, sir, let us now begin the invocation of the Supreme Being." This reply to the *Āhāva* is technically called *Pratigara*. That *Āhāva* is the earliest Mantra is shown by the fact that it contains the Mantra of one letter, viz., *Om* or Praṇava which is regarded as the original Vedic Mantra and called *Akshara* in *Rv.*, x, 13, 3.

'Nivid.' Another early form of the Mantra is known as *Nivid*. Its origin is described in the *Aitareya-Brāhmaṇa*. Prajāpati, filled with desire for creation, gave himself up to *tapas* in silence for a year, and then uttered the first Word twelve times, from which emerged the Universe. This Word of twelve syllables is known as *Nivid*. *Nivids* are described as being 'ancient' (*pūrva*) and "many" in several passages in the Rigveda such as i, 89, 3; i, 96, 2; ii, 36, 63, and referred to in iv, 18, 7 and vi, 67, 10.

'Saṁhitā.' The collection of Mantras is called *Saṁhitā*. For ages the Vedic Mantras remained one and undivided till the needs of worship which became more and more systematized called for an arrangement and a division in accordance with its scheme. Tradition ascribes this division to Krishṇa-Dvaipāyana Veda-Vyāsa, who made a fourfold division of the Vedic Mantras and created out of them four Vedic Saṁhitās known as Ṛik, Sāma, Yajus, and Atharva, which he imparted in the first instance respectively to his pupils named Paila, Vaiśampāyāna, Jaimini, and Sumantu.

The principle of this division rests on that of division of labour among the different classes of *Ṛitvikas* or priests, co-operating in the performance of worship or *Yajña*. It is very well explained by Yāska [*Nirukta*, i, 8] who quotes Rigveda, x, 71, 11, in which it is stated : " One priest nourishes the *ṛiks*."

This means that it is the duty of the priest named *Hotā*, at the time of the sacrifice, to make ready his collection of the *Ṛiks* gathered from different places, and fix it as his *śastra*. Yāska takes the word "*ṛik*" as equivalent to "*archanī*" or invocation of a deity. The Śastra of the Hotā was thus separated and became known as the Rigveda Saṁhitā in which, therefore, were brought together all the *Ṛiks* which were " chhando-vaddha ", i.e. which were in the form of verse or metre.

" Another priest has to sing the Gāyatra as his function at the sacrifice." This priest is called the *Udgātā* whose duty was to *sing* the *Ṛik* verses. The collection of the *Ṛiks* in the form of songs is known as Sāma-Veda Saṁhitā, of which the custodian is the Udgātā.

" The duty of another priest was to measure out the whole structure of the sacrifice (*yajñasya mātrāṁ vimimīta*)." This priest is called the Adhvaryu, literally, one who yokes (*yunakti*) the *adhvara* or sacrifice, one who is the leader (*netā*) of adhvara. He is the custodian of the collection of all the *Ṛiks* that are in prose and suitable for application in the material performance of the Yajña. This collection is known as the Yajurveda Saṁhitā, the term *yajus* being from *yajati*, to sacrifice.

Yāska next points out that the Yajurveda determines the body of the Yajña, of which the other two Vedas serve as limbs and supplements by supplying the required *Stotra* and *Śastra*, hymns and mantras. The Yajurveda is thus the mainstay upon which depend the other Vedas (*Upajīvyasya Yajurvedasya*).

The three Vedic Saṁhitās aforesaid are known as *Trayī*.

But, according to the Rigvedic passage cited by Yāska, the performance of a *Yajña* depends upon a fourth Ṛitvik called *Brahmā* whose duty is to give directions to the other priests regarding their duties and prevent their errors (*sati pramāde samādhātuṁ samarthaḥ*). Therefore, he was one who was proficient in all the three Vedas (*Sarvavidyaḥ . . . Vedatrayoktasarva-karmābhijñaḥ*). Yāska cites Chhāndogya-Upanishad [iv, 16, 1, 2] to explain further the status of the Brahmā priest. " Of Yajña there are two ways, the way of Mind and the way of Words (*Manaścha Vāk cha vartanī Yajñasya*). The way of Mind is cultivated by Brahmā and the way of Words by the three priests, Hotā, Udgātā, and Adhvaryu." This means that the Brahmā priest has to ensure the proper performance of the Yajña as a whole and in parts and to revolve in his mind its entire plan to prevent its errors (*pramādarāhityāya manasā samyaganusandheyaḥ*). The other three priests jointly are responsible for uttering the Mantras of their respective Vedas. The Brahmā alone was responsible for the success and efficacy of the Yajña, its execution in accordance with its inherent purpose and spirit (*Brahmā tu eka eva manorūpaṁ yajñabhāgaṁ saṁskaroti*), while the other three priests looked to its letter, its textual performance, and were responsible for its words as they were needed (*Vāgrūpaṁ yajñamārgaṁ saṁskurvanti*).

It will thus appear that the Vedic Mantras which were later classified into four Saṁhitās were inspired by the needs of prayer and worship in the form of performance of Yajñas or sacrifices. While the Adhvaryu prepared the ground of the Yajña and constructed its altar and platform on which he sat and offered oblations, the *Hotā* uttered the Ṛiks to invoke the deity of worship and the Udgātā would go round the altar chanting the relevant Sāma Ṛiks, while the Brahmā kept the master's eye on every detail of the worship and the fulfilment of its general scheme and underlying spiritual purpose.

The knowledge of a Vedic Mantra should mean the knowledge of its five particulars, viz. (1) the *Ṛishi* to whom the Mantra is ascribed, (2) the Metre (Chhandas) of the Mantra, (3) the Deity to whom it is addressed, (4) the purpose or ceremony for which it is applied (*Viniyoga*), and (5) the meaning of its words (*Śabdārtha* as well as *Adṛishṭārtha*).

'Brāhmaṇa.' Besides the *Mantra* portion, the Veda has also what is called the *Brāhmaṇa* portion. The word Brāhmaṇa is connected with the word *Brahma* which is a synonym of the word *Mantra*. Literally speaking, Mantra is that by which the *manana* or contemplation of God is attempted, while *Brahma* is that by which the worship of God is expanded or elaborated (from *bṛiṁhita*). The literature bearing upon *Brahma* is known as *Brāhmaṇa*.

The controversy regarding the differentiation between *Mantra* and *Brāhmaṇa* portions of the Veda has been settled by the simple solution that the *Brāhmaṇa* portion of the Veda is that which is left over after what the *Yājñikas* (the sacrificial priests) select and count as Mantras [*Tachchodakeshu Mantrākhyā śeshe Brāhmaṇaśabdaḥ* (Jaimini, Sū. ii, 1, 32)].

The Brāhmaṇa texts are marked by a twofold subject-matter, viz. (1) *Vidhi* (Injunction) and (2) *Arthavāda*. As defined by Āpastamba, " Brāhmaṇa texts are those which are injunctive of some action (*Karmachodanā Brāhmaṇāni*) [*Yajña. Pari. Su.*, 32, 33], while their remainder is known as *Arthavāda*." *Vidhis*, again, are of two kinds : (1) *Apravṛittapravartanam*, " enjoining an act which may not be performed," and (2) *Ajñāta-jnāpanam*, " making known what is unknown." Of these, the first kind of *Vidhi* relates to rituals dealt with in the *Karmakāṇḍa* of the Veda. These *Vidhi-Vākyas* are the source of Dharma (*Vidhivākyaṁ Dharme pramāṇam*). The other kind of *Vidhi*, which imparts new knowledge, belongs to the Brahma-Kāṇḍa of Veda, e.g. the knowledge that " Atman alone is the only Reality that existed " (*Ātmā vā idameka evāgra āsīt* in *Ait. Ār.*, ii, 4, 1).

The *Arthavāda*, like *Vidhi*, is equally a part of the Veda. The Arthavāda is really supplementary to Vidhi and is essential to the performance of *Dharma*, one of the objectives of the Veda itself. The *Arthavāda* supplies inspiration and stimulus for worshippers not sufficiently exerting themselves in the execution of *Vidhis*. As is stated in the text, " Vidhi and Arthavāda are mutually dependent (*sākāṁkshau*). Vidhi points out duties, Arthavāda points out their merits (*prāśastya*) and instigates their performance. Therefore, the Veda is made up of three integral parts, *Mantra*, *Vidhi*, and *Arthavāda*.

A part of the Brāhmaṇa literature is distinguished by the name of *Āraṇyaka*. Brahmachārīs, who wanted to continue as such, without marrying, in pursuit of knowledge, were called *Araṇas* or *Araṇamānas*. These *Araṇas* lived in hermitages in the forests outside the villages or centres of population. The forests where these *Araṇa* ascetics lived were called *Araṇyas*. The philosophical speculations of these learned ascetics regarding such ultimate problems as Brahma, Creation, Soul, or Immortality are embodied in works called *Āraṇyakas*.

The last development of the Brāhmaṇa literature is seen in the *Upanishads* which directly expound the knowledge of Brahma and form that portion of *Vidhi* which is described as *ajñātajñāpanam*, as shown above. It is, however, to be noted that the origin of the Upanishads, the roots of their system, are to be found in the Rigveda itself, of which the underlying note and a considerable part are inspired by the conception of Brahma as the sole, ultimate, and all-pervading Reality, rather than Dharma or Yajña. This will be shown in its proper place below.

It may also be noted that the characteristic of Brāhmaṇa literature is its method of deliberation and discussion and that, of its three divisions, the *Brāhmaṇas* were meant for *gṛihasthas*, householders, the *Āraṇyakas* for the *Vānaprasthas* or hermits, and the *Upanishads* for *Sannyasīs*.

'Yajña.' The term *Yajña* is derived from root *yaj*, to worship. Those words by which worship is performed are called *yajus*. Worship was performed in the form of what is called a *Yajña*. As the Veda itself is to serve the purposes of this kind of worship or Yajña which was performed primarily by the use of *yajus*, the *Yajurveda*, as we have seen, counts as the most important of the four Vedas, while some of its parts are also the most ancient.

Its Requisites. The object of *yajana* or worship is called *Yajata* in Vedic language. These *Yajatas* were formless manifestations of the Supreme Being or Brahma for whose worship there was no need of any material temple or shrine. The worshippers were called *Yajamānas*. They performed their worship or *yajña* by means of meditation or *manana* with the aid of the words called *Mantras*. Thus the utterance of the Mantra was essential to the performance of this kind of worship or *yajña* by which the *Yajata* or the deity was approached and invoked by mortals.

Besides the invocation, *āhvāna*, of the deity by the utterance of the proper Mantras, the next requisite of a *Yajña* is what is called *āhuti* or sacrifice of oblations, of something which the worshipper holds dear and valuable. The oblations are offered to Agni or Fire kindled in the altar, *Vedi*, specially prepared for the purpose. Men approached God through Agni who invoked Him on their behalf and is thus called the *Hotā*. The essence of *Yajña* is thus sacrifice or offering as proof of devotion to the Deity.

'Yajña' as Symbol of creation. Vedic thought conceived of Yajña as a symbol or representation of creation and its processes as understood by it. As each individual creature is fundamentally subject to the laws governing Creation as a whole and is a part of the cosmic plan and purpose towards the fulfilment of which it is his supreme duty to contribute by his own self-fulfilment, the Veda invented this most wonderful device of the Yajña as a visible picture of his *Dharma* or religion to remind him of the laws of his being and of his supreme duty aforesaid. The conception of Yajña is thus modelled on that of Creation as presented in Vedic Literature and first indicated in the hymns of the Rigveda, especially the hymns x, 81, 82, 90, 121, 129. Of these, x, 90 is the famous Purusha-Sūkta first presenting the whole process of creation as a *Yajña*. At this primordial and original Yajña, the Creator of the Universe called the *Virāṭ-Purusha* created the universe by offering Himself up as the sacrifice to provide the foundation upon which the structure could rise and rest and the very material out of which it could be constructed. The Śruti text, *Rv.* x, 81, asks the fundamental questions: "Kiṁ svit āsīt adhishṭhānaṁ ārambhaṇam"; "Kiṁ svit vanaṁ ka u sa vṛiksha āsa yato dyāvā-pṛithivī nishṭatakshuḥ"; "Yat adhyatishṭhat bhuvanāni dhārayan"; "Where was the place, what the material, where was the forest, and which the tree, to which the Architect of the Universe resorted in creating it?"

Its Inner Meaning. The Purusha-Sūkta answers this question by stating that the Virāṭ-Purusha, wishing for creation, wishing that the One should create the Many (*āśishā* = vahu syāṁ prajāyeya in x, 81, 1), found in His self-immolation the only means of building up His wished-for creation, for which He sacrificed Himself as the Animal out of Whose body was created the Universe comprising Nature with all its forces and agents like the Sun and Moon, organic and inorganic matter, different forms of life, and Society with its classes. The Animal was tied to a *yūpa* or post before it was sacrificed. The significance of this is that the Infinite chose to become finite, the Immortal mortal, the Great became small. Thus God is in every creature, high or low. This is the essence of Vedic thought or Hinduism. As the Śruti says [*Rv.* x, 81, 1]: "Sa āśishā draviṇamichchhamānaḥ prathamachchhadavarān āviveśa" [Sa Parameśvara āśishā vahu syāṁ prajāyeya ityevaṁ rūpayā punaḥ punaḥ sisṛikshayā draviṇamichchhamānaḥ dhanopalakshitaṁ jagadbhogamākāṁkshamāṇaḥ prathamachchhat prathamaṁ mukhyaṁ nishprapañchaṁ pāramārthikaṁ rūpaṁ āvṛiṇvan avarān svasṛishṭān prāṇihṛidayapradeśānāviveśa" (Sāyaṇa)] "He, the One, again and again, wishing to be Many, wishing for the enjoyment of this world of riches, concealed His primary Self (Absolute and Unconditioned) and created the world of objects and minds into each of which He entered." Man also, like his Creator, has to embrace mortality and the limited life of the world, like the sacrificial animal tied to the *yūpa*. He must bind himself to the ties of relationship, tie the animal in him to the *yūpa* of self-control, and sacrifice that animal at life's *yajña*. Through the limits of individual life, the individual thus attains the Absolute by sacrifice. The Purusha-Sūkta also lays down the doctrine of self-sacrifice as constituting the true worship of the Divine, while the device of Yajña was evolved to give a concrete shape to this doctrine.

Virāṭ Purusha. The Purusha-Sūkta further states that the Virāṭ Purusha sacrificed Himself to Himself. X, 81, 1 makes this clear by stating that the Supreme God chooses (by way of what is called His *līlā*) to offer up the whole Universe as an oblation to Himself. The Universe is periodically dissolved in Him who remains the sole Creator to recreate it: "Ya imā visvā bhuvanāni juhūt Ṛishir Hotā nyasīdat Pitā naḥ." This only means that creation includes a process of evolution and its ultimate dissolution by involution in the Source from Which it arises. As we have seen, Creation originates with the desire of Brahma: "*Saḥ akāmayata bahu syāṁ prajāyeya,*" "Let Me be Many, let Me grow." This indicates three stages in creation, viz. (1) His Will "to be", called *Bhūḥ*, (2) Process of "being", manifestation, called *Bhuvaḥ*, and (3) the manifestations themselves called *Svaḥ*. These three correspond to: (1) *Prāṇa*, the life breathed into creation; (2) *Prakṛiti*, processes of biological evolution; and (3) *Prakriyā*, what *Prāṇa* grows into. These three stages in creation are indicated in the three constituent elements of the word *Yajña*, viz. (1) *Ya* = *saṁyata, antasthaḥ*, implicit, implied; (2) *Jana* = *janma*, manifestation, what is rendered explicit; (3) *As* = the growth itself, the manifested state. Thus the Vedic philosophy of creation is that "we are all evolved out of His will, by His will we are emancipated and merged in Him after growth or expansion": "Yato vā imāni bhūtāni jāyante Yena jātāni jīvanti Yat prayantyabhisaṁviśanti."

Dynamic Universe. It is also to be understood that the world aptly called *Jagat*, "evolving," "moving," is not something that is static or stationary. It is emanating every moment into different objects. It is but the ceaseless working of "the Will of Brahma, the One, to be Many". This Will is being worked out by various agencies and forces like the Sun and Moon, Fire, Storm, Cloud, Rain, and the like, and these are conceived of as so many Manifestations of the Divine, and worshipped as so many deities, the *Adhi-Devatās* behind the cosmic forces shaping Creation. These Devatās are, like His Agents, carrying out the desire of Brahma for creation and are themselves His creation. All individuals thus created are called the *Kshara-purushas*, as distinguished from Brahma, the *Akshara-Purusha* (the Eternal Being) or *Uttama-Purusha* (the Supreme Being) in the Upanishads. These *Devatās* are, therefore, aiding in the evolution of Creation and in the performance of the primeval *Yajña* by which the *Virāṭ-Purusha* outshapes Himself in Creation, as stated in the Purusha-Sūkta.

Prajāpati. We have already seen that the requisites of a *Yajña* are Invocation (*āhvāna*), Fire (Agni), Sacrifice (*āhuti*), and the Altar (Vedi) where oblation is offered to fire. At first the altar was a simple structure but, later, in the *Brāhmaṇa* texts, it is very much elaborated to bring out its underlying spiritual significance. As Eggeling puts it [*SBE*, 43, pp. xiv–xxiv], " in the building of the fire altar, the Brahmans sought to symbolize the constitution of the unity of the universe." As further pointed out by Professor A. B. Keith [*CHI*, i, 142], " in the Purusha hymn of the Rigveda occurs the conception of the creation of the Universe from the Purusha. . . . The Purusha is Prajāpati, ' lord of creatures ' and the sacrifice is conceived as constantly recurring in order to maintain the existence of the Universe. To render this possible is the end of the fire altar, the building of which is the reconstruction of the Universe in the shape of Prajāpati. Prajāpati, again, is identified with Agni, the fire of the altar, and both Prajāpati and Agni are the divine counterparts of the human sacrifice. But Prajāpati is himself Time, and Time is in the long run Death, so that the sacrificer himself becomes death, and by that act rises superior to Death and is for ever removed from the world of illusion and trouble to the world of everlasting bliss. In this the true nature of Prajāpati and of the sacrificer is revealed as Intelligence and the Śatapatha Brāhmaṇa urges the seeker for truth to meditate upon the Self, made up of Intelligence and endowed with a body of spirit, a form of Light and an ethereal nature."

' Sarvahuta ' the Supreme. It is also to be noted that in the Purusha-Sūkta the Supreme Being is called *Sarvahuta*, i.e. He who is invoked by all in whatever Yajñas they perform. He is also called *Yajña*, i.e. as *Yajanīya*, the Object of worship, as explained by Sāyaṇa. The hymn thus makes clear the position as pointed out by Sāyaṇa that though worship or *Yajña* is offered by individuals to different deities, all such worship is fundamentally the worship of the One

Supreme God. As Sāyaṇa states: "Though Indra and other deities are invoked in this and that Yajña, it must be understood that it is the Supreme God who exists in the form of those deities (yadyapīndrādayastatra tatra hūyante tathāpi Parameśvarasyaivendrādirūpeṇāvasthānādavirodhaḥ). Sāyaṇa, to prove his contention, cites *Rv*. i, 164, 46: "*Vipras* (the enlightened Sages) call the One Reality (*ekaṁ sat*) by many names such as Indra, Varuṇa, Mitra, Agni, Yama, Vāyu, or Āditya." And also Bṛihadāraṇyaka Upanishad [i, 4, 6]: "Now, what (the ritualists) say, 'Worship This, Worship That' (thinking Each to be) a different Deity: (it is but a misconception); this multiplicity (of gods) is but His (Manifestation). It is but He who comprehends all the gods." Therefore, Sāyaṇa lays down the fundamental position thus: "In all Yajñas where different deities are invoked, it is the Supreme God who is really invoked (sarvairapi Parameśvara eva hūyate)."

The Rigveda is full of such sacrifices to different deities and they are to be understood as forms of prayer and methods of approach to the Most High. The *Yajñas*, as explained above, were evolved as modes of invocation of the Infinite and possessed of profound spiritual significance and educational value as aids to self-realization.

'Yajña' as Sacrifice. All these Yajñas were modelled on the primordial *Yajña* of the *Virāṭ Purusha* mentioned above, as stated in the text: "Chā kapre tena Ṛishayo Manushyāḥ yajñe yāte Pitaro naḥ purāṇe," "Pitṛis, Men, and Ṛishis performed Yajñas after that primeval Yajña."

This Divine Yajña shows creation in its three processes, *Sṛishṭi* (Beginning), *Sthiti* (Evolution), and *Pralaya* (Dissolution and Emancipation), as indicated in Rigvedic hymns like x, 81 cited above. The human *Yajñas* were so modelled as to symbolize and signify this mystery and meaning of creation. They were based on sacrifice as the essence of Yajña, but man's sacrifice could not be as complete as God's. Instead of offering himself up as sacrifice, he thought of symbolic and vicarious sacrifice. An animal was seized for sacrifice on behalf of the sacrificer. This kind of ceremony was called *Paśu-yāga*. But Vedic religion did not countenance such bloody sacrificing of animals by violence. As the *Chhāndogya Upanishad* [iii, 6] puts it: "Na vai Devā aśnanti na pivanti etadeva amṛitaṁ dṛishṭvā tṛipyanti"; "the gods who do not eat or drink should not be offered meat tainted with violence." Thus sacrifice at a *Yajña* meant self-sacrifice.

Even where animals were sacrificed, only a few select parts of the animals were offered as oblations, but not their blood which was given away to demons. Eventually, the sacrifice of animals was replaced by the offering of *Puroḍāśa*, a cake of vrīhi or yava (rice or barley) and the *Paśu-Yāga* by what was called *Ishṭi-Yāga*. Similarly, there was a third kind of Vedic or Śrauta sacrifice called *Soma-Yāga* where the juice of the Soma plant symbolized and took the place of the blood of animals, just as *Puroḍāśa* stood for their flesh.[1]

Its Varieties. It will also appear that *Yajñas* were necessarily of different kinds according to the different kinds of offering made at them. The offering may be material or spiritual. As is stated in the text: "Dravyayajñāstapoyajñā Yogayajñāstathāpare Svādhyāya-Jñāna-yajñāścha"; "*Yajñas* are of different kinds: (1) *Dravya-yajña* where material objects are offered as oblations, objects which appeal to and indulge the senses; (2) *Tapoyajña* where all desires and out-going activities are offered to be consumed in the fire of asceticism and penance; (3) *Yoga-yajña* where senses are sacrificed at the fire of *saṁyama* or self-control, the practice of detachment; and (4) *Svādhyaya-Jñāna-Yajña*, *Yajña* in the form of study of the Veda and pursuit of knowledge by *brahmacharya*. Rigveda i, 84, 2 mentions the *Yajña* of Ṛishis by means of *stuti* or prayer and of mortals by sacrifice, while i, 18, 7 refers to the *Yajña* of sages in their pursuit of knowledge. These texts thus refer to different kinds of *Yajña* depending on different degrees or kinds of sacrifice to suit different stages or degrees of spiritual progress achieved by the *Yajamānas* concerned. The highest grade of *Yajña* for man is thus described in the *Bhagavadgītā*: "Brahmārpaṇaṁ Brahma-haviḥ Brahmāgnau Brahmaṇā hutaṁ | Brahmaiva tena gantavyaṁ Brahma-karma-samādhinā"; "Life itself is the great sacrifice where Brahma Himself is at once the Yajamāna or sacrificer, the fire where sacrifice is offered, the material of the sacrifice (*havi*), the God to Whom sacrifice is offered, Whom one attains by living his life as if it is *Brahma-karma* or an offering of all its fruits to Brahma in total absence of desire."

[1] One is reminded in this connection of the doctrine of Eucharist Sacrifice in Christian Theology, according to which, Jesus Christ, who took his birth as Man to be his Saviour, on the night before his crucifixion, distributed among his disciples bread and wine as symbolical of his flesh and blood. He gave up his body as sacrifice, washing away by his blood the sins of mankind. The following words are put into his mouth: "I am the bread of Life. He that eateth My flesh and drinketh My blood dwelleth in Me and I in him . . . and hath eternal life."

'Pañcha-Mahāyajñas.' The principle of *Yajña* was that of sacrifice by which man, like his Maker, is to build up and uphold the system he brings into being in this world. He must in his own life go through the eternal creative processes of "Beginning, Development, and Dissolution". Sacrifice is the process of his self-expansion leading to his final dissolution in the Absolute, emancipated from his narrow self. This self-expansion is achieved by a series of *Yajñas* the performance of which Vedic religion makes obligatory upon its votaries. The first of these is called *Deva-Yajña* symbolizing man's approach towards the gods, the creative forces of which he is the outcome. This is called *Svāhā*, expression of *Sva* or Self, which is uttered after the offer of oblations to the *Devatās*. Just as spiritually Man is the outcome of the gods to whom he thus makes sacrifices, physically he is the outcome of his ancestors, the *Pitṛis*, to whom he prays by *Pitṛi-Yajña*, by uttering the word *Svadhā*, "placing of his own self, *Sva*," in the Pitṛis. Then he has to perform what is called *Brahma-Yajña* which consisted, as we have seen, in the study and teaching of Veda and meditation on its Mantras (*Japa*). He has also to perform a fourth *Yajña* called *Bhūta-Yajña* by offering *bali* (oblation) to all created beings with whom he realizes his oneness. "One touch of Nature makes the whole world kin." Lastly, he has to perform the *Nṛi-Yajña* by which he offers worship to all his fellow-men in a spirit of universal brotherhood. This worship is in the form of the offer of daily hospitality by the entertainment of guests as a part of religious duty. It will thus be seen how this hierarchy of five *Yajñas* (known as *Pañcha-Mahāyajñas*) was planned as a scheme of progressive approach towards the Infinite with which they provide so many links with the finite.

'Agnihotra.' We shall now discuss the cultural significance of some of the Vedic *Yajñas* proper. In the Rigveda, as we have seen, *Yajñas* are performed for the worship of God in the forms of Deities like Agni, Varuṇa, Indra, Soma, and the like, each of Whom associated with a particular aspect or representing a particular formative force of creation helps in the contemplation of the Formless Absolute. In the Rigveda, the more important of these *Yajñas* are those in honour of two particular Gods, Agni and Soma. Agni who represents the Energy operating in the whole universe and is the closest approximation to the Formless, the most striking and intimate proof of the power of the Creator in this world-emanation, receives a considerable degree of attention in the Rigveda and his praises are sung in many a hymn. He is worshipped as the Cause of Light and Heat, of Cloud and Rain, of Rain the cause of Food, of Food which sustains Life itself, the all-pervading One Who is both within and without us, Who appears as the Sun on high and opens our eyes as the best avenue of objective knowledge. Thus Agni is at the root of our life, our knowledge, and our bliss (*ānanda*). Therefore, Agni becomes the household deity worshipped in every hearth and home both morning and evening by the *Yajña* called *Agnihotra* by every householder who offers to Him his best as oblation. The offer may be offer of *Śraddhā* instead of a material object, in which case it will be called *Śraddhā-homa* and the ceremony will be performed with the words, " Ahaṁ Śraddhāṁ juhomi," " I offer as sacrifice my reverence." The continuous performance of Agni hotra in a family connotes its perpetuation along with the family fire which is inherited and transmitted.

'**Soma-Yajña.**' A greater prominence is given in the Rigveda to *Soma-yajñas*. Though the word *Soma* is the name of a creeper, it is really used as a symbol for a deep spiritual truth in the Rigveda. This is made clear in several of its hymns. In viii, 48, Soma is addressed as '*Madhu*, the nectar or ambrosia, the drink of Immortality sought by both gods and men. Even the Ṛishi who achieved the greatest fame by his learning and wisdom still prays for something that was lacking, this nectar. He is also addressed as Indu or Aditi, the primordial deity who rules the gods and penetrates into the hearts of all ; the nectar by drinking which mortals become immortal and attain heaven radiant with shining gods ; the vital principle of life.' X, 85 sings in the same strain the praise of Soma. " Soma is the cause of the power of the Ādityas and of the greatness of Pṛithivī (*Somena Pṛithivī Mahī*)." " The Soma whom the worshippers of Brahma know, That is not something to be drunk by the mouth (Somaṁ yaṁ Brāhmaṇo viduḥ na tasyāśnāti kaśchana)." " He cannot be drunk by a materialist (*pārthiva*)." " Some can drink Him but cannot decrease Him by such drink " : for it is a drink of supreme knowledge, a draught of Immortality, which increases by each such drink, because Truth spreads through Its exponents. I, 91 states that " He is to be approached by *manīshā* (effort of mind, meditation) along the path of virtue (*rajishṭhaṁ panthāṁ*) ; the author of cosmic laws (*Vratas*), who is manifest in heaven and earth, in mountains, vegetation, and water." IV, 18, 1, 13, which is the hymn of Ṛishi Vāmadeva, the author of the entire fourth Maṇḍala, relates how the saving knowledge of this *Madhu* or *Soma* doctrine came to him. It relates that he was so poor that he was driven to eat the entrails of a dog (*avartyā śuna āntrāṇi peche*) and could not better his condition by prayers to gods, had to see his wife in a deplorable condition (*apaśyaṁ jāyāṁ amahīyamānām*), until he was saved by God in His mercy bringing to him the nectar (*madhu*) of Soma doctrine in the disguise of a hawk (*śyena*). Thus this supreme knowledge, Madhu- or Soma-Vidyā came to the Ṛishi in a sudden flash in his darkest hour.

We have now considered the typical Vedic Yajñas like the Agnihotra and the Soma-Yāga and their cultural value and spiritual significance. While Agnihotra was a daily *yajña*, some Yajñas were periodical like *Darśayajña* to be performed on new-moon, and *Paurṇamāsa* on full-moon days. *Soma-yāga* had also several varieties the performance of which took one day, or several days like *Jyotishṭoma*, or even a whole year in the form called *Satra*. A description of a *Satra* will show its cultural and social significance.

'Satra.' The *Satra* was a sort of a national festival of the Vedic times and operated as a potent factor for the moral and spiritual uplift of the community, for the progress of its literature and education. All the learned philosophers and Ṛishis of those days gathered at the *Satra* and enchanted the vast audiences of crowds that flocked to it by their thrilling recitation of Vedic Mantras, chanting of Sāmans, and discourses on Brahma. Thus it was a sort of a religious and philosophical Congress that held a continuous session for the whole year and gave scope to the promulgation and propagation of Vedic literature. References to such learned Assemblies or Sabhās in the Rigveda [x, 71, 2, 5, etc.] are dealt with below. But the *Satra* was not also devoid of its social side. The Yajamāna, the householder celebrating the ceremony, would be throughout the year giving generously of his abundance by a free feeding of the poor and lavishly entertaining his learned guests as part of the ceremony. Thus Vedic religion was incentive to social service, sacrifice, and liberality. We may recall in this connection the impassioned Rigvedic hymn in praise of Charity [x, 117].

There were other details of the ceremony, each with its own spiritual value and significance. The *Yāga* was performed in five parts, viz. (1) *Dīkshaṇīya Ishṭi* for the dīkshā or initiation of the Yajamāna for purposes of his second spiritual birth as a *dvija* ("twice-born"); (2) *Prāyaṇīya Ishṭi* or *Ātithya Ishṭi* to indicate that God Soma attended the *Ishṭi* as a guest (*atithi*) and also giving food to the new-born *dvija* ; (3) *Pravarṇya Kriyā* to achieve his spiritual growth ; (4) ***Paśu-yāga***, the sacrifice of the animal in the worshipper ; and (5) *Soma-yāga*, the sacrifice at which Soma is drunk, symbolizing the drink by which the *Dvija* nourishes his soul and attains immortality.

Summary. Now to sum up : The *Yajña* which is the centre of the Vedic system may be thus understood as education of man in self-sacrifice as the law of his being and the only foundation of his religion, self-sacrifice in the form of performance by him of the different classes of duties making up his life in the world by the performance of different kinds of *Yajñas* already explained, such as *Yajñas* of *Tapas* (Penance), *Yoga* (Meditation), *Svādhyāya* and *Jñāna* (Study and Knowledge). The *Aitareya Brāhmaṇa* holds that man is born with three debts, debts to *Pitṛis*, *Ṛishis*, and *Devas*, and these he can discharge only by fatherhood, *yajña*, and study, as " *Putrī*, *Yajvā* and *Brahmachārī*." Thus the *Yajñas* take the individual through a course of self-realization in progressive stages by which he becomes more and more universal in his outlook and interests until he is emancipated and merged in the Absolute. It is the *Yajñas* which lead to *Dharma* and it is *Dharma* which leads to *Brahma*. Thus, as we have seen, the Veda is concerned only with the two subjects, *Dharma* and *Brahma*, treated in its two sections known as *Karma-kāṇḍa* (including *Devatā-* or *Upāsanā-Kāṇḍa*) and *Jñāna-Kāṇḍa*, which are related to each other like two limbs of the structure of Vedic thought and scheme of life.[1]

[1] *References* : two learned works in Bengali, (1) *Yajña-Kathā* by the late Ramendra Sundar Trivedī and (2) *Veda-Praveśikā* by the late Umes Chandra Baṭavyāl ; and Sāyaṇa's Introduction to his commentary on Rigveda. I am also specially indebted to my talented father-in-law, Mr. Dhanapati Banerji, M.A., B.L., and his brother, Mr. Sarat Chandra Banerji, M.A., B.L., both erudite Sanskrit scholars, and members of the Bar at Ranchi, Chhota-Nagpur, for valuable suggestions and notes.

CHAPTER II

RIGVEDIC EDUCATION

The Rigveda as the Source of Hindu Civilization. The Rigveda is established as the earliest work not merely of the Hindus but of all Indo-European languages and of humanity. " One thing is certain," says Max Muller, " namely, that there is nothing more primitive, more ancient than the hymns of the Rigveda, whether in India or the whole Aryan world. Being Aryan in language and thought, the Rigveda is the most ancient of our books " [*Origin and Development of Religion*]. But the great paradox that it presents is that though this is the oldest book of India, it does not mark merely the dawn of its culture, but rather its meridian. " We cannot tell how the religion of the Hindus came into being. When we become aware of it, we find it already complete in its broad outlines, its main principles. Not only is it complete, but the farther back we go, the more perfect it is, the more unadulterated, the more closely related to the loftiest speculations of our modern agnosticism " [Maurice Maeterlinck in *The Great Secret*].

" What we read in the Vedas, those archives of Hindu wisdom, gives us only a faint idea of the sublime doctrines of the ancient teachers, and even so these are not in their original form. Only the gaze of the clairvoyant, directed upon the mysteries of the past, may reveal the unuttered wisdom which lies hidden behind these writings " [Rudolph Steiner quoted in *ib.*, p. 8]. According to the Hindu orthodox view, the Rigveda contains within itself the seeds and sources from which the entire course of Hindu thought through the ages has derived and flowed in so many streams. It lays the foundation upon which Hindu Civilization has been building up through the ages. Broadly speaking, it is on a foundation of plain living and high thinking. Therefore, though ancient India is lacking in great monuments of material progress achieved by some of the early civilizations of the world, like the Egyptian or the Assyrian, she is not lacking in monuments of intellectual or spiritual progress. Life was simple but thought high and of farthest reach, wandering through eternity.

C

Art was late in coming under such conditions, but not the higher art of living. Some of the prayers of the Rigveda, like the widely known Gāyatrī mantram [iii, 63, 10; also found in *Sāmaveda* (*Uttara*, 6, 3) and *Yajurveda* (3, 35; 22, 9; 30, 27)] touch the highest point of knowledge and sustain human souls to this day, while no Hindu, however modernized, will allow a single alteration of their original accents, letters, syllables, or words.

Its Evolution and Contents. The Rigveda itself exhibits an evolution and the history of the Rigveda is a history of the culture of the age. The Rigveda, in the form in which we have it now, is a compilation out of old material, a collection and selection (*saṁhitā*) of 1,017 hymns (or 1,028 hymns, if eleven of Maṇḍala viii, added later, are counted) out of the vast literature of hymns which had been accumulating for a long period. As Macdonell puts it: "Some hundreds of years must have been needed for all the hymns found in the Rigveda to come into being." Bloomfield [*JAOS*, xxix, 288] even considers the so-called oldest parts of the Rigveda as "the last precipitate, with a long and a tangled past behind it of a literary activity of great and indefinite length". Dr. M. Winteritz also concludes: "Centuries must have elapsed between the composition of earliest hymns and the Saṁhitā of the Rigveda." Accordingly, the Rigveda Saṁhitā itself refers to the works of the earlier and later authors [*pūrvaiḥ* and *nūtanaiḥ* (i, 1, 27)], to Agni being worshipped in bygone ages (*pūrve*) by Ṛishis by their hymns (*gīrbhiḥ*) [x, 98, 9] and also to hymns extemporized for the occasion [*stomaṁ janayāmi navyam* in i, 109, 2, etc.].

In dealing with this vast and varied material belonging to different ages, the editors of the Rigveda Saṁhitā were called upon to evolve advanced and comprehensive principles in constructing their work. Firstly, it had to be a representative collection which could reflect the different types and kinds of literary achievements and religious speculation already current in the country. Thus the Saṁhitā is characterized by a remarkable variety in its contents, the topics dealt with in the hymns it brings together, which differ in their appeal and value. Thus there are many hymns which are pure and sublime expressions of faith and poetry, having no connection with any practical purpose or rituals. There are other hymns which are applied for sacrificial purposes. Some again are entirely prompted by the practical needs of the sacrifice and read like sacrificial songs and litanies, arranged in a businesslike manner, by the priestly poets conducting such sacrifices. Much of their poetry again depends upon their subjects. Those addressed to Varuṇa, for example, rank among the highest. Indra again inspires 250 hymns of a different character as the national god of war. These Varuṇa-Indra hymns, however, are marked by great pathos, vigour, and raciness. Agni, again, is the god of the householder, inspiring hymns that touch the heart and rouse tender feelings. There are pearls of lyric poetry in the hymns to Sūrya, Parjanya, Maruts, and Ushas. Among the sacrificial hymns and litanies may be mentioned as the best specimens the famous Āprī Sūktas (propitiatory hymns). Of a different class are what may be called the funeral songs in the tenth maṇḍala of the Rigveda (where there is the interesting reference to the erection of a mound over a corpse) [*Rv.* x, 18, 10–13]. There are also hymns referring to cremation and transmigration [x, 16, 1–6]. The hymn i, 164 reads like a riddle. It refers to a wheel of order with twelve spokes, revolving round the heavens, and holding within it in pairs 720 sons to signify the year of twelve months and 360 days and 360 nights. There is again the long and highly interesting wedding hymn [x, 85]. There are, further, hymns of a somewhat secular character. Instances of these are those called *Saṁvādas*, dialogues or ballads, such as x, 95 on Purūravas and Urvaśī, x, 10 on Yama and Yamī, or x, 85 known as the Sūryā Sūkta. There are also a few didactic poems. One of these, x, 117, is addressed to Dāna (Liberality) as its deity by Ṛishi called *Bhikshu* (Āṅgirasa). It enjoins charity as more meritorious than Yajña, sacrifice. The gift of food is a gift of life, for hunger is a form of death. Friends forsake him who does not help them in need, and leave him homeless, for a home means friends. Fortune also is unstable like the wheels of a rolling chariot. So one must not cling to it as a miser. Nor can it save him from death. Nor should one be proud of it, for a rich man finds another richer. Twins, looking alike, differ in mind (*chit*), strength (*vīrya*), and liberality. So there is no religion higher than charity. Similarly, x, 34, is a pathetic monologue in which a gambler bemoans the ruin he has brought to his wife, mother, and family by dicing, exclaiming: " Play not with dice: ply thy tillage: enjoy and value the property thou hast, thy cattle, and thy wife (*kṛishimit kṛishasva vitte ramasva tatra gāvaḥ tatra jāyā*). There are again some special hymns called *Dāna-stutis*, about forty in number, of which the best is the aforesaid x, 117. Lastly, we ascend to the highest level of philosophy in hymns like the song of creation in x, 129; x, 125 on Logos, or x, 90 on the sacrifice of the Virāṭ Purusha to sustain his creation.

The advance of thought from the concrete towards the abstract is further shown in the conception of abstract deities. We have such names of the Supreme Being as *Dhātā*, *Vidhātā*, *Dhartā*, *Trātā*, *Netā*, *Tvashṭā*, *Savitā*, *Viśvakarmā*, *Hiraṇya-garbha*, *Kaḥ* (for which references are given below). We have also deities comprising personifications of abstract nouns like *Manyu*, Wrath; *Śraddhā*, Faith [x, 151]; *Anumati*, Favour of the Gods; *Aramati*, Devotion; *Sūnṛitā*, Bounty; *Asu-nīti*, Spirit-life; or *Nirṛiti*, Decease; and, lastly, *A-diti*, Liberation or Freedom, the Mother of *Ādityas*, who delivers from the bonds of physical suffering and moral guilt. There is also a goddess called *Araṇyānī* [x, 146], the goddess of Forest Solitude, who is invoked with much feeling: "Araṇyāni! Thou who seemest to lose thyself there, why dost thou not ask the way to the village? Dost not Terror seize thee at thy solitude!" She is described as at once harbouring wild beasts, feeding travellers on fruits, yielding abundant food, and fragrant with flowers!

It will thus be seen that the hymns chosen for the Saṁhitās give a fair picture of the various aspects of a highly advanced cultural life and civilization.

Conservation of its Text. Secondly, besides showing their skill of selection on the basis of their acquaintance with the vast body of hymns then extant, the editors of the Saṁhitā were at pains to think out some mechanical linguistic devices by which the sacred text handed down from time immemorial could be conserved in their pristine purity and original forms and ensured against the interpolations of later ages. The traditional orthodox respect for the sacred word was already responsible for the high standard of verbal authenticity which had been observed in the long interval between the rise of the hymns and the constitution, by grammatical editors, of the extant phonetic text called the Saṁhitā. These editors thus inherited an established tradition and literary practice which they further improved and confirmed. They began by a rigid adherence to the words of the old seers and even to their most minute irregularities of accent or alternate forms not supported by the grammatical rules of a later age, except where changes in phonetic forms were necessary to make them understandable. Thus, to take an instance, the word *sumna* was retained in the Saṁhitā text and not replaced by its later equivalent *dyumna* but the old expression *tuam hi Agne* was changed into *tvaṁ hy Agne,* " For Thou, O Agni."

The principle by which the Saṁhitā text was thus constituted suggested in its turn other devices for its own conservation against changes or corruptions in time. These devices came later. The text of the Saṁhitā was originally presented in the form called *Nirbhuja*-Saṁhitā. It was followed by the formation of a new text of the Saṁhitā called the *Pratṛiṇṇa* Saṁhitā in which every single word is shown in its independent and phonetically unmodified form and compounds are separated into their elements. This is technically called the *Pada-pāṭha,* " Word-text." To make assurance doubly sure, a second device was resorted to in what is called the *Krama-pāṭha,* " Step-text," where every word of the *Pada-pāṭha* appears twice to be pronounced both after the preceding, and before, the following one. Thus *a b c d* as representing the first four words would be read as *ab, bc, cd.* The full scheme of Vedic recitation ultimately developed various forms as means of preserving the purity of the original Vedic texts. The *Saṁhitā* and *Pada* or *krama pāṭhas* are classed under *Prakṛiti,* while the other *Pāṭhas* come under what is called *Vikṛiti* and are of eight kinds, viz. ; (1) *Jaṭā,* (2) *Mālā,* (3) *Śikhā,* (4) *Rekhā,* (5) *Dhvaja,* (6) *Daṇḍa,* (7) *Ratha,* and (8) *Ghana.* Of these, the primary ones are the aforesaid *Jaṭā* and *Daṇḍa.* Under *Daṇḍa* are grouped Nos. (2), (4), (5), and (7), while *Jaṭā* includes (3). In *Jaṭā-pāṭha,* the two words *a b* will be pronounced as *ab, ba, ab,* (as in *Namo Rudrebhyo Rudrebhyo Namo Namo Rudrebhyaḥ*). The *Ghana-Pāṭha* combines the features of both *Jaṭā* and *Daṇḍa* as in *ab, ba* ; *abc, cba, abc.*

These first essays in the editorial art and technique for securing textual purity laid the foundation of Linguistics or Metrics known as *Śikshā* recognized as one of the six sciences which were auxiliaries to the Vedas (Vedāṅgas). This literary art is elaborated in the later *Prātiśākhya* literature in which are presented with examples the euphonic modification necessary for turning the *Pada* into the *Saṁhitā* text, and also in the works known as *Anukramaṇīs,* or Indexes, giving the number of the hymns, verses, words, and even syllables of the sacred text as means of checking its integrity. As Macdonell (*India's Past*) has remarked, " these devices have secured a faithfulness of tradition unparalleled in any other ancient literature."

Arrangement of its Contents. When the Rigvedic text was thus fixed and appropriated for purposes of the *Saṁhitā,* its editors had to think out the principles on which the hymns could be best arranged. These show considerable literary skill, originality of design, and insight into religious needs. First, six representative *Ṛishis* were chosen and their works were utilized to constitute six different *Maṇḍalas*, *Maṇḍalas* ii–vii, of the Rigveda. These Ṛishis are Gṛitsamada, Viśvāmitra, Vāmadeva, Atri, Bharadvāja, and Vasishṭha. To the nucleus of these six Maṇḍalas or "family-books" were added (1) the group of hymns contributed by other families of Ṛishis to form the second part of Maṇḍala i (51–191); (2) other hymns formed into the first part of the same Maṇḍala; (3) the hymns handed down by Ṛishi Kaṇva and his family, which were constituted into Maṇḍala viii; (4) the assignment of all the Soma hymns to one place, Maṇḍala ix, to prevent their being mixed up with other hymns on different subjects; and (5) miscellaneous hymns on a variety of topics brought together in Maṇḍala x, with their number (191) kept same as that of Maṇḍala i and marked by special features of language, metrical form, and contents.

In this way, the whole compilation came to include 1,028 hymns and 10,580 verses in 70,000 lines of 153,826 words. Of these 70,000 lines, 5,000 lines are found to be repetitions. This shows that the makers of later hymns were only drawing upon a common source, the large stock or floating literature of older hymns which had already been in circulation in the country.

Two Ages and Types of Literary Activity. We shall now go behind the Rigveda Saṁhitā into the fundamental question of the method and system of education responsible for the remarkable literary output it presents and also the wider cultural background to which it is related. The Saṁhitā itself indicates that we have to distinguish between two ages of literary and educational activity which were widely separated in both age and character. The first was an age of creation, of the primordial Rigveda which came into being in the original hymns as they were revealed by their so-called seers or Ṛishis. The Vedic Aryans then found it necessary for their work amidst non-Aryans (whom the Rigveda calls Dāsas, Dasyus, or Asuras and distinguishes by several other physical and cultural characteristics) that they should fix their national sacred literature reflecting their own ideals of thought and life as a means of preserving their cultural integrity as a people. Thus was called for the collection and ordering into one body the floating mass of hymns, the composition of the *Rigveda Saṁhitā*. But the production of this work was not a mere religious

PLATE II

No. 1.—Images in stone of seven Vedic Ṛishis..

(1) Vasishṭha (5) Atri
(2) Viśvāmitra (6) Kaṇva
(3) Vāmadeva (7) Gṛitsamada
(4) Bharadvāja

Local tradition names the Ṛishis somewhat differently in the following order: (1) Vasishṭha, (2) Atri, (3) Durvāsā, (4) Bharadvāja, (5) Viśvāmitra, (6) Jāmadagni, and (7) Parāśara. [Found at Rajgir Kund, old Rājagṛiha, in Bihar.]

No. 2.—Another isolated image of a Ṛishi [Rajgir].

[*Facing p. 22*

and political necessity. It was also a literary necessity. It was necessary to preserve the sacred text from the changes to which it was liable in the process of its oral transmission from teacher to pupil and from generation to generation. It was liable to be corrupted, modified, and modernized in the course of such transmission. It had to confront the compelling consequences of a natural linguistic evolution which would make the retention of its pristine purity and original, archaic form more and more difficult, unless it was fixed and standardized. The time soon arrived, as pointed out by Wilson [*Rv. Saṁhitā*, I, xix], " when the antiquity of the hymns, the obscurity of their style, the peculiarities of their language, and the number to which they had multiplied, with the corresponding difficulties of recollecting and teaching them, brought home the supreme necessity of rescuing the dispersed and obsolete Sūktas or Vedic verses from the risk of oblivion and moulding them into some consistent and permanent shape."

Thus the age of the origination of Rigvedic hymns was primarily an age of creation which was necessarily followed by an age of criticism and compilation, of conservation and codification.

Yāska's Comment. These two ages are very well described by the earliest Vedic commentator, Yāska, in his *Nirukta* (*c.* 700 B.C.). There were, firstly, according to Yāska, " the Ṛishis who were the direct seers of Truth. They were followed by the lesser men (*avara*) who were incapable of that direct perception of Truth, which comes from *tapas* or *yoga*, concentrated contemplation. These may be called *Śrutarshis*. The seers, therefore, had to impart their Truths (Mantras) to these inferior people, the Śrutarshis, by means of oral instruction (*Upadeśa*). The Śrutarshis are so called because they became Ṛishis or Seers only through *Śruti* or hearing the truths imparted to them as pupils by their teachers, the Ṛishis (Upadeśena = Śishyopādhyāyikayā vṛittyā) who imparted to them both the words of the Mantras and also their meaning (*granthataḥ arthataścha*). They could not attain to the truths directly by their own powers of *tapas* and insight. These, again, in view of later generations further deteriorating in their powers, as means of facilitating the study of the Veda, compiled the Veda (i.e. the Saṁhitā text), the Nighaṇṭu and the Vedāṅgas [i, 20 with Durga's commentary]." In commenting on Rigveda, x, 98, Yāska defines *Ṛishi* as the person " who is possessed of vision, to whom, practising austerities (tapasyamānaṁ), the self-born Brahma manifested himself" (i.e. "the Vedas revealed their meaning without their study by him", as explained by Durga).

'Tapas' as Method of Learning. Thus the Rigveda Saṁhitā, the form in which the Rigveda is accessible to us, reveals two stages and types of education, and educational method. The matter of the Rigveda, its hymns, are the outcome of the first, the method of the pursuit of the highest Truth and of its direct realization on the basis of ascetic austerities and concentrated contemplation called *Tapas* which marks out the Ṛishi or "Seer". In Rigveda, x, 109, 4, there is mention of seven Ṛishis absorbed in *tapas* (*tapase ye nisheduḥ*) and of the power of *tapas* in raising the lowest to the highest. In x, 154, 2, there is a reference to Tapas of various forms as explained by Sāyaṇa, such as (1) austerities like *kṛichchhra-chāndrāyaṇa* whereby the ascetic is rendered invincible (*anādhṛishya*), (2) sacrifices whereby he attains heaven, and (3) penances of the highest order (*mahat*), e.g. Rājasūya, Aśvamedha, forms of *Upāsanā* (*yoga*) like *Hiraṇyagarbha*. X, 167, 1 refers to the conquest of heaven by tapas (*tapaḥ paritapya ajayaḥ*). X, 136, 2 refers to *Munis* (defined by Sāyaṇa as "the seers of Truths beyond the senses") "clad in barks of trees (*piśaṅgā vasate malā*), shining with the glow of *tapas*, attaining godly forms, and the free movement of the wind". The next verse describes the *Munis* as living in a state of divine afflatus, ecstasy, or supreme bliss (*Unmaditāḥ*) (due to renunciation of the world, as explained by Sāyaṇa), with their souls detached from their bodies which alone are seen by mortals, which means that they lived in a state of *Samādhi*, living in the spirit and not in the body. They are also described as assuming the subtle body resembling the wind (*Vātān ā tasthimā*). The following verse further extols the Muni who becomes all-pervading like the Vāyu, and all-seeing like the sun (by worshipping them), and the equal of the gods (*deva-sakhā*) by *sukṛiti*, pious deeds. The next verse again describes him as attaining to the forms of the gods (Vāyu or Sūrya) or as one whom the gods themselves wish to attain (*deveshita*). I, 55, 4 refers to Ṛishis dwelling in forests (*vane*) in contemplation of God. There is a reference to *Sannyāsa* in viii, 24, 26. The Ṛishi of x, 117 is named Bhikshu and the whole *Sūkta* is in praise of charity and gifts to one who begs in need. X, 190, 1 rises to the culminating conception of *Ṛita* and *Satya*, truth of thought and speech, as the fruit of *Tapas*, and of the whole creation

PLATE III

Ṛishi Atri and his Wife (Anasūyā)

[Facing p. 24

resulting from the *Tapas* of Brahma. Besides *Ṛishi* and *Muni*, other terms indicative of highest spiritual advancement are *Vipra*, *Vedhas*, and *Kavi* [i, 127, 1; 129, 1, 11; 162, 7; iv, 26, 1]. In i, 164, 45, there is a reference to seers called *Manīshīs* who comprehend *Vāk* or speech in all its four forms, Brahma as *Śabda*, as *Yogīs*. Of these four forms of *Vāk*, three are stated to be hidden in *guhā*, i.e. in the depths of the soul, while the fourth is manifest as the speech of man, *laukikī bhāshā*. This states the philosophical position that what is rendered explicit in the creation is only a fragment of the Implicit or the Absolute. A similar idea is contained in the 41st verse describing *Śabda* as Brahma unfolding itself in gradual stages as *Ekapadī*, *Dvipadī*, *Chatushpadī*, *Ashṭapadī*, and *Navapadī* and ultimately pervading the Universe as *Sahasrākshara*. Only a part of this *Śabda* or *Vāk* is captured by man for his use as *laukikī* or *vyavahārikī bhāshā*. This verse also indicates that Vedic Sanskrit grew out of spoken language or popular vernacular Sanskrit.

Method of Learning according to capacity. When highest knowledge was thus built up by these Seers and revealed and stored up in the hymns, there were necessarily evolved the methods by which such knowledge could be acquired, conserved, and transmitted to posterity. Thus every Ṛishi was a teacher who would start by imparting to his son the texts of the knowledge he had personally acquired and such texts would be the special property of his family. Each such family of Ṛishis was thus functioning like a Vedic school admitting pupils for instruction in the literature or texts in its possession. The relations between teacher and taught are well established in the Rigveda. The methods of education naturally varied with the capacities of pupils. Self-realization by means of *tapas* would be for the few.

As the Rigveda itself points out [x, 71, 7]: "Class-mates [*sakhās*, i.e. those of same knowledge (samānaṁ khyānaṁ jñānaṁ yeshām) or who have studied the same *Śāstras* (samāneshu śāstreshu kṛitaśramāḥ)] may have equality in the possession of their senses like the eye and the ear, but betray inequality in respect of their power or speed of mind [asamāḥ manojabeshu = manasāṁ prajaveshu (Yāska, *Nirukta*, i, 9); or the knowledge or wisdom which is attained by the mind (Sāyaṇa)]. Some are like tanks which reach up to the mouth ('unfathomable, i.e. minds whose depths cannot be reached', as explained by Durgāchārya), others up to the breast only (i.e. 'shallow, whose bottom is within sight '). Some are fit for bath, others are to be seen only." As Sāyaṇa points out, this passage refers to three grades of students, the *Mahāprajñān*, the *Madhyamaprajñān*, and the *Alpaprajñān*, students of high, medium, and low ability. In i, 112, 2 there is a reference to pupils (dhiyaḥ) approaching for instruction the teacher called *Vachas*, i.e. one possessed of sound learning. In i, 8, 6 there is a mention of *Vipras* being instructed in supreme knowledge as its seekers (dhiyāyavaḥ).

Recitation of Texts. The subject of learning being these hymns, the first step was naturally to impart the sacred texts to the learners by recitation. The air was resounding with the recitation of the hymns in the Vedic Schools. It was such a familiar phenomenon that it has inspired even a hymn of the Rigveda [vii, 103] which compares the monotonous recitation of words by the teacher and his pupils [yadeshāmanyo anyasya vāchaṁ śāktasyeva (i.e. śaktimataḥ śikshakasya) vadati (anuvadati, repeats) śikshamāṇaḥ (i.e. śishyaḥ)] to the croaking of frogs exhilarated by the approach of rain.

As has been already indicated, recitation of Vedic texts was cultivated as an art by itself. A great value and potency attached to the very sounds of the letters and syllables by which the sacred words were uttered. Such utterance was not left to mere natural or individual pronunciation but was artificially regulated by metres. The passage i, 164, 24 is very explicit on this point. It states how by conjunction of letters (strictly syllables) are produced seven metres [akshareṇa mimate (i.e. nirmāṇaṁ kurvati, makes) *sapta vāṇīḥ* (i.e. sapta chhandāṁsi). These seven metres are known as (1) Gāyatrī, (2) Paṁkti, (3) Anushṭup, (4) Bṛihatī, (5) Virāj, (6) Trishṭup, and (7) Jagatī, being made up respectively of 24, 28, 32, 36, 40, 44, and 48 syllables. The same verse defines a *Chhandas* or *Metre* being made of *Pādas* or divisions and *Pādas* of *Aksharas*. Thus, as explained by Sāyaṇa, the Akshara is the root of the division of the Rigveda into *Varga*, *Sūkta* or *Anuvāka* [Aksharaiḥ pādāḥ parimīyaṁte | Parimitaiḥ pādaiśchhaṁdāṁsi | Tataḥ pādānāṁ chhaṁdasāmaksharaṁ mūlamiti | Tathā Ṛigvargasūktānuvākādīnāṁ chāksharaṁ mūlamiti akshara-praśaṁsā |].

Every day the student started recitation of Vedic Texts 'before birds announced break of day' [*purā-vayabhyaḥ* = pakshyādīnāṁ vāgvadanāraṁbhāt prāk (*Taitti. Saṁ.*, vi, 4, 3, 1)]. The *Aitareya Āraṇyaka* [viii] mentions three ways of reciting the Rigveda, *pratṛiṇṇa*, *nirbhuja*, and *ubhayamantareṇa*, by taking the words singly, as in *Pada* Pāṭha, or in pairs, or in the continuous way, as in *Krama* Pāṭha. There was also already a sound system of phonology. The *Aitareya* and *Śatapatha Brāhmaṇas* distinguish sounds as *ghosha*, *ūshman*, and *vyañjana*, dental and lingual *n*, and the sibilants *ś*, *sh*, and *s*, and also discuss rules of *sandhi* or combinations of words. The Upanishads [e.g. *Taitti*, i, 1, 2] recognize phonological factors like *mātrā* (quantity), *bala* (accent), *sāma* (euphony), and *santāna* (relations of letters).

Evolution of Alphabets. Thus Rigvedic education as its first step comprised the transmission of the sacred texts by the teacher to his pupil by means of regulated recitation and prescribed pronunciation which the pupil had to listen to as *Śruti* and commit to memory. Sāyaṇa [Introduction to Rigveda Commentary] quotes the saying that "the text of the Veda is to be learnt by the method of learning it from the lips of the teacher and not from a MS. (Adhyanavidhiścha likhitapāṭhādivyāvṛitya adhyayanasaṁskṛitatvaṁ svādhyāyasya gamayati)." Because this education was thus primarily a matter of hearing and memorizing by repetition of its texts in the manner of the croaking of frogs, it has been assumed that there was not evolved at that time the art of writing as an aid to memory and education, nor the conception of letters or alphabets as the basis of writing. It has been believed that *Śruti* or Veda should appeal to the ear and not to the eye, and was not to be reduced to writing. No doubt, the tradition of Vedic learning was to impart it to the ear as a secret doctrine to be contemplated and realized, and not to make it a visible object available to all, irrespective of their fitness, and this tradition has been continuing through the ages, even up to the time of Kumārila Bhaṭṭa (of about eighth century A.D.) who has described the writing of Veda as sacrilege. The *Mahābhārata* condemns to hell those who write the Veda (*Vedānām lekhakāḥ*). Kumārila [*Tantra Vārttika*, i, 3, p. 86] states: "That knowledge of the truth is worthless which has been acquired from the Veda, if the Veda has not been rightly comprehended or if it has been learnt from writing." But even if such learning had passed from ear to ear directly under a system of oral tradition and banned the individual method of its transmission through writing, it does not follow that a knowledge of writing or alphabets for use even for secular purposes was not then achieved. Several passages of the Rigveda have been already cited, showing definite reference to *Akshara* as the root [1] of the Rigveda as explained by Sāyaṇa (who considers this verse as intended to be *akshara-praśaṁsā*, stressing the importance of the letter to learning); or i, 164, 41 which refers to the expansion of speech in a thousand (i.e. innumerable) letters (sahasrākshara). Again, the verses vi, 53, 5–8 use metaphors which can only be suggested by the practice of writing then in vogue. In the first two, there is mentioned an instrument of writing called *ārā* which Sāyaṇa explains as a fine-pointed iron-tipped pencil or stylo (*sūkshmalohāgro daṇḍaḥ*) with which hard hearts may be pierced (paritṛindhi = parividhya). In the third verse, the god is asked to "write" (*ārikha* = *ālikha*) on such hard hearts, while in the fourth, the instrument of such "writing" is called again *ārā* or goad. Again, the verse x, 13, 3 refers to the utterance of *Akshara* (known as *Oṁkāra* or Praṇava) required in the performance of sacrifice, while x, 71, 4 refers to both the methods of learning, by *seeing* and *hearing* (Uta tvaḥ paśyanna dadarśa vāchaṁ uta tvaḥ śṛiṇvanna śṛiṇoti enām). Again, a *Yajus* is defined to be "that in which the number of letters is not fixed" by any metre (aniyata-aksharāvasāno yajuḥ). The evolution of letters, alphabets, and writing may, therefore, be assumed as an aid to learning for an age which had paid so much attention to the purity and rules of pronunciation of the texts taught.

Efficacy of Recitation. Thus the first step in Rigvedic education was correct recitation of the texts taught. Jaimini in his *Pūrva-Mīmāṁsā* Sūtra [i, 2, 32], has the dictum *Vākyaniyamāt* which means that the words of Mantras must be recited in the prescribed manner to achieve their full fruit. Mere recitation of the texts in the order prescribed has a spiritual efficacy of its own (Nīyatapāṭhakramasāphalyāya uchhāraṇameva mantraprayojanam). Thus the recitation of Mantras has a mystical use by itself. A spiritual benefit flows from the observance of the strict order of words of the text recited. This tradition of the independent efficacy of the mere word and correct recitation of the Vedic text has found expression in the extreme position stated in a later text [*Pāṇini-śikshā*, v, 52] to the effect that the slightest lapse in uttering a letter or a word of the Vedic mantra on the part of a teacher will spell utter ruin and

[1] According to Max Müller [*Ancient Sanskrit Literature*, p. 507], "*akshara* which is used for letter and syllable means what is indestructible, radical, or an element."

disaster to him [Mantro hīnaḥ svarato varṇato vā mithyāprayukto na tamarthamāha | sa vāgvajro yajamānaṁ hinasti yathendraśatruḥ svaratoparādhāt]. But Jaimini does not deny that Mantras do convey their meaning with reference to the particular sacrifice with which they are connected and states that this function of a Mantra, though a non-spiritual one, should not be left out of account (Sāyaṇa's Introduction to Rigveda].

In this connection Jaimini has an interesting Sūtra [i, 2, 48], *Vidyāvachana-Saṁyogāt*, on which he instances the case of a girl *Pūrṇikā* husking in a room where a student was reciting the words of the Veda without reference to their meaning. Here was thus the operation of husking going on to the accompaniment of the relevant Mantra being recited by a Vedic pupil without any connection between the two operations (Veda-Vidyāgrahaṇa -kāle arthasya yadavachanaṁ tadyajñasaṁyogādupapadyate | Na hi Pūrṇikāyā avaghāto yajñasaṁyuktaḥ | Nāpi māṇavako yajñamanutishṭhati).

Understanding Texts more important than their Recitation. Rigvedic Education, however, was not confined to mere learning by rote the sacred texts. The contemplation and comprehension of their meaning was considered as more important and vital to education than their mere mechanical recitation and correct pronunciation. The Rigveda has several significant passages condemning and holding up to ridicule those whose knowledge is confined only to the repetition of its words without insight into their inner meaning, and emphasizing the supreme need of realizing that meaning by constant and concentrated contemplation.

VII, 103, 1 refers to a period of such contemplation in silence, during which Brāhmaṇas achieve enlightenment. Then they burst out into speech (vāchaṁ avādishuḥ) like frogs quickened into activity by the clouds (parjanya) after a year's slumber. It is this enlightenment which fits the pupils (called *Brāhmaṇā* vratachāriṇaḥ explained by Yāska in his *Nirukta*, ix, 6 as *abruvāṇāḥ*, i.e. maintaining the vow of silence) for the task of expounding the sacred texts.

Again: "I ask: what is the source of *Vāk*, Speech? Speech or Word is God (Brahmāyaṁ Vāchaḥ). That Word I cannot comprehend so long as I am bound by the senses and objectivity (niṇyaḥ sannaddho manasā charāmi). It is the dawn of *Ṛita* (Supreme Knowledge) which alone leads to the comprehension of *Vāk*" [I, 164, 37].

" He who does not realize the ultimate Truth behind the *Ṛik* and *Akshara* (word and letter) in which rest all gods—what will he do by merely reciting and repeating the Ṛiks ? " The Rigveda is *aparā* (inferior) *vidyā* to one who does not go behind its words to their inner meaning (Sāyaṇa) [i, 164, 35, 37, 38]. " (Among pupils studying together) there may be one who merely sees the Word but does not see its meaning. Another hears It, but does not hear It fully. [He only utters the sound without understanding its sense (*dhvanimātramevochchārayati*)]. But to a worthy pupil It fully unfolds Itself like the devoted wife appearing in her best dress before her husband (who can ' see ' and ' hear ' her fully) " [x, 71, 4 as interpreted by Yāska in his *Nirukta*, i, 19, and Durgāchārya].

" He who is established (sthira) and has drunk in supreme knowledge (pītaṁ = pītārthaṁ) is counted as indispensable in the assemblies of the learned seeking such knowledge [sakhye = vidushāṁ saṁsadi, the assembly of those associated with knowledge (Sāyaṇa)]. But he [who merely recites the Word without a knowledge of Its hidden meaning (kevalapāṭhakaḥ)] wanders about with a barren cow (adhenvā), not yielding the milk of desires [nāsmai kāmān dugdhe vāgdohyān (Yāska)], with the mere symbol (māyayā) of speech [vākpratirūpayā (Yāska)], having only grasped its sound (śuśruvān) without its sense, like the tree not bearing any fruit or flower (Vāchaṁ . . . aphalāmapushpām) [ib. 5]. Sāyaṇa (in his Introduction to Rigveda Commentary) takes the *pushpa* (flower) of this passage to mean knowledge of *Dharma* as expounded in the *pūrva-kāṇḍa* of Rigveda and *phalam* (fruit) as knowledge of *Parabrahma* expounded in its *uttara-kāṇḍa*, and further explains that, as fruit brings us satisfaction, knowledge of Brahma fulfils all our desires. He also explains the other simile to mean that the *Veda* or *Vāk*, as a cow, does not yield its milk of Dharma and Brahma-jñāna, Religion and Supreme Knowledge, to one who is given only to recitation of its texts (pāṭhamātraparaṁ prati).

" Those who are devoid of the meaning of the sacred word (arvāk) and of wisdom (aprajajñayaḥ) are fit only, by their cultivation of the imperfect popular speech (*Vāchaṁ abhipadya pāpayā = Vāchaṁ laukikīṁ prāpya tayā pāpayā pāpakāriṇyā vāchā*), to turn the plough or the loom (as peasants or weavers) [ib. 9].

Yāska [*Nirukta*, i, 18] further condemns the mere reciter

of the Veda who does not attend to its meaning by quoting the following two passages as translated below from *Saṁhitopanishad Brāhmaṇa* :

" He is only the bearer of a burden, the blockhead (*sthāṇurayaṁ bhārahāraḥ*), who having studied the Veda does not understand its meaning (like an ass, *sthāṇu*, carrying a load of sandal-wood whose weight it feels without enjoying its fragrance).

" Learning without understanding is called cramming (nigadeṇaiva śabdyate) ; like dry wood on ashes, which can never blaze."

Sāyaṇa [ib.] explains this passage to mean that " the words of the Veda which are received from the teacher without their meaning, and are repeatedly recited as texts, do not kindle, and reveal their inner essence " (yad vedavākyamāchāryāt gṛihītaṁ arthajñānarahitaṁ pāṭharūpeṇaiva punaḥ punaruchchāryate tat kadāchidapi na jvalati svārthaṁ na prakāśayati).

Sāyaṇa cites an opinion that the mere reciter of Vedic Text (kevalapāṭhaka) only does not lose his caste and does not count as a Vrātya. But he is incapable of performing any sacrifice or winning its fruit such as attainment of heaven.

Other passages throw further light on the aims and methods of education in those days. These are mostly to be found in Sūkta 71 of Maṇḍala X.

Evolution of Vedic Sanskrit out of Secular and Spoken Tongue : Work of Learned Assemblies (' Brāhmaṇa-Saṁghas '). X, 71, 1 is itself addressed to the deity named Parabrahmajñāna. The *Bṛihaddevatā* states that " by this hymn Ṛishi Bṛihaspati invokes God as Supreme Knowledge and Blazing Radiance (sujyotiḥ) whom one can attain only through *yoga* ". This hymn points out that the first step in education is the cultivation of popular speech, the spoken tongue or vernacular, by which individual objects are named (nāmadheyaṁ dadhānāḥ). But this language which deals with the objective cannot give expression to what is beyond the objective, the supreme (*śreshṭhaṁ*) and perfect (*aripraṁ*) knowledge hidden in the depths of the heart (*nihitaṁ guhāyāṁ*). That knowledge comes to light by the grace of Sarasvatī through Vedic learning (premnā āvirbhavati).

This passage is also construed to mean that Vedic Sanskrit has grown out of the spoken tongue of the times as its root. This point is discussed by Yāska [*Nirukta*, i, 16]. Yāska quotes the objection of Kautsa that the Vedas have no meaning (anarthakā hi mantrāḥ) and answers it by pointing out that the Vedas *have* meaning because their words are identical with those of the spoken language (*arthavantaḥ śabdasāmānyāt : samāna eva hi śabdo loke mantreshu cha*, " identical are the words of both spoken tongue and the Vedas, e.g. the word *go* which occurs in both "). Words which have meaning in the *bhāshā* (spoken language) must have meaning when used in the Veda. Yāska [xi, 29] also cites Rigveda, viii, 100, 11, which refers to *Vāk* as articulate and understandable in man and inarticulate in the lower creatures" [Tāṁ vāchaṁ viśvarūpāḥ paśavo vadanti—vyaktavāchāścha (manushyādayaḥ) avyaktavāchāścha (gavādayaḥ) (Yāska and Durga's Comment)].

Another passage, x, 71, 2, indicates the method of evolution of Vedic Sanskrit out of the spoken tongue. The learned (dhīrāḥ) meet in their Assemblies where through their discussions language is refined into the language of the Veda, like groats through a sieve (saktumiva tita unā punanto). As fellow-seekers of Truth they are bound by a community of ideas (sakhāyaḥ sakhyāni jānate) to which they give expression in that language, the source of the highest good and knowledge (eshāṁ vāchi bhadrā lakshmīḥ nihitā). Thus this verse indicates that Vedic Sanskrit was hammered into shape out of spoken Sanskrit of the times at learned Assemblies where it was the vehicle of philosophical discussions. It may also be inferred that the Ṛishis used to gather in these Assemblies to disclose and discuss the hymns they had themselves individually attained as the result of their *tapas* and meditation. And this hymn, according to Sāyaṇa, thus refers to what may be called the Conference method, the method of discussion, for the development of this Vedic Language and Knowledge (Vidyat-Saṁghe vāchamakrata).

The next hymn, x, 71, 3, makes the interesting addition that these learned Assemblies were held at the sacrifices. These sacrifices are therefore described as " opening up the way which the wise (dhīrāḥ = viditārthāḥ) tread for finding speech " [yajñena vāchaḥ padavīyam (= mārgaṁ) āyan]. The Ṛishis were the repository of such speech and they revealed it at such sacrificial gatherings of the learned. Their words thus acquired were then collected and spread far and wide. The system adumbrated here is that at the Yājña-Assembly each Ṛishi brought forward his individual contributions to Speech and then these were collected and codified. Then this standardized speech was suitable for being imparted to pupils and was thus propagated through the whole country. The different processes in this method of learning and evolution of Vedic Sanskrit are indicated by the words *āyan*, *avindan*, *ābhṛitya*, and *adadhuḥ*, i.e. " attainment, mastery, collection, and propagation" of the words which were originally confined to the Ṛishis and brought to light by them at the learned assemblies accompanying the sacrifices. The *manner* of learning and teaching this Vedic Sanskrit is also indicated here. It was to be learnt in the form of metres. " Seven metres embraced Vedic speech and made it articulate, like warbling birds flocking to the speechless tree." I, 164, 24 even defines *Arka* or *Mantra* as being in the form of *Chhanda*, and *Sāma* as being made of such *Arka*. The Vedic hymns being thus revealed in the form of metres, it was easier to commit them to memory in that form than if they were in the form of prose. A metre can be more easily memorized than mere individual words in prose.

The next verse, x, 71, 6, repeats the relationship of Vedic to spoken or secular speech. Without Vedic speech and knowledge, all speech is useless (*alakam*) and does not lead to any good in life. The student of the Veda is extolled as its friend (*sachi*) who conserves it by teaching it, and the Veda as the friend (*sakhā*) of man whom it benefits by awakening his insight into truth. The person forsaking these (*tityāja*) misses the way of performing any religious ceremonies or good deeds (*nahi praveda sukṛitasya panthām*). Not knowing Vāk or Vedic speech, " what he hears, he hears amiss ; he cannot ascertain the path of virtue."

The verse x, 71, 8 again mentions the learned Assemblies (*Brāhmaṇa-Saṁghas*, as Sāyaṇa calls them) where Brāhmāṇas united in fellowship in Vedic learning (*sakhāyaḥ*) come together (*saṁyajante*) for the purpose of developing further the truths they had realized in their hearts (*hṛidā tashṭeshu*) or reached by their minds (*manaso javeshu*). They exclude from such assemblies the ignorant who cannot follow their discussions, so that they may have full freedom to wander about unhampered in the realm of speculation (*vicharanti*) and work out their own conclusions (yathākāmaṁ vedārtheshu viniśchayārthaṁ pravartante).

The next verse condemns those who are not fit to move with the Brāhmāṇas (brāhmaṇaiḥ saha na charanti) as being fit only for the plough or the loom, as already stated.

The superiority of Vedic knowledge to all other knowledge is very well expounded by Sāyaṇa (in his Introduction to Rigveda Commentary). "The Veda expounds the truth about gods, *dharma*, and Para-brahma. He who does not recite the Veda but only utters secular speech full of slander, falsehood, and strife cannot have access to true knowledge (Sakaladevatānāṁ Dharmasya Parabrahmatattvasya cha pratipādakaṁ Vedaṁ anuchchārya para-nindā-anṛita-kalahādi-hetuṁ laukikīṁ vārtāṁ sarvatra uchchārayataḥ spashṭa eva vāchi bhāgyābhāvaḥ)." Again: "Let not a man study too many words, for that is waste of words (vācho viglāpanaṁ hi tat). Such a person may listen to poems and plays which lead to no good because they do not know of the right path (yadyapyasau kāvya-nāṭakaṁ śriṇoti tathāpi nirarthakameva tachchhravaṇam)." He also quotes the verse: "The *dvija* who, without studying the Veda, applies his labour otherwise degrades himself to the status of a Śūdra even in this life with his posterity." Sāyaṇa quotes *Purushārthānuśāsana* which points out that the subject-matter of the Veda is twofold: (1) *Dharma* and (2) *Brahma*.

Summary: Highest Knowledge attained by 'Tapas' and revealed in Veda. To sum up: the system of education adumbrated in the Rigveda thus concerns only the acquisition of the highest knowledge and saving wisdom and not of ordinary secular knowledge or intermediate truths for purposes of worldly life. The method of this learning is determined by its aims and contents. The method of attaining the knowledge of the Absolute, "Parabrahma-jñāna," is not the method of acquiring a knowledge of the objective sciences, arts, and crafts. It is the method of realization of the highest and ultimate truths called *Ṛita* and *Satya* by inhibition of the senses and the objective, the method of meditation (*dhyāna*; cf. *dhīrāḥ*) sustained by a life of austerities, *tapas* or *yoga*. In a Rigvedic passage, *Tapas* is described in a literal sense as "the most radiant effulgence coming from the highest knowledge" (*tapaḥ uttamaṁ mahaḥ*), where the worshipper prays for the highest gift, the *light* of supreme knowledge or *Tapas* (the opposite of *Tamas* or ignorance). The vehicle, the language, of this learning, too, is different. The Rigveda describes the popular speech, the spoken tongue, as "imperfect" ("*pāpayā vāchā*") and "untrue" (*alaka*), because it cannot serve as the vehicle of Truth or supreme knowledge. It is the language of the field and factory, a fragment of Vāk or Brahma (*Brahmāyaṁ Vāchaḥ*), which cannot express the truths hidden in the depths of the soul (*nihitam guhāyām*). These highest and ultimate truths are revealed by a different language, the language of the Vedic Mantras evolved out of the popular speech by means of *tapas* and *yoga* by learned men called *Vipras*, *Vedhasas*, or *Kavis*, *Ṛishis*, *Manīshīs*, and *Munis* who live in a state of trance (*unmaditāḥ*) and in the subtle body (*vātān ā tasthimā*) and are worshipped of the gods themselves (*deveshita*). We are further told that these learned men and seers developed Vedic knowledge and speech by their discussions at Assemblies or Conferences meeting on occasions of Sacrifices where this knowledge and speech were " attained, mastered, collected, and distributed ". It was these Academies and learned Assemblies which were thus the agencies for the formulation and propagation of Vedic learning. The members of these bodies are described as *Sakhās*, i.e. those who come together by the bond of fellowship in learning, and are fellow-seekers after Truth.

Mastery of Vedic Texts and their Meaning. When Vedic learning was thus brought to light and fixed in a comprehensible form by its great Masters, the creative geniuses of the Ṛishis, the need arose, and suitable methods were evolved, for conserving and teaching that learning. The first method naturally was that of committing to memory the texts of that learning as they were recited by the teacher. There was a method by which the teacher recited the texts. He recited them in the form of Metres, pronouncing every letter, syllable, and word according to standardized rules regulating accents and stresses and giving scope to the vibrations of every sound so as to call up its inner sense. The young pupils had thus to repeat the letters, syllables, and words of the text, as they fell from the lips of their teachers, with mechanical precision and monotony, like a body of " croaking frogs."

But the mastery of texts was only the first step of learning. The more important step was the mastery of their meaning. As Sāyaṇa puts it by quoting the dictum " Dṛishṭau prāpti-saṁskārau ", the mastery of texts, *akshara-prāpti*, is followed by *artha-bodha*, perception of their meaning [Introduction to Rigveda Commentary]. This mastery of meaning was a difficult and prolonged process, the result of severe thinking and concentration. Pupils had to undergo a proper discipline for it and are described as being *vratachāriṇaḥ*, practising vows. Yāska, as we have seen, interprets this *vrata* or vow as a vow of silence and meditation by which the pupil has to realize the truths imparted to him through the texts. The period of this silent meditation is likened to the season of slumber into which frogs fall till they are quickened into activity by the rains. The pupils also, after achieving enlightenment, burst into activity in discourses (*vācham avādishuḥ*) as teachers. Yāska describes this process of learning by stating that the Ṛishis by their *upadeśa* or teaching lead their pupils to become *Śrutarshis*. They become "seers" of Truth after "hearing" it from the lips of their teacher.

The ideal of this learning was thus the realization of Truth, and not the mere mastery or recitation of its texts. Many passages are cited above from the Rigveda on this point. One of these, a most typical one [i, 164, 39], may be cited again for its profound and emphatic exhortation: "Ṛicho akshare parame vyoman yasmin devā adhi viśve nisheduḥ | yastanna veda kiṁ ṛichā karishyati"; on which Sāyaṇa forcefully comments: "vedanasādhanena Vedena vedyamaviditvā kiṁ sādhayati iti." The Veda is useless learning to him who only recites its *Ṛik* without comprehending its meaning. The Veda is *aparā vidyā*, worthless learning, to him who does not achieve the knowledge of the *Paramātman*, the Reality behind its *Ṛiks* and *Aksharas*, its verses and letters! To such an ignoramus, even the words of the Veda, so big with meaning, are "barren of any fruit or flower" (*vācham aphalāmapushpām*)! The mere crammer of Vedic texts (the *Kevalapāṭhaka* as Yāska calls him), is condemned as *arvāk* by the Rigveda.

'Vratachāri.' We thus get in the Rigveda glimpses of an educational system which comprised the small domestic school run by a teacher who admitted to his instruction resident pupils. These had to live with him under prescribed disciplines or vows as *vratachārīs*. An actual reference to a Brahmachārī and Upanayana ceremony is found in Rigveda,* x, 109, 5 and also iii, 8, 4 and 5. In the primary stage, the school would be marked by noisy recitation and repetition of texts by pupils in the manner of frogs lustily croaking after rain. In the second stage, the collective work of the pupils in a class ceased, and their individual work commenced. Each had to achieve for himself by his individual effort, by his own *tapas* and *yoga*, by his silent and solitary meditation, the truth of the texts which had been taught to the class in common. Very soon differences manifested themselves among these *sakhās* or class-fellows in regard to their mental powers, like tanks of varying depths [x, 71, 7]. The more unfit were weeded out, sent back to the plough or the loom [x, 71, 9]. They were not meant for higher learning and spiritual life. The Rigveda tells of a family where the son was pursuing religious learning (as a *kāru*, "maker of hymns"), the father a practising physician (*bhishak*), and the mother a grinder of corn (*upala-prakshiṇī*) [ix, 112, 3], and of differences of mental aptitudes and occupations among men (*nā nānaṁ dhiyo vratāni janānām*) such as those of the carpenter (*takshā*), physician (*bhishak*), or learned man (*brahmā = brāhmaṇa*) [ib. 1].

'Saṁghas.' The highest stage of education is represented in what are called the *Brāhmaṇa-Saṁghas*, the Assemblies or Academies where the more successful students flocked together, as we have seen, for the advancement of knowledge by discussing their respective contributions to it. Thus the conference method for the promotion and diffusion of learning, the method of discussion in seminars and academies, was first evolved in India, as evidenced by the Rigveda.

Yāska on Vedic Education. Yāska in his *Nirukta* [ii, 3, 4] throws further light on the methods of this Vedic education. He states that the teacher "must avoid teaching (*na nirvrūyāt*) isolated syllables (*eka-padāni*) and should not also teach pupils ignorant of grammar (*avaiyākaraṇāya*) nor any one who is not a regular pupil living with his teacher (*na anupasannāya*). He should teach only such a regular pupil as well as one who is specially qualified by his intelligence (*medhāvī*) or asceticism (*tapasvī*) or thirst for knowledge". This passage shows that Grammar as a subject was evolved as early as the Veda itself, when a knowledge of Grammar was necessary for understanding the text (*padas*) of the Veda. It also shows that the essential of Vedic education was the system of pupils living with their teacher under formal studentship or *brahmacharya*.

Yāska further cites an old text which describes the Vedic educational system thus :—

" Verily, the goddess of Learning (*Vidyā*) approached Brāhmaṇa, saying : 'Protect me : I am thy treasure. Do not expound Me to the following unworthy persons,—him who is jealous (*asūyaka*), who is wanting in simplicity and straightforwardness (*anṛiju*), or who is devoid of self-control (*ayata*). Then alone shall I be potent.'

" 'One should honour him as a father and mother and should never bear ill-will towards the teacher who pierces the ears with (the needle of) Truth without causing pain but giving the boon of immortality by knowledge.

" ' Like teachers who do not feed (but send away) unworthy pupils who do not honour them, though possessed of the highest learning (*viprāḥ* = medhāvinaḥ gṛihītavidyāḥ), by their word, thought, and deed, knowledge also will shun them.

" ' In order to protect thy treasure, O Brāhmaṇa ! expound Me to him alone whom thou knowest to be pure (*śuchi*), devoid of passion (*apramatta*), possessed of intelligence, and established in *brahmacharya*, the discipline of religious studentship (*brahmacharyopapanna*).' "

These verses thus point to the following features of the educational system, viz. (1) the home of the teacher as the school where the pupil had to live with him and was fed by him ; (2) the admission of a pupil on the ground of his moral fitness ; (3) the discipline of *brahmacharya* imposed upon the pupil ; (4) the duty of the pupil to honour the teacher like his father or mother by word, thought, and deed ; and (5) the expulsion of a pupil who does not observe this duty.

Achievements of Rigvedic Education : (a) In Language. We may now comment upon the language and literature that were developed in these Rigvedic Schools as the result of their system of education. The language of the Rigvedic hymns represents the earliest stage of a literary language of which the latest stage is classical Sanskrit as stereotyped and standardized in the epoch-making work, the grammar of Pāṇini who had flourished earlier than 500 B.C. But Rigvedic Sanskrit does not show itself to be a language that is growing. Its entire grammatical mechanism is perfected ; every tense, mood, every number and person of the verb, is fixed, and all the terminations of the cases are firmly established, pointing to the later and more advanced inflectional stage in the life-history of a language. The Rigvedic Sanskrit exhibits a much greater variety of forms than Classical Sanskrit, more numerous case-forms in both nominal and pronominal inflexion, more participles and gerunds, greater evolution of verbal forms as illustrated in the frequent use of the subjunctive, and the infinitive, which alone has twelve forms, of which only one has survived in Classical Sanskrit, and, lastly, a greater elaboration in respect of accent. The Rigvedic accent, like ancient Greek, is of the nature of music, depending upon the pitch of the voice, unlike the stress accent of later Sanskrit, which depends on quantity. Thus Rigvedic Sanskrit is of great importance to Comparative Philology. Indeed, as Bunsen truly remarks, " even these earliest specimens of Vedic poetry belong to the modern history of the human race." Macdonell also states: "Considering their great antiquity, the hymns are composed with a remarkable degree of metrical skill and command of language." He also points out that the Rigveda contains "much genuine poetry", "much beautiful and noble imagery", shows a "remarkably high average of literary merit", and considers that "its most poetical hymns, those addressed to Ushas, are equal, if not superior, in beauty to the religious lyrics of any other literature."

(b) In Thought. It will be out of place in this work to deal with the level of philosophical thought and religious attainments registered in the Rigveda. It may suffice only to cite a few references in this connection. The Rigveda [1] presents the worship of thirty-three gods divided into three groups of eleven each and assigned to the three planes of the Universe, the celestial (*dyuloka*), the intermediate (*antariksha*), and the terrestrial (*bhūrloka*). The celestial gods are Dyaus, Varuṇa, Mitra, Sūrya, Savitṛi, Pūshan, the two Aśvins, and the goddesses Ushas and Rātrī. The gods of the intermediary sphere are Indra, Apāṁ napāt (the lightning form of Agni which lurks in the cloud), Rudra, the Maruts, Vāyu, Parjanya, and Āpas. The terrestrial deities are Pṛithivī, Agni, and Soma.

Each of these three planes or spheres of existence has a presiding deity, Savitā (or Sūrya) for the celestial, Indra or Vāyu for the intermediate, and Agni for the terrestrial sphere. The thirty-three gods are mentioned in the *Śatapatha Brāhmaṇa* [iv, 5, 7, 2] as comprising 8 Vasus, 11 Rudras, 12 Ādityas, together with *Dyau* and *Pṛithivī*. The *eight* Vasus are Dhava, Dhruva, Soma, Āpa, Anila, Anala, Pratyūsha, and Prabhāsa. The *twelve* Ādityas are Dhātṛi, Mitra, Aryaman, Rudra, Varuṇa, Sūrya, Bhaga, Vivasvat, Pūshan, Savitṛi, Tvashṭṛi, and Vishṇu. The *eleven* Rudras are thus named in the *Mahābhārata* [i, 121]: Mṛigavyādha, Sarpa, Nirṛiti, Ajaikapāda, Ahirbudhnya, Pinākin, Dahana, Īśvara, Kapālin, Sthāṇu, and Bhaga. In Rigveda, iii, 9, 9, these thirty-three gods are multiplied into 3,339 gods by way of enumeration of the glories of the original thirty-three, as explained by Sāyaṇa. But the fundamental religious conception in the Rigveda is that of the One emerging as Three, Thirty-three, and in any number to denote the innumerable aspects of the Supreme Being. Each of these gods is worshipped as the Highest

[1] *Rv.*, i, 34, 11; 45, 2; 139, 11; iii, 6, 9; viii, 28, 1; 30, 2; 35, 3; ix, 92, 4.

God, the creator and sustainer of the Universe by turns. Each god is an Aspect of the One God. That is why Yāska in his *Nirukta* emphatically points out that 'the three chief deities aforesaid, viz. Agni of Pṛithivī, Vāyu or Indra of *Antariksha*, and Sūrya of *Dyu* have each many names suggested by their greatness or diversity of functions (*karma-pṛithaktvād*), just as the names of *Hotṛi*, *Adhvaryu*, *Brahmā*, and *Udgāṭri* are applied to one and the same person (according to the particular offices which he happens to be fulfilling)' [vii, 5]. He also states [vii, 4]: "Owing to the greatness of the Deity, the one Soul is celebrated as if It were many. The different gods are separate members of the one Soul. . . Soul is a god's essence (Māhābhāgyād devatāyāḥ ekaḥ ātmā bahudhā stūyate | Ekasya Ātmanaḥ anye devāḥ pratyaṅgāni bhavanti. . . Ātmā sarvaṁ devasya)."

Thus these different deities are worshipped as manifestations of the Supreme Deity in the different aspects and forces of Creation and Nature, aiding in the conception of the Cosmic Power and Order which rule and sustain the Universe, *Viśva*. The hymns addressed to these various deities should not make one miss the fundamental note running through the entire Rigveda, uttering forth the profound conception of the One in the Many. Sayāṇa also explains in his Introduction to the Rigveda already cited that "although Indra and other gods are invoked in many Vedic texts, it is the supreme God who is invoked in the form of Indra and other gods (Yadyapīndrādayastatra tatra hūyante tathāpi Parameśvarasyaīvendrādirūpeṇāvasthānādavirodhaḥ). The Vājasaneyins have the text: 'Some say, Worship This or worship That; but the whole Creation is His, in whom all the gods are comprehended.'" We may also cite the *Bṛihad-Devatā*, i, 70–4: "The Seers in their Mantras say that the Devatās have a common source; they are called by different names according to the spheres in which they are established. . . Because of the magnitude of the Oversoul, a diversity of names is given . . . according to the distribution of their spheres."

We shall now assemble some conspicuous texts which affirm the identity of the One and the Many.

Indeed, in one particular hymn, the Deity it invokes is "directly described as *Parabrahma-Jnāna*, the knowledge of the Absolute [x, 71, 1, already cited]. Sūkta 164 of Maṇḍala I contains many hymns giving striking expressions to the conception of the Absolute. Hymn 46 clearly states that the Vipras (sages) call the One that is by many names such as Indra, Mitra, Varuṇa, Agni, Yama, or Mātariśvāna (Ekaṁ Sat Viprāḥ bahudhā vadanti). Hymn 4 refers to *Ātmā*, the Absolute, as *anasthā*, formless, manifesting Itself in creation (*jāyamānam*) by taking form (*asthi*) and to the unfathomable mystery of creation (Kaḥ dadarśa prathamaṃ jāyamānam) by which Spirit (*Ātmā*) transforms Itself into Matter (*bhūmi*), Life (*asuḥ* = *prāṇaḥ*) and Blood (*asṛik* = *śoṇitam*). Where is the teacher to explain this mystery or the pupil to receive his teaching (Kaḥ vidvāṁsaṁ upagāt prashṭuṁ etat) ? This mystery is not known even to the gods (devānāṁ enā nihitā padāni) [ib. 5]. The next verse states : " I, who am ignorant, shall ask the wise (*Kavi*) to explain the mystery of the One (*Ekaṁ*) who always is, without birth (*Aja* = *gamanaśīla-janma-rahita*)." Another verse refers to the eternally revolving wheel of Time (chakraṁ ajaraṁ vi vāvṛita) [ib. 14]. Another asks : " Whence has sprung the illumined mysterious Mind (*devaṁ manaḥ kutaḥ adhi prajātam*) [18] ? Verse 20 describes the *Jīvātmā* and *Paramātmā*, the soul in the individual, and the Oversoul, as two birds of the same feather (suparṇā sayujā sakhāyā) flocking together on the same tree, one of which eats its sweet fruits but the other only looks on (tayoḥ anyaḥ pippalaṁ svādu atti anaśnan anyaḥ abhi chākaśīti) ! Verse 30 refers to immortal soul (amartyaḥ jīvaḥ) surviving its perishable body (mṛitasya). Verse 34 inquires after the limits of the Earth and the centre of the universe and the supreme source of Speech (Vāchaḥ paramaṁ vyoma). The next verse states that Brahma is the supreme source of speech (Brahmāyaṁ Vāchaḥ paramaṁ vyoma). The next verse points out that one does not realize his oneness with creation as he wanders about in attachment to objects of sense (saṁnaddhaḥ niṇyaḥ manasā charāmi). When supreme knowledge (*Ṛita*) dawns on him, then alone does he realize the meaning of *Vāk*, the ultimate Word or Ātman. Verse 38 states how the Mortal and the Immortal springing from the same ultimate source (amartyaḥ martyenā sayoniḥ) are linked together while people recognize one and not the other. Difficult of realization is the knowledge of the Ātman, as Sāyaṇa remarks. The culminating conception of the Absolute is reached in Verse 39 already cited where it is boldly stated that the Veda itself will avail little to one who does not know its subject, the Supreme Being, in Whom rest the whole creation and the gods, but he who knows Him becomes merged in Him. In i, 22, 20 this Supreme Being is called *Vishṇu* who pervades the universe,

Whose omnipresence is constantly perceived by the *Sūris* or Yogīs, as the unobstructed expanse of the sky is seen by the eyes opened in all directions (divīva chakshurātatam). I, 24, 1 introduces Him as *Aditi* in the sense of universal Nature or the whole Earth (*sakala-jagat* or *akhaṇḍa-nīyā pṛithivī*, as explained by Sāyaṇa). In i, 89, 10 this *Aditi* is described as manifesting Himself in all that is created (*jātaḥ*), in heaven and sky, father, mother, offspring, all the gods, all varieties of being, as the supreme creative principle (janitvam).[1] In i, 90, 6–8 He is conceived of as the Supreme Good, *Madhu*, who brings bliss through the blowing wind, the flowing rivers, the medicinal plants, night and day, the earth and its habitations, sky, forests, sun, and cattle. In ii, 26, 3 Brahmanaspati is described as the parent of the gods. In iii, 55, 11 the different gods are described as springing from a common source (*Hiraṇyagarbha*). III, 62, 10, conveys the famous Gāyatrī Mantram which states: "We meditate (*dhīmahi*) on the Supreme (*Vareṇya*) Essence (*Bharga*) of the One who, self-illumined (*deva*), illumines all, who recreates all, from Whom all proceed, to Whom all return (*Savitā*), Who inspires all our thoughts and deeds (*dhiyo yo naḥ prachodayāt*)." III, 54, 8 contains the significant expression *Viśvam ekam*, pointing to the noble conception of the "integral multiplicity". IV, 26 opens with a description of the One as *Manu* (sarvasya *Mantā* Prajāpati, 'Prajāpati, Lord of created beings, who moves the minds of all'), as *Sūrya*, i.e. One who inspires all as their ultimate source (*sarvasya prerakaḥ savitā*); as *Vipra* (Sage) and *Ṛishi* (Seer); Whom one sees everywhere; the Giver of Space (*bhūmi*), of Rain (*vṛishṭi*), of sounding waters (*vāvaśānāḥ apaḥ*); Whose Purpose the gods follow. IV, 40, 5 is the famous *Haṁsavatī Ṛik* which describes the One as all-pervading (*Haṁsaḥ* from *haṁti* = *gati*), Who penetrates into the mind of man, and the external universe like the Sun, both the subjective and the objective worlds; who fills the realm above (*antariksha*) as *Vasu* or *Vāyu*, Wind (sarvasya vāsayitā Vasuḥ Vāyuḥ); Who is worshipped as Agni at

[1] Max Müller thus comments on this hymn: "*Aditi*, an ancient god or goddess, is in reality the earliest name invented to express the Infinite; not the Infinite as the result of a long process of abstract reasoning, but the visible Infinite, visible by the naked eye, the endless expanse, beyond the earth, beyond the clouds, beyond the sky" [*Rv.*, Translation, i, 230]. Yāska, in his *Nirukta*, describes *Aditi* as the mother of gods [iv, 22]. *Aditi* is contrasted with *Diti* in Rigveda, v, 62, 8, where Sāyāṇa explains *Aditi* as representing the Earth as an invisible whole (*akhaṇḍanīyāṁ bhūmim*) and *Diti* the separate creatures (*khaṇḍitām prajādikām*). His supreme position as deliverer from sin is indicated in several other passages [i, 162, 22; ii, 24, 14; iv, 12, 4; v, 82, 6; vii, 87, 7; 93, 7; x, 12, 8].

every altar (*Vedisat atithiḥ* sarvadā pūjyaḥ Agniḥ) and dwells in every household (duroṇasat) (as fire for cooking food) (duroṇaṁ gṛihanāma tatra pākādisādhanatvena sthitaḥ laukikāgniḥ); who dwells in Man (*nṛi-sat*) (in the form of his consciousness, *nṛishu chaitanya-rūpeṇa sīdati iti nṛi-sat*); who dwells in the solar orb (*Vara-sat*, i.e. *vare varaṇīye maṇḍale* sīdatīti Ādityaḥ); who manifests Himself as *Ṛita* or Truth; as *Vāyu* pervading the sky (*vyoma-sat*); who originates in water (*avjā*) (in the forms of aquatic life), in rocks (*adri-jā*), in light-waves (*go-jā* goshu raśmishu jātaḥ), in Truth (*Ṛita-jā*) (as being visible to all) (Ṛitaṁ Satyaṁ sarvair dṛiśyatvena satya-jātaḥ) and is himself *Ṛita* or Truth, free and all-pervading (Satyaṁ avādhyaṁ sarvādhishṭhānaṁ brahma-tatvam). The deity of iv, 42 declares: "I am Almighty (*Kshatriya*), Ruler of the Universe (*viśvāyaḥ*), Ruler of two worlds (Earth and Heaven), Whom the gods worship as well as men! I am supreme Ruler, Varuṇa, to execute Whose purposes the gods acquire necessary powers! I am limitless in width and depth (*mahitvā urvī gabhīre*)! I am possessed of supreme knowledge (*vidvān*)! I am the Creator (*Tashṭvā*) who breathes life into all creatures (viśvā bhuvanāni tasmairayaṁ saṁprairayam) and sustains the Universe (*rodasī dhārayam*)! I am the author of all actions (*ahaṁ tā viśvā chakaram*) whose power is invincible!" VI, 9 is a hymn in praise of the Supreme God called Vaiśvānara, the Light of the Universe dispelling its darkness, whose appearance causes the rotation of Day and Night by recognized turn (vivartete vedyābhiḥ); Who alone knows what happened before creation and emergence of Time and its sequence; Who alone comprehends the warp and the woof in the fabric of creation (*tantu* and *otu*), i.e. the subtle and the gross in creation (*purusha* and *prakṛiti*), the Immortal (*amṛitasya gopā*) manifesting Itself in mortal forms (*avaḥ charan*) (the Paramātmā appearing as Jīvātmā) till He (as *Guru*, by *Vidyā*) leads back mortals (as *Śishyas*, pupils) to Immortality, and Omniscience (*paśyan*). As Sāyaṇa explains: "He, manifesting Himself, manifests all: His Light illumines all" (Tameva bhātamanubhāti sarvaṁ Tasya bhāsā sarvamidaṁ vibhāti). 'Vaiśvānara is the first Hotā, of Whose Sacrifice the Creation is the outcome. Man must worship Him (Ayaṁ Hotā prathamaḥ paśyata, i.e. bhajata). Himself Immortal, He dwells in every mortal body as *Jyoti*, its soul (or *Jāṭhara*, fire of hunger) (*Idaṁ Jyotiḥ Amṛitaṁ martyeshu*). Himself Motionless (*Dhruvaḥ*), All-pervading (*Ānishattaḥ*), and Immortal (*Amartyaḥ*), He assumes mortal body (*tanu*) and subjects Himself to birth (*jajñe*) and growth (vardhamānaḥ). He, the Motionless (*Dhruvam*), yet swifter than Thought (*manaḥ javishṭham*), dwells in (*nihitam*) every moving (mortal) being (*patayatsu antaḥ*) as the *Jyoti* or Brahma (or *Chaitanya*) to Whom, as showing the way to supreme knowledge (driśaye darśanārthaṁ jñānena hi sarvam jānaṁti), all the senses, together with mind and consciousness (Viśve devāḥ sarvāṇi indriyāṇi samanasaḥ saketāḥ), refer as to the ultimate Cause of Creation (Ekaṁ Kratuṁ abhiviyanti sādhu samyak). His infinite attributes and forms my ears and eyes seek! The light (of intelligence) that is in my heart (*Idaṁ Jyotiḥ āhitaṁ hṛidaye yat*) is seeking to see Him! So also is my mind, that is attached to objects, seeking Him! Little can the finite know the Infinite (Kimu nū manishye)!' VI, 47, 18 describes the Absolute (Paramātmā) as Indra who by His power of *Māyā* assumes different forms and manifests Himself in different bodies (Rūpaṁ rūpaṁ pratirūpo babhūva. . . Indraḥ māyābhiḥ pururūpaḥ īyate); the counter-form of every form, "the single form that is the form of many different things." In vii, 59, 12 Ṛishi Vasishṭha says: "We worship Tryaṁbaka (the parent of the *three* deities, Brahmā, Vishṇu, and Rudra, the god of gods, Mahādeva, as explained by Sāyaṇa), subtle and all-pervading like fragrance (*sugandhiṁ*), the seed of the universe (pushṭi-vardhanaṁ = jagat-bījam). May I (by His grace) be liberated from (the bondage of) Death (mṛityor-mukshīya) like the Urvāruka (Karkatī) fruit from the tree but *not* from immortality (māmṛitāt) (i.e. May I attain immortality by conquering death!)" VIII, 58, 1–2, again, refers to the One whom the Ṛitviks conceive of in many forms (*Yaṁ ṛitvijaḥ bahudhā kalpayaṁtaḥ*) in their meditations (*sachetasaḥ*), the silent Presence at sacrifice (*Yaḥ anūchānaḥ brāhmaṇaḥ* yuktaḥ), of Whom the sacrificer has but little knowledge (*kā svit tatra yajamānasya saṁvit*). That One, as *Agni*, is effulgent in many forms (eka evāgniḥ *bahudhā samiddha*); as *Sūrya* sways the whole universe (*ekaḥ Suryaḥ viśvamanu prabhūtaḥ*); as Ushā, reveals all this. The One became the Many (*Ekaṁ vā idaṁ vi babhūva sarvaṁ*). VIII, 30, 1 states: "Among you, O gods, there is none that is small, none that is young: you all are great indeed." This is the famous hymn to "all the gods", *Viśve Devas*, representing a more advanced stage of thought than the hymns to individual deities. But even where an individual god is worshipped, he is as good as all the gods to the worshipper. As Max Müller points out [*Ancient Sanskrit Literature*, p. 533], "it would be easy to find, in the numerous hymns of the Veda, passages in which every single god is represented as supreme and absolute." It will thus appear that the apparently different deities like Varuṇa, Indra, Sūrya, Savitṛi, and Agni are severally described in strains more suitable to the supreme deity than to subaltern divinities exercising a limited dominion, as having created and as sustaining heaven and earth, and as rulers of the Universe. The notion of particular gods is expanded and all divine attributes are ascribed to particular objects of worship, while the names like Viśvakarmā or Prajāpati do not designate any limited function but the more general and abstract notion of divine power operating in the creation and maintenance of the universe.

These various expressions of the conception of the Absolute reach their culmination in the tenth Maṇḍala of the Rigveda in its hymns, 72, 81, 82, 90, and 129, as the fundamental feature of Rigvedic thought and religion. Hymn 72 describes at length the process of creation, the existent springing from the non-existent (*asataḥ sadajāyata*), the Earth from Uttānapada and the regions from the Earth, Daksha from Aditi, and after Aditi, the gods. It was Brahmaṇaspati who blew forth these births like a blacksmith (*etā saṁ karmāraḥ ivādhamat*). Hymn 81 calls the Absolute as the *Hotā*, the Sacrificer, Who sacrifices the whole Creation to Himself at its dissolution and remains as the sole Father of all, *Pitā*. Then He the One again wishing (*āśishā*) to be Many, wishing (ichchhamānaḥ) for the enjoyment of creation (*draviṇaṁ*), concealed his primary Self (*prathamachchhat*) and created Objects into which He penetrated (*avarān āviveśa*). He the *Viśvakarmā*, Architect of the Universe, the *Ṛishi* All-knowing, the *Viśvachakshāḥ*, All-seeing, created Earth (*Bhūmi*) and Heaven (*Dyā*) by His own power (*mahinā*) out of His own Self, the Self-supporting and Self-sufficient, for Whom there was no external support (*adhishṭhānam*) or material (*ārambhaṇaṁ*). He, the self-shining One (*Devaḥ Etaḥ*), produced Earth and Heaven and comprehended the universe within the reach of His Eye or Mouth, Arm or Foot (*Viśvataśchakshuḥ Viśvatomukho Viśvatobāhuḥ Viśvataspāt*). What was the Wood and what the Tree out of which He, the Divine Carpenter, fashioned out (nishṭatakshuḥ) the Heaven and Earth? Let the wise who have achieved mastery of their minds (*Manīshiṇaḥ*) ask themselves in their own minds by what support He holds the universe (*yat adhi-atishṭhat bhuvanāni dhārayan*). Hymn 82 continues the theme. He, the Creator of the eye, i.e. the objective world (*chakshushaḥ Pitā*), engendered the water (*ghṛitam*) and then the two, Earth and Heaven, floating, undistinguished, on the waters. *Viśvakarmā* is mighty of mind, *Vimanā*, and power, *Vihāyā*, the Maker, *Dhātā*, the Dispenser, *Vidhātā*, the Most High (*Paramā*), and All-seeing, *San-dṛik*, the One beyond all (*Paraḥ Ekam*). He is our Father, *Pitā*, Progenitor, *Janitā*, Dispenser, *Vidhātā*, to Whom are known the different planes of existence (*dhāmāni*), all the worlds (*bhuvanāni*) and the whole universe (*Viśvāḥ*), the One who bears the names of many gods (*Yaḥ Devānāṁ nāmadhāḥ Eka eva*). He, the Unborn, *Aja*, resting upon the waters of His own creation, upon Whose navel was placed the Brahmāṇḍa or Germ of the Universe: Him ye cannot perceive, Him Who is of a different stuff from ye, sentient beings, possessed of individual consciousness (*anyat yushmākaṁ antaraṁ babhūva*). Him they cannot perceive, wrapped up as they are in mists of ignorance (*nīhāreṇa prāvṛitāḥ*), giving themselves up to vain pursuits (*jalpa*), pleasures of life in this world (*asu-tṛipaḥ*) and prayers for gain in the next world (*ukthaśasaścharanti*).

X, 90 is the famous *Purusha-Sūkta*, hymn to the *Ādi-Purusha*, Primordial Being, Who comprehends all that is, has been, or will be (*Purusha eva idaṁ sarvaṁ yat bhūtaṁ yat cha bhāvyam*), the Lord of Immortals and Mortals who grow by food (*amṛitatvasya iśānaḥ yat annena atirohati*). But His greatness is not confined to these limits of Time, past, present, or future: He is beyond Time (*Etāvān Asya mahimā ataḥ jyāyān cha Pūrushaḥ*). For all created beings of past, present, and future only represent a fourth part of Him. The larger part of Him is not manifest in mortal creation (*pādaḥ Asya viśvā bhūtāni tṛipāt Asya Amṛitam*). Three-fourths of Him are in the transcendent state (i.e. above *māyā*) (*tṛipāt ūrdhvaḥ udait Purushaḥ*). A fourth of Him (*māyā-pāda*) came into being in this world again after its dissolution (*pādaḥ Asya iha abhavat punaḥ*). Then He, becoming Many (*Vishvaṁ*), penetrated into all forms, animate and inanimate (*vyakrāmatsāśanānaśane*). Thus the process of creation is that out of the *Ādi-purusha* arises the *Virāṭ-deha* (*vividhāni rājaṁte vastūni atra iti Virāṭ*, "in Whom are contained all objects") the universe-body (*brahmāṇḍa-deha*). Seizing that body, He vitalized it and created out of it the *Virāṭ-purusha* (*Tasmāt virāṭ ajāyata Virājaḥ adhi-Purushaḥ*). The *Virāṭ-purusha*, thus born, extended itself (*atyarichyata* = *atiriktaḥ abhūt*) beyond its original form, covering space on all sides (*bhūmiṁ viśvataḥ vṛitvā*) and also the inner world (*daśāṅgulam*) (i.e. both macrocosm and microcosm), He of countless heads, eyes, and feet (as representing all created beings) (*Sahasraśīrshā Purushaḥ Sahasrākshaḥ Sahasra-pāt*). He then offered up in sacrifice His body as the material out of which the Universe was made, its creatures of the air, of the forests, of the villages, horses and cattle, goats and sheep, the four classes of mankind, Brāhmaṇa, Rājanya, Vaiśya, and Śūdra, the sun and moon, air and sky, the earth and its four quarters, the different worlds, and also supreme knowledge as revealed in Vedic hymns, chants, metres, and sacrificial formulae and the gods themselves.

X, 121 gives another expression to the same conception of a Supreme Creator of the universe. In the beginning, there existed Hiraṇyagarbha, or Prajāpati, 'Lord of all creatures,' who is so called because 'He is all Intelligence up to the depth of His being (*garbha*), the Intelligence that is luminous and illumining like hiraṇya or gold' [Hiraṇyaṁ atyujjvalaṁ prakāśaśīlaṁ jñānaṁ tad garbhaḥ antaḥsāro yasya sa *Hiraṇyagarbhaḥ* (*Bhāsvatī-Pātañjalabhāshya*)].' As soon as He was born, He became the sole Lord of all created beings (*bhūtasya jātaḥ patireka āsīt*). He established in their proper places this earth and heaven above : He, the Oversoul, the giver of individual souls, of life and strength, whose shadow is Immortality : who has conquered Death (*Ātmadā Baladā Yasya Chhāyā Amṛitaṁ Yasya Mṛītyuḥ*) : He who is the sole lord of all animated beings, who are endowed with Motion and Sight, by His innate greatness (*yaḥ prāṇataḥ nimishitaḥ mahitvā Ekaḥ it Rājā jagataḥ babhūva*) : By whose power the Sun rises and shines (*yatrādhi Sūra udito vibhāti*) : He who is the One Supreme Source of Life of all the gods (*Devānāṁ asuḥ Ekaḥ*) : Who arose out of the primeval Agni (Fire) generated in the primeval waters in which the universe was engulfed : the God of gods (*yaḥ Deveshu adhidevaḥ Ekaḥ āsīt*) : the Creator of the Earth (*Janitā Pṛithivyāḥ*), Heaven, and the life-giving waters (*yaḥ cha āpaḥ chaṁdrā bṛihatīḥ jajāna*) : Who holds the universe by His cosmic laws (*Satya-dharmā*) : Prajāpati who alone can comprehend this infinite creation and none else : To that mysterious Deity do we offer worship (*Kasmai Devāya havishā vidhema*).'

Lastly, we come to what is called the Hymn of Creation, x, 129. "Then (*tadānīm*, at the beginning, before creation) there was neither Being (Sat) nor non-Being (*A-Sat*).[1] There

[1] *Sat* is what has form ; *asat* is formless. Or *sat* may stand for the eternally existing, the *Prakṛiti* of Sāṁkhya, and *A-Sat* for the Void of *Śūnyavādīs*.

was neither the atmosphere nor the heavens beyond.[1] What did it contain? Where? And under whose direction? Were there waters, and the bottomless deep? [1]

"There was then neither Death nor Immortality (*Na Mrityuḥ āsīt Amṛitaṁ na tarhi*). The Day was not divided from the Night. Only the One breathed, in Himself, without extraneous breath (*ānīt avātaṁ svadhayā Tat Ekam*). Apart from Him, there was nothing (*Tasmāt ha anyāt na paraḥ kiṁ chanaāsa*).[1]

"In the beginning (*agre*) was Darkness covered by Darkness. Nothing was distinguishable: all was Water (*apraketaṁ salilaṁ sarvam*). All was immersed in a formless void (*tuchchhya*). Out of that void arose the One by power of *Tapas* (meditation, thought of creation).

"Then for the first time Desire came to possess Him (*Kāmaḥ Tat agre samavartata adhi*), Desire that was the first seed of the Spirit (*Manasaḥ retaḥ prathamaṁ yat āsīt*). In that Desire, the Sages (*Kavayaḥ*), pondering in their hearts, with their fully developed mental faculties (*manīshā*), found out the link between Being and non-Being.

"The desire for creating was followed by the emergence of two Agents or principles of creation, the male or active, *Retodhā*, and the female or passive, *Mahimānaḥ*, whose operations, like the

[1] Yāska interprets *raja* as *lokas* or different planes of existence. The term may also imply the *paramāṇu*, the ultimate particle or nucleus of the world, as supposed by *Naiyāyikas*. In that case, *Vyoma* will stand for *ākāśa* as the first creation.

[1] Max Muller [*Ancient Sanskrit Literature*, p. 560], says: "'That One,' the poet says, 'breathed, and lived; it enjoyed more than mere existence; yet its life was not dependent on anything else, as our life depends on the air which we breathe. It breathed breathless.' Language blushes at such expressions, but her blush is a blush of triumph.

"After this the poet plunges into imagery. 'Darkness there was, and all at first was veiled in gloom profound, as ocean without light.' No one has ever found a truer expression of the Infinite, breathing and heaving within Itself, than the ocean in a dark night, without a star, without a torch. . . .

"But now this one had to be represented as growing—as entering into reality. . . As yet, the real world existed only as a germ, hidden in a husky shell; now the poet represents the one substance as borne into life by its own innate heat (*tapas*). . . The question how there was generation in nature was still unanswered. A miracle had to be appealed to: this miracle was Love. 'Then first came Love upon it,' the poet says; a power which arises from the unsearchable depths of our nature, making us feel our own incompleteness, and drawing us, half-conscious, half-unconscious, towards that far-off and desired something, through which alone our life seems to become a reality. . . The One Being which the poet had postulated was neither self-sufficient nor dead: a desire fell upon it—a spring of life, manifested in growth of every kind. . . Here, then, the poet imagines he has discovered the secret of creation—the transition of the nothing into the something—the change of the abstract into the concrete. Love was to him the beginning of real reality, and he appeals to the wise of old, who discovered in Love 'the bond between created things and uncreated'"

Sun's rays (Raśmi), spread in all directions, oblique, above, and below. Creation was the work of *Svadhā* and *Prayati*, Śiva and Śakti, the One manifesting Itself in the Many, the Formless choosing to appear in forms.

" Who knoweth and who can explain whence it originated, whence came this Creation ? Even the gods came after this Creation. Who then knows whence it has arisen ?

" Whence this Creation has arisen ; whether He created it or did not create it : He, the Most High, who oversees all, He only knows, or He may not " ! [1]

(*c*) **In growth of Scientific Spirit.** The Rigveda shows a lively sense of the immutable laws governing Creation. Its best expression is iii, 56, 1, a hymn of Viśvāmitra. It means that the *Vratas* or Cosmic Laws which are at the root of creation (*prathamā*, primeval) operate for all time and regularly (*dhruvāṇi*), which

[1] Commenting on these hymns Maurice Maeterlinck says : " Is it possible to find, in our human annals, words more majestic, more full of solemn anguish, more august in tone, more devout, more terrible ? Where, from the depths of an agnosticism, which thousands of years have augmented, can we point to a wider horizon ? At the very outset, it surpasses all that has been said, and goes farther than we shall even dare to go. No spectacle could be more absorbing than this struggle of our forefathers of five to ten thousand years ago with the Unknowable, the unknowable nature of the Causeless Cause of all Causes. But of this Cause, or this God, we should never have known anything, had He remained self-absorbed, had He never manifested Himself. ' Thus it is,' say the *Laws of Manu*, ' that, by an alternation of awakening and repose, the immutable Being causes all this assemblage of creatures, mobile and immobile, eternally to return to life and to die ' [i, 57]. He exhales Himself, or expels His breath, and Spirit descends into Matter, which is only a visible form of Spirit ; and throughout the Universe innumerable worlds are born, multiply, and evolve. He Himself inhales, indrawing His breath, and Matter enters into Spirit, which is but an invisible form of Matter : and the worlds disappear, without perishing, to reintegrate the Eternal Cause, and emerge once more upon the awakening of Brahma—that is, thousands of millions of years later ; to enter into Him again when He sleeps once more, after thousands of millions of years ; and so it has been and ever shall be, through all eternity, without beginning, without cessation, without end.

" ' When this world had emerged from the darkness,' says the *Bhāgavata Purāṇam*, ' the subtle elementary principle produced the vegetable seed which first of all gave life to the plants. From the plants, life passed into the fantastic creatures which were born of the slime in the waters ; then, through a series of different shapes and animals, it came to Man.' ' They passed in succession by way of the plants, the worms, the insects, the serpents, the tortoises, cattle, and the wild animals—such is the lower stage,' says Manu again, who adds : ' Creatures acquired the qualities of those that preceded them, so that the farther down its position in the series, the greater its qualities ' [i, 20].

" Have we not here the whole of Darwinian evolution confirmed by geology and foreseen at least 6,000 years ago ? On the other hand, is this not the theory of Ākāśa which we more clumsily call the ether, the sole source of all substances, to which our science is returning ? It is true that the recent theories of Einstein deny ether, supposing that radiant energy—visible light, for example—is propagated independently through a space that is an *absolute* void. But the scientific ether is not precisely the Hindu *Ākāśa* which is much more subtle and immaterial, being a sort of spiritual element or divine energy, space uncreated, imperishable, and infinite " [*The Great Secret*, pp. 28, 30, 35, 36, 43, 44].

can never be violated (*adruhā*) by anyone however clever (*māyinaḥ* = *śilpinaḥ*) or wise (*dhīrāḥ*). There is no one in earth or heaven who by his power of supreme knowledge (*Vedyābhiḥ*) can set them at naught. " They cannot bend like mountains " (*parvatāḥ na niname*). The same note is struck in x, 85, 1, stating how the earth remains suspended (*Uttabhita*) in space by the force of *Satya*, and Āditya by the force of *Ṛita* ; and also in x, 190, 1 : " *Ṛitaṁ cha satyaṁ cha abhīddhvāt tapasodhyajāyata* " ; " the whole creation is the outcome of *Ṛita* and *Satya* which are again the emanations of the Light of supreme knowledge called the *tapas* of Brahma." Similarly, vii, 42, 1 refers to the creative agencies called *Vratas*, while i, 25, 8 describes the Creator as *Dhṛitavrata*, the Upholder of Cosmic Order. The Creator is also called in another hymn *Ṛita-dhāman*. We also find such expressions as " guardians of *ṛita* " (*gopā ṛitasya*) and " practisers of *ṛita* ' (*ṛitāyu*). No religion has given a more scientific definition of God so early in man's history. In ii, 12, 5 the atheist unable to find in the Laws of Nature, which are apparently self-sufficient, their Maker, is asked to find Him in those Laws themselves. For *Ṛita* is God : " Ritamekākshararṁ Brahma."

The scientific spirit of the Rigveda is also evident in some amount of free thinking to which it refers at places. Dissenters are denounced as " haters of the Veda " (*Brahma-dvish*), " maligners of gods " (*deva-nid*), or " men devoid of any doctrine ', (*apavrata*). Evidence of heterodoxy and scepticism is also indicated in two hymns, ii, 12 and x, 82. The first is at pains to prove the supremacy of Indra, which is questioned, and the second holds up to ridicule the votaries of the Veda described as " selfish prattling priests plying their business in self-delusion ".

Kshatriyas as Ṛishis. What is known as the caste-system is known to the Rigveda, but it was not known to it in all the rigidity and elaboration marking it in later times. Though its Ṛishis or " Seers " were generally Brahmins, it was not exclusively so. Supreme knowledge was not confined to caste and did not go by birth but by inner worth achieved by *tapas*, as already seen. The Rigveda Saṁhitā preserves the names of several Ṛishis who were kings or kshatriyas. For instance, *Rv*. i, 100 in its 17th verse mentions five kings as Ṛishis, of whom Ambarīsha is also the Ṛishi of ix, 98. Trasadasyu is the royal Ṛishi of iv, 42 and also of v, 27, along with Tryaruṇa and Aśvamedha. Purumilha and Ajamilha are the royal Ṛishis of iv, 43 and 44. VI, 15 has as its Ṛishi King Vītahavya ; x, 9, Sindhudvīpa, son of Ambarīsha ;

x, 75, Sindhukshit; x, 133, the famous King Sudās; x, 134, Māndhātā; x, 179, Śibi as well as Pratardana (King of Kāśī) and Vasumanas, and x, 148 Pṛithi Vairya.

Women as Ṛishis. Women were then admitted to full religious rites and consequently to complete educational facilities. The wife was a regular participator in the sacrificial offerings of the husband [*Rv.* i, 122, 2; 131, 3; iii, 53, 4–6; v, 43, 15; viii, 31, 5; x, 86, 10; etc.]. Women-sages were called *Ṛishikās* and *Brahmavādinīs.* The Rigveda knows of the following Ṛishikās, viz. (1) Romaśā [i, 126, 7], (2) Lopāmudrā [i, 179, 1–6], (3) Apālā [viii, 91, 1–7], (4) Kadrū [ii, 6, 8], (5) Viśvavārā [v, 28, 3], and several others mentioned in the tenth Maṇḍala, such as: (6) Ghoshā, (7) Juhū, (8) Vāgāmbhṛinī, (9) Paulomī, (10) Jaritā, (11) Śraddhā-kāmāyanī, (12) Urvaśī, (13) Śārṅgā, (14) Yamī, (15) Indrānī, (18) Sāvitrī, (19) Devajāmī, while the Sāmaveda adds the following, viz. (20) Nodhā [Pūrvārchchika, xiii, 1], (21) Ākṛishṭabhāshā, (22) Sikatānivāvarī [Uttarārchchika, i, 4], and (23) Gaupāyanā [ib., xxii, 4].

The Brahmavādinīs were the products of the educational discipline of *brahmacharya* for which women also were eligible. Rigveda v, 7, 9 refers to young maidens completing their education as brahmachāriṇīs and then gaining husbands in whom they are merged like rivers in oceans. *Rv.* iii, 55, 16 mentions unmarried learned and young daughters who should be married to learned bridegrooms. Yajurveda [viii, 1] similarly states that a daughter, who has completed her brahmacharya, should be married to one who is learned like her. The Atharvaveda [xi, 6] also refers to maidens qualifying by their *brahmacharya,* the disciplined life of studentship, for married life in the second *āśrama* (*brahmacharyeṇa kanyā yuvānaṁ vindate patim*).

A most catholic passage occurs in Yajurveda [xxvi, 2] which enjoins the imparting of Vedic knowledge to all classes, Brāhmaṇas and Rājanyas, Śūdras, Anāryas, and Chāraṇas (Vaiśyas) (not to speak of women) [*yathemāṁ vāchaṁ kalyāṇīmāvadāni janebhyaḥ Brāhmaṇa-Rājanyābhyāṁ śūdrāya chāryāya cha svāya* (one's own people) *chāraṇāya*].

Education of Non-Aryans and 'Depressed' Classes. The non-Aryans are distinguished in the Rigveda by several characteristics, physical and cultural. They are described as (1) *krishṇa-garbha,* "a dusky brood," and (2) *anāsa,* "snub-nosed," recalling the proto-Australoids, the original inhabitants of India. It was thus a difference of race and colour (Varṇa) between the Aryan and the non-Aryan. The term *Varṇa* later came to be synonymous with caste. Culturally, the non-Aryan differed deeply from the Aryan, because he (1) spoke a different language (*mṛidhravāk*, 'of hostile speech'), (2) did not follow Vedic rituals (*akarman*), or (3) Worship (*abrahman*), or (4) Ordinances (*avrata* and *anyavrata*), or (5) Deities (*adevayu*) whom he even reviled (*devapīyu*), nor (6) performed Vedic sacrifices (*ayajvan*). He was condemned as a worshipper of phallus (*Śiśnadeva*) [*Rv*. vii, 21, 5 ; x. 99, 3].

And yet all these vital differences were rapidly yielding to the process of social assimilation for which the Aryan system stood. At the beginning, the non-Aryan yielded to the Aryan, and was called a Dāsa, Dasyu, Asura, or Piśācha, to signify his political subjugation, but his mark of inferiority was being wiped out under processes of fusion through marriage and alliance. The Śūdra caste was evolved in Aryan Society to receive him. The non-Aryan began to count as an Aryan. A solemn religious recognition is given to this fact in the famous Purusha-Sūkta of the Rigveda where the Brāhmaṇa and Kshatriya, the Vaiśya and the Śūdra are described as limbs of the Creator. In the political field, in the Rigvedic Battle of Ten Kings (Dāśa-rājña), with their following of more than twenty peoples, the non-Aryan figures as the equal and ally of the Aryan, fighting for a common cause. The same equality is seen in the sphere of culture. The author of *Aitareya Brāhmaṇa*, Mahidāsa, had a Śūdra mother, while the Ṛishi, Kavasha Ailusha, was born of a Dāsī, according to that work [viii, 1]. The Rigveda also tells of five peoples who offered sacrifice to Agni [x, 45, 6] (*Janā yadagnim ayajanta pañcha*), and these " five peoples ", according to Yāska [*Nirukta*, vi, 7], included the four castes and the Nishādas. Another Rigvedic passage [ix, 66, 20] describes Agni as " the chief priest of all the races five " (Agnirṛishiḥ pavamānaḥ pāñchajanyaḥ purohitaḥ). On this *Mantra*, the significant comment of Uvaṭa and Mahidhara is that it recognizes the right of the Nishādas, equally and along with the four higher castes, to offer sacrifices [Pāñchajanyaḥ pañchajanebhyo hitaḥ chatvāro varṇā Nishādapañchamāḥ pañchajanāsteshāṃ hi yajñe adhikāraḥ asti (Uvaṭa). Again : Viprādayaśchatvāro Varṇā Nishādaścheti pañchajanāsteshāṁ yajñe adhikārāt]. Again, *Rv*. viii, 65, 23 refers to the participation in Soma-sacrifice by all these five peoples (*janeshu pañchashu*). In *Rv*. vi, 61, 12 the river Saraśvatī is mentioned as " making the five peoples flourish ". The Nishādas in all these passages indicated the non-Aryans and depressed classes of those days who must have had considerable access to Vedic learning to be able to take part in these sacrifices. We may finally cite again the following decisive Mantra of the Vājasaneyi Saṁhitā [xxvi, 2] stating that "all classes have an equal right to study the Veda": "Yathemāṁ Vāchaṁ kalyāṇīmāvadāni janebhyaḥ | Brāhmaṇa-Rājanyābhyāṁ Śūdrāya chāryāya cha svāya chāraṇāya ||

Seats of Learning. We have now to relate the Rigveda to space and locality. Unfortunately, its evidence only indicates in a general way the geographical limits within which the Ṛishis had lived, moved, and had their being, revealing or composing its truths or hymns, and playing their part in the political history of the regions concerned. There is no evidence pointing to individual or particular seats of learning. Rigvedic India is marked out by its rivers, some twenty-five of which are mentioned.

To the west of the Sindhu (Indus) were the rivers Kubhā (= "Kophen" or Kabul), Suvāstu ("of fair dwellings" = Swat), Krumu (Kurram), Gomatī ("abounding in cows" = Gomal) and Mehatnu [*Rv.* x, 75, 6; v, 53, 9; viii, 24, 30; 19, 37]. The Sindhu is mentioned many times [i, 126, 1; 94, 16; 122, 6; ii, 15, 6; iv, 30, 12; v, 53, 9; vii, 33, 3; viii, 20, 25; x, 64, 9; 75, 6.] There are also mentioned the five rivers of the Panjab: Vitastā (Jhelum), Aśiknī (Chenab), Parushṇī (Irāvatī or Rāvi), Vipās (Beas) and Śutudrī (Satlej); and, beyond these, the Sarasvatī, Gaṅgā and Yamunā [*Rv.* x, 75, 5; also Aśiknī in viii, 20, 25; Parushṇī in vii, 18, 89 and 63, 15; Śutudrī in iii, 33, 1; Vipās in iii, 33, 1–3, and iv, 30, 11; Gaṅgā in vi, 45, 31 (Gāṅgya); Yamunā in v, 52, 17 and vii, 18, 19; Sarasvatī in iii, 23, 4 (along with the Dṛishadvatī), vi, 61, 2, 13; vii, 95, 96; etc.]. One hymn [iv, 36, 18] also mentions the river *Sarayu* (in Oudh) which thus marks the easternmost limit of Rigvedic India. It will appear that, of these rivers, the Sarasvatī as well as the Sindhu is mentioned most in the hymns, showing that the easterly regions had already acquired a reputation as the home of Rigvedic learning and culture.

Pargiter has gone so far as to assert that Rigvedic learning had originated in the East and spread to the West on the ground that the rivers mentioned in the famous *Nadī-stuti* are from the east to the west, beginning with Gaṅgā, Yamunā, and Sarasvatī, in accordance with the course of migration of Rigvedic learning from east to west. Hopkins adds to this geographical evidence that of the physical or natural scenery depicted in the Rigveda. A part of the Rigveda and of its highest poetry is inspired by Ushas, the deity of Dawn, whose splendours are best seen in the western parts of the Panjab, to the west of the Indus, which are not troubled much by clouds and rainfall. But the other parts of the Rigveda tell of contrary natural phenomena, of clouds and storms, outbursts of torrential rains, thunder, and lightning, which point to the easterly region between the Sarasvatī and the Dṛishadvatī.

Some further light is thrown on the question of the localization of the Rigveda and its culture by a study of the geographical distribution of its principal peoples, each of whom was distinguished by its association with a particular Ṛishi who acted as the Purohita of its king, invoked its gods, and performed its sacrifices with the hymns of his own creation. Thus the settlement of each such people was also a seat of the learning represented by the Ṛishis moving with them. The chief Vedic settlements are mentioned as follows: (1) The *Gandhāras* (known for the wool of their good sheep); (2) the *Mūjavants* whom Zimmer locates on the south bank of the Kubhā up to its mouth in the Indus and down its east side to some extent; (3) the *Pūrus* settled on both banks of the Sarasvatī [*Rv.* vii, 95, 96]; (4) the *Turvaśas*, with the *Kaṇvas* as their priests, moving about the banks of the Parushṇī [*Rv.* vii, 18]; (5) the *Anus* on the Parushṇī [viii, 74, 15; vii, 18, 14]; (6) the *Druhyus* on the same river, with the *Bhṛigus* as their priests [i, 108, 8; vii, 18, 14; viii, 10, 5]; (7) the *Bharatas* settled in the region of the Sarasvatī, Āpayā, and Dṛishadvatī, with the *Kuśikas* as their priests [iii, 33, 11–12; 53, 9; 12, 24]. Under Ṛishi Viśvāmitra they advance to the Vipās and Śutudrī [ib.] and are defeated and rescued with the aid of Vasishṭha [vii, 8, 4; 33, 6], whence they are probably to be connected with the *Tṛitsus* whose subjects they are stated to be [vii, 33, 6, where the Bharatas are called *Tṛitsūnāṁ Viśaḥ*]; and (8) the Tṛitsus who, led by king Sudās and Ṛishi Vasishṭha, were the victors in the famous Battle of the Ten Kings and settled themselves as the paramount power in all that region between the Yamunā and the Parushṇī.

The Rigvedic hymns, with the learning and culture resulting from them, saw the light in the regions occupied by these peoples led by their respective Ṛishis, the makers of both their political and spiritual well-being.

Secular Learning. Rigvedic Education proper as described above, being purely religious and literary in its character, was for the few who were fit and eager for a dedicated life in quest of the highest truths and supreme knowledge. It was thus not meant for the many or the masses. And yet Rigvedic India did not present a one-sided development.

There must have been a considerable amount of secular non-religious education to build up its economic life. It is known for its progress in all departments of national life, economic, political, or religious, its progress in the various arts and crafts of civilized life, in Agriculture, Industry, and Trade. And this progress must have rested ultimately on the foundation of an appropriate system of technical, industrial, and commercial education, which found its outlet in a corresponding diversity of occupations. The Rigveda itself hardly furnishes any direct evidence on such education, but a glimpse of it may be found in the following hymns throwing light on the economic life of the times [ix, 112] :—

" 1. We different men have different tastes and pursuits (*dhiyo vi vratāni*). The carpenter (*Taskhā*) seeks something that is broken (*rishṭam*), the physician (*Bhishag*) a patient (*rutaṁ*), the priest (*Brahmā*) someone who will perform sacrifice (*sunvantam ichchhati*).

" 2. With dried-up faggots (*jaratībhiroshadhībhiḥ*), with birds' feathers (*parṇebhiḥ śakunānāṁ*), with stones (*aśmabhiḥ*) and fire (?) (*dyubhiḥ*), the artisan (*kārmāraḥ*) continually seeks after (*ichchhati*) a man with plenty of gold (*hiraṇyavantam*).

" 3. I am a poet (Kāruḥ ahaṁ), my father is a physician (Bhishag) and my mother (*nanā*) a grinder of corn (*Upalaprakshiṇī*).

" With our different inclinations (*nānādhiyo*), seeking gain, we run after (our respective objects) as after cattle (*Vasūyavo anugā iva tasthima*).

" 4. The draught horse (*aśvo voḷhā*) wishes for (*ichchhati*) an easy-going chariot (*sukhaṁ rathaṁ*) ; merry companions (*upamantriṇaḥ*) a laugh (*hasanām*) ; the female sex, the male ; and frogs a pond."

This hymn gives a graphic picture of the realities of life in the Rigvedic Age which was not exclusively an Age of Saints and Seers. Even the Ṛishi-head of a family could not secure that all the members of his family should tend towards ṛishi-hood. The mother of a Ṛishi happens to be an illiterate lady who behaves like a good housewife, grinding corn, while his father goes about curing persons not of their spiritual but physical ills, and that for the sake of earning his family's livelihood. Each is after material gain (*vasūyavaḥ*), an ' economic man ', even in the Rigvedic Age resounding so much with the utterance of Mantras. Society thus ridden by economic motives opened up various avenues of employment outside the religious sphere. We come across the woodwright, the metal-worker, the capitalist, wealth in cattle, draught horses, and youths given to gay life and not behaving like severe ascetics.

And in the body of the Rigveda are scattered references [1] to the diverse economic pursuits of the times betokening a diffusion of industrial education in the country. There was considerable progress in Pasture, Cattle-rearing, and Agriculture. The domesticated animals included sheep, goats, asses, and dogs used for hunting, guarding, and tracking cattle, and keeping watch at night. The draught animals were bulls, oxen, as well as horses. Cultivation was highly honoured as an occupation which distinguished the *Ārya* from the *Vrātya*. The plough was drawn by oxen in teams of 6, 8, or 12. There was use of manure (*śakan* or *karīsha*). The water for irrigation came from lakes (*hrada*), canals (*kulyā*), and wells. Water was drawn out of wells by buckets (*kośa*) tied to leather-strings (*varatrā*) pulled round a stone-pulley (*aśma-chakra*) and then emptied into broad channels for irrigation. As regards Industry or Handicrafts, the carpenter was kept busy making carts, chariots, and draught wagons (*anas*), and also artistic carved works. The blacksmith turned out utensils of metal and the goldsmith ornaments of various kinds. Tanning was known and the leatherer was in great request for supplying bowstrings, slings, thongs, reins, whips, and bags. The weaver (*Vāya*) was quite prominent, as Rigvedic India was advanced in textiles. We have already referred to the Rigvedic passage asking those not fit for the higher learning to take to the plough or the loom. The trader and money-lender were in evidence, together with Barter, Debt, Interest, and Money-economy (as shown in the mention of a gift of 100 *nishkas*). We also read of sea-borne trade carried on in boats or ships (*nau* or *plava*) propelled by oars (*nāvaṁ aritraparaṇīm*) and going to sea (*nāvaḥ samudriyaḥ*). There is a reference to a ship with 100 oars (*Śatāritrāṁ nāvam*) by which was rescued a person ship-wrecked on the main " where there is no support, no rest for foot or hand ". The standard of its material civilization is indicated in the architecture and cities of Rigvedic India. Cities or fortified places are called *Pur*. There is a reference to a hundred cities of stone (iv, 30, 20 : *Śatam aśmanmayīnāṁ purām*). These cities

[1] These are fully given in my work *Hindu Civilization* (Longmans, London, 1936).

must have been in localities bordering on hills from which stone could be quarried. Iron cities or fortifications are also mentioned (*puraḥ āyasīḥ* in *Rv.* i, 58, 8 ; ii, 20, 8 ; iv, 27, 1, etc.), as also cities with a hundred enclosures or fortifications (*śatabhujī*, *Rv.* i, 166, 8 ; vii, 15, 14). Probably these forts consisted of a series of concentric walls. All this economic progress was built up by the talent and training produced by schools of craftsmanship, the existence of which we can only infer in the absence of any direct evidence from the Rigveda.

The Vedāṅgas. Orthodox learned opinion describes the Veda as *Shaḍaṅga-Veda,* the Veda of six limbs, and holds that the study of the Rigveda simultaneously gave rise to the six subsidiary studies known as Śikshā, Kalpa, Vyākaraṇa, Nirukta, Chhanda, and Jyotisha. Although these subjects are now extant in the forms of Sūtras belonging to a much later age, their origins must be found in the age of the Rigveda, because the Rigveda could not be properly studied without the aid of these Vedāṇgas. As the Veda was learnt by recitation and proper pronunciation, it was first necessary to learn the science of Śikshā. The word *śikshā* is from the root *śiksh*, to give. The guru was giving the Veda to his pupil by uttering it. Therefore, a knowledge of Śikshā was preliminary to study of Veda, the mastery of which depended upon its proper pronunciation and recitation. This point is made clear in a verse in Hymn vii, 103, in the expression " yadeshāṁ anyo anyasya vāchaṁ śāktasyeva vadati śikshamāṇaḥ ". Here the word *śāktasya* = *śaktimataḥ śikshakasya* refers to the teacher who was possessed of the ability to teach by his knowledge of the science of *Śikshā*, according to which he was uttering and pronouncing the Vedic texts which his pupils were reciting from his lips (*anuvadati*).

It may also be assumed that just as the Veda was recited according to the rules of Śikshā, it was also applied for the performance of Yajña according to the rules of the second Vedāṇga called *Kalpa*. Similarly, the Vedāṇgas, *Vyākaraṇa* and *Nirukta,* had also to be studied as aids to the comprehension of the meaning of the Vedic text upon which so much stress was laid. The mere crammer of Vedic texts (*Kevala-Pāṭhaka*) to whom the Veda merely conveyed a sound without sense (*Nigadenaiva śabdyate*) was condemned as the bearer of a burden, like an ass carrying a load of sandal-wood without relishing its smell.

Similarly, the Vedāṇga called *Chhandas* must have been regarded as preliminary to Vedic chanting. The rules of poetical composition, of versification, and metre, had to be mastered for following the many varieties of metre employed in the Rigveda.

Lastly, a study of *Jyotisha* gave an insight into unchanging and regular laws of nature and kindled the scientific spirit in that age.

It may also be assumed that behind these Vedāṇga sciences there must have been a study of the science of sciences, the science of reasoning or logic. A glimpse of this study is given in Rigveda iii, 26, 9, where the expression "*Vaktvānāṁ Melim*" (= Melakaṁ) refers to one who can reconcile conflicting views advanced by what are called the Pūrva-Paksha and the Siddhāntin.

The scientific spirit of the Vedic age finds expression in the recognition of an immutable cosmic order or the Laws of Nature for which there are employed such terms as *Dhātā*, *Satya*, *Ṛita*, *Dharma*, and *Vrata*. Dhātā refers to what has been, as an accomplished fact, revealing the law of happenings, like the tree growing from a seed, of the sun rising in the east, of Agni always consuming objects thrown into it. Similarly, *Satya* refers to what is (*Sata*) and to what is contributory (*Hita*) to what is happening, the law, for example, by which the sun still rises in the east, fire gives heat, and a plant grows out of a seed. *Dharma* is that which holds in the midst of change.

There may be a doubt whether *Kalpa* as a subject of study is known to the Rigveda. But the doubt is solved by a reference to the Hymn vii, 103, where there is a verse mentioning *Somayājī* Brāhmaṇas, *Satra* continuing for full one year (Parivatsarīṇaṃ) and Adhvaryu. A sacrifice lasting for one year must have required for its performance the services of the full complement of priesthood consisting of sixteen members. There is another verse in the same hymn describing how the Udgātā priests (Gāyatriṇaḥ) were chanting (gāyanti) hymns, how the Arkis (Hotā Priests) were uttering their Arkas (hymns) in praise of the deity (Archanti) and also the Brahmā priests who were supervising the sacrifice. The elaborate scale on which the Soma-sacrifice was performed is also indicated in a passage of Rigveda: "Yat sānoḥ sānuṁ āruhat bhūri aspashṭa-kartvam," implying that it required *bhūri* or elaborate preparation [i, 10, 2].

The same doubt is expressed about the development of *Nirukta* and *Vyākaraṇa* as subjects of study at the time of Rig-Veda. Sāyaṇa cites a text: "Tasmāt Brāhmāṇā ubhayāṁ Vāchaṁ vadanti yā cha devānāṁ yā cha manushyāṇām iti."

This shows that *Deva-bhāshā* or Vedic speech was already separated from the spoken tongue in the time of the *Brāhmaṇas.* There are some passages of the Rigveda which throw light on these linguistic problems. I, 164, 45 refers to four varieties of speech (*Vāk*), of which three were known to Brāhmaṇas, who were Manīshīs, i.e. who had achieved mastery of their minds but not to the ordinary people who knew only the fourth class of speech. Now what are those four varieties of speech ? According to the Yājñikas, these were the languages of (*a*) Mantra, (*b*) Kalpa, (*c*) Brāhmaṇas, and (*d*) that popularly spoken. According to the Nairuktas, the three languages were those of Ṛik, Yajuḥ, and Sāma Veda, and the fourth was the vernacular language of the times. Thus, in this view, the language of the three Vedas was not accessible to the common people.

The same sense is conveyed by *Rv.* x, 71, already cited, where Vedic speech is described as refined (saṁskṛita) speech, speech that is refined and created by the minds of the learned by separating the pure elements from the impure like a sieve. In that refined speech dwells Bhadrā-Lakshmī, the Goddess of Good. It leads to the highest good. This speech was evolved by Ṛishis by employing it at Yajñas where they used to gather. The Yajña was thus the primary centre of learning and education in those days. It provided the sphere where Vedic speech was in circulation, was cultivated and perfected. Vedic speech was the outcome of the Yajña which alone gave the occasion for its use. It had no use in the secular spheres of life. That is why another hymn states how ordinary people only " see " or " hear " the words of the Veda by their mere forms and sounds, but they cannot perceive their sense. The Vedic speech thus originating at the Yajñas was conserved and transmitted through the Vedic schools of the times comprising students called *Sakhās,* those bound by the ties of a common learning (Vidyā-sambandha).

The cultivation of this difficult and refined Vedic speech depended upon the special sciences called *Nirukta* and *Vyākaraṇa.* The Taittirīya Saṁhitā has a story : " Vāg vai parāchī avyākṛitā avadat | Tāṁ Indraḥ madhyataḥ avakramya vyākarot | Tasmādiyaṁ vyākṛitā Vāk udyate," which means that originally Vedic speech was unintelligible like the roar of the ocean till Indra made it intelligible by differentiation of roots, suffixes, and prefixes. This thus refers to the sciences of Etymology and Grammar rendering Vedic speech fit for study. The same meaning is conveyed in *Rv.* x, 71, 1, already cited, where the first stage of

Vedic speech is stated to be "the meaning of objects" (*Nāma dheyaṁ dadhānāḥ*), which must have been the work of the students of *Nirukta* (which collects the various words signifying the same object) and *Vyākaraṇa* throwing light on single and compound words. The second stage of Vedic speech belongs to a different and higher plane and concerns its subtle and spiritual meaning to be attained by meditation, as distinguished from its gross and literal meaning given by the grammarians who understand only the letter but not the spirit of the Vedic speech. For this Bṛihaspati is invoked in the hymn.

Images of Ṛishis. The Ideal of Life and Education as embodied in the Vedic Ṛishis became the established Ideal of the country and finds expression in its Art. I unexpectedly discovered some images in stone of these Ṛishis in the wilds of Rajgir [Plate II]. A proof of the popularity of the Ṛishi type in Indian culture and tradition is to be found in some old Sanskrit works on Tāntrika Buddhism, which were carried to China by the Nālandā scholar, Śubhā Kara Siṁha, in A.D. 716, and translated by him into Chinese in A.D. 730. Thus the original works were much older than their Chinese translations. These works contained portraits of (1) Ṛishi Atri and his wife (Anasūyā) and (2) Ṛishi Vasishṭha in two postures, seated and standing.

These portraits were preserved in a Japanese work called *Hizoki* which was compiled by Kukai who lived about the end of the eighth century A.D. Copies of these are to be found in the published parts of the Dictionary called *Hobogirin*, by S. Levi and Taka Kusu. Plate III is based on drawings of these.

In the picture, Atri holds in his left hand a water-pot and covers his body by the right hand. His wife (Anasūyā) is seated by him.

Vasishṭha is seated on a mat, with his left knee raised, holding a lotus in his right hand and a garland in his left.

The walking Vasishṭha is an emaciated figure of Asceticism leaning on a staff which he holds in his left hand and making a sign by his right hand. The recorded tradition is that he is here represented in the act of constructing a hermitage on Mount Potalaka, the abode of his Deity, Avalokiteśvara.

These Ṛishis are figuring here as Assistants of Agni in the outer courtyard of the *Garbha-maṇḍala*, or 'Mystical Circle', as conceived in Tāntrika Buddhism.

We may note how the Indian Ideal of Asceticism as embodied in the Ṛishi type of character, of which the Buddha was a most powerful example, had had its hold on both China and Japan.

PLATE IV

(*a*) Seated

(*b*) Walking

ṚISHI VASISHTHA

[*Facing p. 60*

CHAPTER III

EDUCATION IN THE OTHER VEDAS

The other Vedic Saṁhitās. These show the trend of learning and educational development as influenced by the trend of religious thought. The three later Vedic Saṁhitās of Sāma, Yajuḥ, and Atharva usher in the age of the *Brāhmaṇas*, a different type of literary activity. The principle governing their compilation is quite different. It follows the order of an established ceremonial pointing to a fixed order of sacrifices. But in the Rigveda Saṁhitā, as we have seen, the order of the hymns has nothing to do with the order of the sacrifices, while it included many hymns which have no use for any sacrifice. The other two Vedic Saṁhitās were compiled exclusively for purposes of ritual application. The fact is that in their time the old Rigvedic religion showed considerable developments of ceremonial and priesthood out of their beginnings in the Rigveda. The priesthood now had a personnel of sixteen members as described below :—

(i) *Hotṛi*, with his Assistants called Maitrāvaruṇa, Achāvāka, and Grāvastut ;

(ii) *Udgātṛi*, with his Assistants, the Prastotṛi, Pratihartṛi, and Subrahmaṇya ;

(iii) *Adhvaryu* assisted by Pratishṭhātṛi, Neshṭṛi, and Unnetṛi ;

(iv) *Brahman*, with Assistants called Brāhmaṇāchchhaṁsin, Agnīdhra, and Potṛi.

All these sixteen priests were called by the general name of *Ṛitvij*. There are also mentioned priests of inferior status who were Assistants of the Adhvaryu, viz. the Śamitṛi, the Vaikarta, and the Chamasādhvaryu. The Kaushītakins added a seventeenth Ṛitvij called the *Sadasya* who is to superintend the whole sacrifice.

Of this full complement of priesthood, the Rigveda [ii, 1, 2] mentions only seven, viz. Hotṛi, Potṛi, Neshṭṛi, Agnīdh, Praśāstṛi, Adhvaryu, and Brahman, besides the institutor of the sacrifice, and the Udgātṛi and his Assistant, Prastotṛi [viii, 81, 5].

Higher education now related itself to the requirements of this priesthood and ritualistic religion. The external, material, and mechanical aspects of worship and sacrifice became now the principal subjects of study which, in their range and complexity, even called for a considerable degree of specialization and division of labour among its students. There were four classes of students and specialists to master the four parts of worship or sacrifice already indicated, viz. (1) recital of hymns in which the *Hotṛi* specialized ; (2) the chanting of hymns requiring a special training for which the *Udgātṛi* equipped himself ; (3) the actual performance of sacrifice involving a number of operations and material details in which the *Adhvaryu* specialized ; and (4) the superintendence and direction of the worship as a whole, for which the *Brahman* priest had to qualify by acquiring proficiency in all the three Vedas so as to be able to correct errors in the performance of the different parts and operations of sacrifice as described above, and to give decision on all doubtful points and disputes, thereby laying the beginnings of what were later developed as the systems of *Nyāya* and *Mīmāṁsā*.

But even this age of ceremonialism was marked by its own creative efforts in different directions.

The Sāma Veda. The *Udgātṛis* contributed some new elements, 78 out of 1,549 verses, to the Sāmaveda. The bulk of the verses of the Sāmaveda is taken out of the Rigveda and mostly from its Maṇḍalas viii and ix. These verses are arranged in the Sāmaveda in two parts : (1) the *Ārchika* of 585 single stanzas or *ṛiks* ; (2) the *Uttarārchika* comprising 400 chants, mostly of three stanzas each. In the Sāmaveda the text is treated only as a means to an end, the learning of melodies. The student whose object was to be trained as an Udgātṛi priest in the schools of Sāmaveda had first to learn the melodies and this he could do with the aid of the Ārchika or the song-book where is given only the text of the *first* stanza of each song as an aid to the recollection of the tune. Here it is not usually the case, as in the west, that a verse is sung to a particular tune. It is the reverse : this or that melody (Sāman) is sung upon a particular stanza. Here the melody arises out of the *Ṛik* or stanza which is thus called the *yoni* of the melody. No doubt a stanza can be sung to various melodies, and one melody can be applied to different stanzas, but certain stanzas are marked out and fixed as the texts or *yonis* for certain melodies. The *Uttārchika* gives the stanzas out of which are formed the *stotras* to be sung at the sacrifices, to the tunes which the *Ārchika* teaches.

It is thus like a song-book giving the complete text of the songs and not merely the text of the first stanza of a song.

Its Musical System. Of course, the *Saṁhitā* can give only the texts as they are spoken. Their melodies were taught by oral and also instrumental rendering. Music is known to the Rigveda, as also the instruments producing music by means of percussion, wind, and string, such as drum (Dundubhi) [i, 28, 5], lute (Karkari, ii, 43, 3), and lyre or harp (Vāṇa) with its seven notes recognized and distinguished [x, 32, 4], together with the flute (of reed) called *Nādī* [x, 135, 7]. The oldest notation for music was probably that indicated by syllables such as *ta*, *cho*, etc. But very often the seven notes were indicated by the figures 1, 2, 3, 4, 5, 6, 7, corresponding respectively to F, E, D, C, B, A, G of our modern scale of music. It may be further noted that the *Ārchika* has got two supplements called *Grāmageya-gāna* (book of songs to be sung in the village) and *Āraṇya-geya-gāna* (book of forest songs). The number of melodies then known was quite large, being computed at 8,000 by R. Simon, while each melody had its own name. The melodies called *Bṛihat* and *Rathantara* are known to the Rigveda.[1]

Some students of Music find in the Vedic *Svaras* called Udātta, Anudātta, and Svarita the origins of the seven Svaras, "Sha-Ri-Ga-Ma-Pa-Dha-Ni" distinguished in modern Indian Music in measuring the gamut. They depend for this view on certain old texts found in Pāniṇi's *Śikshā*, in Nārada's work, and in Yājñavalkya-Śikshā. These may be cited here:

(1) Udātte Nishāda-Gāndhārāvanudātte Ṛishabha-Dhaivatau | Svaritaprabhavā hyete Shaḍja-Madhyama-Pañchamāḥ | "*Udātta* means and includes *Ni* and *Ga*; *Anudātta*, *Ri* and *Dha*; and *Svarita*, Sha, Ma, and Pa."

[1] The Chhāndogya Upanishad marks out five parts in a Sāma-song, viz. (1) *Prastāva* or introduction preceded by the syllable *Hum* sung by the Prastotṛi; (2) *Udgītha* to be sung by the Udgātṛi priest first uttering the sound *Om*; (3) *Pratihāra* ("joining in"), preceded by *Hum*, to be sung by Pratihartṛi who joins in the last syllable sometimes taken in two parts, viz. (4) *Upadrava* or recession, consisting of the last two syllables of the Pratihāra sung by Udgātṛi, and (5) *Nidhana* comprising two syllables or *Om* sung by all the three priests. These five parts may be thus shown in the first verse of the Sāmaveda (taken from *Rv.*, vi, 16, 10):—

1. Huṁ Agne [*Prastāva*].
2. Oṁ āyā hi vītaye gṛiṇāno havyadātaye [*Udgītha*].
3. Ni hotā satsi varhishi Oṁ [*Pratihāra*] to be divided into.
4. Ni hotā satsi va [*Upadrava*].
5. — Ṛishi Om [*Nidhana*].

"The modern Rāgas or arrangements of different notes may be equated to the different Sāmans named after a typical song (the *Chāla* of Indian music); these names are innumerable, such as Vāruṇa, Śaubhara, Brāhma Rathantara, Vinardi, Yajñā-yajñīya, Yodhājaya, and so on" (C. V. Vaidya's *History of Sanskrit Literature*, vol. i, pp. 121 f.].

(2) Uchchau Nishāda-Gāndhārau Nīchāvṛishabha-Dhaivatau | Śeshāstu Svaritājñeyāḥ Shaḍja-Madhyama-Pañchamāḥ ||

"The high-toned (Udātta) means and includes *Ni* and *Ga*; the low toned (Anudātta), *Ri* and *Dha*; while the rest, *Sha-Ma-Pa*."

(3) Gāndharva-Vede ye prayuktāḥ sapta shaḍjādayaḥ svarāḥ | Ta eva Vede vijñeyāḥ traya uchchādayaḥ svarāḥ ||

"The self-same seven Svaras beginning with *Sa* as employed in the Science of Music are to be understood as being implied in the three Svaras of the Vedas, beginning with Udātta."

Experts in Music also hold that Vedic *Udātta* corresponds to modern *Ga* (including within itself its *saṁvādī* or consonant *Ni*), *Anudātta* to *Ri* (including its *saṁvādī Dha*), and *Svarita* to *Sha* (with its *saṁvādīs, Ma* and *Pa*). It will thus appear that the nucleus of the Sāman scale is primarily *Ga-Ri-Sha*, which shows struggles to reach the fourth *Ni*, and even the fifth *Dha* bordering on *Ni*. It is also evident that what we now call the seven *Svaras*, the ancients call the seven *Yamas*, viz. Krushṭa, Prathama, Dvitīya, Tṛitīya, Chaturtha, Mandra, Atisvārya [*Taittirīya-Prātiśākhya*, xxiii, 13], and that while the modern *Svaras* are in the ascending order, the ancient *Yamas* are counted in the descending order. Thus the only light that the Sāmaveda throws on Education is that it was responsible for the development of Indian Music and its School.

The Yajurveda. Just as the Sāmaveda is the song book of the Udgātṛi, the Yajurveda is the prayer-book of the Adhvaryu priest. Prayers were accompanied by sacrificial acts about which differences of opinion were more likely to arise. Any deviation in the ceremonial or in the liturgy led to the formation of a new Vedic School. Thus the Yajurveda lent itself to the formation of numerous schools the number of which was 101 in the time of Patañjali (as stated in the Introduction to his *Mahābhāshya*).

The Yajurveda has two divisions called Black (Kṛishṇa) and White (Śukla), also called Vājasaneyi-Saṁhitā. The white Yajurveda contains only the Mantras, the prayers, and sacrificial formulae which the priest has to utter, while the black Yajurveda contains the Mantras in verse and also a portion in prose, the earliest Indian prose, presenting the sacrificial rites that go with the Mantras along with discussions thereon, anticipating the later Brāhmaṇa literature. Thus from the point of view of education, the Yajurveda has made a material contribution to it by the creation of a prose literature which later culminated in the literary masterpieces of the Upanishads.

The Yajurveda fixes the religious scheme and ordering of Hindu life in the course of ceremonies it prescribes. It prescribes various sacrifices among which may be mentioned those for the New and Full Moon, the Fathers (*Piṇḍa-pitṛiyajña*), Fire (Agnihotra to be performed both morning and evening), seasons (Chāturmāsyas to be performed every four months), Rājasūya (for kings only), Aśvamedha (for a King of Kings), and Agnichayana (ceremony for building the Fire-altar which lasted for a year and was possessed of a mystical significance). This ceremony throws some light upon the architecture of the times. The altar was to be built of 10,800 bricks in the form of a large bird with outspread wings. In its lowest stratum were immured the heads of five sacrificial animals. Their bodies were thrown into water out of which was taken the clay for the manufacture of the bricks and of the fire-pan. Prayers accompanied every process of building, the modelling and baking of the fire-pan and the individual bricks, some of which bore special names. Equally symbolic was the horse-sacrifice of which the purpose was national well-being, as stated below [*Vājasaneyi Saṁhitā*, xxii, 22] :—

" O Brahman ! May in this Kingdom be born the Brāhmaṇa who is radiant with supreme knowledge (Brahmavarchasī jāyatām asmin rāshṭre) ! May here be born the Kshatriya who is a true hero, a good marksman, a skilful shot, and an accomplished charioteer (Mahārathaḥ) ! Also cows which yield plenty of milk, oxen that can draw well, the swift horse, and the good housewife ! May to this sacrificer be born the hero of a son, victorious, a mighty chariot-fighter, and eloquent at Assemblies (*Sabheya*) ! May we get rain according to our needs and our plants yield good fruit and crops ! May there be happiness and prosperity for all ! "

This prayer shows a remarkable appreciation of the factors making for the welfare of a country.

The contents of the Yajurveda show how it gave impetus to the development of new subjects of study, both religious and secular. The need of correct pronunciation of hymns by the Hotṛi priest laid the beginnings of subjects like Śikshā (phonetics) and Chhandas (metrics) treated as Vedāṅgas (parts of Vedic study) and of the elaborate Prātiśākhya literature. And some of the functions with which the Adhvaryu priest was charged in regard to the material performance of sacrifices led to the development of several secular sciences and practical arts. Measuring the ground for sacrifice; building the altar and platform according to area and volume previously determined; ascertaining of proper seasons and moments for the actual performance of the sacrifice: these laid the foundation of geometrical logistics and of *Jyotisha* or astronomy. Some of the Assistants of Adhvaryu again had to cultivate a knowledge of the parts of the bodily frame of the animals to be immolated at sacrifices, and this led to the study of Anatomy (especially Osteology) and to physiological and medical speculations for which the Atharvaveda is chiefly noted.

The Atharvaveda. The Atharvaveda, indeed, contains much new and original matter not to be found in the Rigveda. Of about 6,000 stanzas making up 731 hymns divided into twenty books, some 1,200 are derived from the Rigveda, chiefly from its first, eighth, and tenth Books, and only a few from the other Books. A large part of this Vedic Saṁhitā refers to and mentions appropriate herbs as remedies against diseases like fever, leprosy, jaundice, dropsy, scrofula, cough, ophthalmia, baldness, impotence, and surgical ailments like fractures and wounds, bite of snakes and other injurious insects, and against poison in general, mania, and other complaints. The Atharvaveda is somewhat ungenerous in wishing away some of the ills of life like fever to distant regions and peoples such as the Mūjavans, the Bahlikas or a Śūdra girl whom it is asked to shake —fever, which is " now cold, now burning hot ", which " makest all men yellow ", with its " brother, consumption, and sister, cough, and nephew, herpes " [v, 22]. The Atharvaveda thus ranks as the oldest work of Indian Medicine. Its ninth book anticipates Astronomy by its mention of the lunar mansions. A part of it deals with domestic rites at birth, marriage, or death, thereby anticpating the later Gṛihya Sūtras. Along with spells for warding off evil, it also contains spells for securing good, such as harmony in family and village life, reconciliation of enemies, long life, health, prosperity, safety on journeys, and luck in gambling. There are, again, some hymns giving interesting data, economic [xii, 1], political [xi, 10; vii, 12 on Kings and Assemblies] and philosophical [e.g. iv, 16, exalting divine omniscience].

Thus these later Vedic Saṁhitās, besides extending religious literature in response to the growing needs of worship, gave the start to a variety of speculations which resulted in the growth of a number of secular sciences and arts still subserving the ends of religion.

Evidence on Education. In ancient India, the system of education was fixed and standardized on the basis of certain universally admitted and established ideals and practices connoted by the term *Brahmacharya*. The Atharvaveda is the only Veda which directly extols, exalts, and expounds this fundamental system and institution of *Brahmacharya* which forms the foundation of the entire structure of Hindu thought and life. Subjects and courses of study may vary, but the system of education, its methods of training and discipline, must remain the same under all conditions. Studentship in ancient India was evolved into a science or an art of life which did not admit of any change according to age or clime but was taken to be of universal validity.

The Atharvaveda [xi, 5] contains a separate long hymn describing this system of studentship. The pupil enters upon his stage of studentship through the performance of the ceremony of initiation called *Upanayana* by his chosen teacher called *Āchārya*. The ceremony takes three days (*rātrīstisraḥ*) during which the teacher holds within him the pupil to impart to him a new birth and regenerated life whence the pupil emerges as a *dvija* or twice-born. His first birth he owes to his parents who give him only his body. It is a mere physical birth. His second birth is spiritual. It unfolds his mind and soul [Āchāryaḥ upanayamāno brahmachāriṇaṁ kṛiṇute garbhamantaḥ = Āchāryaḥ *antaḥ* vidyāśarīrasya madhye garbhaṁ kṛiṇute (Sāyaṇa), " the teacher recreates the pupil in a new body of learning " | Taṁ rātrīstisraḥ udare bibharti]. After this *Upanayana* or initiation, the pupil emerges as a Brahmachārī, a new and changed person both externally and internally. He lives according to prescribed regulations governing both his dress and habits by which he is marked out. He goes about wearing a girdle (*mekhalā*) of Kuśa grass, the skin of the black antelope (*kārshṇam*) and long hairs (*dīrghaśmaśru*) and carries fuel which he has to offer to Agni both morning and evening [*Samidhā samiddhaḥ*]. Besides these external marks, he is also distinguished by some inner attributes and disciplines. These are stated to be (1) *Śrama*, self-restraint ; (2) *Tapas*, practice of penance and (3) *Dīkshā*, consecration to a life of discipline through prescribed regulations such as begging and the like (Sāyaṇa). Thus the Brahmachārī is abroad (*eti*), an example of that discipline and detachment which have created and sustain the universe. The Supreme Being Himself is described as the prime Brahmachārī. All creation is the outcome of *Brahmacharya* and *Tapas*. "Through these, a King protects his Kingdom. Through these, the gods have conquered Death . . . All creatures which have sprung from Prajāpati have breath separately in themselves ; all of these are preserved by supreme knowledge (*brahma*) which is produced in the Brahmachārin (Pṛithak sarve prājāpatyāḥ prāṇān ātmasu bibhrati | tān sarvān brahma rakshati brahmachāriṇi ābhṛitam)."

The Āchārya or preceptor is similarly extolled. He is compared to Yama [either the *guru* of Nachiketas or the god of Death killing the sinner (Sāyaṇa)] ; to Varuṇa [either the *guru* of Bhṛigu or the protector against sins (Sāyaṇa)] ; to Sun and Moon as the givers of light and happiness, from whose pleasure is to be derived all prosperity [of which the symbols mentioned are *aushadhayaḥ*, i.e. rice and wheat and *payaḥ* or *kshīram* (Sāyaṇa)]. The Āchārya is also mentioned as being sustained by the devoted disciple performing faithfully his prescribed duties [*Tapasā piparti* = *svanmārga-vṛittyā pālayati* (Sāyaṇa)] and by grateful gifts to him, even as Mitra, the disciple of Varuṇa, gave him presents up to the limit of his resources.

Briefly put, the Brahmachārī, after his initiation into a new life whereby he is recreated by his guru, has to undergo a twofold course of discipline, physical and spiritual. The former comprised (1) wearing the Kuśa girdle and deer skin, (2) letting his hairs grow, (3) collecting fuel and tending the household fire, and (4) begging. The spiritual discipline included (1) offering fuel to and worshipping Agni twice daily, (2) control of senses, (3) practice of austerities, (4) living a dedicated life, and (5) satisfying the teacher by gifts acceptable to him.

Besides this special Hymn in praise of the Brahmachārī, the Atharvaveda contains a few other passages also on the subject. XIX, 41 refers to *Brahmacharya* as a distinct stage in life and as a system of discipline (*tapo-dīkshāmupanisheduḥ*). VII, 105 contains an exhortation to holy life which is quoted in Kauśika Sūtra (55, 16) in connection with the Upanayana ceremony as the teacher takes the pupil by the arm and sets him facing eastward [Praṇītīḥ abhyāvartasva = prakṛishṭanayanādi-veda-brahmacharya-nīyatīḥ (Sāyaṇa)]. The prayers of the Brahmachārī show the high aims for which he stands. He prays for success in his study of the Veda and for its freedom

HERMITAGES IN BHARHUT SCULPTURES (*c.* second century B.C.).

No. 1.—It bears the inscription: *Dighatapasi sise anusāsati*, "the ascetic of long penance instructs his pupils" Cunningham takes some of these pupils to be female Ṛishis. The position of the pupils' fingers shows counting called for in *Sāma-Veda* chanting.

[*Facing p* 68

from interruption [vii, 54, 1–2]; for faith (*śraddhā*), insight (*medhā* = *adhītaveda-dhāraṇam*), progeny (*prajā*), wealth (*dhana*), longevity (*āyu*), and immortality (*amṛitatva*) [xix, 64]. In vii, 61 he claims insight into the Vedas, longevity, and wisdom as the fruits of *tapas*.[1]

Girl-students. It is to be noted that *brahmacharya* was also applicable to girls in those days. X, 5, 18 states how maidens win youths (yuvānam) as their husbands through *brahmacharya*. This probably refers to studentship preceding the married state or second *āśrama* in the case of both boys and girls.

Holidays. Lastly, in connection with the prayer for non-interruption of study, it is interesting to note the holidays observed in these Vedic Schools on occasions of cloudy (*antarikshe* = *meghāchchhanne*) or windy (*vāte*) weather. Vedic study was also not to be under the shade of trees (*vṛiksheshu* = *vṛikshachchhāyāyām*), in sight of green barley (*ulapeshu* = *haritaśasya-sannidhau*) and within hearing of cattle (*paśavaḥ aśravaṇam*) [vii, 66].

Evidence of 'Yajurveda.' The *Yajurveda* [*Taitti. Saṁ.*, vi, 3, 10, 5] contains a reference to this system of studentship which shows that it was an established system for long. It states that man owes three debts which he must repay in three prescribed ways, viz. (1) the debt to Ṛishis to be repaid by *brahmacharya* by which he is to acquire and spread the knowledge he inherits from the Ṛishis; (2) the debt to gods by *yajñas* (sacrifices) to realize his kinship with the spiritual world (of gods); and (3) the debt to ancestors by fatherhood to continue the family in which he is born. The debt to Ṛishis is the debt which one owes to learning in the shape of his cultural heritage. Such an obligation he can only discharge by making his own contribution to learning, which he can achieve only on the basis of *brahmacharya*.

In conclusion, it may be noted that the Yajurveda read as a literary work is not perhaps interesting but it is supremely important and interesting to a student of religion who will find in it a source for the study not only of Indian but also of the

[1] Sāyana describes three kinds of *Tapas*, viz. (1) tending the fires, (2) subduing the flesh by austerities (*kṛichchhrādyācharaṇena śarīra-śoshanam*), and (3) concentration of the mind and senses on the divine (manasaścha indriyāṇāṁ cha aikāgryaṁ tapa uchyate). Sāyana also cites Patañjali-Sūtra which mentions the following four processes of realizing the Divine, viz. (1) *Śaucha* (purity), (2) *Santosha* (contentment), (3) *Tapa* (penance), and (4) *Svādhyāya* (Vedic study).

general science of religion. He will find it specially valuable for a study of the origin, development, and the significance of *prayer* in the evolution of religious ideas. The *Yajurveda* also supplies the key to an understanding of the later literature of the *Brāhmaṇas* of which it contains the origins and also of the *Upanishads* following the *Brāhmaṇas*.

Chapter IV

LATER VEDIC EDUCATION

Sources. We shall now study Education in the light of the data furnished by the vast body of later Vedic literature, comprising what are called the *Brāhmaṇas*, *Āraṇyakas*, and *Upanishads*. In one sense, it may be stated that Indian Education reached its climax and achieved the highest degree of efficiency and success in this period when it could produce a literature like the Upanishads which are universally admitted to record the utmost possibilities of human speculation regarding some of the ultimate problems of life and metaphysical mysteries. Unfortunately, the evidence on the subject is comparatively meagre and not given in any one place in any of the numerous works to be studied for it. One can only find bits of evidence here and there and piece together the scattered bits for constructing a system that may be understood.

An account of these source-books has first to be given in their possible educational bearings and cultural implications.

We have already seen how the Rigveda Saṁhitā presents the two aspects of Religion, the aspect of Thought, Philosophy, Meditation, and Concentration (Tapas) and the practical aspect of Religion as exemplified in external worship of individual deities by means of *Yajñas* or sacrifices. The first aspect is distinguished as *Jñāna-kāṇḍa* and the second *Karma-kāṇḍa*. The *Karma-kāṇḍa*, the practical needs of worship, called for the growth of priesthood and its necessary texts, the two Vedic Saṁhitās of Sāma and Yajuḥ. Religion now began to centre more and more in ceremonial and sacrifice, the details of which were more and more elaborated and called for suitable texts by which they could be regulated, fixed, and conserved. This explains the emergence of a new type of literature, the *Brāhmaṇas*, which is unique in the annals of literature. It is the literature of priesthood and has a very narrow appeal. But like the Yajurveda it is important as a source of religious history, the history of sacrifice and priesthood. Ritualism runs riot in these Brāhmaṇa works. An age of creation is now succeeded by an age of conservation, compilation, and criticism. Poets and Seers are now replaced by Priests and Theologians. A reaction soon followed and expressed itself in the Upanishads which bring back into religion the atmosphere of abstraction and pure thought which the Rigveda breathes.

As has been already explained, the *Brāhmaṇas* are works that deal with *brahma*, i.e. devotion and prayer, and are of the nature of textbooks for rituals or treatises on the "science of sacrifice". They are thus composed in prose. Their main purpose is to explain the relations between the Vedic texts and their corresponding ceremonial and also to explain their symbolical meaning with reference to each other. They are meant not for the lay-worshippers for whom they are too technical, but only for those who are already familiar with sacrificial performances so that the descriptions they give of such performances are not required to be exhaustive. Their subject-matter has been, as we have seen, analysed by Sāyaṇa into (1) *Vidhi* or practical directions for the performance of a *yajña* or sacrifice, and (2) *Arthavāda* or explanations, exegetical, mythological, or polemical, including theological or philosophical speculations on the nature of things (*Upanishad*). While its *Vidhi* portion thus makes of the *Brahmaṇa* a liturgical work concerned with the cult and technique of sacrificial performances, its *Arthavāda* portion is free from the trammels of such technical practicalities of ritualism and freely introduces matters of general interest in the form of legends, ethical teachings, philosophical discussions, historical episodes, etymologies, myths, and the like, covering a wide range of intellectual activity that adds to the value, volume, and variety of this literature.

To each of these *Brāhmaṇas* is also annexed an *Āraṇyaka* or "forest-portion", i.e. the portion to be studied in the forest by those sages who have become its denizens and do not need to perform sacrifices. The idea is that the *Āraṇyakas* are the vehicles of metaphysical and mystical truths which are best studied in the solitude of the forests and not in the distractions of cities. India has thought her highest in the forests, her civilization is sylvan and not urban, the product of out-of-the-way schools or hermitages.

A yet further and more remarkable literary development is registered in what are called the *Upanishads* of which the very title, like that of the *Āraṇyakas*, points to the special educational methods of which they are the fruits. The expression *upa-ni-shad* literally means "sitting down near" and indicated "confidential session" at which the secret or esoteric doctrines of these works were taught to select pupils towards the end of their studentship in discourses from which wider circles were excluded.

The extant *Brāhmaṇas* group themselves round the several Vedas which thus determine their subject-matter. Thus the *Brāhmaṇas* of the Rigveda contain only such explanations of the ritual as are needed by the *Hotṛi* priest in his task of collecting from the total body of the hymns the verses suited to each particular occasion as its *śastra* (canon). Being liturgical works, they follow the order of the sacrificial performance without reference to the sequence of the hymns in their *Veda*. The *Brāhmaṇas* of the Sāman and Yajus confine themselves to the duties of the Udgātṛi and Adhvaryu priests and follow the order of the ritual already established in their respective Vedas.

The literature of the period in its threefold branches of Brāhmaṇas, Āraṇyakas, and Upanishads may be indicated as follows :—

I. THE RIGVEDA

A. **Brāhmaṇas** :

(1) **Aitareya** attributed by Sāyaṇa to Mahidāsa Aitareya, son of Itarā, one of the many wives of a Ṛishi named Viśāla. This Aitareya was probably the founder of a Śākhā or school of Aitareyins whose doctrines, ceremonial, philological, and philosophical, are incorporated in the Brāhmaṇa, Āraṇyaka, and Upanishad attached to his name. These works seem to have been afterwards adopted by the later Śākhās of the Rigveda, for we actually hear of an Āśvalāyana text of the Aitareyakam, Aśvalāyana being the pupil of Śaunaka.

(2) **Śāṅkhāyana**, which cites the views of the two previous authors, Paiṅgya (the sage mentioned in the *Brāhmaṇa* of the White Yajus from whom Yāska Paiṅgī was descended) and Kaushītaka whose views it regards as more authoritative and therefore this *Brāhmaṇa* might be a remoulding of the stock of dogma derived from the Kaushītakins whence it is also known as *Kaushītaki Brāhmaṇa*.

It may be noted in this connection that, along with previous teachers, some previous forms of literary composition are also referred to by both these *Brāhmaṇas* in such terms as *ākhyāna* and *gāthā*, i.e. a kind of memorial verses.

B. **Āraṇyakas :**

(1) **Aitareya**, which lays great stress upon keeping its doctrines secret and the importance of those familiar with them. It gives the extant arrangement of the Ṛik-Saṁhitā with the names of its subdivisions ; mentions the other Vedas ; comments on some hymns on the Rigveda in the manner of a Nirukta ; contains some grammatical matter ; and names many individual teachers among whom are two Śākalyas, a Krishṇa Hārita, and a Pañchālachaṇḍa.

(2) **Kaushītaki**, parts of which correspond to the former Āraṇyaka.

C. **Upanishads :**

(1) **Aitareya.**

(2) **Kaushītaki** in which Ajātaśatru, King of Kāśī, is mentioned as teaching the proud Brāhmaṇa Bālāki ; the wise king, Chitra Gāṇgyāyani, as instructing Āruṇi.

II. THE SĀMAVEDA

A. **Brāhmaṇas :**

(1) **Tāṇḍya**, also called *Pañchaviṁśa*, concerned with the Soma sacrifices in general, ranging from minor offerings to those which lasted 100 days or even several years (called *sattras*, or sessions). It also contains minute descriptions of the sacrifices on the Sarasvatī and Dṛishadvatī and also of *Vrātya-stomas* by which non-Brahmanical Aryans were admitted into the Brahmanical order. It is also hostile towards the Kaushītakins whom it brands as *vrātyas* (apostates) and *yajñāvakīrṇa* (unfit to sacrifice). The name Tāṇḍya is mentioned as that of a teacher in the Brāhmaṇa of the White Yajus.

(2) **Shaḍviṁśa**, a supplement to the former.

(3) **Adbhūta**, a supplement to the former in which are mentioned Uddālaka Āruṇi and other teachers.

(4) **Chhāndogya**, of which the major part is its Upanishad.

(5) **Talavakāra** in five books, of which the first three are connected with sacrificial ceremonial, the fourth is called the *Upanishad* Brāhmaṇa, which contains the *Kenopanishad*, and the fifth is called *Ārsheya Brāhmaṇa* which enumerates the composers of the Sāmaveda.

There are three other short works which are mere *Brāhmaṇas* in name, viz. the *Sāmavidhāna*, showing the uses of chants for superstitious purposes, the *Devatādhyāya*, giving some particulars about the deities of the *sāmans*, and the *Vaṁśa* which gives a genealogy of the teachers of the *Sāmaveda*.

The *Sāmaveda* has no *Āraṇyakas*.

B. **Upanishads :**

(1) **Chhāndogya** known for its mention of the Naimishīya-Ṛishis, the Mahāvṛishas, and the Gāndhāras; of Krishṇa Devakīputra as a pupil of Ghora Āṅgirasa; of Pravāhaṇa Jaivali, a Kshatriya engaged in philosophical discussions; Ushasta Chākrāyaṇa, a teacher; Śāṇḍilya, a teacher; Satyakāma Jābāla, a teacher, the son of a slave girl by an unknown father who was initiated as a Brahmachārin by Gautama Hāridrumata and was also a pupil of Jānaki Āyasthūṇa; Uddālaka Āruṇi; Śvetaketu; and Aśvapati, a prince of the Kekayas who instructed Prāchīnaśāla and other Brāhmins. These names are also mentioned in the *Bṛihadāraṇyaka*. The work also mentions Sanatkumāra, Skanda, Nārada, and subjects like Atharvāṅgirasaḥ, Itihāsa and Purāṇa which probably attained independent forms at the time of this reference. There is also some legal material, e.g. capital punishment for denied theft, trial by ordeal, which points to its comparatively late age. Philosophical doctrines are termed *Upanishad*, *ādeśa*, *guhya ādeśa* (the secrecy of which is repeatedly insisted upon).

(2) **Kena,** remnant of the Brāhmaṇa of the Talavakāras.

III. THE YAJURVEDA

1. **Black :**

A. **Brāhmaṇa :** *Taittirīya*.

B. **Āraṇyaka :** *Taittirīya* in 10 books.

C. **Upanishad :**

(1) **Taittirīya,** books vii–ix of the *Āraṇyaka*;

(2) **Mahā-Nārayaṇa** or *Yājñikī*, book x of the *Āraṇyaka*;

(3) **Maitrāyaṇa** taught to King Bṛihadratha, an Aikshvāku;

(4) **Kāṭhaka** (with the legend of Nachiketas);

(5) **Śvetāśvatara** named after its individual author.

2. **White :**

A. **Brāhmaṇa** : *Śatapatha*, the contents of which will be commented on later.

B. **Āraṇyaka** : the last book of the *Brāhmaṇa*.

C. **Upanishad** : (1) *Bṛihadāraṇyaka* formed by the concluding six chapters of the *Āraṇyaka*; it gives two lists of teachers which, compared with the list attached to Bk. x of the *Śatapatha*, would point to the conclusion that the leading teachers of the ritual tradition (*Brāhmaṇas*) were different from those of the philosophical tradition (Upanishads) [Macdonell, *Sans. Lit.*, p. 235] ; it contains the famous dialogues between King Janaka and Yājñavalkya ; between Yājñavalkya and his wife Maitreyī.

(2) **Īśa** of eighteen stanzas only.

IV. THE ATHARVAVEDA

A. **Brāhmaṇa** : *Gopatha*, the second book of which is based on the Vaitāna Śrauta Sūtra, thus showing a reversal of the usual historical relation between a *Brāhmaṇa* and a *Sūtra*, and other parts of which are derived from other Brāhmaṇas like Aitareya, Kaushītaki, Śatapatha, and Pañchaviṁśa as also the Maitrāyaṇī and Taittirīya Saṁhitās.

B. **Upanishads** :

(1) *Muṇḍaka*, the Upanishad of the *tonsured*, an association of ascetics who shaved their heads.

(2) *Praśna*, treating of questions addressed by six students to the sage Pippalāda.

(3) *Māṇḍūkya*, chiefly known as having given birth to the *Kārikā* of Gauḍapāda, probably the teacher of Govinda, whose pupil was Śaṅkara.

A large and indefinite number of Upanishads is attributed to the Atharvaveda, of which twenty-seven are recognized. Most of them are post-Vedic.

We shall base our study on the ten Upanishads recognized by Śaṅkara in his commentary on the Vedānta Sūtras.

We have now broadly considered the total quantity of literary output of the period, from which we have now to derive the data for the construction of its educational history.

How these works were taught and transmitted. At the outset of this inductive study we should, however, note that the available Brāhmaṇa literature indicated above does not represent the entire literary matter produced. This is clear not merely from the internal evidence of the extant works but also from a consideration of the methods by which the works have been handed down from age to age. From internal evidence we know that to the number of the *Brāhmaṇas*, or recensions of the Saṁhitās, which have been lost to us, belong those of the Vāshkalas, Paiṅgins, Bhāllavins, Śāṭyāyanins, Kālabavins, Lāmakāyanins, Śāmbuvis, Khāḍāyanins, and Śālaṅkāyanins. As regards the circumstances of the origin of these *Brāhmaṇas* and the conditions and methods of their transmission, it may be safely stated that they originated from the opinions of individual sages, imparted by oral tradition, and preserved as well as supplemented in their families and also by their disciples. As these separate traditions grew in number, the necessity was more and more felt for bringing them into harmony with one another. For this purpose learned individuals in different parts who were specially qualified for the task undertook compilations embodying the various traditions and different opinions on each subject and trace them in each case as far as possible to their original exponents. These compilations or digests again in their turn were orally transmitted in accordance with the well-known orthodox predilections on the subject and were not written down. We thus find here and there that of the same work there are two texts entirely differing in their details. Thus would also be produced frequent differences and conflicts between these compilers, as a result of which we find expressions of strong animosity against those whom a particular compilation regards as heterodox. There was also going on among these rival and competing compilations a struggle for existence leading to the survival of the fittest, which became so either by virtue of their intrinsic value, or of the fact that their authors appealed more to the hieratic spirit, the prevailing religious tendencies of the times. Thus we encounter the rather lamentable fact that the works representative of the disputed opinions have for the most part disappeared (with the possibility of mere fragments thereof being recovered here and there) while those which in the end came off victorious have almost entirely supplanted and effaced their predecessors.

Variety of Institutions for propagation of Learning. The peculiar literary processes or movements noticed above bring us to a general consideration of the organization and methods which were evolved in ancient India for the conservation and transmission of her literature from age to age. For what has been described regarding the *Brāhmaṇas* applies also to the Vedic compilations as well as the *Sūtras*. The organization and machinery for the preservation and propagation of the entire Vedic literature which rested on the time-honoured system of oral tradition developed in course of time several types of institutions known as *Śākhās, Charaṇas, Parishads, Kulas, Gotras*, and the like, of which we shall now indicate some particulars. All of these were of the nature of assemblies, academies, literary or religious guilds, serving as Schools of Vedic learning in which that learning was conserved, commented upon, and communicated by successive generations of teachers and pupils gathering round a distinct tradition bequeathed to them by the particular founder of a School named after him.

Śākhās and Charaṇas. The term *Śākhā* was originally applied to the three original Saṁhitās of the *Ṛik*, *Sāma*, and *Yajus* regarded as the three branches or stems of the Veda-tree[1] having the same root, revelation (*Śruti*), and bearing the same fruit, the sacrifice (*karman*) [Kumārila and Āpastamba quoted by Max Müller, *Sans. Lit.*, p. 124]. More frequently, however, the term was used with reference to the different traditionary texts of each of the four Vedas. As Madhusūdana Sarasvatī puts it [ib. 122], " for each Veda there are several Śākhās, and their differences arise from various readings." The growth of a variety of readings in even the sacred texts of the Vedas is of course to be traced to the methods of teaching in vogue in those ancient times. Literary works did not then exist in writing and were devoid of any tangible, external form. The Vedic hymns had no outward existence except through those who heard and remembered them. Thus a book then existed merely as a body of thought handed down in schools or in families. A man who had mastered a book was himself the book. A work once composed might either wither for want of an audience, or grow, like a tree, of which every new listener who would learn it by heart would become a new branch (literally, *śākhā*). But we should not fail to distinguish between the branch, as the book, and the branch, as the reader ; that is to say, between the trust and the trustee. The former is to be designated *Śākhā* and the latter as the reader of a *Śākhā*, while we should also note in this connection that the term *Charaṇa* is to be applied to those ideal successions or fellowships to which all those belonged who read the same *Śākhā*. Thus the analogy of a branch of a tree was employed to convey what we in modern times understand by an edition, say, of a hundred copies. Literary works were handed down by oral tradition in different communities which thus represented, so to say, different works, or even different recensions of one and the same work, like so many MSS. in later times.

The reality of the phenomenon we have been noticing will be more fully realized from the fact that it had led to the growth of the special class of literature called the *Prātiśākhyas*

[1] It is said of Sāyaṇa that he wrote commentaries on each of the *Śākhās* of the Veda.

associated with what are known as the Vedic Śākhās. *Prātisākhya* does not mean a treatise on the phonetic peculiarities of each Veda but a collection of phonetic rules peculiar to one of the different *Śākhās* of the four Vedas, i.e. to one of those different texts in which each of the Vedas had been handed down for ages in different families and different parts of India. The *Śākhās*, as already explained, were not independent collections of the old hymns but different editions of one and the same original collection which in the course of a long continued oral tradition had become modified by slight degrees. The texts of the Veda as they existed and lived in the oral tradition of various sets of people became *Śākhās* differing from other *Śākhās* somewhat in the same way as the MSS. of the New Testament differ from one another. Indeed, most *Śākhas* differ merely in single words or verses, and not materially, in the arrangement of the hymns, and it is only in a few cases that we find one *Śākhā* containing some hymns more than another. Now along with this variety in the texts, there was also an inevitable variety in the methods of their pronunciation pursued by the different *Śākhās* or seats of Vedic learning. There thus grew up a certain number of local varieties in accent and pronunciation and in the recital of hymns, which were strictly and religiously adhered to out of the natural respect paid by each teacher, by each family, and by each Brahmanic community or guild to its own established oral tradition. Thus the *Prātisākhyas*, besides giving general rules for the proper pronunciation of the Vedic language as a safeguard against its further corruption—for already the idiom of the Veda was left far behind the spoken language of India as a kind of antique and sacred utterance so as to need for the preservation of its proper pronunciation a system of rules on metre, accent, and the like—were intended to record what was peculiar in the pronunciation of certain teachers and their schools in the absence of any criterion for determining what was the ancient and most correct way of reciting the sacred songs of the Veda. Even in cases where these Schools had become extinct, we find the names of their founders preserved as authorities on matters connected with the pronunciation of certain letters or words.

We have now considered the origin of the Vedic *Śākhās* which, as we have seen, rested on a variety of both readings and pronunciation. The original sense of the term *Śākhā* takes it to be a literary work, as in the expression *Śākhāṁ adhīte*, " he reads a particular recension of the Veda." But from its original sense of various editions, it soon came to mean the various traditions that branched off from each of the three original branches of the Veda, and in this latter sense it became synonymous with the term *Charaṇa*. The reason of this change in the use of the word seems to be that the *Śākhā* existed in those times not as a written book but only in the traditions of the *Charaṇas*, each member of a *Charaṇa* representing what, in our modern times, we should call the copy of a book. Thus the two terms were used in the same way as we speak of the Jews when we mean the Old Testament or of the Koran when we mean the Moslems.

This was, however, a loose use of the term *Śākhā*, for the real difference between a *Śākhā* and a *Charaṇa* was fully recognized. In a *Vārttika* to Pāṇini [iv, 1, 63] the term *Charaṇa* is taken to mean "the readers of a *Śākhā*" (*Śākhādhyetṛi*). In another place, Pāṇini alludes to *Charaṇas* as consisting of a number of followers [iv, 2, 46]. He also mentions the Kāṭhaka, Kālāpaka and Paippalādaka as Vedic recensions belonging to the *Charaṇas* of the Kaṭhas, Kalāpas, and Pippalādas [iv, 3, 126]. Again, in a Vārttika to Pāṇini [iv, 1, 63], there is a reference to women as belonging to a *Charaṇa*, for a *Kaṭhī* points to a woman who belongs to the *Charaṇa*, or reads the *Śākhā*, of the Kaṭhas. The best definition of a *Charaṇa* occurs in a passage in Jagaddhara's commentary on the *Mālatīmādhava*, where the *Charaṇa* is defined as "a number of men who are pledged to the reading of a certain *Śākhā* of the Veda and who have in this manner become one body" (*Charaṇaśabdaḥ śākhāviśeshādhyayanaparaikatāpanna-janasaṁghavāchī*). Thus, while the Śākhās denoted the texts, their propagators or *pravartakas* were the *Charaṇas*.

Brāhmaṇa-Charaṇas. Thus the *Charaṇas* were practically the Schools for the cultivation and propagation of particular texts of the Vedas. It should, however, be noted that just as the several Vedas under the system of oral tradition developed a variety of texts, so also did the *Brāhmaṇas* which, moreover, being not written in metre, like the Vedas, were more exposed to alteration in that process of propagation. This means that, besides the adoption of a particular text or recension of any of the Vedas, the second factor in the formation of a *Charaṇa* was the adoption of a *Brāhmaṇa* which, be it understood, was not usually or necessarily any independent work but merely one of the various recensions branching out of a common *Brāhmaṇa*. Originally, there was but one body of *Brāhmaṇas* for each of the three Vedas; for the Rigveda, the *Brāhmaṇas* of the Bahvṛichas, for the Sāmaveda, the *Brāhmaṇas* of the Chhandogas, and for the Yajurveda in its two forms, the *Brāhmaṇas* of the Taittirīyas and the Śatapatha Brāhmaṇa. These original *Brāhmaṇas* were compiled out of a floating stock of sayings and discussions which necessarily grew up in connection with the work of the several classes of priests, each specializing in a particular department of the sacrifice. They were, however, from their very character liable to much greater alteration in the course of a long-continued oral tradition than the Saṁhitā texts and were not to be met with very soon in their original forms, but in various recensions creating, and also adopted by, different *Charaṇas* which may be distinguished as *Brāhmaṇa*-Charaṇas from the *Saṁhitā*-Charaṇas. Thus the original Bahvṛicha-*Brāhmaṇa* of the Rigveda appeared in two recensions belonging to the *Charaṇas* of the Aitareyins and the Kaushītakins or Śāṅkhāyanins; the original *Chhāndogyam* appeared as the *Brāhmaṇa* of the Tāṇḍins and as the now lost works belonging to the *Charaṇas* of the Śāṭyāyanins and the Kauthumas; instead of one Adhvaryu-*Brāhmaṇa*, we have the dark code of the old Charakas, or the Taittirīyas and the Kaṭhas, and the new *Brāhmaṇa* of the Vājasaneyins and their descendants, the Kāṇvas and the Mādhyandinas. But the very variations in these *Brāhmaṇa* texts preserved by their respective *Charaṇas* point clearly to one and the same original from which they descended. This is true even of the two *Brāhmaṇas* of the Aitareyins and the Kaushītakins, which exhibit apparently deep differences in respect of ceremonial rules, order in which the sacrifices are described, and even illustrations and legends, but nevertheless show a common origin in their literary coincidence of whole chapters, frequent occurrences of the same sentences, comparisons, and instances, and the like.

There was thus quite a multitude of these *Charaṇas* due to differences in the text of the Vedic hymns as well as to discrepancies in the connected *Brāhmaṇas*, to judge from the numerous and frequent references to them. We can easily recall to ourselves the circumstances under which they arose. A great teacher gathering round him a number of students introduces to his newly-founded colony some sacred text which differs but slightly from the traditional texts kept up in the community to which he originally belonged. But he himself adds some chapters of his own composition or makes other changes in the imported text which in the eyes of the disciples united under his teachings might be sufficient to constitute a new work that should no longer pass under its original title. Thus new *Charaṇas* would be founded and the institutions would multiply, aiding in the propagation of the sacred learning and the extension of the area of its influence. It is thus that Vedic culture radiated in all directions from a comparatively small number of original centres until it spread over the entire continent. It should be noted in this connection that most of these *Charaṇas* differed from one another more in respect of their *Brāhmaṇas* than their Saṁhitās. Students following different *Śākhās*, as far as their *Brāhmaṇa* was concerned, might very well follow one and the same *Śākhā* of the Saṁhitā, though they would no longer call it by its own original name. But in most cases, and particularly in the *Charaṇas* of the Yajurveda, it is seen that a difference in the *Brāhmaṇas* leads to corresponding differences in the Saṁhitā, such as we find, for instance, in the hymns of the Kāṇvas and Mādhyandinas.

Parishads. There was also a third type of institutions developed for the cultivation and propagation of learning. These are known as *Parishads* (lit. sitting round). The term, as used in the Upanishads, means an assemblage of advisers in questions of philosophy. It was a settlement of Brāhmaṇas, a community or college to which members of any *Charaṇa* might belong. It therefore rested on a broader basis than a *Charaṇa* which signified an ideal succession of teachers and pupils who learn and teach a certain branch of the Veda. Thus members of the same *Charaṇa* might be Fellows of different *Parishads* and Fellows of the same *Parishad* might be members of different *Charaṇas*. The Gobhila Gṛihya Sūtra refers to a teacher with his *Parishad* [iii, 2, 40: *Āchāryaṁ saparishatkaṁ = saha parishadā śishyagaṇena vartate iti saparishatkaḥ tam*]. The term *pārshada* is often applied to the Prātiśākhyas [*Nirukta*, i, 17] and is explained by the commentator Durgāchārya to mean "those *pārshada* books by which in a *Parishad* (parish or college) of one's own *Charaṇa* (sect) the peculiarities of accent, Saṁhitā and *krama*-reading, of Pragṛihya-vowels, and separation of words, are laid down as enjoined for and restricted to certain *Śākhās* (branches or recensions of the Veda)". Thus the term *pārshada* is a generic term applied to any work that belonged to a *Parishad*, or formed, so to say, part of the traditional library of the *pārishadyas*, so that the Prātiśākhyas would be a section in the library of the *pārshada* works. Thus, while every Prātiśākhya may be called a *pārshada*, not every *pārshada* can be called a Prātiśākhya. If a follower of the Śākala-Charaṇa was a Fellow of the Vatsa-Parishad, the Śākala-prātiśākhya would necessarily be one of the Pārshada works of the Vatsas, and the Parishad of the Vatsas would through this Fellow be connected with the Śākala-Charaṇa. It should be noted in this connection that in later literature[1] the term *Parishad* does not denote so much an academic institution as a body of advisers on religious topics, also the assessors of a judge, or the Council of ministers[2] of a prince.

To sum up, we may say in modern phraseology that a *Parishat* corresponds to a University comprising students belonging to different colleges called *Charaṇas*.

Gotras. Somewhat akin to the institutions of *Śākhā*, *Charaṇa*, and *Parishad* is that of the *Gotra* or *Kula* which means a family depending on a real or imaginary community of blood and may exist among all the three castes. The *Charaṇas*, confined only to the Brāhmins, depend, as we have seen, not on the community of blood but on the community of sacred texts and were thus *ideal* fellowships held together by ties more sacred than the mere ties of blood. Hence members of different *Gotras* might belong to the same *Charaṇa*, the new *Charaṇa* might bear the name of its founder, and thus become synonymous, but not identical, with a *Gotra*. The names of the *Charaṇas* were naturally preserved as long as the texts which they embodied continued to be studied. The names of the *Gotras* were liable to confusion in later times when their number became too large, but the sacred works preserve the genealogical lists for Brahmins which, considering the respect they pay to their ancestors, may be taken to present a correct account of the priestly families of India. All Brahmin families are

[1] Cf. Manu and Yājñavalkya (i, 9), according to whom the *parishad* should consist of twenty-one Brāhmaṇas well versed in philosophy, theology, and law. Parāśara, however, lays down the following particulars regarding the constitution of *parishads* :

" Four, even three able men from amongst the Brahmins in a village, who know the Veda, and keep the sacrificial fire, may well form the Parishad.

" Or, if they do not keep the sacrificial fire, five or three who have studied the Vedas and Vedāṅgas and know the law.

" Of old sages, who possess the highest knowledge of the Divine Self, who are twice-born, perform sacrifices, and have purified themselves in the duties of the Vedà, one also may be considered as a Parishad.

" Thus five kinds of Parishads have been described by me : but if they all fail, three independent men may form a Parishad."

According to Bṛihaspati, " where seven, five, or three Brahmins who know the customs of the world, the Veda, and its Aṅgas, and the law have settled, that Assembly is like a *yajña* (*yajñasadriśī sabhā*).

[2] The *Kautilīya* uses the term in this sense and refers to the different numbers of members which, according to different political writers, can constitute that administrative council.

supposed to have descended from the seven Ṛishis, viz. Bhṛigu, Aṅgiras, Viśvāmitra, Vasishṭha, Kāśyapa, Atri, Agastya, but the real ancestors are the following eight, viz. Jamadagni, Gautama, Bharadvāja, Viśvāmitra, Vasishṭha, Kāśyapa, Atri, Agastya. The eight *Gotras* descending from these Ṛishis are again subdivided into forty-nine *Gotras* and these forty-nine branch off again into a still larger number of families. The names *Gotra*, *Vaṁśa*, *Varga*, *Paksha*, and *Gaṇa* are all used in the same sense to express the larger as well as the smaller families descended from the eight Ṛishis. A Brahmin, who keeps the sacrificial fire, is obliged by law to know to which of the forty-nine *Gotras* his own family belongs, and, in consecrating his own fire, he must invoke the ancestors who founded the *Gotra* to which he belongs. This invitation or invocation of the ancestors came to be called *Pravara*. Each of the forty-nine *Gotras* claims one or two or three or five ancestors, and the names of these ancestors constitute the distinctive character of each *Gotra*. Lists of these are to be found in the Kalpa-Sūtra works. Their reality is, to some extent, borne out by the fact that they have an important practical bearing upon the two essential ceremonies of Brahmanic society, viz. marriage and consecration of sacrificial fires.

Vedic Schools as Schools of both Law and Learning. We have now gained an insight into the system by which the *Saṁhitās* and *Brāhmaṇas* were handed down from generation to generation, the institutions by means of which Vedic literature was fostered and propagated until it extended to all parts of a vast country. Quite a network of Vedic schools was spread over the country, each of which specialized in particular texts of the Vedas and developed special commentaries of their own and later on even special codes of law so as to become a centre of both life and learning.[1] For in these ancient seats of learning there was no

[1] In the commentary to Parāśara's *Gṛihya Sūtras* (quoted by Max Müller, *History of Ancient Sanskrit Literature*), it is thus stated : " Vasishṭha declares that it is wrong to follow the rules of another *Śākhā*. He says, ' A wise person will certainly not perform the duties prescribed by another *Śākhā* ; he that does is called a traitor to his *Śākhā*. Whosoever leaves the law of his *Śākhā*, and adopts that of another, he sinks into blind darkness, having degraded a sacred Ṛishi.' And in another law book it is said : ' If a man gives up his own customs and performs others, whether out of ignorance or covetousness, he will fall and be destroyed.' And again, in the Pariśishṭa of the Chhandogas : ' A fool who ceases to follow his own *Śākhā*, wishing to adopt another one, his work will be in vain.' " Sometimes, different Brahmanical clans developed different physical marks distinguishing them. In a passage in the Gṛihya-saṁgraha-pariśishṭa (referred to by Max Müller, ibid.), it is mentioned how " the Vāsishṭhas wear a braid on the right side, the Ātreyas wear three braids, the Āṅgirasas wear five locks, the Bhṛigus have their heads quite shaved, others have a lock of hair on the top of the forehead ".

divorce between theory and practice, thought and life, speculation and action. Education, true to its literal sense, meant the development of all the faculties of man and included within its purview the totality of interests which make up life and not merely a section thereof, viz. the interests of intellectual life. It was education not merely in the contents of the sacred lore but also in the methods of living and self-culture according to the ideals embodied therein. Thus these seats of ancient learning were also the centres of life, of all that was best and highest in the community, centres of influence which vitalized the country. These ancient schools were not detached buildings of brick and mortar like modern schools, but were colonies in which were centred the talent, the piety, the culture of the community, from which they radiated in all directions. In them was represented the highest level of life marking the high water-mark of the nation's progress, from which it gradually filtered down to the lower planes of society. The secret of the success of these schools in spreading the learning and culture entrusted to their custody lay in the principle of decentralization, the principle akin to that underlying the domestic system of industrial organization as distinguished from the factory system. In the colonization of a new country the methods of *extensive* cultivation are more appropriate than those of *intensive*. Similarly, in the spread of a new culture and civilization, what is most needed is a multiplicity of centres of the new life and learning, any number of foci from which the new light can shine. Similar indeed are the methods of both physical and spiritual settlement and reclamation, of colonization and civilization.

Thus the numerous Vedic schools which sprang up in the different parts of the country were the chief agents in the Aryanization of the continent, in spreading through it the religion of the Vedas and the social system resulting from it. We shall now adduce some concrete particulars and facts regarding these schools of Vedic learning so as to appraise precisely the part they played in the propagation of the cause they were called upon to serve.

Charaṇas of the Vedas. Though the text of the *Rigveda* has come down to us in a single recension, there is no doubt that its propagation was accomplished in ancient times by the development of a number of *Charaṇas* based on a variety of its *Śākhās*. A comparatively late work belonging to the Sūtra period and known as the *Charaṇa-vyūha* or "Exposition of Schools" mentions as the five *Śākhās* or branches (more properly *Charaṇas*) of the Rigveda, the following, viz. :—

1. The Śākalas.
2. The Bāshkalas.
3. The Āśvalāyanas.
4. The Śāṅkhāyanas.
5. The Māṇḍukeyas.

This list leaves out the names of several old Śākhās such as the Aitareyins, Śaiśiras, Kaushītakins, Paiṅgins. The Śaiśira Śākhā may itself be a subdivision of the Śākala Śākhā, as the Purāṇas mention Śaiśira as one of the five pupils of Śākala like Mudgala, Gokula, Vātsya, Śālīya and Śiśira with the variants of the names in different Purāṇas, each of whom propagated different *Śākhās* of the Rigveda. The largest number of *Śākhās*, said to have been a thousand, is ascribed to the *Sāmaveda* of which the greater part is lost. The *Charaṇa-vyūha* mentions seven *Śākhās* of whom two are now known, viz. the *Kauthumas*, still existing in Gujarat, and the *Rāṇāyanīyas* at one time settled mainly in the Maratha country and now surviving in Eastern Hyderabad, while the Kauthumas themselves had five branches of which that called *Naigeya* is known. The number of *Śākhās* of the *Yajurveda* is stated at eighty six. There are twelve *Charaṇas* comprehended under the common name of *Charakas*. Of these, the *Kaṭhas* together with the *Kapisthala*-Kaṭhas were located in the time of the Greeks in the Pānjab, and later in Kashmir also, where the Kaṭhas are even now to be found, but the Kapisthalas have disappeared. Another branch called the *Maitrāyaṇīyas* is itself subdivided into seven *Charaṇas*. They were originally called *Kālāpas* and appear at one time to have occupied the region around the lower course of the Narmadā for a distance of some two hundred miles from the sea, extending to the south of its mouth more than a hundred miles, as far as Nāsik, and northwards beyond the modern city of Baroda. A few remnants of this School are still to be found in Gujarat, chiefly at Ahmedabad, and further west at Morvi. In the centuries before the Christian era, these two Schools seem to have been very widely diffused throughout India. Patañjali, the grammarian, for instance, refers to the Kaṭhas and Kālāpas as the universally known Schools of the *Yajurveda* whose doctrines were proclaimed in every village. The *Rāmāyaṇa* also tells us that these two schools were highly honoured in Ayodhyā (Oudh). Two new Schools afterwards rose to prominence and supplanted the old ones. These were the Schools of the *Taittirīyas* and the *Vājasaneyins*. The Taittirīyas had two branches, one of which, the *Khāṇḍikīya*, had itself five subdivisions, viz. the *Kāleyas*, the *Śāṭyāyanins*, *Hiraṇyakeśins*, *Bhāradvājins*, and *Āpastambins*. The *Taittirīyas* have been found only to the south of the Narmadā where they can be traced as far back as the fourth century A.D. The *Āpastambas* still survive in the region of the Godāvarī and the *Hiraṇyakeśins* still farther north. The *Vājasaneyins* comprising fifteen subordinate Śākhās spread themselves along the Ganges valley towards the south-east. At the present day they are to be found in North-East and Central India. The number of *Atharvaveda* Śākhās is given as nine including the Paippalādas, Śaunakas, and the like. [See Macdonell, *Sans. Lit.*, pp. 176–7.]

Vedic Charaṇas known to Pāṇini. It is interesting to note that the existence of the following Vedic Schools was known to Pāṇini and his commentators :—

1. Śākalas [iv, 3, 128 ; 2, 117].
2. Āśvalāyanas [iv, 1, 99].
3. Śāṅkhāyanas [iv, 1, 19 ; 1, 119].
4. Māṇḍukāyanas [ib.].
5. Charakas [iv, 3, 107 ; v, 1, 11].
6. Āhvarakas [ii, 4, 20 ; vi, 2, 124 ; iii, 2, 135].
7. Kaṭhās [iv, 3, 107 ; ii, 1, 65 ; vii, 4, 38 ; vi, 3, 42 ; ii, 4, 3 ; i, 3, 49 ; ii, 1, 163].
8. Prāchya-kaṭhas [vi, 2, 10].
9. Kapisthala-kaṭhas [viii, 3, 91].
10. Chārāyaṇīyas [iv, 1, 89 ; iv, 1, 63 ; i, 99 ; 3, 80].
11. Vāratantavīyas [iv, 3, 102].
12. Mānavas [iv, 1, 105].
13. Vārāhas [iv, 2, 80].
14. Haridrāvīyas [iv, 3, 104].
15. Śyāmāyanīyas [ib.].
16. Aukhīyas [iv, 3, 102].
17. Jābālas [vi, 2, 38 ; ii, 4, 58].
18. Baudheyas [ib.].
19. Kāṇvas [iv, 2, 111].
20. Pauṇḍravatsas [vii, 3, 24].
21. Avaṭikas [iv, 1, 17 ; iv, 1, 75].
22. Audheyas [ii, 4, 7].
23. Paippalādas [iv, 2, 66].
24. Śaunakas [iv, 3, 106].

Succession Lists of Teachers. Over and above the *Charaṇas* and other institutions, the *Brāhmaṇas* furnish us with lists of teachers through whom they were handed down. The Chhandogas, for instance, have assigned a separate *Brāhmaṇa* to the list of their teachers, viz. the *Vaṁśa-Brāhmaṇa*. In the *Śatapatha Brāhmaṇa*, these lists are repeated at the end of various sections. The number of teachers in the *Vaṁśa-Brāhmaṇa* amounts to fifty-three. In the *Śatapatha*, there are four *Vaṁśas*, the most important of which stands at the end of the whole work and consists of fifty-five names.

From the methods of the propagation of Vedic literature we now proceed to consider the methods of training, the ideals, rules, and principles regulating the relations between the teacher and the taught.

System of Education : 'Svādhyāya.' As has been already indicated, education was not yet regarded as an end in itself but only as a means to an end, viz. the attainment of *Brahmavarchasa*, i.e. sacred knowledge or knowledge of the Absolute. This is pointed out in numerous passages of Vedic literature.[1] The performance of sacrifice, of specific ritual acts[2] is also mentioned as means to this end of spiritual development but more stress is laid upon the study of the sacred texts. Indeed, the importance of such study is repeatedly insisted upon,[3] for which the technical name *svādhyāya* is applied. The efficacy of *svādhyāya* is pointed out by the *Śatapatha Brāhmaṇa* which regards it as a form of sacrifice to the Brahman by which an imperishable world is gained [xi, 5, 6, 3]. It is also pointed out that by the study and teaching of the Veda, one becomes calm in mind (*yuktamanāḥ*), independent of others, the best physician for himself, with his restraint of the senses, uniformity of mental attitude, growth of intelligence, fame, and the power of perfecting the people [ib., 7, 1]. The *Taittirīya Āraṇyaka* [ii, 9–15] also regards *svādhyāya* as *brahmayajña* or sacrifice of devotion and lays down certain directions as to the exact place and time of study. One should go outside the town or village, north or north-east, until the roofs cease to be seen and after sunrise and then repeat to himself the Vedas (as also other subjects connected therewith such as Brāhmaṇas, Itihāsas, Purāṇas, Kalpa, Gāthās and Nārāśaṁśīs). In times of difficulties the study may be carried on in the town or village during the day or night according to convenience. In that

[1] e.g. *Taitt. Saṁ.*, iv, 1, 7, 1 ; vii, 5, 18, 1 ; *Kāth. Saṁ.*, Aśvamedha, v, 14 ; *Vāja. Saṁ.*, xxii, 22 ; xxvii, 2 ; *Taitt. Br.*, iii, 8, 13, 1 ; *Ait. Br.*, iv, 11, 6–9 ; *Śat. Br.*, xiii, 2, 6, 10 ; x, 3, 5, 16 ; xi, 4, 4, 1 ; *Pañchav. Br.*, vi, 3, 5.

[2] *Kāth. Saṁ.*, xxxvii, 7 ; *Taitt. Br.*, ii, 7, 1, 1 ; *Pañch. Br.*, xxiii, 7, 3, etc. ; *Śat. Br.*, ii, 3, 1, 31, etc.

[3] *Śat. Br.*, i, 7, 2, 3 ; xi, 3, 3, 3–6 ; 5, 7, 10.

case there should be no loud repetition of the texts. In the afternoon one should recite more. When he returns home he is to make a gift. For this kind of study by one's own self without the aid of a teacher there is no *anadhyāya* or prohibition of study except when one is unclean in body or is in an unclean place. Another set of rules of Vedic study is given in the *Aitareya Āraṇyaka* [v, 3, 3]; " When the old water about the roots of the trees has been dried up, he should not study (the time after the full moon of Pausha, i.e. January–February is meant), nor in the forenoon, when the shadows meet, nor in the afternoon, nor when a thick cloud has arisen; and when rain falls out of season he should stop his study of the Veda (but not the study of Vedāṇgas, like Vyākaraṇa, as Sāyaṇa points out) for three nights, nor in this time should he tell tales, nor even at night at this time be fain to set them forth " [Keith's translation]. We may recall in this connection the earlier prohibitions of Vedic study in some specified times, places, and conditions in the Atharvaveda [vii, 66, Harvard ed.], viz. in cloudy weather, in storms, under the shade of trees, in green fields and within hearing of cattle.

Need of the Teacher. The necessity of self-study did not preclude that of the student finding a teacher for himself. The futility of mere self-study is always recognized. The teacher is represented as indispensable to knowledge in *Kaṭha-Upanishad* [ii, 8]: " Apart from the teacher, there is no access here." Simiiarly, the *Muṇḍaka-Upanishad* [i, 2, 3]: " Let him, in order to understand this, take fuel in his hand and approach a Guru who is learned and dwells entirely in Brahman." Again [iii, 2, 3]: " Not by self-study is the *ātman* realized, not by mental power; nor by amassing much information." A teacher is regarded as necessary to disperse the mist of empirically acquired knowledge from our eyes, as explained so beautifully in the following passage from the Chhāndogya Upanishad [vi, 14, 1–2]: " Precisely, my dear sir, as a man who has been brought blindfold from the country of Gandhāra and then set at liberty in the desert, goes astray to the east or north or south, because he has been brought thither blindfold and blindfold set at liberty; but after that someone has taken off the bandage, and has told him, ' In this direction Gandhāra lies, go in this direction,' instructed and prudent, asking the road from village to village, he finds his way home to Gandhāra; even so the man, who in this world has met with a teacher, becomes conscious, ' To this (transitory world) shall I belong only until the time of my release, thereupon shall I go home.' "

In the older Upanishads we repeatedly come across the prohibition to communicate a doctrine or ceremony to anyone except a son or a pupil adopted by the rite of *upanayanam* first mentioned in the Atharvaveda [xi, 5]. In *Aitareya Āraṇyaka* [iii, 2, 6, 9] the mystical meaning of the combinations of the letters must be " communicated to no one, who is not a pupil, who has not been a pupil for a whole year, who does not propose himself to be a teacher " [cf. also v, 3, 3, 4]. Again, the *Chhāndogya Upanishad* [iii, 11, 5] states : " A father may therefore tell that doctrine [i.e. the doctrine of Brahman as the sun of the universe] to his eldest son, or to a worthy pupil. But no one should tell it to anybody else, even if he gave him the whole sea-girt earth, full of treasure." In *Bṛihadāraṇyaka Upanishad* [vi, 3, 12] the ceremony of the mixed drink must be communicated to none but a son or a pupil. Similarly, the *Śvetāśvatara Upanishad* [vi, 22] : " This highest mystery in the Vedānta delivered in a former age should not be given to one whose passions have not been subdued nor to one who is not a son, or who is not a pupil." And the *Maitrāyaṇa-Upanishad* [vi, 29] : " Let no man preach this most secret doctrine to any one who is not his son or his pupil. . . To him alone who is devoted to his teacher only, and endowed with all necessary qualities may he communicate it."

We also find in the Upanishads men and gods taking fuel in their hands and submitting to the conditions of pupilage. The *Chhāndogya Upanishad* [viii] relates how Indra himself was obliged to live with Prajāpati as a pupil for 101 years in order to obtain the perfect instruction. In the *Kaushītaki-Upanishad* [i, 1] Āruṇi takes fuel in his hand and becomes a pupil of Chitra Gāṅgyāyani. In the *Bṛihadāraṇyaka* [ii, 1, 14] Gārgya says to Ajātaśatru : " Then let me come to you as a pupil." In the *Praśna-Upanishad* [i, 1] Sukeśas, Satyakāma, Sauryāyaṇin, Kausalya, Vaidarbhi, and Kabandhin take fuel in their hands to become pupils of Pippalāda [cf. also *Muṇḍ. Up.*, i, 2, 12, cited above].

Instruction without formal pupilage. At the same time the evidence seems to indicate that a formal pupilage was not absolutely binding in the earlier period. The differentiation between the four compulsory *āśramas* or life-stages was a comparatively late growth. Thus in the *Chhāndogya* [iv, 9, 3] it is merely said that " the knowledge which is gained from a teacher (as opposed to supernatural instruction by beasts, fire, geese, or ducks) leads most certainly to the goal." In another passage [v, 11, 7] King Aśvapati instructs six Brāhmaṇas who approach him with the fuel in their hands *anupanīya*, " without first admitting them as his pupils," or " demanding any preparatory rites ". In still another passage [vi, 1, 1] we read : " There lived once Śvetaketu Āruṇeya. To him his father (Uddālaka, the son of Aruṇa) said : ' Śvetaketu, go to school ; for there is none belonging to our race, darling, who, not having studied (the Veda) is, as it were, a Brāhmaṇa by birth only.' " From this remark it may be reasonably inferred that at that time entrance upon the life of a Brahmin-student, while it was a commendable custom, was not yet universally enjoined upon Brahmins. Similarly, the entrance also of Satyakāma upon studentship appears to be his voluntary determination (ib., iv, 4, 1]. Again, in the *Bṛihadāraṇyaka* [ii, 4] Yājñavalkya instructs his wife Maitreyī and King Janaka [iv, 1–2, 3–4] who yet were not strictly his pupils ; he also imparts knowledge on the deepest problems [as, e.g. iii, 8, in the conversation with Gārgī] in the presence of a numerous circle of hearers, and only exceptionally, when he desires to explain to Ārtabhāga the mystery of the soul's transmigration, does he retire with him into privacy [iii, 2, 13].

Father as Teacher. It is also evident from the evidence just cited that it was possible in those days for a man to receive instruction from his father or at the hands of other teachers. Śvetaketu did both [*Chhānd. Up.*, v, 3, 1 ; *Bṛihad.*, vi, 2, 1 ; *Kauṣī. Up.* i, 1 ; and *Chhānd.*, vi, 1, 1]. The *Śatapatha Brāhmaṇa* [i, 6, 2, 4] shows that a Brahmin was expected to instruct his own son in both study and sacrificial ritual, and furnishes an illustration of this in Varuṇa, the teacher of his son Bhṛigu. This fact also is borne out by the evidence of some of the names in the *Vaṁśa Brāhmaṇa* of the *Sāmaveda* and the Vaṁśa or list of teachers of the *Śāṅkhāyana Āraṇyaka* [xv, 1]. It should, however, be noted that these *Vaṁśas* and those of the *Śatapatha Brāhmaṇa* also show that a father often preferred that his son should have a famous teacher.

Admission to Studentship. Studentship is normally inaugurated by the ceremony of *upanayana* or initiation, the significance of which is most beautifully set forth in the *Atharvaveda* in the passage already explained. The spiritual significance of the details of the Upanayana ceremony is also indicated in the *Śatapatha* [xi, 5, 4]. " The teacher lays his right hand on the head of the pupil whereby he becomes pregnant with him (*tena garbhī bhavati*) and then in the third night the embryo issues out of the teacher and, being taught the Sāvitrī, obtains true Brahminhood" [see Sāyaṇa's commentary]. "He is like a divine creature born from his teacher's mouth" [xi, 5, 4, 17]. The request to be received by the preceptor was to be duly made [cf. *vidhivat* in *Muṇḍa. Up.*, i, 1, 3], according to the *Bṛihadāraṇyaka* [vi, 2, 7], with the words—*upaimi ahaṁ bhavantam*. In the *Śatapatha* [xi, 5, 4, 1] the student has to say formally: "May I enter upon brahmacharya", and "Let me be a Brahmachārin". The student has also to take the fuel in his hand as a token that he is willing to serve the teacher, and especially to maintain the sacred fires [see previous passages cited: *Kaushī. Up.*, iv, 19; *Chhānd.*, iv, 4, 5; v, 13, 7; viii, 7, 2; 10, 3; 11, 2; *Muṇḍ.*, i, 2, 12; *Praśna.*, i, 1]. Before receiving him, the teacher makes inquiry into his birth and family. Satyakāma Jābāla going to Gautama Hāridrumata said to him: "I wish to become a Brahmachārin with you, Sir. May I come to you, Sir?" He said to him: "Of what family are you, my friend?'" The manner of the inquiry shows that it was made in a very indulgent fashion and the uncertainty regarding his parentage was not in actual practice admitted as a bar to the teacher's acceptance of the pupil [*Chhānd.*, iv, 4, 4]. In the *Śatapatha Brāhmaṇa* [xi, 5, 4, 1], similarly, the teacher merely asks the name of the intending pupil and then accepts him.

Period of Studentship. The period of studentship was normally fixed at twelve years. Śvetaketu returned home after spending twelve years with his preceptor [*Chhānd.*, vi, 1, 2]. Upakosala Kāmalāyana "dwelt as a Brahmachārin in the house of Satyakāma Jābāla and tended his fires for twelve years" [ib., iv, 10, 1]. There also seem to have been longer terms than twelve years. Satyakāma Jābāla spent "a series of years" with his preceptor during which "four hundred cows had become a thousand" [iv, 4, 5]. The *Aitareya Brāhmaṇa* [xxii, 9] tells of a student named Nābhānedishṭha who had been absent from home on *brahmacharya* under his teacher for such a long time that his father divided up his property among his other sons in the meanwhile. Studentship for thirty-two years is also mentioned (*Chhānd.*, viii, 7, 3] and also for 101 years [ib., 11, 3].

The age at which such studentship commenced is indicated in the case of Śvetaketu who "began his apprenticeship with a teacher when he was twelve years of age" [ib., vi, 1, 2].

We shall now consider the conditions and duties of studentship.

External Duties of Studentship. The first condition, of course, was that the student had to live in the house of his teacher. Even the *Atharvaveda* [vii, 109, 7] refers to this condition in the phrase "if we have *dwelt* in studentship" (*brahmacharyaṁ yadūshima*). It is also referred to in the *Śatapatha Brāhmaṇa* [xi, 3, 3, 2] as also in the *Aitareya*[1] [v, 14] and *Taittirīya*[2] *Brāhmaṇas* [iii, 7, 6, 3]. The *Chhāndogya Upanishad* applies to the student the epithets *āchārya-kula-vāsin* [ii, 23, 2] and *ante-vāsin* [iii, 11, 5; iv, 10, 1]. The latter epithet is also used in *Bṛihadāraṇyaka* [vi, 3, 7] and *Taittirīya Upanishads* [i, 3, 3; 11, 1].

Begging. It was the usual rule of the Brahmachārin to go about *begging* for his teacher. In the *Chhāndogya* [iv, 3, 5] while the householders Śaunaka Kāpeya and Abhipratārin Kākshaseni were being waited on at their meal, a religious student begged of them. The *Śatapatha Brāhmaṇa* [xi, 3, 3, 5] also refers to the Brahmachārin begging for alms, as well as the *Atharvaveda* [vi, 133, 3]. It is also clear from the aforesaid passage of the *Śatapatha* that begging was prescribed for the student to produce in him a proper spirit of humility: "Having made himself poor, as it were, and become devoid of shame, he begs alms."

Tending Fire. Another of his duties was to *tend the sacred fires*. Upakosala tended the sacred fires for twelve years and yet his teacher does not allow him to return home but goes away on a journey without having taught him [*Chhānd.*, iv, 10, 1–2]. Looking after the sacrificial fires is also mentioned in the *Śatapatha Brāhmaṇa* [xi, 3, 3, 4]. Elsewhere in the same work [xi, 5, 4, 5] the duty of the Brahmachārin is stated to be to "put on fuel", the spiritual significance of which is also explained, viz. "to enkindle the mind with fire, with holy lustre."

Tending Cattle. *Tending the house* also was one of his duties. In the *Śatapatha Brāhmaṇa* we read: "Wherefore the students guard their teacher, his house, and cattle" [iii, 6, 2, 15]. In the *Chhāndogya Upanishad* [iv, 4, 5] Satyakāma is sent away with the teacher's herds of cattle into a distant country where he remains for a succession of years during which four hundred cows had become a thousand. The duty of guarding the teacher's cattle grazing on their pasture grounds is also referred to in the *Śāṅkhāyana Āraṇyaka* [vii, 19]. In the *Aitareya Āraṇyaka* [iii, 1, 6, 3–4] Tārukshya guards his teacher's cows for a whole year.

[1] The story of a boy whose brothers divided the paternal property among themselves while he lived with his teacher, studying the Vedas (*brahmacharyaṁ vasantam*).

[2] *Yo vo devāścharati brahmacharyam.*

The Brahmachārin is also enjoined not to sleep in the daytime [*Śatap.*, xi, 5, 4, 5].

On festive occasions, the teacher was accompanied by his pupils who awaited his commands. At the sacrifice of Janaka of Videha, whither had come the Brāhmaṇas of the Kurus and Pāñchālas, when a thousand cows with ten *pādas* of gold attached to each pair of their horns were offered to the wisest Brāhmaṇa, Yajñavalkya stepped forward and asked his pupils to drive them away [*Bṛihad. Up.*, iii, 1, 1–2].

Study. Together with, and after, these acts of service, "in the time remaining over from work for the teacher" [*Guroḥ karmātiśesheṇa*] the pupil prosecuted his studies [*Chhānd.*, viii, 15]. Considering the early age at which students were admitted to study, we should consider what might have been its contents in that primary stage of education. For initiation into such study which was then a study of the Veda, the student should start with a knowledge of the pronunciation of its texts with all that it implied, a knowledge of phonology, metrics, and elementary grammar and etymology. The *Taittirīya* Prātiśakhya [chap. xxiv] states that a student of Veda should first know all about the production of voice or sound: "the degree of effort involved in it, whether it is heavy (*guru*), light (*laghu*) or equal (*sama*), whether it is long (*dīrgha*), short (*hrasva*), or very long or elongated (*pluta*); whether it has undergone elision (*lopa*), addition (*āgama*), or modification (*vikāsa*); its exact nature (*prakṛiti*) and modification (*vikṛiti*), as also stages in the process of its production (*krama*); the degree of its pitch, high (*svarita*), moderate (*udātta*), or low (*nīcha*); the degree of strength of breath in its utterance (*nāda* and *śvāsa*) and also place of its origin (*udgama*)."[1] He should also have a special knowledge (*viśeshajña*) of the *Pada-Pāṭha* and *Varṇa-Pāṭha* (i.e. how each letter is modulated under the influence of each preceding and succeeding letter); the difference between *svaras* (vowels) and the *mātrā* or measure of effort with which they are pronounced.

An idea of the actual regulations governing Vedic studies may be obtained from a passage from the *Aitareya Āraṇyaka* at the

[1] The character of a sound as *a*, *ka*, *cha*, *ṭa*, *ta*, *pa*, *ya*, etc., depends on the place of its origin along the passage of breath used in its utterance within the mouth, whether it is throat (*kaṇṭha*), tip of tongue (*jihvāmūla*), lips (*oshṭha*), etc. From *jihvāmūla*, there are three bifurcations towards palate (*tālu*), *mūrdhā* (head), and teeth (*danta*), producing what are called labial, cerebral, and dental sounds. *Svara* or vowel implies free passage of voice as *a*; it is not free but touches other places in the case of consonants (*vyañjanavarṇa*). If the touch is slight, the result is *antastha-varṇa*. Thus vowel is *a-spṛishṭa*, consonant *spṛishṭa*.

end of its fifth *Āraṇyaka* giving restrictions as to the recitation and teaching of the *Mahāvrata*. The passage gives the following rules among others :

" The teacher and pupil should not stand, nor walk, nor lie down, nor sit on a couch ; but they should both sit on the ground.

" The pupil should not lean backward while learning, nor lean forward. He should not be covered with too much clothing, nor assume the postures of a devotee, but without using any of the apparel of a devotee, simply elevate his knees. Nor should he learn, when he has eaten flesh, or when he has seen blood, or a corpse, or when he has done an unlawful thing ; when he has anointed his eyes, oiled or rubbed his body, when he has been shaved or bathed, put colour on, or ornamented with flower-wreaths, when he has been *writing* or effacing his writing (probably the earliest mention of actual writing in Sanskrit literature)."

Inner Disciplines. By means of these external practices and regulations it was sought to develop in the young pupils those internal conditions [*pratyāsanna, direct*, as opposed to *vādhya*], or mental and moral attributes, which would afterwards fit them for being taught the highest knowledge, the knowledge of the Brahman forming the special subject-matter of the Upanishads. Various presuppositions of Upanishadic instruction, or preparatory means to a knowledge of the Brahman, are laid down in the Upanishads as well as in some earlier works.

Thus the *Gopatha Brāhmaṇa* [ii, 1, 2, 1–9] requires the Brahmachārin to overcome the same passions, viz., caste-pride (*brahmavarchasam*), fame, sleep, anger, bragging, personal beauty and fragrance as are associated respectively with the antelope, the teacher, the boa, the boar, water, maidens, trees, and plants. If he clothes himself in the skin of the antelope he obtains *brahmavarchasam* ; if he works for his teacher, he obtains the latter's fame ; if, though sleepy, he abstains from sleep, he obtains the sleep that is in the boa ; if, humble in spirit, he does not injure anyone through anger he obtains the anger that is in the boar ; if he does not perform braggart tricks in the water he obtains the vanity that is in the water ; if he does not look at a naked maiden he obtains the beauty that is in the maiden ; if he does not smell at plants and trees, after having cut them, he becomes himself fragrant [Bloomfield, *Atharvaveda*, p. 111].

The Upanishads [1] require that the Brahmachārin, before he is taught the highest knowledge, the knowledge of the Brahman,

[1] *Bṛih.*, iv, 4, 23, enumerating all the five attributes.

should show that he is calm and unperturbed in mind (*śānta*),[1] self-restrained (*dānta*), self-denying (*uparata*),[2] patient (*titikshu*) and collected (*samāhita*).[3] To these are sometimes added purity of food and as a consequence purity of nature (*sattvaśuddhi*)[4]; the fulfilment of the vow of the head (*śirovratam*)[5] which indicated either the rite of carrying fire on the head, or, as Deussen[6] suggests, of shaving the head bare (as implied by the term *muṇḍaka*).

Achievement of Highest Knowledge. More often, as might be naturally expected, the realization of the knowledge of Brahman, with its hard conditions and pre-requisites, required the dedication of a whole life and not merely of a part of it. Śvetaketu coming home, after twelve years of studentship, "conceited, considering himself well-read and stern" and ignorant of the knowledge of the Brahman, was probably typical of such students as failed to attain the highest knowledge during the comparatively brief period of their pupilage and were deemed unworthy of that instruction [*Chhānd.*, vi, 1]. Upakosala Kāmalāyana was probably another such case who in spite of his twelve years of austere studentship was not deemed worthy of instruction by his teacher [ib., iv, 10]. Indeed, it is reasonable to assume that some of the moral attributes insisted upon as presuppositions of instruction, being, as they are, but the preparatory means to the highest end of human life—the attainment of the knowledge of the Brahman—belong to the last stages of a disciplined life as the fruit of a long struggle rather than to its first stage. They cannot be regarded as the normal initial endowments with which a youthful student starts in his career. The epithets *śānta*, *dānta*, *uparata*, and the like are hardly applicable, for instance, to an immature stripling who has had no experience of the struggle and temptations of life, of "the ills that flesh is heir to".

Its Pursuit through Life. This view is supported by several passages from the Upanishads in which the conception of the scope of *brahmacharya* is widened so as to embrace not merely the student-period proper but the entire course of life regulated by the disciplines of its four successive *āśramas* or stages as the way that leads to the Ātman. Thus in the *Bṛihadāraṇyaka* [iv, 4, 22] we read : "Brāhmaṇas seek to know Him by the study

[1] *Kaṭha*, ii, 24 ; *Muṇḍ.*, i, 2, 13 ; *Śvet.*, vi, 22 ; *Maitrā.*, vi, 29.
[2] *Kaṭha*, ib. [3] Ib.
[4] *Chhānd.*, vii, 26, 2 ; *Muṇḍ.*, iii, 2, 6 ; cf. also *Mahānār.*, x, 22, and *Kaivalya*, 3, 4. [5] *Muṇḍaka*, iii, 2, 10–11.
[6] *Philosophy of the Upanishads*, p. 73, to which I owe some valuable hints.

of the Veda, by sacrifice, by gifts, by penance, by fasting, and he who knows Him becomes a *muni*. Wishing for that World (for Brahman) only, mendicants leave their homes. Knowing this, the people of old did not wish for offspring . . . and they having risen above the desire for sons, wealth, and new worlds wander about as mendicants." There is here a clear reference to all the four *āśramas* or life-stages. Similarly, in the *Chhāndogya* [ii, 23] we read : " There are three branches of duty. Sacrifice, study, and charity are the first (i.e. the *gṛihastha-āśrama*) ; austerity the second (i.e. *Vānaprastha*, the third *āśrama*), and to dwell as a Brahmachārin in the house of a teacher, always mortifying the body in the house of a teacher, is the third (referring not to the ordinary, but the *naiṣṭhika*, or perpetual, *brahmachārin*). All these obtain the worlds of the blessed ; but the Brahmasaṁstha (referring to the fourth *āśrama*, the sannyāsin or *parivrāj*) alone obtains immortality." A more explicit passage occurs in the same Upanishad [viii, 15] in which the Brahmachārin is exhorted, after completing his studentship, to become a householder and attain fruition in a life of self-study and self-discipline. In another passage [viii, 5], the observances of the last three *āśramas* such as sacrifices, vow of silence, fasting and living an anchorite's life in the forest are recognized as being ultimately but forms of *brahmacharya* as the underlying principle of life. In the *Kena* [xxxiii] asceticism, self-restraint, and sacrifice (*tapas*, *dama*, *karman*) are specified as the preliminary conditions (*pratishṭhāḥ*) for attaining the *Brāhmī Upanishad*, i.e. the mystical doctrine which reveals Brahman. In the *Kaṭha* [ii, 15], all the Vedas, all the practices of *tapas* and *brahmacharyam* are described as means by which *Om* (Brahman) is to be sought as the final aim. In *Muṇḍaka* [ii, 1, 7] the observances of the *āśramas* are referred to as *tapas*, *śraddhā*, *satyam*, *brahmacharyam*, and *vidhi*. The *Praśna* [i, 2] insists on penance (*tapas*), abstinence (*brahmacharyam*), and faith (*śraddhā*). Thus the knowledge aimed at in the Upanishads calls for the application of the whole life through all its stages. It is also clear that the various prerequisites mentioned for that knowledge rest upon a common basis of a life of abstinence and asceticism for which the term *brahmacharya* or *tapas* is generally applied in an extended connotation. Nearly all the Upanishads emphasize the need of asceticism or practice of *tapas* in all stages of life. In the *Bṛihadāraṇyaka* [ii, 4] Yājñavalkya departs into the solitude of the forest in order to practise *tapas* which, by gradually increasing privations and penances, destroys in the ascetic the last links of dependence on earthly existence. In the *Chhāndogya* [iv, 10] Upakosala, the student, is " quite exhausted with austerities, and from mortification was not able to eat ". The *Taittirīya Upanishad* [i, 9] demands of the student asceticism and study of the Veda and quotes the views of two teachers, Taponitya Pauruśishṭhi and Nāka Maudgalya, of whom the former requires " asceticism alone " and the other " study of the Veda ", for " this is asceticism ". Varuṇa repeatedly urges his son Bhṛigu thus : " By *tapas* seek to know Brahman " [ib. iii]. In *Muṇḍaka* [i, 2, 11] the way of the gods is promised to those " who practise asceticism and faith in the forest ". The *Praśna* [i, 10] offers it to those " who have sought the *ātman* by asceticism ". In the *Maitrāyaṇa* [iv, 3] it is stated that " without being an ascetic it is impossible either to attain the knowledge of the *ātman*, or to bring work to fruition ", but asceticism alone does not always secure knowledge of the *ātman*, as in the case of King Bṛihadratha who, renouncing his kingdom, went into the forest and practised highest penance for a thousand days without " knowing the Self " [i, 2].

Examples. That the teaching of the Upanishads was not always confined to the first period of life is also evident from a few concrete examples. Śvetaketu Āruṇeya, on reporting to his father Gautama the imperfect character of the instruction he received from him, as proved by his inability to answer some questions put to him by King (Rājanya) Pravāhaṇa Jaivali, was thus told by his father : " You know me, child, that whatever I know, I told you. But come, we shall go thither, and dwell there as students." Gautama then goes to the king who asks him : " Gautama, do you wish (for instruction from me) in the proper way ? " Gautama replied : " I come to you as a pupil." In the *Chhāndogya* [vi, 1–6] the father of Śvetaketu himself regards his son's education as incomplete when he returns home after twelve years of studentship and is not able to answer his father's question whether " he had that teaching whereby what is not heard of, thought of, or understood becomes so, just as by one piece of clay, copper, or a pair of scissors, everything made of clay, copper, or iron, may be known ". And then the father himself undertakes the further education of his son at home. There are other examples which point to temporary association between teachers, and elderly pupils or householders, for the imparting of knowledge of some special doctrines and truths. In the *Bṛihadāraṇyaka* [ii, 4 ; iv, 1–2, 3–4 ; iii, 8 ; 2, 13, already cited] Yājñavalkya

A MUTTRA SCULPTURE (*c.* first century B.C.).

Showing a typical Brahmanical anchorite with his high chignon, beard, short garments, seat of mat, round leafy hut; four other fellow-denizens of his hermitage, a dove, a crow, a kneeling doe, and a coiled snake, all living at peace as friends in its atmosphere of non-violence

According to Foucher, this sculpture is a product of pre-Gandhāra indigenous school in its simple style of decoration unlike the ornate and foreign style of Gandhāra art

[*Facing p. 98*

instructs Maitreyī, Janaka, Gārgī, and Ārtabhāga. In the *Chhāndogya* [v, 11], "five great householders and theologians"—Prāchīnaśāla Aupamanyava, Satyayajña Paulushi, Indradyumna Bhāllaveya, Jana Śārkarākshya and Buḍila Āśvatarāśvi—first go for some special instruction to Uddālaka Āruṇi and these—all of advanced age—then go to Aśvapati Kaikeya as the best teacher for the purpose. In the *Muṇḍaka* [i, 1, 3] Śaunaka, who is described as a great householder (*mahāśālaḥ*) approaches Aṅgirasa for instruction. In the *Chhānd.* [vii, 1] Nārada approaches Sanatkumāra after completing the period of ordinary studentship during which he has studied a variety of subjects, and says: "I, Sir, have learnt all the *mantras* but do not yet know what *Ātman* is." In another passage [viii, 7–11] Indra grows old in learning at the house of his preceptor. Āpastamba cites the opinion of Śvetaketu that a person who has returned home (*niveśe vṛitte*) after completing his studentship should spend two months every year with his teacher if he wishes to extend his knowledge [*dvau dvau māsau āchārya-kule vaset bhūyaḥ śrutam ichchhan* (i, 4, 13, 19–21)]. But this opinion was against Śāstra (tat śāstraiḥ vipratisiddham | Niveśe vṛitte naiyāmikāni śrūyaṁte), because householders have their own duties to attend to. Nevertheless, Āpastamba accepts this doctrine for a graduate who has need to master a subject, for which he can return to his teacher to complete his unfinished knowledge [ii, 2, 5, 15].

Teacher's Farewell Address to Students. That the period of studentship was regarded as preparatory for the realization of the knowledge of the Absolute is also evident from the following parting words a teacher generally addressed to his student when he was permitted to return home after the completion of his studies and begin the next stage of life as a householder:

"Say what is true! Do thy duty! Do not neglect the study of the Veda! After presenting gifts[1] to thy teacher, take care that the thread of thy race be not broken! Do not swerve from Truth, from duty! Do not neglect your health! Do not neglect your worldly prosperity![1] Do not neglect the learning and teaching of the Veda!

"Do not neglect the (sacrificial) works due to the Gods and Manes! Let thy mother be to thee like unto a god! Let thy father be to thee like unto a god! Let thy preceptor be to thee like

[1] The *Śatapatha Brāhmaṇa* lays down that one must "not beg alms after he has bathed (at the end of studentship)"—a very significant and wholesome restriction for the householder with the responsibilities of his position [xi, 3, 3, 7].

unto a god ! Let thy guest be to thee like unto a god ! Whatever actions are blameless, those should be regarded, not others. Whatever good works have been performed by us, those should be observed by thee—not others. And there are some Brāhmaṇas better than we. These you should show proper reverence. Whatever is given should be given with faith, not without faith—with joy, with modesty, with fear, from sense of duty. If there should be any doubt in thy mind with regard to any sacred act or with regard to conduct,—

" In that case conduct thyself as Brāhmaṇas who possess good judgment conduct themselves therein, whether they be appointed or not, as long as they are not too severe but devoted to duty. And with regard to things that are doubtful, as Brāhmaṇas who possess good judgment conduct themselves therein, whether they be appointed or not, as long as they are not too severe but devoted to duty.

" Thus conduct thyself. This is my admonition. This is the teaching. This is the true purport (*upanishad*) of the Veda. This is the command. Thus should you observe. Thus should this be observed."

These words addressed to the student at the end of his career read almost like the Chancellor's Convocation Address to the students of a modern University passing out of its portals on their admission to their degrees. It will be noticed that in the ancient valedictory address, emphasis is laid upon several interesting points. In the first place, entering upon the householder's life and fatherhood is enjoined as a compulsory religious duty in the interests of the continuity of the race. In the second place is enjoined the duty of studying and teaching the Veda in the interests of the continuity of culture. Indeed, one of the understood conditions of studentship is the obligation to teach and thus transmit learning from age to age [*Ait. Ār.*, iii, 2, 6 : *nāpravaktre* (" don't teach one who won't himself teach ")]. In the third place, the duties of domestic and social life are indicated. They are : to honour [1] father, mother, teacher, and guest as gods ; to honour superiors ; to give in proper manner and spirit, in joy and humility, in fear and compassion, so that it may " bless both him that gives and him that takes " ; to perform sacrifices and, in all doubtful cases, to order himself according to the judgment of approved authorities. Lastly, the pupil is also admonished not to neglect

[1] This anticipates the almost similar language employed in some of the Asokan rock-edicts.

health and possessions [*Taitt. Up.*, i, 11]. In an earlier passage [i, 9] learning and teaching of the Veda are enjoined together with the pursuit of Right, Truth, Penance, Restraint, Tranquillity, Consecration of Fires, Sacrifice, entertainment of guests, social duties, marriage, fatherhood, and grandfatherhood. We may in passing note the spirit of humility characterizing the teacher as shown in his asking his pupil to imitate his good points and ignore his bad ones, and recognizing his superiors.

Relations between Teacher and Taught. The relations between the teacher and the taught were of the happiest kind. The pupil looked up to his preceptor as his father [*Praśna*, vi, 8]. As indicated in the propitiatory verse beginning with *Sahanāvavatu*, which is uttered at the beginning of each day's study, the teacher and his pupil were united by a common aim of preserving and propagating the sacred learning and showing its worth in their life and conduct. Sometimes, the *antevāsins* living in the house of the teacher preferred, and were permitted, to continue that life throughout, because it was so agreeable [*Chhānd.*, ii, 23, 2].

We have now considered the conditions and duties appertaining to studentship. We shall now consider those of the teacher.

Duties of the Teacher. He is to possess the highest moral and spiritual qualifications. "This Truth is not grasped when taught by an inferior man," says the *Kaṭha* [i, 2, 8]. The *Muṇḍaka* [i, 2, 12] requires him to be well versed in the sacred lore (*śrotriya*) and dwelling entirely in the Brahman (*brahmanishṭha*). He must have a conviction based upon realization of the Unity on which he is to enlighten his pupils ; otherwise it would be like the blind leading the blind.

It is the duty of the teacher, when a fit pupil approaches him, to teach him the truth exactly as he knows it [*Muṇd.*, i, 2, 13] without concealing anything from him, for such concealment would spell ruin to him [*Praśna*, vi, 1]. The *Taittirīya Āraṇyaka* [vii, 4] lays down that the teacher must teach with all his heart and soul. He was bound also, according to the *Śatapatha Brāhmaṇa* [xiv, 1, 1, 26, 27], to reveal everything to his pupil who at any rate lived with him for one whole year (*saṁvatsara-vāsin*), an expression which probably hints at possible changes of teachers by students. The teacher, however, was quite free, it must be understood, to impart to his pupil only the knowledge that he was fit for and reserve subjects to which he was not equal. There are on record certain cases of learning kept secret and revealed only to special persons [e.g. the Vasishṭhas and the Stomabhāgas in *Pañch. Br.* xv, 5, 24, *Taitt. Br.*, iii, 5, 2. 1; *Kāṭh. Saṁ.*, xxxvii, 17; Pravāhaṇa Jaivali and his knowledge of Brahman in *Bṛihad. Up.*, vi, 1, 11].

Change of Teacher. Where the teacher found that he was not quite fit to teach a subject, he considered it to be his duty to send up its student to a fitter teacher. An interesting case on this point is mentioned in the *Gopatha Brāhmaṇa* [i, 1, 31]. As a result of discussion between two teachers, Maudgalya and Maitreya, Maitreya found his friend to have a superior knowledge of the subject he was teaching. He was so conscientious that he at once dissolved his class studying that subject and would not resume teaching until he mastered the subject like Maudgalya.

Teacher's Desire for Pupils. This conscientiousness on the part of teachers was, however, consistent with their desire for securing as many pupils as they could teach. This desire was natural in teachers who felt that the truths they had discovered should live after them in their pupils through a succession of teachers, *guru-pāramparya*, keeping up the continuity of culture and an unbroken tradition in knowledge. Every teacher was anxious to assure the continuity of his School of Thought and for pupils who could contribute to that continuity. The *Taittirīya Āraṇyaka* [vii, 4] shows this anxiety of teachers to get pupils and a kind of competition among them for same. A prayer to the same effect is contained in the *Taittirīya Upanishad* (i, 4, 3]: "As water runs downward, as the months go to the year, so, O God, may Brahmachārins always come to me from all quarters!" Very often good teachers were themselves sought after by many pupils, and that from distant places. Patañchala Kāpya was thus sought by "a company of students wandering as far as the land of the Madras (on the Hyphasis or Beas) to learn the Sacrifices" of which he was a master [*Bṛi. Up.*, iii, 3, 1; 7, 1].

Studentship Open to First Three Castes. In connection with these details regarding the religious studentship of the period we have now to consider how far it was thrown open to the other castes and the other sex.

According to the later evidence of the Gṛihya Sūtras, the three twice-born castes were all required to undergo a period of studentship. It was practically a system of universal compulsory education for the Indo-Aryans.[1] The course of training and

[1] This probably explains the ground of the remarkable boast of King Aśvapati Kaikeya in the *Chhāndogya Upanishad* [v, 11, 5]: "In my kingdom there is . . . *no ignorant person*. . . ."

subjects of study were not of course uniform for all the castes. Some scholars support the evidence of the Gṛihya Sūtras by the reference in the *Atharvaveda* [xv, 5, 17] to the king guarding his country by *Brahmacharya*, though it lends itself to a different interpretation. More conclusive, however, is the evidence of the *Kāṭhaka Saṁhitā* [ix, 16] in its reference to the rite intended to benefit one who, although not a Brāhmaṇa, had yet studied (*vidyām anūchya*) but had not acquired fame. We must add to this the evidence of the *Brāhmaṇas* and *Upanishads* regarding learned Kshatriyas and princes who studied the Vedas and attained proficiency in the sacred lore which was the special property of the Brāhmaṇas.

Kshatriyas as Teachers. In the *Śatapatha Brāhmaṇa* [xi, 6, 2, 1] King Janaka of Videha meets with some travelling Brāhmaṇas named Śvetaketu Āruṇeya, Soma-śushma Sātyayajñi, and Yājñavalkya, and asks them how they offered the *agnihotra* oblation. Each of the three answers the question but with regard to the answer of Yājñavalkya the King compliments him by saying : " Thou hast approached very close to a solution of the Agnihotra, O Yājñavalkya," pointing out at the same time the incompleteness of his answer in certain respects. The Brāhmaṇas then said amongst themselves : " This Rājanya has surpassed us in speaking ; come, let us invite him to a theological discussion." Yājñavalkya, however, interposed : " We are Brāhmaṇas and he a Rājanya ; if we overcome him, we shall ask ourselves, Whom have we overcome ? But if he overcome us, men will say to us, A Rājanya has overcome Brāhmaṇas. Do not follow this course." In the end the Agnihotra is explained by Janaka and on Yājña-valkya offering him the choice of a boon he replied : " Let mine be the privilege of asking questions of thee when I list." Hence-forward Janaka became a Brāhmaṇa, i.e. *brahmiṣṭha*, full of divine knowledge.

Janaka was typical of a class of learned Kshatriyas of the period. In the *Kaushītaki Upanishad* [iv, 1] the Brāhmaṇa Gārgya Bālāki " well read in the Veda " is " silenced by the display of superior knowledge on every topic by Ajātaśatru, King of Kāśī. " Then the son of Balāka approached the king with fuel in his hand and said, ' Let me attend thee (as thy pupil) ' [*Samitpāṇiḥ pratichakrame upāyāni iti*]. The king replied, ' I regard it as an inversion of the proper rule that a Kshatriya should initiate a Brāhmaṇa. But come, I will instruct thee then. Having taken him by the hand, he departed " [Pratilomarūpameva tad manye yat Kshatriyo Brāhmaṇaṁ upanayeta]. In the *Śatapatha Brāhmaṇa* [v, 3, 7] nearly the same story is told of Dṛipta-Bālāki Gārgya and also in *Bṛihadāraṇyaka Upanishad* [ii, 1, 1]. Similarly, Pravāhaṇa Jaivali, King of the Pañchālas, silenced Śvetaketu Āruṇeya and his father and treating them as his disciples communicated to them knowledge which "has never heretofore dwelt in any Brāhmaṇa" [*Śatap. Br.*, xiv, 9, 1, 1; *Bṛihad.*, vi, 1, 1; *Chhānd.*, i, 8, 1; v, 3, 1]. Another learned king was Aśvapati Kaikeya to whom came "with fuel in their hands" five learned Brāhmaṇas to become his pupils. The king said: "How is this, venerable Sirs, when ye are learned in the scriptures and sons of men learned in the scriptures?" They replied: "Venerable Sir, thou knowest Vaiśvānara thoroughly: teach us Him!" He said: "I do indeed know Vaiśvānara thoroughly: put your fuel on (the fire), ye are become my pupils" [*Śatap. Br.*, x, 6, 1; *Chhānd.*, v, 11, with slight variations]. Lastly, Nārada is taught by Sanatkumāra, the god of war [*Chhānd.*, vii].

There is a difference of opinion regarding the exact conclusion to which all this evidence should lead. Macdonell and Keith who have carefully considered the subject incline to the view that these cases of Brahmins learning from Kshatriyas or princes have hardly much significance, for "the priests would naturally represent their patrons as interested in their sacred science. It is thus not necessary to see in these notices any real and independent study on the part of the Kshatriyas" [*Vedic Index*, ii, 87]. In any case, the stories refer only to a few selected Kshatriyas of high rank while there is no evidence that the average Kshatriya was concerned with intellectual pursuits. The people who are represented to us as studying and disputing are normally Brahmins, the bearers *par excellence* of Hindu culture; the kings are few and far between, and much of their fame seems to have been due to their generosity in regard to gifts; the *Kaushītaki Upanishad* [iv, 1], indeed, contains a hint that the fame of Janaka's generosity caused Ajātaśatru some embarrassment. The Kshatriya's first care was war and administration which were sufficient to absorb his attention. We may, of course, imagine a king in his spare moments amusing himself with the disputes of ritualists and philosophers and we may even concede that a king might himself be the originator of some philosophic doctrine, especially as we have references to royal sages [*Rājanyarshi* in *Pañch. Br.*, xii, 12, 6] and traditions like the one given in the *Nirukta* [ii, 10] relating how Devāpi, a king's son, became the purohita of his younger brother Śāntanu. But at the same time we must not forget that to attribute wisdom to a king was a delicate and effective piece of flattery when such wisdom was really not held in much respect, as indicated in a passage of the *Śatapatha Brāhmaṇa* [viii, 1, 4, 10]. The real relation between Brahmins and learned Kshatriyas is most clearly indicated in the episode regarding the instruction of Yājñavalkya by King Janaka in the Agnihotra, at the end of which the latter, far from assuming any position of superiority, still looks up to the former as his respected *guru* whom he asks for the following significant boon : " Let mine be the privilege of asking questions of thee when I list, O Yājñavalkya ! " [ib., xi, 6, 2, 10].

Educated Women. The available evidence shows that education was not denied to women. Sometimes they are found to share in the intellectual interests of the day. Of the two wives of Yājñavalkya [*Bṛihad*, iii, 4, 1 ; iv, 5, 1] one takes no unimportant part in the disputations on philosophical topics. Two directions given in the *Aitareya Upanishad* [ii, 1] imply that elderly married women were permitted to hear Vedantic discourses. The Upanishads mention several other women as teachers, but it is not clear whether they were married. The *Bṛihadāraṇyaka Upanishad* [vi, 4, 17] mentions an interesting ritual by which a person prays for the birth to him of a daughter who should be a *paṇḍitā* or a learned lady. The *Kaushītaki Brāhmaṇa* [vii, 6] tells of an Aryan lady Pathyāsvasti proceeding to the north for study and obtaining the title of *Vāk*, i.e. Sarasvatī, by her learning. In this connection, we may note that women were taught some of the fine arts like dancing and singing which were regarded as accomplishments unfit for men [1] [*Taittir. Saṁ.*, vi, 1, 6, 5 ; *Maitrā. Saṁ.*, iii, 7, 3 ; *Śatap. Br.*, iii, 2, 4, 3–6].

Various Classes of Works and Subjects of Study. We now proceed to consider the subjects of study and various forms of literature known and developed during this period.

As has been already indicated, the technical name for study proper, i.e. Vedic study, is *Svādhyāya*, the blessings of which are eloquently described in the *Śatapatha Brāhmaṇa* [xi, 5, 6, 3. 9 ; also *Taitt. Āraṇyaka*, ii, 13]. Elsewhere the bliss of the learned

[1] In the *Śatap. Br.*, xiii, 4, 3, 5, we find a Rājanya as a lute player and singer at the Aśvamedha sacrifice, probably the forerunner of the *Kshatriya* bards from whom sprang the Epic.

The presentation of this subject is based on *JRAS.*, 1908, pp. 868–870 (Keith's comments), and *Vedic Index*, i, 206 ; ii, 87.

Śrotriya or student is deemed equal to the highest joy possible [*Bṛihad. Up.*, iv, 3, 33; *Taitt. Āraṇyaka*, ix, 8]. The object in view was the threefold knowledge (*trayī vidyā*), that of the Ṛik, Yajus, and Sāman [*Śatap. Br.*, i, 1, 4, 2. 3; ii, 6, 4, 2–7; iv, 6, 7, 1. 2; v, 5, 5, 9; vi, 3, 1, 10. 11. 20; x, 5, 2, 1. 2; xi, 5, 4, 18; xii, 3, 3, 2, etc.]. A student of all the three Vedas is called *Tri-Śukriya* [*Kāṭhaka Saṁ.*, xxxvii, 1, 7] or *Tri-Śukra*, "thrice pure" [*Taitt. Br.*, ii, 7, 1, 2].

Besides the three Vedas, there are also mentioned in several works of the period various other subjects of study which may be noticed as follows:—

1. **Anuśāsana**,[1] which, according to Sāyaṇa, is the name given to the six Vedāṅgas, viz. (*a*) Phonetics, (*b*) Ritualistic Knowledge (*Kalpa*), (*c*) Grammar, (*d*) Exegetics, (*e*) Metrics, (*f*) Astronomy.

2. **Vidyā**,[2] which, according to Sāyaṇa, means the philosophical systems of Nyāya, Mīmāṁsā, etc., but it may refer, according to Eggeling [*S.B.E.*, 44, 98, n. 2] to such special sciences as the *Sarpavidyā* (science of snakes) [mentioned in xiii, 4, 3, 9] or *Vishavidyā*, or to the first *Brāhmaṇas* [Geldner].

3. **Vākovākyam**, apparently some special theological discourse or discourses, similar to (if not identical) with the numerous *Brahmodya* disputations on spiritual matters. According to Geldner, it is an essential part of Itihāsa-Purāṇa, the dialogue or dramatic element as distinguished from the narrative portion. In the *Chhāndogya* the term is explained by Śaṇkara as "the art of disputation"[3] (*Tarkaśāstram*).

4. **Itihāsa-purāṇa**.[4] Both are first mentioned in the *Atharvaveda*.[5] *Itihāsa* singly is mentioned in the Śatapatha Brāhmaṇa,[6] the Jaiminīya,[7] Bṛihadāraṇyaka,[8] and Chhāndogya[9] Upanishads. In the latter, it makes up with *Purāṇa* the fifth Veda, while the Śatapatha in one passage[10] identifies both with the Veda. The distinction between the two is not clear. Sāyaṇa (as well as Śaṅkara) understands by *Purāṇa* the cosmological myths or accounts such as "In the beginning this universe was nothing but water", etc., and by *Itihāsa* stories of old heroes and

[1] *Śatap. Br.*, xi, 5, 6, 8. [2] Ib.
[3] *Śatap. Br.*, iv, 6, 9, 20; xi, 5, 6, 8; 7, 5; *Chhānd.*, vii, 1, 2, 4; 2, 1; 7, 1. Sāyaṇa refers as an example of such dialogue to that between Uddālaka Āruṇi and Svaidāyana Gautama in *Śat. Br.*, xi, 4, 1, 4.
[4] See *Vedic Index*, i, 76–7. [5] xv, 6, 4, etc.
[6] xiii, 4, 3, 12. 13, and as compounded in xi, 5, 6, 8; 7, 9.
[7] i, 53. [8] ii, 4, 10; iv, 1, 2; v, 11.
[9] iii, 4, 1. 2; vii, 1, 2. 4; 2, 1; 7, 1. [10] xiii, 4, 3, 12. 13.

heroines (*purātana-purushavṛittānta*) like the story of Purūravas and Urvaśī. Yāska [1] knows only *Itihāsa* and interprets *Aitihāsikas* [2] as those who interpret the Rigveda by seeing in it legends where others see myths. Both, as separate subjects, were probably known to Patañjali.[3]

5. **Ākhyāna.** In the *Aitareya Brāhmaṇa* we have the Śaunaḥśepa *ākhyāna* related at the Rājasūya [vii, 18, 10] and also the *Ākhyānavids* who tell the Sauparṇa legend [iii, 25, 1] which is called a *Vyākhyāna* in the *Śatapatha* [iii, 6, 2, 7]. Stories used at the Aśvamedha during the year of the horse's wandering belong to the series called cyclic (*pariplavam*).

6. **Anvākhyāna,** literally " after-story ", and hence supplementary narrative. In two [4] of its uses, however, in the *Śatapatha Brāhmaṇa*, it merely indicates a subsequent portion of the book, while in the third passage [5] it is distinguished from *Itihāsa* proper.

7. **Anuvyākhyāna** (glosses) is a species of writing referred to in the Bṛihadāraṇyaka Upanishad [6] which Śaṅkara interprets as " explanation of the Mantras ".

8. **Vyākhyāna** used in the sense of " commentary " (*Arthavādāḥ*) in the Bṛihadāraṇyaka [7] and in some passages [8] of the *Śatapatha Brāhmaṇa* but in another passage [9] of the latter it means only a " narrative ", e.g. that of the dispute of Kadrū and Suparṇī. Śaṅkara connects it with *Sūtras* and *Anuvyākhyāna* with Mantras or *Slokas*.

9. **Gāthā,** a Rigvedic [10] term meaning " song or verse ", in one place [11] is classed with *Nārāśaṁsī* and *Raibhī*. The *Aitareya Āraṇyaka* [12] regards it as a form of verse with Ṛik, Kumbyā, while the *Aitareya Brāhmaṇa* [13] regards *Ṛik* as divine and *Gāthā*, human. Several *Gāthās* epitomizing the sacrifices of famous kings are preserved in the *Śatapatha Brāhmaṇa*,[14] some of which are of the nature of Dānastutis [15] or praises of gifts like Nārāśaṁsī verses as defined in the *Bṛihaddevatā*, iii, 154. Sāyaṇa [16] identifies the two but refers to the other view that *Gāthās* are verses like that about " the great snake driven from the lake " [*Śatap. Br.*, xi, 5, 5, 8] while *Nārāśaṁsīs* (verses

[1] *Nirukta*, ii, 10 ; 24 ; iv, 6 ; x, 26 ; xii, 10. [2] Ib., ii, 16 ; xii, 1.

[3] Vārttika on Pāṇini, iv, 2, 60, and *Mahābhāshya*, 2, 284. *Purāṇa*, according to Śaṅkara (on *Bṛihad*., ii, 4, 10), thus means cosmogonies (making up one of the five traditional elements of the later Purāṇas), while *Itihāsa* means legends.

[4] vi, 5, 2, 22 ; 6, 4, 7. [5] xi, 1, 6, 9.

[6] ii, 4, 10 ; iv, 1, 2, ; 5, 11. [7] ii, 4, 10 ; iv, 1, 6 ; 5, 11.

[8] vi, 1, 27, 33 ; vii, 2, 4, 28. [9] iii, 6, 2, 7.

[10] i, 43, 4 (gātha-pati); i, 7, 1 (gāthin) ; i, 190, 1 (gāthā-nī) ; v, 44, 5 (ṛijugātha).

[11] ix, 85, 6. [12] ii, 3, 6. [13] vii, 18.

[14] xiii, 5, 4, etc. [15] xiii, 4, 2, 8. [16] On xi, 5, 6, 8.

" telling about men ") would be such as that regarding Janamejaya and his horses [ib., xi, 5, 5, 12].

10. **Nārāśaṁsī** occurs first in the Rigveda [x, 85, 6] and is distinguished from *Gāthā* in later works [*Av.*, xv, 6, 4 ; *Taitt. Saṁ.*, vii, 5, 11, 2 ; *Ait. Br.*, vi, 32 ; *Kaushī. Br.*, xxx, 5 ; *Kāṭha. Saṁ.*, v, 5, 2 ; *Taitt. Āraṇyaka*, ii, 10, etc.]. The *Kāṭhaka Saṁhitā* [xiv, 5], while distinguishing the two, affirms that both are false (*anṛitam*), while the *Taittirīya Brāhmaṇa* [i, 3, 2, 6] has the phrase " a *Gāthā* celebrating men " (*Nārāśaṁsī*).

11. **Brāhmaṇa,** " religious explanation " [*Ait. Br.*, i, 25, 15 ; iii, 45, 8 ; vi, 25, 1, etc. ; *Taitt. Saṁ.*, iii, 1, 9, 5 ; 5, 2, 1 ; *Śatap. Br.*, iii, 2, 4, 1, etc.], is the title of a class of books mentioned as such in the *Nirukta* [i, 15, 5 ; ii, 36, 5] and also in the *Taittirīya Āraṇyaka* [ii, 10].

12. **Kshatravidyā,** the science of the ruling class, is mentioned in the *Chhāndogya Upanishad* [vii, 1, 2. 4 ; 2, 1 ; 7, 1]. Śaṅkara glosses the term with *Dhanur-veda,* the science of the bow.

13. **Rāśi** [*Chhānd.*, vii, 1, 2. 4, etc.] is explained by Śaṅkara as *Gaṇitam*, science of numbers or arithmetic.

14. **Nakshatra-Vidyā,** the science of the lunar mansions, astronomy, is mentioned with other sciences in the Chhāndogya [ib.] which Śaṅkara explains as *Jyotisham.*

15. **Bhūta-vidyā,** which Macdonell takes as the science of creatures that trouble men and of the means of warding them off, and hence it may be " demonology ". It is also one of the sciences mentioned in the *Chhāndogya* [ib.]. Śaṅkara explains it as *Bhūtatantram*, literally *the science of life.* Raṅgarāmānuja, however, takes it as " the art of controlling " [*Vaśīkaraṇa-vidyā*]. We may note in this connection the art termed *Māyā* in the *Śatapatha Brāhmaṇa* (xiii, 4, 3, 11] which corresponds to the *Asura-Vidyā* [= *Indrajālavidyā*, magic art, trickery (by sleight of hand, " *aṅgulinyāsarūpam* ")] according to the commentator of the Śāṅkhāyana [x, 7] and Āśvalāyana [xiii, 4, 3, 11] Śrauta Sūtras.

16. **Sarpa-vidyā,** the science of snakes, is mentioned in the *Chhāndogya* as well as the *Śatapatha Brāhmaṇa* [xiii, 4, 3, 9], by which the commentator on Āśvalāyana Śrauta Sutra [x, 7, 5] understands the *Kāśyapīya* and other treatises (tantra) on venoms. That it was a well-developed science is evident from the fact that a section (*parvan*) of it is required to be recited. The *Gopatha Brāhmaṇa* has the form *Sarpa-veda.* Śaṅkara explains it as *Gāruḍa-vidyā.*

17. **Atharvāṅgirasaḥ** is the collective name of the Atharvaveda in some of the *Brāhmaṇas* [e.g., *Taitt.*, iii, 12, 8, 2 ; *Śatap.* xi, 5, 6, 7 ; *Bṛihad. Up.*, ii, 4, 10 ; iv, 1, 2 ; 5, 11 ; *Chhānd. Up.*, iii, 4, 1. 2 ; *Taitt. Up.*, ii, 3, 1 ; *Taitt. Āraṇyaka*, ii, 9 ; 10]. The term occurs once in the Atharvaveda itself [x, 7, 20]. The first part of the name probably refers to the auspicious practices of the Veda (*bheshajāni*, *Av.*, xi, 6, 14) and the second to its hostile witchcraft [*yātu* (*Śatap. Br.*, x, 5, 2, 20) or *abhi-chāra* (Kauśika Sūtra, 3, 19)] associated repectively with the two mythic personages Ghora Āṅgirasa and Bhishaj Ātharvan.

18. **Daiva** appears in the list of sciences in the *Chhāndogya Upanishad* (in the passages cited above) where Śaṅkara explains it as *Utpātajñāna*, the knowledge of portents.

19. **Nidhi** also appears in the list of sciences of the *Chhāndogya Upanishad* and is taken by Śaṅkara to mean *Mahākālādinidhi-śāstram* and by Raṅgarāmānuja as *Nidhi-darśanopāya-śāstram* which is probably some science of divination.

20. **Pitrya** appears in the *Chhāndogya* list of sciences and is taken by Śaṅkara to mean rituals so far as they concern the worship of the manes (*śrāddha-kalpa*).

21. **Sūtra** (prose formulae) used in the *Bṛihadāraṇyaka Upanishad* [ii, 4, 10 ; iv, 1, 6 ; 5, 11] in the sense of a book of rules for the guidance of sacrifices and so forth.

22. **Upanishad** as a class of literature is mentioned first in the *Bṛihadāraṇyaka Upanishad* [ii, 4, 10 ; iv, 1, 2 ; 5, 11]. Some of the sections of the *Taittirīya Upanishad* also end with the words *ityupanishad*, while the *Aitareya Āraṇyaka* [iii, 1, 1] commences its third part with the title "The Upanishad of the Saṁhitā" which also occurs in the *Śāṅkhāyana Āraṇyaka* [vii, 2].

23. **Śloka** in the *Bṛihadāraṇyaka* [ib.] is rendered by Śaṅkara as those Mantras which are to be found not in the Vedas but in the *Brāhmaṇas* (*brāhmaṇaprabhavāḥ mantrāḥ*).

24. **The Veda of Vedas** (*Vedānāṁ Veda*) in the *Chhāndogya* is explained by Śaṅkara to mean "grammar of old Sanskrit", through which the five Vedas are to be understood [Vedānāṁ Bhārata-pañchamānām (cf. Vedānadhyāpayāmāsa Mahābhārata-pañchamān) Vedaṁ Vyākaraṇamiti].

25. **Ekāyana** in the *Chhāndogya* is explained by Śaṅkara as *Nīti-śāstram*, or science of conduct ; literally, "the only, and narrow and right path of morality."

26. **Deva-vidyā** in the *Chhāndogya* is taken by Śaṅkara

to mean *Nirukta* or Exegetics but Raṅgarāmānuja explains it as "the science of the worship of gods" (*devatopāsanāprakāra-vidyā*).

27. **Brahma-Vidyā** in the *Chhāndogya* is explained by Śaṅkara to mean the Vedāṅgas of Śikshā (pronunciation), Kalpa (ceremonial), and Chhandas (prosody).

28. **Deva-jana-vidyā,** the last in the *Chhāndogya* list of subjects of study, means, according to Śaṅkara, the arts affected by the lesser gods such as the making of perfumes [*Gandhayukti* which the commentator on Śaṅkara explains as *kuṅkumādi-saṁpādanam*, which may mean *dyeing*], dancing, singing, playing on musical instruments, and other fine arts [*Nritya-Gīta-Vādya-Śilpādi-Vijñānāni*]. Raṅgarāmānuja, however, splits up the compound into two parts, viz. *Deva-vidyā* = the arts of the Gandharvas, and *Jana-Vidyā* = Science of Medicine (*Āyurveda*).

Supreme Knowledge. Besides indicating these branches of knowledge, arts, and sciences, the Upanishads speak of the supreme or highest knowledge technically called *parā vidyā* as distinguished from all other knowledge termed *aparā* [*Muṇḍa.*, i, 1, 4]. The *Muṇḍaka* [i, 1, 5] defines *aparā vidyā* as comprising the four Vedas and the six Vedāṅgas or ancillary subjects of Phonetics, Ritualistic Knowledge, Grammar, Exegetics, Metrics, and Astronomy. By the *parā vidyā* the *Muṇḍaka* understands that knowledge through which the Ultimate Reality is known. All knowledge, *parā* or *aparā*, is opposed to Ignorance or *avidyā*. It is, however, this *parā vidyā* or highest knowledge which forms the real subject matter of the Upanishads. It is extolled as *sarva-vidyā-pratishṭhā*, the foundation of all arts and sciences [*Muṇḍa.*, i, 1, 2], as *Vedānta*, the final and highest stage of Vedic wisdom [ib., iii, 2, 6], and as, verily, the science of sciences wherein lies implicit the knowledge of everything [ib., i, 1, 3]. On account of the emphasis thus laid upon this particular type of knowledge, all other subjects of study are thrown into the background and even branded as *avidyā* in some of the Upanishads. A few citations will show clearly how the insufficiency of even the knowledge of the Vedas and indeed of all existing knowledge is recognized in the Upanishads.

In the *Chhāndogya* [vii, 1], Nārada acknowledges to Sanatkumāra :

"I have studied, most reverend Sir, the Rigveda, Yajurveda, Sāmaveda, the Atharvaveda as fourth, the epic and mythological poems as fifth Veda, grammar, necrology, arithmetic, divination, chronology (?), dialectics, politics (?), theology, the doctrine of prayer (?), necromancy, the art of war, astronomy, snake-charming (?), and the fine arts—these things, most reverend Sir, have I studied ; therefore am I, most reverend Sir, learned indeed in the scripture [*Mantra-vid*) but not learned in the *Ātman* (*Ātma-vid*). Yet have I heard from such as are like you that he who knows the *Ātman* vanquishes sorrow. I am in sorrow—lead me then over, I pray, to the farther shore that lies beyond sorrow."

" Sanatkumāra said to him : ' Whatever you have studied is but words.' "

Similarly, in the *Chhāndogya* [v, 3–10], *Bṛihadāraṇyaka* [vi, 2], and *Kaushītaki* [i], treating of the same topic, Śvetaketu professes to have been taught by his father Āruṇi, but fails to answer the eschatological questions propounded by King Pravāhaṇa [in the *Kaushītaki*, Chitra], and returning in anger to his father, reproaches him : " So then, without having really done so, you have claimed to have instructed me " [*Chhānd.*, v, 3, 4] ; " it was imagination, then, when you previously declared that my instruction was complete " [*Bṛihad.*, vi, 2, 3].

Again, in the *Chhāndogya* [vi, 1] it is shown how Śvetaketu's " thorough " study of " all the Vedas " for full twelve years leaves him only full of conceit and confidence in his study and wisdom, but ignorant of the questions put to him by his father regarding the One and the Self-existent with whose knowledge everything is known.

Accordingly, we find several emphatic declarations of the principle pointed to by these examples. " Therefore let a Brāhmaṇa, after he has done with learning, wish to stand by real strength (knowledge of the Self which enables us to dispense with all other knowledge)," says the *Bṛihadāraṇyaka* [iii, 5, 1]. " He should not seek after the knowledge of the books, for that is mere weariness of the tongue " [ib., iv, 4, 21]. " Before whom words and thought recoil, not finding him " [*Taitt.*, ii, 4]. " Not by the Veda is the *Ātman* attained, nor by intellect, nor by much knowledge of books " [*Kaṭha*, i, 2, 23].

In this view, the *Kaṭha* [i, 2, 4–5] regards even *aparā vidyā* as *avidyā*, and emphasizes its essential inferiority and worthlessness, although the *aparā vidyā* means, according to the *Muṇḍaka* [i, 1, 5], the four Vedas together with the six Vedāṅgas.

Similarly, Kalpa or ritualism comes in for its special share of condemnation from the standpoint of this uncompromising idealism.[1] The *Muṇḍaka* [i, 2, 7] openly brands as fools those that seek to perform mere rites and ceremonies. The *Bṛihadāraṇyaka* [i, 4, 10] in a spirit of depreciation thinks it fit to compare those who, instead of knowing and recognizing the *Ātman* as the only Reality, merely offer sacrifices to the gods, to domestic animals ministering to the comforts of their owners. In i, 5, 16 we have: "By sacrifice the world of the Fathers, by knowledge the world of the gods, is gained." In the *Aitareya Āraṇyaka* we find the following: "To what end shall we repeat the Veda, to what end shall we sacrifice? For we sacrifice breath in speech, or in breath speech" [iii, 2, 6]. In the later Upanishads, however, we find a more friendly attitude towards the sacrificial cult. In *Kaṭha* [i, 17] the performance of certain ceremonies and works leads to the "overstepping of birth and death" and to "everlasting rest". This reaction attains its climax in the *Maitrāyaṇa Upanishad*, of which the very first passage affirms that the laying of the sacrificial fires leads to a knowledge of Brahman, while in iv, 3 it is expressly laid down that a knowledge of the Veda, observance of caste-duties, and *āśrama*-duties are all essential to the emancipation of the natural *ātman* and its reunion with the supreme *ātman*. It should be noted, however, that orthodox and traditional Brahminical opinion does not find any real antagonism between the sacrificial cult, the scheme of practical life, under the orders of caste and *āśrama* on the one hand, and the Upanishadic spirit of the quest of the Brahman on the other. The one is taken as a preliminary to the other and the intention of such passages is only to emphasize the supreme importance and worth of *parā vidyā*.

Methods of Study. From the subjects of study we now pass on to the methods of study prevailing in the period. The Upanishads often fall into the form of a dialogue which shows that the method of teaching was catechetical, the method of explaining a subject by an intelligent and graduated series of questions and answers, anticipating the method of the great Greek teacher, Socrates. The pupils asked questions [there was no lack of boldness in some of them; e.g. *Praśna*, iii, 2] and the teacher discoursed at length on the topics referred to him [e.g. *Kenopanishad*, *Kaṭha*]. In these discourses are found utilized all the familiar devices of oral teaching such as apt illustrations [*Praśna*, ii], stories [*Kaṭha*], and parables [*Kena*, iii]. The *Taittirīya Brāhmaṇa* uses the technical terms, *Praśnin*

[1] For the entire evidence see Deussen's *Philosophy of the Upanishads*, p. 63.

(questioner), *Abhi-praśnin* (cross-questioner), and *Praśna-vivāka* (answerer), while the Atharvaveda knows of the *Prāvāchika* or expounder (whence *Nirvachana* and *Niruka*). The use of discussion as a method of study led to the development of the Science of Logic called *Vākovākyam*, as we have seen, by which Śaṅkara understands *Tarka-Śāstra*, the Science of Disputation. Thus it was in these Vedic Schools that the foundation was laid of a science which later attained remarkable developments in the many works of Nyāya.

It should not be understood that these discourses leave nothing for the pupil to think out for himself. The need for introspection and contemplation on his part is never overlooked. *Manana* or cogitation as a means of convincing oneself of the truth of what he has learnt and thus fortifying himself against possible future doubts is specifically prescribed [cf. *Bṛi. Up.*, ii, 4]. Even as regards the initial teaching it is usual for the preceptor to furnish only broad hints and ask the pupil to work them out fully. The most interesting instance of this method of teaching is found in the *Taittirīya Upanishad* [iii] where Varuṇa, in instructing his son Bhṛigu, contents himself with indicating in only general terms the features of the Absolute and leaves to his son the discovery by reflection of Its exact content. This method of giving general hints and directions is repeated four times and it is only in the fifth turn that Bhṛigu is able to comprehend the nature of the Absolute. Another interesting instance of the same method is contained in *Chhāndogya* [vi], where Śvetaketu's father, in teaching his son how the Mind and its faculties depend for their functioning upon the body, how psychological conditions are bound up with the physiological, puts his son through a course of actual fasting so that he may achieve a direct perception of that truth by his own experiments and experiences. He makes him fast for fifteen days, cutting off all food except drinks of water, to show that life (*prāṇa*) depends on water. After this fast, his father asks him to recite the Vedas. The son, to his surprise, finds that that knowledge has vanished from his mind (*na pratibhāta*). It began to dawn on his mind, as he began to take food. By this experiment he realized the truth that *Manas*, Mind, depended upon *Anna*, Food. It could not function except in a body that is nourished and not famished. Similarly, the faculty of speech, *Vāk*, depends upon *tejas* or heat of the body (its element of calories coming from food to give it energy). His father concluded by saying : " Just as by covering it with a piece of straw (*tṛiṇa*), one may make a single small spark (*khadyot*) left in it to blaze up, so is it with you ! "

Indeed, the main part of education was the work of the student and not of the teacher. The *Bṛihadāraṇyaka Upanishad* clearly states that education in the highest knowledge depends upon the three processes following one another, viz. (1) *Śravaṇa*, (2) *Manana*, and (3) *Nididhyāsana*. *Śravaṇa* is listening to what is taught by the teacher, but even for this there are specified six aids (*liṅgas*, signs or phases), such as (*a*) *Upakrama*, a formal ceremony to be performed before reading the Veda ; (*b*) *Abhyāsa* constant practice or recitation of the texts taught ; (*c*) *Apūrvatā*, immediate apprehension of the meaning. (*d*) *Phala*, comprehension of results, (*e*) *Arthavāda*, study of explanatory texts, the *Brāhmaṇa* texts ; and (*f*) *Upapatti*, attainment of conclusions. *Manana* is defined as constant contemplation of the One Reality in accordance with the ways of reasoning aiding in its apprehension. *Nididhyāsana* is concentrated contemplation of the truth so as to realize it.

Need of Renunciation (Sannyāsa) and Meditation (Yoga) for Highest Knowledge. Study and teaching can, however, only lead to a mediate knowledge. For an immediate knowledge of the Ultimate Truth and Reality, the pupil must depend upon himself. The whole of the empirical knowledge which Nārada has acquired is declared by Sanatkumāra as mere words when he begins his instruction. For the knowledge of Brahman was essentially of a different nature from that which we call " knowledge " in ordinary life. Nārada with all his familiarity with the then conceivable branches of knowledge and empirical science finds himself in a condition of ignorance (*avidyā*) as regards the Brahman. The knowledge of the Real cannot grow out of the knowledge of the unreal, of the realm of experience, which is the realm of ignorance. The knowledge of the Ātman cannot be gained by mere speculation (*tarka*) concerning it, but only by revelation as the result of the proper degree of self-growth. The acquisition of such knowledge which means emancipation is not a matter of study but of life. It presupposes two things : (1) annihilation of all desire, (2) annihilation of the illusion of a manifold universe, of the consciousness of plurality. The means evolved to secure these two ends were what are popularly known as the systems of (1) *Sannyāsa*, which means the " casting off " from oneself of his home, possessions, and family and all that stimulates desire. It thus " seeks laboriously to realize that freedom from all the ties of earth in which a deeper conception of life in other ages and countries also has recognized the supreme task of earthly existence, and will probably continue to recognize throughout all future time ". The system of Sannyāsa as a means to the knowledge of the Brahman and to emancipation is completely developed in a series of later Upanishads (such as *Brahma*, *Sannyāsa*, *Āruṇeya*, *Paramahaṁsa*, etc.), with which we are not concerned for the present.

(2) **Yoga** which, by withdrawing the organs from the objects of sense and concentrating them on the inner self, endeavours to shake itself free from the world of plurality and to secure union with the *Ātman*.

In post-Vedic times the practice of *Yoga* was developed into a formal system with its own textbook (the *Sūtras* of Patañjali). Its first beginnings are, however, shown in *Kaṭha* [iii and vi], *Śvet.* [ii], and *Maitrā.* [vi]. The system implies the following eight members (*aṅgas*) or external practices : (1) *Yama*, discipline (consisting in abstinence from doing injury, truthfulness, honesty, chastity, poverty) ; (2) *Niyama*, self-restraint (purity, contentment, asceticism, study, and devotion) ; (3) *Āsanam*, sitting (in the right place and in the correct bodily attitude) ; (4) *Prāṇāyāma* [*Bṛihad.*, i, 5, 23], regulation of the breath ; (5) *Pratyāhāra*, suppression (of the organs of sense) [*Chhānd.*, viii, 15] ; (6) *Dhāraṇā*, concentration of the attention [*Kaṭha*, ii, 6, 10–11] ; (7) *Dhyānam*, meditation ; (8) *Samādhi*, absorption.

As has been already indicated, both the systems are a perfectly intelligible consequence of the doctrine of the Upanishads according to which the highest end is contained in the knowledge of self-identity with the *Ātman*. As means to the attainment of that end, we must purposely dissolve the ties that bind to the illusory world of phenomena (*Sannyāsa*) and practise self-concentration (*Yoga*). Thus arose two remarkable and characteristic institutions of Indian culture through which emancipation was sought to be attained and expedited by processes and disciplines invented by the spiritual genius of the people. The first seeks by calculated methods to suppress desire and the second the consciousness of plurality and the entire practical philosophy and morality of the Hindu is comprehended in these two methods of self-realization pursued separately or in combination.[1]

[1] In treating of this topic I have largely followed Deussen's truly Indian presentation in his *Philosophy of the Upaniṣads*.

Eligibility for Highest Knowledge. We thus see that the instruction of the teacher is as necessary for Upanishadic studies as the self-exertion of the student in developing a spirit of self-sacrificing asceticism and the power of self-concentration in the pursuit of knowledge. Accordingly, we frequently find the striking feature constantly recurring in the Upanishads that a teacher refuses to impart any instruction to a pupil until he has proved to his satisfaction his competence, mental and moral, to receive the instruction, especially when that instruction is connected with the highest truths of life. The typical instance of this kind of pupil is Nachiketas in the *Kaṭha* approaching Yama for instruction on the nature of the Soul and its destiny when Yama first satisfies himself as to his sincerity and zeal in the pursuit of Truth by offering him the strongest temptations that might divert him from his end—viz. " sons and grandsons who shall live a hundred years, herds of cattle, elephants, gold and horses, sovereignty of the wide abode of the earth, fair maidens with their chariots and musical instruments, and control over death ". Nachiketas answers like a true *Sannyāsin* : " Keep thou thy horses, keep dance and song for thyself. No man can be made happy by wealth." Then Yama is compelled to admit : " I believe Nachiketas to be one who desires Knowledge, for even many pleasures did not tear thee away." Indra deals similarly with Pratardana by asking him to choose a boon, but Pratardana is wise enough to leave the choice to Indra [*Kaushī*, iii, 1]. King Janaśruti Pautrāyaṇa similarly approaches Raikva for instruction with 600 cows, a necklace, and a carriage with mules, whereupon Raikva answers : " Fie, necklace and carriage be thine, O Śūdra, together with the cows " [*Chhānd.*, iv, 2]. Satyakāma Jābāla did not impart instruction to Upakosala Kāmalāyana even after his tending his fires for twelve years [ib., iv, 10, 2]. Pravāhaṇa, approached by Āruṇi for instruction, says to him : " Stay with me sometime " [ib., v, 3, 7 ; *Bṛihad.*, vi, 2, 6]. Similar is the treatment meted out by Prajāpati to Indra and Vairochana [*Chhānd.*, viii, 8, 4], and by Yājñavalkya to Janaka [*Bṛihad.*, iv, 3, 1 f.], and by Śākāyanya to King Bṛihadratha [*Maitr.*, i, 2]. All these cases but emphasize the pupil's own efforts along with those of his teacher as factors in education. The Vedic teacher imposed exacting moral and mental tests for admission of pupils ; he refused to work with inferior and unsuitable material. Nārada is admitted as a pupil by Sanatkumāra when he has mastered all the arts and sciences of his times by which he qualified himself for the knowledge that was above the empirical and experimental.

Wandering Teachers ('Charakas'). Instruction was derived not merely from the regular teachers settled in their homes of learning where they admitted pupils, but also from other sources. Such were *Charakas*[1] or wandering students who, though not normally competent as teachers, are yet regarded as possible sources of knowledge by the *Śatapatha Brāhmaṇa* [iv, 2, 4, 1]. This institution of peripatetic teachers was thus another useful agency for the spread of learning and culture. They were the real educators of thought. These bands of wandering scholars went through the country—the *Bṛihadāraṇyaka* refers to one such band wandering as far North as the land of the Madras [iii, 3, 1; 7, 1]—and engaged in disputes and discussions at which prizes were staked by the parties. In the *Śatapatha Brāhmaṇa* [xi, 4, 1, 1 f.] Uddālaka Āruṇi, a Kuru-Pañchāla Brahmin, goes to the North where he offers a gold coin as a prize "for the sake of calling out the timid to a disputation". Seized with fear, the Brāhmins of the northern people challenged him to a disputation on spiritual matters with Svaidāyana Śaunaka as their champion. In the end, Uddālaka finds himself unable to answer the questions put to him by Śaunaka, "gave up to him the gold coin," and became his pupil to study those questions. Such discussions were also encouraged and organized by the more intellectual and spiritually-minded kings. Thus in the *Śatapatha Brāhmaṇa* [xi, 6, 2, 1 f.; 3, 1; also *Bṛihad.*, iv, 1, 1–9, 20, 29] Janaka, King of Videha, having come across some travelling Brahmins, arranges a discussion with them on the *Agnihotra* as a result of which he makes liberal gifts to the most successful of the disputants. Indeed, the literary patronage of Janaka made his contemporary Ajātaśatru, king of Kāśī, admit that he could hardly find any learned man to patronize, because all learned men were running after Janaka and settling at his court [*Bṛihad,* ii, 1, 1]. Discussion with Yājñavalkya was the chief means adopted by Janaka for his education in spiritual lore, at the conclusion of which he says to his teacher: "Sir, I give you the Videhas, and also myself, to be together your slaves" [ib., iv, 4, 23]. Further examples of such learned

[1] According to Śaṅkara, they were called *Charakas* because they were observing (*char*) a vow for the sake of study. The word occurs in one of the inscriptions of Uṣavadāta at Nasik—"*charaka parshabhyaḥ*"—where there is a reference to Brahminical schools at four places named in the record [*IA.*, 1883, p. 30].

debates are those between Yājñavalkya and Gārgī Vāchaknavī [ib., iii, 8] and between him and Vidagdha Śākalya [Ib., iii, 9; *Śatap. Br.*, xi, 6, 3, 3].

A similar agency for the spread of education was the institution known as *Brahmodya* (riddle poetry). It was a special form of theological discussion for which a regular place was assigned at the Aśvamedha [*Śatap. Br.*, xiii, 5, 2, 11] and at the Daśarātra, ten-day festival [ib., iv, 6, 9, 20].

Representative Teachers of the Times.—We shall now give an account[1] of some of those representative teachers and pupils in whom were embodied the learning and culture of the period. They are named as follows in the alphabetical order:

1. **Ajātaśatru,** a king of Kāśī who instructs the proud Brāhmin Bālāki as to the real nature of the Self. It has been already stated how he became jealous of his contemporary Janaka who collected in his court all the learned men of the times by his lavish patronage [*Bṛihad.*, ii, 1, 1, etc.; *Kaushī*, iv, 1.] Gārgya Bālāki was himself "famous as a man of great reading" in the entire literary world of the day, for "he lived among the Uśīnaras, Satvat-Matsyas, Kuru-Pañchālas, and Kāśī-Videhas" and Ajātaśatru was only honouring himself by honouring such a far-famed scholar [ib.].

2. **Aṇichin Mauna,** an authority on ritual and a contemporary of Jābāla and Chitra Gauśrāyaṇi in the *Kaushītaki Brāhmaṇa* [xxiii, 5].

3. **Atidhanvan Śaunaka,** the teacher of an *udgītha* of his pupil Udara-Sāṇḍilya in the *Chhāndogya* [i, 9, 3].

4. **Atyaṁhas Āruṇi,** a teacher in the *Taittirīya Brāhmaṇa* [iii, 10, 9, 3–5], who sent a pupil to question Plaksha Dayyāṁpati as to the Sāvitra (a form of Agni), for which his pupil was severely rebuked.

5. **Abhipratārin Kāksha-seni** is mentioned in several works as engaged in discussions on philosophical topics [*Jaiminīya Up. Br.*, i, 59, 1; iii, 1, 21; 2, 2, 13; *Chhānd.*, iv, 3, 5 (where he refuses alms to a religious student); *Pañcha. Br.*, x, 5, 7; xiv, 1, 12, 15]. The *Jaiminīya Brāhmaṇa* gives the further fact that there was a division of his property among his sons in his life-time, he being a Kuru and a prince [iii, 156].

6. **Aruṇa Aupaveśi Gautama,** which is the full name of a famous teacher whose son was the more famous Uddālaka

[1] This account has been written with the indispensable aid of Macdonell and Keith's *Vedic Index*.

Āruṇi. He was himself the son of Upaveśa and a contemporary of King Aśvapati Kaikeya whom he approached for instruction on a particular spiritual topic [*Taitt. Saṁ.*, vi, 1, 9, 2; 4, 5, 1; *Maitr. Saṁ.*, i, 4, 10; iii, 6, 4, 6; 7, 4; 8, 6; 10, 5; *Kāṭh. Saṁ.*, xxvi, 10; *Taitt. Br.*, ii, 1, 5, 11; *Śatap. Br.*, ii, 2, 2, 20; x, 6, 1, 2; xi, 4, 1, 4; 5, 3, 2; *Bṛihad. Up.*, vi, 5, 3].

7. **Aśvapati Kaikeya,** a learned prince, and an ideal king who could boast: "In my kingdom there is no thief, no miser, no drunkard, no man without an altar in his house, no ignorant person, no adulterer, much less an adulteress." He was pre-eminent in both politics and religion. Five great Brahmin theologians, viz. Prāchīnaśāla, Satyayajña, Indradyumna, Jana, and Buḍila under the leadership of Uddālaka Āruṇi approached him for instruction regarding the mystery of the Vaśvānara Self, which he was the only man of his times to master [*Chhānd.*, v, 11, 1–5; *Śatap. Br.*, x, 6, 1, 1, 2, where the name Mahāśāla appears instead of Prāchīnaśāla]. Regarding Aśvapati's special knowledge of the doctrine of Vaiśvānara, the Brahmins said: "Venerable Sir, thou knowest Vaiśvānara thoroughly: teach us Him" [*Śatap.*, ib.]; and in the *Chhāndogya*: "Sirs, Aśvapati Kaikeya knows *at present* that Self called Vaiśvānara, etc."

8. **Aśvala,** the Hotṛi priest of Janaka, king of Videha, who figures as an authority at the sacrifice of Aśvamedha to which the king invited the Brahmaṇas of the Kurus and Pañchālas. The king offered precious gifts to the Brahmin who was the "best read" of them. Yājñavalkya stepped forward, asserted his superiority, and asked his pupils to carry away the gifts, whereupon the other priests headed by Aśvala tested his superiority by questions [*Bṛihad.*, iii, 1, 2, 10].

9. **Ahinā Āśvatthya,** a sage (*muni*) who achieved immortality by knowledge of the special rite called *sāvitram* [*Taitt. Br.*, iii, 10, 9, 10].

10. **Āktākshya,** the name of a teacher whose views are quoted on a point bearing on the *Agnichiti* or piling of the sacred fire, but are stated to be different from the "settled practice" [*Śatap. Br.*, vi, 1, 2, 24].

11. **Āruṇeya Svetaketu** or **Auddālaki** is mentioned repeatedly in the *Śatapatha Brāhmaṇa* [x, 3, 4, 1; xi, 2, 7, 12; 5, 4, 18; 6, 2, 1; xii, 2, 1, 9; *Auddālaki* in iii, 4, 3, 13; iv, 2, 5, 14], the *Bṛihadāraṇyaka* [iii, 7, 1; vi, 1, 1] and *Chhāndogya* [v, 3, 1; vi, 1, 1; 8, 1] Upanishads. As a student, he became known for his insistence on the eating of honey which a Brāhmachārin

was not permitted to take. He was the contemporary of the Pañchāla king, Pravāhaṇa Jaivali, who also gave him some instruction. He was also a contemporary of the Videha king, Janaka, whom he met while travelling about with two other companions and participated in the discussion started by the king. One of these companions was Yājñavalkya with whom he had on another occasion a discussion at which he was defeated [*Bṛihad.*, iii, 7, 1]. At another time, he went to the *Samiti* or *parishad* (assembly) of the Pañchālas where he failed to answer any of the five questions put to him by the King Pravāhaṇa Jaivali. It is also recorded that his career as a student was begun when he was twelve years old and ended when he was twenty-four and during this period though he studied all the Vedas under *several* teachers [*Chhānd.*, vi, 1, 7] the study did not produce the desired and expected effect on his character, for he returned home "conceited, considering himself well-read and stern," until his father brought his ignorance home to him by questions he could not answer. Thus his entire intellectual career was marked by a series of discomfitures. The *Kaushītaki Brāhmaṇa* refers to him as an authority on the intricate subject of the duty of the seventeenth priest called Sadasya at the ritual of the Kaushītakins, whose function was to exercise a general superintendence over the ceremony and notify errors in its performance.

12. **Āsuri** appears as a ritual authority in the first four books of the *Śatapatha Brāhmaṇa* and as an authority on dogmatics, specially noted for his insistence on truth in the last book [i, 6, 3, 26 ; ii, 1, 4, 27 ; 3, 1, 9 ; 4, 1, 2 ; 6, 1, 25. 33 ; 3, 17 ; iv, 5, 8, 14 ; xiv, 1, 1, 33].

13. **Indrota Daivāpa Śaunaka** is mentioned in the *Śatapatha Brāhmaṇa* as the priest who officiated at the Aśvamedha of Janamejaya [xiii, 5, 3, 5] and in the *Jaiminīya Upanishad Brāhmaṇa* as a pupil of Śruta [iii, 40, 1].

14. **Udaṅka Śaulbāyana,** a contemporary of Janaka of Videha, who was taught by him the doctrine that "*prāṇa* is Brahman" [*Bṛihad.*, iv, 1, 3]. He was also known for his opinion that the Daśarātra ceremony was the best part of the *sattra* ("sacrificial session").

15. **Uddālaka Āruṇi,** the son of No. 6, Aruṇa Aupaveśi Gautama and father of No. 11, Śvetaketu. His, therefore, was one of the most cultured families of the period whose literary fame extended over several generations. He was "a

Kurupañchāla Brahmin[1]" [*Śatap.*, xi, 4, 1, 2] whose *son* Śvetaketu attended the Pāñchāla Parishad. His *teachers* were (1) Aruṇa, his father [*Bṛihad.*, vi, 4, 33]; (2) Patañchala Kāpya of *Madra* [ib., iii, 7, 1]. His *pupils*[2] were (1) Proti Kausurubindi of *Kauśāmbī* [*Śatap.*, xii, 2, 2, 13]; (2) the famous Yājñavalkya Vājasaneya [*Bṛihad.*, vi, 3, 7; 4, 33] who was afterwards clever enough to beat his guru [ib., iii, 7, 31]; (3) Kaushītaki [*Śāṅkhāyana Āraṅyaka*, xv]. His *opponents* in academic disputations whom he defeated were (1) Prāchīnayogya Śaucheya [*Śatap.*, xi, 5, 3, 1, etc.] and probably (2) Bhadrasena Ājātaśatrava [ib., v, 5, 5, 14] (apparently son of Ajātaśatru, king of *Kāśī*, the contemporary of King Janaka, the patron of Yājñavalkya whom he bewitched), and (3) Svaidāyana Śaunaka [*Śatap.*, xi, 4, 1, 1, 9], the champion of the northern Brahmins, challenged by Uddālaka to a disputation at which Uddālaka had to yield to him a gold coin as token of his superiority and wanted to become his pupil, but Śaunaka said he would teach him without his becoming his pupil. His *contemporaries* were (1) Divodāsa Bhaimaseni [*Kāṭhaka Saṁhitā*, vii, 8] and (2) Vāsishṭha Chaikitāneya, his patron [*Jaim. Up. Br.*, i, 42, 1]. He was chosen as the *chief priest* by Chitra Gāṅgyāyani for the performance of a sacrifice to which he deputed his worthy son Śvetaketu. But Chitra puts to him a question regarding future life which neither he nor his father to whom it is referred can answer, and in the end both the son and father go as pupils to Chitra for instruction which is at once given because "they were worthy of Brahman, being free from pride" [*Kaush. Up.*, i, 1]. To Āruṇi also is attributed the formula with which the morning and evening sacrifice is celebrated [*Śatap.*, ii, 3, 1, 34] and in several other Yajus formulae are found traces of Āruṇi's hand [ib., iii, 3, 4, 19]. His place in the history of Indian culture is thus indicated by Oldenberg: "When the time shall have come for the inquiries which will have to be made to create order out of the chaotic mass of names of teachers and other celebrities of the *Brāhmaṇa* period, it may turn out that the most

[1] The *Mahābharata* [i, 682], describes him more closely as a Pāñchālya.

[2] The Mantha-doctrine was first taught by Uddālaka and transmitted by a succession of pupils which may be shown thus: Uddālaka-Vājasaneya Yājñavalkya-Madhuka Paiṅgya-Chūla Bhāgavitti-Jānaki Āyasthūṇa-Satyakāma Jābāla [*Bṛihad.*, vi, 3, 7–12]. Thus in the person of Uddālaka meet the most divergent lines of tradition: he is named as the teacher of Yājñavalkya [*Śat.*, xiv, 9, 3, 15; 9, 4, 33; v, 5, 5, 14]; of Kaushītaki and Śāṅkhāyana [*Kaush. Ār.*, xv]; and of Madhuka Paiṅgya, the head of another branch of Rigvedic school tradition.

important centre for the formation and diffusion of the Brāhmaṇa doctrine will have to be looked for in Āruṇi and in the circles which surrounded him" [*Buddha*, p. 396 n.]. Most of the important works of the period constantly refer to him as a recognized authority on rituals and philosophy [e.g. *Śatap.*, i, 1, 2, 11; ii, 2, 1, 34; iii, 3, 4, 19; iv, 4, 8, 9; xi, 2, 6, 12; *Bṛihad.*, iii, 5, 1; *Chhānd.*, iii, 11, 4; v, 11, 2; 17, 1; vi, 8, 1; *Ait. Br.*, viii, 7; *Kaushī. Br.*, xxvi, 4; *Ṣaḍviṁśa Br.*, i, 6; and *Kaushī. Up.*, i, 1, etc.].

16. **Upakosala Kāmalāyana**, who was a student in the house of his teacher Satyakāma Jābāla for twelve years [*Chhānd.*, iv, 10, 1] and then, instructed by Agni, became himself a teacher [ib., iv, 14].

17. **Ushasti Chākrāyaṇa** was one of the disputants at the court of Janaka on the occasion of his Aśvamedha, who tried to question the superiority asserted by Yājñavalkya and was forced to "hold his peace" [*Bṛihad.*, iii, 4, 1]. He is also mentioned as living as a beggar with his wife at Ibhyagrāma "when the Kurus had been destroyed by hailstones" and the resulting famine, until he presented himself at the sacrifice of the king where he is thought fit to "take all the sacrificial offices" [*Chhānd.*, i, 10, 1; 11, 2, 3].

18. **Kahoḍa Kaushītaki** or **Kaushītakeya** is mentioned as a teacher contemporary with Yājñavalkya with whom he once disputes [*Śatap.*, ii, 4, 3, 1; *Bṛihad.*, iii, 5, 1; *Sāṁkhāyana Āraṇyaka*, xv].

19. **Kuśri Vājaśravasa** is a teacher concerned with the lore of the sacred fire in the *Śatapatha Brāhmaṇa* [x, 5, 5, 1].

20. **Kusurubinda Auddālaki,** probably a brother of Śvetaketu (No. 11), is mentioned as an authority on rituals in several works [e.g. *Pañchav. Br.*, xxii, 15, 1. 10; *Taitt. Saṁ.*, vii, 2, 2, 1; *Jaimi.*, i, 75; *Shaḍ. Br.*, i, 16; cf. No. 15—Proti Kausurubindi].

21. **Kṛishṇa Devakīputra**, mentioned in the *Chhāndogya* [iii, 17, 6] as having learnt a particular view of the sacrifice from Ghora Āṅgirasa, is regarded as the person deified later as the god Krishṇa by both tradition and modern scholars like Weber [*Ind. Lit.*, pp. 71, 148, 169], Grierson [*Encyclopædia of Religion and Ethics*, *Bhakti*] and Garbe. In the Upanishad, he "is but a scholar, eager in the pursuit of knowledge, belonging, perhaps, to the military caste" [Weber].

22. **Kauravyāyaṇi-putra** is mentioned as a teacher to whom is attributed the doctrine of *ākāśa* or ether in the *Bṛihadāraṇyaka* [v, 1, 1].

23. **Kraushṭuki** is mentioned as a grammarian in the *Bṛihad-devatā* [iv, 137] and *Nirukta* [viii, 2] but as an astrologer in a Pariśishṭa of the Atharvaveda.

24. **Khaṇḍika Audbhāri** is mentioned as a teacher of Keśin in the *Śatapatha Brāhmaṇa* [xi, 8, 4, 1] and as having been defeated by him as a sacrificer in *Maitrāyaṇī Saṁhitā* [i, 4, 12].

25. **Gardabhī-vipīta**, a Bhāradvāja, was one of the teachers from whom King Janaka learned a particular doctrine, viz. that "*Śrotra* is Brahman" but whose limitations are pointed out by Yājñavalkya [*Bṛihad*., iv, 1, 5].

26. **Gārgī Vāchaknavī**, a learned lady, was one of the circle of disputants who questioned the superior knowledge claimed by Yājñavalkya at the court of Janaka on the occasion of his Aśvamedha. In the end she admits: "No one, I believe, will defeat him in any argument concerning Brahman" [*Bṛihad*., iii, 6, 1; 8, 12].

27. **Gotama Rāhūgaṇa**, first mentioned in the Rigveda [i, 78, 5], figures in the *Śatapatha Brāhmaṇa* as the Purohita or family priest of King Māthava Videgha and as a bearer of Vedic civilization in the famous passage in which Weber finds depicted three successive stages of the eastward migration of the Brahminical Hindus. At the time of the hymns of the Rigveda the Aryan settlements extended over the Panjab as far as the Sarasvatī, the Yamunā, and the Gaṅgā. Thence the Aryans pushed forward, led by the Videgha Māthava and his preceptor Gotama Rāhūgaṇa as far east as the river Sadānīrā, i.e. Karatoyā [Sāyaṇa], forming the eastern boundary of the Videhas, or Gaṇḍakī [Eggeling] forming the boundary between the Kosalas and Videhas. The progress beyond this limit was stopped for some time by the "very uncultivated, very marshy" land east of it, but at the time of the *Śatapatha*, "there are many Brahmans to the east of it" and the land was "very cultivated" [i, 4, 1, 10–16].

28. **Gauśla** is a teacher represented as in disagreement with Buḍila Āśvataraāśvi in the *Aitareya Brāhmaṇa* [vi, 30].

29. **Glāva Maitreya**, also known by the name of Vaka Dālbhya, is mentioned as going out to repeat the Veda in a quiet place in the *Chhāndogya* [i, 12] in connection with the *udgītha* of the dogs. He appears as Pratistotṛi at the snake festival of the *Pañchaviṁśa Brāhmaṇa* [xxv, 15, 3] and is mentioned also in the *Shaḍviṁśa Brāhmaṇa* [i, 4]. He is defeated in a scholastic disputation with Maudgalya in the *Gopatha Br*. [i, 1, 31].

30. **Chākra**, whose full name is Revottaras Sthapati Pāṭava

was the *sthapati* [a royal official, a governor (cf. Nishāda-Sthapati in *Āpas. Śr. Sū*, ix, 14, 12) or a chief judge (*Vedic index*, ii, 486)] of the exiled Dushṭarītu Pauṁsāyana, a king of the Sṛiñjayas, and succeeded in restoring him to his royal dignity, despite the opposition of the Kauravya King Balhika Prātipīya by performing the Sautrāmaṇī, and hence he must have been a sage rather than a warrior [*Śatap. Br.*, xii, 8, 1, 17 ; 9, 3, 1, etc.].

31. **Chitra Gāṅgyāyani** or Gārgyāyaṇi is mentioned as a contemporary of Āruṇi and Śvetaketu in the *Kaushītaki Upanishad* [i, 1].

32. **Chitra Gauśrāyaṇi** is mentioned as a teacher in the *Kaushītaki Brāhmaṇa* [xxiii, 5].

33. **Chelaka Śāṇḍilyāyana** is mentioned as a teacher of one of the " doctrines of mystic imports " [" upanishadāmādeśāḥ "] in the *Śatapatha* along with Śāṭyāyani [x, 4, 5, 1, 2, 3,].

34. **Chaikitāneya Brahmadatta** is brought into connection with the Soma in *Bṛihadāraṇyaka* [i, 3, 24]. In the *Jaiminīya Upanishad* [i, 38, 1 ; 59, 1] his patron is the Kuru King, Abhipratārin.

35. **Chailaki Jīvala** is a teacher in the *Śatapatha* [ii, 3, 1, 34] which quotes his views. He is represented as reproving Takshan.

36. **Jana Śārkarākshya** is one of the five disputants who, under Uddālaka Āruṇi, went to Aśvapati Kaikeya for instruction [*Chhānd.*, v, 11, 1 ; 15, 1 ; *Śatap.*, x, 6, 1, 1].

37. **Janaka,** king of Videha, is one of the most prominent figures of the period, whose court was practically the centre of Vedic culture and civilization. Though a Videhan, he is always found to associate with the Brahmins of the Kuru-Pañchālas, like the sages Yājñavalkya and Śvetaketu, which probably indicates that the seat of the Upanishadic philosophy and Vedic learning was in the Kuru-Pañchāla country rather than in the east. Janaka is mentioned for his learning and encouragement of learned men in several works [e.g. *Śatap.*, xi, 3, 1, 2 ; 4, 3, 20 ; 6, 2, 1, etc ; *Bṛihad.*, iii, 1, 1 ; iv, 1, 1 ; 2, 1 ; 4, 7 ; v, 14, 8 ; *Jaimin. Br.*, i, 19, 2 ; *Kaushī. Up.*, iv, 1, etc.]. These references will show that discussion was the method of instruction conveniently adopted by the king who could thus count quite a number of teachers, viz. (1) Yājñavalkya, though he was himself in his earlier years once taught by the king [*Śatap.*, xi, 6, 2], (2) Jītvan Sailini, (3) Udaṅka Śaulbāyana, (4) Barku Vārshṇa, (5) Gardabhīvipīta Bhāradvāja, (6) Satyakāma Jābāla, and (7) Vidagdha Śākalya.

38. **Jala Jātūkarṇya** achieved the pre-eminent position of being the Purohita of three different peoples and kings, viz. those of Kāśi, Videha, and Kosala [*Śāṅkhāyana Śrauta Sūtra*, xvi, 29, 6].

39. **Jāta Śākāyana** is an authority on rituals in the *Kāṭhaka Saṁhitā* [xxii, 7].

40. **Jāratkārava Ārtabhāga** is one of the eight disputants with Yājñavalkya at the Aśvamedha of Janaka [*Bṛihad.*, iii, 2, 1 ; also *Śāṅkhāyana Āraṇyaka* (vii, 2)].

41. **Jitvan Śailini,** a teacher who taught Janaka that *Vāk* (Speech) was Brahman [*Bṛihad.*, iv, 1, 2].

42. **Taponitya Pauru-śishṭi** is the name of a teacher in the *Taittirīya Upanishad*, who believed in the supreme value of *tapas* or penance as contrasted with " learning and practising the Veda " [i, 9, 1].

43. **Tāṇḍya** is the name of a teacher in the *Śatapatha* [vi, 1, 2, 25] quoted on a point bearing on the *Agnichiti* or piling of the sacred fire. The school of the Tāṇḍins had the *Tāṇḍya Mahābrāhmaṇa* or *Pañchaviṁśa Brāhmaṇa* of the Sāmaveda.

44. **Tumiñja Aupoditi** is mentioned in the *Taittirīya Saṁhitā* [i, 7, 2, 1] as a Hotṛi priest at a Sattra or sacrificial session and as having been engaged in a discussion with Suśravas.

45. **Tura Kāvasheya** is the teacher of the doctrine regarding the fire-altar set forth in the tenth book of the *Śatapatha Brāhmaṇa*. Śāṇḍilya refers to him also as having erected a fire-altar on the Kārotī [ix, 5, 2, 15] and in that connection he makes the significant remark : " Let there be no bargaining as to sacrificial fees, for by bargaining the priests are deprived of their place in heaven." As a purohita, he consecrates as king Janamejaya Pārikshita [*Ait. Br.*, iv, 27 ; vii, 34 ; viii, 21]. He is supposed to be mentioned in the *Pañchaviṁśa Brāhmaṇa* [xxv, 14, 5] as Tura, the *deva-muni*, the saint of the gods.

46. **Tura-śravas** is the name of a seer in the *Pañchaviṁśa Brāhmaṇa* [ix, 4, 10] as having, by the composition of two Sāmans (chants), pleased Indra who in return gave him the oblation of the Pārāvatas on the Yamunā.

47. **Tri-śaṅku** in the *Taittirīya Upanishad* [i, 10, 1] has his teaching of the Veda quoted and is called a poet.

48. **Dīrgha-śravas** (far-famed) is the name of a *royal seer* mentioned in the *Pañchaviṁśa Brāhmaṇa* [xv, 3, 25] as having been expelled from his kingdom and reduced to starvation till he obtained succour from his being able to reveal or " see " a certain Sāman.

49. **Dṛiḍhachyut Āgasti** was the Udgātṛi priest at the sattra (sacrificial session) of the Vibhindukīyas [*Jaimi. Br.*, iii, 233].

50. **Deva-bhāga Śrautarsha** was the Purohita of the two peoples, the Sṛiñjayas and Kurus [*Śatap.*, ii, 4, 4, 5]. He is said to have taught Girija Bābhravya the science of the dissection of the sacrificial animal (*paśor vibhakti*) in the *Aitareya Brāhmaṇa* [vii, 1], while in the *Taittirīya Brāhmana* [iii, 10, 9, 11] he is deemed an authority on the Sāvitra Agni.

51. **Nāka Maudgalya** is cited as a teacher in the *Śatapatha* [xii, 5, 2, 1] in connection with ceremonies concerning the death of the Agnihotrin and in the *Taittirīya Upanishad* [i, 9, 1] for his view that learning and practising the Veda are the true *tapas* or penance and also in the *Bṛihadāraṇyaka* [vi, 4, 4].

52. **Nārada**, first mentioned as a *seer* in the Atharvaveda [v, 19, 9; xii, 4, 16, 24, 41] figures in the *Aitareya Brāhmaṇa* as *priest*, with Parvata, of Hariśchandra [vii, 13], as a *teacher* of Somaka Sāhadevya [vii, 34] and as anointing Āmbashṭhya and Yudhāṁśraushṭi [viii, 21]. He is mentioned as a teacher also in the *Maitrāyaṇī Saṁhitā* [i, 5, 8] and as a *pupil* of Bṛihaspati in the *Sāmavidhāna-Brāhmaṇa* [iii, 9] and of Sanatkumāra in the *Chhāndogya Upanishad* [vii, 1, 1].

53. **Patañchala Kāpya,** a famous teacher in the land of the Madras and a specialist in sacrificial lore whose reputation drew renowned pupils from the south like Uddālaka Āruṇi and Bhujyu Lāhyāyani [*Bṛihad.*, iii, 3, 1; 7, 1].

54. **Pippalāda** is a great sage in the *Praśna Upanishad* [i, 1] whose instruction was sought by six advanced students named Sukeśas, Satyakāma, Sauryāyaṇin, Kausalya, Vaidarbhi, and Kabandhin, who were themselves "devoted to Brahman, firm in Brahman", but "seeking for the Highest Brahman", they "thought that the Venerable Pippalāda could tell them all that" and so approached him with fuel in their hands. The Ṛishi, however, insisted on their year's stay with him with penance, abstinence, and faith as qualifying them for his instruction.

55. **Pravāhaṇa Jaivali** is one of the learned princes of the day whose instruction was sought by noted Brahman scholars like Śvetaketu Āruṇeya and his father Uddālaka [*Bṛihad.*, vi, 2, 1-7]. He was a leading figure in the Academy (*Samiti*, Parishad) of the Pañchālas [*Chhānd.*, v, 3, 1]. He was famed for his special knowledge of *udgītha* (i.e. *Om*) along with two other Brāhmaṇa scholars, Śīlaka Śālāvatya and Chaikitāyana Dālbhya, with whom he had once a discussion in which he seems to have come out

victorious [ib., i, 8]. He was also a specialist in the subjects connected with the mystery of life, death, and immortality of the soul, on which he put five questions which could not be answered by Śvetaketu and his father [see *infra*].

56. **Prāti-bodhi-putra** is the name of a teacher in the *Aitareya* [iii, 1, 5] and *Śāṅkhāyana* [vii, 13] *Āraṇyakas*.

57. **Priyavrata Somāpi or Saumāpi** is the name of a teacher in the *Aitareya Brāhmaṇa* [vii, 24] and *Śāṅkhāyana Āraṇyaka* [xv, 1]. Priyavrata Rauhiṇāyana is the name of a teacher in the *Śatapatha* [x, 3, 5, 14].

58. **Babara Prāvāhaṇi** is the name of a person whose ambition was to become an *orator* and by the use of the Pañcharātra sacrifice he acquired rhetorical powers [*Taitt. Saṁhitā*, vii, 1, 10, 2].

59. **Babhru Kaumbhya** is the name of a seer to whom a Sāman or Chant is attributed in the *Pañchaviṁśa Brāhmaṇa* [xv, 3, 13].

60. **Babhru Daivāvridha** is mentioned in the *Aitareya Brāhmaṇa* [vii, 34] as a pupil of Parvata and Nārada.

61. **Barku Vārshṇa** is a teacher in the *Bṛihadāraṇyaka Upanishad* [iv, 1, 4] who taught Janaka Videha the doctrine that *chakshus* (sight) is Brahman. He is also mentioned in the *Śatapatha* [i, 1, 1, 10] where his views are regarded as wrong.

62. **Basta Rāmakāyana** is a teacher in the *Maitrāyaṇī Saṁhitā* [iv, 2, 10].

63. **Bādhva** is the name of a teacher whose views are cited in the *Aitareya Āraṇyaka* [iii, 2, 3] on "the four persons", viz. those of the body, the metres, the Veda, and the great person.

64. **Buḍila Āśvatarāśvi** is one of the six Brahmins who had a discussion with King Aśvapati Kaikeya regarding "that Self called Vaiśvānara" [*Chhānd.*, v, 11, 1; 16, 1; *Śatap.*, x, 6, 1, 1]. His views are cited in another place in the *Śatapatha* as those of an authority on rituals [iv, 6, 1, 9]. The *Bṛihadāraṇyaka Upanishad* makes him a contemporary of Janaka Videha who puts a question to him "as knowing the Gāyatrī" [v, 14, 8].

65. **Bhima Vaidarbha** is mentioned in the *Aitareya Brāhmaṇa* [vii, 34] as having received instruction regarding the substitute for the Soma juice through a succession of teachers from Parvata and Nārada.

66. **Bhujyu Lāhyāyani** was one of the eight disputants who questioned the intellectual superiority claimed by Yājñavalkya at the horse-sacrifice of Janaka Videha [*Bṛihad.*, iii, 3].

67. **Madhuka Paiṅgya** is a teacher in the *Śatapatha* [xi,

7, 3, 8] whose views are quoted on a point regarding animal sacrifice.

68. **Mahāśāla Jābāla** is a teacher to whom Dhīra Śātaparṇeya repairs for instruction and has a discussion with him on Agni [*Śatap.*, x, 3, 3]. He himself goes along with five other Brahmins including Uddālaka for instruction to the Kshatriya, King Aśvapati [*Śatap.*, x, 6, 1, 1 ; *Chhānd.*, v, 11, 1].

69. **Mahidāsa Aitareya** (according to Sāyaṇa, the son of Itarā) is the sage from whom the *Aitareya Brāhmaṇa* and *Āraṇyaka* take their names as being compiled by him. The references to him and to his views in the *Āraṇyaka* [i, 1, 1 ; ii, 1, 8 ; 3, 7] indicate that he was its editor and not its author and was also a philosopher of distinction. His exceptional longevity (of 116 years) is referred to in the *Chhāndogya Upanishad* [iii, 16, 7] as the result of his special spiritual practices and also in the *Jaiminīya Upanishad Brāhmaṇa* [iv, 2].

70. **Mākshavya** is a teacher in the *Aitareya Āraṇyaka* [iii, 1,] who defines *ākāśa* as the union of earth and heaven.

71. **Māhāchamasya** is the patronymic of a teacher to whom the *Taittirīya Āraṇyaka* [i, 5, 1] ascribes the addition of *Mahas* to the triad *Bhur Bhuvas Svar*.

72. **Māhitthi** is the patronymic of a teacher mentioned in the *Śatapatha* whose views are cited in several places [vi, 2, 2, 10 ; viii, 6, 1, 16, etc. ; ix, 5, 1, 57 ; x, 6, 5, 9].

73. **Maitreyī** was the learned wife of Yājñavalkya who "was conversant with Brahman" while his other wife Kātyāyanī "possessed such knowledge only as women possess". When Yājñavalkya was about to renounce the life of a householder for that of a hermit, Maitreyī insists on his giving her instruction in spiritual wisdom.

74. **Yājñavalkya** is a prominent authority on rituals in the *Śatapatha Brāhmaṇa* and on philosophy in the *Bṛihadāraṇyaka Upanishad*. In the *Śatapatha* he, however, appears exclusively and very frequently in the first five and the last four *Kāṇḍas* as a noted teacher whose opinion is appealed to as the decisive authority, although in one place he is said to be in contradiction with the Rigveda [ii, 5, 1, 2] and in another [iii, 8, 2, 24] with the Charaka-Adhvaryus, one of whom curses him. It may also be noted that these books associated with him mention only the races settled in eastern or central Hindusthan such as the Kuru-Pañchālas, Kosala-Videhas, Śviknas, and Sṛiñjayas [with the exception of the following peoples mentioned only *once*

in them, viz. the *Vāhīkas* (western tribes) as opposed to the *Prāchyas* (eastern tribes), *Udīchyas* (northern tribes), and the *Nishādhas* (southern tribes), alluded to in the name of their king, Nala Naishadha], while the other Kāṇḍas [vi–ix] recognize Śāṇḍilya as the final authority and mention only the *north-western* peoples, viz. the Gāndhāras, with their King Nagnajit, the Śalvas, and the Kekayas. This shows which part of India Yajñavalkya came from. His association with the Kuru-Pañchāla Brahmins, Uddālaka, and his son Śvetaketu, points more definitely to his place of origin. Uddālaka was one of his *teachers* from whom he learnt the Mantha-doctrine [*Bṛihad.*, vi, 3, 7]. Śvetaketu was one of his fellow-disciples with whom, and another fellow-disciple, Somaśushma Sātyayajñi, he wanders about, until he meets King Janaka of Videha, driving in a car, who stops and invites the party to a discussion on Agnihotra. The king, dissatisfied with the Brahmins' wisdom, mounted his car and drove away. The discomfited Brahmins, finding themselves out-talked by a Kshatriya, wanted to challenge him to a disputation, but Yājñavalkya, preferring knowledge to rivalry, mounted his car, drove after the king, and overtook him, and made him teach the Agnihotra [*Śatap.*, xi, 6, 2]. Yājñavalkya afterwards grows up to be one of the most learned teachers of the times. His own *guru* Uddālaka Āruṇi could not hold his own in a disputation with him [*Bṛihad.*, iii, 7, 1] in a vast assembly or Congress of scholars of the entire Kuru-Pañchāla country, which was summoned by King Janaka of Videha in connection with his celebration of the horse-sacrifice. In that Assembly, Yājñavalkya asserted and maintained his superiority in the knowledge of sacred writ against all the renowned scholars of the age such as (1) Aśvala, the Hotṛi priest of Janaka, who put to him no less than eight knotty questions regarding sacrifice; (2) Jāratkārava Ārtabhāga, who put five questions; (3) Bhujyu Lāhyāyani, who questioned him regarding the destiny of the Pārikshitas who perpetrated the crime of *brahmahatyā* but performed Aśvamedha; (4) Ushasta Chākrāyaṇa, regarding the Self who is within all; (5) Kahola Kaushītakeya, who put a similar question; (6) Gārgī Vāchaknavī, the learned lady, who engaged in repeated disputations at the end of which she publicly declared before the Assembly: "Venerable Brahmins, you may consider it a great thing if you get off by bowing before him. No one, I believe, will defeat him in any argument concerning Brahman"; (7) Vidagdha Śākalya, who started a discussion on the gods at the end of which, for his impertinence, he lost his life.

In conclusion, Yājñavalkya said: "Reverend Brāhmaṇas whosoever among you desires to do so, may now question me Or question me, all of you. Or whosoever among you desires it, I shall question him, or I shall question all of you." But those Brāhmaṇas durst not say anything. Thus Yājñavalkya justified his initial appropriation of the prize of victory offered by the king, viz. 1,000 cows to each pair of whose horns were fastened ten *pādas* of gold, when he said to his pupil: "Drive them away my dear" (*Bṛihad.*, III; cf. *Śatap.*, xi, 6, 3]. His whilom teacher, Janaka, also figures as his most important pupil later on. He learns from him the Agnihotra for which he gives him 100 cows [*Śatap.*, xi, 3, 1, 2, 4]. On another occasion the king descended from his throne to receive instruction from him as his formal pupil, for otherwise he would not accept any reward which the king would fain give. Then Yājñavalkya, after testing the knowledge previously imparted to the king by other teachers, delivers his discourse on Brahman, at the end of which the king says: "Sir, I give you the Videhas, and also myself, to be together your slaves" [*Bṛihad.*, iv, 1–4]. Janaka also recognized Yājñavalkya's special knowledge of the Mitravindā sacrifice [*Śatap.*, xi, 4, 3, 20]. Yājñavalkya was also noted as an authority on the way in which the oblation is to be treated [ib., xi, 4, 2, 17], on the expiatory ceremonies in connection with the Agnihotra, and on the offering of the omenta [ib., xiii, 5, 3, 6]. He had two wives, Maitreyī and Kātyāyanī, the former being learned, conversant with Brahman, and the latter like other women. He has a discourse on Brahman with Maitreyī on her insistence, after which he bids adieu to the world to spend the last days of his life in contemplation in the solitude of the forest after making a due settlement between the two wives [*Bṛihad.*, iv, 5]. The concluding passage of *Bṛihadāraṇyaka* [vi, 5, 4] attributes to him the *White Yajus* [*Śuklāni yajūṁshi*]. In the *Śatapatha Brāhmaṇa*, Yājñavalkya is represented as a somewhat recalcitrant priest to whom are attributed some new views and doctrines. He protested against the priest's new demand that the benefit of the sacrifice should accrue in part to the priest, and said: "How can people have faith in this? Whatever be the blessing for which the priests pray, this blessing is for the worshipper (sacrificer) alone" [i, 3, 1, 26]. His comparative nobility of heart is apparent from his prayer to the Sun: "Give me light, *varcho me dehi*" instead of the usual "Give me cows" [i, 9, 3, 16].

75. **Raikva** is the name of the person whom the pious King

Jānaśruti Pautrāyaṇa, famed for his liberality in "always keeping open house and building places of refuge everywhere so that people should everywhere eat of his food", approached for instruction with the present of "600 cows, a necklace, and a carriage with mules". But Raikva replied: "Fie, necklace and carriage be thine, O Śūdra, together with the cows." Then the king "took again 1,000 cows, a necklace, a carriage with mules, and his own daughter", whereupon Raikva relented and gave him the instruction, viz. that Vāyu (air) and Prāṇa (breath) are to be meditated upon as Brahman [*Chhānd.*, iv, 1. 2. 3].

76. **Vatsapri Bhālandana** is a seer to whom is attributed the Vātsapra Sāman [*Taitt. Saṁ.*, v, 2, 1, 6; *Kāṭha. Saṁ.*, xix, 12; *Maitr. Saṁ.*, iii, 2, 2; *Pañchav. Br.*, xii, 11, 25; *Śatap.*, vi, 7, 4, 1].

77. **Vātavant** is a Ṛishi in the *Pañchaviṁśa Brāhmaṇa* [xxv, 3, 6] who, commencing a certain Sattra or sacrificial session, did not finish it and hence came to grief, while his colleague, Dṛiti, carried it through, whence the Dārteyas were more prosperous than the Vātavatas.

78. **Śilaka Śālāvatya** was a contemporary of Chaikitāyana Dālbhya and Pravāhaṇa Jaivali who were all well-versed in the Udgītha (*Om*), on which they had a discussion in which the Kshatriya proved his superiority to the Brahmins and taught them the knowledge [*Chhānd.*, 1, 8].

79. **Śaunaka** is a common patronymic. It is applied to Indrota and Svaidāyana [*Śatap.*, xiii, 5, 3, 5, in connection with the offering of the omenta; xi, 4, 1, 2, where Svaidāyana is a champion of the northern Brahmins who were challenged to a disputation by the famous Kuru-Pañchāla scholar, Uddālaka Āruṇi (see No. 15). It is also applied to Rauhiṇāyana [*Bṛihad.*, ii, 5, 20; iv, 5, 26 (Mādhyaṁdina)], Atidhanvan [No. 3], and Kāpeya [*Chhānd.*, iv, 3, 5, 7; *Jaimi. Up. Br.*, iii, 1, 21] while a Śaunaka appears as a great authority on grammatical, ritual, and other matters [*Bṛihaddevatā*, 1, xxiii].

80. **Saṁśravas Sauvarchanasa** is a teacher who has a discussion on a point of ritual with Tumiñja [*Taitt. Saṁ.*, i, 7, 2, 1].

81. **Satyakāma Jābāla** has an interesting history. Wishing to become a Brahmachārin he asked his mother: "Of what family am I?" The mother replied: "I do not know, my child, of what family thou art. In my youth when I had to move about much as a servant (waiting on the guests in my father's house) I conceived thee. I do not know of what family thou art. I am Jabālā by name, thou art Satyakāma. Say that thou art

Satyakāma." The boy then approached for instruction Gautama Hāridrumata who asked him, "Of what family are you, my friend?" He reported fully what his mother had said and on this Gautama exclaimed: "No one but a true Brāhmaṇa would thus speak out. Go and fetch fuel, friend, I shall initiate you. You have not swerved from the truth." Thus his truthfulness dispelled all doubts as to his origin and caste and admitted him to studentship. As a student he was equally true and dutiful. The first duty prescribed for him by his teacher was to tend his cows, 400 lean and weak ones. But Satyakāma resolved within himself: "I shall not return unless I bring back a thousand" and so dwelt a number of years in the forest till the number of cattle grew into his calculated figure. In the meanwhile, in the solitude of the forest, he acquires a knowledge of Shoḍasha-kalāvidyā, the sixteen parts of Brahman, and, on his return home, his teacher says to him: "Friend, you shine like one who knows Brahman. Who then has taught you?" Satyakāma replied: "Not men (it is an offence to have instruction from any other man than his accepted teacher). But you only, Sir, I wish, should teach me." Then the teacher gave him full instruction—"nothing was left out." With his studentship thus nobly spent, Satyakāma grew up to be a famous teacher. One of his pupils mentioned is Upakosala Kāmalāyana whom he makes tend his fires for twelve years. To him is attributed the famous parable of the rivalry of the organs in which the *prāṇa* proves its superiority to the other vital organs (eye, ear, speech, manas, etc.) and this doctrine (*prāṇasaṁvāda*) he communicated to another pupil named Gośruti Vaiyāghrapadya [*Chhand.*, iv, 4, 1, etc; 5, 1; 6, 2; 7, 2; 8, 2; 9, 10; 10, 1; v, 2, 3]. King Janaka Videha also seems to have been one of his pupils to whom he imparted the doctrine that *manas* (mind) is Brahman [*Bṛihad.*, iv, 1, 6]. One of his teachers was Jānaki Āyasthūṇa from whom he learned the Mantha-doctrine handed down from Uddālaka Āruṇi through a series of teachers and pupils [vi, 3, 12].

82. **Satya-vachas Rāthītara** is the name of a teacher who holds that truthfulness is the one thing needful in a Brahmachārin [*Taitt. Up.*, i, 9, 1].

83. **Sukeśin Bhāradvāja** was one of a circle of six Brahmin students who approached the Ṛishi Pippalāda for instruction regarding the Highest Brahman. The reason of his seeking that instruction was his failure to answer the question on the subject put to him by the prince of Kosala (Ayodhyā) named

Hiraṇyanābha. The Ṛishi insisted on their staying with him for one full year in penance, abstinence, and faith, and then imparted the instruction [*Praśna Up.*, i, 1, 2,; vi, 1].

Three Types of Educational Institutions : (1) Homes of Teachers as Schools. From the evidence adduced so far regarding the educational conditions of the period, it will be seen that, broadly speaking, there were evolved three different types of institutions for the spread of learning.

Firstly, there was the normal system under which the teacher, as a settled householder, admitted to his instruction pupils of tender age who, on the first dawn of consciousness, leave the home of their natural parents where their body was cared for and nurtured for that of spiritual parents where their mind and soul would be nourished. This entry into the preceptor's home was a sort of spiritual birth and hence a *rebirth* whence the brahmachārin becomes a *dvija* and an *antevāsin*. The admission of the pupil was formally made by the celebration of the specific ceremony of *upanayana* or initiation, the details of which declare the essentially *spiritual* character of the process as distinguished from the *mechanical* character of its modern substitute under which a pupil is admitted into a school on payment of a fee securing the registration of his name on its rolls. Details regarding this kind of studentship have been already given. A typical instance of this institution may be again conveniently cited of Satyakāma Jābāla going to his preceptor's house as a young boy where he spends several years tending his cattle and later on he himself, as a teacher, admits to his house as his pupil Upakosala Kāmalāyana who tends his fires for twelve years.

(2) Debating Circles and Parishads (Academies). Secondly, there was another type of institutions which ministered to the never-to-be-satisfied needs of the advanced students whose quest of Truth and Knowledge did not cease with the period of formal studentship and necessarily elementary education but was continued into the householder's state. Such students improved their knowledge by mutual discussions or by the instruction of renowned specialists and literary celebrities in search of whom they wandered through the country.

Examples. Uddālaka Āruṇi, from the Kuru-Pañchāla country, goes to the north where in a disputation to which he challenges the northern scholars he has something to learn from their leader, Svaidāyana Śaunaka [*Śatap. Br.*, xi, 4, 1, 2 f.]. Similarly, Śvetaketu Āruṇeya, Somaśushma Sātyayajñi, and Yājñavalkya, while travelling about, were met by Janaka of Videha who raised a discussion at which the Brahmin scholars learnt something from the Kshatriya [ib., xi, 6, 2]. Śilaka Śālāvatya, Chaikitāyana Dālbhya, and Pravāhaṇa Jaivali had a discussion on *Udgītha* in which the Brahmins learnt something from the Kshatriya Pravāhaṇa Jaivali [*Chhānd.*, i, 8]. King Jānaśruti Pautrāyaṇa sought instruction on a special topic from Raikva [ib., iv, 2, 3].

King Pravāhaṇa Jaivali was a member of the Pāñchāla Parishad, an academy of advanced scholars, which he went out of his palace every morning to attend. In one of the meetings of the academy, Śvetaketu could not answer the questions raised by the king which brought home to his mind that his education was not quite complete. Śvetaketu went back sorrowful to his father's place and pointed out the insufficiency of his teaching though at first he held it to be sufficient. The father, also finding himself incompetent to answer the king's questions, goes with his son to the king's palace where they are treated with proper respect and asked to stay for some time [ib., v, 3; *Bṛihad.*, vi, 2, 1-7]. "Five great householders and theologians came once together and held a discussion as to what is our self and what is Brahman," and then went together to the famous sage Uddālaka Āruṇi "who knows at present that Self, called Vaiśvānara", but Uddālaka "recommended to them another teacher", viz., King Aśvapati Kaikeya, to whom all the six went. They are respectfully treated with proper presents by the king who "without demanding any preparatory rites" indicative of formal pupilage proceeded straightway to give them the instruction asked for [*Chhānd.*, v, 11; *Śatap.*, x, 6, 1, 1-2]. Śvetaketu, returning home after completing his education during a twelve years' studentship, has his knowledge tested by his father in a discussion in which it is found to be wanting and further instruction is imparted to him by his father [*Chhānd.*, vi, 1]. Nārada, an advanced student, who mastered all the arts and sciences of the times, has his knowledge further extended and improved in a discussion with Sanatkumāra [ib., vii, 1 f.]. Uddālaka and his son Śvetaketu had another discussion with King Chitra Gāṅgāyani from whom they receive further knowledge [*Kaush. Up.*, i, 1]. Dṛiptabālāki Gārgya, whose fame "as a man of great reading" was known to several countries and peoples such as those of the Uśīnaras, Satvat-Matsyas, Kuru-Pañchālas, and Kāśī-Videhas, is still beaten at a disputation with Ajātaśatru, King of Kāśī, who knew the Brahman in its true character "as something not ourselves", while Bālāki worshipped the Brahman as the Sun, Moon, etc., i.e. as limited, active, and passive [*Kaush.*, iv, 1; *Bṛihad.*, ii, 1, 1, etc.]. Yājñavalkya teaches his learned wife, Maitreyī, by means of a discussion [*Bṛihad.*, ii, 4; iv, 5]. The principal means adopted by King Janaka of Videha for his instruction was to invite the learned men of his times to discussion in his court. [ib.; iv, etc.]. The venerable saint Śākāyana was moved by the thousand days' penance of King Bṛihadratha who renounced the world for the sake of knowledge which is then imparted by the Ṛishi [*Maitr. Up.*]. We thus see that, along with the settled homes of learning in which education was begun and imparted under a regular system of rules and discipline governing the entire life of the Brahmachārin as a whole-time inmate of his preceptor's house, there was this system of academic meetings for purposes of philosophical discussions among advanced scholars wandering through the country in quest of knowledge and of the teacher who was able to impart it. It was in these learned debates of fluctuating bodies of peripatetic scholars that the truth about the Ātman, the Ultimate Reality and foundation of things, was thoroughly threshed out and the study and wisdom of the elementary schools were tested and matured through the ordeal of criticism and friction of minds.

The Upanishads as the outcome of such discussions. It may be noted in this connection that the Upanishads themselves are in a sense to be regarded as the record and outcome of such academic disputations, the transactions, so to speak, of the philosophical societies or circles of the literary celebrities of the times. They represent the results of the researches of advanced scholars with whom the pursuit of Truth, the quest of the Ātman, superseded all other pursuits and quests and who frequently met together to discuss and compare the results of their independent investigations. They constitute a kind of knowledge, a body of truths, which could not usually and naturally be attained in the preliminary and preparatory period of formal pupilage under a system in which the student was to "sit down near" (*upa* + *ni* + *sad*, to sit down) his teacher for instruction. And yet that is the system or institution supposed to be implied by the term *upanishad* in the prevailing acceptation of the term based on its derivation. But though this particular derivation of the word is grammatically sound, it does not make other derivations impossible. While nearly all Western scholars are agreed about the aforesaid derivation, Indian scholars led by Śaṅkara derive the word from the root *sad*, in the sense of destruction, or from the root *sad*, in the sense of approaching.[1] In the former case, the word would mean the knowledge which destroys all worldly ties and thence the treatises which embody that knowledge, while in the latter case it would indicate the means by which the knowledge of Brahman comes near to us or by which we approach Brahman. Sāyaṇa suggests another derivation according to which the *Upanishad* would be that "wherein the highest good is embedded" (*upanishaṇṇamasyām param śreyaḥ*). The derivation given by the Indian scholars has at least the merit of explaining the various primary senses in which the word is used in the Upanishads themselves, whereas Max Müller himself admits that "it is strange that *upanishad*, in the sense of session or assembly, has never, so far as I am aware, been met with" [*S.B.E.*, i, lxxx]. I am tempted to think that if the word is at all to mean "sitting down near", it was sitting down near the sacrificial fire and not near a teacher. The connection of the Upanishads with sacrificial celebrations is amply borne out by the evidence of the

[1] The original use of the word seems to have been in the sense of sitting down near somebody to listen or to meditate and worship as in *Rv.*, ix, 11, 6; x, 73, 11; i, 65, 1, and in *Chhānd. Up.*, vi, 13, 1; vii, 1; and vii, 8, 1. In the *Trikāṇḍaśeshakosha* the word is explained as sitting down near a person [*samīpasadana*; cf. *Pāṇini*, i, 4, 73 (*upanishatkṛitya*), and iii, 4, 72, commentary)]. It has thus been taken to express the idea of session or assembly of pupils sitting down near their teacher to listen to his instruction and also the idea of a confidential secret sitting in contrast to *parishat* or *saṁsad* (assembly). It has also been suggested that the contents of the Upanishads were thought to be so esoteric that they could not be taught publicly to a miscellaneous assembly but only to a son or a regular pupil who would approach very near the teacher to hear those subtle doctrines. The Upanishads themselves contain restrictions in this regard [e.g. *Ait. Up.*, iii, 2, 6–9; *Chhānd.*, iii, 11, 5; *Bṛih.*, vi, 3, 12; *Śvet.*, vi, 22; *Muṇḍ.*, iii, 2, 11; *Maitr.*, vi, 29]. These explanations of the word are, however, not accepted by any orthodox Indian scholar from Śaṅkara downwards, nor are they supported by the passages in which the word occurs in the Upanishads themselves where it has been used in one or other of the following meanings, viz.:—

(1) Secret or esoteric explanation [e.g. *Ait. Ār.*, iii, 1, 6, 3; *Taitt. Up.*, i, 3; *Ait. Ār.*, iii, 2, 5, 1; *Chhānd.*, i, 13, 4; iii, 11, 3; viii, 8, 4]. [Cf. also *Śatap.*, x, 3, 5, 12; 4, 5, 1; 5, 1, 1; xii, 2, 2, 23.]

(2) Knowledge derived from such explanation [*Chhānd.*, i, 1].

(3) Special rules or observances incumbent on those who have received such knowledge [*Taitt. Up.*, ii, 9; iii, 10, 6].

(4) Title of the books containing such knowledge [*Bṛihad. Up.*, ii, 4, 10; iv, 1, 2; 5, 11]. [See on the whole subject, *SBE.*, i, lxxx, etc.]

Oldenberg traces the use of the word to the earlier sense of worship as in *upāsanā*. But Deussen points out [*Philosophy of the Upaniṣads*, p. 13 f.] that in the Upanishads *upa* + *ās* is always "to worship", never "to approach for instruction" and *upa* + *sad* always "to approach for instruction", never "to worship". He agrees with such Indian scholars as explain the word *upanishad* by *rahasyam*, i.e. secret, and points for support to such expressions as *guhyādeśāḥ* [*Chhand.*, iii, 5, 2], *paramaṁ guhyam* [*Kaṭha.*, iii, 17; *Śvet.*, vi, 22], *vedaguhya-upanishadsu gūḍham* [*Śvet.*, v, 6], and *guhyatamam* [*Maitr.*, vi, 29].

Śatapatha Brāhmaṇa, the Brihadāraṇyaka, and Chhāndogya Upanishads. The various conversations reported in such works mostly took place in the course of the celebration of big sacrifices. For instance, in the *Chhāndogya* [i, 10, 11] Ushasti Chākrāyaṇa went to a king's sacrifice and, having challenged the *Prastotṛi*, the *Udgātṛi*, and the *Pratihartṛi* to explain the nature of the various deities they were severally concerned with, explains it himself and concludes with a praise of the Udgītha which forms the burden of the whole chapter. In the fifth chapter there is the typical story of five learned scholars headed by Uddālaka Āruṇi going to King Aśvapati Kaikeya to have instruction regarding Vaiśvānara, Self, and the king before instructing them proposes to hold a sacrifice. The various discussions of philosophical problems now embodied in the Upanishads originally took place during the celebration of a great sacrifice. Literary disputations have always been the characteristic feature of such festive occasions. It was during such sacrificial sessions that Śukadeva recited the *Bhāgavatam* to Janamejaya and Sūta recited other Purāṇas to Ṛishis.[1]

(3) Conferences : An Example. This brings us to the third type of institutions developed for the spread of learning in these ancient times. Besides the small circles of philosophical disputants and *parishads* or academies of different localities, there was occasionally summoned by a great king a national gathering or Congress in which the representative thinkers of the country of various Schools were invited to meet and exchange their views. One such Congress of Ṛishis (the first of its kind in history) is reported in the *Bṛihadāraṇyaka Upanishad*, the *Śatapatha Brāhmaṇa*, and the *Vāyu Purāṇa*. King Janaka Videha performed a horse-sacrifice to which he invited all the Brāhmaṇas of the Kuru-Pañchāla country. The king offered a special prize of great value (1,000 cows with horns hung with gold) to the person, " the best read," " the most learned in sacred writ," and " the wisest ", and the prize was at once appropriated by Yājñavalkya. This was the signal for the great tournament of debate to begin, and Yājñavalkya's assumed superiority was challenged by seven representative scholars of the age who began to put a series of perplexing problems to Yājñavalkya requiring him to explain a

[1] Bodas in *JBRAS.*, XXII, 71, has a clever suggestion that the word *Āraṇyaka* might be traced to *araṇi* or wooden sticks by rubbing which the sacrificial fire is produced which may therefore be called *araṇya* and the discourses compiled in the presence of, or relating to, the sacrificial fire may have come to be called *Āraṇyaka*.

large variety of points concerning the ritual, the gods, the soul, the supreme cause of the world and the soul of all, good deeds, bad deeds, etc. The satisfactory answer that Yājñavalkya was able to give to each and all of the numerous questions by which his boasted and assumed supremacy was questioned at once won for him a country-wide fame [cf. *Bṛiha.*, iii, 8, 12] and demonstrated the versatile character of his learning and wisdom whereby he felt quite at home in problems ranging from the domain of the most practical and petty details of rituals to that of the most abstract and subtle philosophy and eschatology. It is worthy of note that in these learned debates in the midst of the gorgeous [1] sacrificial solemnities at the courts of kings, there flocked with Brahmans eager for the fray learned Brahman ladies not less eager for the contest to cross lances in argument regarding the Ātman or the Highest Truth. The wise Gārgī, one of the interlocutors of Yājñavalkya, says to him : " As an heroic youth from Kāśī or Videha bends his unbent bow and takes two deadly arrows in his hand, I have armed myself against thee with two questions, which solve for me." Not less bold and piercing was the thrust of another opponent : " When anyone says ' that is an ox, that is a horse ', it is thereby pointed out. Point out to me the revealed, unveiled Brahma, the Ātman which dwells in every thing : the Ātman which dwells in everything, what is that, O Yājñavalkya ? "

Was Sanskrit spoken language ? It may be presumed that the language of these debates, the medium of instruction in these times, was Sanskrit which was a spoken language then. During the *Brāhmaṇa* period and down to later times, there is no doubt that, as F. W. Thomas has pointed out [*JRAS.*, 1904], " Sanskrit was the language of public religious rites, of domestic ceremonies, of education, and of science." In the *Śatapatha Brāhmaṇa* [xiii, 4, 3] is given a vivid picture of the Brahman priest teaching the people (men, householders unlearned in the scriptures, old men, handsome youths, maidens, evil-doers, usurers, fishermen, etc.) the Pāriplava legend, the Rigveda, the Yajurveda, the Atharvaveda, the Āṅgirasa, the Sarpavidyā, the Devajanavidyā, Magic, Itihāsa, Purāṇa, the Sāmaveda. Some of the sacred works of the

[1] Be it noted that, as Oldenberg so forcibly points out [*Buddha*, p. 32], side by side with these highly-coloured court scenes where renowned masters from all lands, who have knowledge of the Ātman, contend with each other for fame, patronage, and reward, the texts give us another very different picture : " Knowing Him, the Ātman, Brahmans relinquish the desire for posterity, the desire for possessions and worldly prosperity, and go forth as mendicants." This was what even the victorious Yājñavalkya did.

period distinguish two kinds of speech, divine (*daivī*) and human, which probably stand for the Sanskrit of the hymns and ritual, the language of divine service, and the Sanskrit of ordinary conversation respectively, and not, as Sayāṇa suggests, for Sanskrit and Apabhraṁśa [ib., vi, 3, 1, 34; *Kāth. Saṁ.*, xiv, 5; *Maitr. Saṁ.*, i, 11, 5 (*yaś cha veda yaś cha na*); *Ait. Br.*, vii, 18, 13 (*om iti vai daivam tatheti mānusham*, etc.); *Ait. Ār.*, i, 3, 1]. Both kinds of speech are known to the Brahmin [*Kāṭh.*, ib., *Maitr.*, ib.]. Reference is also made to *Āryan* [*Ait. Ār.*, iii, 2, 5 (*āryā vāchaḥ*)] and to *Brāhmin* [ib., i, 5, 2, which Sāyaṇa vaguely comments on as *vedasambandhi vākyam*] and these distinctions represent an early piece of evidence for the existence of several dialects of the ancient Indian language. As yet the opposition meant seems to be to the non-Aryan tongues of the period [cf. *Taṇḍya Mahā. Br.*, xvii, 1, 2, 9]. In Keith's opinion [*Ait. Ār.*, p. 196 n.], whatever be the history of Vedic and Sanskrit, it is difficult to believe at this date (800–700 B.C.) in very much development of Prākritic forms so as to render contrast with them natural, though no doubt such forms existed. Thus a twofold linguistic differentiation was known in the period, viz. (1) *Sanskrit* designated as Āryan or Brāhmin speech to distinguish it from non-Aryan tongues, (2) within the domain of Sanskrit, the *daivī* or sacerdotal forms of Sanskrit as distinguished from its popular forms. In the *Sundarakāṇḍa* of the *Rāmāyaṇa*, Hanumant in choosing the language in which he should speak to Sītā mentions as his alternatives the above two varieties of Sanskrit (*vāchaṁ mānushīṁ saṁskṛitām* or *dvijāter iva vāchaṁ saṁskṛitām*). By the time of Daṇḍin, the term *daivī vāch* had come to be used for Sanskrit [*Kāvyādarśa*, i, 33].

The best Sanskrit of the times seems to have been current in the country of the Kuru-Pañchālas and probably also of the Uttara-Kurus in Kashmir and men went there to study the language [*Śatap.*, iii, 2, 3, 15 (a passage difficult, however, to construe); *Kaushītaki Br.*, vii, 6]. The *Śatapatha* [iii, 2, 1, 23. 24] also refers to barbarisms in speech which were to be avoided. These barbarisms were probably characteristic of the Vrātyas who are described in the *Pañchaviṁśa Brāhmaṇa* [xvii, 1, 9] as speaking the language of the initiated (*dīkshita-vāch*), though they, uninitiated (*a-dīkshita*), do so with difficulty for "they call what is easy of utterance (*a-durukta*) difficult to utter". This shows that the Vrātyas were very probably

Aryans who had been already developing prakritic forms of speech.[1]

Geographical Background. We shall now proceed to consider the geographical background of this many-sided culture of the *Brāhmaṇa* period and bring together the available data for the purpose.

Kuru-Pañchāla, Kosala, Videha. The most important work to be considered in this connection is the *Śatapatha Brāhmaṇa*, the geographical data of which point to the land of the Kuru-Pañchālas as being still the home and headquarters of Brahmanical culture. The kings of these parts who performed the horse-sacrifice are all eloquently extolled under what appears to be " a still fresh feeling of gratitude " [Weber, *Ind. Lit.*, 125]. We have mention of the Kuru King Janamejaya Pārikshita with his three brothers who by means of horse-sacrifice (performed at his capital, Āsandīvant) were absolved from the guilt of *brahmahatyā*. The sacrificial priest was Indrota Daivāpa Śaunaka, who is once mentioned as coming forward in opposition to Bhāllaveya and to Yājñavalkya who rejects his view. We have mention of the Pāñchāla kings Kraivya (the Pāñchāla overlord of the Krivis, formerly called the Pañchālas) and Sātrāsāha ; of Bharata Dauḥshanti (born of Śakuntalā at Nāḍapit, the hermitage of Ṛishi Kaṇva) and Śātānīka Sātrājita, king of the Bharatas and enemy of the Kāśī king ; of Purukutsa Aikshvāka ; Dhvasan Dvaitavana, king of the Matsyas ; Ṛishava Yājñatura, king of the Śviknas. The renowned scholars Uddālaka and Śvetaketu,

[1] The claim that Prākritic dialects became very early the ruling speech of the people superseding Sanskrit cannot be well supported. They were subsequent to the Mantra literature and to the earliest epic (not mere *ākhyānas* or *itihāsas*), Brāhmaṇas, Upanishads, and Āraṇyakas (800–600 B.C.). The necessary interval of time is to be allowed for the complete separation of the literary and vulgar speech. The place of the Epic must be found either before the decay of speech had rendered Sanskrit unintelligible to the warrior classes of the populace or after the general revival of Sanskrit in the second and third centuries A.D. The latter view is not quite in accord with our conception of the history of language and literature. Besides, we have references to the *Mahābhārata* and *Ramāyaṇa* in the *Kautilīya* (300 B.C.) and the *Mahābhāshya* (150 B.C.). The fact, besides, cannot be doubted that the Epics constituting the fifth Veda were meant to be studied by ordinary worldly people, warriors, husbandmen, and ladies, just as the four Vedas and the Brahmanical literature founded on them were studied by the priests. The Prākrits were certainly posterior to Pāṇini (350 B.C. at the latest) who distinguishes the *laukikabhāshā* or the spoken Sanskrit of ordinary life from *chhāndasa* or poetical language of the Vedas. Again, since Patañjali knew the drama we must assign to his period the separate use of Sanskrit and Prākrit for the different characters when Sanskrit could be used by kings and nobles as intelligible to their inferiors. [On the whole subject see Macdonell, *Vedic Index* (on *Vācha* and *Vrātya*) ; *Sans. Lit.*, pp. 20–4 ; *JRAS.*, 1904, pp. 435 f. ; Keith, *JRAS.*, 1906, p. 2 ; and *Ait. Ār.*, pp. 179, 196, 255 (notes). I have here adopted Dr. Keith's conclusions.]

father and son, who figure prominently in the *Śatapatha* are expressly stated to be Kuru-Pañchāla Brahmins. Nevertheless, it is clear that the Brahmanical system had also by this time spread to the countries to the east of Madhyadeśa, to Kosala with its capital, Ayodhyā, and Videha with its capital, Mithilā. Among the horse-sacrificers, the Kausalya king, Para Āṭṇāra, is mentioned. The court of King Janaka of Videha figures, as we have seen, as the centre of the culture of the times which drew to itself the learned Brahmins of the Kuru-Pañchāla country in literary Congresses and Conferences summoned on important sacrificial occasions. The neighbouring kingdom of Kāśī was devoid of learned men who were all attracted to Janaka for his lavish patronage and, accordingly, Ajātaśatru, the Kāśī king, could not but envy his great contemporary. Yājñavalkya was the hero of the tournaments of debate held at Janaka's court and was himself probably a Videhan, and the fact that he is represented as getting the better of the most distinguished teachers of the West in argument probably shows that the redaction of the White Yajurveda took place in this eastern region [Macdonell, *Sans. Lit.*, p. 214]. The earlier stages of this movement of Vedic culture towards Videha and the eastern regions are allegorically represented in the legend of Māthava, King of Videgha, and his preceptor, Gotama Rāhūgaṇa, which has been already referred to. It has also been stated that a part of the *Śatapatha*, Books vi–x, where Śāṇḍilya is regarded as the highest authority, and where the north-western peoples alone are mentioned, viz. the Gāndhāras, Śalvas, and Kekayas, has a *north-western* origin, while the remainder, where Yājñavalkya is the authority and the peoples of central and eastern Hindusthan alone are consequently mentioned, viz. the Kuru-Pañchālas, Kosala-Videhas, Śviknas, and Sṛiñjayas, belongs to those parts.

Vaśa-Uśīnara, Kāśī. Most of the geographical data, together with really historical statements, are to be found in the last books of the *Aitareya Brāhmaṇa* from which it at any rate specially follows that their scene is the country of the Kuru-Pañchālas and Vaśa-Uśīnaras. The ethnological table given in viii, 14 is sufficiently clear on this point. In the middle [" *asyāṁ dhruvāyāṁ madhyamāyāṁ pratishṭhāyāṁ diśi* " in which the use of the word *asyāṁ* as distinguished from *etasyāṁ* used in respect of other territories shows that the compiler of the text belongs to this very territory] lie the realms of the Kuru-Pañchālas together with Vaśas and Uśīnaras. To the south of this Land of the Middle there dwell the Satvats, eastward the Prāchyas (i.e. the Kāśī, Kosala, Videha, and Magadha peoples), westward the Nīchyas, Apāchyas. In the north the Middle Land is bounded by the Himālaya, beyond which (*pareṇa Himavantam*) dwell the Uttara Kurus and Uttara Madras. This sketch of the distribution of Indian peoples points to the land which formed the centre of genuine Vedo-Brahmanic culture from which it radiated in all directions. This land was later known (cf. Manu) as the land of the Brahmarshis whose customs and rites are taken as a model, whose warriors are the bravest, the land of Kurukshetra and of the Matsyas, Pañchālas, and Śūrasenas [ii, 19 ; vii, 193] corresponding to what is set down in the *Aitareya* as *madhyamā diś* and as south ; but what is regarded in the *Aitareya* as west and east, above all, the land of the eastern peoples of Kāśī, Kosala, Videha, and Magadha, is by Manu excluded from the land of the Brahmarshis.

The *Śāṅkhāyana* (or *Kaushītaki*) *Brāhmaṇa* gives the interesting information that the northern parts of India were then famous as seats or centres of linguistic studies and people resorted thither in order to become acquainted with the language and on their return came to be regarded as authorities and specialists on linguistic questions.

Matsya. The *Kaushītaki Upanishad* knows only of the territory enclosed between the northern (Himavant) and southern (Vindhya) mountains and mentions a list of peoples in accord with this, viz. the Vaśas, Uśīnaras, Matsyas, Kuru-Pañchālas, and Kāśī-Videhas.

Places of Sacrifice. The *Tāṇḍya* or *Pañchaviṁśa Brāhmaṇa* contains a variety of interesting geographical data. In the first place, we have minute descriptions of sacrifices on the Sarasvatī and Dṛishadvatī. Secondly, we have descriptions of *Vrātyastomas* or sacrifices by which Aryan but non-Brahmanical Indians were admitted into the Brahmanical order. Thirdly, the great sacrifice of the Naimishīya Ṛishis is mentioned, along with the river Sudāman. Weber concludes from these data that they point to an active communication with the west, particularly with the non-Brahmanic Aryans there, and, consequently, to the fact that the locality of its composition must be laid more towards the west. But there are other data which point us to the east such as the mention of Para Āṭṇāra, King of the Kosalas, of Namī Sāpya, King of the Videhas (the Nimi of the Epic), of Kurukshetra, Yamunā, etc., of the Vedic name Trasadasyu Purukutsa (connecting it with the earlier Ṛishi period) and the significant absence of any allusion to the Kuru-Pañchālas or to Janaka (showing probably its origin in a different locality or its priority to the flourishing epoch of the Kuru-Pañchālas).

The *Chhāndogya Upanishad* mentions the Naimishīya, the Mahāvṛishas, and the Gāndhāras which would make its origin more western, while the *Bṛihadarāṇyaka* to which it is more akin [1] in other respects belongs distinctly to the eastern part of Hindusthan.

The general conclusion drawn by Oldenberg from the geographical data of the literature of the period is that the culture of the Vedas was indigenous to but one portion of the Aryan peoples of Hindusthan and from them reached the other afterwards only at second hand ; that the home of Brahmanic civilization has been with the Kuru-Pañchālas and the stocks of the west standing in closer union with them who, as the qualified champions of Aryan culture, are to be distinguished from those who were not regarded as equally accredited partakers in this culture. Though this conclusion seems to be contradicted by the fact that our *Brāhmaṇa* texts like the *Śatapatha*, for instance, do not mention the western peoples to the exclusion of the eastern (as have been already shown), we should, however, bear in mind that the cases of their being mentioned, specially of the Kurus and Pañchālas, and, in a second degree, of the Bharatas, surpass at once in frequency the mentioning of the eastern peoples ; and that the texts frequently attribute to the western peoples unmistakably the weight of an older and higher sacral authority than to the eastern groups, which latṭer are plainly named in a hostile or contemptuous tone, or at least appear as peoples who have received from the west instruction in the spiritual knowledge which has its home there.

Kurukshetra. Oldenberg has adduced a body of select evidence on the point which may be set forth after him. The Kurukshetra is the place of sacrifice of the gods [*Śatap.*, iv, 1, 5, 13 ; xiv, 1, 1, 2]. From the Chamasa which the gods used in the sacrifice was produced the sacred tree Nyagrodha ; the first-born of the Nyagrodha trees grew on the Kurukshetra [*Ait. Br.*, vii, 30]. In the tale of Purūravas and Urvaśī, the Kurukshetra plays

[1] The two have in common the following names: Pravāhaṇa Jaivali, Ushasti Chākrāyaṇa, Śāṇḍilya, Satyakāma Jābāla, Uddālaka Āruṇi, Śvetaketu, and Aśvapati. The somewhat late date of *Chhāndogya* may be inferred from the mention of Atharvāṅgirasaḥ, Itihāsas, and Purāṇas as existing in independent forms (though Śaṅkara regards them as parts of the *Brāhmaṇas*) ; of legal cases recalling Manu's Code, viz. infliction of capital punishment for denied theft, trial by ordeal (carrying red-hot axe) ; and of the doctrine of transmigration of souls (also mentioned in the *Bṛihadāraṇyaka*).

a part [*Śatap.*, xi, 5, 1, 4]. The offerings which must be made on the Sarasvatī, Dṛishadvatī, and Yamunā are known [*Pañchav. Br.*, xxv, 10; *Śāṅkh. Śr.*, xiii, 29; *Kāty.*, xxiv, 6]. In the north, among the Kuru-Pañchālas, is the country where the Vāch has her peculiar home; the Vāch, as she there is, is truly (*nidānena*) to be called a Vāch [*Śat.*, iii, 2, 3, 15]. Some prefer the Pañchāvattam to the Chaturavattam, but the Chaturavattam follows the custom of the Kuru-Pañchālas; "therefore, let it be given the preference" [ib., i, 7, 2, 8]. There are other references to the Kurus or Pañchālas showing their relative importance, e.g. a saying of the Kuru-Pañchālas with reference to such of their kings as have performed the Rājasūya [*Śat.*, v, 5, 2, 5]; a form of Vājapeya offering called Kuru-Vājapeya [*Śāṅkh. Śr.*, xv, 3, 15]; a disaster of a shower of stones to the Kurus [*Chhānd.*, i, 10, 1]; an old verse, "the mare saves the Kurus" [ib., iv, 17, 9]; a Brahmin's threat that the Kurus shall be obliged to fly from Kurukshetra [*Śaṅkh. Śr.*, xv, 15, 10].

Equally significant is the brilliant part played by the Kuru King, Janamejaya, in a series of *Brāhmaṇa* texts, as well as that noble ode in praise of his father, Pārikshita [*Av.*, xx, 127, 7].

As Parikshita and Janamejaya among kings, so Āruṇi Uddālaka among those versed in sacred writ stands on a high, perhaps on the highest platform, as will be evident from the details of his life and work given above.

Certain peculiarities of recitation are attributed to the Pañchālas among whom probably arose the method of Vedic recitation [*Śāṅkh. Śr.*, xii, 13, 6; *Ṛik-Prātiś. Sūtra*, 137 and 186].

The land of the Bharatas. A similarly important position attaches to the Bharatas in the texts. We have already referred to two Bharata princes in the *Śatapatha* list of Aśvamedha offerers and their greatness is stated in the accompanying verses to be as far beyond that of other mortals as the heavens are above the earth. In other places, the Bharatas are regarded as the exemplars of correct conduct, the knowledge of whose customs is stated to be something which not everyone has [*Śat.*, v, 4, 4, 1; *Ait. Br.*, ii, 25; iii, 18]. According to Oldenberg, the testimony of the Rigveda shows the Bharatas emerging, out of the struggles in which the migratory period of the Vedic stocks was passed, as the possessors of the regions round the Sarasvatī and Dṛishadvatī on whose banks the Bharata princes perform their sacrifices. The weapons of the Bharata princes and the poetical fame of their Ṛishis may have co-operated to acquire for the cult of the Bharatas the character of universally acknowledged rule and for the Bharatas a kind of sacral hegemony: hence Agni as friend of the Bharatas, the goddess Bhāratī, the sacredness of the Sarasvatī and Dṛishadvatī. Then came the period when the countless small stocks of the Saṁhitā age were fused together to form the greater peoples of the Brāhmaṇa period. The Bharatas found their place, probably together with their old enemies, the Pūrus [cf. the vanishing enmity in *Rv.*, i, 112, 4; vii, 19, 3], within the great complex of peoples now in process of formation, the Kurus; their sacred land now became Kurukshetra.

Videha under Janaka. To the evidence here adduced (partly from the *Śatapatha*) of the pre-eminence of the Kuru-Pañchālas in the Vedic world may be opposed, however, the evidence of the same text itself regarding the important part played by the people of Videha living far in the east and their king Janaka. In the literary Congress held by Janaka who invited to it the entire body of Kuru-Pañchāla Brahmins, the palm of victory belongs to Yājñavalkya, a *Videhan* scholar [xiv, 6, 1, 1–3; especially 6, 9, 20]. This shows, firstly, that Vedic culture was held in honour at a place far east from the land of the Kuru-Pañchālas—a shifting, so to speak, of the literary centre of gravity—and, secondly, the most important figure in that Congress of Brahmins, whose authority on spiritual questions is regarded as decisive, belongs to that eastern region. This fact, however, has to be considered along with other facts related about the Congress in order to get at the truth of the matter. For the *Śatapatha Brāhmaṇa* itself shows clearly that Brahmanic culture among the Videhas is only an offshoot from the Kuru-Pañchālas. Yājña-valkya himself, as we have seen, is a pupil of Āruṇi, a Pāñchāla. Next, the Brahmans whom Janaka invites to his Congress are all —except Yājñavalkya—*Kurupañchālānāṁ brāhmaṇāḥ*. The king of the east, with his regard and partiality for the culture of the west, pays homage to that culture by collecting at his court the literary celebrities of the west—much as the intellects of Athens gathered at the court of Macedonian princes. Over and above this stands the evidence already cited, showing how the authority of the west, of the Kuru-Pañchālas, is felt and acknowledged throughout the text and how the land of the Videhas was once a stranger to the sacrificial system as it flourished on the Sarasvatī.

Position of Magadha. Farther off from the old centres

of Vedic culture than the Kosalas and Videhas stood the Magadhas to whom along with the Aṅgas in the farther east and the Gandhāris [1] and Mūjavants in the far north-west fever is wished away, as we have seen, in a well-known passage of the Atharvaveda [v, 22, 14]. That Magadha Brahmins were held in light esteem is evident from other passages in Vedic literature [e.g. *Vāja. Saṁ.*, xxx, 5, 22], but the reason for it is their imperfect brahminization and not, as surmised by Weber, the success of Buddhism in their country.

We thus find that the literature of the *Brāhmaṇas* points to a certain definitely circumscribed circle of peoples as its home, as the home of genuine Brāhmaṇism, corresponding to the region held noted for its purity by Manu. This community, a complex of peoples of earlier Rigvedic stocks (like the Pūrus, Turvaśas, Bharata-Tṛitsus), is to be distinguished from the Kosalas, the Videhas, and the Magadhas, who were pressing forward farther to the east down the Ganges, as the former peoples were pressing forward through the Panjab towards their later habitations.

Seats of Sacrifice as Seats of Learning. We have now had an idea of the general geographical background of the culture of the *Brāhmaṇa* period, but regarding the actual seats of this ancient learning we have unfortunately but little evidence. Nowhere in the entire range of this vast and varied literature do we find any direct mention of the locality of any of the numerous schools through which that literature was preserving and propagating itself except in one solitary passage in the *Chhāndogya Upanishad* [v, 3, 1] repeated in the *Śatapatha Brāhmaṇa* [xiv, 9, 1, 1] testifying to the Assembly or Parishat of the Pāñchālas which counted among its members the distinguished scholars, the Brahmin Śvetaketu and the Prince Pravāhaṇa Jaivali. If we, however, proceed on the assumption that the places celebrated for sacrifices were also those celebrated for learning, then we can avail ourselves of some additional evidence. Nor is the assumption far from truth. It has been already shown how the

[1] The Gandhāras in the north-west will have to be regarded also as standing outside the pale of Vedic culture, despite the reference to Gandhāra in the *Chhāndogya Upanishad* [vi, 14], which proves, according to Oldenberg, neither the northern origin of its compiler, nor the antiquity of the text, as supposed by Max Müller, but rather the contrary, as will appear from the context and contents of the passage where there is a comparison of a man who is led (*āntya*) away by the Gandhāras with closed eyes and who then inquires his way back from village to village. Thus in the passage the Gandhāras are made to reside the farther from the land where the statement of the passage may have been made.

culture of the Upanishads centred round the sacrifice which was made the occasion for learned debates in meetings of scholars well versed in the wisdom of the age. One of the most renowned places of such sacrifice in these ancient times was the far-famed Naimisha forest. The Ṛishis of the Naimisha forest and their sacrificial festivals are frequently mentioned in the literature of the period [e.g. *Kāth. Saṁ.*, x, 6 ; *Pañchav. Br.*, xxv, 6, 4 ; *Jaimi. Br.*, i, 363 ; *Kaush. Br.*, xxvi, 5 ; xxviii, 4 ; *Chhānd. Up.*, i, 2, 13, where the Udgātṛi of the Naimishīya sacrificers is mentioned, viz. Vaka Dālbhya]. It may be noted, too, in this connection that one of the sacrificers in this Naimisha forest was Śaunaka at whose sacrificial feast Sauti, the son of Vaiśampāyana, is said to have repeated before the assembly of Ṛishis the *Mahābhārata* recited by his father on an earlier occasion to Janamejaya (the second) together with the *Harivaṁśa.*

It is also to be noted that these sacrifices were celebrated in a great variety of ways. According to the *Pañchaviṁśa Brāhmaṇa*, the Soma sacrifices extended over one day or several, or finally over more than twelve days. The latter were known as *Sattras* or sessions which Brahmins alone could perform and that in considerable numbers. These might last 100 days or even several years. It is thus clear how these sacrificial sessions would naturally be the occasions for learned discussions by the concourse of Brahmins engaged therein. Like the Soma sacrifices, the horse-sacrifices which only great kings were entitled to perform were also accompanied by gatherings of learned men, the most typical instance of which is the Aśvamedha of Janaka of Videha who brought together for the occasion a vast assembly of Brahmins from the Kuru-Pañchāla country.

Some of these horse-sacrifices are described in a few of the sacred texts.

At *Āsandīvant*, the capital of the kingdom of the Kuru king Janamejaya, a horse-sacrifice was performed by the Ṛishi Indrota Daivāpa Śaunaka [*Śat.*, xiii, 5, 4]. The *Aitareya Brāhmaṇa* mentions Tura Kāvasheya as the Ṛishi of Janamejaya [viii, 14, 4 ; 19, 2]. At the sacrifice of Kraivya, " the Pañchāla king," at a place called *Parivakrā*, the immense offering was divided " among the Brahmins of the Pañchālas from every quarter " so that it must have been the occasion for a great gathering of learned men [*Śat.*, ib.]. Near the lake of *Dvaitavana* in the country of the Matsyas was the scene of the sacrifice of its King Dhvasan Dvaitavana [ib.]. Then there were the sacrifices of Bharata

Dauḥshanti with his priest Dīrghatamas Māmateya in the country of *Mashṇāra* where he distributed as gifts inumerable elephants with white tusks and golden trappings; innumerable cows to 1,000 Brahmins of the country named *Sāchīguṇa*; and kept 78 steeds in a place on the *Yamunā* and 55 in the place named *Vṛitraghna* on the *Gaṅgā* [ib.; *Ait. Br.*, ib.]. At the sacrifice of Ṛishabha Yājñatura, king of the *Śviknas*, the Brahman-folk assembled divided between them the offering-gifts [*Śat.*, ib.]. At the sacrifice of the *Pāñchāla* King Śoṇa Sātrāsāha, the assembled Brahmins became satiated with wealth [ib.]. There were sacrifices performed on the *Sarasvatī* and *Dṛishadvatī* of which minute descriptions are given [*Pañchav. Br.*].

Courts of Kings as Centres of Learning. Besides the noted seats of sacrifice which were also, on the view taken here, the seats of learning, we are able to trace some definite Schools in the sense of circles or associations of learned men, of teachers and pupils, flourishing independently or in connection with the courts of kings. Proceeding from the periphery of Brahmanical culture in the east, we find a centre of learning in the court of Ajātaśatru, king of Kāśī, associated with the famous scholar, the proud Bālāki Gārgya, whose fame was spread through the entire land of the Uśīnaras, Satvat-Matsyas, Kuru-Pañchālas, and Videhas. Bhadrasena Ajātaśatrava who was a contemporary of Uddālaka and was defeated by him in argument was probably a son or descendant of the Kāśī king.

Another easterly centre of learning was the court of King Janaka of *Videha*. Janaka himself was the centre of a distinguished literary circle. Many learned scholars of the day revolved round him like satellites, among whom are mentioned Yājñavalkya, Śvetaketu, Jitvan Śailini, Udaṅka Śaulbāyana, Barku Vārshṇa, Gardabhīvibhīta Bhāradvāja, Satyakāma Jābāla, and Vidagdha Śākalya. The learned men of the *Kuru-Pañchāla* country were also associated with the court of Janaka through the tournaments of debate accompanying his horse-sacrifice, and we have the names of their representatives who took part in that debate, viz. Aśvala, Jāratkārava Ārtabhāga, Bhujyu Lāhyāyani, Ushasta Chākrāyaṇa, Kahoḍa Kaushītakeya, Gārgī Vāchaknavī.

Next to Videha, we have *Kosala* also figuring as a seat of culture. The Prince of Kosala (with his capital called Kosala, i.e. Ayodhyā) was a learned man who sought instruction from the Ṛishi Sukeśin Bhāradvāja. We have also seen that another Kosala king Para Āṭṇāra Hairaṇyanābha performed Aśvamedha.

In the country of the *Pañchālas* the court of King Pravāhaṇa Jaivali was another centre of culture on account of the wisdom of the king himself, which attracted to him scholars like Śvetaketu Āruṇeya, and his father, Śilaka Śālāvatya, and Chaikitāyana Dālbhya.

Similarly, the court of King Aśvapati Kaikeya was another such centre in the far north. The circle of scholars that gathered round that learned king included the famous Uddālaka, Prāchīnaśāla, Sātyayajña, Indradyumna, Jana, and Buḍila. If the kingdom of *Kekaya* is to be placed between the Vitastā and Sindhu, the court of Aśvapati must be deemed to have been far-famed as a seat of learning to attract thither scholars from the distant Kuru-Pañchāla country.

The north was also famous for other renowned teachers and centres of learning. For we find Patañchāla Kāpya as a famous teacher in the land of the *Madras* and round him gathered an association of scholars from distant parts like Uddālaka Āruṇi and Bhujyu Lāhyāyani.

The centre of another circle of learned scholars in the north [1] was the famous Svaidāyana Śaunaka, the champion of northern scholars, whose superiority was acknowledged by the great scholar of the Middle Country named Uddālaka who went to him to test his knowledge, just as the superiority of the great eastern scholar, Yājñavalkya, was admitted by him.

Lastly, we have scholars of the eminence of Yājñavalkya, Uddālaka, or Pippalāda who were institutions by themselves. The circles of scholars that gathered round them and the contributions they made to the advancement and diffusion of culture have been already indicated in the notices of their respective careers given above.

Sylvan Schools. In this connection a reference may also be made to the type of schools implied in the literature of the

[1] In this connection we may recall the evidence already cited regarding the reputation of the northerners or *Udīchyas* for learning and scholarship. In the *Śatapatha Brāhmaṇa* [iii, 2, 3, 15] we have a reference to the speech of the north as being similar to that of the Kuru-Pañchālas. Indeed, the Northerners' speech was so well known for its purity that, according to the *Kaushītaki Brāhmaṇa* [vii, 6], scholars from other parts used to go to the north for linguistic studies. According to Franke [*Pāli and Sanskrit*, 88, 89], Sanskrit was specially developed in Kāśmīra. It may be also noted that Takshaśilā (in Gandhāra) was one of the most famous centres of learning in India according to Buddhist and Brahmanical texts.

Āraṇyakas. According to Sāyaṇa,[1] the *Āraṇyakas* are so called because they had to be read in the forest. In another place, Sāyaṇa defines an *Āraṇyaka* as a Brāhmaṇa appointed for the vow of the anchorite. Oldenberg [*Prolegomena*, p. 291] holds that the *Āraṇyaka* is so called because the mysterious or mystical character of its contents requires that it should be imparted to the pupil in the solitude of the forest (*araṇye*) outside the busy haunts of men and far from the madding crowd's ignoble strife. Perhaps an instance of this may be found in the *Bṛihadāraṇyaka* [iii, 2, 13] where Yājñavalkya with reference to the discussion of a secret doctrine with another scholar in a public meeting says: "Take my hand, my friend. We two alone shall know of this; let this question of ours not be discussed in public." "Then these two went out and argued." [Cf. the terms *rahasyam*, *upanishad* as explained above.] Deussen accepts the second interpretation of Sāyaṇa because, as he states, the *Āraṇyakas* consist mainly of all kinds of explanations of the ritual and allegorical speculations embodied in the *Brāhmaṇas* which would serve as a substitute in the life of the forest for the actual sacrificial observances. Max Müller also opines that it might almost seem as if the *Āraṇyakas* were intended for the *Vānaprasthas* only, people who, after having performed all the duties of a student and a householder, retire from the world to the forest to end their days in the contemplation of the Divine, as Yājñavalkya is said to have done in the *Bṛihadāraṇyaka* [iv, 5]. Indeed, it is even explicitly stated in the *Āruṇikopanishad* that the *Sannyāsin*, the man who no longer recites the Mantras, and no longer performs sacrifices, is bound to read, out of all the Vedas, only the Āraṇyaka or the Upanishad.

Keith [*Ait. Ār.*, p. 15], however, holds this view as far-fetched, for originally the *Āraṇyaka* was meant to give secret explanations of the ritual and hence presupposed that the ritual was still in use and known. The tendency was of course for the secret explanation to grow independent of the ritual until the stage is reached where the Āraṇyaka passes into the Upanishad, and, by that time too, there grew up the order of dividing the life of the Hindu into the four stages or Āśramas.

[1] Araṇye eva pāṭhyatvāt Āraṇyakam (Preface to *Aita. Āraṇyaka*). Āraṇyavratarūpam Brāhmaṇam (ib.).

Again: "Araṇyādhyayanāt etat Āraṇyakam iti" [*Taitti. Āra.*]. Also: "Etat Āraṇyakaṁ sarvaṁ nāvratī śrotumarhati" [ib.].

Pāṇini [iv, 2, 129] uses the word *āraṇyaka* in the sense of "a *man* living in the forest", but the author of the *Vārttikas* remarks that the same word is also used in the sense of "that which is *read* in the forest".

Thus the *Āraṇyaka* represents the "forest-portion" of the *Brāhmaṇa* and points to the development of forest life as an institution by itself in the social life of the community. It is to this forest-life and to the solitary little sylvan seats of learning that, as Weber so rightly points out, we must chiefly ascribe the depth of speculation, the complete absorption in mystic devotion by which the Hindus are so eminently distinguished, and, accordingly, we find the *Āraṇyakas* bear this character impressed upon them in a most marked degree. In harmony with their prevailing purpose, to offer to the Vānaprastha an equivalent for the sacrificial observances, for the most part no longer practicable, they indulge in mystical interpretations of these, which are then followed up in some of the oldest Upanishads. It should, however, be remembered that, as Max Müller points out, as sacrifices were performed long before a word of any *Brāhmaṇa* or *Sūtra* had been uttered, so metaphysical speculations were carried on in the forests of India long before the names of *Āraṇyaka* or *Upanishad* were thought of.[1]

Education of Castes other than Brāhmaṇa. An account of the education of the *Brāhmaṇa* period will not be complete without a reference to the position of the castes other than the Brāhmaṇa in respect of same. But, unfortunately, as the literature of the period from which we have to derive our evidence is almost exclusively religious in its character and, as such, is only concerned with that caste to which society committed the care and ministrations of its religion, we can hardly expect to find much evidence on the subject. Macdonell and Keith frankly admit [*Vedic Index*, i, 207] that "of the training and education of Kshatriya we have no record". The education of a caste in those days was necessarily determined to a large extent by the particular occupations and functions assigned to it in society. But the

[1] Cf. Max Müller: "The very fact that the *Āraṇyakas* are destined for a class of men who had retired from the world in order to give themselves up to the contemplation of the highest problems shows an advanced . . . society. . . . The problems, indeed, which are discussed in the *Āraṇyakas* and the old *Upanishads* are not in themselves modern. They had formed the conversation of the old and the young, of warriors and poets, for ages. But in a healthy state of society these questions were discussed in courts and camps: priests were contradicted by kings, sages confounded by children, women were listened to when they were moved by an unknown spirit. This time, which is represented to us by the early legends of the *Āraṇyakas*, was very different from that which gave rise to professional anchorites, and to a literature composed exclusively for their benefit. . . We must carefully distinguish between a period of growth and a period which tried to reduce that growth to rules and formulae. . . The generation which became the chroniclers of those Titanic wars of thought was a small race; they were dwarfs, measuring the footprints of departed giants."

degree of the separation of castes did not in the earlier stages quite correspond to that of the separation of functions. Accordingly, in the earlier literature, we find sometimes a variety of occupations for each caste. The most glaring instance of such variety in respect of the Brāhmaṇa caste is given by a Rigvedic passage [ix, 112] already cited, where the author of the hymn says he is a poet, his father a physician (Bhishaj), and his mother a grinder of corn (Upala-prakshiṇī). This would seem to show that a Brahman could practise medicine while his wife would perform the ordinary household duties. So we find a Purohita accompanying the king in battle, and, like the medieval clergy, not unprepared to fight as Vasishṭha and Viśvāmitra seem to have done and as priests do even in the Epic from time to time [*JAOS.*, 13, 184], while Dīrghaśravas in the Rigveda [i, 112, 11] is taken as the example of a Brahmin turning merchant through poverty. All this, however, does not by any means establish that the priests normally fought or that they were normally agriculturists [cf. Brahmachārin tending cattle of his teacher (*Chhānd.*, iv, 4, 5 ; *Ait. Ār.*, iii, 1, 6)] and merchants, though they could on occasions turn to agricultural or mercantile pursuits. The Brahmin represented the intellectual and spiritual interests of the community and "was required not merely to practise individual culture but also to give others the advantage of his skill either as a teacher or as a sacrificial priest [at least for the more important (śrauta) rites] or as a purohita guiding the king in secular, political matters. Similarly, the normal duties of the Kshatriya were administration and war. The bow is his special attribute, as shown in a number of passages in Vedic literature.[1] There is hardly any reference to Kshatriyas engaging in agriculture, trade, or commerce. We have already discussed the question how far the evidence regarding the exercise of the priestly or Brahminical functions of learning and teaching or officiating as Purohita justifies the theory advanced by some scholars that the distinction between the Kshatriya caste and Brāhmaṇa was not yet. The stories of such priestly functions assumed by the Kshatriyas refer only to a few selected Kshatriyas

[1] The *Vedic Index* gives the following references on the point : *Av.*, xviii, 2, 60 ; *Kāṭh. Saṁ.*, xviii, 9 ; xxxvii, 1 ; *Śat. Br.*, v, 3, 5, 30 (" the bow truly is the nobleman"'s strength ") ; *Taitt. Ār.*, vi, 1, 3. In the *Aitareya Brāhmaṇa* [vii, 19], the list is longer—chariot, breastplate (*kavacha*), bow and arrow (*ishu-dhanvan*)—and in the prayer for the prosperity of the Kshatriya (*rājanya*) at the Aśvamedha, the Rājanya is to be an archer and a good chariot-fighter [*Taitt. Saṁ.*, vii, 5, 18, 1 ; *Maitr. Saṁ.*, iii, 12, 6; *Kāṭh Saṁ.*, Aśvamedha, v, 14; *Vājas. Saṁ.*, xxii, 2].

of high rank, while there is no evidence that the average Kshatriya was concerned with intellectual pursuits when there were other engrossing duties connected with the protection of the people to absorb his attention. It is thus a fair deduction that the royal caste did not much concern itself with the sacred lore of the priests, though it is not unlikely that individual exceptions occurred.

Thus the Kshatriya was normally and primarily concerned with those subjects of study which would give him a training in the occupations he had to follow. In the lists of subjects of study referred to in the literature of the period (as discussed above), those termed *Kshatravidyā* (the science of the ruling class, of polity or administration), *Ekāyana* (as interpreted by Śaṇkara, viz. *Nīti-śāstram*) or *Dhanur-veda* were therefore suitable for the Kshatriya. But it would appear from the evidence that the Kshatriya had to depend upon Brahmin teachers even for instruction in those subjects. Nārada, when he approaches Sanatkumāra for instruction, informs him of his mastery of those subjects [*Chhānd.*, vii, 1], while the Brahmin priest is elsewhere [*Śatap. Br.*, xiii, 4, 3] represented as teaching the people (irrespective of classes and castes) even such subjects as Sarpa-vidyā, Magic, Devajanavidyā or fine arts.

The admittedly close connection between the Brahmins and the Kshatriyas of the highest rank—the kings—rested on a community of culture and intellectual equipment. The link of connection was of course the sacrifice. The sacrifices special for kings were the Rājasūya, Vājapeya, and Aśvamedha in which they had naturally to take an active part with the officiating priests and this participation implied their knowledge of the sacred lore which enabled them to utter the various Mantras used by the priests in the performance of the sacrifices.

The Vaiśya plays singularly little part in Vedic literature, which has so much to say of Kshatriya and Brāhmaṇa. Accordingly, there is hardly any evidence to show how he was educated. And yet the definite and important part he played in the economic life of the community implies that he must have received the required training for it. Agriculture was his chief pursuit. The goad of the plougher was the mark of a Vaiśya in life [*Kāṭh. Saṁ.*, xxxvii, 1] and in death [*Kauśīika Sūtra*, lxxx]. Probably the trade of the country was in his hands, for the *Vaṇij* is known to the Rigveda [i, 112, 11; v, 45, 6] and later [*Av.*, iii, 15, 1; *Śat. Br.*, i, 6, 4, 21; *Pañch. Br.*, xvii, 1, 2 (vāṇijya)]. He also took part in wars under Kshatriya leaders, for in several passages of the Rigveda there is a reference to the people (*viś*) fighting [i, 69, 3 ; 126, 5 ; iv, 24, 4; vi, 26, 1 ; vii, 79, 2 ; viii, 18, 18 ; 96, 15 ; vii, 33, 6 (*Tritsūnāṃ viśah*, the subject-peoples of the Tritsu princes) ; cf. also *Av.*, ix, 7, 9, where the people are designated as *balam* which in later literature is the term for armed force]. But his chief ambition in life was to attain to the position of a *Grāmaṇī*, or village headman, which he regarded as the summit of his prosperity [*Taitt. Saṁ.*, ii, 5, 4, 4 (*gataśrī*) ; *Maitr. Saṁ.*, i, 6, 5]. There is no evidence to show that he played any part in the intellectual life of the times, as did the Kshatriya king.

Similarly, there is but little evidence regarding the character of the education that the Śūdras received, although there is much evidence pointing to the undoubted results of such education in the economic development of the country as regards agriculture, pasture, cattle-rearing, and the numerous arts and crafts of civilized life.[1] In the list of subjects, too, for the period, we find mention of one termed *Deva-jana-vidyā* which, according to Śaṅkara, included some of the fine arts like dancing, singing, playing on musical instruments, perfumery, dyeing and the like, and, therefore, just the subjects in which the Śūdra was interested. The evidence seems also to point out that the teachers of those subjects were the Brahmins themselves, for the *Chhāndogya* mentions Nārada as a master of same, while, in the *Śatapatha* passage already referred to, the Brahmin is stated to be teaching similar secular subjects to circles of pupils that included even usurers (probably Vaiśyas), fishermen, snake-charmers, bird-catchers (Śūdras), and men unlearned in the scriptures.

It may be finally noted that it was probably the culture and importance of the Vaiśya and Śūdra alike which entitled them to a place in the ceremony of Ratnahavīṁshi or jewel-offerings in connection with the Rājasūya. Among the recipients of these offerings (the Ratninaḥ) we find the *Grāmaṇī*, the *Go-nik-artana* (Superintendent of games and forests), and the *Pālāgala* (Courier) [*Śatapatha. Br.*, v, 3, 1, 3, etc.], or the *Vaiśya-grāmaṇī* and *Taksha-rathakārau* (the carpenter and the chariot-maker) [*Maitr. Saṁ.*, ii, 6, 5 ; iv, 3, 8], along with the other principal officers of the State (lit. the " jewels " in the crown of sovereignty) such as the *Senānī* (commander-in-chief), the *Purohita*, the queen-consort (*Mahishī*), the *Sūta* (court minstrel and chronicler),

[1] See my *Hindu Civilization* for an account of economic life in Vedic India.

the *Kshattṛi* (chamberlain), the treasurer (*Saṁgrahītṛi*), the collector *Bhāgadugha*), and the superintendent of dicing (*Akshāvāpa*). The Atharvaveda [iii, 5, 7] gives a list of the *Rāja-kartṛis* or *Rāja-kṛits* who, not themselves kings, aided in the consecration of the king and these were the *Sūta*, the *Ratha-kāra* (the representative of the industrial population), the *Grāmaṇī* and the *Viśaḥ* (the people generally).

We have now concluded our account of education in the *Brāhmaṇa* period, and it may be well to sum up here some of its general and principal features. The Brahmaṇas were the real intellectual leaders controlling education. We must assume among them a very stirring intellectual life which really accounts for the supremacy established and exercised by them over the rest of the people. Wide was the scope of their intellectual interests and activities; it embraced the whole range of Brahmanical theology, extending in like manner to questions of worship, dogma, and philosophical speculation, all of which were closely interwoven with each other. Not merely did they teach fixed groups of students settled in their homes as "*internal*" students (to use a modern expression), but they also had to admit "external" students pursuing advanced ("post-graduate") studies after completing their normal period of studentship. There were circles formed around them of *travelling* scholars, who made pilgrimages from one teacher to another according as they were attracted and led by the fame of the special learning they were seeking. Nor did the military caste hold aloof from the intellectual activities of the time when they had already earned for themselves a time of repose from external warfare. Neither did the women, who are found to be partners of their husbands in every department of life. We have here, indeed, a close correspondence to the scholastic period of the Middle Ages in Europe; "sovereigns whose courts form the centres of intellectual life; Brāhmaṇas who, with lively emulation, carry on their inquiries into the highest questions the human mind can propound; women who with enthusiastic ardour plunge into the mysteries of speculation impressing and astonishing men by the depth and loftiness of their opinions. . . As to the quality of their solutions (of philosophical problems) and the value of all these inquiries generally, that is another matter. . . It is only the striving and the effort which ennobles the character of any such period" [Weber, *Ind. Lit.*, p. 22].

Summary. We shall now sum up the principal features of

Education and Culture in this most important period in the history of Indian Civilization, the period of the Brāhmaṇas and Upanishads.

The Twofold Path. The Upanishads tell of the twofold path pursued by man in life, the Path of *Preyas*, of worldly life, pleasure, and prosperity; to be achieved by *Karma* and *Dharma*, deeds and rituals, the fruits of which will accrue to him in this life and extend beyond it to its later incarnations in other worlds. The other Path is the Path of *Śreyas* by which Man seeks the sole and ultimate Reality, the everlasting Good, in a life of sustained and strenuous meditation on the *Ātman*. We have already seen that there is no inherent conflict between the two Paths, between *Karma* or *Dharma*, and *Jñāna*, in the Vedic scheme of life, as the one Path leads to the other, and *Jñāna* or realization of the Ātman is the fruit of Dharma and Karma. Ultimately, as the *Kaivalya Upanishad* puts it, " neither through rituals (*Karma*) nor through progeny or wealth, but renunciation alone, persons attain to Immortality."

The two Paths only imply the two phases of life, social and spiritual. There is the outer and external life of man as a member of society which imposes upon it its rules and regulations, conventions and obligations, ultimately based on morality. But behind this external, social life, there is the inner life of man as an individual, his spiritual life, which is regulated and shaped in the Upanishads by *Upāsanā* (worship) and *Yoga* (psychic control) whereby *Anubhūti* and *Moksha* are attained.

Morality. There is a view that morality or ethics has no place in the teaching of the Upanishads, which concentrate only on the Ātman or the Absolute as the sole Reality, whereas ethics implies social relationships, a world of plurality. This is mistaking the truth of the Upanishads which always take morality as the only foundation of spirituality. The *Muṇḍaka*, for instance, states that " spiritual truths can be imparted only to the pupil who approaches the teacher with proper respect, whose thoughts are not deflected by desire and are completely composed " [i, 2, 13]. Similarly, the discussion between Yama and Nachiketas shows that Yama considered Nachiketas as fit for the highest knowledge only when the pupil proved to him that he was above all desire, desire for " hundred sons and grandsons, many cattle, elephants, gold, and horses, wealth and long life, lovely maidens with chariots, with lyres—whatever desires are hard to get in the mortal world ", which Yama promised him to

HERMITAGES IN BHARHUT SCULPTURES (*c.* second century B.C.).

No. 2.—The ascetic, clad in birch bark, with his matted hair bound up into a knot, leaning and grieving over his dead pet antelope.

[*Facing p.* 157

wean him away from the pursuit of Truth. Nachiketas answered Yama: "Thine be the vehicles (*vāha*), the dance and song, ephemeral things!" We have also seen how the Upanishads are always insisting that the pupil must be *śānta*, *dānta*, *uparata*, possessed of *dama*, *dāna*, *dayā*, *śraddhā*, and *satyam*, the essential virtues. Besides, the very doctrine of the One Ultimate Reality is the strongest support and foundation of morality and the social sense or feeling. As the *Bṛihadāraṇyaka* points out [ii, 4, 5], "all others are dear to us not for their sake but for our own sake. It is the love of the Self that causes love of husband, wife, son, love of all beings. Not for love of all is all dear, but for love of the Self, all is dear." Thus, as Patañjali states in his *Yoga-Sūtras* [ii, 36], spiritual life is to be built up on the basis of "these universal moral practices which are not confined to any particular people, country, time, or age". The position is thus clenched in the *Chhāndogya* [viii, 5, 1]: "Continence is the only *yajña* and the only worship (*ishṭa*) through which one can attain Brahma."

Āśrama. The Upanishads know of the four *Āśramas* of life, as already indicated. The Brahmacharya-āśrama has been fully described. The duties of the Gṛihastha are detailed in the *Taittirīya* [i, 2, 1–7] already cited. As regards the third Āśrama, that of Vānaprastha, we may recall the example of King Bṛihadratha who, "establishing his son in the kingdom, went forth into the forest where he performed extreme austerities" [*Maitri*, i, 2]. As an example of the fourth Āśrama, we may cite the case of Yājñavalkya who renounced the world and embraced *sannyāsa*, or the life of a *parivrājaka* [*Bṛihad.*, ii, 4, 1; iv, 5, 1], declaring that "Brāhmaṇas knowing the Ātman overcome the desire for sons, for wealth, for worlds, and live the life of mendicants". The words, however, do not indicate clearly whether they refer to the third or fourth *āśrama*.

Varṇa. The Upanishads know of what is called *Varṇāśrama-dharma*, the system of Caste and Āśrama. As we have seen, Caste is first adumbrated definitely in the Purusha-sūkta of Rigveda [x, 90] where the four castes are described as the four limbs of the Purusha, related to one another as parts of a common organism. This idea is fully developed in the *Bṛihadāraṇyaka* [i, 4, 11 f.]: "Verily, in the beginning, this world was Brahma, one only. Being One, He did not flourish. He projected an excellent form, the Kshatriya, gods like Indra, Varuṇa, Rudra, Īśāna. . . Yet He did not flourish. He projected the Vaiśya, even gods like the Vasus, the Ādityas, the Viśvadevas. He did not yet flourish. He then created the Śūdra caste, Pūshan. This earth is Pūshan, for she 'nourishes' (root *push*) everything that is." This passage shows that the completeness of social life requires a variety of groups and functions, all of which are necessary for it. The Śūdra is aptly called Pūshan, as he is a child, a thorough-bred, of the soil, rooted in the mother-earth, supporting society by production of food. The tiller of the soil is the foundation of the social structure and remains so to this day. Thus *Śruti* or Veda does not differentiate between the different castes but treats them as equally indispensable as members of the social organism, like the limbs of the body. Even the gods could not complete creation till the Pūshan was forthcoming, springing out of the mother-earth, to lay the foundations of economic and social life in agriculture. The paramount conception of functions in Caste without any suggestion of social inequalities in status or dignity is also indicated in other significant passages. In the *Chhāndogya* [vi, 1, 1], Uddālaka Āruṇi reprimands his son Śvetaketu Āruṇeya for his disinclination for learning, the prescribed function of a Brāhmaṇa, saying, "Verily, my dear, from our family there is no one who is not learned (*ananūchya*) and is a Brāhmāṇa by mere birth (*Brahmabandhu*)." In the same strain, the *Bṛihadāraṇyaka* [ii, 4, 6] states that "Brāhmaṇahood deserts him who knows Brāhmaṇahood in aught else than the Self." Again [iii, 5, 1]: "By what means would he become a Brāhmaṇa? By that means by which he does become such a one." Further [iii, 8, 10]: "If one performs sacrifices and worship and undergoes austerity in this world for many thousands of years, but without knowing that Imperishable, limited, indeed, is that work of his."

Process of Knowing. Broadly speaking, the Upanishads prescribe *Upāsanā* and *Yoga* as the means of acquiring the highest knowledge, the knowledge of the Ātman. *Upāsanā* or worship refers itself to the *Saguṇa* aspect of Brahma as distinguished from *Nirguṇa*. The conception of these two aspects of Brahma is indicated in the *Bṛihadāraṇyaka* in the discussion between the Brahman scholar, Dṛiptabālāki Gārgya, and Ajātaśatru, King of Benares. Bālāki defined Brahma by His manifestations like the Sun, Moon, Lightning, Space, Wind, Fire, Water, Sound, and the like. Ajātaśatru stated that there were two aspects of Brahma, one with form (*Mūrta*) and the other without any form (*Amūrta*), mortal and immortal, stationary and moving. Wind and atmosphere is formless Brahma, while the sun is Brahma in form. Brahma the Formless can only be indicated by a negative process of elimination to the effect that It is "Not thus! Not so!" (*Neti Neti*).

But the Upanishads recognize the steps by which the mind can fix itself on *Nirguṇa* Brahma, the need of *Upāsanā* or worship of symbols of God. This is called the *Pratīka-upāsanā*. Various symbols are prescribed to suit persons in different stages of spiritual progress. As many as twenty such symbols were suggested by Sanatkumāra in teaching Nārada the knowledge of Brahman, starting with meditation on Name as Brahman, and ending with meditation on the Great (*Bhūman*), the Supreme Bliss, as Brahman.

The most important of such symbols is the mystic syllable *Om*. The syllable is made up of three parts, *a*, *u*, *m*, corresponding to the three states of consciousness, waking, dreaming, and deep sleep, which have for their objects the gross, the subtle, and the causal world. Through the meditation of these three parts is reached the highest plane, the fourth (*Turīya*) "which is imperceptible, not subject to any development, is blissful, without a second." The *Om* thus meditated upon is "verily the Self. He who knows this, with his self, enters the Self" [*Māṇḍūkya*, 12]. The process of this meditation is further described in *Muṇḍaka*: "*Om* is the bow, the self is the arrow, Brahma is its mark. It is to be hit by a man whose thoughts are composed. Then, as the arrow becomes one with the target, he will become one with Brahma."

This *Pratīka-upāsanā* includes the worship of God in the forms of different deities like Brahmā, Vishṇu, Rudra, Prajāpati, Agni, Varuṇa, or Vāyu as mentioned in the *Maitreyī Upanishad* v, 1. In such prayers may be seen the beginnings of the Bhakti cult.

The Upanishads also pave the way of the worship of *Saguṇa* Brahma merging in the meditation of *Nirguṇa* Brahma. This is effected by the direction that he who worships God must think of Him as his own self in the spirit of the doctrine, *Tat Tvam Asi*, or the other doctrine, *Ayam Ātmā Brahma* or *Aham Brahmāsmi*. The Upanishad condemns the worshipper who keeps up a sense of duality in *Upāsanā*: "Now if a man worships another deity, thinking the deity to be one, and himself another, he does not know."

Yoga. It has been already indicated in a general way that the system of discipline for which the Upanishads stand is based upon that of *Yoga* as has been elaborated later in the *Yoga-sūtras* of Patañjali, of which some of the most important concepts and terms are derived from the Upanishads.

A start is made with the statement that it is the *Chitta* alone which is *Saṁsāra* (*Maitreyī. Up.*, i, 5). Again: "Whatever his *chitta* thinks, of that nature a man becomes" [ib.]. Further: "If his *chitta* is so fixed on Brahman as it is on things of the world, who would not then be freed from bondage?" [ib., i, 7]. This means that the process of Yoga is *chittavṛitti-nirodha*, as defined by Patañjali, to detach the mind from the objects of senses so as to inhibit all its creative ideations and concentrate it on God.

Much of Yoga psychology is anticipated in the Upanishads. *Kaṭha*, iii, 3, 6, 10, 13 defines the terms Ātmā, Śarīra, Buddhi, Manas, and Indriya. The *Ātmā* is described as riding in the chariot of *Śarīra*, of which the driver is *Buddhi*, the horses are the *Indriyas*, *Manas* as the reins, and the objects of sense what the horses range over. When *Purusha* is joined to *Indriya*, and *Manas* becomes the *Bhoktā*, the *Indriyas*, out of control, are like the vicious horses of a chariot-driver.

Thus, according to this analysis, higher than the senses are the objects of sense (*Artha*); higher than these is *Manas*; higher than mind is *Buddhi*; higher than *Buddhi* is the great Self.

Kaṭha, vi, 10, 11 defines Yoga as firm control of the senses (*Taṁ yogaṁ iti manyante sthiraṁ indriyadhāraṇaṁ*). The Yogī is *Apramatta*, undistracted.

"When one ceases the five kinds of knowing through the senses, together with the mind, and Buddhi (intellect) also is inoperative (*na vicheshṭate*), that is called the highest course (*Paramā gati*)."

Prāṇāyāma is referred to in *Bṛihadāraṇyaka*, i, 5, 23. Again, the same Upanishad [iv, 4, 23] uses the following significant terms of Yoga, viz. *Śānta-dānta-uparata-titikshā-samāhita*.

Chhāndogya [vi, 8] uses the term *Pratyāhāra* and defines it as making all the senses rest in *Ātmā* (*Ātmani sarvendriyāṇi sampratisṭhāpya*).

Muṇḍaka [ii, 2, 3, 4], as already cited, describes *Praṇava* as the bow, *Ātmā* the arrow, *Brahma* the mark (*Laskhya*). One should shoot undistracted (*Apramatta*) at the mark and be merged in it like the arrow and the mark (*śaravat tanmayo bhavet*).

Maitri [vi, 18] refers to *Shaḍaṅga*-yoga as comprising Āsana (posture), Prāṇāyāma (Restraint of breath), Pratyāhāra (Withdrawal of the senses), Dhyāna (Meditation), Dhāraṇā (Concentration), Samādhi (absorption).

The process of Yoga is further described in vi, 19–29. Yoga (joining) is defined as oneness of mind and the senses.

" If a man practises yoga for six months,
And is constantly freed [from the senses],
The infinite, supreme, mysterious Yoga is perfectly produced.

But if a man is afflicted with Passion (rajas) and Darkness (tamas),
Enlightened as he may be—
If to son and wife and family
He is attached—for such a one,

No, never at all ! "

The *Śvetāśvatara* [ii] describes how the Yogī acquires lightness of body, freedom from diseases, calm of mind, radiant countenance (*varṇaprasāda*), and pleasant voice (*svarasaushṭava*), anticipating the *Bibhūti-pāda* of *Yogasūtras*.

The same Upanishad mentions how the pursuit of Yoga should be undertaken in a congenial physical environment which it thus describes : " In a clean (*śuchau*) level (*same*) spot, free from pebbles (*śarkarā*), fire (*vahṇi*), and gravel (*bālukā*), by the sound of water and other propinquities favourable to meditation (*manonukūle*), and not offensive to the eye (*na chakshupīḍane*), in a hidden retreat, one should practise Yoga (*prayojayet*).

CHAPTER V

THE PERIOD OF SŪTRA LITERATURE

Changing Conditions. We now leave the period of the *Brāhmaṇas* and come to that of the *Sūtras* which introduce us to new types and forms of literary activity called forth by the requirements of the times, by new social, religious, and political conditions. The rise of the Sūtra literature is connected with the necessities of self-defence and self-preservation of the old Vedic religion. We have already seen how in the first or *Chhandas* period the Vedic bards or Ṛishis, by giving free and full utterance to their inner intuitions and revelations, their inspired thoughts and sentiments, were giving to the Indians a new world of religious, moral, and political ideas ; how in the second or *Mantra* period all that rich harvest was being garnered and preserved ; and how the literary activity of the third or *Brāhmaṇa* period chiefly occupied itself in systematizing and interpreting the precious poetry of the earlier age which had already become unintelligible and sacred. The result was the growth of a vast and varied literature of commentaries round the original kernel of religion which none but specialists could extract and unfold, of a complicated system of theology and ceremonial of which the knowledge became more and more the exclusive property of particular families (of priests) in which it became hereditary.

Need of simplified Literature. There was, however, a natural limit to this exuberant growth of literature in particular directions. The mass of matter became too vast ; there appeared the risk of the substance of religion, the tenor and spirit of the whole, being lost in the details. Diffuse discussion of details had to be replaced by their concise collective summaries. The result was the creation of a new type of literature, the *Sūtras,* which were all thus written with a practical object. The Sūtra-kāras claim no inspiration for themselves. They made a scientific study of the literature handed down to them from previous times and they wanted to make the contents of that literature more easily accessible through the results of their own studies. Thus the style of composition which they necessarily adopted for that purpose was businesslike in the extreme. The utmost brevity was required in comprising within the smallest compass the vast mass of literary material that had to be handled in order that the memory might not be overburdened. Brevity was the soul of this new literary style and there is a proverbial saying (taken from the *Mahābhāshya*) that "an author rejoiceth in the economizing of half a short vowel as much as in the birth of a son". Thus arose in pursuit of this ideal of brevity a remarkably condensed and enigmatical style which was more and more cultivated as the literature of the Sūtras became more independent and popular with the growing appreciation of its advantages.

Conditions created by Buddhism. Apart, however, from pedagogic considerations and educational requirements, there seems to have been in operation another factor connected with the political history of the period, which was contributing towards the growth of this new literature. That factor was connected with the rise of a new school of thought, viz. Buddhism, whereby Brahmanism was called upon to meet a novel situation to which it had never been accustomed before. It is, however, to be borne in mind that Buddhism, as Weber rightly points out, originally proceeded purely from theoretical heterodoxy regarding the relation of matter to spirit and similar questions. The early Buddhism was but one out of many sects then existing. There was as yet no schism but mere controversy such as we find in the *Brāhmaṇas* themselves between different schools of thought. Buddha himself, according to his own canonical biographer, learned the Rigveda and was well versed in the various branches of Brahmanic lore. Many of his pupils were Brahmins and no hostile feeling against the Brahmins finds utterance in the Buddhist canon, nor any slur cast on the gods and songs of the Veda. Matters, however, gradually became different in course of time when Buddhism addressed itself to practical points of religion, worship, and life, and ceased to concern itself with the settlement of mere theological or speculative issues. Then there began a real conflict between the two systems, a struggle for self-preservation and supremacy. At first the position of Brahmanism was seriously imperilled by certain disadvantageous circumstances of its own creation. For Buddhism developed into a system of easy devotion which was naturally resorted to with considerable eagerness and a sense of relief by that vast majority of people whom Brahmanism alienated and frightened away by the inaccessibility of the literature in which it was embodied, by its difficulty and complexity. At the same time that Buddhism attracted the ignorant among the Brahmins, it received with open arms the poor and the miserable of all classes. Thus Brahmanism was forced to forge a suitable weapon of defence against the onslaught which a new religion directed against its weak points. It was forced to find an easier and more popular medium for the imparting of its instruction and thereby remove the difficulties in the way of its propagation. Changes in the sacred literature of a people never take place except under the pressure of a grave necessity such as that of its self-preservation, and the object which the *Sūtras* were created to serve could be no other than to offer practical manuals to those who were discouraged by the too elaborate treatises of the *Brāhmaṇas* and yielded themselves as willing recruits to a rival faith that opened out to them easier means of religious instruction and ways to salvation.

The Sūtras a more suitable Vehicle of Old Knowledge. These historical facts are, indeed, indicated by the internal evidence, the style, of the *Brāhmaṇas* and *Sūtras* themselves. The deliberately popular style of the *Sūtras* shows that the time was now gone when students would spend ten or twenty years of their lives in fathoming the mysteries and mastering the intricacies of the *Brāhmaṇa* literature. We miss, too, in the *Sūtras* that self-complacent spirit which pervades the *Brāhmaṇas.* It seems as if the authors of the *Sūtras* feel that their reading public will no longer be satisfied with mere endless theological swaggering but will demand something else. There may be deep wisdom in the previous literature but they feel that the people will not appreciate or accept wisdom unless it is clothed in a garb of clear argument and imparted in easier language. Thus their words contain all that is essential in the *Brāhmaṇas*, but they give it in a practical, concise and definite form. They represent in fact the quintessence of all the knowledge previously acquired and accumulated by the study and meditation of centuries. Their language is also firm, though no longer inflated, indicating a spirit of self-confidence that did not quail before the first attacks levelled by a popular religion. Lastly, a part of the *Sūtra* literature (the *Gṛihya-Sūtras* treating of the ceremonies of domestic life such as those relating to birth, death, and marriage) goes by the name of *Smṛiti*, i.e. that which is the subject of *memory*, as distinguished from *Śruti*, i.e. that which is the subject of *hearing*, in so far as the former impresses itself directly on the memory, without special instruction and provision for the purpose. It belongs to all, it is the common possession, the property, of the whole people; it is supported by the consciousness of all and does not therefore need to be specially inculcated. Not so is ritual which, in spite of its origin in the common consciousness, was developed in its details by the speculations of a special class which owned it as its exclusive property and monopoly, while custom and law were thrown open to all as common property. It is for this reason also that we find in these works a rich treasure of ideas and conceptions of extreme antiquity. Domestic manners and customs have been left untouched and handed down in their ancient form; there was no interest in changing them, for they were devoid of all political bearings [Weber, *Ind. Lit.*, p. 19].

We shall now consider the evidence of the *Sūtra* literature regarding the education of the period.

Classes of Sūtra Works: New Subjects of Study. In the first place, it gives us an idea of the number and variety of the *subjects of study* then existing. The *Śrauta Sūtras* are a continuation of the *Brāhmaṇas* on their ritual side, as the Upanishads are on their speculative side. The rites they deal with are never congregational but are always performed on behalf of a single individual called *Yajamāna* (sacrificer). The second branch of ritual Sūtras are the *Gṛihya Sūtras* treating of numerous ceremonies applicable to the domestic life of a man and his family from birth to death. Since these lay outside the scope of the *Brāhmaṇas*, the authors of the *Gṛihya Sūtras* had to rely on popular tradition in dealing with observances of daily life. The third branch of the Sūtra literature, based on tradition or Smṛiti, are the *Dharma Sūtras* which deal with the customs of daily life (*Sāmayāchārika*) and are thus our earliest legal literature. There is lastly a division of the Sūtras called the *Śulva Sūtras* connected with religious practice; they are practical manuals giving the measurements necessary for the construction of the *vedi*, of the altars and so forth. They show quite an advanced knowledge of geometry and constitute the oldest Indian mathematical works [Macdonell, *Sans. Lit.*, p. 264].

The Vedāṅgas. The entire body of the Vedic works composed in the style of the Sūtras is according to the Indian traditional view divided into six branches called *Vedāṅgas* (members of the Veda). The names of these six subjects are first mentioned in the *Muṇḍaka-Upanishad* [i, 1, 5]. A consideration of the contents of these Vedāṅgas will give us an idea of the multiform literary activity of the period and the subjects of study then prevailing.

Śikshā. *Śikshā* is defined by Sāyaṇa as the science of the pronunciation of letters, accents, and the like. Some of the headings in the seventh book of the *Taittirīya Āraṇyaka* are: "On Letters," "On Accents," "On quantity," "On the organs of pronunciation," "On delivery," "On Euphonic Laws." It was thus an important branch of knowledge which was necessary for the right understanding of the sacred texts, especially of the philosophical parts of the Veda as distinguished from the ceremonial parts (Karma-Kāṇḍa). Originally a part of the *Brāhmaṇas*, the subject came to be treated in independent scientific treatises called the *Prātiśākhyas* which, besides giving general rules for the proper pronunciation of the Vedic language in general, were intended to record what was peculiar in the pronunciation of different Vedic schools. A *Prātiśākhya* is thus a collection of phonetic rules peculiar to a *Śākhā* of a Veda, i.e. to one of the different texts in which each of the four Vedas had been handed down for ages in different families and different localities. Thus ancient dialectical differences, and even irregularities and exceptions, created by the freedom of a spoken language, were preserved and rescued from oblivion; general laws were derived from the collection of a large number of similar passages; and a start was thus given to that scientific study of language which reached its perfection in the grammatical masterpiece of Pāṇini.

Chhandas. The second Vedāṅga is *Chhandas* or Metre, to which there are many scattered references in the *Brāhmaṇas*. But it is in the *Sūtras* (e.g. the *Śāṅkhāyana Śrauta Sūtra*, the *Rigveda Prātiśākhya*, and the *Nidāna Sūtra*) that an attempt is made to arrange the archaic metres systematically.

Vyākaraṇa. *Vyākaraṇa* or Grammar was the third subject developed. The foundation was already laid in the *Padapāṭhas* which distinguish parts of compounds, prefixes of verbs and suffixes and terminations of nouns, in a word, the four parts of speech. The most important information regarding pre-Pāṇinean grammar is to be derived from Yāska's work.

Nirukta. The fourth Vedāṅga is *Nirukta* or Etymology as represented in the work of Yaska, which is a sort of an etymological lexicography of Vedic terms. The *Nirukta* together with the *Prātiśākhyas* and Pāṇini's Grammar supplies the most interesting and important information on the growth of grammatical science in India. The *Nirukta* is in reality a commentary on the *Nighaṇṭu*, a collection of Vedic words and synonyms which, by virtue of their arrangement, largely explain themselves. Yāska had before him five such collections of which the first three contain synonyms, the fourth a list of specially difficult Vedic words, and the fifth, a classification of the various divine personages who figure in the Veda.

Kalpa. The fifth Vedāṅga is the *Kalpa* or ceremonial of which we have already treated. The *Kalpa-Sūtras* are based entirely on the *Brāhmaṇas* of which they presuppose not only three distinct collections but also different *Sākhās* or recensions which in course of time had branched off from each of them. It is also to be noted that the Sūtras were intended by their authors for more than one *Charaṇa* or adapted to more than one *Śākhā*. No single *Śākhā* contained a complete account of the ceremonial and a reference to other *Śākhās* was absolutely necessary. Even if a Brahmin had studied the Saṁhitās and *Brāhmaṇas* of the three Vedas according to their various *Śākhās*, he would still have found it difficult to learn from them the correct performance of each sacrifice. To remove this difficulty the Sūtras were composed as a kind of grammar of the Vedic ceremonial useful for members of all *Charaṇas*. There were, of course, Kalpa Sūtras for the different classes of priests, viz. those for the Hotṛi, the Adhvaryu, and Udgātṛi priests. Another point to be noticed in this connection is that different communities, after adopting a collection of Sūtras as the highest authority for their ceremonial, became naturally inclined to waive minor points of difference in the *Saṁhitās* and *Brāhmaṇas* and thus coalesced into a new *Charaṇa* under the name and sanction of their *Sūtrakāra*. When once these new *Sautra-Charaṇas* were started, even the Saṁhitās and *Brāhmaṇas* which were current among their members came to be designated by the name of the new *Charaṇas*.

Jyotisha. The last of the Vedāṅgas is called *Jyotisha* or Astronomy, of which the literature available is very scanty. As is always the case, the growth of this subject was due to religious requirements. The knowledge of the heavenly bodies was necessary to fix the days and hours of the Vedic sacrifices. The first impulse to astronomical studies came from the establishment of a sacred Calendar. Even in the *Brāhmaṇas* and *Āraṇyakas* we come across references to astronomical subjects, and the Vedic hymns point to observation of the moon as the measurer of time [cf. *Rv.*, viii, 3, 20 ; ii, 32 (phases of the moon) ; i, 25, 8 (intercalary or thirteenth month) ; *Vāja. Saṁ.*, vii, 30 ; xxii, 31 ; xxx, 10 ; 20 (*gaṇaka*) ; *Taitt. Br.*, iv, 5 (***nakshatra-darśa***).

Other Supplementary Studies. There were also other minor subjects of study developed during this period. The Sūtras had their supplements called *Pariśishṭas* which form an extensive literature. There were also developed for the proper understanding of the sacrificial ceremonial special types of literature called *Prayogas* or Manuals which describe the course of each sacrifice and the functions of the different classes of priests with reference to its practical performance and *Paddhatis* or Guides which follow the systematic accounts of the Sūtras and sketch their contents. There were also versified accounts of the ritual called *Kārikās*. There were further the *Anukramaṇīs* or Vedic Indices giving lists of hymns, the authors, the metres, and the deities in the order in which they occur in the various Saṁhitās.

Specialization. It may also be as well noted in this connection that the age of the Sūtras was an age of scientific study and specialization. As will be explained more fully later on, at first the study of these Aṅgas was strictly subservient to the primary needs of the Veda-study, and education meant only the transmission of traditions from the teacher to the pupil and the committing to memory the sacred texts. In course of time, however, the content of this education began naturally to widen out, and each one of the several Aṅgas of the Veda began to develop, snapping the bonds of its connection with the Veda-study and declaring its independence in special Schools. Thus arose the special sciences and specialists. The sacrificial ritual itself led to the growth of some of the sciences. Geometry and Algebra arose out of the elaborate rules for the construction of altars. Sometimes it was necessary to erect a round altar covering the same area as a square one, giving rise to problems like squaring the circle. Astronomy and Astrology grew out of the necessity of finding out the proper times and seasons for sacrifice and other purposes. The foundation of Anatomy was laid in the dissection of sacrificial animals. Grammar and Philology had their origin in the care to preserve the sacred texts from corruption and fix the methods of their proper pronunciation. Thus each of the original Vedic Aṅgas was giving rise to a number of allied sciences through its specialized and scientific study in special Schools. Pāṇini's work is to be treated as the final outcome of a long process of grammatical development. New subjects also began to develop as a result of this freedom of thought and study. Law was the most important of them. The different legal Schools came to be represented on the Parishads regulating the life of the community. Experts in the new subjects like Nyāya, Mīmāṁsā,

Nirukta, and Law are placed side by side with those proficient in the Vedas and Aṅgas as members of the same Parishad. The specialists were as necessary to the community as the Vaidikas. The latter possessed a complete verbal knowledge of the sacred texts but had an imperfect understanding of the meaning thereof and were like walking libraries. The former reduced the quantity of the sacred texts to be committed to memory and devoted the mental energy thus saved to specialized study of other subjects like sacrifices, grammar, law, or astronomy. Questions bearing on these could no longer be solved by the Vaidikas who were not fitted to put their learning to practical use. The performance of sacrifices needed the services of the Śrauti, the expert in sacrificial literature. The Jurist alone could decide doubtful points of law. Grammar in its developed form was adequate by itself to absorb the entire mental energy of a student. Thus the expansion of learning brought in the system of specialization.

Religion still shaping Literature. The brief and broad survey we have made of the literary activity of the period shows to what a large extent that activity was still determined and shaped by the dominant considerations of religious needs. The variety of literary productions was but answering the variety of religious interests developed. Intellectual life was but the handmaid of the life spiritual. It had no independent course of its own. The mind was but a means of ministering to the spirit. Much of the literature of the period, as we have already seen, is but founded essentially on the *Brāhmaṇas* and must be considered as their necessary supplement as a further advance in the path struck out by the latter in the direction of a rigid ritualism and formalism. The stimulus to the growth of this literature came, as has been explained, from the needs of the preservation and propagation of the religion which was being assailed by a new and rival religion working on more proper lines. As regards that part of Sūtra literature which has no direct connection with the *Brāhmaṇas*, we shall still find that it has a *direct* connection with religion and such of its aspects as are not treated of in the *Brāhmaṇas*. The *Gṛihya-sūtras*, equally with the *Dharma-sūtras*, only aimed at giving its final form and shape to the Brahmanical polity or system of social life expressive of the individuality of the Vedic civilization which was thus secured against all attacks levelled by heretical religions. Similarly, the very advances in linguistic research for which the age of the Sūtras is so much noted received their impetus from the needs of religious life. The various works making up the linguistic part of Sūtra literature will be found to be connected with one or other of the following necessities for safeguarding the interests of religion : firstly, there was the need to fix the text of the Vedic prayers ; secondly, to establish a correct pronunciation and recitation ; thirdly, to preserve the tradition of their origin ; and lastly, when in course of time the literal sense of the old texts became more and more foreign to the current language, or the spoken dialects of the day, to take precautions whereby the original sense might be secured and established and not lost. It is thus that we find that even the linguistic Sūtras stand on the same basis on which the *Brāhmaṇas* themselves stand. While the *Brāhmaṇas* are concerned with the elucidation of the relation of the prayer to the sacrifice, the Sūtras are concerned with the form in which the prayer itself was drawn up.

Upa-Vedas. Regarding the subjects of study, it is interesting to note that some of the Sūtra works furnish evidence showing the growth of a few secular subjects. There is a passage in Āpastamba [*Dh. Sū.*, ii, 11, 29, 11–12] which states : " The knowledge which Śūdras and women possess is the completion of all study. They declare that this knowledge is a supplement of the Atharvaveda." According to the commentator, " the knowledge which Śūdras and women possess " is the knowledge of dancing, acting, music, and other branches of the so-called Arthaśāstra, the science of useful arts and of trades. The object of the Sūtras is to forbid the study of such matters before the acquisition of sacred learning. The same forbiddal is given also by Manu [ii, 168 (" other and worldly study " forbidden)] and by Vasishṭha [iii, 2] and Vishṇu [xxviii, 36]. It may be noted that Āpastamba knew the division of Hindu learning as taught in the Prasthānaveda of Madhusūdana Sarasvatī who points out that each Veda had a *Upa-Veda* or supplementary Veda and that the *Upa-Veda* of the Atharvaveda is the Arthaśāstra. It may also be noted that outside the circle of Brahminical studies there were thus existing the secular arts and sciences which were normally to be studied by the women of all castes and by the Śūdras, but it is also implied that they were not unworthy of study by the men of the three twice-born castes, provided they first completed their normal course of sacred studies. It may be further presumed that it was possible to find Brahmin teachers of these secular arts and sciences comprising the Arthaśāstra or *Upa-Veda* of the Atharvaveda, and we may compare in this connection the references given above from the Upanishads on this subject. Lastly, the theory of the *Upa-Vedas* is a clever way of connecting all branches of human knowledge with the Vedas as their ultimate and common source on which Hindu orthodox opinion is unanimous through the ages.

Sūtra Schools and Teachers. We shall now consider the evidence available regarding the geographical background of the Sūtra literature and the noted teachers of the period.

Firstly, we shall consider the evidence of the Sūtras connected with the Rigveda. The *Āśvalāyana Śrauta Sūtra* gives us some particulars. The name Āśvalāyana is probably to be traced back to Aśvala, the Hotṛi priest of Janaka, king of Videha, of whom we have already given a notice. Again, the formation of the word by the affix *āyana* probably points to the time of established schools (*ayana* ?). Names formed in this way occur but seldom in the *Brāhmaṇas* and only in their later portions and may be taken to betoken a late period. Among the teachers quoted is an Āśmarathya referred to by the scholiast on Pāṇini [iv, 3, 105]. Another teacher quoted is Taulvali expressly mentioned by Pāṇini [ii, 4, 61] as belonging to the *prāñchas* or "dwellers in the east". At the end, there is an interesting enumeration of the various Brāhmaṇa-families distributed among the family stems of Bhṛigu, Aṅgiras, Atri, Viśvāmitra, Kaśyapa, Vasishṭha, and Agastya. The sacrifices on the Sarasvatī are also briefly touched upon. Lastly, it may be noted that Āśvalāyana is the author of the fourth book of the *Aitareya Āraṇyaka*; that he was the pupil of Śaunaka who is stated to have destroyed his own Sūtra in favour of his pupil's work which he considered to be so good. According to Weber, the Sūtra of Āśvalāyana along with the *Aitareya Brāhmaṇa* belonged to the eastern part of Hindusthan.

The *Śāṅkhayana Śrauta Sūtra* wears in general a somewhat more ancient aspect, particularly in its fifteenth and sixteenth books where it assumes the appearance of a *Brāhmaṇa*. There is a *paddhati* to the *Śāṅkhāyana-Gṛihya* by Rāmachandra who lived in the Naimisha forest in the middle of the fifteenth century, and Weber holds that this Naimisha forest was the birthplace of the *Sūtra* itself.

The *Gṛihya* Sūtras of the Rigveda are also those of Āśvalāyana and Śāṅkhāyana. They introduce us to *three female sages*: Gārgī Vāchaknavī, the familiar figure of the Upanishads; Vaḍavā Prātitheyī; Sulabhā Maitreyī (cf. *Saulabhāni Brāhmaṇāni* quoted by the scholiast on Pāṇini, iv, 3, 105). Again, the *Śāṅkhāyana-Gṛihya* mentions the following names: Sumantu-Jaimini-Vaiśampāyana-Paila-Sūtra-bhāshya[-Gārgya-Babhru]...; while the *Āśvalāyana* mentions: Sumantu-Jaimini-Vaiśampāyana-Paila-Sūtra-Bhārata-Mahābhārata-Dharmāchāryāḥ. We may notice here the tradition of the Vishṇu Purāṇa which assigns the Atharvaveda compilation to Sumantu, the Sāmaveda to Jaimini, the Yajurveda to Vaiśampāyana, and the Rigveda to Paila.

Secondly, we shall consider such of the Sūtras of the Sāmaveda as give us evidence on the points we are dealing with. The *Lāṭyāyana Śrauta* Sūtra is probably connected by its very name with the country of Lāṭa lying quite in the west, directly south of Surāshṭra, and its western origin is borne out by other data too. Among the teachers cited are Śāṇḍilya (mentioned in the Chhāndogya), Dhānañjapya, and Śāṇḍilyāyana as expounders of the *Pañchaviṁśa Brāhmaṇa*; Gautama Sthavira; Śauchivṛikshi (a teacher known to Pāṇini), Kshairakalambhi, Kautsa, Vārshagaṇya, Bhāṇḍitāyana, Lāmakāyana, Rāṇāyanīputra, etc.; the Śāṭyāyanins and Śālaṅkāyanins (of the western part of India). There is also a reference to the Śūdras and the Nishādas (i.e. the Indian aborigines) who are treated better than later, being allowed to attend in person at the ceremonies although outside of the sacrificial ground. The general name given to these western, non-Brahminical Aryan tribes is *Vrātīnas* (cf. Pāṇini, v, 2, 21], and they are put on a par with the non-Brahminical peoples of the eastern parts, for we are told by Lāṭyāyana that the converted Vrātyas must transfer their wealth (and thereby their own former impurity) to such of their brethren as abide by the old mode of life or else to a " Brahmabandhu Māgadhadeśīya ".

The Sūtras of the Black Yajus do not give much evidence, except the *Prātiśākhya-Sūtra*, which mentions some peculiar names of teachers such as Ātreya, Kauṇḍinya (once by the Buddhist title of Sthavira), Bhāradvāja, Vālmīki, Āgniveśya, Āgniveśyāyana, and Paushkarasādi (cited in the *Vārttikas* to Pāṇini by Kātyāyana). The two last names as well as that of Kauṇḍinya are mentioned in Buddhist works as those of pupils or contemporaries of the Buddha. There is also an allusion for the first time to the Mīmāṁsakas and Taittirīyakas and to a distinction between two types of Sanskrit, Chhandas (Vedic) and Bhāshā (ordinary).

Among the Sūtras of the White Yajus the first to be

considered is the *Śrauta Sūtra* of Kātyāyana which mentions the following teachers : Laugākshi, Bhāradvāja, Jātūkarṇya, Vātsya, Bādari, Kāśakṛitsni, and Kārshṇājini, of whom the three last appear in the *Vedānta-Sūtra* of Bādarāyaṇa, while Bādari is also mentioned in the *Mīmāṁsā Sūtra* of Jaimini. Among other particulars given may be mentioned the reference to the custom of *dig-vijayas* [xx, 4, 26], to the sacrifices on the Sarasvatī, and the Vrātya-sacrifices at which figure the Māgadhadeśīya Brahmabandhu [xxii, 4, 22]. Next, in the *Prātiśākhya Sūtra* of the White Yajus are mentioned three grammarians, Śākaṭāyana, Śākalya, and Gārgya (all mentioned by Yāska and Pāṇini) ; also Kāśyapa (mentioned by Pāṇini) ; and, lastly, Dālbhya, Jātūkarṇya, Śaunaka, Aupaśivi, Kāṇva, and the Mādhyaṁdinas.

Educational System of the Sūtras. We now proceed to consider the educational system and organization as reflected in the Sūtra literature which fortunately furnishes ample evidence on the subject. It is to be remembered at the outset that the Sūtra works do not introduce any innovations but only continue and embody the older traditions started from the Vedic age to which they only give their final form and shape in an age in which they were liable to be affected by the growth of differing systems of religion and social life. They sum up the entire previous development, and codify pre-existing traditions, unwritten laws, and customs as indicated in the sacred texts on which they are essentially based. They usher in the age of social legislation, of a rigid system of rules, regulations, and restrictions for the sake of the preservation of the culture they represent.

Vidyārambha. The pupil's first introduction to education was made by his performance of a ceremony called *Vidyārambha* (also called *Akshara-svīkaraṇam*) at which he was to commence the learning of the alphabets for the first time. The ceremony was to be performed when the child attained his fifth year (*prāpte tu pañchame varshe*) and was open to children of all the castes. It consisted in the child offering worship to the deities (1) Hari, (2) Lakshmī, and (3) Sarasvatī (the goddess of learning), and also to (1) the *Vidyā* cultivated by his family, or ancestral learning (*sva-vidyā*), (2) the *Sūtra-kāras* of that particular *Vidyā* or subject, the sages who have promulgated that learning and in particular (3) the *Vidyā* or subject of his choice [*Smṛiti-Chandrikā*, Mysore ed., pp. 66–67].

The ceremony of *Vidyārambha* followed that of *Chūḍākaraṇa* or tonsure, and was followed by *Upanayana*. According to Kauṭilya [*Arthaśāstra*, i, 2], the *Vidyārambha* for a Prince who was duly tonsured (*vṛitta-chaulakarmā*) meant that he was to learn Writing (*Lipi*) and Numbers (*Saṁkhyā*).

Upanayana. The formal and regular introduction to education was, however, made by the ceremony of *Upanayana*, which was ordained for all the castes,[1] Brāhmaṇa, Kshatriya, and Vaiśya, though under different rules. Members of these castes, however, who committed sinful deeds, as also the Śūdras, were not eligible for this ceremony [ib.].

Eligibility of Śūdras for Upanayana. But it may be noted that Baudhāyana [*Gr. S.*, ii, 5, 8–9], alone among the law-givers, admits the Śūdra, Rathakāra, to the ceremony of Upanayana. He says : " Let him initiate a Brāhmaṇa in spring, a Kshatriya in summer, a Vaiśya in autumn, a Rathakāra in the rainy season ; or all of them in spring." Baudhāyana here follows Vedic tradition. The ancient Vedic ritual in certain cases admitted Śūdras, and, particularly, the Rathakāra or carpenter who, according to all accounts, had Śūdra blood in his veins, to a participation in the Śrauta rites. The *Taittirīya-Brāhmaṇa* even mentions certain Mantras which are to be recited by the Ratha-kāra at the *Agnyādhāna* sacrifice. Baudhāyana [*Dh. S.*, i, 9, 17, 6] defines the Rathakāra as the offspring of a Vaiśya male and Śūdra female, and the hostility shown against the mixed castes, and the exclusion of the carpenter from the privilege of initiation or Upanayana (which is an expression of that hostility), as shown in the works of the Sūtra-kāras like Āpastamba, are to be regarded only as the outcome of the later doctrines of later ages.

Age and Time of Upanayana. The normal age for Upanayana is 8 for a Brāhmaṇa, 11 for a Kshatriya, and 12 for a Vaiśya [Manu and Yājñavalkya]. Logākshi makes it 7, 9, and 11 respectively for these three castes. But these normal ages are different where the Upanayana is performed with reference to a particular aim (*kāmya*), as stated by Gautama. For a Brāhmaṇa whose aim is *Brahmavarchasa*, the age of Upanayana is 5 [Manu and Āṅgirasa]. Brahmavarchasa is the divine glory and spiritual pre-eminence or sanctity resulting from proficiency in *Brahma* or Veda. Where his aim is *Āyu* or longevity, the age of Upanayana should be 9 [Āṅgirasa]. For a Kshatriya whose aim in life is increase (vṛiddhi) of Power (Bala) and Life (Āyu), the age of Upanayana should be 12 [ib.]. A Vaiśya whose ambition in life is the attainment of Āyu, longevity, and *Īha*, " prosperity in

[1] *Baudhāyana, D.S.*, i, 2, 3, 10 ; *Āpastamba*, i, 1, 1, 6.

Agriculture and other pursuits" (*Kṛishyādivishaya-cheshṭā*) should perform his Upanayana at the age of 14 [ib.]. These variations of age according to those of castes and aims are brought under a general rule applicable to all by Āpastamba [i, 1, 1, 21–6] as follows : " The age of Upanayana is to be 7 where the objective is *Brahma-varchasa* ; 8 where it is *Āyu* ; 9 where it is *Teja* or physical vigour ; 10 where it is livelihood (*annādi*) ; 11 where it is vital force (*indriya*) ; and 12 where it is increase of live stock (*pashu*).

It will appear that the ages are fixed in accordance with the different capacities and aptitudes for learning in the pupils and the studies of their choice determining the periods required for their completion. The age of admission to learning is, for instance, the lowest for a Brāhmaṇa in view of his high aims, and the difficult and extended course of study and discipline required for their realization. Where a pupil's paramount aim in life is its longevity, he should pay more attention to his body than his mind and begin study later. Education similarly begins later and is shorter in length where worldly aims are sought after.

It is also to be noted that the maximum limit of age of Upanayaya is also fixed on the basis of the same considerations. It is 16 for a Brāhmaṇa, 22 for a Kshatriya, and 24 for a Vaiśya [Āpastamba, *Dh. S.*, i, 1, 1, 27 ; Gautama, i, 5, 11 ; Baudhāyana, i, 2, 3, 7–9 ; etc.]. The age of 16 is none too high for a Brāhmaṇa who has completed his preliminary training as preparation for Vedic study which is not elementary but advanced study. The age for higher study is always stated to be 16 in the Jātakas referring to admission of students at Taxila. The age of 16 is also considered as the maximum for a Brāhmaṇa from the moral point of view for which he stands. This point is brought out by Jaimini [*Gṛihya Sūtra*, i, 12] who forbids Upanayana after 16 on the ground that a pupil older in years will find Vedic study difficult and mind prone to sexual distractions for want of an earlier discipline by *brahma-charya* [*na atishoḍaśavarshaṁ upanayīta* | *prasṛishṭavṛishaṇaḥ hi eshaḥ vṛishalībhūto bhavati*].

Besides the age of Upanayana, its time also is different for different castes. According to Āpastamba, the Upanayana of a Brāhmaṇa should be performed in the season of Spring (*Vasanta*), that of a Kshatriya in Summer (*Grīshma*), and that of a Vaiśya in Autumn (*Śarat*). In the Jyotisha-śāstra, the general rule is stated that the Upanayana for all the castes should be performed in the five months from Māgha, perhaps because these constitute the auspicious portion of the year, known as Uttarāyaṇa. Āpastamba

[*D.S.*, i, 19] also specially recommends the season of Spring for the Upanayana of Brāhmaṇas belonging to Yajuḥ-Śākhā.

Defaulters of Upanayana. The defaulters, those who do not have their Upanayana performed within the age-limits prescribed, are condemned as *Sāvitrī-patita* and *Vrātya*, " devoid of Sāvitrī Mantra and the *vrata* or vow of Brahmacharya, and hence degraded, degenerate, and unclean." These persons are, therefore, to be " shunned with care " (parihāryāḥ prayatnataḥ) [Vyāsa]. This implies, as stated by Vasishṭha, that " no one should have any dealings with them (na abhivyavahāreyuḥ) such as teaching them or performing sacrifices for them ", to which another text adds even matrimonial connections (adhyāpanaṁ yājanaṁ cha vivāhādi cha varjayet). This implies their complete social boycott and ostracism. Manu calls them *apūrta*, " unclean," with whom there can be no " brahma-saṁbandha ", relationship by learning or religion [ii, 39, 40 ; x, 20 ; *Śāṅkhā. G.S.*, ii, 1, 9–13 ; *Āśvalā*. i, 19, 8–9, etc.].

Their Redemption. These sinners are not, however, past redemption. They are reclaimed by performances of certain expiatory ceremonies and penances. Yājñavalkya prescribes the ceremony (*Kratu*) called *Vrātya-stoma*. Āpastamba [i, 1, 1, 28] prescribes an easier penance of observance of all restrictions which are imposed upon a Brahmachārī, such as continence and the like, for a period of two months. Vishṇu [liv, 26] prescribes three Prājāpatya penances, and Manu three Kṛichchhra penances [xi, 192]. Vasishṭha [xi, 76, 77] prescribes that " the *Patita-Sāvitrīka* must perform *Uddālaka Vrata*, subsisting for two months on barley-gruel (*yāvakena vartteta*), one month on milk (*payasā*), half-month on *āmiksha* (the solid part of milk extracted from its liquid, Bengali *chhānā*), eight days on *ghṛita*, six days on alms given without asking, three on only water, and one without any food or drink, by complete fasting. Or he may perform the Aśvamedha sacrifice or Vrātya-stoma " [*Smṛiti Chandrikā*, pp. 67–74].

Education Compulsory. These penances and penalties attaching to the violation of this primary obligation of Upanayana only show to what extent education was valued by Hindu society and how it was sought by law to make education universal and compulsory among all the three castes which made up Aryan society in those days. They also imply by contrast the supreme efficacy of Upanayana as a purifying influence, a factor of moral and spiritual uplift.

Education a Second Birth. The texts describe with great feeling how Upanayana accomplishes a second birth which is purer in its origin than man's natural birth. Here, as Manu says [ii, 146, 148], his mother is Sāvitrī, and father the Āchārya who imparts to him what is higher than the body, the Veda or Knowledge which builds up his mind and soul. "That birth which the teacher procures for him through the Sāvitrī is exempt from age and death." As Āpastamba states, "this birth is the superior birth, as it originates from knowledge. What father and mother generate is the mere body." Thus all are "twice-born" by Upanayana and become known as *Dvijas*. "The first birth is due to the mother, the second to *mauñjī-bandhana*" [Vasishṭha and Yājñavalkya]. Thus man is "reborn" by education in the life spiritual aptly called *Brahma-janma* by Manu. With this high conception of education and its effects by which man is refined (*saṁskṛita*) and spiritualized, there is no wonder that the man not taking education is deemed unworthy of social intercourse and an outcast.

Details of the Ceremony: Meaning of the term 'Upanayana'. We shall now go into the details of the important ceremony of Upanayana and bring out their full educational significance.

The term *Upanayana* (from *upa* + *ni*) literally means the introduction of the pupil, but it is not the introduction of the pupil to the teacher by his father or any other relation. The texts imply that it is the introduction of the pupil to *brahmacharya* by the teacher himself. The pupil enters upon (*upaiti*) *brahmacharya* or enters *with* the teacher and he who has thus entered upon studentship is designated *upeta* [*Śāṅkhā*. iv, 8, 1; Pāraskara, iii, 10, 10]. In this sense, the word *Upāyana* is sometimes used for the more usual term Upanayana [*Smṛiti-Chandrikā*, pp. 67, 68]. This sense is anticipated, as we have seen, in the *Śatapatha Brāhmaṇa* where [xi, 5, 3, 13] Śaucheya says to Uddālaka Āruṇi: "I will enter as a student with the reverend one (*upāyāmi bhagavantam*)." Āruṇi replies: "Come, enter (with me) (*ehyupehi*)," and "he initiated him" (*taṁ hopaninye*). In another passage [xi, 5, 4, 16], it is stated that, according to some, a teacher who has initiated a Brāhmaṇa as a student (*brāhmaṇaṁ brahmacharyaṁ upanīya*) should abstain from sexual intercourse, because a student who enters upon *brahmacharya* becomes as it were a *garbha* [*SBE.*, xxix, p. 58].

The later text *Vīramitrodaya* describes Upanayana as "the ceremony by which a *dvija* is brought into contact with the following, viz. Guru, Vrata, Veda, Yama, Niyama, and the Devatās ".

The Student's Uniform. The first step in Upanayana is to impose upon the pupil certain external marks of differentiation concerning his dress, equipment, and appearance by which he is singled out and recognized.

'Ajina.' The Brahmachārī is to wear *Ajina* or upper garment of the skin of certain animals. It should be the skin of *Krishṇa* or *Eṇa*, black buck, for a Brāhmaṇa ; of *Ruru*, or spotted deer, for a Kshatriya ; of *Vasta* or *Aja*, goat, for a Vaiśya [Bṛihaspati ; Yama ; Śaṅkha]. It may also be the skin of the cow (*gavyam*) for all, according to Pāraskara (*sarveshāṁ vā gavyam*).

'Vāsa.' Vāsa is the lower garment which may be made of the following materials, viz. (1) *śāṇa*, hemp ; (2) *kshauma*, fibre of *atasi* plant ; (3) *chīra*, *darbha*, or kuśa grass ; (4) *kutapa*, wool derived from mountain goats and used to make *kambala* or blankets ; and (5) *kārpāsa*, cotton. According to Vasishṭha, it may be only woven cotton cloth (*tāntavam*). But it should be woven or manufactured in the home of the pupil for purposes of the ceremony [*Vāsaḥ sadyaḥ kṛittotam* (Baudhāyana, *G.S.*, ii, 5, 11)]. This shows the use of loom and *khaddar* in every household in those days. According to *Taittirīya Āraṇyaka* [ii, 1], cloth could alternate with skin (*ajinaṁ vāso vā dakshiṇataḥ upavīya*).

According to Manu, the Brāhmaṇa should use *Vāsa* of *Śāṇa*, the Kshatriya of *Kshauma*, and the Vaiśya of *Avika* or goat's wool. But most texts agree that different castes should use *Vāsa* of different colours. The Brāhmaṇa should use his *Kārpāsa* which is white, clean, and fresh, and coloured red with *manjishṭhā*. The Kshatriya should have his *Kshauma* cloth coloured yellow, and the Vaiśya *Kauśeya* cloth [Vasishṭha]. According to Āpastamba, the Brāhmaṇa should use cloth coloured with *kashāya*, a vegetable dye (vṛiksha-kashāya-nirmitaṁ vārksham), the Kshatriya *māñjishtha* cloth, and the Vaiśya *hāridra* cloth.

'Daṇḍa.' The Brahmachārī is also to be equipped with a *daṇḍa* or staff of wood of lengths which are different for different castes. The different woods mentioned are Bilva, Palāśa, Vaṭa, Khadira, Pilava, Udumbara, Plaksha, Nyagrodha, Vetasa, Aśvattha, and, failing these, any wood fit for use in sacrifice (*yajñīya*). It should reach up to head in length for a Brāhmaṇa, up to forehead for a Kshatriya, and up to nose for a Vaiśya.

But in all cases, it should be straight, beautiful, non-terrifying (*anudbegakara*), unburnt, and in its natural condition (*satvacha*) [Yama].

'Mekhalā.' The Brahmachārī's uniform also comprises a *mekhalā* or girdle made of different materials for different castes. It is *muñja* grass for the Brāhmaṇa, *jyā* (bowstring) for Kshatriya (symbolizing his military avocation), and *śaṇa*, thread for the Vaiśya. It may also be of rope used for yoking the oxen to the plough (symbolical of agriculture as his occupation).

Symbolism of Uniform. There is spiritual significance behind each of these external marks prescribed for the Brahmachārī. Āpastamba states [*D.S.*, i, 1, 3, 9] : " He who wishes the increase of Brāhmaṇa power shall wear *Ajina* (skins) only ; he who wishes the increase of Kshatriya power shall wear cloth only ; he who wishes the increase of both shall wear both [cf. *Gopatha Brāhmaṇa*, i, 2, 4]. Hiraṇyakeśin [i, 1, 4, 6] calls the skin as " a chaste, mobile vesture ". The symbolism of *Vāsa* or garment is thus explained by Pāraskara [ii, 2, 7] : " In the way in which Bṛihaspati put the garment of immortality on Indra, thus I put (this garment) on thee, for the sake of long life, of old age, of strength, of splendour." Hiraṇyakeśin [i, 1, 4, 2–3] extends still further this symbolism by stating that the student puts on the garment that he may be clothed " with long life, in the increase of wealth, and be a protector of human beings against imprecations ".

The *Mekhalā* was made of a triple chord to indicate the protection of the three Vedas encircling the child. It was tied round his waist to the recitation of verses stating that it was a daughter of the deity *Śraddhā* (Faith) and a sister of the sages (*svasā ṛishīṇām*), born of *tapas* (*tapaso'dhijātā*) [*Av.*, 133, 4], the protector of purity (*ṛita*), and asceticism (*tapas*), against evil [Varāha, *Gṛ. S.*, 5]. Hiraṇyakeśin calls the *Mekhalā* " the blessed one who has come to us, who drives away sin, purifying, our guard, and our protection " [i, 1, 4, 4]. Gobhila [ii, 10, 37] and Pāraskara [ii, 2, 8] also call the *Mekhalā* the girdle of protection.

The *Daṇḍa* also has a spiritual meaning. According to Pāraskara [ii, 2, 12–13], the student is to be equipped with it " for the sake of long life, holiness, holy lustre ", or because " he enters upon a long Sattra " [cf. *Śatapatha*, xi, 3, 3, 2 ; Kātyāyana, *Śr. S.*, vii, 4, 1–4]. *Mānava Gṛ. S.*, i, 22, 11 takes the staff as an aid to the traveller on the quest of Truth. *Varāha Gṛ. S.*, 6 takes it to indicate that, armed with it, the Brahmachārī will guard the Vedas. Aparārka (on Yājñavalkya, i, 29) takes a materialistic view of it as a weapon of defence to the Brahmachārī when he is out in the forests to collect firewood, in darkness, or unknown places like a tank or river.

'Yajñopavīta.' The equipment of the Brahmachārī is completed by the *Yajñopavīta* or sacred cord to be worn by him in three sets of three threads each. These nine threads (*tantu*) are consecrated to the following nine deities who impart to them their own potency, viz. (1) Oṁkāra, (2) Agni, (3) Nāga, (4) Soma, (5) Pitṛi, (6) Prajāpati, (7) Vāyu, (8) Sūrya, (9) All Deities together. The thread is to be made of cotton (kārpāsa) for a Brahmaṇa, of *śaṇa* for a Kshatriya, and of goat's skin for a Vaiśya [Manu]. "He who does not know the divine origin and significance of the Upavīta will have all his religious ceremonies such as Snāna, Dāna, or Japa fruitless." [See *Smṛiti-Chandrikā*, pp. 68–85, for most of above references.]

Dressing of Hair. There are rules for the arrangement of the *hair* which were determined not by the individual choice of the student but by the custom of his family, school, or country. The following ways of arranging the hair are mentioned, viz. shaving the head, wearing the hair tied in a braid, or keeping merely a lock on the crown of the head tied in a braid (shaving the other portions of the head) [*Āpa.*, i, 2, 31–2; 30, 8, etc.].

Preliminary Queries. When the intending pupil is thus properly dressed, he had to satisfy some preliminary queries put to him by the teacher before he initiates him. The first query was as regards his name and lineage. The second asked him to declare formally that he wants admission as a disciple. The form of the declaration is thus prescribed by Hiraṇyakeśin [i, 2, 5, 2]: "I have come hither to be a student. Initiate me! I will be a student, impelled by the god Savitṛi." Pāraskara makes the teacher ask the pupil, "Whose pupil art thou?" and the pupil answer, "Yours" [ii, 2, 19–20]. The object of this was probably to make the pupil promise that he would abide by the rules of *brahmacharya* upon which he would be presently entering. According to Vishṇu [xxix, 5, 9, 10] the teacher must not admit to his teaching one whom he does not know. There are also laid down certain moral conditions qualifying a pupil for admission. "He must not be a scorner, a wicked man, or one of uncontrolled passions; he must be pure, attentive, possessed of a good memory, and chaste, who will not grieve nor revile the teacher, to whom the sacred knowledge can be revealed as to a keeper of one's gem" [cf. Manu, ii, 109 (ten persons eligible for Vedic instruction), 112–15].

Invocations. The student is then committed to the charge of the gods with prayers varying also with his caste. The Brāhmaṇa is committed for the sake of great learning, the Kshatriya for great royalty, and the Vaiśya for great wealth [*Hiraṇya.* i, 1, 4, 8]. According to Śāṅkhāyana [ii, 2, 13–14], "those who are desirous of a host of adherents should be initiated with the verse: 'Thee, the Lord of Hosts' [*Rv.*, ii, 23, 1]," and "warriors, with the verse: 'Come here, do not come to harm'" [*Rv.*, viii, 20, 1].

Prayers. Some of the prayers used in the performance of the ceremony indicate the objects of education. They are both religious and secular and such as are necessary for the harmonious development of a man's nature. The pupil prays to the gods for insight, offspring, splendour, strength, and vigour [*Āsval.*, i, 21, 4]. The gods invoked are named Bhaga, Yama, Aryamā, and Savitṛi. Savitṛi was invoked to ward off evils like disease and death [ib., *Gṛ. S.*, i, 20, 6 (*Deva Savitaresha Te Brahmachārī sa mā mṛitaḥ*)]. In the Śāṅkhāyana [ii, 3, 1] he prays for long life, offspring, and strength, increase of wealth, mastery of all the Vedas, fame, and bliss. Pāraskara [ii, 4, 3] makes him worship Agni with the following poetic prayer: "To Agni have I brought a piece of wood. As thou, Agni, art inflamed by wood, thus am I inflamed by life, insight, vigour, offspring, cattle, holy lustre." Hiranyakeśin [i, 2, 5, 13] has the prayer for offspring, valiant sons, splendour, wealth, wisdom, and pupils (for the student must develop into a teacher and help forward the spread of learning). There is also a special prayer for intelligence [i, 2, 6, 4]. He has also a similar prayer to Agni: "As thou art inflamed, Agni, through that piece of wood, thus inflame me through wisdom, insight, offspring, cattle, holy lustre, and through the enjoyment of food" [i, 2, 7, 2].

'Aśmārohaṇa.' After prayers came the ceremony of the Brahmachārī being made to stand on stone as a symbol of steadfastness at study [*Mānava Gṛ. S.*, i, 22, 12], or strength and invincibility [*Bhāradvāja Gṛ. S.*, i, 8].

Admission. The teacher's formal acceptance of the pupil is made with the following words which indicate the sacred and inviolable character of the spiritual bond that connected them: "Thy heart shall dwell in my heart; my mind thou shalt follow with thy mind; in my word thou shalt rejoice with all thy heart ; to me alone thou shalt adhere ; in me thy thoughts shall dwell ; upon me thy veneration shall be bent ; when I speak thou shalt be silent." [*Hiraṇya*. i, 2, 5, 11 ; *Śāṅkh*., ii, 4, 1 ; *Pārask*., i, 8, 8 (formula for marriage) ; *Āśval*., i, 21, 7.] The pupil was also formally asked the question, " Whose Brahmachārī art thou ? " When he answered, " Thine," the preceptor stated : " Thou art the Brahmachārī of Indra, Agni is the Āchārya, I am thy Āchārya " [*Pārask. Gr. S*., ii, 3]. He also stated that he was admitting him as a pupil under god Savitṛi [*Āśva. Gr. S*., i, 20, 4].

Admonition. The ceremony of initiation concludes with the following charge laid upon the Brahmachārin : " A Brahamachārin art thou ! Drink water. Do the service. Do not sleep in the day-time. Devoted to the teacher, study the Veda " [*Āśval*., i, 22, 2]. The Śāṅkhāyana [ii, 4, 5] adds the further duty—" Put on fuel " [cf. also *Pārask*., ii, 3, 2 ; *Gobhila*, ii, 10, 34 ; *Hiraṇya*. i, 2, 5, 11].

The first observance of Brahmacharya: Sāvitrī Vrata. The Brahmachārī now starts on his career by taking on the *Sāvitrī Vrata* as a part of the Upanayana ceremony. Brahmacharya literally means " attendance on *Brahma* or Veda " and involves the observances which the student has to keep through certain periods of time before the different Vedic texts which he has to learn can be taught him. Thus the study of the Veda is opened by the Sāvitrī [cf. *Śatap. Br*., xi, 5, 4, 6 f.]. The Brāhmaṇa student is to be taught the Gāyatrī which belongs to Viśvāmitra [*Rv*., iii, 62, 10] ; the Kshatriya is to be taught the Trishṭubh which is a verse ascribed to Hiraṇyastūpa [*Rv*., i, 35, 2][1] ; the Vaiśya is to be taught the Jagatī which is a verse ascribed to Vāmadeva [*Rv*., iv, 40, 5] or to Hiraṇyastūpa [*Rv*., i, 35, 9].[2] The Sāvitrī Vrata which the student observes as a preparation for that instruction might last for one year or three days or the Sāvitrī can be taught immediately after the initiation [*Śāṅkh*., ii, 5, 1–6 ; 7, 11]. According to Pāraskara [ii, 4, 3, 6], the Sāvitrī Vrata may last for one year, six months, twenty-four days, twelve days, six days, or three days. [For teaching the Sāvitrī, cf. Gobhila, ii, 10, 39 ; *Hiraṇya*., i, 2, 6, 11 ; *Āp. Gr*., iv, 11, 9 f. ; *Kh*., ii, 4, 20 ; *Āśv*., i, 21, 5 f. ; 22, 29.] The normal period

[1] Or *Rv*., i, 35, 9, according to Nārāyaṇa commenting on Śāṅkhāyana Gr. S., ii, 5.

[2] Or *Rv*., v, 81, 2, according to Medhātithi (on Manu, ii, 38), Śatātapa (cited by Vīramitrodaya) and Laugākshi (cited by Aparārka on Yājña, i, 15) ; or *Rv*., v, 81, 1, according to *Āśva. Gr. S*., iii, 7 and *Vārāha. Gr S*., 6.

set for this, the first of the Brahmacharin's *vratas* or special observances, seems to have been three days. During this time, the student had to live on special food, which was not to be either pungent or saline, or milk, according to Khādira [ii, 4, 32], and to beg that food, firstly, of his mother, and "of two other women friends or of as many as there are in the neighbourhood" [Gobhila, ii, 10, 43] or "other houses where they are kindly disposed towards him" [*Hiraṇya.*, i, 2, 7, 17], or of "a woman who won't refuse" [*Śāṅkh.*, ii, 6, 6; *Āśval.*, i, 22, 7], or "from three women who will not refuse or from six, twelve, or an indefinite number" [*Pārask.*, ii, 5, 5, 6]. Manu [ii, 50] makes the pupil beg food first of his mother, then of his sister, then of his own maternal aunt and then of a female who will not disgrace him by a refusal. The alms were to be collected in a bowl given to the pupil by his teacher [*Hiraṇya.*, i, 2, 7, 14].

'Medhājanana.' After three days' observance of the Sāvitrī Vrata, the ceremony of *Upanayana* is ended by the performance of the *Medhājanana* rite whereby the gods are invoked for the development of the Brahmachārī's mental powers [*Bhāradvāja Gr. S.*, i, 10]. Then Brahmacharya or studentship formally begins under prescribed conditions governing the life and studies of the pupil dwelling in his teacher's house.

Food. The restrictions of Upanayana ceremony as regards *food* are withdrawn, and the student is allowed to eat pungent and saline food and vegetables [*Hiraṇya.*, i, 2, 9, 9]. Manu forbids the taking of honey, meat, substances used for flavouring food and substances turned acid [ii, 177; cf. *Baudh.*, i, 3, 23–4; *Pārask.*, ii, 5, 12; *Gobhila*, iii, 117, 19, 23]. According to Āpastamba, also, the Brahmachārin shall not eat food offered at a sacrifice nor pungent condiments, salt, honey, or meat [i, 1, 2, 22, 23; i, 1, 4, 6]. Āpastamba, appealing to the Mīmāṁsists, combats the doctrine implied in the injunctions of Baudhāyana that pupils may eat forbidden food, such as honey, meat, and pungent condiments, if it is given to them as leavings by their teacher. For the general rule is that students should eat the fragments of food given to them by their teachers and to obey their teachers except when ordered to commit crimes which cause loss of caste and such crimes, according to Baudhāyana, did not include eating forbidden food. Gautama [ii, 13], prohibits honey and meat. The *hour* of eating is also prescribed: it is the fourth, six, or eighth hour of the day [Vasishṭha, vii, 8]. The *manner* of eating is thus laid down: "he shall eat in silence, contented and without greed" after receiving permission to eat from his teacher [*Gautama*, ii, 39, 41]. Manu prescribes eating with a concentrated mind, a pleased face, and without contempt, after meditating on the food as the sustainer of life and forbids eating between the two meal-times, over-eating, and giving to any man the food that is left [ii, 53–7 ; cf. *Baudh.*, ii, 3, 5, 21 ; ii, 12, 7, 9 ; ii, 13, 11 ; *Gaut.*, ix, 59 *Vishṇu*, lxviii, 34–5 ; 42–3 ; 48 ; *Vasishṭha*, iii, 69 ; *Āp.*, ii, 1, 2, 3]. Āpastamba requires the pupil to clean his dish after he has eaten [i, 3, 36].

Though there is restriction as to food and drink for the Brahmachārī, there was no restriction as to quantity of these he should consume. He could take as much nourishment as was necessary for his health. "The *Muni* (of the fourth *āśrama*) should restrict his food to only eight mouthfuls ; the Hermit (of the third *āśrama*) to sixteen mouthfuls ; the Householder to thirty-two ; but there was no limit for a Brahmachārī." This rule is based on that of health which requires that the quantity of food must be largest for youths and decrease with age. The same text forbids the penance of fasting for both a Brahmachārī and a Gṛihastha [Baudhāyana, ii, 7, 31–3 ; *Smṛiti-chandrikā*, p. 114].

Begging. One of the standing duties of the Brahmachārin was to go out *begging* for alms. Generally, the women were to be addressed in prescribed terms varying according to the caste of the begging student. A Brahmin is to use the word "Lady", at the beginning, a Kshatriya, in the middle, and a Vaiśya, at the end, of the sentence prescribed for asking for alms [*Pārask.*, ii, 5, 2–4 ; *Āpastamba*, i, 1, 3, 28–30]. The student had to go out for begging twice a day, in the morning and evening [*Āp.*, i, 1, 3, 25 ; *Āśval.*, i, 22, 4]. According to *Gopatha Brāhmaṇa* [i, 2, 1–8], and Baudhāyana-Dharma-sūtra [i, 2, 52], a pupil must perform a prescribed penance for his omission to beg at least once a week. This rule indicates (1) that begging was enjoined mainly as a measure of discipline for its educative value, and (2) that it was not a compulsory daily duty. According to Āpastamba [ib.] the student may beg of "everybody except low-caste people unfit for association with Āryas and Abhiśastas". Gautama [ii, 35] also forbids the students begging of "abhiśastas and outcastes", while Vishṇu [xxviii, 9] restricts the begging to "the houses of virtuous persons, excepting those of the Guru or his relatives". Where, however, no alms could be obtained by aforesaid means, the student might beg in his own house, or in that of his teacher or his relations [Gautama, ii, 37). According to Manu, the proper persons to be approached for alms are those who are not deficient in the knowledge of the Veda and in performing sacrifices, and who are noted for adhering to their lawful occupations [ii, 183–5; also Baudhāyana, i, 2, 3, 18]. Manu also condemns a student as guilty of theft if he gathers by begging more food than he needs and sells the surplus [cited in *Vīramitrodaya*, p. 486]. Begging was also not permitted to a *Snātaka* [*Samāvṛittasya bhikshā aśuchikarā* (Baudhāyana, ii, 1, 63)]. The student shall not beg for his own sake alone [*Āp.*, i, 1, 3, 35], but submit the proceeds of his begging to his teacher [ib., 31; *Āśv.*, i, 22, 10; *Vasishṭha*, vii, 14; *Vishṇu*, xxviii, 10]. If the proceeds are other than food, such as cattle or fuel, they are to be offered to the teacher as rewards given to priests for the performance of a sacrifice [*Āp.*, i, 1, 4, 3]. Baudhāyana [i, 2, 4, 7] points out the virtues of begging, viz. that by this the student makes himself poor and humble in spirit. It was thus valued as a method of moral discipline.

Service to Teacher. The life of the student was regulated on the principle that he must do what is pleasing and serviceable to his teacher [Gautama, ii, 30; Vishṇu, xxviii, 7]. One text sums up the position by stating that the pupil is to serve his teacher as a son, supplicant, or slave (Putravat dāsavat arthivat cha anucharatā tvayā). Charaka [Vimānasthāna, viii, 4] states that "the pupil should serve his teacher as he serves Agni, Deva, King, Father, and Master, with steady devotion" As Āpastamba puts it more definitely, the pupil shall "assist his teacher daily by acts tending to the acquisition of spiritual merit and of wealth" [i, 1, 4, 24]. The former class of acts will comprise collecting sacred fuel, kuśa grass, cow-dung, earth, and flowers for sacrifice, as also fetching a pot full of water, while the latter class implies gathering fuel for cooking, begging alms, etc. [Manu, ii, 182].

But this relationship of service must always rest on a moral foundation. If the teacher goes wrong, the pupil should first complain to him in private [Pramādān āchāryasya *rahasi* bodhayet (Āpastamba, i, 2, 6, 13)]. Gautama terminates this relationship where the teacher indulges in *adharma* or sinful conduct [iii, 1, 15].

Fetching Water, Flower, Fuel: Tending Fire. Thus the next important class of duties after begging is that connected with fuel and fire. The pupil is to fetch fire-wood out of the forest without damaging the trees [*Pārask.*, ii, 5, 9] and before sunset

[*Āp.*, i, 1, 4, 15]. The fuel thus fetched daily from the forest is to be placed on the floor of the teacher's house. After having kindled the fire, and swept the ground around the altar the pupil is to place the sacred fuel on the fire every morning and evening. He shall sweep the place around the fire after it has been made to burn (by the addition of fuel) with his hand, and not with the broom (of Kuśa grass) but before adding the fuel, he is free to use the broom at his pleasure [ib., 16–19].

Besides fetching fuel and tending the fire twice daily, the pupil was to fetch water in a vessel for the use of his teacher both in the morning and evening [ib., 13].

Thus the standing duties to be performed by the student in the interests of his teacher and of his own discipline and moral life were begging, fetching fuel, water, and flowers and other articles for sacrifice, and tending the sacred fire. These duties were more of the nature of services rendered to the teacher, but there were others more directly connected with his own life. We have already considered the regulations prescribed regarding the student's diet. We shall now consider those regarding his dress, the luxuries he must avoid, his general behaviour, the habits he must eschew or cultivate, and the like.

Duties of Student. According to Āpastamba [i, 2, 5, 9–10], the duties of a student consist in acts pleasing to the spiritual teacher, the observance of rules conducive to his own welfare and industry in studying. "Acts other than these need not be performed by a student" (such as pilgrimages and the like, according to the commentator, thus showing the puritanic austerity of the discipline which won't allow even these innocent diversions because they are for the householders and aged people). We have already considered the first class of these duties, viz. the services to be rendered to the teacher. Now we shall consider the second class of duties connected with the student's own welfare, from which we can gather his daily routine.

His Daily Routine of Duties. The student is to rise from his bed before his teacher [1] and before sunrise [2] in the last watch of the night.[3] Penances are prescribed for the sin of sleeping when the sun rises, or sets, or when the teacher is awake.

Then he is to bathe and purify himself.[4] He is not to sport

[1] *Vi.*, xxviii, 13; *Ba.*, i, 3, 21.
[2] *Āp.*, ii, 12, 13–14; *Ga.*, xxiii, 21; *Vas.*, xx, 4; *Ba.*, ii, 7, 16; *Vi.*, xxviii, 53; *Manu*, ii, 220.
[3] *Āp.*, i, 5, 12.
[4] Manu, ii, 176; *Ga.*, ii, 8–9.

in the water whilst bathing, but must swim motionless[1] or plunge into the waters like a stick.[2] He must not wash his body with hot water for pleasure, but if it is soiled by unclean things, he might clean it with earth or water in a place where he is not seen by a guru.[3] He is not to use any bathing powder or the like for cleaning himself. The bath has to be taken three times a day.[4]

His next duty is to perform his morning devotions (*sandhyā* or muttering the Sāvitrī). This must be done with a concentrated mind in a pure place outside the village, and in a standing posture, and in silence. The prayer is to begin from the time when the stars are still visible, and to end when the sun rises. The evening prayer is also to be similarly performed from the time when the sun still stands above the horizon until the stars appear.[5]

Returning home after his twilight devotions, the student is to offer libations of water to gods, sages, and manes, worship the images of the gods, and place fuel on the sacred fire.[6]

Restrictions. He must avoid the following *luxuries*: perfumes, garlands, anointing his body, applying collyrium to his eyes, use of shoes, umbrella, parasol, and carriage, and sleep in the day-time.

There are laid down many *moral* injunctions which the student must obey. He must avoid singing, playing musical instruments, and dancing, at which he must not even look [Āp., i, 3, 11]. He must not go to the assemblies (for gambling, etc.), nor to crowds assembled at festivals.

Certain virtues or moral qualities are specified for his cultivation and practice. He must avoid idle disputes and gossiping, backbiting and lying. He must be free from sexual desire, anger, envy, covetousness. He must not injure animate beings. He must talk with women only so much as his purpose requires. He must be forgiving, untired in fulfilling his duties, modest, possessed of self-command, and devoid of pride.

Behaviour towards Teacher. There are rules regulating the behaviour of the student towards his teacher. He must always obey his teacher except when ordered to commit crimes which cause loss of caste. He must not contradict him. He must occupy a couch or seat lower than that of his teacher. When he meets his teacher after sunrise (coming for his lessons),

[1] *Āp.*, i, 2, 30; *Ba.*, i, 3, 39–40.
[2] *Āp.*, i, 2, 28–9.
[3] Manu, ii, 101, 222; *Ga.*, ii, 10–11; *Va.*, vii, 16; *Āp.*, i, 30, 8; *Ba.*, ii, 7, 13–14.
[4] *Vi.*, xxviii, 5.
[5] *Va.*, vii, 17; *Ga.*, ii, 8.
[6] Manu, ii, 176.

he shall embrace his feet, and shall study, after having been called by the teacher, and not request the teacher to begin the lesson. He must not stretch out his feet towards him but, according to some, he may, if the teacher be lying on a bed. He shall not address the teacher whilst he himself is in a reclining position, but he may answer the teacher sitting, if the teacher himself is sitting or lying down. And if the teacher stands, he shall answer him after having risen also. He shall walk after him if he walks, and run after him if he runs. He shall not approach his teacher with shoes on his feet, or his head covered, or holding implements in his hand, except when on a journey, or occupied in work. He shall approach his teacher with the same reverence as a deity, without telling idle stories, attentive, and listening eagerly to his words. He shall not sit either too near to, or too far from, his teacher, nor with his legs crossed. In the presence of his guru, he is to avoid covering his throat, leaning against a wall, stretching out his feet, spitting, laughing, yawning, and cracking the joints of his fingers. He must not sit with his teacher to the leeward or to the windward of him, but may sit with his teacher in a carriage drawn by oxen, horses, or camels, on a terrace, on a bed of grass or leaves, or a mat, on a rock, on a wooden bench or in a boat.

Rules of Study. From the regulations governing the life of the student in the home of his preceptor, we now pass on to the regulations governing his studies.

The student must commence his study in the morning, embracing the feet of his teacher both at the beginning and end of his lesson. After having received permission, he will sit down to the right of his teacher, turning his face towards the east or towards the north. Then the Sāvitrī is to be recited, together with the syllable *Om* before the instruction in the Veda is begun. The student must be very attentive the whole day long, never allowing his mind to wander from the lesson during the time devoted to studying. During the time for rest (which he has, after attending to his studies and the business of his teacher, as has been indicated above), the pupil is to give his mind to doubtful passages of the lesson learnt.

Courses of Study. The courses of study included the " *whole* Veda ", together with " the Rahasyas " as stated by Manu [ii, 165]. There were also accompanying various kinds of austerities and vows prescribed by the rules of Vedic study. By the " *whole* " Veda, as already stated, the commentators understand the four Vedas with the six *Aṅgas* or the *ritualistic* treatises comprising Phonetics (Śikhshā), Rituals proper (Kalpa), Grammar (Vyākaraṇa), Etymology (Nirukta), Prosody (Chhanda), and Astronomy (Jyotisha), and the *esoteric* treatises such as the Upanishads; or one entire Śākhā of Veda, consisting of the Mantras and the *Brāhmaṇa*. By the term *Rahasyas* are meant esoteric treatises, the Upanishads, or the secret explanations of the Veda. According to Vishṇu [xxviii, 34–5], the student must first acquire by heart one Veda, or two Vedas, or all the Vedas, and thereupon the Vedāṅgas. If, without studying the Veda, he applies himself to another study, he degrades himself and his progeny to the state of a Śūdra. In another place, he discusses the comparative merits of the different subjects of study which include the hymns of the Ṛigveda, the Yajus texts, the Sāman melodies, the Atharvaveda, as well as the Purāṇas, Itihāsas, Vedāṅgas, and the Institutes of Sacred Law [xxx, 34–8]. In yet another passage [ib., 43], the knowledge imparted to the pupil is stated to be of three kinds, viz. worldly knowledge (relating to poetry, rhetoric, and the like subjects), sacred knowledge (relating to the Vedas and Vedāṅgas), and knowledge of the Supreme Spirit.

Special Observances ('Vratas') for Special Subjects of Study. It has been already indicated that there were prescribed some special *Vratas* or observances which the student had to keep through certain periods of time before the different texts appointed in the course of Brahminical studies could be taught him. We have already referred to the first of these, the *Sāvitra Vrata*, by the observance of which the student is introduced to the Sāvitrī verse. Then follows the *Śukriya Vrata* (duties of holiness) to be kept for three days, or twelve days, or one year, or any other period of time, according to the teacher's discretion [*Śāṅkh. Gṛ. Sū.*, ii, 11, 10]. By this *Vrata*, the student is enabled to study the main portion of the Veda. Next follows the *Anuvāchana*, or the way of studying the Veda "which can be done only after the Śukriya Vrata has been enjoined on the student. Before that nothing but the Sāvitrī can be taught to him" [ib., p. 69, note, *S.B.E.* ed.]. Finally come the *Śākvara*, *Vrātika*, and *Aupanishada* observances, each of which has to last one year, and which refer to the different parts of the Āraṇyaka. These three are special *Vratas* connected with the character of mystical secrecy attributed to the Āraṇyaka. After the lapse of the year through which the Vrata is kept, a ceremony is performed called

Uddīkshaṇikā, i.e. the giving up of the Dīkshā or preparatory observance for the study of the Āraṇyaka texts. This *Uddīkshaṇikā* consists chiefly in the teacher's ascertaining whether the student has fulfilled the duties involved by the Vrata. Besides that, a repetition of the Upanayana also formed part of the preparatory rites for the study of the Āraṇyaka.[1] After this, the teacher goes out of the village in a north-eastern direction and sits down on a clean spot, turning his face to the east. Then when the sun has arisen, he recites in the way prescribed for the Veda-study (i.e. the *anuvāchana*) the Āraṇyaka texts to the student or the "*Rahasya*", as termed by Manu.

These Vratas which the student has to undergo in the time of his studentship are those of the Rigvedins. There are some different Vratas for the followers of the Sāmaveda, which are thus explained by the commentator on Gobhila Gṛihya Sūtra, iii, 1, 28: "The *Upanayana* Vrata has been declared to refer to the study of the Sāvitrī; the *Godāna* Vrata, to the study of the collections of verses sacred to the gods Agni, Indra, and Soma Pavamāna (this is the Pūrvārchika of the Sāmaveda); the *Vrātika*-vrata, to the study of the Āraṇyaka, with the exclusion of the Śukriya sections; the *Āditya*-vrata, to the study of the Śukriya sections; the *Aupanishada*-vrata, to the study of the Upanishada-Brāhmaṇa; the *Jaishṭha-sāmika*-vrata, to the study of the Ājya-dohas" [*SBE.*, xxx, p. 69 *n*].

It is thus clear that the graduated course of studies corresponded to a graduated course of special observances or practical disciplines, whereby the gradual development of the inner capacities answering to the growing difficulty of the subjects of study was sought to be secured.

Period of Studentship. All the Sūtras are agreed as to the length of the period of studentship. It is to consist ordinarily of twelve years for the mastery of each Veda. "Twelve years lasts the Brahmacharya for each Veda, or until he has learnt it" [Āśvalāyana]. "The studentship lasts for forty-eight years, or twenty-four years, or twelve years, or until he has learnt the Veda" [Hiraṇyakeśin]. "He who has been initiated shall dwell as a religious student in the house of his teacher for forty-eight years (if he learns all the four Vedas), or a quarter less (i.e. for thirty-six years), or less by half (i.e. for twenty-four years), or three-quarters less (i.e. for twelve years), but twelve

[1] According to Āpastamba, a fresh initiation is necessary for the study of the Atharvaveda but not of other Vedas [see *Vaitāna-Sūtra*, i, 1, 5].

years should be the shortest time for his residence with his teacher" [Āpastamba]. Manu, however, recognizes only the three Vedas for study, and permits thirty-six years, or half that time, or quarter, of the period required by the student to learn them perfectly [iii, 1]. Baudhāyāna, prescribing the same time-limits, calculates that, at the least, one year will be required for the study of each Kāṇḍa (of the seven Kāṇḍas of the Taittirīya-saṁhitā) [i, 2, 3, 3]. The rather excessive length of the period of studentship under the scheme of the Sūtras is also noticed by Baudhāyana who says that life is uncertain (Life is short, Art long), and quotes a passage from the Śruti which declares, "Let him kindle the sacred fires while his hair is still black." This means that the period of studentship must not be protracted too long.

Academic Session : 'Upākarma' and 'Utsarjana' Ceremonies. In connection with the length of the period of studentship, we have to consider the length of what may be called the academic session, i.e. the number of days of actual teaching done in these Brahminical schools in the year. The school-term opens solemnly with the performance of a special ceremony called the *Upākarman* on the full moon of the month of Śrāvaṇa (July–August). From this opening day, for a month, study in the evening is not permitted (though, according to Haradatta, the commentator, it is not sinful to study later in the night after evening). The term then continues until the full moon of the month of Pausha or the Rohiṇī day when it is solemnly closed by the performance of the *Utsarjana* ceremony after which the student has to leave off reading the Veda. Thus the term comprises five months in the year, viz. latter half of Śrāvaṇa, Bhādrapada, Āśvina, Kārttika, Mārgaśīrsha, and the first half of Pausha [see *Āpas.*, i, 3, 9]. Manu [iv, 95–6] makes the academic session comprise four months and a half by prescribing for the *Upākarman* ceremony the alternative date of the full moon of Bhādrapada, and for the *Utsarjana*, the Pushya (or sixth) day of Pausha or the first day of the bright half of Māgha. Thus the interruption of Vedic teaching lasts for six months and a half or five months and a half [*Śāṅkh.*, iv, 6, 7–8]. During this period, though the teaching was not done, the private study of students was, however, not to be interrupted. Manu [iv, 98] lays down the rule that, after the performance of the *Utsarjana* ceremony, the student is to study the Veda during the light nights of each month until the full moon of Śrāvaṇa in order to fix in his mind the part learned already ; and in the dark fortnight of each month he is to study all the Vedāṅgas, grammar, and the rest [Haradatta's commentary quoted in *SBE.*, ii, 33]. With the commencement of the next academic session the student will begin the study of a fresh part of the Veda.

Their Details. Some of the ritualistic details of these ceremonies of *Upākarma* and *Utsarjana* are worth noting for their educational bearings. The term *upākarma* is part of the full expression *Chhandasāṁ upākarma*, showing that *upākarma* was meant for study and conservation of Vedic texts. The ceremony is also known as *Śrāvaṇi*, as it began in Śrāvaṇa when the rains set in and keep the people out of work after the sowing of harvest is over. It was celebrated by the teacher uttering the Sāvitrī Mantra before his assembled pupils [*Khādira*, iii, 2, 18, 19] ; praying for pupils by uttering a suitable Mantra [*Pāras.*, ii, 10 ; *Vārāha Gṛ. S.*, 7 (*antevāsīnāṁ yogamichchhannatha japati*)] ; and giving a feast to his pupils [*Jaimini Gṛ. S.*, i, 14 (*Sabrahmachāriṇaścha upasametān bhojayedāchāryaḥ*)]. *Upākarma* also included invocation of appropriate deities. The Rigvedins worshipped Sāvitrī, Śraddhā, Medhā, Prajñā, Dhāraṇā, and the Ṛishis of the Veda, and then recited the first and last stanzas of the ten Maṇḍalas of the Rigveda, offering oblations of curds and *saktu* to Agni. The Yajurvedins first offered oblations to the sacrificial deities for success in the performance of sacrifices in which they wanted to specialize, and then they invoked the deities of the Saṁhitās and their Ṛishis. Next, the four Vedic Saṁhitās, together with Itihāsa and Purāṇa, were reverently recalled. In this connection, the Yajurvedins also paid their homage to the memory of scholars who had built up their studies: Krishṇa Dvaipāyana, Vaiśampāyana, Tittiri (author of Black Yajurveda), Ātreya (author of Yajurveda Pada-pāṭha), Kauṇḍinya the *Vṛittikāra*, Baudhāyana the *Pravachana-kāra*, Āpastamba the *Sūtrakāra*, and also to Satyāshāḍha, Hiraṇyakeśin, Vājasaneya, Yājñavalkya, Bhāradvāja, and Agniveśya. The Sāmavedins in their turn recalled such names as Jaimini, Tālavakāra, Rāṇāyani, Bhāguri, and the like [*Aśva. Gr. S.*; *Baudhā. Gṛ. S.*, iii, 1]. This ritual of recalling with worshipful gratitude on the opening day of the school the names of those who have contributed to its studies and traditions was the best inspiration to its pupils to keep up the culture now committed to their care, to keep burning the torch of learning left to them. A sense of *Guru-pāramparya*, of succession of teachers, creates a sense of responsibility to learning in its new devotees who are thus inspired to do their best for it as their worthy successors. Such a significant ritual should have its modern substitute.

Holidays. The academic session is punctuated by numerous holidays. Interruptions of study were allowed for a variety of causes and circumstances. The *first* cause of such interruption is the occurrence of certain natural phenomena. These include the following: wind whirling up dust in the day-time (dust-storm) or audible at night; sky flaming red; rainbow; hoar frost settling on the ground; clouds out of season; thunder, rain (sufficiently heavy to cause dripping of water from the edge of roof) and lightning out of season or in season (in which case the study is to stop for the remaining hours of the day or night); Jupiter, Venus, Sun, and Moon surrounded by a halo; thunder, earthquake, eclipse, and fall of meteors (to stop study until the same time next day, i.e. for 24 hours); simultaneous rain, thunder and lightning (to stop study for three days). *Secondly*, the standing list of holidays included the following: new moon (two days' leave); full moon days of the months of Kārttika, Phālguna, and Āshāḍha; eighth and fourteenth days of each half-month and full-moon days of every month [Manu, iv, 113]; certain other days set apart for religious ceremonies, e.g. three Ashṭakas (involving three days' leave for each); Upākarma and Utsarjana (with three days' leave for each); spring festival (which, according to Haradatta, falls on the thirteenth of the first half of Chaitra), and the festival of Indra in the month of Āshāḍha (when the study of an Anuvāka [1] is forbidden, according to Āpastamba); and, lastly, festive days (the day of the initiation and the like) [*Gaut.*, xvi, 43]. *Thirdly*, study is forbidden in the case of certain political or other events taking place, e.g. invasion of the village [Gautama, xvi, 34; Manu, iv, 118]; when the cows are prevented from leaving the village due to cattle-lifting by robbers and the like [*Āp.*, i, 3, 9, 25]; or during a battle [Vishṇu, xxx, 11]; if outcasts [" robbers such as Ugras and Nishādas " (Haradatta on *Āp.*, i, 3, 9, 18)] have entered the village or if *good men have come*) or when a king or a learned Brahmin (who has mastered one Veda; or a cow, or a Brahmin in general has met with an accident; if there is an outbreak of fire in the village; or when the king of

[1] According to Haradatta, Āpastamba uses the word Anuvāka in order to indicate that smaller portions of the Veda may be studied. Others think that by Anuvāka the Saṁhitā and Brāhmaṇa are meant and that the study of the Aṅgas is permitted [*SBE.*, ii, p. 42 *n.*].

the country has died [Gautama, xvi, 32] or has become impure through birth or death in his family (cf. modern "court mourning") [Manu, iv, 110]. *Fourthly*, study is to be stopped when certain sounds are heard, e.g. howling of jackals, barking of dogs, braying of donkeys, grunting of camels, cry of a wolf, screeching of an owl; the sound of an arrow, of a large or small drum; the noise of a chariot; the wail of a person in pain or weeping.

Places banned for Study. There are specified certain circumstances under which study is not permitted. One must not study in the following *places*: a burial ground, extremity of a village, a high road, a village in which a corpse lies or Chaṇḍālas live, or a forest if a corpse or a Chaṇḍāla is in sight. Nor must one study during impurity when his near relations have died, or when he has partaken of a funeral repast or of dinner on the occasion of a sacrifice offered to men (when the study is stopped for a day and a night). Considerations of health dictate stoppage of study under certain circumstances, e.g. when the pupil has vomited or emits a foul smell or suffers from sour eructations, or when he has taken his evening meal.

Lastly, there is an interesting regulation of a different kind for the stoppage of study. "If some of his fellow-students are away on a journey, he shall not study during that day the passage which they learn together" [*Āp.*, i, 3, 11, 11]. "If one pupil has gone on a journey and another stays with the teacher, the study of the Veda shall be 'interrupted until the absentee returns'" [Gautama, xvi, 33].

In connection with some of these rules for interruption of study, it should be noted that they seem to apply to the study of new parts of the Veda and not of the parts already learnt nor to the study of the Aṅgas of the Veda. This is clear from Manu [ii, 105–6]: "Both when one studies the supplementary treaties of the Veda and when one *recites* the daily portion of the Veda, no regard need be paid to forbidden days, likewise when one repeats the sacred texts required for a burnt oblation. There are no forbidden days for the daily recitation, since that is declared to be a Brahmasattra (an everlasting sacrifice offered to Brahman); at that the Veda takes the place of the burnt oblations, and it is meritorious even when natural phenomena requiring a cessation of the Veda-study take the place of the exclamation, *Vashaṭ*." The same view is held by Āpastamba [i, 4, 12, 9], according to whom these various cases for the prohibition of study refer only to the repetition of the sacred texts in order to learn them and not to their application at sacrifices. He quotes *Vājaśaneyi-Brāhmaṇa* which declares that Vedic recitation is a sacrifice and must be done when it thunders, or a thunderbolt falls, or lightning flashes, for these sounds are like *Vashaṭ* (which, when pronounced by the Hotṛi-priest, serves as a signal for the Adhvaryu to throw the oblations into the fire) which must not be heard in vain.

Rules of Vedic Study. We shall now consider the methods of teaching, the rules of Vedic study implied by what is technically termed *Anuvāchana*. These rules are best explained in the *Śāṅkhāyana Gṛihya Sūtra* [ii, 7, 18–27]. In the first place, the text of a hymn of the Rigveda is taught the student. Secondly, the Ṛishi, Deity, and Metre of the hymn are indicated to him. In this way the teacher is to go on reciting the hymns, belonging to each Ṛishi, or each Anuvāka, which make up the lesson for each day. There seem to have been, however, shorter lessons for the students of other castes who had no intention of becoming Vedic scholars. For these students, a day's lesson might comprise an Anuvāka of the Kshudrasūktas or short hymns of the Rigveda (i.e. the tenth Maṇḍala); or as much as the master may think fit for them; or it was still further whittled down to the first and last hymn of a Ṛishi or an Anuvāka, the study of which would by a sort of fiction be regarded as the study of the whole portion belonging to that Ṛishi or the entire Anuvāka; or, lastly, it might be even only one verse of the beginning of each hymn (of the collection belonging to a Ṛishi or making up an Anuvāka).

Hiraṇyakeśin [i, 2, 8, 16] lays down that at the beginning and on the completion of the study of a Kāṇḍa (i.e. of the Black Yajur Veda which is divided into books called Kāṇḍas), there is to be performed a special ceremony or a sacrifice for which a verse is prescribed, in which the student prays for the gift of insight. Āpastamba [i, 3, 11, 6–7] also refers to the ceremony for beginning a Kāṇḍa and also to ceremonies prescribed on beginning or ending the recitation of one entire Veda. He further lays down the rule that when the student studies the index of the Anuvākas of a Kāṇḍa (i.e. completes the study of the Kāṇḍa), he shall not study that Kāṇḍa on that day nor in that night. In another place [i, 4, 13, 10], he enjoins that without a vow of obedience a pupil shall not study nor a teacher teach a difficult new book with the exception of the texts called *Triḥ-Śrāvaṇa* and *Triḥsahavachana* ; but he quotes the contrary opinion of Hārīta who does not allow that exemption but insists on a vow of obedience for the study of the whole Veda. This shows also that the Aṅgas or works explanatory of the Veda need not be studied under a vow of obedience.

Uśanā [81–2] states that mastery of the mere text of Veda is to be followed up by that of its meaning. " The mere recitation of the Vedas becomes useless like a cow in mire. He who studying duly the Veda does not discuss the Vedānta becomes like a Śūdra with his whole family." Daksha [ii, 27] refers to the five-fold practice of Vedic study comprising (*a*) admission of the superiority of Vedic study, (*b*) discussion on Vedas, (*c*) study and (*d*) recitation of Vedas, and (*e*) imparting lessons to disciples. These five limbs of Vedic study are stated by Vāchaspati Misra to be (1) *Adhyayana* (hearing of words), (2) *Śabda* (apprehension of meaning of words heard), (3) *Ūha* (reasoning leading to generalization), (4) *Suhṛitprāpti* (confirmation by friend or teacher), and (5) *Dāna* (application). Dhīguṇa enumerates the following steps of Vedic study : (1) *Śuśrūshā*, (2) *Śravaṇam*, (3) *Grahaṇam* (apprehension), (4) *Dhāraṇam*, (5) *Ūhāpoha* (discussion), (6) *Arthavijñānam*, and (7) *Tattvajñānam* (knowledge of ultimate truth) [*Smṛiti-Chandrikā*, pp. 131–3 ; S. K. Das, *Educational System of the Ancient Hindus*, pp. 127–8]. Manu puts the matter in a nut-shell thus : " The student learns a fourth from his Āchārya, a fourth by his own intelligence by himself, a fourth from his fellow-pupils, and the remaining fourth in course of time, by experience."

A few more rules of Vedic study are laid down by Āpastamba [Ib.]. Out of term the student must not study any part of the Veda which he has not learnt before. Nor shall he study during term some new part of the Veda in the *evening*. That which has been studied before must never be studied during the vacation or in the evening. According to Vishṇu [xxx, 27], a student must not lie down to sleep again when he has begun to study in the second half of the night. This is, of course, study by himself and not with his teacher.

According to Gautama [xvi, 21] and also Vishṇu [xxx, 26], the Rigveda and Yajurveda must not be studied while the sound of the Sāmans is heard, while, according to Āpastamba [i, 3, 10, 20], if another branch of the Veda is being recited in the neighbourhood, the Sāman melodies must not be studied. A student must also first master the *Śākhā* of the Veda which belongs to his family and forms its heritage from its ancestors [Svakula-paramparāgatā Śākhā adhyetavyā (Vasishṭha)]. One who forsakes the study of his own *Śākhā* is to be ostracized (*vahishkārya*) like a Śūdra and is called a *Śākhāraṇḍa* [ib.]. According to Nārada, a student must study under a teacher and not from mere books. Otherwise he is not recognized in any *Sabhā* (Pustaka-pratyayādhītaṁ nādhītaṁ guru-sannidhau | Bhrājate na sabhā-madhye jāragarbha iva striyaḥ).

Lastly, there are mentioned six hindrances to study, viz. (1) Gambling (*dyūta*), (2) Dependence on MSS. (*pustaka-śuśrūshā*), (3) Addiction to dramatic art (*nāṭakāsakti*), (4) Women, (5) Lethargy and (6) Sleepiness (*nidrā*).

Description of actual Teaching in a Vedic School. Details of the methods of oral instruction pursued by these ancient teachers are furnished by a Prātiśākhya of the Rigveda [cited by Max Müller in his *History of Ancient Sanskrit Literature* (pp. 503–6)]. They show how the teaching of the Vedic Texts was conducted in the Lecture-rooms of these Brāhmanic colleges: "The Guru, who has himself formerly been a student, should make his pupils read. He himself takes his seat either to the east, or the north, or the north-east. If he has no more than one or two pupils, they sit at his right hand. If he has more, they place themselves according as there is room. They then embrace the feet of their master, and say, 'Sir, read!' The master gravely says, '*Om*,' i.e. 'Yes'. He then begins to say a Praśna (Question) which consists of three verses. In order that no word may escape the attention of his pupils, he pronounces all with the high accent and repeats certain words twice, or he says 'so' (*iti*) after these words.

"The chief difficulties in the pronunciation of the Veda are changes of the final and initial letters. The pupils are instructed in these euphonic rules independently (the *Śikshā*), but whenever a difficult case of *sandhi* occurs, the Guru examines his audience and explains the difficulties. And here the method followed is this. After the Guru has pronounced a group of words, consisting of three or sometimes (in long compounds) of more words, the first pupil repeats the first word, and when anything is to be explained, the teacher stops him, and says, 'Nirvāchyetu,' 'explain it.' After it has been explained by the pupil who is at the head of the class, the permission to continue is given with the words, 'Well, Sir.' After the words of the teacher have thus been repeated by one, the next pupil has to apply to him with the word, 'Sir.' When there is no difficulty, the rule seems to be that the Guru says two words at a time, which are then repeated by the pupil. If it is a compound, one word only is to be pronounced by the Guru, and to be repeated by the pupil. After a section of three verses has thus been gone through, all the pupils have to rehearse it again and again. When they have mastered it, they have to recite the whole without any break, with an even voice, observing all the rules of Sandhi, marking slightly the division in the middle of compounds, and pronouncing every syllable with the high accent. It does not seem as if several pupils were allowed to recite together, for it is stated distinctly that the Guru first tells the verses to his pupil on the right, and that every pupil, after his task is finished, turns to the right, and walks round the tutor. This occupied long hours every day, considering that a day's Lecture consisted at least of sixty and more *Praśnas*, or of about 180 verses. The pupils were not dismissed till the Lecture was finished. At the end of the Lecture, the tutor, after the last half-verse is finished, says, 'Sir'; the pupil replies, 'Yes, sir.' He then repeats the proper verses and formulas, which have to be repeated at the end of every reading, embraces the feet of his tutor, and is allowed to withdraw."

Life-long Studentship. We have now completed the consideration of the various regulations governing the life and studies of the Brahmachārin during the period of his stay at his teacher's house. But some students would elect to make the period of that stay life-long without any desire for the householder's life or the married state. Such students are known as *Naishṭhika* Brahmachārins as distinguished from the others called *Upakurvāṇas*. It is probably for these that such long periods of studentship as 24, or 36, or 48 years are meant. Those who would be householders would have to confine their studentship to a period of twelve years, and naturally to satisfy themselves with the mastery of a portion of the prescribed studies. There is a most interesting saying quoted by Āpastamba [i, 4, 13, 19–22] in which the famous scholar Śvetaketu of Upanishadic fame is made to declare: "He who desires to study more after having settled as a householder shall dwell two months every year with collected mind in the house of his teacher. For by this means I studied a larger part of the Veda than before (during my studentship)." But Āpastamba does not approve this practice because it would interfere with the duties belonging to a householder's life, though he makes the concession that it could be allowed where a graduate

PLATE VIII

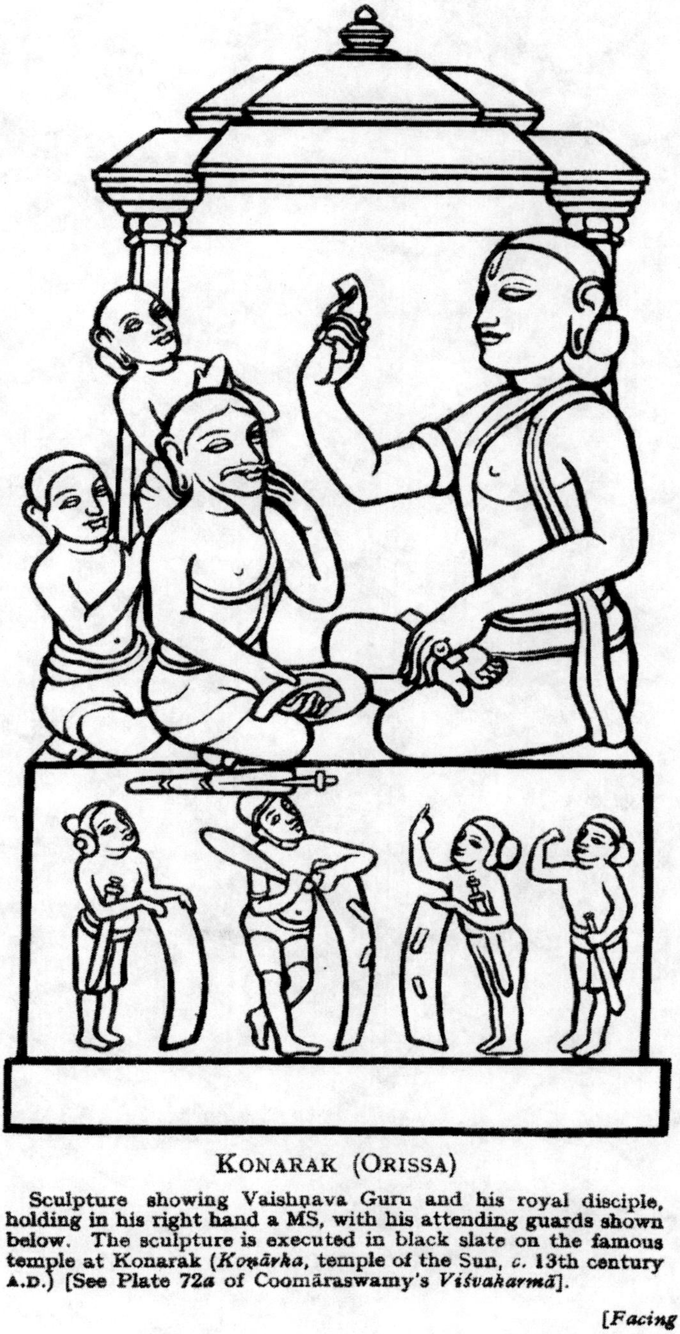

KONARAK (ORISSA)

Sculpture showing Vaishṇava Guru and his royal disciple, holding in his right hand a MS, with his attending guards shown below. The sculpture is executed in black slate on the famous temple at Konarak (*Koṇārka*, temple of the Sun, *c.* 13th century A.D.) [See Plate 72*a* of Coomāraswamy's *Viśvakarmā*].

[*Facing p.* 198

felt his study was not adequate, in which case he could return to his teacher to complete it under prescribed discipline [ii, 2, 5, 15 : *yayā vidyayā na virocheta punarāchāryamupetya niyamena sādhayet*]. In another place Āpastamba [i, 2, 5, 6] refers to the same Śvetaketu as a rare example amongst the men of later ages (when rules of studentship are always transgressed) of a scholar who became a Ṛishi by his knowledge of the Veda, but, be it noted, that, as shown in the previous passage, he acquired that knowledge as a householder by observing the vow of studentship for some months in the year. This is another confirmation of the conclusion already stated that in what has been called the Brāhmaṇa period, there were agencies and arrangements for the continuance of studies beyond the normal period of formal studentship,

Plurality of Teachers. The Sūtras also continue the tradition of the Upanishads in another respect. They point to a plurality of teachers for the student. Young Brahmins in olden times, just as now, went from one teacher to the other, learning from each what he knew. Each such teacher would generally know and teach only one Veda and a student would have to learn several Vedas from several teachers. The rules which seemingly require a pupil to stay with one and the same teacher refer only to the principle that the pupil must stay with his teacher until he has learnt the subject which he began with him. This is evident from the following passage of Āpastamba [i, 2, 7, 14] : "If a pupil has more than one teacher, the alms (collected by him) are at the disposal of him to whom he is just then bound." Another passage [i, 2, 8, 26] expressly refers to a pupil "attending to two teachers", while, according to another [i, 2, 7, 26], the student is permitted, in the event of the incompetence of his teacher, "to go to another and study there." Sometimes, the regular teacher may appoint another to do his work. So long as his instruction lasts, the new teacher is to be treated with the same respect as the principal but, according to some, only if he is a worthy person in point of learning and character. In any case, obedience as towards the teacher is not required to be shown towards his substitute. We are also told of teachers younger than their pupils who are not, of course, to show him the obedience proper for the regular teacher. One such teacher was "young Kavi, the son of Aṅgiras, who taught his relatives who were old enough to be fathers, and as he excelled them in sacred knowledge he called them 'Little sons', for a man destitute of sacred knowledge is indeed a child" [Manu, ii, 151–3]. Lastly, three are mentioned persons teaching each other mutually different redactions of the Veda, in which case obedience towards each other is not ordained for them [see Āpastamba, i, 4, 13, 13–17].

Change of Teacher. But teachers could be changed not merely on intellectual grounds. The obedience of the pupil was limited by the conduct of the teacher. We have already adverted to the rule that a pupil is not to obey his teacher if he asks him to commit such crimes as cause loss of caste. But we have again the further regulation that where a teacher transgresses his duties through carelessness or knowingly, the pupil will first point it out to him privately. But if, in spite of this, he does not amend his conduct, the pupil shall either himself perform the religious acts omitted by his teacher or he may forsake him and return home [*Āp.*, i, 1, 4, 25–7].

Qualifications and Duties of Teachers. This leads us to a consideration of the qualifications and duties of the teacher. According to Āpastamba [i, 1, 1, 12–17], he should be a man in whose family sacred learning is hereditary, who himself possesses it, and who is devout in following the law. Under him the sacred science must be studied until the end, provided the teacher does not fall off from the ordinances of the law. He from whom the pupil gathers (*āchinoti*) the knowledge of his religious duties (*dharmān*) is called the Āchārya whom he should never offend, as he is his spiritual father who, by imparting to him the sacred learning, gives him a new life, a second birth which is the best.

Grades of Teachers. There seem to have been different classes or grades of teachers. The *Āchārya* is defined by Manu [ii, 140 f.] to be one who initiates a pupil and teaches him the Veda, together with the *Kalpa* (the Sūtras referring to sacrifices), and the *Rahasyas* [lit. the secret portions, i.e. the Upanishads and their explanation (Medh., Gov., Kull., Rāgh.), or the extremely secret explanation of the Veda and Aṅgas, *not* the Upanishads, because they are included in the term *Veda* (Nār.)]. According to Gautama [i, 9–10] the title *Āchārya* belongs to one who initiates a pupil and teaches him the Veda. According to Vishṇu, the *Āchārya* is he who, having initiated a pupil, instructs him in the Vratas,[1] teaches him *one branch* [2] of the Veda, together with

[1] As already mentioned, the Vratas are certain observances to be kept by him before he is admitted to the regular course of study of the Veda, and again before he is allowed to proceed to the study of the Mahānāmnī verses and to the other higher stages of Vedic learning [*SBE*, vii, p. 121 *n*.].

[2] This is in accordance with the provision by which the studentship is allowed to terminate after twelve years, the period ordinarily taken for learning one Veda.

its Aṅgas. Vasishṭha [iii, 21], however, insists on the teaching of the *whole* Veda for the *Āchārya*. One who teaches only a portion of the Veda or who teaches the Aṅgas of the Veda is to be called *Upādhyāya* (sub-teacher) according to him. Manu [ii, 141] and Vishṇu [xxix, 2], however, regard the *Upādhyāya* as the person who teaches the aforesaid subjects " for a fee " or " for his livelihood ". The *Āchārya* is ten times more venerable than the *Upādhyāya* [Manu, ii, 145]; he is chief among all Gurus [Gautama, ii, 50]; he is called an *Atiguru*, along with father and mother [Vishṇu, xxxi, 1–2].

Obligations of Teacher to Pupil. There are prescribed regulations governing the teacher's relations with, and duties towards, his pupil. The teacher is to adopt and love the pupil as his own son so that Baudhāyana [*Dha. Su.*, i, 2, 48] considers a teacher devoid of a natural issue as not issue-less if he has a pupil. He should teach him the sacred science with whole-hearted attention without withholding from him any part of the whole Law. He is described as leading the pupil from darkness of ignorance to the light of learning [*Āp. Dh. S.*, i, 10, 11] and uncovering that light hidden in a cover [Aparārka on *Yājña.*, i, 212]. A teacher who neglects the instruction of his pupil ceases to be his teacher [*Āp.*, i, 2, 8, 27]. Such neglect is described as giving the pupil work which interferes with his studies (Na cha cnaṁ adhyayanavighnena ātmārtheshu uparundhyāt anāpatsu). Thus, though it is the duty of the pupil to render services to the teacher to please him, the teacher must be careful to see that the pupil is not exploited for his own purposes to the detriment of his studies. Such services are meant for the pupil's own moral improvement and not solely for the economic advantages of the teacher. In times of distress, however, the teacher was permitted to accept the assistance of his pupil [*Āp.*, ib., 24–5].

Punishment of Pupils. These old-world teachers were against hard punishments being inflicted on their young pupils. According to Gautama, " as a rule the pupil shall not be punished corporally. If no other course is possible, he may be corrected with a thin rope or cane. If the teacher strikes him with any other instrument, he is liable to punishment by the king (i.e. under the law) " [ii, 42–4]. Manu [viii, 299–300] allows a pupil who has committed faults to be beaten with a rope or split bamboo but only on the back part of the body, never on a noble part. The teacher who strikes him otherwise will incur the same guilt as a thief. Gautama, as we have seen, permits bodily punishment only as the last resource, when other means of reformation fail. These other means are defined by Āpastamba to consist, first, of reproof by the teacher, and then of " frightening, fasting, bathing in cold water, and banishment from the teacher's presence ", which are to be applied according to the magnitude of the pupil's fault until the pupil is completely corrected and leaves off sinning [i, 2, 8, 28–9].

Teacher's Remuneration. We have already seen that the teacher proper who was called the Āchārya did not accept any remuneration for his work. He did the work of teaching as a matter of religious duty. The admission of a pupil was not a source of income to the teacher but an addition of a member to his family like that caused by the birth of a son. The teacher and the pupil were not connected with each other by the " cash-nexus " but by ties of spiritual relationship whereby both were repaying the debt they owed to the Ṛishis by the pursuit of knowledge. Manu says that a student should not pay anything to his teacher before he finishes his education [ii, 245]. A teacher teaching for fees is condemned as being guilty of a sin, *upapātaka* [*Vishṇu*, xxxvii, 20, 21, 34 ; *Yājña*, iii, 236, 242]. Uśanā [iv, 24] brands him as a *Vṛittika*. The *Smṛiti-chandrikā* (p. 140) not merely condemns the acceptance of a fee by the teacher but also any proposal for it as a condition of the pupil's admission. The *Saura Purāṇa* [x, 42] condemns to hell teacher and pupil working on the basis of any fees fixed. This tradition receives its classic expression in the *Mālavikāgnimitram* [i, 17] where Kālidasa condemns the learning which is sold as an article of merchandise and means of livelihood (*yasyāgamaḥ kevalajīvikāyai taṁ jñānapaṇyaṁ vaṇijaṁ vadaṁti*). The teacher who imparts instruction for a fee would be called an *Upādhyāya*. But though the *Āchārya* could not accept a fee from a pupil *under* instruction, he could accept the same from the pupil whose instruction was completed. In fact, it was one of the obligations of the Brahmachārin to bring to a close the period of his formal pupilage by making presents to his teacher. Of course, in the majority of cases it could not be expected that such presents would be at all any adequate remuneration for the amount of labour and expense involved in supporting and educating a student for a minimum period of twelve years. It was a case, in modern parlance, of free board, lodging, medical aid, clothing, and tuition given to the student during a continuous and long period exceeding a decade, the cost of which could not be properly assessed and much less paid in the shape of parting presents, especially in the case of a student of the Brahmin caste which was distinguished for its phenomenal poverty. It is, therefore, a misconception to argue that these parting gifts of a student to his teacher after completion of his studies disprove the honorary character of the work of the teacher and show the incorrectness of the prevailing assumption which makes it out to be a labour of love, a virtue which is its own reward, while it is essentially, looking beneath the appearances, a mere economic transaction.

A Pupil's presents to his Teacher after end of Pupilage. According to Manu, "he who knows the sacred law must not present any gift to his teacher before the *Samāvartana* (rite performed by student to end his studentship); but when, with the permission of his teacher, he is about to take a final bath, let him *procure* a present for the venerable man according to his ability, viz. a field, a cow, a horse, a parasol and shoes, a seat, grain, even vegetables, and thus give *pleasure* to his teacher" [ii, 245–6]. The word "procure" implies that the student is ordinarily of such circumstances that he has to collect the gifts for his teacher by begging. This supposition is indeed clearly confirmed by a passage in Āpastamba [i, 2, 7, 19–21] in which he enjoins that the student "shall procure in a righteous manner the fee for the teaching of the Veda to be given to his teacher according to his power". The "righteous manner" means that unless his teacher is in distress and need of immediate relief, the student is not to take a fee from an Ugra ["either the offspring of a Vaiśya and of a Śūdra woman or a twice-born man, who perpetrates dreadful deeds" (Haradatta quoted in *SBE.*, ii, p. 27)] or from a Śūdra, though "some declare that it is lawful at any time to take the money for the teacher" from such persons. Efforts of poor students to procure such fees for their teachers are mentioned in the *Jātakas*, as stated below [e.g. No. 478] or in the *Raghuvaṁśa* of Kālidāsa in the story of Kautsa [Canto v]. The *Mahābhārata* mentions a typical case of King Poshya asking his wife to make a gift of her precious *kuṇḍala* (ear-rings) to the poor Snātaka, Utaṅka. It will thus appear that the payment of the fee is enjoined more as a religious act formally bringing to a close the period of studentship and marking the fulfilment of a sacred vow than as any kind of material remuneration for useful services rendered. Indeed, one text emphasizes the ideal position that "there is no object in the world by the gift of which a pupil can discharge his debt to his teacher, even if he has taught him only one letter [Ekam api aksharaṁ yastu guruḥ śishye nivedayet | Pṛithivyāṁ nāsti tad dravyaṁ yad dattvā so'nṛiṇī bhavet]. But this rule did not apply to the exceptional cases of the rich. In the *Mahābhārata*, Bhīshma appointed Droṇa as the teacher of the Kaurava princes by first paying him a handsome fee [i, 142, 1]. The *Jātakas*, as cited below, are full of cases of rich and royal guardians paying in advance the whole remuneration to the teachers of their wards. In the *Milinda Pañha* [i, 17], the father of Nāgasena pays to the teacher first, as he sends his son to him for Vedic study. But the idealist monk, Nāgasena, refuses the lavish gifts of his royal pupil, Menander, who humbly urges their acceptance to escape from the scandal of not paying his teacher [ib., i, 134–5]. Along with rich students thus paying their teacher in advance, the Buddhist works tell of poor students who were admitted by their teachers as "free" students, so that poverty was not allowed to operate as a bar to education in the system of the times. But such students were differently treated from the regular students. They were employed on manual work for the school in the daytime when the teacher was occupied in instructing the other students. He would, however, give the evenings to their instruction [cf. Dhammāntevāsikā āchāriyassa kammaṁ katvā rattiṁ sippamuggaṇhaṁti āchāriyabhāgadāyakā gehe jeṭṭhaputtā viya hutvā sippameva uggaṇhaṁti (*Tilamuṭṭhi Jātaka*, No. 252)].

Freedom of Honorary Teachers. It may also be noted in this connection that, on account of the absence of any economic relationship between the teacher and the taught, the independence of the former as regards the choice and admission of the latter was complete and absolute. A most thoroughgoing test of mental and moral fitness was imposed on the student whose fulfilment of same gained him admission and not any other consideration. The spirit of the system is beautifully expressed in the following passages from Manu [ii, 112–15] : "*Even in times of dire distress, a teacher of the Veda should rather die with his knowledge than sow it in barren soil.* Sacred Learning approached a Brāhmaṇa and said to him : 'I am thy treasure, preserve me, deliver me not to a scorner' [nor to a wicked man, nor to one of uncontrolled passions' (Vishṇu, xxix, 9 ; Vasishṭha, ii, 8] ; so (preserved) I shall become strong. But deliver me, as to the keeper of thy treasure, to a Brāhmaṇa whom thou shalt know to be pure, of subdued senses, chaste and attentive." The same spirit is expressed by Baudhāyana [i, 2, 4, 2]: "As fire consumes dry grass, even so the Veda asked for but not honoured destroys the inquirer." In a word, the passport for admission to such Brahmanical schools was constituted by the inherent fitness of the pupil for the Vedic studies, a fitness of which the recognized tests were a desire and aptitude for learning and a spirit of obedience and discipline. Before admitting the student, the teacher would satisfy himself that he has in him the vital principle of growth, an inherent responsiveness to moral stimulus and that he is not like dull, dead, inert matter incapable of any expansion.

Main Aim of Education was Development of Personality. These tests for admission and the regulations governing the life of the student after the admission during the period of his education were no doubt determined by the very ideals and aims of that education. We have already seen how in the scheme of this ancient education moral training fills a scarcely less important part than mental training. The development of the inner nature or character of the student was deemed as one of the essential objects of education. The value attached to this aspect of education is apparent from the following significant declaration of Manu [ii, 97] in the chapter treating of the rules of studentship. "Neither the study of the Veda nor liberality nor sacrifices nor any self-imposed restraint nor austerities can ever procure the attainment of rewards to a man whose heart is contaminated by sensuality." This definitely and emphatically lays down the ancient view that mere intellectual development without the development of character, learning without piety, proficiency in the sacred lore with a deficiency in the practices it implies, will defeat the very ends of studentship. Thus the part of education that deals with the *life* of the students probably fills a larger place in the ancient pedagogic scheme than the part that deals with the mere intellect. Indeed, as the elaborate regulations we have already considered show us, the intellectual part of education covered only a part of the year; the lecture of the Vedic Professors continued during about half the year, the term practically beginning with the rainy season, while even from this comparatively short period we have to deduct the time taken by a fairly numerous list of holidays. But the strict and rigid rules governing the daily life of the student knew of no relaxation or interruption; the course of moral training provided for no holidays; the disciplinary regulations acted unceasingly as impersonal teachers, exercising a sleepless vigilance and control over the elastic and tender natures committed to their care. Daily has the student to get up early in the morning before sunrise, failing which he has to perform a penance [fasting the next day and muttering the Sāvitrī (Manu, ii, 220)]. He has to say his prayers twice a day at sunrise and sunset. Every morning and evening he has to go round the village begging and whatever is given him he has to hand over to his master. He is himself to eat nothing except what his master gives him. He has to fetch water, to gather fuel for the altar, to sweep the ground round the hearth, and to wait on his master day and night. This looks like menial service interfering with the student's studies according to our modern ideas, but we must bear in mind the accompanying explanatory regulation that the teacher is never to utilize the labour of his pupil for his own selfish, household purposes and Āpastamba's definite declaration that the observance of those rules is in the interests of the student's own welfare [i, 2, 5, 9]. Nor must we forget to consider that along with a progressive course of studies was prescribed a progressive course of austerities and discipline in the form of the various Vratas to be observed for promotion to higher stages of learning. The growth of the whole nature of the boy, and not the growth of his intellect merely, was the objective of this ancient pedagogy. The raw material is received into the workshop after due examination as to its soundness ; it is then treated to different processes of manufacture ; and finally sent out to the world as a finished product. The making of the nation or the country was in the charge of these schools. Their aim was to produce not mere recluses or scholars but whole men, ideal householders who would perfect family, society, and country.

Higher Education open to first three Castes. It has been first stated that the nation was in the making in these schools. But a doubt is sometimes expressed that the nation as a whole did not benefit by such schools which were close corporations not open to all but only to a select class, the Brahmins. The evidence adduced above will show the falsity of this charge. But let a higher authority speak on the point. The following remarks are made by Max Müller [*Lectures on the Origin of Religion*, p. 349] : "Before the ancient language and literature of India had been made accessible to European scholarship, it was the fashion to represent the Brahmins as a set of priests jealously guarding the treasures of their sacred wisdom from the members of all the other castes and thus maintaining their

PLATE IX

POLANNĀRUVA

A Sage reading a palm-leaf MS; supposed by O. C. Gangoly to be the Vedic Ṛishi Pulastya after whom is named the city Pulasta-nagara = Polannāruva in Ceylon [Plate 51 of Coomaraswamy's *Viśvakarmā*].

[*Facing p. 206*

ascendancy over an ignorant people. It requires but the slightest acquaintance with Sanskrit Literature to see the utter groundlessness of such a charge. One caste only, the Śūdras, were prohibited from knowing the Veda. With the other castes, the military and civil classes, a knowledge of the Veda, so far from being prohibited, was a sacred duty. All had to learn the Veda; the only privilege of the Brahmins was that they alone were allowed to teach it. It was not even the intention of the Brahmins that only the traditional forms of faith and the purely ritual observances should be communicated to the lower castes, and a kind of esoteric religion, that of the Upanishads, be reserved for the Brahmins. On the contrary, there are many indications to show that these esoteric doctrines emanated from the second rather than from the first caste."

The view which Max Müller thinks was in vogue before the discovery of Sanskrit Literature unfortunately still persists with great vigour in some quarters even in this country and it is necessary in the interests of truth to combat it. Indeed, one passage of Manu [ii, 165] proves conclusively that the rules of studentship applied not merely to the highest caste, but practically to the entire Indo-Aryan people: "An Āryan must study the whole Veda together with the Rahasyas, performing at the same time various kinds of austerities and the vows prescribed by the rules of the Veda." It is to be noted that the *Āryas* were made up of the three twice-born classes and the Śūdras making up the lowest castes were outside the pale of Aryan society.[1] Regarding the other feature or fact noted by Max Müller in our ancient educational system, viz. that it was a system of compulsory universal education, we may bring together a few select passages from the Sūtra works. "A twice-born man who, not having studied the Veda, applies himself to other (and worldly

[1] See the account of social divisions of Ancient India in my *Local Government in Ancient India*. Cf. Max Müller [*Lectures on the Origin of Religion*, p. 350 f.]: "We find the old Indian Society divided, first of all, into two classes, the *Āryas* or nobles born, and *Śūdras*, the servants or slaves. Secondly, we find that the Āryas consist of Brāhmaṇas, the spiritual nobility, the Kshatriyas or Rājanyas, the military nobility, and the Vaiśyas, the citizens. . . A much more important feature, however, of the ancient Vedic society than the four castes consists in the four āśramas or stages. A Brāhmaṇa, as a rule, passes through four, a noble man through three, a citizen through two, a Śūdra through one of these stages [*Āryavidyā-sudhānidhi*, p. 153]. . . As soon as the child of an Ārya is born, nay, even before his birth, his parents have to perform certain *saṁskāras*. As many as twenty-five *saṁskāras* are mentioned, sometimes even more. Śūdras only were not admitted to these rites; while Āryas who omitted to perform them were considered no better than Śūdra. (According to Yama, Śūdras also may receive these sacraments *up to the upanayana* but unaccompanied by Vedic verses)."

study) soon falls, even while living, to the condition of a Śūdra and his descendants after him" (Manu, ii, 168). We have already cited other passages [e.g. Manu, ii, 39] in which it is laid down that persons who do not initiate themselves within the periods fixed for their castes "become Vrātyas (outcasts), excluded from the Sāvitrī and despised by the Aryans". It was not, however, mere social degradation with which breaches of the sacred and compulsory duty of a man to educate himself were punished. Vasishṭha [iii, 4] quotes a very remarkable passage from Manu in which it is laid down that "the king shall punish that village where Brāhmaṇas, unobservant of their sacred duties and *ignorant of the Veda*, subsist by begging; for it feeds robbers". Thus the state enforced this wholesome law of compulsory education framed by society by penalizing a village that even acquiesced in the culpable ignorance of Brahmins by giving them alms to which they were not entitled, and such Brahmins were to be treated not merely as *Śūdras* but also as *robbers*, thus meriting both social and moral odium. It is thus that we can also very well realize the force and truth of the following legitimate boast of a king in the Upanishads: "In my kingdom there is no thief, no miser, no drunkard, no man without an altar in his house and no ignorant person" [*Chhānd.*, v, 11, 5].

Education of Women. The Vedic tradition was continued as regards education of women. The *Bṛihat-devatā* calls the Rigvedic Women-Ṛishis (such as Ghoshā, Romaśā, Lopāmudrā, or Viśvavārā) as *Brahma-Vādinīs*. Some of the Smṛiti texts understand by a *Brahma-Vādinī* a Kumārī who does not marry. Hārīta [xxi, 23] says: "Women are of two classes: (1) *Brahma-Vādinī*, (2) *Sadyo-badhū*. The former is eligible for Upanayana, Agnyādhāna (Sacrifice to Fire), Veda-Study, and practice of begging within the household. The *Sadyo-badhū* had only to perform Upanayana in some form before she is married." Yama also says: "In times of yore, girls were eligible for (1) *Mauñjī-bandhana* (i.e. Upanayana), (2) study of Veda, and (3) *Sāvitrī-vāchana* (use of Sāvitrī Mantra)."

The Śrauta or Gṛihya Sūtras mention Vedic Mantras being uttered by the wife at ceremonies along with her husband [e.g. Āśvalāyana *Śr. S.*, i, 11; *Gobhila Gr. S.*, i, 3; ii, 3; *Āpas.*, xii, 3, 12; *Pārask.*, ix, 2, 1]. Gobhila [*Gr. S.*, i, 3] states that the wife should be educated to be able to take part in sacrifices (*nahi khalu anadhītya śaknoti patnī hotumiti*). Again, Adhikaraṇa III of Chapter I of Jaimini's *Pūrva-Mīmāṁsā* is taken by Sabara Swāmī to deal with the *equal* rights of men and women in the performance of sacrifices, while Madhavāchārya (*Nyāya-Mālā-Vistara*, p. 335), commenting on same states: "Asyaivādhikaraṇasya anusāreṇa ashṭavarshaṁ brāhmaṇaṁ upanayīta taṁ adhyāpayīta ityatrāpi striyopi adhikāraḥ": "Brāhmaṇa boys of eight years are to be initiated and taught and the same right also belongs to girls." Lastly, we may cite the statement of Hemādri that "Kumārīs, unmarried girls, should be taught Vidyā and Dharmanīti. An educated Kumārī brings good to the families of both her father and husband. So she should be married to a learned husband (*manīshī*), as she is a *vidushī*."

Non-Brahmin Teachers. There is one other statement of Max Müller which also requires to be qualified. He says that the teachers were recruited only and exclusively from the Brahman caste. Exceptions were, however, allowed to this rule. Baudhāyana [i, 2, 3, 41] permits "study under a non-Brahmin teacher in times of distress". This is confirmed by Āpastamba [ii, 2, 5, 25], who says that "in times of distress a Brāhmaṇa may study under a Kshatriya or Vaiśya" and also by Gautama [vii, 1]. Such a non-Brahmin teacher was to be paid due honour by the Brahman student throughout the long period of his studentship. He must "walk behind him and obey him" [ib.]. The same injunction is also given by Manu [ii, 241]: "he shall walk behind and serve such a teacher, as long as the instruction lasts." The supply of non-Brahmin teachers in the country was, of course, created by the system which freely admitted them to the Brahminical schools and made education compulsory for all. We may in this connection recall the eminence achieved by Kings and Kshatriyas in the realm of highest knowledge of which they figure as teachers in the *Brāhmaṇas* and Upanishads, kings like Janaka, Ajataśatru, Aśvapati, or Jaivali, and also a significant passage in the *Kāṭhaka Saṁhitā* [ix, 16], prescribing a ceremony by which a non-Brahmaṇa who had mastered the Vedas but was not faring well in life could achieve his due reputation and affluence (*yaḥ abrāhmaṇaḥ vidyāmanūchya naiva rochate sa etānśchaturhotṟīn vyāchakshīta*).

Ceremony ending Studentship; 'Samāvartana' (graduation). The studentship was brought to a close by what has been termed the *Samāvartana* (lit. the returning home of the student) ceremony to be performed by the pupil. It included a number of acts signifying the end of the austerities imposed upon the condition of studentship. First, the Brahmachārī was confined in a room in the morning lest his superior lustre puts to shame the sun who shines in the lustre borrowed of him [*Bhāradvāja Gṛi. S.*, ii, 1, 8]! No higher compliment to education can be conceived. Coming out of the room at midday, he shaved his head and beard and cut off all marks of his studentship. Then followed the bath accompanied by the use of powder, perfumes, ground sandalwood, and the like to be presented by the friends and relations of the student, and then were also thrown into the water all the external signs of his *brahmacharya* such as the upper and lower garments, girdle, staff, skin. After the bath, he becomes a *Snātaka* wearing new garments, two ear-rings, and a perforated pellet of sandalwood overlaid with gold at its aperture—the gold which brings gain, superiority in *battles* and in *assemblies*—and he prays that he may be loved of all, Brahmins, Kshatriyas, Vaiśyas, Śūdras, and Kings [see *Hiraṇyakeśin*, i, 3, 9–11]. Some of the Sūtras distinguish three kinds of *Snātakas* [Gobhila, iii, 5, 21–3; Pāraskara, ii, 5, 3, 32–5]. "He who performs the Samāvartana ceremony after having finished the study of the Veda but before the time of his vows has expired is a *Vidyā-snātaka*. He who performs the Samāvartana after his vows have expired but before he has finished the study of the Veda is a *Vrata-snātaka*. He who performs the Samāvartana after having finished both is a *Vidyā-Vrata-Snātaka*." "Of these the last ranks foremost; the two others are equal to each other." Thus a *Snātaka* (one who has bathed) or a *Samāvṛitta* (one who has returned home) would be, according to modern ideas, one who had taken his degree. A *homa* or sacrifice was performed with a prayer that the *Snātaka* will have any number of pupils to teach in his turn [*Baudhā. Gṛi. S.*, ii, 6]. Then he, donned in his new robes, was to pay a visit to the local learned Assembly in a chariot or on an elephant to be introduced to them as a full-fledged scholar by his teacher [*Drāhyāyana Gṛi. S.*, iii, 1, 26; Āpa. *Gṛi. S.*, i, 11, 5].

A Snātaka, however, was permitted to return to his teacher and live with him for purposes of further study for a period not exceeding four months [*Baudhāyana*, ii, 1, 46]. This shows that facilities for study did not end with studentship. At the same time, studentship was not to be unduly prolonged. Baudhayāna enjoins that one must marry in youth before he grows grey hairs [i, 2, 31]. Śukra prescribes deportation or imprisonment of persons who continue a life of asceticism and celibacy to escape from their social obligations [iv, 1, 105]. At the time of parting, the teacher would say to the Snātaka the following valedictory words: "Apply thyself henceforth to other duties" [*Āpaś.*, i, 2, 8, 30]. The teacher's valedictory message is given in a more elaborate form in one of the Upanishads (cited above).

The Rule of Oral Teaching. We have now considered the salient features of the educational system of ancient India as exhibited in the Sūtra literature. There is one fundamental aspect of that system which clearly distinguishes it from the modern system of education, viz. its complete independence of the external aids given to learning by the art of writing. This basal factor will easily explain the characteristic features of the ancient Indian educational methods which almost follow from it as corollaries. It is not yet definitely known when the art of writing itself was evolved in India. But the point to be noted in this connection is that even when the art of writing was completely prevalent in the country, the indigenous teachers and educationists deliberately omitted to take advantage of it for purposes of instruction. The Vedic system of oral teaching, like everything else to be found in the Vedas, was the first and last word on the subject of pedagogic methods; that was the only authoritative system to be pursued through the subsequent ages in spite of all material facilities they might bring in their course. It is hardly to be doubted that by about 500 B.C. at the latest there must have been developed the complete Sanskrit alphabet on phonetic principles, the alphabet assumed in the grammar of Pāṇini (giving him the latest possible date, viz. fourth century B.C.) and yet it was a long time before writing was used for the preservation and propagation of our sacred literature, for it was relegated to the sphere of business or secular life. There was a traditional opinion absolutely condemning the acquisition of knowledge from written sources. This opinion has been already cited from the *Mahābhārata* and *Tantra-Vārttika* of Kumārila.

This view is only consistent with, and indeed the natural outcome of, that held regarding the Veda itself which has thus been elaborated by Kumārila: "The Veda is distinctly to be perceived by means of the senses. It exists, like a pot or any other object, in man. Perceiving it in another man, people learn it and remember it. Then others again perceiving it, as it is remembered by these, learn it and remember it, and thus hand it on to others. Therefore, the theologian concludes, the Veda is without a beginning." And again: "Before we hear the word *Veda*, we perceive, as different from all other objects, and as different from other Vedas, something in the form of the Rigveda that exists within the readers, and things in the form of *Mantras* and *Brāhmaṇas*, different from others." From these explanations it is clear that when a material existence is attributed to the Veda, it is conceived of as existing only in the minds of men, written if at all on the tablets of their hearts—and not as something written on paper. It is also clear how this conception determines the method by which the Vedic learning has to be preserved and propagated. It is held to be too holy to be left to exist as an external object; it must live in the memory of man as a part of him to be cherished dearly in his heart, and not as something external or foreign to him. It is thus that the Smṛitis constantly refer to Vedic knowledge as the cause of a man's second birth, because its assimilation is supposed to effect a radical transformation of the student's nature.

Cultivation of Memory. Thus this view of the subject-matter of learning necessarily moulded the methods and system under which it was to be imparted. Hence we find that the preliminary stage of learning was the learning by heart the sacred texts through indefinite repetition and rehearsal by both the teacher and the taught. This means that the cultivation of memory was accorded a most important place in the ancient system of education. The powers of verbal memory were accordingly developed to a degree almost incredible in modern times. As Max Müller well puts it: "We can form no opinion of the power of memory in a state of society so different from ours as the Indian Parishads are from our universities. Feats of memory, such as we hear of now and then, show that our notions of the limits of that faculty are quite arbitrary. Our own memory has been systematically undermined for many generations. To speak of nothing else, one sheet of *The Times* newspaper every morning is quite sufficient to distract and unsettle the healthiest memory." As Max Müller has further stated in some of his writings, this dependence on verbal memory for the transmission of sacred literature has continued to this day in a sense. "Even at the present day when MSS. are neither scarce nor expensive, the young Brahmins who learn the songs of the Veda, the Brāhmaṇas, and the Sūtras, invariably learn them from oral tradition and know them by heart. They spend year after year under the guidance of their teacher, learning a little, day after day, repeating what they have learnt as part of their daily devotion until at last they have mastered their subject and are able to become teachers in turn." Max Müller himself arranged to collect various readings for his edition of the Rigveda not from MSS. but from the oral tradition of Vaidik Śrotriyas who are fittingly described by the Indian scholar, Mr. Shankar Pandurang, who was entrusted with the work, in the following passage: "*I am collecting a few of our walking Rigveda MSS.*, taking your text as basis." We may also have in this connection some idea of the quantity of literary burden and matter carried in the small heads of these young learners. The Rigveda alone, as we have already stated, consists of 1,017 (1,028) poems, 10,580 verses and about 153,826 words. But besides the Rigveda, the Sūtra works mention a number of other subjects to be learnt by the student. An Indian scholar informed Max Müller that even so late as the early 'seventies, the Vedic curriculum comprised the following: (1) The *Saṁhitā or hymns*; (2) The *Brāhmaṇa*; (3) The *Āraṇyaka*; (4) The *Gṛihya Sūtras*; (5–10) The six *Vedāṅgas*.

Max Müller calculates that these ten books contain nearly 30,000 lines, with each line reckoned as thirty-two syllables. According to his informant, this course was to be finished in eight years. Now, "a pupil studies every day during the eight years except on the holidays, the so-called *anadhyāya*, non-reading days. There being 360 days in a lunar year, the eight years would give him 2,880 days. From this 384 holidays have to be deducted, leaving him 2,496 work-days during the eight years." On this computation, a student of the Rigveda has to learn about twelve slokas a day, a sloka of thirty-two syllables.

Different Forms of Vedic Texts as Aids to Memory. This vast literary matter was memorized by suitable mechanical methods invented for the purpose. The system of rote-learning has been well described in the Ṛik-Prātiśākhya we have already cited, but the description implies a variety of methods naturally evolved under the system. These methods aim at different arrangements of the words of the texts, and each such arrangement is given a distinct name. We take the following from the account of Sir R. G. Bhandarkar in the *Indian Antiquary* (1874): "In the *Saṁhitā text*, all words are joined according to the phonetic rules peculiar to Sanskrit. In the *Pada* text, the words are divided and compounds also are dissolved. In the *Krama* text, suppose we have a line of eleven words, they are arranged as follows, the rules of Sandhi being observed throughout for letters and accent : 1, 2 ; 2, 3 ; 3, 4 ; 4, 5 ; 5, 6 ; 6, 7 ; 7, 8 ; etc. The last word of each verse, and half-verse too is repeated with *iti* (*veshṭana*). In the *Jaṭā*, the words are arranged as follows : 1, 2, 2, 1, 1, 2 ; 2, 3, 3, 2, 2, 3 ; 3, 4, 4, 3, 3, 4 ; etc. The last word of each verse and half-verse is repeated with *iti*. In the *Ghana*, the words are arranged as follows : 1, 2, 2, 1, 1, 2, 3, 3, 2, 1, 1, 2, 3 ; 2, 3, 3, 2, 2, 3, 4, 4, 3, 2, 2, 3 ; 2, 3, 3, 2, 2, 3, 4, 4, 3, 2, 2, 3, 4 ; 3, 4, 4, 3, 3, 4, 5, 5, 4, 3, 3, 4, 5 ; etc. The last two words of each verse and half-verse are repeated with *iti*, as, e.g., 7, 8, 8, 7, 7, 8 ; 8 *iti* 8 ; and again, 10, 11, 11, 10, 10, 11 ; 11 *iti* 11. Compounds are dissolved (*avagraha*). The object of these different arrangements is simply the most accurate preservation of the sacred text. Nor is the recital merely mechanical, the attention being constantly required for the phonetic changes of final and initial letters, and for the constant modification of the accents. The different accents are distinctly shown by modulations of the voice."

Merits of the Method. Thus this wonderful mnemonic system was developed to aid the memory in its responsible work of preserving the nation's sacred literature, and there is no doubt that it admirably achieved its work. As remarked by Max Müller, "the texts of the Veda have been handed down to us with such accuracy that there is hardly a variant reading in the proper sense of the word, or even an uncertain accent, in the whole of the Rigveda. There are corruptions in the text which can be discovered by critical investigation ; but even these corruptions must have formed part of the recognized text since it was finally settled. Some of them belong to different Śākhās or recensions, and are discussed in their bearings by ancient authorities.

"Thus, as far back as we know anything of India, we find that the years which we in modern times spend at school and at university were spent by the sons of ancient India in learning, from the mouth of a teacher, their sacred literature. Thus the Vedic succession was never broken—for this oral learning and teaching came to be one of the compulsory religious duties of the people, one of the great *yajñas* or sacrifices."

Personal Touch in Education. Education has been aptly defined as the transmission of life from life to life. This ideal seems to have been literally realized under this ancient pedagogic system which did not permit the introduction of any dull, dead, inert matter—the written literature—as an instrument of education. Some of the Indian religions provide for intermediaries between God the Most High and sinful humanity below to work out the latter's salvation, but in the educational organization there was no intervening medium between the guru and his disciple. The teacher was the direct and sole source of light and life and the pupil must depend upon him absolutely for his educational salvation, for there was no other source of knowledge available in the country. Thus there was always a personal touch, a human element, a living inspiration in such instruction which helped to make it a vital and not a mechanical and monotonous process: it was a commerce of life, a communion of souls.

Teacher's control over spread of Knowledge. We may now trace the further consequences and corollaries of this system of oral tradition under which the education was imparted. The deliberate adhesion to the principle of confining the sacred texts to memory instead of trusting them to writing produced certain characteristic results. In the first place, the spread of the sacred texts was completely controlled by those to the keeping of whose memory they were committed. Written works, like most other material things, are economic goods, traffic in which cannot be controlled. But the knowledge that is carried in the head is a monopoly of the knower and is devoid of that externality and materiality which would make it capable of appropriation by others. The spread of such knowledge is thus absolutely determined by the choice and sweet will of the knower who has the liberty to dictate on what terms he would exercise his choice. In the inner chambers of his soul have been stored up the literary treasures to which no one can have access unless he consents to unlock them with the key he holds. Thus the system could logically lay down conditions of admission which would eliminate all those who were not deemed to be sufficiently qualified, by aptitude, temperament, and character, to receive instruction in the sacred learning. Thus undeserving persons would be naturally and automatically excluded from the study of the sacred texts which stood in no fear of being misused, reviled, and desecrated. Thus the very conditions of teaching helped to make the teacher absolutely independent as regards the selection of his pupils.

Knowledge insured against risks. Secondly, the system contributed to the preservation and propagation of its literature in a most remarkable and unique manner. Nowadays human knowledge is stored up for the most part in books stocked in libraries, and is thus made liable to all those risks to which all material things are liable. History records many an instance of political vandalism which has deliberately destroyed valuable libraries under a spirit of bigoted animosity against the knowledge they stored up and preserved. Many a library, if not a victim to human malice, has succumbed to nature's destructive agencies or physical accidents such as earthquake, deluge, or fire. Recently, the destruction of Louvain has beaten the record of the horrors of war and barbarism. But the knowledge and culture of ancient India were not left from the very outset to the tender mercies of these risky and precarious, faithless and unreliable agencies. The human mind—and no perishable material storehouse—was the repository of our ancient, accumulated wisdom. And, if the individual dies, the nation lives. Thus Indian culture has been immortally preserved through an unbroken succession of teachers. Every literary man of ancient India was himself a living library, so to speak. Thus the storage and preservation of the learning of the country were effected by means of what were practically immaterial and immortal agencies. It would appear as if the Vedas which, according to orthodox traditional opinion, are not perishable books but eternal verities have also evolved their appropriate methods of transmission from age to age. There were no centralized libraries wherein was accumulated the wisdom of the ages, so that to strike at them would mean striking at the sources of knowledge. There was the widest possible diffusion of learning through the millions of the "living libraries" and domestic schools of ancient India that helped to insure her culture against the risks alike from Nature and Man—from the destructive effects of physical accidents and political revolutions. And the result of this remarkable system is, as has been well pointed out by Max Müller, that at the present moment if all the MSS. of the Vedas were lost we should still be able to recover the whole of them from the memory of the Śrotriyas of India; and that, further, "if writing had never been invented, if printing had never been invented, if India had never been occupied by England, young Brahmins in their hundreds and thousands would probably have been engaged just the same in learning and saying by heart the simple prayers first uttered on the Sarasvatī and the other rivers of the Panjab by Vasishṭha, Viśvāmitra, Śyāvāśva, and others."

A feat of memory in spreading Knowledge. A remarkable example of a feat of memory and of the way in which this system of oral tradition could achieve the spread of learning from one province of India to another through her "moving libraries" is furnished by the history of the rise of the Navadvīpa school of Logic in Bengal. The founder of that school was Vāsudeva Sārvabhauma who, having completed his study of the Upanishads at Benares, sought the instruction of the renowned scholar Pakshadhara Miśra of Mithilā which was then (in the fifteenth century) the most important centre of learning in Northern India. It was a condition imposed by Pakshadhara Miśra upon his pupils that they were not to transcribe any copy of *Chintāmaṇi* by Gaṅgeśa Upādhyāya, the best work on Logic, of which the only MS. was in his possession, so that the college of Mithilā might enjoy its monopoly in regard to instruction of Logic. Equally valuable were also the interpretations and commentaries of Pakshadhara. This monopoly was, however, broken down by the memory of the pupil Vāsudeva who got by heart the four Parts of *Chintāmaṇi*, its annotations, and also a greater part of the famous work *Kusumāñjali*, and came to Nadia where he established a School which soon outrivalled Mithilā as a centre of learning. Thus the spread of learning overcame its physical barriers.

A Teacher's obligation to conserve and spread Knowledge as its Custodian. Thirdly, this particular system of transmitting knowledge had the natural effect of producing a keen sense of responsibility in those who came to be the custodians and guardians of that knowledge. Every teacher felt that his primary and paramount duty was to discharge himself of the sacred obligation he owed to the *Ṛishis*, to the cause of culture and learning, by finding proper pupils to whom he might communicate the knowledge borne by him. That knowledge he could not permit by any means to die with him. Thus a serious and solemn responsibility attached to the position of a teacher as the trustee of the nation's culture, and the violation or non-fulfilment of that sacred trust was one of the gravest of sins. Indeed, every teacher took to his profession as a supreme religious duty and as he used to take a number of pupils he would have the satisfaction of finding that he has been able to create in them several centres and sources of knowledge where there was only one such centre and source, and that he has, by his personal contribution, amply repaid the debt he owes to the cause of the culture of his country.

Teacher's Home as School. Fourthly, the system of oral tradition rested upon a continuous personal connection between the teacher and the taught which could be cultivated only in the home. The domestic system of education was the inevitable consequence of the particular pedagogic methods employed. Memorizing a vast quantity of texts with absolute accuracy in the pronunciation of every accent and word thereof implied the ready and constant supervision on the part of the teacher such as can be exercised only in the teacher's home upon pupils who would live there at all hours. This result could not be achieved under a system of temporary connection for a few hours only between the teacher and the taught as in modern schools and colleges. Thus the ancient educational arrangements insisting on the residence of the pupil in the home of his teacher were demanded by the very system of rote-learning in vogue in the country.

Oral Teaching determines its Period. Fifthly, the period of such residence and studentship, the time required for the completion of the study of the normal curriculum were also determined on similar principles. The minimum period of twelve years prescribed for studentship was none too long if we consider the quantity of literature which had to be assimilated by the memory (of which an account has been already given), and the number of non-reading days allowed and the prescribed length of the academic term during which lectures and new lessons were given.

Study of One Subject the Rule. Sixthly, the system had the merit or demerit of being able to produce only specialists, mere masters of one subject. As Max Müller justly remarks, " the ambition to master more than one subject is hardly known in India." We have already referred to the evidence showing how pupils had to go from one teacher to another for instruction in different branches of sacred learning. Generally, a teacher was the master of one particular Veda, and, even of that, he specialized in a particular *śākhā* or recension.

Teaching was Individual. Lastly, the system of teaching was necessarily individual. The teacher had to address himself separately to the instruction of each pupil. The occasions when anything was explained to all the pupils together were comparatively few in number. The need of bestowing individual attention upon the pupils placed a natural limit to the number of such pupils which a teacher could accept and hence determined the size of these domestic schools of Ancient India. Sometimes, as is indicated in a passage in Manu [ii, 208], the son of the teacher would help his father by undertaking some of his work and there was also the custom in later times of senior pupils doing the same, but these makeshifts did not materially alter the conditions which limited the number of admissions to such schools. Even the physical capacity of the preceptor's home to accommodate pupils must have operated as a material factor in determining the number to be admitted.

Education under 'Āchārya'. We have now seen that the normal type of educational institutions as evidenced in the Sūtra literature is that represented by an Āchārya or Preceptor admitting, according to his unfettered discretion, a number of pupils who would have to live with him at his own house as members of his own family under the discipline of a system of rules and regulations governing their life and studies for a minimum period of twelve years. The Āchārya would not accept any fees from the pupils under his instruction and the only condition imposed upon their tenure of studentship was the pleasure of the teacher produced by a conformity to its rules. The progress shown by the pupil was the only factor that determined the continuance of his apprenticeship.

Education under 'Upādhyāya'. We have, however, other types of educational institutions indicated by the evidence of the period. We have already referred to the schools conducted by teachers technically called *Upādhyāyas* who would admit to their instruction on payment of fees temporary pupils who sought lessons in particular subjects. Generally speaking, the Upādhāyas provided supplementary instruction and were proficient only in the Vedic Aṅgas or a part of the Veda.

'Parishad.' The Sūtra works, however, reveal a third type of educational institutions, the scope and purposes of which make it radically different from the other two types of institutions. Every educational colony or settlement in ancient India had within itself an academy of learned and religious men called a *Parishad*. According to Gautama [xxviii, 49], a *Parishad* should consist at least of the ten following members, viz. four men who have completely studied the four Vedas, three men belonging to the three Orders enumerated first (viz. a student, a householder, and an ascetic), and three men who know three different Institutes of Law. Vasishṭha [iii, 20] and Baudhāyana [i, 1, 1, 8] lay down the same definition of a *Parishad* but instead of the three members knowing three different Institutes of Law they specify one who knows the Mīmāṁsā, one who knows the Aṅgas, and a teacher of the sacred law. Manu [xii, 111] gives a somewhat different composition of the *Parishad*. According to him, the *ten* members include *three* persons who each know one of the three principal Vedas, *one* logician, *one* Mīmāṁsaka, *one* who knows the Nirukta, *one* who recites the Institutes of the sacred Law, and *three* men belonging to the first three Orders (which do not include the hermit who cannot enter a village). Manu also permits a *Parishad* to be constituted by three members learned in the three Vedas. It will also be observed that the eligibility for the membership of such an authoritative academic body did not rest on mere intellectual qualifications. " Even if thousands of Brāhmaṇas who have not fulfilled their sacred duties are unacquainted with the Veda and subsist only by the name of their caste meet, they cannot form a *Parishad* " [Manu, xii, 114 ; Baudhāyana, i, 1, 1, 16]. And again : " Whatever an assembly consisting either of at least ten or of at least three persons who follow their prescribed occupations declared to be law, the legal force of that one must not dispute " [Manu, xii, 110]. Or again : " There may be five or there may be three or there may be one blameless man who decides questions regarding the sacred law. But a thousand fools cannot do it " [ib., 113 ; *Baudh.*, i, 1, 1, 9].

Thus the *Parishad* was a distinctive and higher type of institution which was meant to give instruction regarding doubtful points of law. There are distinguished in the Sūtras three sources [1] of sacred law, viz. (*a*) the Veda or *Śruti*, (*b*) the *Smṛiti* (i.e. the sacred law as explained by tradition), and (*c*) the practices of the *Śishṭas*, i.e. those who are free from the ordinary human passions (such as envy, pride, covetousness, prudence, hypocrisy, anger, etc.), and who in accordance with the sacred law have studied the Veda together with its appendages and are able to draw inferences from same and adduce proofs perceptible by the senses from the *Śruti* or revealed texts. On failure of these, a

[1] Cf. Baudhāyana [i, 1, 1, 12] : " Narrow and difficult to find is the path of the sacred law, towards which many gates lead." The " gates " of the Sacred Law are many, because the redactions of the Vedas and Smṛitis are numerous and the practices vary in different countries.

Parishad is to decide disputed points of law [*Baudh.*, i, 1, 1, 1–7; *Manu*, xii, 106–9]. Hence the *Parishad* was intended to be an academy of experts from whom emanated authoritative interpretations and decisions on doubtful points in the sacred texts which would be as binding on the community as the sacred texts themselves. Āpastamba refers to a *Parishad* as a Brahminical school which studies a particular redaction of the Veda. He refers us to the teaching and works of other *Parishads* for "further particulars regarding the interruption of the Veda study" [i, 3, 11, 38].

Therefore, the composition or constitution of the *Parishad* was quite in keeping with the gravity of the functions and responsibilities entrusted to it. Because it had to direct the life of the community, it was at once the most representative and authoritative body that the community could think of. The highest talent and character in the community were represented on this Committee. In the first place, there was an adequate representation of Vedic learning which was the fountain of all law. By this feature the *Parishad* is easily distinguished from the ordinary domestic school of the period presided over by an Āchārya who was normally an expert in only one of the Vedas. The *Parishad* included four experts in the four Vedas. Secondly, there were, in the words of Manu [xii, 106], those who could explore the Śruti and Smṛiti by modes of reasoning not repugnant to the Veda-lore. The "modes of reasoning" as mentioned here are, according to Medhātithi and Kullūka, the Mīmāṁsā of Jaimini to be distinguished from philosophical Schools like the Bauddhas, Nirgranthas, and Lokāyatikas, who deny the authority of the Vedas. Thirdly, there were those who were experts in what may be called the secular law, the Dharma and Gṛihya Sūtras, of which the different Schools were represented on the *Parishad*, whereas the ordinary school of an Āchārya was connected with one particular School of Sūtras determined by the particular Vedic Śākhā to which that Āchārya belonged. Fourthly, the *Parishad* represented the particular wisdom and the experience belonging to each of the three Orders or Āśramas, viz. the student, the householder, and the Vānaprastha or the ascetic, but not the hermit who had no concern for secular matters at all and would not pass through human habitations. The representation of the student community on such an authoritative body shows a degree of recognition of their special interests and status which is not allowed even in modern educational organizations professing advanced democratic ideals. As the commentator Govinda [on *Baudhāyana*, i, 1, 1, 8] points out, professed students are declared to be particularly holy in the *Dharmaskandhabrāhmaṇa*. The Brahmachārin was a " well of wisdom undefiled " by contact with the world, which a body like the *Parishad* could ill afford not to take advantage of. Besides there might crop up disputed points regarding the laws of studentship itself on which an actual student or Brahmachārin might throw much light from his fresh experience and place before the *Parishad* the student's point of view. Like the student, the householder by himself claimed a special representation, although, perhaps, except the student, and the ascetic members, the other eight members were all householders themselves. Similarly, the ripe wisdom and experience of one who passed from the householder's state to that of an ascetic detached from the world constituted a valuable asset which society had a right to utilize. The ascetic was a good judge of the doubtful points of law not only on account of his seniority and superior experience of life but also on account of his judicial temperament, disinterested attitude, and impartial outlook that are the natural characteristics of a man in the third āśrama of life no longer affected by its passions or problems.

Thus the *Parishad* was an academic institution of a composite or federal type on which were represented the different faculties or departments of the learning of the times, together with the different classes of experience and interests in society. Thus constituted and composed, it was competent to discharge its high and responsible functions sometimes as a judicial assembly and sometimes like an ecclesiastical synod. It was also an association of teachers and students and other learned men, and would thus form the nucleus of something corresponding to a University.

The composition of the *Parishad* is also interesting from another point of view. It shows the progress of specialization in Vedic study achieved during this period. According to Gautama, as we have already seen, there were, firstly, four specialists in the four Vedas of the " walking library " type. Next, there were three others who specialized in the three different Institutes of Law, besides another three who were proficient in the laws relating to the three āśramas of life. Vasishṭha and Baudhāyana refer, however, to specialists in the Mīmāṁsā, in the Aṅgas, and in sacred law. Manu wants three specialists in the three Vedas, and specialists in Logic, Mīmāṁsā, Nirukta, and Law. It will be noted that all these references point to the early development of special law Schools. Vasishṭha and Baudhāyana mention side by side with one who knows the Aṅgas the reciter or teacher of the sacred law (*Dharma-pāṭhaka*), who must therefore be a person who specially devotes himself to the study of that subject and knows more than one Dharma-sūtra. He is, so to speak, the *Law Member* of the *Parishad* and to speak of *one* legal expert means that special law Schools were already existing, the collective literature of which had to be mastered by that expert. Gautama, however, constitutes his *Parishad* rather differently: he does not create a special seat in it for an individual law member; he requires three persons knowing three different Dharma-sūtras and says nothing of any experts specially devoted to the study of the sacred law. Manu's *Parishad*, however, knows of an individual law member like that of Vasishṭha and Baudhāyana.

Special Sūtra Schools. Thus the evidence regarding the constitution and function of the *Parishads* introduces us to the more general and fundamental question[1] regarding the special Sūtra Schools that grew out of the original and primary Vedic Schools or *Charaṇas*, and thus constitute the fourth type of educational institutions characterizing the period.

It will appear that in the original and primary Vedic schools, the principal objective of instruction was a full and accurate knowledge of the sacred texts. Thus the curriculum, as has been already noted, comprised the Saṁhitā texts of the Mantras and *Brāhmaṇas*, together with their Pada, Krama, and other still more difficult *pāṭhas* or modes of recitation added in the later age when these were devised. To complete this course would require a considerable time and must have fully occupied the twelve terms of four and a half or five and a half months which the Smṛitis give as the average duration of the studentship for the acquisition of one Veda [see *ante*]. Besides the Veda, the student had also to learn the Aṅgas, and as long as these consisted of short simple treatises, it was possible for him to commit them to memory in the time prescribed for it, viz. the seven or eight dark fortnights from the month of Pausha to that of Vaiśākha, though, according to some Smṛitis, the Aṅgas might be studied at any time out of term [cf. *Vas.*, xiii, 7]. The literature of the Aṅgas was not,

[1] This subject has been discussed in the learned Introductions prefixed to the translations of the various Sūtra works in the Sacred Books of the East Series and most thoroughly and exhaustively in the Introduction of Bühler to his translation of Manu. The remarks that follow are largely based on the facts and arguments set forth in these Introductions.

however, stationary but was growing. In course of time one of its branches, the Kalpa or Ritual alone, reached large dimensions as seen in the Sūtras of the Baudhāyanīyas and Āpastambīyas. Another branch, Vyākaraṇa or Grammar, also developed similar proportions and a scientific system of treatment as reflected in the final work of Pāṇini. But the Aṅgas were developing not merely in bulk but also in number. Thus Nyāya or Pūrva Mīmaṁsā, the art of interpreting the rules of the Veda, was added to the list of the auxiliary sciences which had to be studied in connection with the sacred texts. It was thus becoming a matter of sheer impossibility for a student to commit to memory the vast literature that was meant by these sacred texts together with the Aṅgas in their developed forms. The fact of the matter was that though it was in the Vedic schools that the study of the Vedāṅgas was first started as a supplement to the study of the Vedas, the impetus given to their cultivation gradually and naturally resulted in the production of a literature which could no longer be contained within the purview of the original Vedic schools. Thus these Vedic schools lost their old monopoly as centres of the intellectual life of the Āryas, for new special schools of science grew up in response to the requirements of a growing culture. There was a large accumulation of material for each of the Aṅgas, requiring a more specialized study and scientific treatment than was possible in the Vedic schools proper. The quantity of the matter to be learnt and the natural difficulty of its acquisition necessitated a readjustment of educational arrangements. The expanding culture of the country was outgrowing its old trappings.

Thus two alternatives presented themselves before the members of the Vedic schools. They might either commit to memory all the Vedic texts of their Śākhās together with the Aṅgas without aiming at their complete understanding, or they might reduce the quantity of the matter to be memorized for the sake of a thorough mastery of what they learnt. Those who adhered to the former course became what we have already called "living libraries" but lacked the power of putting their learning to much practical use. Those who followed the latter course became specialists in the auxiliary Sciences of Sacrifice, Grammar, Law, or Astronomy, though, of course, they could not hold their own against the other class of students in respect of the verbal knowledge of the sacred books. Thus these special Schools of Science grew out of the original Vedic Schools which, by themselves, could no longer minister to the expanding educational needs and enjoy the monopoly in the spread of learning.

Separate Schools of Kalpa, Vyākaraṇa, and Jyotisha, apart from Vedic Schools. We have some evidence in the Sūtra literature by which we can trace the process of this change whereby the Vedic *Charaṇas* were depressed from their old position by special Schools which took over the scientific cultivation of some of the most important portions of the Aṅgas. Some of these special Schools grew up even before the age of Yāska's Nirukta which, for instance, mentions *Vaiyākaraṇas* or grammarians, *Nairuktas* or etymological exegetes, and *Yājñikas* or ritualists and even contrasts their conflicting opinions. The very fact of the disputes between these Schools regarding grammatical or exegetical questions demonstrates that these subjects were not taught as auxiliary branches of the Vedic lore to the students of a common school, but that each of these subjects was attaining independent development through treatment in a special School. This view is confirmed by the actual conditions in which the various Aṅgas have been preserved. It shows that two at least, Vyākaraṇa and Jyotisha, slipped away from the control of the Vedic Charaṇas in very early times. For we hardly know of any grammatical or astronomical work belonging to any of the Vedic Schools whose textbooks have survived. The works embodying the earliest speculations on grammar as an auxiliary of Vedic study in the Vedic Schools have no doubt been lost to us. But we have clear evidence to show that grammar won for itself an independent status in fairly early times. It declared its independence long before the days of Pāṇini. Pāṇini's *Ashṭādhyāyī* itself is now the sole representative of the Vyākaraṇa branch of the Aṅgas acknowledged equally by the followers of all the Vedas. But it is to be noted that the subject, as treated by Pāṇini, is no longer completely subservient to the needs of mere Veda-study but has an independent life and destiny of its own, though it does not exclude the Veda from its purview. It is no longer a " mere handmaiden of the Vedavidyā ". It is a distinct science laying down the laws applicable to the entire Sanskrit language, of which the typical form assumed is what we call classical Sanskrit regarded as the standard of Āryan speech, the Vedic forms being treated as anomalies. Thus the work of Pāṇini is to be regarded as the final outgrowth of a long scientific development achieved in the special Schools of Grammar, the earliest phases of which are represented by the various older Schools and teachers referred to not only in Pāṇini's work but also in the Prātiśākhyas and in Yāska's Nirukta.

Similarly, the growth of Astronomy is far less indebted to the Vedic Schools. Its existence as an Aṅga of the Veda is to be traced only in the small treatise entitled Jyotisha, of which, as Bühler states, two slightly different recensions are extant, one belonging to the Rigveda and the other to the Yajurveda. All the famous works on the subject like the Gārgī Saṁhitā or the later Vāsishṭha Saṁhitā and Siddhānta show no connection with the Veda or Vedic schools except that their authorship is attributed to Ṛishis or descendants of the families of Ṛishis.

Dharma-Sūtras included longer in the studies of Veda and Brāhmaṇa 'Charaṇas'. As regards *sacred law*, however, there is no doubt that it formed part of the curriculum of the Vedic Schools for a much longer time. At first each Vedic Charaṇa or School developed its own Dharmasūtra or body of rules for the guidance of its own pupils. All the Dharmasūtras were originally the property of particular Vedic Schools, were held to be authoritative in restricted circles, and were later on acknowledged as sources of the sacred law applicable to all Āryas. It is also to be noted in this connection that the rise of Sūtra literature (under circumstances already explained in detail) meant the rise of Sūtra-Charaṇas which supplanted the earlier Vedic and Brāhmaṇa Charaṇas based on the texts of the Saṁhitās and Brāhmaṇas. The founder[1] of a Sūtra-Charaṇa did not claim to have received a revelation of Vedic Mantras or of a Brāhmaṇa text but merely gave a new systematic arrangement of the precepts regarding sacrifices and the sacred law. The members of these new Sūtra-Charaṇas would preserve the text of the Saṁhitā and Brāhmaṇa of an earlier Charaṇa from which they originally branched off. It is also clear that the ground of distinction among these Sūtra-Charaṇas being in the Sūtras, they would naturally make light of the minor differences between the texts of the Saṁhitās and Brāhmaṇas which, in previous times, were deemed to be all-important and there was even a tendency to reunite different Vedic Śākhās into one, as a result of which many old Śākhās have been actually lost. It was these Sūtra-Charaṇas that first commenced the systematic cultivation of the sacred sciences; they first collected the fragmentary doctrines, scattered in the

[1] For instance, Āpastamba [*Dh. Sū.*, i, 2, 5, 4–5] clearly disclaims any right to the title of Ṛishi or inspired seer of Vedic texts, for he belongs to the age of the *Avaras* as a child of the Kali Yuga.

older Vedic works, and arranged them for the convenience of oral instruction in Sūtras or strings of aphorisms. Among the subjects which these Schools chiefly cultivated were included the several Vedāṅgas like ritual, grammar, phonetics, to which was added the sacred law too. Thus each Vedic School or Charaṇa possessed a peculiar work on Dharma and this view is also supported by the tradition of the Mīmāṁsā school. The Mānava Sūtra-Charaṇa, for instance, which was a subdivision of the Maitrāyaṇīya School connected with a redaction of the Black Yajur-veda, developed a Dharma-Sūtra of its own, of which the extant *Mānava Dharma-śāstra* is considered to be a recast and versification. Similarly, the *Gautamīya Dharmaśāstra* is believed to have been originally the exclusive property of a school of Sāmavedins. Further, the *Āpastambīya Dharma-Sūtra*, as Bühler points out, forms part of an enormous Kalpa literature or body of aphorisms, which digests the teaching of the Veda and of the ancient Ṛishis regarding the performance of sacrifices and the duties of twice-born men, Brahmins, Kshatriyas, and Vaiśyas, and which, being chiefly based on the second of the four Vedas, the Yajurveda in the Taittirīya recension, is primarily intended for the benefit of the Adhvaryu priests in whose families the study of the Yajurveda is hereditary. Thus Hindu sacred law has its source in the teaching of the Vedic Schools, the Sūtra-Charaṇas, of which the teachers composed prose works or manuals that were meant to be committed to memory by the young Āryan students and to teach them their duties. Every School had its own code of manners and morals, so to speak. Sometimes the same code or Dharma-Sūtra might be adopted by several Sūtra-Charaṇas [e.g. the Dharma-Sūtra which both the Āpastambīyas and Hairaṇyakeśas study or the Chayana-Sūtra which the Bhāradvājas and Hairaṇyakeśas have in common (Bühler, *S.B.E.*, 14, xiv)] and in such cases we must assume that the later School did not care to compose a treatise of its own on a certain subject but preferred to adopt the work of an earlier teacher.

Formation of special Law Schools, apart from purely Vedic Schools or Charaṇas, on the basis of Dharma-Śāstras such as those of Manu and Yājñavalkya. Sacred Law, like Grammar and Astronomy, had also to part company with the Vedic schools in the interests of its own development. It demanded an independent treatment uncontrolled by the needs of Veda-study. Special Law Schools grew up even in the time of the two Dharma-Sūtras of Vasishṭha and Baudhāyana, as we have already seen. The formation of special Law Schools was, however, but the first step: the second step was the composition of Manuals for their use, of that class of secondary Smṛitis the chief surviving representatives of which are the Dharma-śāstras of Manu and Yājñavalkya. The original Dharma-sūtras with which these special Law Schools started offered copious materials for special study, as also grounds for it. Most of their topics were connected with the moral duties of the Āryas, of which detailed rules are given, but the rules are not systematically arranged. They also treat of the legal procedure, the civil and criminal law, but the treatment is unsatisfactory except that of the law of inheritance and partition. From the standpoint of the Vedic Schools a more detailed and orderly treatment of such matters was irrelevant, as they were more concerned with the means of acquiring spiritual merit and warning to pupils against commission of sins. Some of their members might, of course, be called upon to assist the administration as Dharmādhikārins or legal advisers or as judges and to settle the law between man and man, but for this purpose a mere knowledge of the general principles was sufficient in an age which recognized the great authority of local customs. The case, however, was quite different when sacred law came to be studied as a separate science by specialists who would naturally seek to remedy the deficiences of the older books either by remodelling them or composing new works. In general the first alternative would commend itself to them more. Thus the first work of the special Law Schools was the production of the secondary Smṛitis on the basis of older Dharma-sūtras and the consequent conversions of locally authoritative Sūtras of mere School-books into works claiming the allegiance of all Āryans.

Time of these Developments. That these processes accomplished themselves before the time of the grammarian Patañjali is shown from some of his allusions. He mentions Dharma-sūtras and also refers to the formation of the special word "*Dhārmavidyā*" which denotes "a person who studies or knows the *dharmavidyā*, the science of the sacred law". The word *Dharma-śāstra* which also occasionally occurs in his *Bhāshya* may perhaps point to the Manuals composed and studied in the special Schools, which were distinct from the Dharma-sūtras.

Their modern Remnants. A picture of these processes is afforded to some extent by the conditions of sacred learning even in modern times. The true modern representatives of the ancient *Charaṇas* are the so-called Vaidiks of whom an interesting account is given by Sir R. G. Bhandarkar [" The Veda in India ", in the *I.A.*, iii]. A Vaidik of the Āśvalāyana school knows by heart the Rigveda according to the Saṁhitā, Pada, Krama, Jaṭā, and Ghana pāṭhas, the *Aitareya Brāhmaṇa*, and *Āraṇyaka*, the ritualistic Sūtras of Āśvalāyana, Śaunaka's *Prātiśākhya*, and the Śikshā, Yāska's *Nirukta*, Pāṇini's Grammar, Jyotisha, Chhandas, Yājñavalkya's Dharma-śāstra, portions of the *Mahābhārata*, and the philosophical Sūtras of Kaṇāda, Jaimini, and Bādarāyaṇa. Similarly, the Vaidiks of the Yajus, Sāman, and Atharvan schools are expected to recite all the works of their respective Śākhās together with certain other non-Vedic works. Now those who carry in their head such a vast quantity of learning cannot be expected to be experts in its exposition or practical application. A professional Vaidik, as Bühler points out, is not the person who can be trusted with the proper performance of the sacrifices according to the Śrauta-Sūtras, or with the interpretation of the intricate system of Pāṇini's grammar or even decision of knotty points of Law according to the Dharma-Sūtra or the secondary Smṛiti which he knows by heart. Each of these subjects can be dealt with only by specialists. The Śrotriya or Śrauti is the man for sacrifices: he knows by heart the sacred texts of his Śākhā, understands fully the meaning of the Śrauta-sūtras and has a practical knowledge of the actual *Kriyā* or manual work described in the *Prayogas*. His colleague, the Yājñika, is similarly a specialist in the Gṛihya Sūtras and domestic ceremonies. But these two will thus have their knowledge confined only to a few branches of the entire literature of the Aṅgas such as Kalpa or parts of it, and perhaps the Śikshā. Similarly, those who would specialize in the other Aṅga subjects such as Grammar, Law, or Astronomy, will have to reduce proportionately the quantity of learning related to the Veda and its auxiliary subjects. Their obligations in respect of Veda-study, for instance, would be fulfilled by their committing to memory a few important sections of the Vedas such as the Pāvamānī-hymns of the Rigveda or the Śatarudriya of the Yajurveda or the verses occurring in the Brahmayajña and the Sandhyāvandana.

CHAPTER VI

EDUCATION IN THE TIME OF PĀṆINI

Education as revealed in the grammatical Sūtras of Paṇini, together with the works of Kātyāyana and Patañjali. The account of education in the Sūtra period will not be complete without the consideration of the evidence of the grammatical literature as represented in the works of Pāṇini and of his two famous commentators, Katyāyana and Patañjali. That evidence is indeed unique in its interest and importance. It may be further noted that, chronologically speaking, the entire Sūtra period may be roughly considered to lie between the time of Pāṇini with whom it begins and the time of Patañjali with whom it ends. Accordingly, some of the chief characteristics of the educational system and conditions of the period are reflected in the literature that grew round the grammar of Pāṇini. It may also be easily understood that, on account of the inevitable and vital connection that must exist between a grammatical work and the standing language and literature and the established forms and usages of speech upon which it is based, grammatical works must always be a fertile source of social and political history, abounding in references to contemporary and pre-existing institutions, ways of life, and conditions of culture.

Literature known to Pāṇini. Pāṇini throws light on the literature of his times. Four classes of literature are distinguished. The first is that which is "seen" (*dṛishṭam*) or revealed, e.g. the Sāmaveda. Some of the "seers" of the Sāmaveda are also mentioned, viz. Vāmadeva [iv, 2, 7, and 8]. Kātyāyana and Patañjali add the names of Kali, Agni, Uśanas, and Aupagava. The second is that which is "enounced" [iv, 2, 63; iv, 3, 101 (*proktam*)]. To this class would belong the *Veda* or *Chhandas* enounced by Tittiri, Varatantu, Khaṇḍika, and Ukha [1]; works by the Ṛishis like Kāśyapa and Kauśika; the *Chhandas* works of Śaunaka and others [2]; of Kaṭha and Charaka; of Kalāpī and

[1] Patañjali mentions the works called Kāṭhaka, Kālāpaka, Maudaka, and Paippalādaka [iv, 3, 101 (3)].

[2] As "others" the *Kāśikā* mentions Kaṭha, Śāṭha, Vājaśaneya, Sāṅgarava, Śārṅgarava, Sāṅpeya, Śākheya, Khāṇḍāyana, Skandha, Skanda, etc. The *Śaunaka* of this rule is taken by Goldstucker on the authority of Sāyaṇa to be the Ṛishi who is supposed to be the author of the second Maṇḍala of the Rigveda as we now have it. Accordingly, since this Maṇḍala is classified by Pāṇini under

Chhagalī ; and of the *direct* pupils of Kalāpī[1] and Vaiśampāyana. In this class are also included such *Brāhmaṇa*[2] and *Kalpa*[3] works as are enounced by the ancient sages, thereby excluding, according to Kātyāyana and Patañjali, the works of later sages[4] like Yājñavalkya and Sulabha. Lastly, Pāṇini mentions as examples of this class of literature the *Bhikshu-sūtras* as enounced or originally propounded by Pārāśarya and Karmanda as well as the *Naṭa-sūtras* as propounded by their founders mentioned as Śilālin and Kṛiśāśva. The *Bhikshu-sūtra* means a collection of rules or precepts for mendicants, while the *Naṭa-sūtra* means a collection of rules for actors [iv, 3, 101–111]. The third class of literature distinguished by Pāṇini is that which is " discovered " and not handed down by tradition [ii, 4, 21 ; iv, 3, 115 ; vi, 2, 14 (*Upajñā*)]. As examples of this class the *Kāśikā* mentions the works of such original authors as Pāṇini, Kāśakrishṇa, Āpiśali, and Vyāḍi. The fourth class of literature comprises the ordinary compositions of ordinary writers on any subject [iv, 3, 87 and 116]. As examples, Patañjali mentions the books of *Story* (*ākhyāyikā*) such as *Vāsavadattā*, *Sumanottarā*, *Bhaimarathī*, to which the *Kāśikā* adds *Urvaśī*. The *Kāśikā* mentions *mythological* works like *Saubhadra*, *Gaurimitra*, and *Yāyāta*. In iv, 3, 88 Pāṇini refers to works on such peculiar subjects as the child's cry (*Śiśukrandīya*) or the court of Yama (*Yamasabhīya*) to which the *Vārttika* adds the works bearing on the wars between gods and demons such as *Devāsura*, *Rākshosura*, and the *Kāśikā* adds the works called *Agnikāśyapīya*, *Śyenakapotīya*, *Indrajananīya* (also mentioned by Pāṇini) and *Pradyumnāgamanīya*. Patañjali further mentions under this class the *Kāvya* or poetical works of *Vararuchi* and the *Slokas* known as *Jālūka* [iv, 3, 101 (3)]. Pāṇini also refers to *Ślokas* as eulogistic verses [iii, 1, 25] and to their author as *Ślokakāra* [ib., 2, 23]. There is also a reference to

prokta (proclaimed) as distinguished from the *dṛishṭa*, literature, it is to be regarded in Goldstucker's opinion as being later in Pāṇini's view than the other Maṇḍalas. Goldstucker further argues that the very first hymn of the second Maṇḍala fully confirms this impression, for, by speaking of Hotṛi, Potṛi, Neshṭṛi, Agnīdhra, Praśāstṛi, Adhvaryu, and Brahman priests, it certainly betrays a very advanced development of sacrificial and artificial rites. According to the *Kāśika*, Śaunaka is the reputed author of the *Rik-prātiśākhya* which is thus considered to be anterior to Pāṇini.

[1] According to the *Kāśikā*, there are four such pupils of Kalāpī, viz. Haridru, Chhagalī, Tumburu, and Ulapa, while there are *nine* of Vaiśampāyana, viz. Ālambi, Palaṅga, Kamala, Ṛichāva, Āruṇi, Tāṇḍya, Śyāmāyana, Kaṭha, and Kalāpī.

[2] E.g. those of Bhāllava, Śāṭyāyana, and Aitareya [*Kāśikā*].

[3] E.g. those of Paiṅga and Aruṇaparāja [ib.]. Patañjali also mentions *Āsurīya Kalpa* [iv, 1, 19 (2)].

[4] The *Kāśikā* adds the Kalpa work of Āśmaratha.

Gāthās [ib.], to a composer of *Mantras* (*Mantrakāra*), and to the author of Padapāṭha (*Padakāra*). Pāṇini also mentions a Mahābhārata [vi, 2, 38] and the followers of Vāsudeva and Arjuna [iv, 3, 98]. Yudhishṭhira also is mentioned [viii, 3, 95], while Patañjali mentions Yudhisṭhira and Arjuna as elder and younger brothers respectively [ii, 2, 34]. Non-ṛishi families of Vṛishṇi and Kuru are also mentioned [iv, 1, 114], as members of which Patañjali instances Vāsudeva, Vāladeva, Nākula, Sāhadeva, and Bhaimasenya. In addition to the above four types of literature, Pāṇini mentions separately the literature of *Commentaries* [iv, 3, 66 (*Vyākhyāna*)], as examples of which Patañjali mentions the commentaries on *Nirukta* and *Vyākaraṇa* and also on *Kalpa* works such as *Agnishṭoma*, *Rājasūya*, and *Vājapeya*. Pāṇini refers to commentaries on Soma sacrifices (*kratu*) and other sacrifices (*yajña*), as examples of which Patañjali mentions *Pākayajñika*, *Nāvayajñika*, *Pāñchaudanika*, *Sāptaudanika*, *Śātaudanika* [iv, 3, 68]. Commentaries on sections of grammar alluded to by Pāṇini are mentioned by *Kāśikā* as *Saupa* (on case-affixes), *Taiṅga* (on verbal affixes) and *Kārta* (on *kṛit* affixes), also *Shātvaṇātvikam* and *Nātānatikam* [iv, 3, 66, 67]. Pāṇini [ib., 69] refers to commentaries on chapters (*adhyāyas*) of works of Ṛishis, as examples of which the *Kāśikā* mentions *Vāsishṭhika-adhyāya*, *Vaiśvāmitrika*. Pāṅini refers to commentaries on the verses or mantras on *Puroḍāśa* (sacred cake) as *Puroḍāśika* and *Pauroḍāśika*. He refers to the formations *Chhandasya* and *Chhāndasa* as commentaries on *Chhandas*. He refers to the commentaries called Brāḥmaṇika, Ārchika, Prāthamika, Ādhvarika, Pauraścharaṇika, Nāmika, Ākhyātika, and Nāmākhyātika, as also to commentaries of which the *Kāśikā* gives the names as Aishṭika, Pāśuka, Chāturhotṛika, Pāñchahotṛika. Lastly, he refers to commentaries on certain classes of works belonging to the category called *Ṛigayanādi* which, according to *Kāśikā*, included a great variety of subjects such as Chhandobhāshā, Chhandovichiti, Nyāya, Vyākaraṇa, Nigama, Vāstuvidyā, Aṅgavidyā, Kshatravidyā, Upanishat, Śikshā, etc. [iv, 3, 703].

We thus see that Pāṇini was acquainted with a wide range of subjects, religious and secular. He knew the *Rigveda* [vi, 3, 55, 133 ; vii, 4, 39] and refers to its *Pada* [vi, 1, 115 ; vii, 1, 57 ; viii, 1, 18, etc.] and *Krama pāṭha* [iv, 2, 61], while the division into Adhyāyas and Anuvākas was also known [v, 2, 60]. He also uses the word *Chhanda* in the sense of Metre [viii, 3, 94]. He knew the *Sāmaveda* [i, 2, 34 ; iv, 2, 7, and 60 ; v, 2, 59 ; etc.]. He knew also of a Yajurveda [ii, 4, 4; iv, 2, 60; v, 4, 77; vi, 1, 117; vii, 4, 38; viii, 3, 104; etc.]. All the three Vedas are referred to in one Sūtra [iv, 3, 129] together with the Schools or Charaṇas based thereon. The *Śākala* Śākhā of the Rigveda is also referred to [ib., 128]. Regarding his knowledge of the *Atharvaveda,* there is no positive evidence as the word occurs only in the Gaṇas to the Sūtras or in the Vārttikas [see iv, 2, 38 and 63; iv, 3, 133; etc.]. Nor do we know definitely whether the White Yajurveda was known to him, because it was left to a Vārttika [to iv, 3, 105] to refer to its author Yājñavalkya as a comparatively later Ṛishi (probably a contemporary of Pāṇini, as I interpret the Vārttika) than those contemplated in the said Sūtra. It is also uncertain whether Pāṇini knew the *Āraṇyakas* on account of his rather significant omission to refer to that meaning in explaining the formation, *Āraṇyaka* [iv, 2, 129]. The omission was left to be supplied by Kātyāyana. On this supposition the *Upanishads,* as we have them now, were not probably known to him because these were developed out of the *Āraṇyakas.* Pāṇini mentions the word *Upanishad* only once and *that* probably in the sense of a secret [i, 4, 79] (though the *Bālamanoramā* takes it to mean the literary work, *Vedāntabhāga*), but the word occurs twice in the Gaṇas [iv, 3, 73 (in the sense of a literary work) and iv, 4, 12]. There is, however, no doubt that he knew of the *Brāhmaṇas* [ii, 3, 60] and *Kalpa* works and also of *Sūtras* [iv, 2, 65] (which are interpreted to mean grammatical Sūtras by Kātyāyana and Patañjali). He definitely mentions *Brāhmaṇa* works of thirty and forty *adhyāyas* or chapters [v, 1, 162]. Lastly, he refers to works which are similar to the *Brāhmaṇas* and called *Anu-Brāhmaṇas* [iv, 2, 63], while there was something like the Indexing of the Mantras for convenient reference at the time of sacrificial performances [iv, 4, 125–7] by different classes of priests which are also known to Pāṇini [v, 1, 135 and 136].

The range of secular literature in Pāṇini's times seems to have been remarkably wide and varied, considering that he discusses grammatical formations connected with such subjects as those bearing upon the rules and practices of actors and mendicants, and upon the treatment of children's cries, or the seasons [iv, 2, 64],[1] or fables and stories [ib., 102].

[1] The growth of such a varied profane literature as is indicated by these casual references inclines one to doubt the correctness of the supposition that such ancient religious texts as the Atharvaveda, the Āraṇyakas, the Upanishads, the Vājasaneyi Saṁhitā, or the Śatapatha Brāhmaṇa were unknown to Pāṇini. The matter requires to be carefully considered by more competent scholars.

Literature known to Kātyāyana and Patañjali. We notice a considerable advancement of learning in the subsequent ages of Kātyāyana and Patañjali. The advancement is shown in regard to both depth and width, i.e. in the growth of the literature bearing on the old traditional subjects and the growth of *new* subjects in the process of time. We have already cited above the evidence proving it. But there is some further evidence to be considered in that connection. For instance, there is to be noticed a considerable growth of grammatical literature. Pāṇini mentions among his predecessors Āpiśali, Kāśyapa, Gārgya, Gālava, Chākravarmana, Bhāradvāja, Śākaṭāyana, Śākalya, Senaka, Sphoṭāyana, and also those authors designated by the collective appellation of eastern [ii, 4, 60 ; iii, 4, 18 ; iv, 1, 17. 43. 160, etc.] and northern grammarians [iii, 4, 19 ; iv, 1, 130. 157 ; etc.]. To this list of names Patañjali makes his own additions. In one place he mentions the four landmarks in the history of grammar, viz. those represented by the schools of the four Āchāryas, Āpiśala—Pāṇini—Vyāḍi—Gautama [vi, 2, 36], the order of the mention being, according to a Sūtra [the *Vārttikas* to ii, 2, 34], that of chronology. He mentions also grammarians of the School of the Bhāradvājīyas [iii, 1, 89 (1) ; iv, 1, 79 (1) ; vi, 4, 47 (1) ; ib., 155 (1)], and Saunāgas [ii, 2, 18 (1–4) ; vi, 3, 44 (1)], as also Kuṇaravāḍava [vii, 3, 1 (6)], Sauryabhāgavat [viii, 2, 106 (3)], and Kuṇi [Kaiyyaṭa's gloss on i, 1, 75]. There is also an indefinite number of grammarians designated under the words "some" and "others" (*Kechit* and *Apare*) [see Goldstucker's *Pāṇini* for these references]. There is also a reference to those who study or understand the Vārttikasūtra and Saṁgrahasūtra.[1] Besides grammar, there is a number of other secular subjects mentioned. A person well-versed in the science of (augury from observing) crows is called *Vāyasavidyika*. Similarly, there are references to experts in sciences bearing upon cows (Gaulakshaṇika) and horses (Āśvalakshaṇika), upon interpretation of signs (Lākshaṇika), upon dyes of lac (Lākshika ?). There is a reference to a subject called *Anusū* (the meaning of which I cannot ascertain). Next we have references to *Aṅgavidyā* (knowledge of lucky or unlucky marks on the body), *Kshatravidyā* (military science or *Dhanurvidyā*, the science of the bow, archery) and *Dharmavidyā*

[1] There was indeed a considerable growth of Vārttika literature, of which we may distinguish three distinct and different strata : (1) The *Kārikās* or Śloka-vārttikas, (2) *Traditional* Vārttikas which end in the expression "it is remembered", and (3) *Opposition*-Vārttikas which dictate a rule in the style of the Sūtras.

(Law). Patañjali distinguishes between *Ākhyānas* (historical stories), e.g. those connected with Yavakrīta, Priyaṅgu, Yayāti, and *Ākhyāyikās* (works of fiction), e.g. those connected with Vāsavadattā or Sumanottarā, and refers to *Itihāsa* and *Purāṇa* [iv, 2, 60]. A Vārttika mentions Vyāsa whose son is named Śuka by Patañjali [iv, 1, 97]. The story of Kaṁsa being killed by Krishṇa is referred to by Patañjali as being very popular [iii, 1, 26 (6)].

Popular Literature. Patañjali's was indeed an age of popular literature, of Ākhyānas, Ākhyāyikās, Itihāsas, Purāṇas, of recitations from the Epics of the Mahābhārata and Rāmāyaṇa [Vālmīki being mentioned in the earlier *Taittirīya Prātiśākhya* (v, 36)], of homely slokas, of vocal and instrumental musicians, of actors and the like. The spread of popular education due to this growth of a vast and varied popular literature may be inferred from one of the typical illustrations of Patañjali (in his gloss to Vārttika on ii, 4, 56). He there describes a dialogue between a grammarian and a coachman in which the latter gets the better of the former in regard to the accuracy of a grammatical formation. An extract from the dialogue will be interesting: "A certain grammarian asked, 'Who is the *Pravetā* (driver) of this chariot?' The Sūta (charioteer) answered: 'Sire! I am the *Prājitā*.' The learned grammarian said: 'This word (Prājitā) is grammatically incorrect.' The Sūta retorted: 'The fool knows the rule (of Pāṇini) but not the *ishṭi* of the teachers.' The grammarian answered: 'Oh! how troubled are we by this *opposite* of a Sūta [*Duruta* = Dur + ve (weave) + kta = ill-woven, to which the grammarian thinks Sūta is a cognate].' This answer provokes a stronger retort from the coachman who says: 'You think that *Sūta* is derived from the root *ve*, whereas it is really derived from the root *sū*, to propel. If, however, you wish to use a correct term of contempt for me you must use the form *Duḥsūta*.'"

Rules of Education. We shall now consider the evidence regarding the conditions and regulations of education. The ceremony of initiation is referred to as Āchārya-karaṇa [i, 3, 36] and *Upanayana*. The sense of the latter term, according to Pāṇini, is that the teacher, by bringing, according to religious rules, the pupil unto himself, brings himself up as a teacher through instruction, whence the expression, *Māṇavakaṁ Upanayate*. The *Bālamanoramā* cites an interesting verse defining an Āchārya as one who, receiving unto himself (*upanīya*) a pupil, teaches him the Veda together with the Kalpas and Rahasyas.

Relations between Teacher and Pupil. Next, we have certain expressions indicative of the relations between the teacher and pupil. The same affix is applied to their relationships as to that of blood [iv, 3, 77 and vi, 3, 23]. The pupil is called a *Chhātra* [iv, 4, 62] because, as explained by Patañjali, the preceptor is like an umbrella sheltering the pupil or covering his defects, or the pupil is like an umbrella maintaining his preceptor. The pupil must secure the affection of his teacher for the sake of his own welfare both here and hereafter [Patañjali on iii, 1, 26 (15)].

Marks of Pupilage. All the well-known marks of pupilage are known to Pāṇini. The pupil is to live with his teacher (*ante-vāsī*) but there is also a reference to day-scholars, the common mark of both classes of pupils being the carrying of the *daṇḍa* or staff [iv, 3, 130]. Another mark of the pupil is the bowl in his hand [i, 4, 84 (2)—*Kamaṇḍalu-pāṇiṁ chhātraṁ*]. The most important mark of the pupil was his going on begging rounds to approved householders for food and other necessaries [Patañjali on i, 1, 56 (1)]. There were several pupils thus serving their common teacher, as indicated by the special term applied to the boarder-pupils of the same school [iv, 3, 107 (*satīrthya*)]. Special *vratas* or vows of the Brahmachārin are also referred to [v, 1, 94] as well as the ceremony of Anupravachana [v, 1, 111].

School Regulations. We have also a glimpse into some of the regulations of the school. The Āchārya is stated by Patañjali to sit with sacred grass in his hand at a pure moment with his face towards the east and then commence teaching with great care [i, 1, 1 (7)]. The pupils reciprocated the treatment of their teacher. There is a reference to studious pupils working night and day [Patañjali on ii, 4, 32]. Some, when they could not get oil for their lamps, would even burn dried cow-dung and study by themselves in an isolated corner by the light thereof, so zealous were they [Patañjali on iii, 1, 26 (2)]. There is also a reference to prescribed times and places of study [iv, 3, 71].

Unworthy Pupils. Unworthy pupils and teachers were not unknown. Some pupils found study too painful and difficult and abstained. Sometimes the rough manners of a teacher might also repel them [i, 4, 26, together with Patañjali's gloss]. Sometimes a pupil would not have the courage to face his teacher who would rebuke and dismiss him for some offence committed [ib., 28]. Or a pupil would not have the patience to complete his full period of studentship and leave it prematurely for the life of ease of the householder without his teacher's permission or the performance of the concluding purificatory bath. For such a person the standing contemptuous epithet was *Khatvārūḍha*, i.e. one who begins sleeping on a cot without being entitled to it by a completed studentship when he ought to sleep on the ground [ii, 1, 26, with Patañjali's gloss]. Sometimes a pupil would change teachers and schools too frequently, in which case the contemptuous epithet, *Tīrthakāka*, would be applied to him, because he is as fickle as a crow that does not stop long at a place of pilgrimage [ii, 1, 41, with Patañjali's gloss]. Other contemptuous epithets are contemplated in another Sūtra of Pāṇini [vi, 2, 69] with reference to an *antevāsin* and a *māṇava* when they become pupils for reprehensible motives. As examples the *Kāśikā* mentions the term *Kumārī-Dākshāḥ*, which means those who study the works, or make themselves pupils, of Daksha for the sake of girls, and also the term *Bhikshā-māṇava* which applies to a person entering upon studentship for the sake of the proceeds from begging it brings. Similar terms mentioned by Patañjali are *Odana-Pāṇinīyāḥ*, i.e. those who become pupils or study the work of Pāṇini only for the sake of securing boiled rice, *Ghṛita-Rauḍhīyas* (the Rauḍhīyas desirous of *ghṛita*), and *Kambala-Chārāyaṇīyas* (the Chārāyaṇīyas desirous of blankets) [see Patañjali on Vārttika 6 to i, 1, 73 and *Kāśikā* on vi, 2, 69]. Thus there was not always the pursuit of knowledge for its own sake, and deviations from the ideal were so common or general that special epithets were evolved requiring grammatical explanations for their formation. Be it, however, considered that students pursuing studies for worldly advantages accruing therefrom earned a legitimate social opprobrium, and this in a manner testifies to the strict insistence upon the true ideals of studentship. Nowadays most persons acquire knowledge because it brings *odana*, *ghṛita*, and *kambala* but escapes the application of epithets expressive of social censure.

'Yaujana-Śatika.' The *Bṛihadāraṇyaka Upanishad* (see *ante*) mentions a famous teacher in the land of the Madras to whom came pupils from distant countries. We have an interesting confirmation of this evidence regarding the existence of such far-famed teachers in the *Mahābhāshya* [v, 1, 74 (2)] which explains the grammatical formation *Yaujana-śatika* as the designation applied to a *guru* whom pupils seek from distances of hundreds of miles (*yojanaśatādabhigamanamarhati*).

'Varṇī.' Pāṇini gives evidence of the fact that studentship was open to all the three twice-born castes in the grammatical formation *Varṇī* which is explained as a general term for a Brahmachārī [v, 2, 134].

Gifts. Patañjali mentions the gift of cows to the teacher [i, 4, 32].

Father as Teacher. He refers to a pupil having his father as his teacher [i, 4, 51].

Terms for Teachers. Four terms are used to indicate the teacher, viz. *Āchārya, Guru, Śikshaka,* and *Upādhyāya.* It may be noted that the term *Āchārya* is reserved by Patañjali for application to the highest type of teacher, to an original thinker and master like Pāṇini, while the other three terms he uses with reference to the ordinary teachers.

Methods of Study. There is some evidence available regarding the methods of study and instruction. These were, of course, necessarily determined by the character of the curriculum. Where only Vedic texts were the subject of study, rote-learning was the suitable method. It is this method of study that Pāṇini refers to in his Sūtra—*Śrotriyaśchhandodhīte* [v, 2, 84], which means that the Śrotriya is he who learns by heart the Chhandas or Veda. Patañjali refers to "reading aloud" and "reading low" [ii, 1, 2 (7)]. Examinations in the recitation of texts seem to be contemplated in two Sūtras of Pāṇini [iv, 4, 63 and 64] upon which Patañjali unfortunately does not comment, so that we have to depend upon the *Kāśikā* for information on the point. The examinee who made a single mistake in the pronunciation of sacred texts[1] was designated *Aikānyika,* i.e. pupil of one error. We have similar epithets based on the number of lapses thus committed which might be even twelve, thirteen, and fourteen. These epithets which became so common and important as to deserve the notice of Pāṇini indicate that there were different grades or classes according to which the examinees were ranked in the order of merit on the results of their oral examination. In this connection we may also refer to a Sūtra [v, 1, 58] in which the practice of learning by repetition seems to be alluded to. Thus *Pañchakodhītaḥ* means "what is studied five times" [*Kāśikā*].

But rote-learning was not of course the only method of study. There were indeed various subjects of study in the learning of which memory played a far less important part than understanding. Pāṇini's grammar was itself one of the most conspicuous

[1] Yasyādhyayane niyuktasya parīkshākāle pāṭhataḥ skhalitamapapāṭharūpamekaṁ jātaṁ sa uchyate Aikānyika iti *Kāśikā.* Bhaṭṭojidīkshita explains the mistake as *viparītochchāraṇarūpam,* i.e. as one of pronunciation.

of such subjects, demanding a most sustained exercise of the reader's reasoning faculty in comprehending the orderly evolution of a perfectly scientific system on the basis of a combined application of approved deductive and inductive methods. Thus the methods of both mechanical and critical study are explicitly referred to by Pāṇini in his Sūtra [iv, 2, 59]—*Tadadhīte tadveda* upon which the gloss of Patañjali is equally explicit. The term *adhīte* in the Sūtra refers to studies which depend upon memory, i.e. texts which have to be learnt by heart, while the other term, *veda*, applies to studies depending upon understanding. Patañjali distinguishes a pupil who simply commits to memory texts, without understanding their meaning (*saṁpāṭhaṁ paṭhati*), from one who elects studies that involve the exercise of intelligence. The *Bālamanoramā* (a commentary on Bhattoji-dīkshita's *Siddhāntakaumudī*) defines the technical term *adhyayana* as used by Pāṇini in the sense of the repetition by the pupil of the syllables in the order in which they issue from the lips of his teacher, while the term *vedanam* is explained as the knowledge of the meaning of the words heard.[1]

The currency of the two methods of study in times anterior to Pāṇini may be taken for granted. This is indeed proved by the very fact that it has formed the subject-matter of a Pāninean Sūtra. We are not, therefore, suprised at the emphatic protest of Yāska (already mentioned) against the method of rote-learning as generally applied to Veda-study. He strongly condemns those who would make the Vedic texts a mere matter of memory, not of an intelligent and critical study. In the words of Yāska [*Nirukta*, i, 18] : " The person who is able only to recite the Veda (*adhītya*) but does not understand its meaning is like a post or a mere load-bearer ; but he who understands the meaning will attain to all good here and hereafter, being purged of sins by knowledge. For the words that are simply memorized and not understood will merely sound when uttered, and not enlighten, just as wood, be it never so dry, will not blaze if it is put into what is not fire." Thus, in Yāska's opinion, the words of the Vedic texts were not more important than their meaning and hence the Vedas should be treated to both mechanical and rational methods of study. Yāska has also sought to discharge the responsibility of his opinions by composing a work which contributes towards a comprehension of the meanings of Vedic texts as distinguished

[1] Gurumukhādaksharānupurvīgrahaṇamadhyayanam | Śabdārthajñānaṁ vedanam |

from their proper pronunciation which is the exclusive objective of the Prātiśākhya literature. It may be also supposed that this spirit of reaction against the excessive dominance of mechanical methods of study to which we owe the preservation of the sacred texts was due to the intellectual tendencies of the age towards critical thinking and philosophical speculation which culminated in the Upanishads and Āraṇyakas.

Different Classes of Literary Men. Pāṇini acquaints us with different classes of literary men. These may be inferred from the different classes of literature mentioned in his Sūtras which have been already noticed. At their head is the Ṛishi whose literary work, as we have already seen, is not created or composed ("*kṛita*") but "seen", revealed, inspired. We have already noticed the names of some of the Ṛishis mentioned by Pāṇini. To these we may add the names of Praskaṇva, Maṇḍūka, and Hariśchandra [vi, 1, 153; iv, 1, 19]. The manner of the mention [e.g. iv, 3, 105] shows that the age of the Ṛishis was long gone. Pāṇini has to take note of the distinction between *ārsha* and *anārsha* (non-ṛishi) literature [i, 1, 16]. We have some Sūtras explaining formations that only apply to non-Ṛishis [e.g. iv, 1, 104 (*anṛishi*)]. Next comes the promulgator of original works. The works thus promulgated ("*prokta*" and not *dṛishṭa* or revealed) might be Chhandas, Brāhmaṇa, and Kalpa works. We have already noticed the authors of these three different classes of religious literature as mentioned by Pāṇini. Some of them might be *Ṛishis* [iv, 3, 103]. From the manner of Pāṇini's mention it is clear that the age of these promulgators was long past [iv, 3, 105], though there were still some later representatives of the class as noticed by Kātyāyana, viz. Yājñavalkya and Sulabha. The original works promulgated might also be in the domain of secular learning. Pāṇini refers to the originators of literature bearing upon ascetics (*bhikshus*) and actors (*naṭas*), as we have already seen The third type of men of letters is the discoverer of original systems, who brings to light *new* knowledge as distinguished from the knowledge that is handed down [iv, 3, 115]. The fourth type was the ordinary author of ordinary works (which were neither *dṛishṭa*, nor *prokta*, but *kṛita*). Kātyāyana mentions the formation *Śāstrakṛit* [Vārttika to iii, 1, 85]. The fifth type was the commentator [see *ante* for these references]. Thus Pāṇini practically refers to all possible varieties of literature and literary men that would all be connected with one or other of the following, viz. (*a*) *inspired* literature, (*b*) *original* works connected with

PLATE X

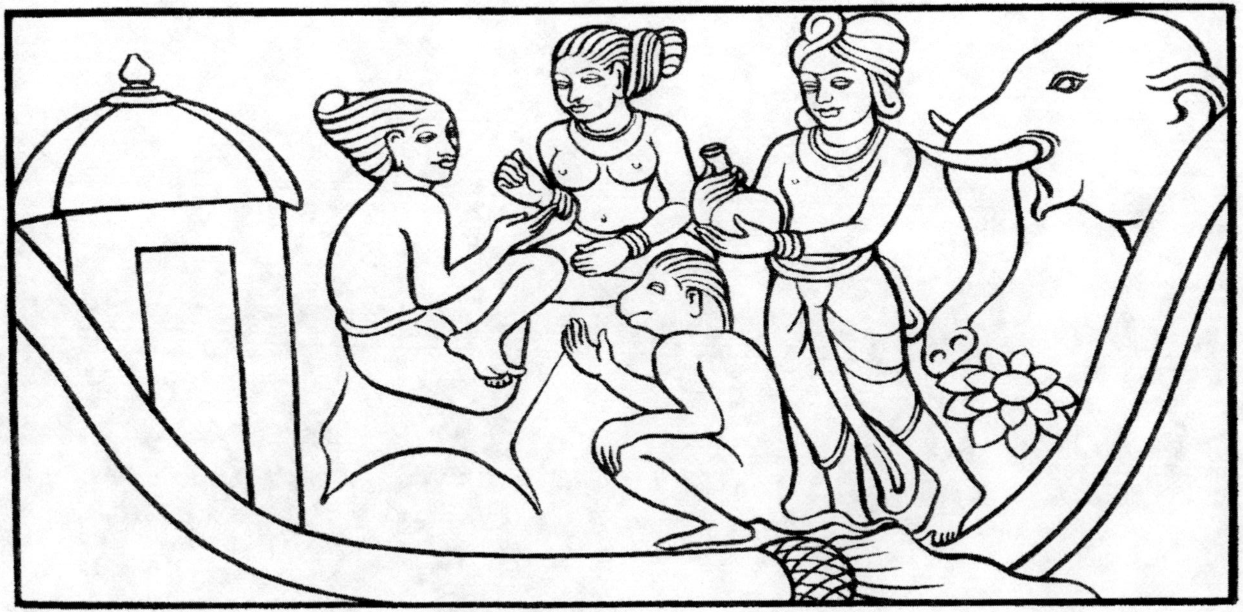

BHARHUT : A HERMITAGE SCENE [No. 3]

[Facing p. 241

traditional literature, sacred and profane, (*c*) *original* works embodying *new* knowledge, (*d*) *commentaries*, (*e*) *ordinary* compositions. Besides these classes of authors, Pāṇini refers also to thinkers and teachers who might not be the authors of actual works themselves. Three different types of philosophical thinkers are distinguished, viz. (1) the *Āstika*, who believes in the life after death, (2) the *Nāstika*, who has no such belief, and (3) the *Daishṭika*, a rationalist (according to the *Kāśika*) or a fatalist, a predestinarian (according to Bhattojidīkshita [iv, 4, 60]). There are also two other references to the prevalence of similar beliefs [v, 2, 92 ; vi, 1, 49]. Besides thinkers and philosophers, Pāṇini mentions teachers of the first rank who, though not themselves famous for any works of their own, were famous for the works of their pupils. Kalāpa and Vaiśampāyana were teachers of this type whose discourses were so fruitful that they gave rise to different schools of thought, all within the domain of the subject-matter of those discourses. Each of the several pupils of those great instructors became the founder of an independent system, so vital and varied were the seeds of thought implanted in their minds [iv, 3, 104]. In this connection we may also refer to the *Brahmavādins* who, according to Kātyāyana [Vārttika 2 on iii, 2, 78], *discoursed* on sacred texts, though they might not themselves be authors of independent works.

Classes of Ascetics. There were also other educators of thought in the country. Pāṇini refers to the class of *Parivrājakas* or religious mendicants of the last Āśrama or fourth stage of life who were also called *Maskariṇaḥ* [vi, 1, 154]. They were so called because, as explained by Patañjali, they preached thus to the people : " Perform ye no works (i.e. sacrifices) : seek ye peace as the highest end." Thus these wandering preachers, renouncing the world, went about the country teaching doctrines which preferred the pursuit of inner peace as being more religious than the disquieting performance of external ceremonies. Pāṇini alludes to two classes of ascetics [iv, 4, 73], viz. those called *Āraṇyakas* who, according to the rules of their order, must dwell at least two miles away from human habitations and those called *Naikaṭika* bhikshus who are permitted to live in the vicinity of society [*Kāśika* ; but, according to the *Bālamanoramā*, the *Naikaṭikas* do so in violation of rules].

Thus the spread of learning was being promoted by the co-operation of various agencies, by books and men, by literature and instruction, by authors and teachers, by regular training and occasional discourses.

Variety of Educational Institutions. Pāṇini indicates the variety of institutions in the country through which its learning and culture were promoted. There were firstly, of course, the schools proper of the residential type where the householder-teacher would regulate the life and studies of a number of boarder-pupils he could conveniently manage. But, as has been already explained in some of the earlier chapters, the precise character of the work of these schools cannot be properly appreciated without a reference to their social and cultural background. We must view them not by themselves as isolated institutions out of touch with the larger life of the community but as parts of the entire organization of learning and culture which the country developed. That organization was made up of several typically Indian institutions which were known as *Kula*, *Gotra*, *Charaṇa*, and *Parishad*. We have already dealt with the distinctive character, scope, and functions of these institutions and are here concerned only with what we may know of them from the Pāṇinean literature. It is, however, to be noted once again that these institutions are primarily concerned and connected with the social life of the community, but they have certain important cultural and educational aspects which cannot be ignored.

'Gotra.' The *Gotra* may be defined as a system of relations based upon community of ancestors. In the earlier stages of the history of the institution, the joint-membership in any given *Gotra* seems to have been determined less on the grounds of mere physical descent than on those of spiritual connection and inheritance. The Vedic mantras, religious traditions, and sacrificial customs which came to be associated with the name of a particular Ṛishi became the property of the *Gotra* in later times. Its physical aspects were strengthened by the connected ceremony of the *pravara* by which Agni had to be invoked under the names of three or five ancestors. Thus a knowledge of ancestors descended from generation to generation and helped to impart a certain degree of stability or definiteness to the genealogical relations of various families. Pāṇini has quite a number of references to the *Gotra* [ii, 4, 58–61, 63–70 ; iv, 1, 78, 79, 89–94, 98–112, 162–7 ; iv, 2, 111 ; iv, 3, 80 and 126]. They give numerous well-known Gotra-names, e.g. Paila, Taulvali, Yāska, Atri, Bhṛigu, Kutsa, Vasishṭha, Gotama, Aṅgiras, Tika, Kitava, Āgastya, Kauṇḍinya, Kuñja, Harita, Śaradvat, Śunaka, Darbha, Droṇa, Parvata,

Jīvanta, Garga, Madhu, Babhru, Kapi, Bodha (an Āṅgirasa), Vataṇḍa, Aśva, Śiva, Kaṇva. They also give us a glimpse of the system of social organization. It was made up of patriarchal families. Three forms of surnames are mentioned by Pāṇini as denoting the Gotra or family. The first was the patronymic by which the head of the united family, the patriarch, was known. Thus Garga or Gargāchārya was the recognized head of the united family of all the Gargas who may be more than a hundred. The second form of the surname was applied to his eldest son and heir who was called Gārgi, while the third form was applied to his grandsons, called Gārgyas. On the death of the patriarch his eldest son, Gārgi was to be called Garga, and his eldest grandson Gārgi, while the great-grandsons, who were called Gārgāyaṇas, were now to be called Gārgyas. It may be also noted that on the death of the patriarch, the other sons designated *youths* (*yuvan*) were subordinate to his authority. On the failure of a direct descendant in the line, the paterfamilias passed on to a collateral relation, but a position of superiority attached to the oldest surviving member, be he an uncle of the surviving representative of the Gotra or the elder brother of his grandfather. Pāṇini also notices the term *Kula* [iv, 1, 79 and 139], which is explained by the commentators to be the non-famous Gotras or families, e.g. Puṇika, Bhuṇika, Mukhara as instanced by *Kāśikā* and Gārgya, Vaida, and Āṅgas as instanced by Patañjali [gloss on ii, 4, 64].

'Charaṇas.' These *Gotras* or close corporations of culture could not, however, remain as such for ever. The special body of knowledge, of traditions, doctrines, and customs which was vested in each as its exclusive property could not long continue in its necessary narrowness, but had to be thrown open to the community in the interests of its own growth and of public instruction. Thus the *Gotras* came to be federated together for their common good. Out of this federation arose that peculiar synthesis or institution known as the *Charaṇa*. Members of different *Gotras* with their particular culture-traditions now united in the *Charaṇas* to widen their culture. The *Gotra* became more and more indicative of the blood-relationship, while the *Charaṇa* indicated a spiritual relationship, an ideal fellowship. Every pupil had thus a double relationship, what Pāṇini calls *Vidyā-yoni-sambandha*, i.e. relationship in learning and blood. As every person was bound to seek an *Āchārya* for instruction, he was considered to be his descendant in a spiritual sense [i, 3, 36 (*āchāryakaraṇa*)].

The *Charaṇas* in Pāṇini's times had a much wider basis

than before. Two elements are distinguished in that basis by Kātyāyana [Vārttika, 11, to iv, 2, 120], viz. (1) *Āmnāya*, i.e. the sacred texts handed down by repetition, and (2) *Dharma*, i.e. the laws peculiar to the Charaṇa. Thus each *Charaṇa* had its own particular set of traditional texts and customs or practical usages and regulations [see also iv, 1, 63].

Variety of ' Charaṇas '. Thus the *Charaṇas*, from their very constitution, promoted a considerable degree of specialization. The specialization was also necessarily carried in a double direction, theoretical and practical. Pāṇini thus refers to a wide variety of such special schools.

Schools based on different Vedic texts are mentioned. Thus *Śākala* or *Śākalaka* is the name of the *Saṁgha* or *Charaṇa* for the study of the Śākala *Śākhā* or recension of the *Rigveda* [iv, 3, 128]. Pāṇini also refers to the schools of Kaṭha, Charaka, and Kalāpin [ib. 107, 108], to which Patañjali adds Kauthuma [gloss on ii, 4, 3], Maudaka, and Paippalādaka [iv, 3, 120 (11)]. According to Patañjali, the Kāṭhaka and Kālāpaka recensions were very popular, being taught in every village. *Paippalādaka* refers to a recension of the Atharvaveda, while the other terms are connected with the Śākhās of the Yajurveda. Kātyāyana refers to the School of the *Ātharvaṇas* [Vārttika 2 to iv, 3 (131)]. We may also note in this connection the different Vedic *Charaṇas* founded by each of the *four* immediate pupils of Kalāpī and of the *nine* of Vaiśampāyana as indicated by Pāṇini [iv, 3, 104].

Special Schools. Specialization was also achieved in the domain of priestly literature and practices. Pāṇini mentions the special schools of the *Chhāndoga* priests (who sang in metre, i.e. the Udgātṛi priests) and also of the *Ukthikas* [who recited certain verses called *Ukthas* to be distinguished from *Sāman* verses which are chanted and from Yajus verses which are muttered sacrificial formulas (Monier Williams)]. There are also mentioned the schools of the Yājñikas and Bahvṛichas (i.e. priests connected with the Yajurveda and Rigveda, the latter being the Hotṛi priests who represent the Rigveda in sacrificial ceremonies). The Schools of these classes of priests were the custodians of the texts and rules which they had to study to qualify themselves for their work [iv, 3, 129].

There was also progress of specialization in other departments of knowledge not directly connected with religion. Pāṇini refers to the School of the *Naṭas*. The formation *Nāṭyam* connotes the literature and practices bearing on the dramatic art [ib.]. Patañjali mentions specialists in instrumental music like the

Mārdaṅgika [iv, 4, 55]. Pāṇini mentions the specialist in the art of story-telling [*Kāthika*, iv, 4, 102]. Patañjali mentions specialists like the *Aitihāsika* and *Paurāṇika* [iv, 2, 60], the *Vaiyākaraṇa*, and *Mīmāṁsaka* [gloss on ii, 2, 29]. He mentions grammarians of the school of Śākalya [iv, 1, 18 (1)]. He also refers to military schools where the science of the bow was taught [*Dhanushi śikshate*, i, 3, 21 (3)]. It may be noted that he mentions fight with cavalry (*aśvairyuddham*) and with weapons (*asiviryuddham*) [v, 1, 59 (4)].

'Parishads.' Lastly, we have also references to the *Parishads*. We have already examined in an earlier chapter their constitution, composition, and functions. They were of the nature of an executive council regulating the relations between different *Charaṇas* and giving authoritative and binding decisions on the doubtful points in the general social laws. Pāṇini refers to the Institution in two Sūtras [iv, 4, 44 and 101]. In the one, the formation *Pārishadya* is explained as one who attends a meeting, and therefore is a member of the *Parishad*, and in the other, the formation *Pārishada* is explained as one who is clever at debates in the meetings of the *Parishad* [*Parishadi sādhu*]. The term *Sabhya* was used to signify the specialist in oratory [iv, 4, 105].

Women and Education. Women were not denied education. The Vārttika on iv, 1, 48 makes this quite clear. Women teachers, not their wives, are called *Upādhāyī* or *Upādhyāyā*, *Āchāryā*. Bhattojidīkshita [1] explains these terms to mean ladies who are themselves teachers, while the *Bālamonoramā* quotes an interesting old verse to show that in earlier times there were women who were well versed in Vedic literature and were called *Brahmavādinīs*.[2] Women-students of Vedic Śākhās are referred to by Pāṇini [iv, 1, 63]. Thus *Kaṭhī* means the female student of the Kaṭha *Śākhā* ; *Bahvṛichī* means the student who studies many hymns, i.e. the Rigveda [*Bālamonoramā* and *Kāśikā*]. Women seem also to have been admitted to military training, as indicated by the formation, *Śāktikī*, mentioned by Patañjali [iv, 1, 15 (6)], which means a female spear-bearer, and in this connection we may indeed refer to the Amazonian bodyguard of armed women which Megasthenes noticed in the palace of the emperor, Chandragupta Maurya.

1 Yātu svayamevādhyāpikā.

2 Yugāntare Brahmavādinyaḥ striyaḥ santi tadvishaye idam | Purā yugeshu nārīṇāṁ mauñjībandhanamishyate | Adhyāpanaṁcha Vedānāṁ Sāvitrī vachanaṁ tathā || iti smaraṇāt | This shows that the women were admitted to the discipline of *brahmacharya* as indicated by the binding of the muñja girdle and to the studies of the Vedas and repetition of the Sāvitrī mantra, so that they would afterwards be qualified teachers.

CHAPTER VII

EDUCATION IN KAUṬILYA'S 'ARTHAŚĀSTRA'

Kauṭilya's 'Arthaśāstra'. The conditions of education in the Sūtra period are very clearly, if somewhat succinctly, indicated in that famous work, the *Arthaśāstra* of Kauṭilya, which is now regarded almost unanimously by all scholars as the work of the minister of the emperor, Chandragupta Maurya. Kauṭilya indicates the entire circle of the then knowledge as being made up of four divisions called (1) *Ānvikshakī*, (2) *Trayī*, (3) *Vārtā*, (4) *Daṇḍanīti*. Each of these divisions comprises a number of subjects or sciences.

Subjects of Study. The name *Ānvikshakī* stands for the sciences derived from subjective or metaphysical speculation involving keen introspection. Three such different subjects or systems of thought and philosophy are known to Kauṭilya, viz. *Sāṁkhya*, *Yoga*, and *Lokāyata*.

The division called *Trayī* is, of course, made up of the three Vedas, Sāma, Ṛik, and Yajus. The Atharvaveda and Itihāsaveda are also known as Vedas. The Vedāṅgas are also enumerated, viz. Śikshā, Kalpa, Vyākaraṇa, Nirukta, Chhandas, and Jyotisha.

The rules of studentship are clearly mentioned.

Studentship was open to the first three castes. The first Āśrama or stage of life obligatory upon all the three castes was that of studentship.

The duties of the student comprised (1) repetition of sacred texts, (2) worship of fire, (3) ablution, (4) observance of the vow of begging, (5) service to the teacher to the end of his life and in his absence to his son or to the fellow-disciple.

Certain moral and mental qualities are insisted upon as constituting the eligibility for studentship, implying the duties as mentioned above. Learning is regarded as a process of discipline which cannot operate successfully except upon suitable material [*Kriyāhi dravyaṁ vinayati nādravyam*]. Learning cannot train up any student unless he is intent upon or keen about the following requisites thereof, viz. (1) desire to learn, (2) receiving the lessons duly, (3) understanding them, (4) retaining them in memory, (5) reflection upon them, (6) exercise of judgment or discrimination, and (7) love of truth.

The need of a teacher is emphasized. The regulations regarding instruction and discipline will be determined by him according to the subjects of study.

The *Kauṭilīya* gives some new information regarding the preliminary training to be given to a child before he is old enough to be admitted to formal studentship. After the ceremony of tonsure was over, the child was to be taught Writing (*lipi*) and Numbers (i.e. arithmetic, *saṁkhyā*).

The studentship begins with the ceremony of Upanayana. Then the student is introduced to the different subjects of study connected with the four principal divisions of knowledge mentioned above under competent teachers.

The *Kauṭilīya* is primarily concerned with the education of the prince belonging to the ruling Kshatriya caste for which the following details are given.

The studentship of a prince is to continue only up to his sixteenth year when he must marry. During this necessarily short term [1] of his studentship, he is to pursue a threefold course of studies. The first course is in the department of the *Trayī* and *Ānvikshakī*, i.e. religious and philosophical subjects. The teachers of this course must be *Śishṭas*, i.e. teachers whose authority was acknowledged as much for their character as for their learning. The second course of studies was connected with *Vārtā*, i.e. subjects relating to agriculture, cattle-rearing, and trade. These subjects the prince must study under practical experts, viz. the heads of the several actual government departments administering the interests pertaining thereto. The third course for the prince was in *Daṇḍanīti* or the science and art of government. The teachers should be those who were equally proficient in the theory and practice of administration.

Even after his marriage the prince was to continue his studies, for which a time-table is given. In the forenoon he is to receive training in the military arts connected with the four departments of the army, viz. the elephant, the horse, the chariot, and the infantry (which implies training in the art of handling various weapons of war). The afternoon he is to spend in listening

[1] Considering that the Dharma-sūtras prescribe the eleventh year as the age when the Kshatriya is to commence studentship, its term for the prince would thus comprise only six years.

to discourses on *Itihāsa*, which included, according to Kauṭilya, the following subjects, viz. Purāṇa, Itivṛitta, Ākhyāyikā, Udāharaṇa, Dharmaśāstra, and Arthaśāstra. During the available intervals of day and night he is to acquire new and revise old knowledge. In the case of lessons not grasped, he must listen to repeated instruction. Besides these studies, companionship with men of ripe wisdom and culture is also prescribed for the prince as the root of mental and moral growth. In the case of a king, such companionship was afforded by his *Purohita* whom he is to obey as the pupil his preceptor, the son his father, or the servant his master. As regards the qualifications of the *Purohita*, it is stated that he must have the culture and character of a family well versed in traditional learning, fully educated in the Vedas, the six Vedāṅgas, the science of portents and omens, the art of administration, and able, by his knowledge and application of the Atharvan remedies, to ward off calamities due to divine and human agencies.

Schools of Arthaśāstra. That the Sūtra period was an age of specialization leading to the growth of numerous schools of thought in various subjects of study then known is also shown by the evidence of Kauṭilya. In connection with the special subject of the Arthaśāstra with which alone he is concerned in the book, he refers to a number of Schools named after their founders which all grew up long before his time. These Schools are called the Mānavāḥ, Bārhaspatyāḥ, Auśanasāḥ, Pārāśarāḥ, and Āmbhīyāḥ. Besides Schools, individual specialists are also mentioned, viz. Bhāradvāja, Viśālāksha, Parāśara, Piśuna, Kauṇapadanta, Vātavyādhi, Bāhudantīputra, Kātyāyana, Kaṇiṅka-Bhāradvāja, Dīrgha-Chārāyaṇa, Ghoṭamukha, Kiñjalka, and Piśunaputra.[1]

[1] A convenient list of these names is given in Professor D. R. Bhandarkar's *Carmichael Lectures*, 1918, pp. 89, 90.

In this connection we may note the exact significance of the name *Arthaśāstra* as defined by Kauṭilya himself. *Artha* = the source of livelihood of men = the earth as peopled by men whom it supports. The *Artha-śāstra* is the science (and art) dealing with the means by which the earth of human beings is to be acquired and maintained. Thus it comes to mean the science and art of government [p. 426 of Dr. Shama Sastri's edition of the *Kauṭilīya*].

It may also be pointed out that though the evidence of the *Kauṭilīya* has been considered here in connection with the Sūtra period, that work is not a typical Sūtra work, made up as it is of both *sūtras* and *bhāshyas* or commentaries, as Kauṭilya himself reminds us at the end of the book.

CHAPTER VIII

THE LEGAL ASPECTS OF EDUCATION

Legal Evidence. We may conveniently deal here with the very interesting educational evidence furnished in the *Smṛitis* or the Hindu legal literature proper. The evidence is very fully presented in the *Digest of Hindu Law* prepared by Colebrooke, upon which the following account is based.

Litigation between Teacher and Pupil. The law-books have to discuss the relations between the teacher and the taught in connection with the question, To what extent, or under what circumstances, those relations can become the subject-matter of suits or legal proceedings ?

According to Nārada, " When a man yields not the obedience he has promised, it is called a breach of promised obedience, which is a title of law." " Persons bound to obedience are in law declared by the learned to be properly of four kinds, viz. those for science, human knowledge, love, or pay " (Bṛihaspati). Of these, the first class is comprised by the pupils proper who seek the acquisition of the knowledge of " science ", i.e. of the Vedas and the like, while the second class by the apprentices or technical students who seek the acquisition of skill in arts or " human sciences " (Nārada).

" The wise have declared their general dependence " (ib.), which means that they are not their own masters but are themselves subject to masters. This may further mean that they are incapable of acquiring wealth for themselves as pupils, or are liable to punishment for violation of their master's commands.

Bṛihaspati describes the subjects of study of the pupil proper to be the triple science, Ṛik, Yajus, and Sāma-Vedas. " For these let him pay obedience to a spiritual teacher, as directed by the law." This means that, as the commentator points out, " he who yields it not may be reproved or chastised by the teacher, and the preceptor offends not."

The infliction of punishment as a disciplinary measure on the pupil by his teacher is held to be perfectly legal. " In case of strife between teacher and pupil . . . their mutual litigation is not legal " (*Smṛiti*). The teacher's right to punish is also emphasized by Manu who also gives directions for its exercise by way of indicating its limiting conditions which it would be illegal for the teacher to transgress. " A pupil may be corrected when he commits faults with a rope or the small shoot of a cane but on the back part only of his body, and not on any noble part by any means." Says Gautama : " The correction of a pupil for ignorance or incapacity should be given with a small rope or shoot of a cane ; the teacher shall be punished by the king, if he strike with any other instrument."

The law-books contemplate the contrary possibility of the case of a pupil striking his preceptor. Such an offending pupil will, according to Yājñavalkya, have his punishment equal to that of the highest scale of crime.

The meaning of these regulations is very well explained by Vijñāneśvara. According to one regulation cited above, *all* litigation between teacher and pupil is illegal. The fact of the matter is " that a suit preferred before the king is irregular, and, preferred by the teacher against his pupil, is forbidden. But if the pupil violate his duty, and the teacher being weak is not able to correct him, it is consistent with common sense that he should then apply to the king ; for, by violating his duty, the pupil absolutely becomes *pāshaṇḍa* or irreligious ". " The litigation of teachers and the rest is not laudable, either in a moral or civil law ; therefore pupils and others should, in the first instance, be discouraged by the king or the court. But in very important cases, the suits of pupils may be entertained in the form mentioned." Thus, in regard to punishment, " if a teacher, from an impulse of wrath, strike his pupil with a great staff on a noble part (of his body), then should the pupil, hurt in a mode contrary to law, complain to the king, there exists a subject of litigation."

The duties of studentship are thus stated. " Until he acquires the science, let the pupil diligently obey his preceptor ; his conduct should be the same towards the preceptor's wife and his son : *Afterwards*, performing the stated ceremonies on his return home, and giving to his instructor the gratuity of a teacher, let him return to his own house. This conduct is prescribed to the pupil " (Nārada). Violation of duties under these injunctions cannot be subject-matter of litigation. The commentator has the following explanation : " The suit of a teacher, if his gratuity be not paid, is not mentioned by any other author ;

but hell is the pupil's fate, if he pay not a gratuity to his instructor." Obedience to the teacher implies the pupil's dependence on him, so that " he should not go anywhere, nor consume anything, without his preceptor's orders ; and what he acquires by labour should be delivered to the teacher ". As Yājñavalkya puts the matter : " When called, let him study ; and deliver what is gained to his teacher." The commentator takes this to be a moral ordinance. The pupil has the legal right to give away to anyone he pleases either his paternal property or property acquired by him during his minority, though if it is given away without the knowledge or the consent of his teacher there will be a violation of his moral duties. " The pupil must also perform other labour in his preceptor's house." As Yājñavalkya puts it, " Let him constantly promote his teacher's benefit, by every exertion of mind, speech, body, and action."

Rights of Property in respect of Gains of Learning. We have in the legal literature another kind of interesting educational evidence in connection with the discussion of property which is not subject to partition. An example of such property is " wealth acquired by learning " as stated by Manu. Other law-givers describe the various means by which wealth can be acquired by learning and the description thus necessarily acquaints us with some typical facts and features in the intellectual life of the times and some characteristic educational institutions.

The following texts of Kātyāyana will speak for themselves :

What has been acquired by learning, after instruction received from a stranger and a maintenance provided by one of a different family, is called wealth gained by learning (1).

What is gained by proving superior learning, after a prize has been offered by some third person, must be considered as the acquisition of a scholar, and ought not in general to be divided among co-heirs (2).

So what has been received as a gift from a pupil, as a gratuity for the performance of a sacrifice, as a fee for answering a question in casuistry, or for ascertaining a doubtful point of law ; or what has been gained as a reward for displaying knowledge, or for victory in a learned contest, or for reading the Veda with transcendent ability (3).

Such wealth have the sages declared to be the acquisition of science, and not subject to distribution ; and the law is the same in regard to liberal or elegant arts, and to increase of price from superior skill in them (4).

A prize which has been offered for the display of superior learning and a gift received from a votary for whom a sacrifice was formerly performed, or a present from a pupil formerly instructed, sages have declared to be the acquisition of science : what is otherwise acquired is the joint property of the co-heirs (5).

Even what is won by surpassing another in learning, after a stake has been deposited, Bṛihaspati pronounces the acquisition of knowledge and impartible (6).

What is obtained by the boast of learning, what is received from a pupil, or for the performance of a sacrifice, Bhṛigu calls the acquisition of science (7).

Yet Bṛihaspati has ordained that wealth shall be partible if it was gained by learned brothers who were instructed in the family by their father, or by their paternal grandfather or uncles (8).

In case of increment to paternal wealth, the acquirer gets a double share according to the following text of Vasishṭha :

He among the brothers who singly acquires wealth shall take a double share of it (9).

Nārada mentions a distinction in the case of *Vidyādhana* (gains of learning) of a certain kind :

He who, be he ever so ignorant, maintains the family of a brother while engaged in study will share the wealth which that brother may gain by his learning (10).

Variety of Educational Institutions. Thus these texts point to a variety of institutions through which the spread of learning and culture was promoted.

In (1) we have a reference to the normal method of imparting instruction to a pupil who has to leave his parental home and maintenance and live with his chosen preceptor who gives him free board, lodging, and tuition. But though usual and ordinary, this particular mode of acquisition of learning in which the pupil is not supported during the period of his tuition by his paternal property has, as shown in the text, important legal consequences to the material gains which he may subsequently realize from his learning.

In (8) is indicated the parallel practice of giving to boys education in their own homes, the preceptor being their father, grandfather, or uncle. The special proficiency shown by a particular son with the necessarily superior earning power it gives him is duly recognized by law, as shown in (9).

In (10) we have a reference to the third variety in the methods of educational organization. Where a preceptor would not admit a pupil for his inability to maintain him and yet is regarded as indispensable for his education, the pupil was allowed to bring his own means of maintenance with him and become a paying member of his preceptor's family. The text pictures to us a dutiful brother, himself devoid of learning, being anxious for the learning of a more promising brother whom he supports at school by his own self-sacrifice which is duly recognized and rewarded in law.

Presents to Teacher. In (3) and (5) is indicated the time-honoured Hindu institution of paying voluntary fees to the preceptor for all the pains and expenses he undergoes in educating his pupil. In fact the usual source of the preceptor's property and maintenance is the presents of his pupils whether just discharged from their studentship or formerly instructed. In the case of the latter we have another proof of the abiding cordiality of the relations between the teacher and the taught which are cultivated with so much care under so many regulations during the period of the tuition and are expected to continue beyond it and indeed lasted through life.

Higher Academic Activities. Besides the school for the young or the pupils proper, we have in the other texts references to institutions of a higher type meant for the advancement of learning of and by the elderly and mature scholars through the opportunities they afford of varied and vital academical intercourse. The friction of minds is necessary for sharpening their powers and strengthening their grasp of truth which must not remain only as a matter of one's subjective realization. The mastery of truth has to be proved by objective standards and established against external criticism. It is this sound principle of pedagogics on the basis of which the Nyāya philosophy has laid down *Suhṛitprāpti* as one of the aids to the acquisition of knowledge. Truth must triumph over all attacks. Hence the remarkable development in all ages of Indian culture-history of these characteristically Hindu institutions of academic gatherings for the purpose of holding intellectual tournaments, those Philosophical Conferences and Science Congresses which were known to India as early as 1000 B.C., as shown by the evidence of the *Brāhmaṇas* and Upanishads already dealt with.

In the texts (2)–(6) are indicated various types of learned debates and dialectical contests with the different forms of recognition given to intellectual primacy.

Upanyāsa. According to (2), the intellectual contest or examination is held, and the superiority of learning is proved, in the field of *Upanyāsa* which is " explained in the *Madanaratna* to be the recitation of the Vedas in the several modes of stringing together the different *padas* or words such as *Krama*, *Jaṭā*, etc. Others say it means the exposition of abstruse topics in an assembly " [*Vyāvahāra-Mayūkha* [1]]. The prize of victory offered is in accordance with established tradition and approved precedent and practice as shown in the *Śatapatha Brāhmaṇa* already referred to.

Praśna ; Vāda. In (3), there is a reference to various kinds of intellectual competition and competence. The principal sources of the preceptor's property are indicated. They are the presents of pupils and the fees for performing sacrifices paid by a votary. Thus the two normal occupations of a learned Brahmin were teaching and priestcraft. Next, there is a reference to controversial social questions (*praśna*) in the solution of which learned men found opportunities of proving their merit and honourably earning money. According to the *Smṛiti-Chrandikā*, the *Praśna* as a source of the gain of learning is that relating to the determination of the suitable atonement or *prāyaśchitta* for the minor sins (*upapātaka*). This indicates the specialization of some learned men in social legislation. Thirdly, there is a reference to the settlement of doubts of a person regarding the meaning of a particular ordinance or deciding a question of law between two contending parties who apply for an award (*Mitākshara*). Thus some learned men would specialize in law and serve on the Parishads and find ample means of livelihood from a legal career, either from arbitration or giving " consultations " and opinions (somewhat like the " Chamber practice " of lawyers in modern times). Sometimes again a young scholar would have his learning and ability recognized by others and so would be selected for gifts by the wealthy acting on the public opinion about him. Sometimes victory in a *Vāda* explained as a " contest relative to sacred literature or any other learned controversy " would be amply rewarded.

Prādhyayanam. There is again a reference to cases where something is proposed to be given away for which there are many deserving competitors. In such cases *Prādhyayanam*, i.e. ability

[1] Kramajaṭādīnāṁ saṁkalitānāṁ pāṭha iti *Madanaratne* | Sabhāyāṁ gūḍhaprameyavivṛiti iti kechit | The *Smṛiti-Chandrikā* explains it as ' Vargatyāgādivaichitryeṇa upanyaste '.

in reciting the Veda would be adopted as the standard for determining superiority of learning. Some take *Prādhyayanam* to be not superior recitation of the Veda but "the excellent lecture of it", such as "the recital of one *Śākhā* of the Veda in one day". It may also mean recital of the Purāṇas and the like. As regards intellectual contests, the commentators draw attention to the fact that sometimes a prize may be previously announced for victory or "display of superior learning", or sometimes though no such prize may be offered the victor may win his due reward from a rich man in the assembly moved to make a gift by "the satisfaction afforded to him by overcoming an adversary in disputation". Such kinds of spontaneous literary patronage must have been of very usual occurrence in the academic life of the country when they have been noticed in the law-books as constituting a source of income to the learned men. Wealth could always be depended upon to come forward in support of learning. Again, "a fee for answering a question in casuistry (*praśna*)" is sometimes explained as "a reward received on account of the gratification afforded by the solution of a question. For instance, a man possessing immense knowledge attends a universal monarch and discusses a question proposed by him; though he do not gain the victory (for even in controversy a conqueror of worlds is invincible) yet, spreading lustre over the assembly, he receives a reward from the monarch". Regarding *Prādhyayanam*, some commentators take objection to its meaning as merely "reading the Veda with transcendent ability". Their view is that "the wages of mere transcribers, and generally the fee received from the audience for reading the Veda, Purāṇas, and the like, without transcendent skill in poetry, and in explaining the sense of poems: this, and other similar gains, according to Chaṇḍeśvara and the rest, are not the acquisition of science. In fact in all cases whatsoever wherein superior skill is required the wealth gained is technically denominated the acquisition of science. Otherwise it is simply wealth acquired by the man himself". The fees from *Prādhyayanam* (whatever may be the right meaning of the term) regarded as a source of income to the learned point without doubt to that remarkable agency of popular education under which readings in the Vedas, Purāṇas, and other sacred literature were organized by means of circles of competent scholars who specialized in such readings before the larger assemblies of the common people.

Appliances of Learning Impartible. In (4) we see how property in the special gains derived from superior technical skill (' such as that of painters, goldsmiths, and the like, and even of gaming ') is governed by the same laws as those applying in the sphere of liberal learning.

Along with the *Vidyādhana* or gains of learning as acquired in the various ways explained above, the necessary implements or appliances of learning or of arts are also to be deemed impartible, e.g. " books and the like in the study of the Vedas, etc. ", or " pencils and tools " for the study of the fine arts. Books are " not to be shared by ignorant brethren. So what is adapted to the arts belongs to artists, not to persons ignorant of the particular art ".

Teacher as Heir of Pupil. The relationship of a teacher, a pupil, or a priest has been given a distinct legal value in Hindu Law. According to Baudhāyana, on failure of all heirs claiming any sort of blood-relationship, "the spiritual preceptor, the pupil, or the priest engaged to perform sacrifices, shall take the inheritance." The *Āchārya*, spiritual preceptor, is defined by Baudhāyana as " he who girds the pupil with the sacrificial cord and instructs him in the Vedas ". On failure of these heirs the succession passes on to the fellow-student " who studies the Veda under the same teacher ". According to the law as laid down by Gautama, the legal heirs may also include " persons allied by funeral oblations, family name, and by patriarchal descent ", but commentators differ as to whether this remote relationship in blood has precedence over the relationship in learning. At any rate it must be observed that the law accords a lower status to the spiritual relationship through learning than that given to it by the rules relating to Brahmacharya under which the preceptor is to be regarded as the equal of the pupil's parents as regards the reverence and obedience due from him. This equality, as has been already pointed out, was emphasized in a much earlier age when we find its recognition in a Sūtra of Pāṇini relating to the relationship of blood and learning—*vidyāyonisaṁbandha*—to which is to be applied the same grammatical suffix.

Property accruing to a person in pupilage. The institution of the young pupil leaving his home and parents to live with his preceptor for education had its own legal consequences which are duly provided for. For it may so often happen that during this period of the pupil's tuition, " wealth may descend to him by inheritance and become his property." In such a case Manu thus lays down the law: "The king should guard the property which descends to an infant by inheritance until he returns from the house of his preceptor."

Property of Ascetics. Lastly, the law relating to the inheritance of anchorites and devotees gives some interesting evidence. According to Yājñavalkya [ii, 137] the heirs who take the wealth of a *Vānaprastha* (a hermit), of a *Yati* (an ascetic), and a *Brahmachārī* are in their order the preceptor, the virtuous pupil (*Satśishya*), and one who is a supposed brother and belongs to the same order (*dharmabhrātā* and *ekatīrthī*). Here we have a reference to some typical Hindu institutions. The term *Brahmachārī* points to the institution of perpetual studentship. The pupil who adopts this vow (of continuing as a student through life without marrying and entering upon the householder's state) is technically known as *Naishṭhika*, the temporary student being called an *Upākurvāṇa*. Next we have the term *Dharmabhrāta*, the spiritual brother, the brother by religious duties. The term *Ekatīrthī* means one resident in the same holy place, i.e. the same hermitage, and hence pupil of the same preceptor [*Vīramitrodaya*]. The *Satśishya*, the virtuous pupil, is he who is "versed in the study of revelation concerning the supreme soul and in preserving that sacred science". Such a man is the most suitable for inheriting the effects of one whose teachings and practices and way of life would have a chance of surviving him through his successor. The wealth of the deceased is best utilized when it is consecrated to the ideals and purposes for which he lived and worked.

Chapter IX

PHILOSOPHICAL SŪTRA LITERATURE

The Sūtras of Six Systems of Philosophy : their Origins. The account of Education in the Sūtra period will not be complete without a consideration of what may be gathered about it from a special type and class of Sūtras or aphorisms presenting what are known as the six systems of philosophy. In the history of Hindu thought, and also from the educational point of view, these philosophical Sūtras are possessed of a singular significance and value.

It is, however, to be noted that these do not represent the very first fruits of Indian philosophical speculation which had been in progress from time immemorial. This is seen in the large stock of ideas and technical terms upon which, as the common inheritance from a bygone age, the different Schools of Philosophy have freely drawn in constructing their own systems. The philosophical Sūtras systematize and codify the speculation which is exhibited in an exuberant growth in the *Brāhmaṇas* and older Upanishads, while that growth itself has sprung out of germs contained in a still earlier literature. Indian Philosophy has had, indeed, a very old and continuous history. The early streaks, the dawn of philosophy, are to be discovered in the Vedic Mantras, while the Upanishads show the meridian. The Upanishads contain many technical terms like Brahman, Ātman, Dharma, Vrata, Yoga, Mīmaṁsā, and the like, which point to the activity of speculation in the previous ages, a vast accumulation of religious and philosophical thought upon which they are able to draw. The Upanishads themselves picture the stirring intellectual activity of which they are the products, an activity which, as we have already seen, passed from the solitary hermitages in forests of isolated Brāhmaṇa ascetics to the busy haunts of men, the courts of kings, where it became almost a national concern, a fairly popular pursuit, and not the monopoly of a special caste. The Upanishads, indeed, as Max Müller remarked, represent India as a nation of philosophers with innumerable centres of intellectual activity scattered throughout the country, so that we find men of practically all castes and classes—men and women, Brāhmaṇas, Kshatriyas, and even Śūdras—sharing in that activity, as is seen, for instance, in the anecdotes already related of Satyakāma Jābāla of unknown parentage and of Raikva called a Śūdra, both of whom made their mark in philosophical studies. But the starting-point of all this activity is to be found in the Rigveda itself where we already see speculation earnest on solving the riddle of creation by grasping the Unity behind its diversity. A sense of diversity in the world of appearances expresses itself in the creation of a richly varied Vedic pantheon, of gods like Agni, Indra, Varuṇa, and Vāyu, but behind this variety is the underlying conception of the One "extending as a god to the gods from afar and embracing this universe" [*Rv.*, ii, 24, 11], who is called in His different aspects as Hiraṇyagarbha, Prajāpati, Viśvakarmā [viii, 89, 3], Bṛihaspati, or Brahmanaspati, the god of all gods, culminating in Brahman and Ātman. Lastly, it may be noted that this nascent philosophic thought handed down by oral tradition or embodied in what Max Müller has well called Mnemonic literature produced an extraordinary volume and variety of opinions long before the rise of the philosophical Sūtras or systems. Some evidence of this luxuriant growth of speculation is furnished by one of the Suttas or Sermons supposed to have been preached by the Buddha himself, viz. the *Brahma-jāla-sutta* (literally, the net of Brahma in which all philosophical theories are caught up like fishes in a net). In that work, the Buddha mentions as many as sixty-two different schools of philosophy prevailing in the country even in that early age, together with many subdivisions of such schools which he criticizes and condemns in his pursuit of Truth.

Their Ages. In the midst of this multiplicity of schools of thought, the six systems of philosophy have stood out and held their own as the most typical and representative of them all. The six systems have come to be distinguished as orthodox systems from the heterodox systems of the Buddhists, Jains, and Chārvākas, because they are all somehow reconcilable with the Vedic system, though they mutually differ in their relations to the same. The six systems are known as (1) the *Sāṁkhya* of Kapila, (2) *Yoga* of Patañjali, (3) *Nyāya* of Gautama, (4) *Vaiśeshika* of Kaṇāda, (5) *Karma* or *Pūrva Mīmāṁsā* of Jaimini, and (6) *Śārīraka* or *Uttara Mīmāṁsā* or *Vedānta* of Bādarāyaṇa. It is to be noted that the philosophers to whom these systems are ascribed were not necessarily their originators. They gave the final form to the Sūtras which themselves refer to older philosophers. Some of the Sūtras, again, refer to the opinions of other Sūtras, which shows that the different philosophical Schools were already in existence before the final redaction of the Sūtras took place. It may further be noted that the extant literary works in which the doctrines of the six systems are embodied are themselves much later in date than their original founders. Thus the *Sāṁkhya-Kārikā* of Īśvara Krishṇa, giving the best exposition of the Sāṁkhya system, which was taken by Paramārtha to China in A.D. 546, is generally considered to be not older than the fourth century A.D., the period of Indian literary revival under the Gupta emperors. Similarly, Bādarāyaṇa, Jaimini, Kaṇāda, or Patañjali are to be regarded as mere eponymous founders of their respective philosophical schools, so that whatever might be the date of the actual composition of the Sūtras embodying their systems, they were ascribed to them in accordance with the characteristic and time-honoured Hindu literary practice of fathering the subsequent works of disciples upon their *gurus* (though there might be occasionally exceptions to this practice, as in the case of Śaunaka suppressing his own work in favour of his disciples). Thus though, on grounds of rigid chronological standard, the philosophical Sūtras do not come within the Sūtra period proper, they may be justifiably considered as belonging to that period on the basis of what Max Müller aptly calls "the chronology of thought" by which we are able to distinguish between the three phases of Vedic thought represented by Mantras, Brāhmaṇas, and Upanishads, followed by the period of the Sūtra literature, during which even the Buddhists were composing their *Suttas* after the literary fashion of the times.

Systems of Philosophy as Systems of Discipline and Education. These systems of philosophy insist on their own ideas and systems of discipline by which the pupil has to acquire and fulfil those qualifications and conditions that are required of him by way of *adhikāra* or eligibility for his chosen philosophical studies. This course of arduous preparatory discipline is dictated by the typical Hindu point of view which treats philosophy not as a mere subject of study through books but as something to be lived, like religion, as truth to be realized. It was studied as a means for the attainment of the highest truth or *mukti*, emancipation which one is to attain by stages of experience, each representing a specific degree of conquest achieved over the body and the material world. A system of philosophy is a system of Release. Thus philosophical study is bound up with a system of discipline.

At the outset it is to be noted that the different Schools of Philosophy rest on a common system of discipline as their foundation. This system is known as *Varṇāśramadharma*, the regulations belonging to the different castes and *āśramas* of life. These comprise the various *saṁskāras* or sacraments prescribed for the different stages of life: *Upanayana*, *Brahmacharya*, and *Samāvartana* (graduation) for its first stage, that of Studentship; the various sacrifices prescribed for the householder's life (already described); the rules for the gradual detachment from the world in the third stage of the forest-dwelling hermit; followed by the last stage of a wandering mendicant to be devoted wholly to meditation [for details see my *Hindu Civilization*, London, 1936, pp. 128–133].

All these sacraments are intended to equip the finite self with a suitable physical body which might sustain the burden of the arduous pursuit of knowledge through life. The *Chhāndogya Upanishad* [viii, 15] thus describes the life of the ideal householder brought up under this system. " He who returns home from the family of his teacher, after the prescribed study of the Veda carried on in the time remaining over from his work for the teacher, and continues the private study of the Veda in his own household in a pure neighbourhood, trains up pious sons and pupils, subdues all his organs in the soul, and injures no living beings except for a sacred purpose—he, in truth, if he maintains this manner of life all his days, enters into the world of Brahman and does not return." Even such a householder by way of further purification and progress has to retire from his household, renounce the world, and take to the forest to live the life of an anchorite in meditation, penances, fasts, living on food that is not the outcome of cultivation, and offering a few select sacrifices, then, in the last stage, performing the *prājāpatya* sacrifice at which he gives away all his meagre belongings as the sacrificial fee, he wanders about as a mendicant, conquering Desire and attaining Brahman.

On the basis of this common foundation of a disciplined life, each of these systems of philosophy has built up its own methods of education, training, and discipline. This is indicated by the use of the word *atha* with which the different philosophical

Sūtras begin. The word is used in two senses, the first by way of auspicious beginning and a literary formality and the second to indicate the continuity of the exposition, presupposing a course of preparatory training. This sense is called *ānantaryārtha*. This course of preparatory training is different in different schools of philosophy.

The Discipline of Vedānta. As the best example of these special systems of discipline, we shall begin with that of the Vedānta which describes it more fully than the other schools of philosophy, while it is also described by no less an authority and philosopher than Śaṅkara in his *Bhāshya* on the Vedānta-Sūtras, and also in his *Upadeśasāhasrī*. The following account is based on these works.

Views of Śaṅkara. Śaṅkara begins by defining the subject-matter of Vedānta. It is *Brahma-jijñasā*, " an inquiry into Brahman," and not *Dharma-jijñāsā*, " the inquiry into Dharma," which is the subject of *Pūrva-Mīmāṁsā*.

Study of Texts. The student of Vedānta will thus study those Vedic texts which deal with *Brahman*, excluding those which deal with *Dharma* and the acts or rituals which are prescribed for purposes of Dharma. These are not his concern, because they lead only to transitory felicity, and not to eternal bliss which is his objective. Of the Vedic texts, Śaṅkara says that the teacher should first teach those bearing upon the unity of Self and then those containing definitions of Brahman, the Supreme Self.

The study of these select Vedic texts is to be carried out in the prescribed manner under the discipline of *brahmacharya*. Mere desire for philosophical study is not enough qualification for it. One must acquire an inner capacity for it, and this can be acquired only by a preliminary study of the Veda as a Brahmachārī.

Discipline of Āśramas. The discipline of the other *āśramas* of life is also necessary for the purpose. It is necessary for purifying and preparing the mind so that it can grasp Brahman as the only and ultimate Reality. This means that the mind must be able to discriminate between the eternal and the non-eternal (*nityānitya-viveka*), to perceive the ephemeral character of the world so as to detach itself from it and ultimately to renounce it in an utter indifference to all enjoyment both here and hereafter (*ihāmutrabhoga-virāga*). Then alone will be awakened in the disciple the desire to know the Brahman (*brahma-jijñāsā*). One must be fired with the desire for self-realization as the only way to salvation (*mumukshutva*).

Steps of Self-realization. For this self-realization the following steps are thus prescribed :—

(1) *Śravaṇa*, " hearing of Vedānta texts as expounded by the teacher " ;

(2) *Manana*, " reflection on their meaning " ;

(3) *Nididhyāsana*, " constant meditation on the Self described in those texts."

This process is to be continued until the immediate apprehension of Reality is achieved.

Meditation and its Stages. Constant practice of meditation is required to develop the faculty whereby the Self can be realized, just as constant practice alone can awaken the musical faculty which enables a perception of the niceties of sound and tone.

But it is not easy to meditate on and realize the Self at once. A start may be made by taking Him as the Sun (as his most conspicuous manifestation) and then as *Ākāśa*.

These minor Meditations will lead up to the final Meditation on the true Self.

Meditation is always to be practised in a sitting posture or one conducive to its uninterrupted continuance, for which the best time and place should be selected.

This Meditation as a means and process of self-realization presupposes much preparation. First, the body as the vehicle of mind is to be purified by penances. Then, the mind has to be cleansed by Restraints (*yama*), Observances (*niyama*), and Austerities (*tapas*). For the Mind, the most important discipline is its one-pointedness (*ekāgratā*) or concentration, the best of virtues, to be achieved by overcoming its usual states defined as (1) *Kshipta*, " distraction " ; (2) *Vikshipta*, " lack of continuous concentration " ; (3) *Mūḍha*, " sluggishness." *Ekāgratā* then leads to the final stage of mental discipline, the stage of *Nirodha* or total suspension of mental activity (*vṛitti*). The Mind is also to be further purged of its notions of " I " and " Mine " as impurities so as to enable it to receive the knowledge of the Self.

Śaṅkara marks out three stages in this Meditation leading up to a knowledge of the Self, viz. (1) the seeker after Truth is to start by meditating anything he chooses either within his own " heart " (as representing a specific centre of experience in spiritual discipline), or outside his body as apart from its name and form ; (2) the second stage is that of uninterrupted meditation upon the One Entity, Absolute, Impartite, of the nature of *Sat-Chit-Ānanda*, " the Supreme and only Reality, Self-luminous Consciousness, and Bliss " ; (3) in the third stage the *sādhaka* remains completely immobile in rapturous self-realization, in which all notion of " *mine* " with reference to the body (*dehātma-bodha*) has melted away and the Higher Self is realized. He henceforth passes all his time in meditation.

It will thus be apparent that such supreme knowledge can come only to one who has conquered desire for son, wealth, and fame, has renounced the world, and is in the fourth *āśrama* of life, as a wandering mendicant marked by the virtues known as *Śama*, " control of the overt behaviour." *Dama*, " regulation of the inner impulses," *Samādhāna*, " attention and concentration of mind," *Śraddhā*, " faith," *Titikshā*, " ability to bear with equanimity the tensions caused by the operation of stimuli coming from antagonistic qualities, and by the appetites of the body," and, lastly, *Uparati*, " ability to withdraw one's mind completely from the external stimuli."

In fine, Śankara's scheme of Vedantic discipline is that thought and feelings, attitudes and dispositions, impulses and behaviour, are all to be shaped into new configurations. Conscious reflection on the background of these mental patterns brings home to the disciple a new order of values, other than those of ordinary life. Thus the study of the Vedānta is to proceed on the basis of such a re-oriented personality.

Views of other Philosophers : Sureśvara. Sureśvara presents his scheme as follows. To achieve liberation (*naishkarmasiddhi*), one must destroy his ignorance which is non-realization of the unity of Self. This cannot be done by performance of religious rites which can, however, help it indirectly by purifying the mind by detaching it from all pleasures of this world or the next, as they are found to be ephemeral. Thence arises *vairāgya*, renunciation, followed by meditation on Vedic texts like " *Tat Tvam asi* ". Another help towards this consummation is stated to be *ashtāṅga-yoga* by which consciousness of external objects is lost. These eight *aṅgas* or factors of *Yoga* are (1) *Yama*, " restraints in the form of virtues like *ahiṁsā*, non-violence, and *santosha* or *aparigraha*, continence " ; (2) *Niyama*, " observances like cleanliness, *śaucha*, sacrifices, repeating of Mantras, pouring of libations into fire, offerings to forefathers, charity, fasts, etc." ;

(3) *Āsana*, postures for meditation ; (4) *Prāṇāyāma*, " regulation of breath by its inhalation, inhibition, and exhalation " ; literally, " control of *prāṇa*, the vital plane, i.e. control of springs of impulses " ; (5) *Pratyāhāra*, " detachment " ; (6) *Dhāraṇā*, " retention and elaboration " ; (7) *Dhyāna*, " contemplation of divinities like Śiva, Vishṇu, and the like " ; and (8) *Samādhi*, " absorption in meditation."

Vidyāraṇya. In his *Anubhūtiprakāśa*, Vidyāraṇya repeats the three means of attaining knowledge, viz. *Śravaṇa*, *Manana*, which he defines as reflection on what has been heard to remove doubts, and *Nididhyāsana*, defined as constant meditation to check tendency to error. He further points out that renunciation is indispensable to such meditation, because property entails activity. Therefore, property, i.e. all longing for progeny, wealth, fame, has to be given up for attaining knowledge. This implies the life of a householder which alone can make such renunciation possible. Meditation is possible only where there is no thought except thought of Self.

Sadānanda. To Sadānanda we owe the interesting addition in his *Vedāntasāra* that students of Vedānta must guard against four obstacles to meditation, viz. (1) *Laya*, mental inertia or laziness of mind, (2) *Vikshepa*, distraction, turning of mind on things other than Truth, (3) *Kashāya*, passion which impedes the proper functioning of mind by kindling lust or other desires, and (4) *Rasāsvāda*, " tendency towards emotive enjoyments."

Rāmānuja. While Śaṅkara eschews the study of Vedic texts relating to *Dharma* and concentrates on those relating only to *Brahma*, Rāmānuja does not believe in such restriction. His scheme includes a course of study of the whole Veda with its Karma-Kāṇḍa, because he believes that such a study will lead to the knowledge that the results of rituals are uncertain and transient. This disillusionment will be followed naturally by the desire for that which can secure permanent results. Thence arises *brahmajijñāsā*, the earnest quest of Brahman. Thus, in the opinion of Rāmānuja, " the inquiry into the nature of Brahman " may be preceded by a study of Dharma and practice of Vedic rituals so as to rate them at their proper worth and produce a sense of the eternal.

Nimbārka. Nimbārka follows the line of thought indicated by Rāmānuja. He interprets the term *atha* to include a study of Dharma and performance of its rituals and argues thus : (1) A study of the Veda with all its six limbs (Vedāṅgas) leads to

(2) reflection on the true nature of *Karma* and its results which are perceived to be ephemeral and not as aids to salvation. (3) The result of this reflection kindles a desire for a truer understanding of the Veda by (4) a study of *Pūrva-Mīmāṁsā*. This study gives an insight into Dharma in all its phases and consequences as a system of ultimate laws. Then comes (5) a lively realization of the futility of Karma, of the method of rituals in the religious sphere, and of a life of objective activity and energy in the secular sphere. When the life of Karma is thus valued and exposed, (6) the problem of salvation reappears as the problem of problems, and (7) rouses fully " the inquiry into Brahman ".

The scheme of Nimbārka is ultimately an interpretation of the Vedānta Sūtras from the standpoint of devotional love. First, the resources of ritualistic religion must be fully exploited, their elements of devotion, and incentives to energy and activity, by means of a thorough Vedic study and intellectual culture. It is then only that one can take advantage of the higher spiritual discipline which takes possession of the total trends of the personality. Hindu thought takes philosophy in the sense of a totalitarian discipline and education.

It is to be noted that in all these authoritative expositions of the system of training and education suitable for the study of Vedānta, a very minor part is assigned to study proper, i.e. study of the prescribed texts or literature to which so much importance is attached in modern and secular education. The pivot of this ancient system is not study of literature but an arduous struggle for realization of truth, a process of the gradual transformation of the mental plane through a progressive purification of the springs of action or action-tendencies (*chittaśuddhi*) as a means of meditation on the heights of which settle the eternal sunshine of the verities of Being. Education here is a living process of growth and not an ' additive ' process.

Social Implications of Vedantic Education. The dependence of Vedantic education on a study of the Veda raises some social issues which are indicated in the Sūtras and fully commented upon by Śaṅkara. The question is, since the study of Veda must await *upanayana* and other purificatory ceremonies from which the Śūdras are excluded, whether the Śūdras could be eligible for study of the Vedānta. Upanayana as a pre-requisite of Vedic study is recognized in Vedic literature [e.g. *Śata. Br.*, xi, 5, 3, 13 ; *Chhān. Upa.*, v, 11, 7 ; vii, 1, 1 ; *Praś. Upa.*, i, 1], while the Smṛitis do not consider Śūdras eligible for it [e.g. Manu, x, 4, and 126], prohibit their hearing and studying the Veda, and understanding and performing Vedic ceremonies. What they are entitled to is a knowledge of the Purāṇas and Itihāsas, which is open to all the castes.

The Pūrvapakshin (critic), however, would maintain the eligibility of the Śūdras for the study of the Vedānta on the grounds that (*a*) they desire that knowledge, (*b*) they are capable of it, (*c*) there is no scriptural prohibition analogous to the text, " Therefore the Śūdra is unfit for performing sacrifices " [*Taitti. Saṁ.*, vii, 1, 1, 6, 7]. Bādarāyaṇa's reply to these arguments as interpreted by Śaṅkara is that mere desire for knowledge does not mean capacity for it ; mere temporal capacity is nothing ; spiritual capability is required in spiritual matters ; and spiritual capability is absent in the Śūdras for their exclusion from study of Veda ; while the Vedic prohibition of the performance of sacrifices by the Śūdras is due to their exclusion from the legitimate study of the Veda under a *guru*, through which alone a knowledge of the Veda can be acquired.

Next, the Pūrvapakshin cites certain cases found in the Veda itself which seem to point to the imparting of Vedantic doctrines to a Śūdra or a man of doubtful caste, e.g. Jānaśruti and Jābāla. Appropriate answers are indicated in the Sūtras and explained by Śaṅkara.

In the *Chhāndogya Upanishad*, iv, 1–3, Raikva first calls Jānaśruti a Śūdra, and then imparts to him the Saṁvarga-Vidyā (" a theory of Vāyu and Prāṇa as *samvargāḥ*, absorbers of the elements and life-organs "). The reply is that a single case does not make a rule ; that the claim to one particular Vidyā does not mean claim to all Vidyās ; and that the epithet Śūdra was applied by the Ṛishi in its etymological sense (viz. " one who rushes into grief ", *śuchāṁ abhidudrāva*) to the sorrowful Jānaśruti by virtue of his supernatural insight into the king's mental state. Besides, in the story, Jānaśruti, being praised for the same Vidyā with the Kshatriya Abhipratārin, shows that the former was really a Kshatriya and not a Śūdra. To this Śaṅkara adds the further proof of his Kshatriyahood from the fact that he had a steward and other similar signs of power. This, as aptly pointed out by Deussen, itself shows that " for the time of Śaṅkara and also for that of Bādarāyaṇa it was by no means self-evident that a man of princely pomp and wealth like Jānaśruti could not have been a Śūdra ", which is interesting from the point of view of both political and cultural history.

As regards the story of Jābāla Satyakāma [*Chhā.*, iv, 4], it points to the other conclusion: "on account of Gautama proceeding to initiate Jābāla on the ascertainment of his not being a Śūdra [i, 3, 37] ['from his speaking the truth' (Śaṅkara)]." Śaṅkara quotes the following passage [*Chhā.*, iv, 4, 5], on the point: 'None who is not a Brāhmaṇa would thus speak out. Go and fetch fuel, friend, I shall initiate you. You have not swerved from the truth.'

This way of taking the passage points to another significant fact that in those days "there was a disposition to let alone the question of Brāhmanhood by birth where a Brāhmanhood of heart and mind existed" [Deussen, *Philosophy of Vedānta*], a breadth of view and catholicity which recognized character as much as caste, and took liberties, when needed, with the social distinctions based on birth.

Thus the Vedānta-Sūtras exclude the Śūdra from the study of the Veda to which they admit only the three twice-born classes. Brahmavidyā is for these fit persons, and the Ṛishis and gods themselves.

The last point of educational and social interest discussed in the Vedānta-Sūtras is the question, How far the seeker after the highest Truth, the Knowledge of Brahman, is bound by the regulations of social life. We have already seen how the Vedānta, while mentioning the antecedent conditions of its study, has excluded the inquiry into *Dharma* or ceremonial religion as being unnecessary. The question is, Whether this exclusion means that the Vedāntin is not to continue even as a member of society, subject to the laws of caste and *Āśramas* and the obligations they prescribe. The conclusion of the matter is that he who has attained to the knowledge of the Brahman may at his option concern himself with such duties, but on him who has not yet attained it, such duties, the obligations of the four *Āśramas*, are ordinarily binding. This is clear from certain scriptural texts cited in the Sūtras, e.g. "The Brāhmaṇas seek to know this (the supreme soul) by reading the Veda, by sacrifice, by gifts, by penance, by fasts [*Bṛi. Upa.*, iv, 4, 22]." These conditions apply only to those who are striving after knowledge and are called *Vāhya*, external, conditions, to be distinguished from the other more immediate, *pratyāsanna*, means of acquiring Vedāntic knowledge (such as *śama*, *dama*, etc., already described), which should not be given up by those who have even acquired that knowledge. Thus there are interesting instances quoted of men performing sacrifices even after their attainment of the knowledge of Brahman, and of others abstaining from them. Among the former are mentioned Aśvapati Kaikeya who, when approached for instruction by three Ṛishis, told them: "I am about to perform a sacrifice, Sirs" [*Chhā. Upa.*, v, 11]; also Janaka and other princes regarding whom it is said: "By Dharma only Janaka and others attained to perfection" [Śaṅkara on *Sūtra*, iii, 4, 3]. As regards men who, knowing Brahman, abandoned all work, Śaṅkara [on iii, 4, 4], cites texts such as: "The Ṛishis, descended from Kavasha, said: 'For what purpose should we study the Veda? For what purpose should we sacrifice?'"

Other Features. From the evidence adduced above we may gather the following facts and features regarding the education of the times: (1) The intellectual life of the country did not always centre round rituals but grew up independently in the atmosphere of free and pure thought. The Vedāntin has nothing to do with Karma-Kāṇḍa or *Pūrva-Mīmāṁsā*.

(2) The condition precedent of all higher studies was the study of the Veda, the mastery of its words. Then follows bifurcation of or specialization in studies. To use the words of Śaṅkara [on iii, 4, 12]: "A man who has thus mastered the words of the Veda apprehends therefrom that it makes statements as to rituals producing certain results, and then on his own account applies himself to the inquiry into the meaning of those declarations; he who desires to follow the path of action applies himself to the knowledge of Dharma; he who is desirous of Release applies himself to the knowledge of Brahman. This knowledge is something different from mere cognition of sense."

(3) The study of the Vedānta or the inquiry into Brahman is necessarily for the few and spiritually advanced who can devote themselves to it in complete detachment from the world or the objects of sense. This detachment can only be the outcome of the process of discipline pertaining to the four *Āśramas* of life or stages of its growth. This shows that the Vedānta was not for the novitiate; it was rather a part of the post-graduate course taken up either by the Naishṭhika or perpetual brahmachārin who would renounce the world for the sake of that knowledge or by the man of the world fitted for it by the purifying discipline and experience through which he has passed. Thus

there were various grades of culture in the country suited to its different classes and ranks. The progress of a country depends largely upon the endowment of research maintaining a group of thinkers who would extend the bounds of knowledge. Such a class of seekers after truth, scientists, or philosophers did exist in ancient India, where students alone were not trusted to take care of the culture of the country. There was a vigorous intellectual life, apart from students and schools, which invaded the courts of kings (as evidenced in the Upanishads) and claimed even the aged householders as its votaries.

(4) As to the education of the Śūdra, the Vedānta Sūtras imply a distinction between the Vedic texts and the wisdom or knowledge which they are meant to convey. The Śūdra is excluded from the former but not from the latter. The " saving " knowledge is not denied to him. It is, on the contrary, made accessible to him in easier works specially composed for him in a popular style and manner, such as the *Mahābhārata* and the *Purāṇas* sometimes called the fifth Veda. There are also on record examples of Śūdras attaining to the highest knowledge such as Vidura and Dharma-Vyādha [*Mbh.*, iii, 206 f.] [Śaṅkara on i, 3, 38]. The eligibility of the woman for the highest knowledge [and therefore of the Śūdra too (?), for the Śūdra and the woman are given practically equal status by the Smṛitis] is again emphasized in a later *Sūtra* [iii, 4, 36], where Śaṅkara cites the example of Vāchaknavī. But the example would seem to prove more than is perhaps intended in this particular *Sūtra*. For it might be recalled that Vāchaknavī was as competent a Vedic scholar as anybody else. She put herself forward as an opponent of the sage Yājñavalkya, and by virtue of her erudition and wisdom, dared challenge his assertion of pre-eminence in the great philosophical Congress which assembled at the court of King Janaka. Vāchaknavī was thus as much a student of the Veda as anybody else, and if the woman and the Sūdra are equal in status, privileges, and disabilities, it may be legitimately inferred that the study of the Veda itself (and not merely the acquisition through other works of the knowledge conveyed by the Veda) was open to the Śūdra too. The position is made still clearer by Śaṅkara in his comment on iii, 4, 38, where he quotes Manu [ii, 87], to show that the highest knowledge is even attainable through such special acts as praying, fasting, worshipping, and the like, which have nothing to do with *Varṇa* or *Āśrama* duties. Śaṅkara concludes with the statements:

" Knowledge is open to anyone who is desirous of it," and " prayer alone qualifies for knowledge ". Rāmānuja [on i, 3, 39] also seems to hold Śaṅkara responsible for the view that the Śūdra is not excluded from the highest knowledge (" cognition of Brahman ") and tries to prove the error of the view. But Śaṅkara's real position (which he seems to misunderstand) is that it is the qualification which matters, and not the accident of birth and that the qualification once acquired (as the result of Vedic study) can never be lost in any subsequent birth. No kind of obstacle (e.g. Śūdrahood) can prevent Vedic study (made in a previous life) from producing its own fruits [Śaṅkara on i, 3, 38].

It is to be noted in conclusion that the *Vedānta-Sūtras* were preceded by considerable speculation on similar lines, the results of which are referred to in the *Sūtras* themselves. Bādarāyaṇa refers to the opinions associated with the following earlier masters, viz. Ātreya, Āśmarathya, Auḍalomi, Kārshṇājini, Kāśakṛitsna, Jaimini, and Bādari. It would appear, too, that these Doctors of the Vedānta differ among themselves considerably not merely upon minor points, but also upon essential doctrines of the system. This shows only the vitality and vigour of Vedāntic thought which has a history of its own. The work of Bādarāyaṇa occupies a central place in that history. While it summarizes the results of antecedent speculation, it has become also the source of much subsequent speculation flowing in an ever-broadening stream down to this day, with yet a future before it.

Pūrva-Mīmāṁsā and its System of Discipline. The subject of *Pūrva-Mīmāṁsā* is the *Karma-Kāṇḍa* or *Dharma* of Veda, as that of *Uttara-Mīmāṁsā* is *Jñāna-Kāṇḍa* or *Brahma*. The *Uttara-Mīmāṁsā* seeks to evolve a system out of the Upanishads. The *Purva-Mīmāṁsā* seeks to reconcile the divergent ceremonials and customs as preserved in the *Brāhmaṇas* by evolving a general and rational scheme, a philosophy of ritualism showing the place and justification for each particular rite by the method of *mīmaṁsā*, " investigation, examination, consideration."

The very first sentence of the Pūrva-Mīmāṁsā is " *Athāto Dharma-jijñāsā* ", " Now therefore the desire of knowing Dharma or duty." *Dharma* here refers to prescriptive observances comprising sacrifices in the main as enjoined in the *Brāhmaṇas*. The *Sarva-Darśana Saṁgraha* finds in this first sentence the suggestion of several complicated issues which are pertinent to the present inquiry for their educational interest. They may be presented as follows after Mādhava: The main issue is, whether the study of Dharma as proposed by Jaimini's *Mīmāṁsā* is to be undertaken or not. To settle it, we must answer the possible objections to it. Study of *Mīmāṁsā* is not implied by the command that the Veda is to be read (*Vedodhyetavyaḥ*).

The meaning of this injunction may be twofold. The Veda is to be studied and understood as well, like any other book we read. This can, however, be done by studying the Veda under a qualified teacher. But there is no injunction to study the *Pūrva-Mīmāṁsā* as a means of knowing the sense of the Veda. The second meaning of the Vedic injunction is that the Veda is merely to be learnt by heart, which " merely enjoins the making oneself master of the literal words of the Vedic text without any care to understand the meaning which they may convey ", regarding the Veda simply as a work good in itself with its reward in heaven.

We have already seen how popular was this view of the methods of Vedic study in earlier times according to which the mastery of the mere sound of the Vedic words was meritorious acquisition or accomplishment and the Veda committed to memory would be more efficacious than if it is rationally read and understood. This view of the injunction enjoining the study of the Veda thus leaves no room for the study of *Mīmāṁsā* at all, which concerns itself with the meaning of the Vedic texts. There is, however, a third objection taken to the study of *Mīmāṁsā* and that is based on the Smṛiti rule that " having read the Veda, let him bathe ". For this rule clearly implies that no long interval must elapse between reading the Veda and the student's return to his home. This rule, however, would be violated if after completing the study of the Veda in either of the senses aforesaid, the student would still have to continue in his preceptor's place for the intervening study of the *Mīmāṁsā*, Thus it is argued that for these three reasons, viz. (*a*) that the study of *Mīmāṁsā* is not enjoined, (*b*) that heaven can be obtained by the simple memorizing of the Vedic text, and (*c*) that the rule for the student's return to home is thus fulfilled, it is to be maintained that the study of the Mīmāṁsā discussions on Dharma is not to be undertaken.

This position is now met by the Siddhāntin. The study of Mimāṁsā is no doubt not enjoined as a *Vidhi* but necessary as a *Niyama*. The injunction " the Veda is to be read " shows that it is regarded as a means to some end and that end is the knowledge of the meaning as obtained by carrying out the sense of the words of the injunction. Now the knowledge of the meaning cannot be obtained by reading the simple text of the Veda even under an authorized teacher. It may, however, be said that he who reads the Veda along with its *Aṅgas*, grammar, etc., may attain to this knowledge and that the study of *Mīmāṁsā* is uncalled for. The reply is that he may thus attain to a mere simple knowledge of the literal meaning, while for all deeper investigation he must depend upon the Mīmāṁsā discussions, which thus constitute a means towards the highest end of Vedic study, viz. the proper performance of its commands. As regards the violation of the Smṛiti rule that " having read the Veda, let him bathe ", the words do not necessarily imply that the return to the paternal roof is to follow immediately on his having read the Veda ; but only that it is to follow it at some time, and that both actions are to be done by the same person. Hence the Smṛiti injunction does not rule out the study of the Mīmāṁsā.

When the necessity of a study of *Pūrva-Mīmāṁsā* as a part of " the inquiry into Dharma " is thus established, the next point to be considered is, what is the kind of preliminary and preparatory training contemplated by the Pūrva-Mīmāṁsā ? According to Prabhākara (in his *Bṛihatī* commentary on *Pūrva-Mīmāṁsā* Sūtras), such preparation means the study of the Veda. Kumārila in his *Tantravārttika* goes a little farther and holds that for a study of Dharma or acquisition of knowledge of Self, the performance of Vedic rituals is a necessity, and such performance depends on a study of the Veda, and that under the prescribed system of *Brahmacharya*. Thus the point of view advanced here is (1) that for the knowledge of Self the proper performance of sacrificial ceremonies is essential and is thus a means to that end ; and (2) that this knowledge of Self is achieved by a process of worship led up to by inquiry and understanding undertaken by the *Pūrva-Mīmāṁsā*.

Śavara Svāmī, however, holds a completely contrary view. He does not admit that a study of the Veda is at all a preparatory requisite for the study of *Mīmāṁsa*. In his view the *Mīmāṁsā* by itself is a self-sufficient system like *Yoga* and itself leads to a proper understanding of the Veda (Vedavākyānāṁ anekavidho vichāra iha vartishyate).

It is to be noted that the importance of Mīmāṁsā is due more to its method than to the matter to which the method is applied. The Mīmāṁsā method of intellectual discipline is possessed of a larger appeal than its subject of inquiry which is of more limited interest. Its logical apparatus, its methods and canons of criticism and interpretation have received a wider application and especially in the sphere of Law where they are utilized to settle disputed points. The old Hindu Courts of Justice always included as Judges what are called *Mīmāṁsakas*.

Eligibility of Women and Śūdras for Education. The *Mīmāṁsā* throws some light on the status of women and Śūdras and their place in the intellectual and religious life of the country. In discussing the *adhikāra vidhis* or the eligibility for the performance of sacrifices, Jaimini is led on to discuss whether women are to be considered to have that eligibility. The objections to it (the Pūrvapaksha) are thus stated: "Women have no property. What they have rests in the husband. They are bought and sold like goods." To this the answer of the Siddhāntin is to the following effect: Women are as good as men in point of the desire and capacity for performing sacrifices. They may not own property but have control over it. For their consent is obtained to the men's gifts. As regards the payment of dowry by the bride's father, it is made in accordance with the rule of Smṛiti and not as a commercial transaction. For otherwise the amount of the dowry would vary with the merits of the bride. Besides, it is expressly laid down that the husband and wife must jointly perform the *Yāgas* or sacrifices. Similarly, as regards the status of the Śūdras, Jaimini shows a very liberal spirit. He begins by postulating that sacrifices must not be mechanically but intelligently performed to be efficacious. Thus emphasis is laid upon a man's merit rather than his caste. The disability of the Śūdras is limited only to the Āgneya Yāgas and due to some express texts (viz. that of the Ṛishi Ātreya) [Jaimini, vi, i, 1–7]. Jaimini takes his stand upon the opinion of Bādari that all without any distinction desiring heaven can perform sacrifice. Thus the religious life was open both to women and Śūdras according to the *Mīmāṁsā* which means that they could acquire the necessary intellectual equipment for it.

The Nyāya System of Discipline. Although the Nyāya Philosophy does not encourage mysticism and the consequent moral disciplines, yet it does not dispense with these altogether.

The structure of its reasoning may be briefly presented thus. A true knowledge of the Self is necessary to achieve the highest good or *mukti*, but this knowledge does not come at once. It has to be acquired by stages. First, it comes from the Scriptures, that is, what the Vedānta calls *Śravaṇa*. Next, it is confirmed by reasoning, what Vedānta calls reflection or *Manana*. Then follows direct cognition of Self, or self-realization through concentrated contemplation and meditation. When all these stages are gone through, then alone is Ignorance, the root of all defects, removed [*Nyāya Sūtra*, i, 1, 1–2 ; *Nyāya-Vārttika*, Translation, p. 93, note].

It is to be noted, however, that concentrated contemplation and meditation as a step towards true knowledge is not at all possible for a man until he has shed his defects.

These *Defects* have been thus classified :—

A. *Rāga*, Desire, as expressed in the forms of *Kāma* (lust), *Matsara* (selfishness), *Spṛihā* (greed), or *Tṛishṇā* (wish to possess others' property lawfully or unlawfully).

B. *Dvesha*, Hatred, expressed as *Krodha* (anger), *Īrshā* (jealousy), *Asūyā* (envy), *Droha* (malice), and *Amarsha* (impatience).

C. *Moha*, defective outlook in its different forms like *Mithyājñānam* (error), *Vichikitsā* (doubt), *Māna* (egotism), or *Pramāda* (inattentiveness) [*Nyāya Sūtra*, iv, 1, 2].

These various basic Defects are rooted in Ignorance, i.e. a wrong conception of the objects of cognition [ib., iv, 1, 68]. This Ignorance is to be dispelled or destroyed by true Knowledge. And true Knowledge can only come from Meditation [iv, 2, 35 ; 3, 38]. Meditation means (1) that the mind is withdrawn from the sense-organs, and (2) is kept steady by effort towards concentration, and then (3) it comes into contact with the Self, and (4) is filled with an eagerness to get at the Truth. Such Meditation will not allow any cognitions with reference to the objects of the external world.

Such Meditation is, however, always hindered by physical as well as moral obstacles. The practice of *Yoga* is necessary to overcome such obstacles. Thus to achieve success in Meditation, one should equip himself by *Yoga*, i.e. *Yama* (restraints), *Niyama* (observances), and other prescribed methods of internal discipline such as penance, breath-regulation (*prāṇāyāma*), abstraction (*pratyāhāra*), contemplation (*dhyāna*), and concentration of mind (*dhāraṇā*).

The *Nyāya Sūtras* further recommend as aids to learning (1) continuous study of philosophy, (2) discussion with persons learned in philosophy, especially with the teacher, the pupil, and one's fellow-pupil, and (3) even disputations and controversies which have their uses in thrashing out the Truth [iv, 2, 38–50].

Lastly, the *Nyāya* position is that knowledge comes when *Defects* are rooted out and all *Activity* ceases, both righteous and unrighteous. *Activity*, righteous or unrighteous, is described as being of three kinds, viz. Verbal, Mental, and Bodily.

Unrighteous *Verbal* activity is of four kinds : (1) *Anṛita* (lying), (2) *Parusha* (harsh speech), (3) *Asūyana* (back-biting), and (4) *Asaṁbaddha* (irrelevant talk).

Righteous *Verbal* activity will be of four kinds, *Satya-Priya-Hita-Vachana*, "truthful, agreeable, and wholesome speech," and *Svādhyāya-Pāṭha* (reciting the Veda).

Unrighteous *Mental* activity is of three kinds: (1) Thought of injuring others (*paradroha*), (2) Longing for others' belongings (*paradravyābhilāsha*), and (3) Irreverent attitude (*nāstikā-nudhyāna*).

Mental activity of the right kind will have three forms: (1) *Aspṛihā* (freedom from desire), (2) *Anukampā* (compassion), (3) *Paralokaśraddhā* (belief in the other world).

Unrighteous *Bodily* activity is of three kinds: (1) *Hiṁsā* (killing), (2) *Steya* (stealing), and (3) *Pratishiddhācharaṇa* (doing what is forbidden).

Righteous *Bodily* activity is of three kinds: (1) *Dāna* (Charity), (2) *Paritrāṇa* (Protection), and (3) *Parichāraṇa* (Service) [*Nyāya-Mañjarī*, p. 499, ed. Gaṅgādhara Śāstrī in Viziānagram Sanskrit Series].

Besides the general scheme of discipline and training implied by Nyāya Philosophy, we shall now consider other special points of education brought out in its Sūtras.

Elements of Knowledge. According to Gautama, Knowledge is made up of a comprehension of sixteen *padārthas* or topics, the discussions of some of which have a bearing upon education.

Pramāṇa. The first topic is *Pramāṇa* or means of knowledge which are described as fourfold, viz. (1) *Pratyaksha*, sensuous perception, (2) *Anumāna*, inference, (3) *Upamāna*, comparison, and (4) *Śabda* or the Word, particularly that of the Veda. This shows that *Nyāya*, far from repudiating the Veda, acknowledges it as a source of knowledge itself.

Śabda including non-Vedic Revelation. *Śabda* is explained as *Āptopadeśa* [i, 1, 7], i.e. as a precept of one worthy to be trusted, or a right precept. It refers to both visible and invisible objects. It is noteworthy that the commentator holds that it is possible even for the Mlechchhas or barbarians as well as for Ṛishis and Āryas to be regarded as *āpta* or those whose authority is to be followed. This shows the broad catholicity and toleration of the philosophers who, on grounds of dry and dispassionate reason, could not but accord the same place to non-Vedic as to Vedic revelation, the growth and importance of which are also clearly indicated by the Sūtra and its commentary in question. There were other worlds and systems of thought than the Vedic in ancient India, claiming numerous followers of their own.

As regards the merits of this analysis of the sources of valid knowledge, the following remarks of Max Müller are very appropriate [*Six Systems*, p. 374]: "It seems to me highly creditable to Indian Philosophers that they should have understood the necessity of such an analysis on the very threshold of any system of philosophy. How many misunderstandings might have been avoided if all philosophers had recognized the necessity of such an introductory chapter? If we must depend for all our knowledge, first on our senses, then on our combinatory and reasoning faculties, the question whether Revelation falls under the one or the other, or whether it can claim an independent authority can far more easily be settled than if such questions are not asked *in limine*, but turn up casually whenever transcendental problems come to be treated."

Anumāna. Secondly, it may also be noted that, while accredited authority is regarded as a source of knowledge whose findings have to be taken for granted, a due emphasis is also laid upon the positive methods and objective standards for the investigation of truth.

The first source of knowledge is *Pramāṇa*, observation or perception, direct, personal, and independent. As pointed out by Dr. B. N. Seal [*Positive Sciences of the Ancient Hindus*, ch. vii], "the entire apparatus of scientific method proceeded on the basis of observed instances carefully analysed and sifted." The second means of knowledge is *Anumāna* (Inference), which is the process of ascertaining, not by perception or direct observation, but through the instrumentality or medium of a mark that a thing possesses a certain character.

Inference is, therefore, based on the establishment of an invariable concomitance (*Vyāpti*) between the mark and the character inferred. The Hindu inference is, therefore, neither merely formal nor merely material, but a combined Formal-Material Deductive-Inductive process. It is neither the

Aristotelian syllogism (Formal Deductive process) nor Mill's Induction (Material-Inductive process) but the real Inference which must combine formal validity with material truth, inductive generalization with deductive particularization.

Thus it is clear that the achievements of the Hindu mind in the domain of positive science to which history so amply testifies were ultimately due to the development of a rigorous scientific method [see Dr. Seal's book for fuller information].

Objects of Knowledge. The next topic of educational interest discussed is that on the objects of knowledge which are limited to twelve, viz. (1) soul or self, (2) body, (3) senses, (4) objects of sense, (5) intellect, (6) mind, (7) activity (Will), (8) fault, (9) transmigration, (10) fruits of actions, (11) suffering, (12) final beatitude. It is clear from this list how frankly spiritual were the aims of education or the ideals dominating the pursuit of knowledge.

Need of Discussion in Learning. The Nyāya Sūtras also indicate their own appropriate pedagogic methods. The knowledge that is derived from the four aforesaid sources of Observation, Inference, Comparison, and Trustworthy Testimony is further put to the test of objective standards in the shape of discussion of various forms such as (1) *Vāda*, i.e. ' Argumentation, consisting of objections and answers, both disputants, however, caring only for truth.' (2) *Jalpa*, ' Sophistry or attacking what has been established, by any means.' (3) *Vitaṇḍā*, ' Cavilling.' The importance of Discussion to the investigation of truth led to a definition of the errors to be avoided. Thus we find an elaborate study of the fallacies of reasoning, such as *Hetvābhāsaḥ* and *Chhalam* ' quibbles '.

Hetvābhāsa means " specious arguments, paralogisms, and sophisms. These are *Savyabhichāra*, arguments that prove too much ; *Viruddha*, arguments which prove the reverse ; *Prakaraṇasama*, that tell equally on both sides ; *Sādhyasama*, that stand themselves in need of proof, and *Kālātīta*, mistimed " [Max Müller].

There is also referred to a kind of argument characterized as *jāti*, which means futility arising from false analogies (' change of class '), as well as another, which renders a disputant unfit for discussion and deserving of rebuke (*nigrahasthānam*) when, by misunderstanding, or not understanding, he still continues to talk.

The methods of discussion are disapproved only when the disputants seem to care more for victory than truth.

It is also laid down that discussion for the sake of reaching truth should be carried on only with those who do seek the truth and not victory (i.e. *anasūya*, 'unenvious'), viz. disciples, preceptors, fellow-students, and seekers after emancipation. When the investigation of truth requires it, discussion may be held even without an opposing side. Even *Jalpa* ('disputation characterized by overbearing reply, and disputed rejoinder') and *Vitaṇḍā* ('idly carping at the arguments or assertions of another without attempting to prove the opposite side of the question') are regarded as necessary to keep alive the zeal for truth, just as thorny boughs are useful for safeguarding the growth of seeds [iv, 2, 98–50]. The circles of disputants are called *Parishads* [v, 2, 17].

Spheres of Faith and Reason. As has been already pointed out, the Nyaya Sūtras at the outset clearly distinguish between the spheres of reasoning and faith. The sphere of faith lies beyond the ken of the senses and the knowledge derived therefrom is not to be tested by the application of those logical methods which appertain to that derived from ordinary observation or perception by the senses. The Nyāya Sūtras instance the Veda as a source of such revealed or valid knowledge and are at pains to defend it against the attacks of the sceptics who doubt the authority of the Vedas. Both the attack and the defence are interesting as showing the place occupied by Vedic studies and religion in the intellectual life of the times and also the growth of schools of thought (headed by the Buddhists) which stood up for other sources and systems of revelation than the traditional and time-worn Vedic. These dissenters hold the Veda as unreliable because they find in it the three defects of untruth, contradiction, and tautology. As an instance of untruth, the commentator points to the statement of the Veda that a son is produced when a particular sacrifice for that purpose is performed, whereas it often happens that the performance of that sacrifice is not followed by the promised result. To this objection the reply of the Nyāya is that the so-called untruth of the Veda is due to some defect in the act (e.g. sacrificing not according to rules), operator (e.g. the priest not being a learned man), and materials of sacrifice (e.g. fuel being wet, butter being not fresh, remuneration to the officiating priest being small, etc.).

As regards contradiction, such statements are instanced

as "let one sacrifice when the sun has risen" and "let one sacrifice when the sun has not risen". The reply is that here the Veda only prescribes alternative courses for the convenience of the sacrificer.

As regards tautology, the reply is that the re-inculcation is of advantage and is done either for completing a certain number of syllables or explaining a matter briefly expressed. The entire Vedic literature is classified according to its several purposes, such as those of *Vidhi* (injunctions pointing to certain courses of action), *Arthavāda* [persuasion through *stuti* (extolling the consequences of a certain course of action), *nindā* (pointing out the consequences of neglecting it), *parakṛiti* (precedent), *purākalpa* (prescription)], and *Anuvāda* (repetition of what has been enjoined by injunction). Lastly, it is stated that the Veda is reliable like the Mantra and Āyurveda, because of the reliability of their authors. The commentator explains that the authors are reliable because they were Ṛishis who had (1) an intuitive perception of truth, (2) love of living beings, and (3) the desire to communicate their knowledge of the truths for the common good [ii, 1, 57–68].

Vaiśeshika Discipline. The Vaiśeshika view of discipline may be gathered from the *Nyāya Kandalī*. A man's experience will bring home to him the truth that his Self is quite distinct from external objects or internal processes which are sources of pain and suffering. Then he develops an attitude of detachment from life, and even its pleasures. His sole aim in life is now to know the means of removing pain. He approaches a teacher to learn the means. "He hears the knowledge from the lips of his teacher, but it is pointed out that he must carry out *Manana* and *Nididhyāsana* for a direct perception of Truth."

The direct educational evidence of the Vaiśeshika Sūtras of Kaṇāda is meagre. There are several Sūtras giving arguments to establish the authority of the Veda as source of valid knowledge [i, 1, 3; vi, 1, 1–4; x, 2, 8–9]. The contents of those arguments need not concern us. Secondly, there is an interesting reference to *brahmacharya* (in the sense of observance of *dharma* in general according to the commentator) and *gurukulavāsa* (residence in the home of the teacher of a student for the purpose of studying the Veda, the twelve-year vow called *Mahāvrata* as explained by the commentator) as productive of invisible fruits [vi, 2, 2]. Thirdly, the distinction is explained between *Avidyā* and *Vidyā*. The former is defined as *dushṭajñānam* or vitiated knowledge due to the imperfection of the senses as a venue of knowledge and the imperfection of impressions received by them. The latter is defined as *adushṭajñānam* or perfect knowledge. The term *Vidyā* also applies to the cognition of the Ṛishis and the vision of the perfected (*siddhadarśanam*) [ix, 2, 10–13].

Sāṁkhya Discipline. The Sāṁkhya discipline aims at the realization of the self-conscious Principle (*Purusha*) as distinct from the mental states, the bodily functions, and the events of the external world, subsumed under the term *Prakṛiti* or Nature. This can be achieved by Virtue and Wisdom, by dispassion and clarity of consciousness. Passionate attachment leads to transmigration. *Sāṁkhya* also recognizes that Error has to be removed before supreme wisdom or *mukti* can be attained. Error (*viparyaya*) is of five forms, viz. Ignorance, Egotism, Passion, Hatred, and Attachment to the body as also to the objects of sense [*Kārikā*, 44–7].

Some Special Features. We have seen that all the *Darśanas* start from a common assumption that it is ignorance of one kind or another which is the root cause of all misery in life. Hence the need of discovering the true knowledge as the only way of escape from the ills which flesh is heir to.

As aids to the acquisition of this knowledge, the *Darśanas* lay stress upon moral purity, unswerving faith in *guru*, and spiritual truths and an overmastering passion for knowledge. The different *Darśanas* pursue Truth by different ways and methods and arrive at different views of Reality. Each system then represents a bold spirit of inquiry, a freedom from bias and "idols", and stands for its own scheme of ideals and values.

The Sāṁkhya Method of Study. The new intellectual note of the age is struck by the *Sāṁkhya-Kārīkā* at its very beginning. The efficacy of Vedic religion as a means of escape from the misery inherent in human life is questioned. It is found to have three defects, viz. (1) it is impure (*a-viśuddhi*), because, as the commentator explains, of its connection with sacrifice and slaughter of animals; (2) it is terminable (*kshaya*) because the practice of Vedic religion can secure only transitory results and not a final release; (3) it admits of gradation of happiness (*atiśaya*), for "all men are not wealthy enough to offer costly sacrifices to the gods and thus the rich man may have more and the poor less" (Davies). Hence final emancipation is to be attained not by Vedic ceremonies but by knowledge as explained by Kapila. We may also refer in this connection to the expression *dākshiṇaka-bandha* which, according to the *Tattva-Kaumudī*, is one of the three classes of the *bandha* or bondage mentioned in the *Kārikā*, 44. The expression condemns worship for personal ends, for which fees to priests are paid, as a kind of impediment to emancipation.

Some of the features of the prevailing system of instruction are also referred to in *Kārikā*, 51, in which *Śabda*, *Adhyayana*, and *Suhṛit-prāpti* are mentioned among the eight means of attaining perfection. *Adhyayana*, or study, as explained in the *Tattva-Kaumudī*, means receiving the syllables (and the words) of the spiritual sciences as they fall from the lips of the Guru according to prescribed regulations. The effect of *Adhyayana* is *Śabda*, i.e. comprehension of the meanings of the words learnt and hence oral instruction. Next to the *Śabda* comes *Ūha* or reasoning which consists in the examination of the meaning of *Śruti* or scripture by a process of dialectics not opposed to the scriptures themselves, and hence it means supporting the scriptures by solving all doubts and objections regarding them. *Ūha* is also called *Manana* by Vedic writers. Next comes *Suhṛit-prāpti*, literally, acquisition of friends. Its real meaning is that though one may arrive at truth by his individual process of right reasoning, yet he has no faith in his conclusions until he has discussed them with his " friends ", i.e. his guru, his pupils, and his own fellow-disciples. " Nyāyena svayaṁ parīkshitamapy-arthaṁ na śraddadhate na yāvad-guru-śishya-sabrahmachāri-bhissaha saṁvādyate " [*Tattva-Kaumudī*]. Thus discussion or debate was rightly recognized as the concluding stage in the process of the study and investigation of philosophical truths.

There is another work on the *Sāṁkhya* which, though of a comparatively modern date and inferior in some ways to the *Kārikā* as an exposition of the system, is worthy of consideration for considerable old matter which it may contain. The Sūtra is at pains to prove the harmony of its views with scriptures and emphasizes conformity to Vedic practices as a means of securing emancipation. The Sūtra also emphasizes the need of the really competent teacher possessed of supreme enlightenment securing him final release in death and of the practice of *Vairāgya*. The value it attaches to asceticism is derived from the Yoga, and there is a view that both Sāṁkhya and Yoga are fundamentally parts of a common system. It also points out the insufficiency of the mere listening to the teaching of truth which must be supplemented by reflection and meditation to which the Yogic practices are recommended as being contributory.

Caste and Education. On the general question as to how far education in Ancient India was available for all castes, we have important evidence furnished by the works on the Sāṁkhya which may be best set forth in the words of Dr. A. B. Keith [*Sāṁkhya System*, p. 100]: "It is characteristic of the Sāṁkhya that it does not restrict, like the Vedānta,[1] the saving knowledge to the three upper classes of the Aryan community to the exclusion of the Śūdras. This generosity of outlook is seen already in the great Epic [xiv, 19, 61], where the result of Yoga is distinctly declared to be open even to women and to Śūdras, and the same sentiment can doubtless legitimately be recognized in the fact that the system, despite its fondness for subdivisions, actually classes, in its theory of the kinds of living creatures, men in one division only, while divine beings fall under no less than eight. The motive for the difference of treatment doubtless lies in the fact that the Sāṁkhya, like the Yoga, does not build on the Veda as an exclusive foundation, and, therefore, unlike the Vedānta, they do not fall under the rule which excludes Śūdras from even hearing the Veda recited. The fact that the Veda formed one of the sources of proof of the system was not any more inconsistent with the system being made available to all, than the fact that the Epic which contains Vedic quotations was equally open to Śūdras to hear."

In conclusion, it may be noted that the *Sāṁkhya Kārikā* gives the *paramparā* or the list of teachers and disciples through whom the doctrines were handed down. The founder of the system was that *Muni* Kapila who, out of compassion, imparted this supremely purifying science to Āsuri, and Āsuri imparted it to Pañcha Śikha from whom it spread in many directions. Handed down by the tradition of pupils it has been compendiously written in Āryā metre by the pure-souled Īśvarakṛishṇa who has thoroughly mastered the truth.

Non-Vedic Āgamas. Besides this Āgama of the *Sāṁkhya*, the *Kārika* hints at systems of *Āgama* unconnected with the *Vedic Āgama*. The latter is described as *Āptaśruti* and *Āptavachana* in *Kārikā*, 5, and in the next *Kārikā* as *Āptāgama*, i.e. as true,

[1] Even the Vedānta, as already shown, does not prescribe the restriction referred to here. In considering these questions, the sacred Vedic *texts* are to be regarded as distinct from the "saving" *knowledge* they are meant to convey.

trustworthy, or approved revelation, to be distinguished, as explained by Vāchaspati Misra, from the systems of Āgama followed by the Śākyas, Bhikshus, Nirgranthakas, and other classes of ascetics, which are branded as spurious revelations. Their existence, however, proves that the prolific power of Hindu thought has produced not merely a single Vedic world or system of culture but also other worlds and systems round other centres than the time-honoured Veda. And these had their own outlook upon life and corresponding systems of training.

Yoga System: its Self-sufficiency. The Yoga system is more self-contained and self-sufficient than the other systems and does not prescribe or depend very much on any elaborate preparatory training. Its own measures of self-discipline are calculated to develop the outlook that is necessary for the comprehension of its philosophical theory and for the application of that theory to life. The system by itself prescribes the means and methods by which is to be achieved its aim and object, viz. the orientation of the whole life with reference to one idea and the emotional transformation corresponding to this focussed state.

Yoga implied in other systems. As we have seen, the Yoga discipline is implicated in all other systems and methods of training. As stated in an old text: "As the Gaṅgā and other rivers are merged in the ocean as its parts, the Sāṁkhya and other systems are involved in Yoga."

We have already seen how Yoga is implied in the Vedic system in spite of its ritualism. The Rigveda is full of references to *tapas* and to its culmination in a state of ecstasy and trance. The Atharvaveda refers to supernatural powers one can obtain by austerities. The Upanishads take the Yoga practice as the way of achieving the knowledge of Ātman or Reality [*Bṛi.*, iv, 14; iii, 5; iv, 4; *Taitti.*, i; *Kaṭha*, iii, 12; *Praśna*, v, 5]. The *Kaṭha* more explicitly assumes the Yoga discipline in the following passage [ii, 2]: "The Being, who has emerged out of Himself, has created the senses (*Khāni*), focussing them on the external objects (*parāṁ*). Therefore, they see (know) only the things outside, and not the Self within. One who attains peace and quiet (*dhīraḥ*) sees the individual self within himself [*pratyagātmā*; cf. *Yoga-Sūtra*, i, 29], when he seeks the life immortal and turns his gaze inwards (*āvṛitta-chakshuḥ*)." The *Śvetāśvatara* not only mentions the term Yoga, but explicitly refers to its practices and the experiences arising therefrom as preliminary to the revelation of Brahman (*Brahmaṇyābhivyakti-karāṇi Yoge*).

Coming now to the later philosophical systems, we find they all imply the Yoga system. The *Nyāya-Darśana*, for instance, mentions *Samādhi* as the means of attaining *tattvajñāna*, true knowledge [iv, 3, 36]. It also mentions the obstacles to *Samādhi*, such as hunger, thirst, and disease [iv, 3, 40], and the *Bhāshya* on iv, 2, 38 mentions *pratyāhāra* and *abhyāsa* as aids to *Samādhi*, as also *Yama* and *Niyama* as means of self-purification (*ātma-saṁskāra*). Again, iv, 2, 42 refers to a forest, cave, or river-bank, as helpful for the practice of Yoga. *Vaiśeshika* also refers to Yama, Niyama, Śuchi, and the like as aids to Yoga, which it thus defines [v, 2, 16]: "Tadanāraṁbha ātmasthe manasi śarīrasya duḥkhābhāvaḥ saṁyogaḥ"; "Yoga consists in cessation from action, rest in self, and freedom from feeling of pain of body and mind."

It is, however, to be noticed that Yoga itself depends to some extent on *Nyāya*, and, particularly, on *Sāṁkhya*. Indeed, Nyāya gives to all the Schools of Philosophy its logical technique, while Yoga gives them its technique of spiritual discipline. Each System of Philosophy has its own views in regard to the sources of valid knowledge (*Pramāṇas*) and Yoga, too, pursues its own theories concerning the *Pramāṇas* but, like other systems, it grounds itself on *Nyāya* in regard to the methods and terminology of Logic.

Sāṁkhya and Yoga. But the relations between Sāṁkhya and Yoga are much closer and deeper. There is a tradition ascribing them both to a common originator, Ṛishi Kapila. The *Bhagavat-Gītā* states that "it is the ignorant who take Sāṁkhya and Yoga as separate systems"; that "the end which Sāṁkhya seeks is also pursued by Yoga, and those who perceive them to be one are possessed of the true insight".

While *Sāṁkhya* treats of *Jñāna-Yoga*, the path of knowledge, Yoga concerns itself with the ways and means of achieving such knowledge and presents a scheme of life, *Kriyā-yoga*. Its interest is not metaphysical but practical. Its theoretical background is furnished by Sāṁkhya whose philosophy, categories, and concepts it accepts, without developing its own theory of knowledge like other systems.

But though Yoga follows the Sāṁkhya in its ideology, theory of knowledge, and its metaphysics, there is an important difference between the two. While the Yoga scheme has a place for the conception of God and of Divine Grace [i, 23, 24], the Sāṁkhya has no place for these. Sāṁkhya is accordingly described as

Nirīśvara-Yoga, non-theistic Yoga, while Yoga is *Seśvara-Sāṁkhya*, theistic Sāṁkhya. Yoga, as a consequence, gives great value to the doctrine of self-surrender to the Divine, which is inculcated in the spiritual discipline of many schools of religious thought. It is the acceptance by Yoga of these principles and methods which has made it possible for all theistic schools of thought to adopt Yoga as the universal method of discipline common to all. Yet it must be noted that since the God-concept and the doctrines it implicates count as optional categories in Yoga, the Yoga is capable of assimilation even in the absolutistic and atheistic schools of thought. This flexibility of Yoga thought further expresses itself in its treatment of the doctrine of *adhikāra* or gradations of capacity. This doctrine which is accepted in all schools of orthodox religious thought implies that each individual should pursue a course of discipline suitable to his nature. This gives ample scope to variations of practices to suit individual needs. Accordingly, different aspects of spiritual culture are differently stressed by different Schools in the context of their special theories. The *Yoga-Sūtras* have gathered together these various practical measures and built them into a system.

Yoga-Sūtras. In course of time the Science of Yoga, presented differently by different teachers through the ages, became complicated and difficult of comprehension, until it was given to Patañjali to present it in the simple and comprehensible form of *Sūtras*. The *Sūtra* is " that literary form which is known by the following marks, viz. (1) economy of words, (2) absence of ambiguity, (3) use of words that are absolutely necessary, strictly relevant, and full of meaning, (4) what may be understood from all points of view, (5) absence of superfluous or unnecessary words, and (6) absence of any flaws " (Svalpāksharaṁ asaṁdigdhaṁ sāravat viśvatomukham| astobhaṁ anavadyaṁ cha sūtraṁ sūtravido viduḥ).

Patañjali also begins his *Yoga-Sūtras* with the Sūtra : " *Atha Yogānuśāsanam.*" Here the prefix *anu* before the word *Śāsana* or " instruction in Yoga " indicates that it is not the first or original instruction in that subject but only its ' repetition ', i.e. handed down from earlier times.

Yoga aims at treatment of Mind. The Yoga scheme of education has for its object " the purification of Mind, just as the Āyurvedic science of Charaka treats of the Body, and the grammatical science presented in the *Mahābhāshya* treats of *Śabda* or speech." There is even a tradition that all these three Sciences were the work of a single author, Ṛishi Patañjali. The Science of Yoga prescribes the course of this treatment of Mind.

The Terms Yoga and Samādhi. The word *Yoga* and its meaning have a history behind them. It is from the root *yuj* " to join together ", yoking, and is applied in the Rigveda to indicate the yoking of steeds. The term was soon applied from the control of steeds to the control of senses, as in the *Kaṭha-Upanishad* [iii, 4] (indriyāṇi hayānāhuḥ vishayāṁsteshu gocharān) or *Maitr.*, 2, 6 (Karmendriyāṇyasya hayāḥ, " the organs of actions are the horses "). In the time of Pāṇini, the spiritual sense of the word was established to indicate *samādhi*, as seen in his Sūtra, "*yuj samādhau,*" while its physical sense of " joining together " is separately explained in the Sūtra "*yujir yoge*" (root *yujiḥ* = connecting). The sense of " joining together " lent itself also to spiritual application. The whole philosophy of the Upanishads, for instance, traces the root of sin, sorrow, and suffering, the ills to which flesh is heir, to the separation of the individual from the supreme soul. Accordingly, Yājñavalkya defines *yoga* to be " the bringing together of the individual and supreme souls " [Saṁyogo Yoga iti ukto jīvātmāparamātmanor iti (*Sarvadarśana Saṁgraha*, xv)]. Even Patañjali himself seems to take *yoga* in the sense of *union* and is concerned more with the fact of *viyoga* (as explained by the commentator, Bhoja) or separation between *Purusha* and *Prakṛiti* and the sustained effort necessary to get over that separation, so that *yoga* practically means this effort, a course of strenuous and sustained endeavour after the restraint of the senses and control of mind whereby *Samādhi* or the union above referred to may be attained.

It may thus be noted that the term *yoga* from its root meaning " to join " has developed three connotations : (1) It signifies a process by which the individual self is brought into contact with the Brahman, the Absolute, the realm of the spirit ; (2) it stands for *Samādhi* which is a condition of integration, of " joining together " all the mental functions ; (3) it stands for a primary stage of disjunction (*viyoga*) of desires from their objects. The inner impulses, disoriented from the external world, amalgamate into a single stream of psycho-vital impulse that seeks its kinship with the higher spiritual life. The first of these meanings implicates a metaphysical doctrine ; the second is based upon the facts of transformation that the mind undergoes ; and the third is formulated on the ground of the practices of the Yoga system.

The term *Samādhi* also, like Yoga, has both a general and technical sense. Its general meaning is "collectedness and calm of mind" (*Samyakādhāna*). Such *Samādhi* or Chitta-samādhāna is described as *Sārvabhauma*, i.e. as being implicit in all states (*bhūmi*) of mind as its innate characteristic. Its more specific meaning as used in Yoga will be explained later.

Assumptions. Thus the Science of Yoga seeks so to treat the Mind as to render it the vehicle and instrument of supreme knowledge by relieving it of the tension and depression, both physical and mental, arising from the continuous process of sensory and motor adjustments to stimuli, to which it is normally exposed. The Mind is thus led to a state of equipoise and placidity which belong to its true nature and is restored to its innate strength and clarity of vision. Thus the scheme is to effect a complete change in the trends and activities of the mind, a transformation of the psychic organism, so as to raise the level of consciousness. Thus the fundamental assumption of *Yoga* is that mental life is not entirely bound up with or completely dependent upon the realm of objects, and that our faculties of perception are not necessarily confined to the five senses. It thus seeks to open up other avenues of knowledge than the mere brain, or the outer senses, through sustained concentration and meditation, in silence and solitude, in the life of the spirit, which is dead to the external world of objective realities. In a word, Yoga believes that the universe is not what is revealed by our bodily senses which we share with the lower animals, and that man is capable of infinite development by tapping the limitless resources of the soul.

Thus the Yoga discipline seeks to release the Mind from its connections with objects (*vishaya*) and to make the psychic life self-sufficient, so that objects cease to convey any meaning.

It may be noted that the Doctrine of Dialectic of Devotion known as *Bhakti-yoga* holds that there can be no form of consciousness which is objectless. As Rāmānuja says: *Na hi nirvishayā kāchit saṁvit asti*. For the devotional feeling must be always directed to the Divine. On the other hand, the *Yoga* proper points to a consummation in which the sense of object and individuality entirely disappear (Asaṁprajñāta-Samādhi).

Theory of Knowledge. Yoga formulates its system of practical discipline and training in accordance with a definite theory of knowledge or a scheme of interpretation of life and experience. It has, therefore, to be studied in this philosophical setting for which it has depended upon Sāṁkhya, as has been already stated.

Sāṁkhya analyses experience into different planes or stages which it arranges in the following descending order in which each arises from the other, giving to each such stage a specific name in a well-defined scheme of categories or concepts :—

1. Purusha
2. Prakṛiti or Pradhāna
3. Mahat = Buddhi
4. Ahaṁkāra
5. Manas
6. Tanmātras (five)
7. *Jñānendriyas* (five sensory organs)
8. *Karmendriyas* (five motor organs)
9. Bhūtas (five)

Purusha. The first stage in the above scheme is that of Pure Consciousness called *Purusha* which is described as content-less (*amūrta*), conscious (*chetana*), the principal enjoyer of the whole range of experiences (*bhogī-sukhyahaṁ duḥkhyahaṁ ityupacharyate*), eternal (*nityaḥ*), present everywhere (*sarvagataḥ*), devoid of any impulse to action (*akriyaḥ*), incapable of being the subject of knowledge (*akartā*), incapable, either, of being the object of experience (*sūkshma*), unitary and individual [*Shaḍdarśana-samuchchaya*].

The *Purusha*, then, is the primal consciousness, the *Bewusstsein überhaupt*, which is reflected in every type of conscious experience that we observe in daily life.

Prakṛiti. To such a Consciousness is set a Reality which is external to It, as a sense of pure objectivity. It is called *Prakṛiti*, the source from which all objects of knowledge arise (*mūla-rūpā*), the source of the stages of experience that gradually emerge.

According to Sāṁkhya authorities, the two Principles, Purusha and Prakṛiti, stand together like a lame and a blind person. *Purusha* as an inactive principle is lame. *Prakṛiti*, as devoid of consciousness, is blind (*Prakṛiti-Purushayor-vṛittirvartanaṁ paṅgvandhayoriva*).

The relation between the two, Purusha and Prakṛiti, is

analogous to that between Form and Matter as conceived by Aristotle. Purusha, like God in Aristotle's system, is the "unmoved mover". Modern thought, too, has derived its theory of *Vitalism* from Aristotle's concept of *Entelechy*. The conception in all these systems is that the living organism is guided and co-ordinated by a principle which is not itself a part of the physical processes; it is the latent purpose that shapes the form and growth of the organism. The concept of Purusha is in a similar sense "the goal and destiny" of the world of nature that evolves and proliferates into manifoldness.

Mahat-Buddhi. The pure consciousness is reflected in the object-world which it lights up with consciousness. This inflow of Psyche results in the rise of experience in which things are discriminated. This stage presents itself as a conscious effort to discriminate the various objects and to reach a state of decision and certainty (Niśchayatvena padārthapratipatti heturyodhyavasāyaḥ sā Buddhiḥ). In so far as we view an individual case, it is called *Buddhi*. When we view it in its general aspect, it is called *Mahat*.

The Sāṁkhya authorities compare this consciousness to a two-faced mirror, of which one face is turned towards and reflects pure consciousness (Purusha), and the other towards Prakṛiti or objects (Buddhi-darpaṇasaṁkrāntamarthavipratívimbakaṁ Dvitīyadarpaṇakalpe purushe hi adhirohati).

Ahaṁkāra and Manas. These two aspects in Sāṁkhya Phenomenology, the subject-ward and the object-ward forms of consciousness, develop into two strands of experience. The subject-ward pole, the pole of pure consciousness, develops into (1) *Ahaṁkāra* or Self-consciousness. From this again develops (2) *Manas* or Mind. The function of Mind is to connect the senses with the sense-impressions which the senses convey. The other aspect of consciousness directed towards objects develops into the experience of the external world, in the form of what are called the *Tanmātras* and the *Bhūtas*, the subtle and gross elements.

That *Ahaṁkāra* is the product of *Buddhi* is evident from the fact that discriminative experience which Buddhi represents must needs implicate a self-conscious and individual subject. At every moment of comparing things, there arises the consciousness of *I*. This stage is called that of *Ahaṁkāra* (*Sachābhimānātmakaḥ | Yathā ahaṁ rase raktaḥ ahaṁ śabde saktaḥ ahaṁ Īśvaraḥ asau mayāhataḥ*).

From this stage of self-consciousness (*Ahaṁkāra*), says the *Sāṁkhya-Kārikā*, there emerge two orders of phenomena (*tasmāt dvividhaḥ pravartate sargaḥ*).

One of these leads to the apprehension of the world as a subjective experience. The other concerns itself with its objective aspects in which things appear to be independent of the self.

Under *Ahaṁkāra*, the individual subject in fact stands in twofold relationship to the world of objects. In the first case, the self ceases to be centred in itself, as it is set against and affected by a world of objects, something which is other than itself. The object-world first appears as an assemblage of qualities comprising vision, sound, taste, smell, and touch. These qualities or sense-data appear blended with one another and convey the first impressions of the objective world.

Thus the consciousness involved at this stage (*Ahaṁkāra*) tends to lose its ego-centric character and becomes transformed into a fusion of sensory experiences. The consciousness " *I* feel this taste " changes into an indeterminate manifold of vision, taste, smell, touch, and sound, which cannot at the outset be discriminated or described. It is a stage of ineffable sensory experience, in which substantives and adjectives, similar feelings and opposites, are all in an inchoate mass (*asti hi ālochanaṁ jñānaṁ prathamaṁ nirvikalpakam*). Thus, as the self-conscious ego senses a reality other than itself, it is overwhelmed by an inflow of sensory intimations, a mass-attack, as it were, of the other upon the self.

Sensory and Motor Organs. *Manas* (Mind) now emerges and analyses this manifold into classes and in accordance with their resemblances [*Viśeshaṇa-viśeshya bhāvena vivechayati* | *samānā samāna-jātīyābhyāṁ vyavachchhindan mano lakshayati* (Commentary to *Kārikā*, 27)]. The *Manas* resolves into order what James calls " the blooming, buzzing confusion ". In it enter not only the sensory experiences but also the impulses that activate the organs of action. It is also possible that the organic sensations which arise from activities have a place in this blend.

It is, however, conceivable to picture a stage of experience in which simple sensory qualities appear as solitary moments of awareness. As James says : " Only new-born babes or men in semi-coma may experience such sensations." One of the commentators on the *Kārikā* points out that though the breeze carries fine particles of water and odorous particles, the sense of contact brings home to man only the sensation of cold. The stage of sensory experience, then, presents its several qualities, one at a time, each in isolation from the rest. Each of these, again, is limited only to the moment at which it appears in consciousness [*vartamānakālaṁ vāhyamindriyam* (Vāchaspati Misra on *Kārikā*, 33)].

In a similar manner, the impulses that work through the organs of action, and the sensations that arise from the operation of each of the organs, may be separately experienced. As the text states: "Karmendriyāṇi yathāyathaṁ vachanādīn padārthān utpādayanti tataścha teshu padārtheshu teshāṁ ālochanātmakaṁ jñānaṁ jāyate." This is probably what the Sāṁkhya authorities describe as the emergence of the organs of action (*Karmendriyas*) from the plane of *Manas*.

Tanmātras. We shall now turn to the second order and series of experiences that emerge from the plane of the ego (*Ahaṁkāra*). Here the apprehension of the object ultimately resolves itself into a series of irreducible units. The concrete initial experience of colour or sound, for instance, no longer persists. This passes into a generalized awareness of each sense department, visual or auditory, gustatory, olfactory, or tactual. These are residua of sense-experiences which the Mind cannot completely assimilate by conscious manipulation. The world, therefore, appears to the self, on the one hand, as a system of mental objects, and, on the other hand, as a system of physical objects.

At this stage, then, the self feels itself limited by generalized sensory data external to itself. This is probably analogous to Fichte's conception of the opposition between the Ego and the Non-Ego. In Fichte's philosophy, the Non-Ego is given in one block, as it were; in the Sāṁkhya, the Non-Ego is given divided into generalized sensory qualities, vision, sound, smell, taste, and touch (*tanmātrāṇi aviśeshāḥ, Kārikā*, 38). The sense of the external has divided itself as it were into these five basic qualities.

Bhūtas. In what way do these five sensory qualities differ from what are conceived in Sāṁkhya as the five great elements (*Bhūtas*), viz. *Kshiti* (Earth), *Ap* (Water), *Teja* (Fire), *Marut* (Wind), and *Vyoma* (Ether), the constituents of the external world? In the first place, the generalized qualities (*Tanmātras*) are said to be "subtle", that is, difficult of perception (*sūkshmaṁ = durlakshyam*, as Vāchaspati says). In the second place, these "elements" are said to be specified (*viśeshāḥ*). Such

" specification " consists in that they are capable of being " experienced " and " enjoyed " [*Upabhogayogyaḥ viśeshaḥ* (Vāchaspati Misra on *Kārikā*, 38)].

Thus, according to Sāṁkhya scheme, consciousness traverses the diverse realm of experience, from the level of " pure consciousness " (*Purusha*) to the concrete material entities (*Bhūtas*).

It will, therefore, be observed that the Sāṁkhya educes the course of phenomenal consciousness from the basic reality of Pure Consciousness (*Purusha*) and of the Principle of Objectivity (*Prakṛti*). As has been already explained, the course of this consciousness leads from the subtle to the grosser forms of experience by an order of *descent*.

The problem of Yoga is to *ascend* from the plane of daily life to that of pure consciousness.

We may now sum up the workings of the process of perception as follows :—

(1) Perception is related to a real object and is thus distinguished from *Viparyaya* (illusion).

(2) The real object is immediately apprehended by its corresponding sense-organ.

(3) The Mind (*Manas*) seizes this immediate apprehension of the sense-organ, reflects upon it, and makes it definite by assimilation and discrimination.

(4) The *Ahaṁkāra* (empirical ego) appropriates to itself this determinate apprehension of the mind, and assimilates it as a part of the empirical unity of apperception, that is to say, a part of its own history.

(5) The *Buddhi* (intellect) decides what is to be done towards the object perceived ; it is the will to react to the object perceived.

(6) The *Purusha* (Self) " enjoys " the perception of the object. It is the transcendent principle of Intelligence (*Chiti-Śakti*) which intelligizes the unconscious *buddhi* and makes perceptive consciousness possible.

These processes are well illustrated by Vāchaspati-Miśra as follows : The village headman collects taxes from the villagers, and delivers them over to the next higher authority, the Governor of the province, who hands them over to the Minister, and the Minister to the King. In a similar manner, the sense-organs, obtaining an immediate apprehension of external objects, passes the immediate impressions on to the Mind (*Manas*), and the Mind in its turn, reflecting on them, transmits them to *Ahaṁkāra* which appropriates them to itself by its unity of apperception and hands over these self-appropriated apperceived impressions of external objects to *Buddhi* which resolves what action is to be taken on them.

It is only when the Mind renders, by its powers of assimilation and discrimination, definite and determinate the immediate and indeterminate apprehension of the sense-organs, that *Ahaṁkāra* can appropriate such apprehension to itself and transform the impersonal apprehension of the object into a personal experience suffused with egoism.

This self-appropriation (*abhimāna*) is the function of *Ahaṁkāra*. Vāchaspatimiśra illustrates it as follows, putting the following words into the mouth of *Ahaṁkāra :* " It is I alone who presides over the object that is intuited by the sense-organ and is then definitely perceived by the mind. I wield power over all that is perceived and known, and all objects thus perceived are for my use. There is no other superior except ' *I* '. *I am.*"

He also describes the function of *Buddhi* thus : " The sense intuits an object ; *Manas* reflects on it ; *Ahaṁkāra* appropriates it to itself ; *Buddhi* resolves, ' this I should do by it,' and then one proceeds to action." And again : " In dark a person at first apprehends an object as something undifferentiated, then reflects upon it, and determines it to be a dangerous robber by his bow and arrow, then thinks of him in relation to himself, e.g. ' he is rushing to attack me ', and then resolves or determines, ' I must run away from this place.' "

Thus Manas, Ahaṁkāra, and Buddhi are parts of one, viz. Antaḥkaraṇa or *Chitta* [Chittaśabdena antaḥkaraṇam buddhim upalakshyayati (Vāchaspati)], though performing different functions. *Manas* achieves *niśchaya-jñāna* (definite knowledge of an object) which *Ahaṁkāra* appropriates to itself and produces what is called *abhimāna*. Then *Buddhi* steps over to determine what action to take on it and how to react to this knowledge.

Further, the external organs are called the gateways of knowledge, while the internal organs the gate-keepers [*Sāṁkhya-kārikā*, 35]. The external organs receive immediate impressions from external objects and communicate these to the *antaḥkaraṇa* which by reflection (*manana*), ego-consciousness (*abhimāna*), and determination (*adhyavasāya*) makes them definite and determinate and receives them for the enjoyment of the Purusha (Self).

It is also held that both the external and internal organs thus operating in perception are themselves insentient principles, and, as such, are incapable of conscious apprehension of objects. It is the *Purusha* that makes them apprehend objects. Thus, according to Sāṁkhya-Yoga, perception implicates two epistemic factors, (1) the existence of an extra-mental object, and (2) the existence of the Purusha (Self).

Like these external and internal organs, the *Chitta*, too, being itself an object of consciousness, is not self-luminous (natat svābhāsaṁ dṛiśyatvāt). The Mind is not self-conscious (svābhāsa), as it is the outcome of the unconscious Prakṛiti, as explained above. In this sense, the Mind is itself a form, the highest form, of Matter. It is the Purusha which is the cognizer and enjoyer of the Mind. The essence of the Purusha is consciousness. The self-luminous Purusha is reflected upon the unconscious Mind and mistakes the state of the Mind for its own state. Thus in the Sāṁkhya dualism of conscious *Purusha* and unconscious *Prakṛiti* or primal nature, there is a place for an intermediate reality, the Buddhi, as the highest form of evolution from Matter or Prakṛiti in the infinite series of its modifications of different grades and as approximating most to Purusha at the other end. Buddhi is thus the missing link between Spirit and Matter, the conscious Purusha and unconscious Prakṛiti.[1]

Yoga Scheme of Discipline. Yoga describes the measures by which the ascent of man can be achieved. It retraces in the reverse order the stages of experience as described in the Sāṁkhya system. It starts from the lowest level where the Mind is held in the grip of Matter by the operations of the senses. Yoga, therefore, begins with making the organs of knowledge and action abandon their operations so as to free the Mind from the clutches of Matter (*Yoga-śchitta-vṛitti-nirodhaḥ*). The idea is that such inhibition closes the avenue of the senses and, therefore, empties the mind of its content of all sensory experience.

[1] It may be noted that the theory of perception in Western Psychology is based on the assumption that the sense-experiences are entirely different in their nature from the objects which they represent. This has given rise to a number of problems in the Western theory of knowledge, which are yet to be solved. The doctrines of Representationism and of Relations are some of the outstanding issues even in contemporary thought. The philosophical solution offered to these questions to-day mainly follow two leading ideas: (1) That the interests, attention, and apperception-mass lead the mind to the object, so that its external character becomes entirely hypothetical. We do not know how much of matter or external reality enters into knowledge. (2) That there is no duality between the sense-experience and the sense-object. There is merely the world of sense-data which through analytical reasoning is divided into two spheres of sense-experience and sensory objects. Some of the Indian theories offer a solution in which the first of these views is anticipated. This is, however, systematized in terms of certain metaphysical assumptions.

'Chitta-bhūmi.' Yoga elaborates this process of the discipline and purification of *Chitta* or Mind. *Chitta* is recognized as exhibiting five patterns or *bhūmis*. A *Chitta-bhūmi* is defined as " the condition in which the Mind has a natural tendency to rest, and to which it habitually reverts by the momentum of its dispositions and aptitudes established by accumulated experience " (*saṁskāra*-vaśāt yasyām avasthāyāṁ chittaṁ prāyaśaḥ *saṁtishṭhate* sā eva chitta-bhūmiḥ). The Mind moves in its accustomed grooves co-related to corresponding configurations.

Its Five Phases. The five patterns or states of Chitta are described as follows: (1) *Kshipta*, restless, distracted, wandering (*bhramati*) from one object to another; (2) *Mūḍha*, absorbed in *vishaya* or pleasures, blinded by passion like anger; (3) *Vikshipta*, a state of distraction occasionally broken by lucid intervals of concentration, a state in which the mind generally cultivates the pleasant and avoids what is unpleasant; (4) *Ekāgra*, 'one-pointed thinking,' focussed state where the mind concentrates on the thought of one object; (5) *Niruddha*, " concentration, and inhibition of conflicting functions, so that the mind is left with the substratum of its innate dispositions as its only content (niruddhasakalavrittikam saṁskārāvaśesham).

'Yoga-bhūmi.' The aim of Yoga is to lead the mind away from the first three conditions which are not congenial to concentration and fix it on the last two states which constitute the *Yoga-bhūmi*, the plane favourable to the practice of Yoga or concentration. Concentration or *samādhāna* of Chitta is possible in all states (*sārva-bhauma*), including the first three. For instance, " a Jayadratha blinded by hostility to the Pāṇḍavas was yet able to concentrate on worship of Śiva. One may also concentrate on pleasures, on wealth or women." But such *samādhi* is short-lived, not stabilized, liable to be disturbed by distractions and gusts of passion. It is the *ekāgra* state in which the mind is intent on an object which leads to *saṁprajñāta samādhi*. It is so called because in that state " the object of concentrated contemplation is directly apprehended " (saṁprajñāyate sākshāt kriyate dheyasvarūpamatra). The object of such contemplation can only be an object to which the mind will cling with a longing, as the bee seeks honey. Such object is supreme truth or knowledge. The mind that has once tasted Truth will not have any liking for untruth. Therefore, " concentrated contemplation brings to light the ultimate meanings and values (*sadbhūtaṁ arthaṁ pradyotayati*), causes sorrows to dwindle, loosens the bonds of action, cuts at its springs or roots, and leads to the next stage of supra-conscious contemplation (nirodha-samādhi = asaṁprajñāta samādhi)."

The Five Afflictions. The 'sorrows' (*kleśas*) that dwindle are described to be the five following, viz. (1) *Avidyā*, ignorance; (2) *Asmitā*, sense of individuality; (3) *Rāga*, passion; (4) *Dvesha*, hatred; and (5) *Abhiniveśa*, instinctive clinging to life, instinct of self-preservation.

Stages of 'Samādhi'. The *Samādhi* that is attained in the *ekāgra* condition of Chitta is attained by a series of graduated stages marked out as follows: (1) *Vitarka*, where contemplation has for its object a form "like the four-handed deity"; (2) *Vichāra*, where the subtle as the cause of the gross is contemplated; (3) *Ānanda*, where there is a sense of joy; and (4) *Asmitā*, where there remains a feeling of self-hood.

Progress from Concrete to Abstract. The principle involved in the differentiation of these stages is that the progress of psychic life is from the more concrete modes of experience to its subtle forms and ways.[1] In *Vitarka* and *Vichāra*, for instance, the Mind is concerned with objects and actions, their causes, properties, and implications. In the third stage of *Ānanda*, there remains simply a feeling of bliss, an objectless emotion, while, in the last stage called *Asmitā*, only the sense of selfhood persists. When this sense also ceases, the Samādhi is called *Asaṁprajñāta* as distinguished from its previous state called *Saṁprajñāta* Samādhi.

The Three 'Guṇas'. A deeper analysis explains the different states of Chitta as being influenced by one or other of the three *Guṇas*, *Sattva*, *Rajas*, and *Tamas*, the elemental laws governing all existence and activity. The three Guṇas mark out the corresponding conditions of Chitta to be those of (1) *Prakhyā*, (2) *Pravṛitti*, and (3) *Sthiti*. *Prakhyā* is characterized by *prakāśa*

[1] These Yoga stages of *Samādhi* may be compared with the *Koshas* of the Upanishads. The doctrine of *Koshas* is mentioned in the *Taittirīya* Upanishad [ii, 1–5], according to which there are five *Koshas* or "sheaths" enfolding the soul. The outermost *Kosha* is called *Annamaya* signifying the body or physical covering of the *Jīva* and the natural aspect of individual existence. Next comes the *Prāṇamaya Kosha* representing the vital or organic side of an individual's existence. Then come the higher levels of life, the conscious (*Manomaya*), and the self-consciousness (*Vijñānamaya*), crowned by the *Ānandamaya Kosha* marked by bliss, and peace, and *rasa*. *Brahma* Itself is described as "*Raso vai saḥ*" [ib., ii, 7]. The body, *prāṇa*, and *Manas* may be thus taken to constitute a sort of 'empirical home' for the soul. Only conscious activity is taken over by *Manas*. It may also be noted that the Upanishads anticipate the Sāṁkhya-yogic terms *vijñāna* or *ahaṁkāra* [cf. *Bṛi. Upa.*, i, 5, 3].

and *prasāda*. *Prakāsa* indicates that, being itself luminous, it lights up objects by its own light. *Prasāda* is the *ānanda* or bliss of equipoise. This mental stage is further marked by *prīti*, fellow-feeling, and *khyāti*, discrimination.

The second state of *Pravṛitti* is marked by activity stimulated by desire which is the cause of suffering.

The third state of *Sthiti* is marked by inertia and darkness eclipsing knowledge and obstructing manifestation (*prakāśa*).

It will be seen that of the five aforesaid conditions of mind, the *Kshipta* is the outcome of *Raja*, the *Mūḍha* of *Tama*, and the *Vikshipta*, the result of a mixture of both *Sattva* and *Raja*. When *Sattva* is mixed up with *Raja* and *Tama*, the character of the mind degenerates and, instead of *Prakhyā*, the mind runs after *Aiśvarya* and *Vishaya*, after power and pleasures of the senses (Rūpa, Rasa, Gandha, Sparśa, and Śabda). There is a further deterioration of the mind under *Tamas* when it is immersed in the darkness of sins.

'Chitta-vṛitti' : Its Five Ways. But the Mind or Chitta is to be studied not merely in its various possible patterns or conditions (*bhūmi*) but also in its processes and ways of working. All possible mental processes are grouped into the following five classes :—

1. **'Pramāṇa.'** *Pramā* means 'true knowledge' and *Pramāṇa*, 'what produces such knowledge, the means of achieving such knowledge.' *Pramāṇa* therefore stands for the usual ways of knowing through (*a*) *Pratyaksha* (direct perception), (*b*) *Anumāna* (Inference), and (*c*) *Āgama* (Authority). *Pratyaksha* is defined as *indriyajanyā* (outcome of the senses), *Anumāna vyāptijñāna-janyā* (outcome of a knowledge of generic qualities), and *Āgama* as *śabdajñāna-janyā* (caused by knowledge of what is heard) *chitta-vṛitti*.

Its Three Forms : (a) 'Pratyaksha'. The Mind is driven to seek the first method of knowledge by the senses conveying to it a taste of objects (*vishaya*). It is a direct contact between Mind and Matter. The characteristic of *pratyaksha-jñāna* is that it comprehends an object by its tangible qualities. It also comprehends objects as individuals by their specific (*viśesha*) qualities and not by their generic (*sāmānya*) ones by which individual objects are seen to belong to classes or groups.

(b) Anumāna. *Anumāna* is the method whereby the knowledge of one object is derived from the knowledge of another, as fire is known from smoke ; where the object of knowledge cannot be directly perceived but may be understood as the effect of a cause (*hetugamya*). *Anumāna* reveals the generic attributes of an object rather than its specific ones, 'as in the case of the inference that Moon and Stars have motions because they change places, or that the Vindhya hills are devoid of motion because they are unable to change places.'

(c) **Āgama.** *Āgama* is what proceeds from the lips of a person considered as an *āpta* or unimpeachable authority by the person listening to it and accepting it with implicit faith without arguing or doubting it. "Such a person imparts to the other what he has himself seen or inferred by uttering words with the intention that such words may produce a like sense in him." Such verbal instruction is *Āgama*. The value of *āgama* as a source of knowledge depends on the character of the person imparting such knowledge. Such a person should be absolutely above board, 'free from foibles like unsound views, erroneous perception, deceit, defective organs of sense, and should be possessed of insight, charity, and soundness of perception.' That *Āgama*, however, cannot rank as *Pramāṇa* or a source of valid knowledge which is expounded by a person whose words cannot be taken for granted (*aśraddheyārtha*) and who has not even directly obtained the knowledge he expounds by his own perception or inference. The objection may be taken that Śāstras like Manu, Smṛiti, and the Purāṇas, which only recall and repeat the words of the Veda, should not count as *Āgama*. The reply is that the Veda is revealed by an unimpeachable authority, viz. Íśvara Himself Who is perfect, and so the Śāstras, like Manu, based on Veda, are *Āgama*. The texts of systems which do not believe in God cannot count as *Āgama* or *Pramāṇa*.

Its Two Features. It is to be noted that *Āgama* is marked by two features: (1) that it comprises words which are actually uttered, and (2) that the words should be those of an admitted authority (*āpta-vākya*). The knowledge that is derived from a study of books (*pāṭhaja-niśchaya*) is not *Āgama*.

Its Attributes. The sound or Word that counts as *Āgama* cannot be understood without a knowledge of its four attributes, viz. (1) *Śakti* (implication), (2) *Lakshaṇā* (what it symbolizes), (3) *Vyañjanā* (allusion), and (4) Inner Sense or gist (*Tātparya*). Sound will convey its sense only to one who has desire for learning (*ākāṅkshā*), fitness (*yogyatā*), devotion (*āsakti*), and insight (*tātparya-jñāna*).

2. **'Viparyaya'.** *Viparyaya* is illusory perception, "like

the mistaking of a rope for a serpent or shell for silver." The mind is prone to both *viparyaya* and *saṁśaya*, misconception and misgivings. The difference between the two is that while the former starts with a sense of certainty of knowledge which is later corrected, the latter starts with a doubt about its position. The causes of such misconception are stated to be five: avidyā (undifferentiated consciousness), asmitā (sense of self-hood), rāga (passion), dvesha (hatred), and abhiniveśa (attachment to life, the will to live).

3. **Vikalpa.** *Vikalpa* is 'use of words not corresponding to reality', where knowledge of an object is imagined (*vikalpita*). 'A sound or word has the power of calling up a sense of something which may not exist' (atyantamapi asati arthe śabdo jñānaṁ karoti hi), as the Mīmaṁsakas say. A reality may be defined by the following three marks, viz. *Śabda* (name or word indicating it), *Artha* (actual existence), and *Jñāna* (meaning, what it indicates or stands for). In the case of *Vikalpa* method of knowing, only the *Śabda* or Sound and the Jñāna or the sense it conveys, remain, without any *Artha* or correspondence to reality.

4. **Nidrā.** *Nidrā* is 'lapse of consciousness, sleep'. *Nidrā* or sleep is also a form of mental activity, because its results or effects can be recalled after sleep. Otherwise, "how can one reflect thus in the waking state? I have slept well, my mind is at ease, it makes my understanding clear. Or, I have slept in deep stupor, I feel my limbs to be heavy, my mind is fatigued, not refreshed, it is languid, as if it does not exist." Therefore, Sleep is a kind of presented idea (*pratyaya*) or experience (*anubhava*) and is to be considered as a *Chitta-vṛitti* and, as such, is to be resisted in *Samādhi*.

5. **Smṛiti.** *Smṛiti* means 'recalling the past, memories'. Smṛiti works on the basis of previous experience which it recalls, "just as a son may possess himself of the property of his father wholly or in part by virtue of his right to it, and is not accused of theft for it." Similarly, Smṛiti works within the limits of experience or *anubhava* and does not go beyond them. It works on the basis of the known, while *anubhava* is experience of what was unknown. *Anubhava* or experience makes and leaves an impression (*saṁskāra*) on the mind and *Smṛiti* takes its rise from such *saṁskāras*.

Two Classes of 'Chitta-vṛitti'. The above five *Vṛittis* of *Chitta* are brought by Vyāsa under two classes with reference to their effects. These are called (1) *Klishṭa-vṛitti*, 'out-going activities or movements of the mind resulting in *Kleśa* or suffering,' and (2) *Aklishṭa-vṛitti*, 'which leads to bliss.' These correspond respectively to what are known as *Pravṛitti-mārga*, 'way of action,' and *Nivṛitti-mārga*, 'way of cessation of activities.'

Process of Yoga in Outline : Meaning of Chitta, Vṛitti, and Saṃskāra. As already stated, Yoga means the *nirodha* or inhibition of the *vṛittis* of *Chitta*. The *Vṛitti* is the reaction of Mind to Matter, of Subject to Object. This reaction is effected through the senses, the five senses of cognition and the five of action ; those of Eye, Ear, Nose, Tongue, and Skin enabling vision, audition, smell, taste, and touch ; and the organs of speech, hands, feet, evacuation, and generation. Through the operation of these two classes of organs, the Mind comes into contact with Matter and is transformed by it. This transformation of the Mind by which the Mind takes on the form of a material object in apprehending it is called *Vṛitti* (vishayākāreṇa chittasya pariṇāmaḥ = Vṛittiḥ).

Vāchaspati Misra takes the *Chitta* of Yoga to be the same as the *Buddhi* of Sāṁkhya (Chitta-śabdena Antaḥkaraṇaṁ Buddhiṁ upalakshayati). *Buddhi* or *Chitta* signifies an act, the mental act of apprehension (Buddhiḥ *grahaṇa-rūpā*). According to the *Bhāsvatī*, this act of apprehension or knowing is blended with the content apprehended, the object known, of which it is a constituent. But the act of apprehension can be by itself, separately, grasped. It further points out that such apprehension or knowing leaves behind it its traces called *saṁskāra* (grahaṇaṁ cha prādhānyāt agṛihītasya upādānaṁ | tasya upādānasya api asti anubhavaḥ saṁskāraḥ). These traces or impressions of previous experience, these *saṁskāras*, constitute an element in the consciousness of objects, in being indirectly in the objects that are remembered ; they also colour the ways of knowing or sources of cognition ; and they thus influence the operation of the Buddhi (Chitta) (tādṛiśa saṁskārāṇāṁ smṛitiḥ gauṇa-bhāvena upādānarūpe anadhigata-vishaye pramāṇe buddhau vā tishṭhati). *Saṁskāras*, therefore, complete knowledge and give it a form.

'All these acts of knowing, Pramāṇa, Anumāna, and the like, on the part of the *chitta* are called its *Vṛittis*, because by these the *Chitta* lives, just as the twice-born classes live by performing sacrifices' (yaiḥ pramāṇādi-lakshaṇa-vyāpāraiḥ chittaṁ jīvaṭi te tad-vṛittaya uchyante dvijādīnāṁ yājanādivat).

Process of 'Chitta-vṛitti-nirodha': its different Stages. It is to be noted that the process of Yoga which is defined to be *Chitta-vṛitti-nirodha* does not mean the annihilation of Chitta. For Chitta cannot be annihilated according to Sāṁkhya-Yoga logic, the doctrine of *Satkārya-vāda* which holds that the effect is latent in the cause, 'like oil in the seeds.' Besides, Chitta = Buddhi is, as we have seen, an evolute of Prakṛiti which is eternal. The Yoga process of *Chitta-vṛitti-nirvodha*, therefore, signifies (1) the process by which the cognitive operations of the mind by which it is brought into touch with matter or objects, physical and mental, past and present, cease, and the mind is emptied of its contents of sensory experience. Only the innate qualities of psychic life, its awareness (*prakhyā*), its impulses (*pravṛitti*), and the impressions of past experience (*sthiti* = *saṁskāra*) remain as grist for the mill of the mind. (2) These subjective processes are, however, readily projected to the external world. When the sense-organs reveal the realm of independent realities, impulses (*pravṛitti*) seize upon them; the vestiges of past experience (*saṁskāra*) impart to them familiar forms; and awareness (*prakhyā*) pervades the object in such a manner that no line can be drawn between that which comes from without and its conscious apprehension. If the world of objects can be rendered into nothingness, if the sense that there are external and independent objects ceases altogether, the emanations of consciousness recoil on the self. The vestigial dispositions are no longer felt as qualities of the object; the impulses turn on the self and blend with the self-feeling; the quality of awareness itself becomes an attribute of the self. This is the condition described as that of oneness of the mind with self (*sārūpya*). (3) The mind is now left alone with its own innate tendencies which now require to be regulated in their turn. This end can be achieved by steady and strenuous cultivation of the placid states of mind and inhibition of those that promote inertia or action (*avṛittikasya* = rājasa-tāmasa-vṛittirahitasya praśāntavāhitā = vimalatā sāttvika-vṛitti-vāhitā ekāgratā = sthiti). This placid state is the state of what is called *Sthiti* which leads (4) to that of *Vairāgya* in which the mind has acquired control over the impulses that are directed to objects of enjoyment (dṛishṭānuśravika-vishayavitṛishṇasya vaśīkārasaṁjñā vairāgyam).

But the state of *Vairāgya* is, after all, a negative phase which only prepares the way for a positive phase, a higher plane of consciousness (5) where it is now devoid of all states and trends, and persists only as a placid expanse of the Psyche (vyaktāvyaktebhya dharmakebhya sarvathā viraktaḥ sattva-purushānyatākhyātau api guṇātmikāyāṁ yāvat viraktaḥ). At this stage, the mind, however, still owns to some intellectual functions called *Vitarka* and *Vichāra*, a sense of joy (*ānanda*), and a sense of the self (*asmitā* = jñātāhaṁ iti asmitāmātrasaṁvit), as already explained. The mind is still troubled by its innate dispositions, and inherited tendencies. Mental life still pursues a latent course. A state of *samādhi*, of continuous absorption in the object of contemplation, now sets in. But the factors that may lead the mind back to the world of things are not yet eliminated. This can be achieved only by a persistent process of self-regulation and control, continuous contemplation, and practice of recital of the mystic syllable *Om*, the verbal translation of Brahma (tajjapaḥ tadarthabhāvanam) whereby (6) the mental plane can be transcended. These will end the career of *Manas* (or Chitta) and bring into play (7) the principle of Ego or self-consciousness (*ahaṁkāra*-tataḥ pratyakchetanādhigamaḥ).

But like Manas, the Self, too, must cease to operate as a centre of experience. This end is to be pursued by several processes: (i) Elimination of all negative feelings (*antarāya*), of sorrow (*duḥkha*) and melancholy (*daurmanasya*) that usually cling to the ego-feeling [i, 31]; (ii) cultivation of a sense of universal sympathy (*maitrī*), a feeling of kindliness for all (*karuṇā*), and an attitude of indifference to joys and sorrows (*upekshā*) [i, 32, 33].

(8) In this way, says the Yoga-Sūtra [i, 36], there grows up in the mind 'a placid, griefless, and radiant consciousness' (*Viśokā vā jyotishmatī*).

Further, the world of objects may be viewed in two ways. (*a*) We may think of it as a complex of sense-qualities, as a system built out of the combination of vision, sound, touch, smell, and taste. (*b*) We may think of it as a manifestation of independent realities. We have so far traced the course of the Psyche from the plane of sense-qualities to the inwardness of self-conscious life. We may also lead back from the realm of gross material realities (*mahābhūta*), through the subtler forms of material entities (*tanmātra*) to the self. (9) The latter appear as shadows of the material world in the form of generalized sensory phenomena (vishayavatī vā pravṛittirutpannā) [i, 35].

Finally, another level of contemplative life becomes necessary. Consciousness must be trained to contemplate objects both gross and subtle. This process develops (10) a plasticity of consciousness which routined rites so far followed have tended to circumscribe. This is called *Vaśīkāra*, a state of psychic self-sufficiency and freedom [avyāhata prasāra (*Bhāsvatī*); sthūla-sūkshma-rūpaṁ paksha dvayaṁ charataḥ asya chittasya yaḥ apratighātaḥ kenāpi aprativaddhatā (*Vārttika*)]. The psyche thus achieves a freedom to reflect in itself with equal success the nature of pure consciousness, of the act of knowing, as also of the object known (grahītṛi-grahaṇa-grāhyeshu tadañjanatā). It is the plane of pure cognition (*Samāpatti*) [i, 41].

The Yoga-sūtras describe two principal stages of such cognition. In the first of these, the sense of interval between the word, its meaning, and its general significance disappears (*saṁkīrṇā*). It may be called discursive apprehension (*savitarkā samāpatti*). When the meaning is apprehended (*arthamātra-nirbhāsā*) without the aid of words (vāk-viyukto jñāyate), it is called non-discursive cognition (nirvitarkā samāpatti) [i, 43].

The latter mode of insight, again, has its own dialectic. (i) When the meaning thus grasped leads to concrete phases of experience that distribute themselves in time and space (deśa-kāla-nimitta-anubhava-avachchhinna) [i, 44 (*Bhāsvatī*)], it is called discriminative insight (*savichāra*). (ii) Where the meanings are apprehended without any reference to the space-time and the cause-effect schema, in the manner of Platonic ideas, it is called non-discursive insight (nirvichāra-samāpatti).

(11) As consciousness progresses into subtler ways, meanings appear merely as qualifying a subject, without words, without objects (asmītimātra-prabodhasvarūpam). This is called *savīja-samādhi*, the stage of contemplation that carries a sense of *reference*. For, all meanings lead to objects other than the self. A reference, then, conveys a sense of things other than pure consciousness, of the object-world (dhyeyarūpeṇa pṛithak jñāyamāṇaṁ-vastu) [*Bhāsvatī*, i, 44].

(12) This residuum of the external passes away in the translation of consciousness into pure inwardness. Then there emerges a clear uninterrupted flow of pure consciousness (*svachchhaḥ sthiti-pravāhaḥ*) which rejects all references to the sense of the object-world (bhūtārtha-vishaya-kramānurodhī). It represents a clarity of insight and placidity of inward life (sphuṭaprajñālokaḥ adhyātma-prasādaḥ). This is called the stage of spiritual mastery (*vaiśārada*) [*Yoga-Sūtra*, i, 47]. (13) There is an inflow, into this plane of life, of the eternal verities that reject all knowledge

HERMITAGE SCENES FROM MUTTRA SCULPTURES (*c.* first century B.C.).

A pre-Gandhāra sculpture showing two monks, the older feeding a bird, the younger one, a new arrival, resting against his baggage-basket hung on a pole ; an altar and a water-pot (*kamaṇḍalu*) shown in the field ; some trees and a pair of deer running over a rocky surface, symbolical of the sylvan environment ; the third panel shows the young monk alone.

[*Facing p. 305*

alloyed with the secular. The insights of this plane supersede the total range of experience (anyasaṁskāra-pratibandhī) and establish themselves. This is called *Ṛitambharā Prajñā*, the stage of Insight of Verity [ib., i, 50].

(14) This plane of the spirit, too, like the preceding planes, gives rise to a new cycle of insights, each of which may leave its traces on the life-history of consciousness (tataḥ navo navaḥ saṁskārāśayo jāyate). When the progress of the spirit stops, the sprouting of consciousness even in this form ceases, and the final stage, that of 'seedless contemplation' (*nirvīja-samādhi*), matures.

Moral Practices and Technique of Yoga. From the outline of the process of Yoga and its general view, we shall now pass on to a consideration of the practices aiding in the accomplishment of that process and of its success in self-fulfilment.

Yoga or *Chitta-Vṛitti-Nirodha* depends on two fundamental factors: (1) *Abhyāsa* (Practice) and (2) *Vairāgya* (Freedom from passion or objectivity).

Abhyāsa. The aim is to inhibit those activities (*Vṛittis*) of the mind (Chitta) which are dictated by *Raja* or *Tama*. When the Chitta is thus rendered free of its vṛittis (*avṛittika*), it attains a state of equipoise (*sthiṭi*), flowing on in undisturbed calm (praśānta-vāhitā) under the influence of *Sattva-guṇa*. To achieve this mental *sthiti*, effort (*prayatna*) is needed. *Prayatna* implies (*a*) *Vīrya* (energy) and (*b*) *Utsāha*, enthusiasm, persevering struggle. This *prayatna* or effort is to be directed towards the strenuous pursuit (*anusṭhāna*) of the external and internal practices laid down in Yoga, to be explained below. An old text states: "*Ichchhā* (desire) is created by knowledge (*ātmajanyā*); *Kṛiti* (prayatna = effort) by *Ichchhā*; *Cheshṭā* (bodily exertion) by *Kṛiti*; and *Kriyā* by *Cheshṭā*." Thus *Abhāyāsa* means the energetic and enthusiastic pursuit of the practices enjoined by Yoga.

This *Abhyāsa* must not be spasmodic, but must be "confirmed and established on a stable basis (*dṛiḍha-bhūmiḥ*) by its prolonged and continuous cultivation (*dīrghakāla-nirantarā sevitaḥ*) with *satkāra*, i.e. with *tapasyā* (penance), *brahma-charya* (continence), *vidyā* (knowledge of ultimate truth), and *śraddhā* (devotion)".

Vairāgya. *Vairāgya* (passionlessness) is defined as the consciousness (*saṁjñā*) of mastery of thirst (*tṛishṇā*) for seen (*dṛishṭa*) and unseen, revealed (*ānuśravika*) objects (*vishaya*).

The things of this world are stated to be Woman, Food, Drink, and Power, comprising both animate and inanimate objects. The things of the other world of which one 'hears' from the Vedas comprise attainment of *svarga* (heaven), *vaidehya* (freedom from birth), and *prakṛiti-laya* (resolution into primary matter). *Svarga* is defined as 'pure happiness unalloyed by any touch of sorrow'. Thus in *Vairāgya* the *Chitta* will be unmoved (*anābhogātmikā*) by contact with objects seen and unseen, considering their inadequacy (*vishaya-dosha-darśī*). The mind will be devoid of any desire either to reject, or accept (*heyopādeya-śūnya*) objects. It perceives their deficiencies such as 'the trouble to acquire them, to preserve them, and their inevitable decline' (*arjana-rakshaṇa-kshaya*, etc.). This indifference to objects results from *prasaṁkhyāna*, the constant contemplation of the inadequacy of all objects followed by a lively sense of their innate worthlessness.

Four Stages of Vairāgya. *Vairāgya* is to be achieved in four stages of consciousness: (*a*) *Yatamāna-saṁjñā*. This stage is marked by the effort (*yatna*) to purge the mind of its impulses or impurities (*mala*) like attachment or hatred which stimulate the senses and drive them towards objects. (*b*) *Vyatireka-saṁjñā*. In this stage is to be examined to what extent the senses are withdrawn from objects so as to find out by elimination the remaining objects to which the senses are still drawn. (*c*) *Ekendriya-saṁjñā*. This refers to the stage where, even when the senses are all withdrawn from objects, the *Chitta*, as the sole sense left operative, still thinks of objects with zest, which thus still persist and find a habitation there. (*d*) *Vaśīkāra-saṁjñā*. The last and highest stage of *Vairāgya* is marked by a complete conquest (*vaśīkāra*) of all faint or latent desire.

Apara- and Para-Vairāgya. This fourth stage of *Vairāgya* is not the final stage. *Vairāgya* in its four stages as described above is *Apara*-Vairāgya, which ripens into the final stage called *Para*-Vairāgya. *Apara*-Vairāgya is negative. Here the mind turns away from (*virakta*) objects, those of daily life (*dṛishṭa*) and those prescribed as ultimate ends (*ānuśravika*). This detachment from objects is due to perception of their inherent imperfections (*vishaya-dosha-darśī*) which are three-fold, comprising the three afflictions (*tritāpa*) of spiritual baffle-ment (*ādhyātmika*), sorrows arising from the material world (*ādhibhautika*), and those that are inflicted by chance and super-natural agencies (*ādhidaivika*) [*Bhāsvatī*]. On the mind thus detached from the realm of desired ends dawns the 'awareness of Purusha' (*purusha-khyāṭi*). In this state of detachment which is also one of purity (*śuddhi*), the *Buddhi* (intellect) achieves equipoise and placidity (*tatśuddhiviveka-āpyāita-buddhi*). Out of this state of *apara-vairāgya* arises that of *para-vairagya* marked by a serene insight, self-fulfilling, and self-fulfilled (*jñāna-prasāda*). In it, "all that is worthy of attainment has been attained; all that has to be given up has been rejected; the links in the chain of births and deaths have been broken. This *Vairāgya* marks the highest point of knowledge (*jñānasya parākāshṭhā*), and holds within it *Kaivalya* (mukti, salvation)."

When the mind is thus brought under control by the inhibition of its objective tendencies (*Chitta-vṛitti-nirodha*) through the two processes (*upāyadvayena*) of *Abhyāsa* (exertion) and *Vairāgya* (detachment), *Samādhi* is attained. We have already seen how *Samādhi* comprises two stages called *Saṁprajñāta* and *Asaṁprajñāta* and how they are distinguished.

Five Means of Samādhi. The following five means (*upāya*) are enumerated for the attainment of Asaṁprajñāta-Samādhi (literally, "concentration not conscious of objects") by Yogins. These are (1) *Śraddhā* defined as the contentment (*saṁprasāda*) of mind with truth which it seeks with the greatest zeal. This spirit of devotion to truth keeps up the Yogī in his quest thereof, like the well-wishing mother (*jananīva kalyāṇī*). It is to be observed that the mind cannot remain contented with anything except the ultimate Truth (*Ātman*). (2) *Vīrya*, strenuous exertion; (3) *Smṛiti*, mindfulness; (4) *Samādhi*, collectedness and concentration; and (5) *Prajñā*, discriminating insight whereby things are perceived as they truly are. By practice (*abhyāsa*) of these means coupled with *vairāgya* or detachment from objects, *Samādhi* of the highest stage is attained.

The speed of attainment of this *Samādhi* depends upon the degree of devotion or zeal (*saṁvega*) with which the above five measures are pursued. Such zeal may be mild (*mṛidu*), moderate (*madhya*), or intense (*adhimātra*).

The Sixth Means: Devotion to God, or 'Īśvara' (*Īśvara-praṇidhānam*). "Īśvara blesses with success (*anugṛihṇāti*) the Yogī when confronted (*āvarjjita*) by his profound devotion (*abhidhyāna*)."

Who is Īśvara? Īśvara is defined as a *particular* Purusha (distinct from the Purusha and Pradhāna or Prakṛiti of Sāṁkhya) who is not subject to (1) the five afflictions (*Kleśas*, such as

Avidyā, Asmitā, Rāga, Dvesha, and *Abhiniveśa*), (2) to *Karma*, (3) to the fruits of *Karma* (*vipāka*) such as birth (*jāti*), length of life (*āyu*), and experience (*bhoga*), and (4) to the springs of desires corresponding to these fruits (*āśaya*). He is also to be distinguished from the many *Mukta-Purushas* or *Kevalins* who have achieved their salvation by breaking the bonds of threefold existence, of the phenomenal world, material and mental (*prākṛitik*); of the realm of concrete realities so as to dwell in the region of generalized matter gross and subtle (*vaikārika*, cf. *bhūta-tanmātrādi-dhyāyinām*); of attachment to heavenly and other objects (*dākshiṇikaḥ bandho divyādivyavishaya-bhājām*). Further, God or Īśvara is not subject to history like these other emancipated *purushas* who are bound to their past and dragged to their future fate, however high their spiritual attainment may be. Lastly, Īśvara represents eternal perfection (*śāśvata utkarsha*) and the absolute wealth of attributes (*aiśvarya*). He represents the limit of knowledge, omniscience (*sarvajña*). But he is marked by one desire, 'to lift up living beings who are whirled in the vortex of existence' and assumes attributes and forms for the purpose, as the prime Teacher of Truth which must survive dissolution [Tasya ātmānugrahābhāve api bhūtānugrahaḥ prayojanaṁ jñānadharmopadeśena Kalpa-pralayamahāpralayeshu saṁsāriṇaḥ purushān uddharishyāmīti | Tathāchoktaṁ—'Ādi Vidvān nirmāṇachittamadhishṭhāya kāruṇyāt Bhagavān paramarshiḥ Āsuraye jijñāsamānāya Tantraṁ provācha iti' *Vyāsa-Bhāshya*].

Method of approaching God. God or Īśvara is indicated by the Mystic Syllable known as *Praṇava* or *Omkāra* which is to be taken as His symbol. The Yogī should repeat the syllable and reflect upon its meaning (Tajjapastadarthabhāvanam), i.e. should practise *svādhyāya* or study of Veda (of which the *Praṇava* is the root) and *yoga* or concentration on its import which is God Himself. As the *Chhāndogya Upanishad* states: "*Oṁ iti aksharaṁ udgīthamūpāsīti*—the letter *Om* is to be uttered and worshipped."

By this method of worshipping God (*Īśvara-praṇidhānāt*), the Yogī gets over all obstacles in his way and attains to a sight of his own real self (*svarūpa-darśanam*). "He has the right knowledge which sees that as the Īsvara is a Purusha who is undefiled (*śuddha*, not subject to growth and decay), unafflicted (*prasanna*), devoid of attributes (*kevalaḥ anupasargaḥ*), so also is he a self, conscious by reflection of its thinking-substance."

MAMALLAPURAM

Bhagīratha in Meditation [Pallava relief of 7th–8th century A.D.]. The Yogī (who was a King) appears petrified by his prolonged penance and has become a part of the rocks round him. His penance moves Goddess Gaṅgā who melts and descends from Heaven to Earth, pouring out Her bounty in streams of plenty [See Plate 61 of Coomāraswamy's *Viśvakarma*].

[*Facing p. 308*

Obstacles to Samādhi. These are the nine distractions of mind (*chitta-vikshepāḥ*) which are hindrances (*antarāyāḥ*) to concentration. They are (1) *Vyādhi*, Sickness. It is defined as a disorder in the humours of the body (*dhātu* = *vāyu*, wind; *pitta*, and *śleshmā*, bile and phlegm), or in the secretions (*rasa*), or in the organs (*karaṇa* = *indriya*). *Dhātu* is so called because it *sustains* (*dhāraṇa*) the body. A *rasa* is a special kind of mutation (*pariṇāma*) undergone by nourishment eaten or drunk. A disorder is a state of defect or excess in these.

Sickness is cited as the first of these obstacles to meditation. An old text states: "*Dharmārtha-kāma-mokshānām ārogyaṁ mūlam uttamam*; Health is the prime root of Dharma, Artha, Kāma, Moksha, the four ends of life."

(2) *Styāna*, languor, lack of activity, incapacity for action in the mind (*Chittasya akarmaṇyatā*).

(3) *Saṁśaya*, doubt, which is a kind of thinking which touches both alternatives of a dilemma, so that one thinks, 'This might be so; might not be so.'

(4) *Pramāda*, heedlessness, which is a lack of reflection upon the means of attaining concentration.

(5) *Ālasya*, listlessness, a lack of effort due to excess of *tama* guṇa in the mind and of humours like phlegm in the body so as to produce its heaviness.

(6) *Avirati*, thirst after the objects of sense.

(7) *Bhrānti-darśana*, erroneous perception, thinking of misconceptions, taking one thing for another.

(8) *Alabdha-bhūmikatva*, failure to attain any stage of concentration (such as the stage of Madhumatī and the other three).

(9) *Anavasthitatva*, instability in the state of concentration attained, failure of Chitta to remain in the stage attained. If, after attaining a given stage, the Yogī should remain content with only so much progress, there would be a break in the concentration and a resulting retrogression, or fall from even that stage. Therefore, the Yogī must stabilize his mind in the stage of concentration. When concentration is completely achieved (*samādhi-pratilaṁbha*), it means the direct perception of the object contemplated, so that the mind gets fixed on it and has no tendency to withdraw from it.

Further Distractions. The above nine hindrances have their other accompaniments or consequences. These are stated to be (1) *Duḥkha*, or Pain. Pain is that by which living beings are stricken down (*abhihata*) and to avert (*upaghāta*) which they strive (*prayatante*). This pain comes from three sources: (*a*) From self (*ādhyātmika*), such as bodily pain due to sickness, or mental pain by virtue of such things as passion (*kāma*); (*b*) From living creatures (*ādhibhautika*), such as the pain inflicted by a tiger for instance; (*c*) From chance or accident, acts of God or Nature (*ādhidaivika*), the baleful influence of planets.

(2) *Daurmanasya*, or Despondency, due to inhibition of desire through impediment to its fulfilment (*ichchhāvighātāt Chittasya kshobhaḥ*).

(3) *Aṅgamejayatva*, unsteadiness of the body and its trembling.

(4) *Śvāśa-praśvāśa*, inspiration and expiration. This refers to the practice of *prāṇāyama* or regulation of breath as an aid to concentration. Drawing in the breath is *pūraka*; holding it within is *kumbhaka*; and expelling it is *rechaka*. The natural respiration disturbs this process of regulation of breathing.

All these distractions, which are hindrances to concentration (*samādhi-pratipakshāḥ*), are to be conquered by the aforesaid two fundamental accomplishments of Yoga, viz. *Abhyāsa* and *Vairāgya*. *Abhyāsa* should be the practice of concentration on one entity such as Īśvara aforesaid (ekatatvābhyāsaḥ = ekasmin tattve Īśvare abhyāsaḥ chittasya punaḥ punaḥ niveśanam).

Moral Means of Yoga. The pre-requisite of Concentration of Mind is its purification (*parikarma* = *chitta-pariśuddhi*). 'One whose *antaḥkaraṇa* or heart is unpurified and full of such feelings as jealousy cannot successfully (*saṁpatti*) effect concentration and the means of concentration aforesaid. Therefore, the Sūtra-kāra now proceeds to set forth the means by which the placidity, undisturbed calm of the mind (*chitta-prasādanam*) may be secured.' These consist of the cultivation of the following moral attitudes or virtues: (1) *Maitrī*, desire for and enjoyment of the happiness of others so as to shut out the taint of envy (*īrshā* or *paraśrīkātaratā*); (2) *Karuṇā*, or Sympathy for the suffering. One must treat another's suffering as his own and exert himself to remove it as if it is own suffering. This is called *Karuṇā* or compassion. This virtue is an antidote to the taint of a desire to injure others. (3) *Muditā*, happiness at seeing the virtues of others. This wards off the taint of *asūyā* which finds fault in virtue. (4) *Upekshā*, indifference towards the sinful by shunning their company. This will overcome the taint of *krodha* or wrath at the sight of sin.

Regulation of Breath. The steadiness of mind (manasaḥ *sthitiḥ*) is to be achieved by the process called *Prāṇāyāma*, consisting of the two functions called (1) *Prachchhardanam*, the gradual ejection (vamanam) of the abdominal wind (*koshṭhasya vāyuḥ*) through the apertures of the nose by a special kind of effort as described in books of Yoga ; (2) *Vidhāraṇam*, retention or restraint of breath. By this process the body becomes light and *antaḥkaraṇa*, stable.

" The word *or* (*vā*) as used here in the Sūtra [i, 34] signifies that there is a choice with regard to other means now to be stated but there is no such choice as regards the cultivation of aforesaid virtues which are indispensable to Yoga." Thus Yoga is primarily a matter of moral discipline.

Contact with steady Minds. An aid to concentration is stated [i, 37] to be the companionship of those ' who are freed from passion, such as Krishṇadvaipāyana, Sanaka, and others '. The Yogī, by bringing his own mind into contact with the steadied minds of these, moulds it into the shape of these minds (Vītarāga-chitta-avalambana-uparaktaṁ vā yoginaḥ chittaṁ sthitipadaṁ labhate).

Measures for achieving 'Abhyāsa' and 'Vairāgya'. Practice of concentration and an attitude of detachment from the world are the two principal means by which the Yogī is to achieve his progress towards *Samādhi*. But for those who are not yet yogīs but are mere novices and beginners, these two means have to be acquired by much preliminary discipline. The measures of this discipline are elaborated in the Sādhana-Pāda of the *Yoga-Sūtra*.

Kriyā-Yoga. Beginners in Yoga are to pursue what is called *Kriyā-yoga*, comprising the three requisites of (*a*) *Tapaḥ*, (*b*) *Svādhyāya*, (*c*) *Īśvara-praṇidhāna*.

(*a*) *Tapas*. *Tapasyā* is needed to purge the mind of the impurities accumulated in it from the beginning of time by the effects of *karma*, *kleśa*, *vāsanā*, covering the mind by a net-work of objectivity (*vishayajāla*). But this process of purification of mind (*chitt ι-prasādanam*) must be so practised that it is not interrupted by illness (*abādham*).

(*b*) *Svādhyāya*. This is repetition of purifying formulae such as the *Praṇava* (Praṇavādi-pavitrāṇāṁ japaḥ), or study of the literature on liberation (Moksha-śāstrādhyayanam). As samples of this literature, Vāchaspati Misra cites the Purusha-Sūkta [*Rv.*, x, 90], the Rudra-maṇḍala [*Taittirīya Saṁhitā*, iv, 5], or the *Brahma-pārāyaṇa* of *Vishnu Purāṇa*, i, 15.

(*c*) *Īśvara-praṇidhāna*. This is devotion to the Īśvara to whom, as the supreme Teacher, are offered up all actions and dedicated the fruits thereof (sarva-kriyāṇāṁ paramagurau arpaṇam tatphala-saṁnyāso vā).

The Five Afflictions (Kleśas). The aforesaid *Kriyā-yoga* is the means of annihilating the five primary impurities of human nature. They are called *Kleśas* because they stimulate action (Karma) and produce its fruits of happiness and sorrow to be experienced. These are :—

1. **Avidyā.** There are four forms in which *Avidyā* or Ignorance manifests itself, viz. :

(*a*) " Recognition of the permanent in a transitory effect," for example, that the earth is eternal (*dhruvā*), as also the sky with the moon and stars, etc." Under this Ignorance, " some deeming the elements permanent and longing to attain to their form, pay devotion to them, to the Paths, the Way of the Fathers, and the Way of the gods " [Vāchaspati].

(*b*) Recognition of purity in the impure (*aśuchau*) and highly repulsive (*parama bhībhatse*) body. The body is impure at its origin, at its first abode in the mother's womb, in its food converted into blood, in its exudation or sweat, and, lastly, at its death as an untouchable corpse. And yet such an impure body is loved, the body of a girl described as " beautiful like the sickle of the new moon (*naveva śaśāṅkalekhā*), whose limbs are fashioned of honey and nectar, eyes large as the petals of the blue lotus (*nīlotpala-patrāyatākshī*), who has burst forth from the moon (*chandraṁ bhitvā niḥsṛitā*) to bless the living world by the significant message of her eyes (*hāvagarbhābhyāṁ lochanābhyāṁ jīvalokamāśvā-sayantī*). This is the result of *avidyā*, of a misconceived idea of the pure in the impure (*Evaṁ aśuchau śuchirviparyāsa pratyayaḥ*). Similarly, there is a wrong ascription of merit to demerit, of the useful to the useless."

(*c*) Recognition of pleasure in pain.

(*d*) Recognition of the self in the not-self. The ignorant person identifies his self with external objects, animate, such as son, wife, or cattle, and inanimate, such as bed, seat, or food, and is affected by these.

Thus *Avidyā* is not a *pramāṇa*, a source of valid knowledge, nor its negation, but is a different kind of thinking, the reverse of knowledge (*vidyā-viparītaṁ jñānāntaram*).

2. **Asmitā.** It is the consciousness of identity between Purusha and Prakṛiti (or Buḍdhi), Self and Not-self. Purusha

animates and enjoys ; Buddhi is inanimate (*achetana*) and enjoyed (*bhogya*). To distinguish between the two is *mukti*. *Purusha* is marked out by its *ākāra* which is pure white, its *śīla*, its detachment, and its *vidyā* which is *chaitanya* or consciousness. *Buddhi* or *Prakṛiti* stands for impurity, attachment, inertia, and bondage.

3. **Rāga.** It is passion, greed (*garddha*), thirst (*tṛishṇā*), or lust (*lobha*), for pleasure or the means of attaining pleasure on the part of one already acquainted with it. The passion for pleasure is roused in such a person by his recollection of pleasure previously experienced.

4. **Dvesha.** It is aversion, repulsion (*pratigha*), wrath (*manyu*), anger (*krodha*), vengeance (*jighāṁsā*), kindled in a person who has experienced pain and resists it and its cause.

5. **Abhiniveśa.** It is the instinctive love of life or fear of death present in both the worm and the wise man. It is due to the previous experience of death. All living beings are affected by this vision of extermination (*uchchheda-dṛishṭi*) and alike wish that they may not cease to live.

The Eight Aids to Yoga. These are stated to be (1) Yama, (2) Niyama, (3) Āsana, (4) Prāṇāyāma, (5) Pratyāhāra, (6) Dhāraṇā, (7) Dhyāna, and (8) Samādhi. The *Yogāṅgas* are helpful in dissociating the mind from its impurities (*viyoga-kāraṇa*) and leading it on to the highest knowledge (*āptikāraṇa*).

1. **Yama,** Abstention. This comprises the following five abstinences, viz. (a) *Ahiṁsā*, which means "abstinence from malice towards all living creatures in every way and at all times" (sarvathā sarvadā sarvabhūtānāṁ *anavidrohaḥ*). This is the root of all other virtues (*yama niyamāḥ stanmūlāḥ*). The *Yogi-yājñavalkyam* makes it abstinence from causing pain (*kleśa-jananam*) by body, mind, or speech. (b) *Satya*, "truth of speech and thought (yathārtha-vāṅmanaḥ) corresponding to what is seen, inferred, or heard." Truth of speech means that the person hearing it is not deceived by it, does not mistake its meaning and implications, and that it is not purposeless (*na vañchitā bhrāntā vā pratipatti-bandhyā vāguktā sā*). Truthfulness is also to be limited by a higher consideration for the good of all beings and should not be to their ruin (sarva-bhūtopakārārthaṁ na bhūtopaghātāya). Truth is limited by Non-violence (*ahiṁsā*). From violence springs wrong, not right or truth (bhūtopaghātaḥ syāt na satyaṁ bhavet pāpameva-bhavet). Therefore, one should speak the truth which is consistent with universal good (*Tasmāt parīkshya sarvabhūtahitaṁ*

satyaṁ brūyāt). The *Yogi-Yājñavalkyam* states: "Satyaṁ bhūtahitaṁ proktaṁ na yathārthābhibhāshaṇam"; "Truth is what is good for all living beings and not merely a statement of fact."

(c) *Asteya*, abstention from theft. Theft is defined as unauthorized appropriation of things of value from another. It should also mean that one must be even free in thought from a desire for another man's property. The *Yogi-Yājñavalkyam* defines it as indifference shown by body, mind, and speech towards another's property (Kāyena manasā vāchā paradravyeshu nispṛihā).

(d) *Brahma-charya*, or continence.

(e) *Aparigraha* abstinence from acceptance of gifts, and also from appropriating objects. One can cultivate this virtue, when he sees the disadvantages in the trouble to acquire objects, to keep them, the chance of losing them, or of getting attached to them, or as a source of envy to others.

When all these five Abstentions are practised, irrespective of the limits of caste (Jāti), region (Deśa), time or even vows, and in every way and always, they rank as *Mahāvratas*. The *Bhāsvatī* cites instances where these abstentions are limited. A fisherman injures only fishes and none else. A butcher may say, 'I will not slay in a holy place.' Or one may say, 'I will not slay on the fourteenth day nor on an auspicious day.' Or another may say, 'For the sake of gods and Brāhmaṇas, and not otherwise, I will slay.' The Kshatriyas will also say that they will practise violence only in battle. But the Yogī is not bound by these social conventions and considerations. His practice of virtue is unqualified and absolute.

2. Niyama. The Niyamas, or observances, are five in number, namely:—

(*a*) *Śaucha*, purity, *external*, with reference to body and food, and *internal*, i.e. purging the mind of its impurities such as arrogance, pride, and jealousy.

(*b*) *Santosha*, contentment, which means the desire to take no more than is necessary for the bare maintenance of life (cf. *aparigraha*, abstention from acceptance of gifts).

(*c*) *Tapas*, penance, which means the capacity for enduring extremes, hunger and thirst, cold and heat, standing and sitting, stock-stillness (where no intention is expressed even by a sign) and silence (without speech). Certain *Vratas* or vows are enjoined for cultivation of these, viz. Kṛichchhra, Chāndrāyaṇa, and other mortifications of flesh (sāntapana).

HERMITAGES IN BHARHUT SCULPTURES (*c.* second century B.C.).

No. 4.—A five-hooded snake paying homage to an ascetic.

[*Facing p. 314*

(*d*) *Svādhyāya*, study of Moksha literature, and repetition of the mystic syllable, as already explained.

(*e*) *Īsvara-praṇidhāna*, consecration of the fruits of all action to God, the prime Guru, i.e. living absolutely as the merest instrument of God with no sense of any independent and individualist activity.

If the suggestions of passion supervene and hinder the pursuit or practice of the various prohibitions or *Yamas* aforesaid, they are to be subdued by reflection on their consequences, viz. misery and ignorance with their endless train of evils. The glories of success in the *Yamas* are described to perfection. Like the sun illumining his system, the Yogī's purity purifies his surroundings. Malice (*hiṁsā*) is shamed in his presence, and is converted into its opposite, *Vairāgya*. Horse and buffalo, mouse and cat, snake and mongoose, lose their eternal enmity before that All-mighty Presence of Peace and Universal Forbearance. The leopard changes its spots under that supreme influence. Through his always telling the truth, whatever he tells turns out to be truth. Through not hankering after others' wealth, he becomes master of all wealth. Through his confirmed continence, he grows in power and competence to instruct pupils in the eight practices of Yoga. Lastly, through non-acceptance of gifts, he attains complete enlightenment regarding the mysteries or problems of existence.

Similarly, the perfection of the practice of observances or *Niyamas* is also described. Bodily purity makes him abhor his own body with its inherent offensiveness and abhor still more the bodies of others. The purging the mind of its impurities restores the inherent strength of the mind, softens it, and from that results singleness of intent whence mastery of passion and capacity for self-realization. Contentment results in supreme happiness. Penance destroying impurities makes the body and its organs perfect. *Svādhyāya* or study as defined above is followed by a communion with the chosen deity. And, lastly, the devotion to God produces a perfection of Samādhi which enables the Yogin to know correctly whatever he wishes to know in other times, other places, and other beings.

3. **Āsana** or prescribed postures which prevents the Yogin from being affected by the extremes of temperature and the like.

4. **Prāṇāyāma** or regulations of the breath.

5. **Pratyāhāra** or withdrawal of the senses from their object.

6. **Dhāraṇā** (fixation of attention).
7. **Dhyāna** (contemplation).
8. **Samādhi** (absorption).

Without going any further into the details or doctrines of the Yoga system, the bare outline of it as given above shows the distinctive system of training which it introduces with its corresponding aims, ideals, and methods in education.[1]

A General View. We shall now sum up the general features of the educational system adumbrated in these six Systems of Philosophy, having now given an account of the educational bearings of each system separately.

Different Philosophical Systems have a Common Scheme of Discipline. It will be seen that while each System presents its own view of the Universe, this is to be realized by a common scheme of discipline implied in all the Systems. That scheme involves, as we have seen, (*a*) a course of study of select texts and the intellectual discipline that such a study involves ; (*b*) reflection on the inner meaning of the texts studied, coupled with the achievement of a moral discipline resulting in (*c*) a re-orientation of the desires and impulses and (*d*) a transformation in the character of behaviour. As has been already pointed out, each System of Philosophy prescribes its own course of preliminary and preparatory training which is differently emphasized in the different Systems. For instance, the Yoga and the Pūrva Mīmāṁsā present themselves as more self-contained systems which do not depend upon much of preliminary training. On the contrary, they proceed directly from the third and fourth stages of the above scheme to an enunciation of their special philosophical outlook.

Its Common Aim. It may also be noted that the different Systems agree as to the end of all education and knowledge, the attainment of *mukti* or final release from the bonds of existence. They insist in common on this, the only, aim of learning. Each System is at pains to discover its own way and approach to that common goal and presents its own view and definition of that goal. Thus there is a choice of roads opened up by several independent lines of investigation, but all roads lead to one goal about which there is no choice. The very growth of such a varied

[1] *References.*—Ganganath Jha's Philosophical Discipline (Calcutta University Kamalā Lectures) ; philosophical works of Professors S. N. Das Gupta and Sir S. Radhakrishnan ; Dr. J. N. Sinha's work on Hindu Psychology (from which I derived special help in both thought and expression) ; Professor N. N. Sengupta's MSS. and Notes specially prepared for my needs.

and valuable crop of philosophical speculation points to the intellectual tendencies of the times, to the existence of any number of circles or schools of thinkers who concerned themselves with the Quest of the Ātman, to the exclusion of the pursuit of other interests or secondary and intermediary truths.

Differences of Pedagogic Method : the Method of Faith and that of Reason. We may also note that the philosophical Systems, from the pedagogic standpoint, exhibit, broadly speaking, a twofold method, though the two methods are not mutually exclusive in all stages of education. Firstly, there are some Darśanas which stand for the principle that the disciple should receive on trust what is taught. Thus the *Yoga* begins with the following distinctive dictum: *Atha Yogānuśāsanam*, "Now follows the *injunction* of Yoga." Secondly, there are other Darśanas which take their stand upon the contrary principle. They expect the disciple to raise all possible objections, the answers to which build up the systems. Except the Yoga, all the Darśanas are of the latter type. This, therefore, shows that the method of education which was generally followed was not at all mechanical and dogmatic, but absolutely rational and critical. It gave scope to doubt, debate, and discussion. Although, according to the orthodox view, the originators of the Systems obtained a *darśana*, a "vision" of Truth, through their Yogic powers, they would not promulgate their teachings on mere authority, but depended upon and appealed to the ordinary reasoning powers of their disciples to grasp the truths they proclaimed. They refused to build upon blind faith and suspend the critical faculty.

Debate the traditional Method of Indian Education. Indeed, the outstanding tradition of Indian Education is to give the fullest scope to differences of opinion and to debate and discussion at which such differences were freely fought out, thrashed out, and solved. It is never to take anything on trust, but each must test and discover for himself afresh, and in his own way, the truth he is taught. The "direct perception of truth" was both the means and end of education. This has been the time-honoured traditional method of Indian Education through the ages since the days of the Vedas and Upanishads, as we have amply seen.

This method of interrogation, cross-examination, debate, and discussion among fellow-seekers of Truth (whom the Rigveda describes as *Sakhās* meeting for the purpose in *Saṁghas*) was later elaborated into a Science, and exalted into an Art, to teach the principles and practices of debate or argument as a means of knowledge or education. It reached its culmination in the age of the Philosophical Systems, and in one of the Systems, *Nyāya* or Logic. It will, therefore, be useful to bring together some of the typical texts and data showing how Debate was practised as a Fine Art in the sphere of learning and education.[1]

Treatises on Debate: Tantra-yukti (*c.* 600 B.C.). We find that as early as about 600 B.C., a special treatise called *Tantra-yukti*, a manual of debate, was in existence for its use in conducting debates and arguments at Parishads and learned Assemblies. In the *Suśruta-Saṁhitā* [Uttaratantra, ch. lxv], it is stated that by the aid of *Tantra-yukti* a person can establish his own position and overthrow that of his opponents who are unfair in debate. *Tantra-yukti* is the oldest work in the history of Logic (*Hetuvidyā*) and is referred to in the Saṁhitās of both Suśruta and Charaka, in Kauṭilya's *Arthaśāstra*, and in the commentaries of Vātsyāyana and others on the Nyāya-Sūtra.

Terms of Scientific Argument. *Tantra-yukti* presents the forms of scientific argument under thirty-two topics as mentioned below :—

(1) *Adhikaraṇa*, subject.
(2) *Vidhāna*, arrangement.
(3) *Yoga*, union of words.
(4) *Padārtha*, category.
(5) *Hetvārtha*, implication.
(6) *Uddeśa*, enunciation.
(7) *Nirdeśa*, declaration.
(8) *Upadeśa*, instruction.
(9) *Apadeśa*, specification.
(10) *Atideśa*, extended application.
(11) *Pradeśa*, determination from a statement to be made.
(12) *Upamāna*, analogy.
(13) *Arthāpatti*, presumption.
(14) *Saṁśaya*, doubt.
(15) *Prasaṅga*, a connected argument.
(16) *Viparyaya*, reversion.
(17) *Vākya-śesha*, context.
(18) *Anumata*, assent.
(19) *Vyākhyāna*, description.

[1] *References.*—Dr. S. C. Vidyābhushana's erudite works, *Mediaeval Indian Logic* and *History of Indian Logic.*

(20) *Nirvachana*, etymological explanation.
(21) *Nidarśana*, example.
(22) *Apavarga*, exception.
(23) *Sva-saṁjñā*, a special term.
(24) *Pūrva-paksha*, question.
(25) *Uttara-paksha*, reply.
(26) *Ekānta*, certain.
(27) *Anāgatāvekshaṇa*, anticipation.
(28) *Atikrāntāvekshaṇa*, retrospection.
(29) *Niyoga*, injunction.
(30) *Vikalpa*, alternative.
(31) *Samuchchaya*, aggregation.
(32) *Ūhya*, ellipsis.

The *Tantra-yukti* of Charaka-Saṁhitā comprises thirty-four terms which include the following new ones, viz. :

(1) *Prayojana*, purpose.
(2) *Nirṇaya*, ascertainment.
(3) *Anekānta*, uncertain.
(4) *Pratyuchchāra*, repetition.
(5) *Uddhāra*, citation.
(6) *Sambhava*, probability.

The Work of Medhātithi Gautama. Besides *Tantra-yukti*, there is another early work on *Ānvikshikī* attributed to Medhātithi Gautama of about the sixth century B.C., whose doctrines are embodied in the Charaka-Saṁhitā of Charaka, as also in the Nyāya-Sūtra of Akshapāda. According to tradition, it was Punarvasu Ātreya (*c.* 550 B.C.) who was the original author of the so-called Charaka-Saṁhitā or Āyurveda-Saṁhitā, and the name *Charaka* might be that of a sect [*Chārakāḥ*, according to Pāṇini, iv, 3, 107] or a physician who was the redactor of the Ayurveda Saṁhitā, as stated in the *Nyāya-mañjarī* [iv, 249], or the court-physician of Kanishka, as stated in the Chinese Tripiṭaka [Jolly, *Medicine* (Bühler's Grundriss, iii, 10), p. 11]. While Charaka-Saṁhitā utilized the doctrines of Medhātithi Gautama in their crude forms, Akshapāda pruned them fully before incorporating them into the Nyāya-Sūtra.

These doctrines as preserved in the Charaka-Saṁhitā deal with three themes, viz. (1) *Kāryābhinirvṛitti*, "the aggregate of resources for the accomplishment of an action," such resources being numbered ten, including Deśa, Kāla, Pravṛitti, Upāya, and the like ; (2) *Parīkshā*, or "the standard of examination", such as *āptopadeśa*, "reliable assertion or testimony," *prataksha*, "perception", *anumāna*, "inference", and *yukti*, "continuous reasoning"; and (3) *Saṁbhāshā* or *Vādavidhi*, "the method of debate."

Its Chapter on Method of Debate. We are concerned here more with this third theme of Medhātithi Gautama, giving the rules of debate.

First, the utility of this practice of debate in learning is explained. "It increases the knowledge and happiness of those carrying on a debate, produces dexterity, bestows eloquence, brightens reputation, removes misapprehension, kindles zeal for further study. Therefore sages applaud debate with fellow-scholars."

Secondly, a Debate may be of two kinds, friendly and congenial (*sandhāya*) or hostile (*vigṛihya*).

There is mentioned an Assembly or Council (Parishad) of Debate where Debate is to be held. This Assembly may be a learned body or ignorant, and may also be friendly, strictly impartial, or hostile, being committed to one side.

Then there are mentioned what may be called the Expedients of Debate (*vādopāya*), explaining the ways and means of (*a*) vanquishing a person of blazing reputation, (*b*) arguing with an opponent who is superior, or inferior, or equal in merit, and (*c*) influencing the Parishad hearing the Debate.

Next is explained the *Vāda-mārga*, the Course of Debate comprising several categories which must be studied as preparation for debate.

A debate may degenerate into mere (*a*) Wrangling (*Jalpa*) for the purpose of defence or attack, or (*b*) *Vitaṇḍā*, Cavil, for the purpose of attack for its own sake.

Then one must understand the other important elements of Debate, such as (1) the Issue or Proposition called *Pratijñā*, the definition of the subject to be debated upon; (2) *Sthāpanā*, 'the establishment of a Proposition through the process of a reason, example, application, and conclusion'; (3) *Pratishṭhāpana*, 'establishment of counter-proposition'; (4) *Hetu*, Reason, the source of knowledge such as *pratyaksha*, perception; *anumāna*, inference; *aitihya*, scripture; and *aupamya*, comparison; (5) *Upanaya*, application; (6) *Nigamana*, conclusion; (7) *Uttara*, rejoinder; (8) *Dṛishṭānta*, example; (9) *Siddhānta*, 'the truth or tenet established on examination by experts or on proof by reasoning'; (10) *Saṁśaya*, doubt or uncertainty;

(11) *Prayojana*, purpose for the accomplishment of which an action is undertaken ; (12) *Jijñāsā*, inquiry or investigation ; (13) *Vyavasāya*, 'determination, e.g., that disease is due to the disturbance of wind in the stomach, and this is the medicine' ; (14) *Artha-prāpti*, 'presumption, the knowledge of a thing implied by the declaration of another thing' ; (15) *Vākyadosha*, 'defects of speech such as inadequacy, redundancy (in the form of irrelevancy or repetition), meaninglessness, incoherence (combination of words which do not convey a connected meaning), and contradiction (opposition to the tenet, example, or occasion or a statement inconsistent with the occasion)' ; (16) *Chhala*, quibble (in respect of a word or a generality) ; (17) *Ahetu*, fallacy such as (*a*) Begging the question (*prakaraṇa-sama*), when what is to be proved is taken as the reason, (*b*) Assumption based on doubt (*saṁśaya-sama*), (*c*) Balancing the subject (*varṇya-sama*), where the example is not different from the subject in respect of its questionable character ; (18) *Atīta-kāla*, inopportune, 'when that which should be stated first is stated later' ; (19) *Upālambha*, imputation of defect to the reason adduced ; (20) *Hetvantara*, shifting the reason ; (21) *Arthāntara*, shifting the topic ; and (22) *Pratijñāhāni*, abandonment of a proposition.

A person who is acquainted with all these points or turns that may crop up in argument will be strongly fortified for purposes of both offence and attack in the course of a debate.

Most of these terms of Medhātithi Gautama were later incorporated into the Nyāya-Sūtra of Gautama (Akshapāda ?) and its commentaries which deal with *Vāda* or Discussion as one of its five main subjects. The Nyāya-Sūtra treats of sixteen Categories which comprise all the topics of *Vāda-mārga* (course of debate) as enumerated in the Charaka-Saṁhitā. Only it arranges these topics in a more systematic and scientific manner. It arranges them under stages marked out in the development of a debate. Thus the first stage of a debate, its starting-point or basis, is the thesis to be proved, which is brought under the two Categories, (1) *Pramāṇa*, means of knowledge, and (2) *Prameya*, implying objects of knowledge. These two Categories constitute the basis of Debate. After this, the Debate opens and enters upon its third stage called *Saṁśaya*. The disputant in pursuit of his *prayojana* (purpose) first tries to answer the doubt of his opponent by citing a *drishṭānta* or a parallel case which is not so open to doubt. Then the next stage in the Debate is reached when the case, free of doubt, is shown to rest on *siddhāntas* (conclusions or tenets) accepted by both parties. The validity of the case is then further proved by analysing it into its five constituent parts called *avayava*. Thus another stage, that of *nirṇaya* (certainty), is reached when the disputant has successfully carried on the *tarka* (confutation) against all contrary arguments. But the Debate may take a different turn, in case the respondent, not satisfied with the process of argument, presents an antithesis. This will lead to another stage of the Debate, that of *Vāda* proper, which may degenerate into *Jalpa* or *Vitaṇḍā* and even to the use of shady casuistry in the forms of *hetvābhāsa* (fallacious reasons), *chhala*, *jāti* (analogues, far-fetched analogies). The exposure of these falsehoods will bring about his defeat (nigraha) and terminate the debate.

Conclusion. We conclude this account of the philosophical Sūtras by the following vivid presentation of some of the characteristic aspects of this ancient Indian education by Max Müller [Royal Institution Lectures on Vedānta Philosophy]: "The study of philosophy in India was not only an integral part of the religion of the Brāhmaṇas but it was based from the very beginning on a moral foundation. We saw already that no one was admitted to the study of the Upanishads who had not been properly initiated and introduced by a qualified teacher, and who had not fulfilled the duties, both civil and religious, incumbent on a householder. But even that was not enough. No one was supposed to be fit for true philosophical speculation who had not completely subdued his passions. The sea must no longer be swept by storms, if it is to reflect the light of the sun in all its divine calmness and purity. Hence even the hermit in the forest was expected to be an ascetic, and to endure severe penances as a help for extinguishing all the passions that might disturb his peace. And it was not only the body that had to be subdued and hardened against all external disturbances such as heat and cold, hunger and thirst. Six things had to be acquired by the mind, namely, tranquillity, restraint, self-denial, long-suffering, collectedness, and faith [Śama, Dama, Uparati (often explained as relinquishment of all sacrificial duties), Titikshā, Samādhi, and Śraddhā]. It has been thought [Deussen, *System*, p. 85], that this quietness is hardly the best outfit for a philosopher who, according to our views of philosophy, is to pile Ossa on Pelion in order to storm the fortress of Truth and conquer new realms in earth and heaven. But we must remember that the object of the Vedānta was to show that we have really nothing to conquer but ourselves, that we possess everything within us, and that nothing is required but to shut our eyes and hearts against the illusion of the world in order to find ourselves richer than heaven and earth. Even faith, Śraddhā, which has given special offence as a requisite for philosophy, because philosophy, according to Descartes, ought to begin with *de omnitus dubitare*, has its legitimate place in the Vedānta philosophy, for, like Kant's philosophy, it leads us on to see that many things are beyond the limits of human understanding, and must be accepted or believed, without being understood.

"How seriously and religiously philosophy was taken up by the Vedāntists we see from what are considered the essential requisites of a true philosopher. He ought to have surrendered all desire for rewards in this life or in the life to come. He ought, therefore, never to dream of acquiring wealth, of founding a school, of gaining a name in history; he ought not even to think of any recompense in better life. . . And so we have the extraordinary fact that, after 2,000 years, their works are still able to rivet our attention, while with us, in spite of advertisements, of friendly and unfriendly reviews, the philosophical book of the season is often the book of one season only. . . I believe much of the excellency of the ancient Sanskrit philosophers is due to their having been undisturbed by the thought of there being a public to please or critics to appear. They thought of nothing but the work they had determined to do: their one idea was to make it as perfect as it could be made. . . The ancient Upanishads describe the properly qualified student of philosophy in the following words [*Bṛihad. Upa.*, iv, 4, 23]: 'He, therefore, who knows the Self, after having become quiet, subdued, satisfied, patient, and collected sees Self in Self, sees all as Self. Evil does not overcome him, he overcomes all evil. Evil does not burn him, he burns all evil. Free from evil, free from spots, free from doubt, he becomes a true Brāhmaṇa'" (ib., pp. 36–40].

To sum up: the study of philosophy is by itself a complete and self-sufficient scheme of education and discipline. Philosophy with Hindus is not what William James called "Logic-chopping". It was severely practical in its aim, which was no less than to mould life, its outlook and activities, in accordance with its scheme of values and view of the Universe, its theory of Reality. Its study, therefore, depends, firstly, on some amount of intellectual training and reading of texts by which its particular outlook, aim, technique, and system can be understood. But it depends also on an amount of moral preparation by which is to be created the atmosphere conducive and congenial to the cultivation of a new way of life with its new pattern of conduct and view of values. It must be an atmosphere of peace and quiet, where the mind can remain unperturbed, and is not distracted by unwholesome stimuli, or the crises and turmoils to which life is exposed in its ordinary environment. Such an environment the student of philosophy, the seeker after truth, must create for himself. He must create this heaven on earth by the power of a newly oriented mind, a new world of thoughts, feelings, and attitudes, where he remains unmoved by the facts and events, men and things, of ordinary daily life. He remains oriented to other realities. As De Caussade puts it: "The divine action can only take possession of a soul in so far as that soul is empty of all confidence in her own action." This is an echo of some of the prayers of pupils contained in the Upanishads: "Let my ears listen only to what is noble, and let my eyes see only what is good and pure. Let my body be controlled and my mind be in perpetual prayer, so that I may serve the gods, who represent the glory of the life of the spirit, throughout my earthly career." Again: "May Mitra, Varuṇa, Aryamā, Indra, Bṛihaspati, and Vishṇu give me their blessings that I may fare well on my way to this knowledge. I shall utter only what is in accordance with cosmic law (Ṛita). I shall only state the Truth. Protect me, O God, protect this speaker."

CHAPTER X

EDUCATION IN THE EPICS

The Epics as Sources of History. We shall now discuss the evidence of the Epics, the *Rāmāyaṇa* and the *Mahābhārata*.

The value of the Epics as sources of history is somewhat affected by the uncertainty of the dates of the works in their present forms and the difficulty of distinguishing the various strata contributed in different periods to these composite literary structures. According to Hopkins, " upon the original story, the *Bhārata*, have been grafted many ' secondary tales ' (*upākhyāna*), and upon these, and apart from these, have been inserted whole poems of romantic, ethical, and theological character, having nothing to do with the course of the Epic itself. We must, however, remember that our Epic has been enlarged in two ways : first, by a natural expansion of matter already extant ; secondly, by unnatural addition of new material. The twelfth book may serve as a type of the latter ; the eighth, of the former ". Hopkins's conclusion is that " even the modern Epic, the full completed work, is not as a whole unimportant in the elucidation of the customs of India in the Middle Ages, reaching back more than 2,000 years ".

We may recall in this connection the references to the story of the two Epics in our earlier literature. Pāṇini, as has been already indicated, mentions the word Mahābhārata [vi, 2, 38] and the formation Yudhishṭhira [viii, 3, 95]. He also mentions Vāsudeva and Arjuna as heads of sects [iv, 3, 98]. But, as Hopkins points out, " Pāṇini's evidence is negative, mentioning characters but not the poem by name." By the time of Patañjali, however, the Mahābhārata, as a poem, must have existed, considering his references to some of its typical characters like Vasudeva and Vāladeva, Nākula, Sāhadeva, and Bhaimasenya who are mentioned as descendants of Vṛishṇi and Kuru families [see the references given before]. Another early reference to the story of the two Epics is in the *Kauṭilīya* which mentions how the two kings, Rāvaṇa and Duryodhana, came to grief for their sins, the former in not restoring another man's wife (*paradāränaprayachchhan*) out of conceit and the latter another man's legal share of the kingdom [i, 6].

Their interest mainly military. The purely educational evidence of the Epics is, however, very meagre in comparison with the sizes of the works or the vast quantity of sociological data they furnish. This is of course due to the interest of the two Epics lying mainly in the realm of action and not in that of thought. The military interest of the Epics predominates over the intellectual. The predominant part in their history is also taken by the military and ruling caste. The bulk of the intellectual life of the country centred in the hermitages and homes of Ṛishis and Brahmins, which do not receive notice in the Epics except when they are connected with the course of their story.

Meagre educational material. Nevertheless, we can wring out of such unpromising sources some quantity of interesting information bearing upon matters educational. There are some general discourses bearing on the duties of the first Āsrama of life, the life of studentship. Secondly, there are accounts of some ideal students and schools or hermitages, the centres of learning in those days. Thirdly, there are accounts given of the education that was imparted to the princes or the children of the Kshatriya caste who were meant for the military and political career.

Principles underlying Castes and Āśramas. If we may use a metaphor, the different Āśramas or stages of life are mutually related in the same way as the bud, the flower, and the fruit. The tender youth is first subjected to a process of rigorous discipline and training the aim of which is to purge him of all the impurities and imperfections, physical and moral, which obstruct the free operation of the vital principles of growth of the individual. Thus endowed with a sound mind in a sound body, the budding youth blossoms into a noble manhood which then reproduces itself in the householder's state and through the experience of an active life ripens into the fruit of mature wisdom and moral steadfastness which are dedicated in the third Āśrama of life to the advancement not of the *individual* but the *collective* life. The *Vānaprastha* must detach himself from personal interests centring in his individual home and family. He must wander from home into homelessness, cut himself off from his old moorings of self-interest to sail on the open main towards the Universal and the Absolute, and feel that " one touch of Nature which makes the whole world kin ".

Thus the first period of life is that of preparation through education. But this means that we must know what it is a preparation for. The preparatory processes, the contents and methods of education, will thus vary with the ultimate ends in view. The education of the Brahmin is to be such as can prepare him for the duties and vocations laid down as legitimate for him. Similarly, the education of the Kshatriya, the Vaiśya, and the Śūdra, too, will have to be such as can fit each for his respective career in life. All education thus becomes in a sense vocational or practical.

Duties of different Castes according to Mahābhārata. The duties of the several castes which thus determine the kind of training suitable for them are laid down in some passages of the Mahābhārata. One such passage has them as follows [xvi, 60] :—

" Self-control is the first duty of the Brāhmaṇas. Study of the Vedas and patient practice of austerities are also their other duties. By practising these two, all their acts are done.

" If, while engaged in the observance of his own duties, without doing any unlawful act, riches come to a peaceful Brāhmaṇa endued with knowledge, he should then marry and beget offspring and should also practise charity and perform sacrifices. He should also share the enjoyment of this wealth with the worthy.

" But by Vedic study alone will a Brāhmaṇa's duties be done. Whether he does anything else or not, he will be regarded as a true Brāhmaṇa, the friend of the universe."

Thus practically the life of a Brahmin is the life of study whereby he becomes the custodian of the nation's culture to the promotion of which he has to consecrate his whole life.

Regarding the duties of the Kshatriya, it is laid down that he " should give but not beg ; should himself celebrate sacrifices but not officiate as a priest in the sacrifices of others ; should never teach the Veda but study the same with a Brāhmaṇa teacher (*dadyāt na yācheta* ; *yajeta na yājayet* ; *nādhyāpayeda-dhīyīta*) ; should protect his people, being always ready to kill robbers and show his mettle in battle ; for there is no higher duty of a Kshatriya than checking the wicked. While gifts, study, and sacrifices bring him prosperity, the Kshatriya who wishes for spiritual merit can realize it only by doing his duties as a warrior (rājñā viśesheṇa yoddhavyaṁ dharmamīpsatā). No true Kshatriya should leave a battle unscathed. The proper duty of a king is to defend his people and keep them to their duties and when that is done, it does not matter if he does anything else or not. The best of kings is distinguished by three attributes, viz. performance of sacrifices, knowledge of the Vedas, and victory in wars.

Regarding the *Vaiśya*, he should make gifts; study the Vedas, perform sacrifices, and acquire wealth by fair means.

It is thus evident that while study is binding upon all belonging to the three twice-born castes (making up the majority of the entire Indian population), a life of learning or an intellectual career is not prescribed for all. The Kshatriya is destined for the political, and the Vaiśya for the economic career. In Adam Smith's phraseology, the former is for "defence" and the latter for "opulence".

The status of the Śūdra in this ancient society has been much misunderstood. It would be irrelevant to our present purpose to go into the question thoroughly. We are only concerned with its educational or cultural aspects which are very well indicated in some passages of the Mahābhārata [ib.]. It may be recalled that much of the intellectual life and culture of the community centred round sacrifice which had thus a very great educative influence. From such influence the Śūdra was not excluded. The privilege of performing or participating in sacrifices was not denied to him. Of course, these sacrifices were of a kind, other than the strictly Vedic sacrifices for which the higher castes alone were eligible. The sacrifices for which the Śūdra is eligible are called *Pākayajñas*. But the Mahābhārata is very particular in pointing out that the highest of all sacrifices is open to all including the Śūdra. That sacrifice is devotion, what is called *Śraddhā-yajña*, performed by the mind (*manīshayā*). "Even gods do not disdain to share the offerings of sacrifices of Śūdras when performed in such spirit." "Therefore all the four castes are equal." "That person who desires to worship God through sacrifice is considered virtuous, even though he happens to be a thief or the worst of sinners."

We have now roughly indicated the legitimate careers marked out for the four castes for which they must prepare in the period of their education. It is, however, to be noted that though the lines of differentiation of occupations normally followed those of caste, the lines were not at all rigid and inelastic. They were departed from under difficulties, distress, or emergencies. Under the pressure of necessity which has no law, the promiscuous pursuit of occupations is permitted, thus exposing the real character and significance of caste as determining the destiny of labour. As a matter of fact, the social and economic divisions were not always coinciding. On this point,[1] "the text of Yājñavalkya is pertinent: 'a Śūdra should serve twice-born men; but if he cannot thus subsist, he may become a trader'; and the profession of a husbandman is allowed to the Śūdra by the *Narasiṁha Purāṇa*, 'let him rely on agriculture for his subsistence.' On this ground, the practice of money-lending by a Śūdra has been mentioned" [Colebrooke's *Digest of Hindu Law*, vol. ii, p. 356].

Education of Brahmins. We now proceed to discuss the Epic evidence regarding the kind and methods of education prescribed for the members of the different castes to qualify them for their respective careers or callings in life.

As has been already indicated, the evidence regarding the education of Brahmins and the centres of Brahminical learning is comparatively very meagre in the Epics and is forthcoming only in an indirect fashion in connection with episodes or stories or dialogues, and not with the general course of their narrative.

Regarding the education of Brahmins, it is indicated in several passages which summarize the duties and rules relating to the first Āśrama or stage of life and applicable to the three twice-born classes on the lines laid down in the Dharma-Sūtras dealt with above. In xii, 191 we have the following:

"Of the four modes of life, to live in the house of the preceptor is the first. In this mode of life one should have his soul cleansed

[1] Cf. *Mbh.*, xii, 78, 2, which permits a Brahmin in distress to take to agriculture and tending cattle like a Vaiśya, if unable to perform the duties of a Kshatriya, and also to trade (4–6), but not in certain prohibited articles. In xii, 76, a Brahmin is described as degraded by the pursuit of the following occupations, viz. accepting office in law-courts for summoning people (the office meant for a Śūdra), performing worship for others for money, officiating in sacrifices for a village, making sea-voyages, foretelling from the stars, acting as Ritvijas, Purohitas, counsellors, envoys, and messengers, or engaging in the army as a horseman, or a fighter on elephant or chariot, or as a foot-soldier. In another passage, there is the interesting injunction that the Brahmins should take up arms to protect the people when they are left unprotected. Even a Śūdra who affords such protection to helpless people deserves to be adored by all [xii, 78, 29–40]. It is thus quite apparent that the division of occupations or the distribution of careers in life was not at all rigid and immutable like that of castes. We should note in this connection the remarkable passage [xii, 85, 7–11] which lays down that the king's Ministry should be constituted by four Brahmins, eight Kshatriyas, twenty-one Vaiśyas, three Śūdras, and one Sūta, and all of fifty years of age. Thus the highest post in the administration was thrown open to all the castes, and the Śūdra did not labour under any disqualification. We may also recall the passage of Manu [ii, 241; *Āp.*, ii, 4, 25; *Gaut.*, vii, 1–3; *Baudh.*, i, 3, 41–3], which permits a Brahmin student, "in times of distress," to "learn the Veda" from a non-Brahmin teacher whom he must duly respect—"walk behind and serve"—"as long as the instruction lasts"

(*viniyatātmā*) by purity of conduct, by Vedic rites, by restraints, vows, and humility. He should adore the morning and evening twilights, the sun, his own consecrated hearth, and the gods. He should shake off procrastination and idleness. He should purify his soul by saluting his preceptor, by studying the Vedas, and by attending to his preceptor's instructions. He should perform his ablutions thrice. He should lead a life of celibacy ; attend to his consecrated hearth ; serve his preceptor dutifully ; daily go out for alms, and give ungrudgingly to his preceptor the whole of what is got in alms. Carrying out willingly the behests of his preceptor, he should be ready to receive such Vedic instruction as his preceptor may give him as a favour."

The following passage [xii, 242] still further elaborates the rules of studentship :

" While living in the preceptor's house, the Brahmachārin should seek bed after the preceptor has gone to his, and rise therefrom before the preceptor rises from his. He should do all such acts again as a disciple or a menial servant should do. Doing these, he should humbly stand by his preceptor.

" Having performed all acts, he should study, sitting at the feet of his preceptor, with anxious desire to learn. He should always behave with simplicity, avoid evil speech, and take lessons only when his preceptor asks him for it.

" He should never eat before his preceptor has eaten ; never drink before his preceptor has done so ; never sit down before his preceptor has sat down ; and never go to bed before his preceptor has gone.

" Having thus spent a fourth part of his life in the study of the Vedas and observance of vows and fasts, and having given the preceptor his fee, the disciple should, according to the ordinance, bid adieu and return home for becoming a householder."

Another passage [xii, 66] points out " study of the Vedas every day, forgiveness, worship of preceptors, and services rendered to one's own teacher as securing the attainment of the object of *brahmacharya* ".

Four Duties of Studentship. The following passage [v, 44] throws further light on the system of studentship and the sacred relations obtaining between the teacher and the taught :—

" The father and the mother only create the body ; but the condition derived from the instructions of the preceptor is sacred, undecaying, and immortal.

"The preceptor is to be regarded as father and mother, and must not be sinned against."

A disciple should every day pay respect to his preceptor and engage in study with a pure mind and concentrated attention. He should never feel annoyed or angry (at the humble or hard services he is called upon to perform at his preceptor's house). This is the first step of studentship.

He who acquires learning and maintains himself by the proceeds of his begging in the morning and evening and not by depending upon the preceptor's means—such a dutiful student completes the first step of studentship.

The second step of studentship is the performance of acts desired by the preceptor at all costs and by all means—at the cost of life or the last penny, by body, mind, and speech.

This devotion should be observed even towards the preceptor's wife or his son.

The third step towards the fulfilment of studentship consists in the proper realization by the pupil of the benefits his preceptor confers on him by imparting to him the knowledge which annihilates pain and brings on bliss, the peace that passeth all understanding, so that in exaltation of heart he may thus think always of his preceptor, "By him have I been so developed."

The fourth and last step of studentship consists in the pupil not leaving the preceptor's home without first paying off the debt he owes to his preceptor for his gift of knowledge by suitable presents. The pupil must make the presents also in due humility and a spirit of self-effacement, not thinking at all that he is making a gift to his teacher, much less speaking about it.

In trying to make presents, whatever wealth the pupil acquires must be given to his teacher.

These four steps of studentship are acquired (*a*) in course of time, i.e. by the natural growth of one's mental powers, (*b*) by contact with the preceptor, (*c*) by the pupil's own endeavours or mental capacity, and (*d*) by discussion with fellow-pupils. Thus the four factors of education are a suitable period of time, individual earnestness, and capacity, the aid of the teacher and the aid of associates in study.

Eligibility for education. The eligibility for studentship is strictly laid down. The teaching of the Vedas must not be imparted to one who has not formally become a disciple, who has not observed vows or who is of impure soul. No knowledge should be imparted to one whose character is not previously known. As pure gold is tested by heating, cutting, and rubbing, so should disciples be examined with reference to their birth and qualities. There is, in addition, the very remarkable injunction that persons of *all the four castes* are competent to listen to discourses on Vedas or Vedic recitations (*śrāvayechchaturo varṇān*) [xii, 327].

Lastly, the pedagogic principle is laid down that the studies prescribed should be according to capacity, for " one's knowledge is always proportionate to his understanding and diligence in study " [xii, 327].

Examples of Ideal Students. Both the general course of the narrative and the episodes or stories of the Mahābhārata introduce us to ideal students, teachers, schools, and hermitages and other centres of learning.

Āruṇi. Takshaśilā was a noted centre of learning. The story is told of one of its teachers named Dhaumya who had three disciples named Upamanyu, Āruṇi, and Veda. Āruṇi hailed from Pañchāla and was an ideal student in respect of devotion to his teacher, under whose orders to stop a breach in the watercourse in his field, Āruṇi, finding every other means unavailing, threw his own body into the breach. His devotion was recognized by his teacher by giving him the appellation of *Uddālaka* [1] (from *uddāraka*).

Utaṅka. The traditions and ideals of Dhaumya were continued by his pupils. His other pupil, Veda, became a successful teacher noted for the devotion displayed by one of his pupils, Utaṅka, who in the story encounters every variety of experience and danger to procure for his preceptor the presents of his choice before he was free to leave his preceptor's home on completion of studentship.

Upamanyu. This story confirms the traditions of the Upanishads and other literature regarding the regulations of the system of studentship, such as the duty of the student to tend the preceptor's cattle (Upamanyu in the story being entrusted with this work), take care of his fields, serve him at the cost of his life, if necessary, and give him pleasing presents at the end of the pupilage [i, 3].

Kacha. Another picture of ideal studentship is called up by the story of Kacha and Devayāni. Kacha himself gives the following description of the life he lived in that sylvan retreat

[1] Uddālaka and his son Śvetaketu of the Upanishadic fame are also referred to in the Mahābhārata [i, 122].

PLATE XIV

HERMITAGES IN BHARHUT SCULPTURES (*c.* second century B.C.).

No. 5.—Supposed by Cunningham to be the hermitage of Kapila who gives it away to four exiled Ikshvāku princes.

[*Facing p. 333*

of learning: "Carrying the burden of sacrificial wood, Kuśa grass, and fuel, I was coming towards the hermitage and, feeling tired, sat for rest under the shade of the banyan tree, along with my companions, the kine, under my charge" [i, 76, 35, 36]. One of the traditional duties of the student was to tend his preceptor's cattle, and collect wood for fire and sacrifice, and this brought him into intimate touch with Nature and subjected him to Nature's influence and educational processes working through "silent sympathy", as Wordsworth puts it. The outdoor life and fellowship with the lower animals had also their own advantages to the student.

Failures of Scholarship : Yavakrīta. The story of Yavakrīta [iii, 135] emphasizes the indispensable need of a teacher in the acquisition of knowledge which the Upanishads also insist upon. In the story, Yavakrīta engaged in the severest asceticism for obtaining the knowledge of the Vedas, because he thought that study under a teacher would require a long time for the purpose. Indra admonished him by saying: "The way you have adopted is not the proper way. Go and learn the Vedas from a preceptor." Finding his advice still going unheeded, he conveyed to Yavakrīta a sensible image of his folly by attempting the impossible feat of bridging the river Gaṅgā by means of hands.

Ārshṭisena. The story of Ārshṭisena illustrates the limitations of the doctrine aforesaid. It shows how in spite of his long continued residence at his preceptor's house, and regular instruction day by day, he could not master any branch of learning or the Vedas. It was only after his practice of austere penances that he achieved success [ix, 40].

Hermitages. The Mahābhārata tells of numerous hermitages where pupils from distant parts gathered for instruction round some far-famed teacher. A full-fledged Āśrama is described as consisting of several Departments which are enumerated as follows: (1) *Agnisthāna*, the place for fire-worship and prayers; (2) *Brahma-sthāna*, the Department of Veda; (3) *Vishṇusthāna*, the Department for teaching Rāja-Nīti, Arthanīti, and Vārttā; (4) *Mahendrasthāna*, Military Section; (5) *Vivasvata-sthāna*, Department of Astronomy; (6) *Somasthāna*, Department of Botany; (7) *Garuḍa-sthāna*, Section dealing with Transport and Conveyances; (8) *Kārtikeya-sthāna*, Section teaching military organization, how to form patrols, battalions, and army.

Naimisha. The most important of such hermitages was

that of the *Naimisha*, a forest which was like a university. The presiding personality of the place was Śaunaka, to whom was applied the designation of *Kulapati*, sometimes defined as the preceptor of 10,000 disciples. Śaunaka attracted to Naimisha a vast concourse of learned men by his performance of a twelve years' sacrifice, of which the most essential *aṅga* or accompaniment was the discourses and disputations of learned men on religious, philosophical, and scientific topics. In one place [ix, 37] we read of " ascetics living at Naimishāraṇya being engaged in a sacrifice lasting for twelve years ", on completion of which they set out in large numbers for visiting the various sacred shrines of the country. In another place [ib., 41] we have the same reference with the interesting additional information that in the course of that twelve years' sacrifice, when a particular one called *Viśvajit* had been completed, the Ṛishis started for the country of the Pañchālas, and reaching there, requested the king to give them twenty-one strong and healthy calves to be given away as *dakshiṇā* for the sacrifice they had finished.

Hermitage of Kaṇva. The hermitage of Kaṇva was another famous centre of learning, of which a full description is given [i, 70]. It is situated on the banks of the Mālinī, a tributary of the Sarayū River. It was not a solitary hermitage, but an assemblage of numerous hermitages round the central hermitage of Ṛishi Kaṇva, the presiding spirit of the settlement. The entire forest was full of hearths where sacred fire was burning, and resounding with the chanting or recitation of sacred texts by learned Brahmins. The wide range and variety of their studies is also indicated. There were specialists in every branch of learning cultivated in that age; specialists in each of the four Vedas; in sacrificial literature and art; Kalpa-Sūtras; in the art of reciting the Saṁhitās according to the *Paḍa* and *Kramapāṭha*, and in Orthoepy generally, and in Śikshā (Phonetics), Chhanda (Metrics), Śabda (Vyākaraṇa), and Nirukta. There were also the philosophers well versed in Ātma-Vijñāna (Science of the Absolute), in Brahmopāsanā (Worship of Brahma), in Mokshadharma (the way to salvation), and in Lokāyata (*Vaiśeshika*). There were also Logicians knowing the principles of *Nyāya*, and of Dialectics (the art of establishing propositions, solving doubts, and ascertaining conclusions). There were also specialists in the physical sciences and arts. There were, for example, experts in the art of constructing sacrificial altars of various dimensions and shapes (on the basis of a knowledge of Solid Geometry) ; those who had knowledge of the properties of matter (*dravyaguṇa*) ; of physical processes and their results, of causes and their effects ; and zoologists having a special knowledge of monkeys and birds. It was thus a forest University where the study of every available branch of learning was cultivated.

Other Hermitages. The hermitage of Vyāsa was another seat of learning. There Vyāsa " taught the Vedas to his disciples. Those disciples were the highly blessed Sumanta, Vaiśampāyana, Jaimini of great wisdom, and Paila of great ascetic merit ". They were afterwards joined by Śuka, the famous son of Vyāsa [xii, 328].

Among other hermitages noticed by the Mahābhārata may be mentioned those of Vasishṭha and Viśvāmitra [ix, 42], and that in the forest of Kāmyaka on the banks of the Sarasvatī [iii, 183]. But a hermitage near Kurukshetra [ix, 54] deserves special notice for the interesting fact recorded that it produced two noted women hermits. There " leading from youth the vow of brahmacharya, a Brahmin maiden was crowned with ascetic success and ultimately acquiring yogic powers, she became a *tapassiddhā* ", while another lady, the daughter not of a Brahmin but a Kshatriya, a child not of poverty but affluence, the daughter of a king, Śāṇḍilya by name, came to live there the life of celibacy and attained spiritual pre-eminence.

Learned gatherings at Sacrifices. Along with the hermitages in these sylvan retreats which were the stationary seats of learning, another great educative influence in the country was the occasional concourse of learned men gathered together at the courts and palaces of kings by the sessions of sacrifices they used to celebrate with due pomp and liberality. The Upanishads, as we have already seen, are full of pictures of such learned congregations which in ancient India played the principal part in the advancement and diffusion of knowledge. As may be expected, the Mahābhārata does not fail to notice this important type of educational institutions which constitute such a characteristic feature in the history of Indian pedagogic theory and practice, organization and achievements.

Mahābhārata recited at the Sacrifice of Janamejaya. The Mahābhārata itself composed by Kṛishṇa Dvaipāyana was fully recited from day to day by Vaiśāmpāyana at the sacrifice of Janamejaya, son of Parikshit, which was attended by thousands of learned Brahmins. Again, it was at the sacrifice of Śaunaka at Naimishāraṇya that the Mahābhārata was repeated by Ugraśravā Sauti. Thus the celebration of these royal sacrifices was the principal agency for the promulgation and popularization of original literary works of national interest and importance.

Sacrifice of Janaka. The Upanishads also emphasize the other feature of these learned gatherings, viz. that they provided the arena where scholars seeking to establish their intellectual position entered the lists in tournaments of debate. This feature is also noticed by the Mahābhārata [iii, 132–4], where it is stated how learned Brahmins were flocking to the sacrifice of Janaka "for the purpose of listening to controversies" (and also to Brahmaghosha, recitation of the Vedas). Thither came Ashṭāvakra, eager to assert and establish his intellectual primacy, but the entrance to the Congress was barred by the gate-keeper who, under orders of the learned chief Vandī, was to admit "only old and learned Brahmins". Ashṭāvakra had thus first to convince the gate-keeper of his eligibility for membership of that learned Assembly, and addressed him as follows: "O Gate-keeper, you will to-day see me engaged in a controversial fight with all the learned men and get the better of Vandī himself in arguments." In the end Ashṭāvakra came out victorious with his supremacy acknowledged by the entire Assembly. Lastly, in this connection we may also note the different classes of learned men distinguished [xii, 236, 18–20]. "Those who are acquainted with the Vedas are of two sorts, viz. those who lecture on the Vedas (Pravaktṛi) and those who are otherwise (i.e. mere preceptors). . . The preceptors of the Vedas are of two sorts, viz. those who are conversant with the Self and those that are otherwise."

Education of the Kshatriya with reference to his occupations. We shall now discuss the Epic evidence regarding the education of the Kshatriya. Both law and legend are at one in making studentship the first stage in the life of every member of the three twice-born classes. But, as has been already stated, the course of studies may be naturally assumed not to have been uniform for all the classes, but determined by the ultimate ends and careers prescribed for each class. This *a priori* assumption seems to be borne out by the evidence of the Epics as a whole, though there are some passages in that evidence liable to give a contrary impression.

It is necessary at the outset to recall how the position is

defined in law. The three occupations common to all the twice-born classes as stated therein are "studying, sacrificing, and giving ". To these three occupations are added as special to the Brahmin " teaching, performing sacrifices for others, and receiving gifts ", and as special to the Kshatriya, " defence or protection of his people." It is also to be noted that such study as was enjoined for the Kshatriya might make him sufficiently proficient in the Veda to be able to teach, and teach a Brahmin student who should not go without education for failure of a Brahmin teacher. Thus normally the Kshatriya was only to study, and the Brahmin to study as also to teach and perform sacrifices for others. It is thus evident that the study as a qualification for the high, responsible, and practical function of teaching and direction of religious practices will be different in scope and method from that which is followed by occupations not directly depending on or connected with it. Some law-givers expressly point out that it is the king alone who is expected to commit to memory the Vedas, like the Brahmin, and not the ordinary members of his caste [*Gaut.*, xi, 3 ; *Manu*, vii, 43].

Bhishma as Teacher of Kuru and Pāṇḍu Princes. Let us now examine the Epic evidence on the education of the princes. The Pāṇḍus are described as " having studied *all* the Vedas and the various Śāstras or treatises on duty, etc. " [i, 1, 122]. Dhṛitarāshṭra, Pāṇḍu, and Vidura " brought up from their very birth by Bhīshma as if they were his own sons " are described as " being purified by the ceremonies of their order, disciplined by study and the vows and practices of studentship, and emerging into manhood skilled in ' studies ' (*Śrama*, as explained by Nīlakanṭha) and ' hand to hand fights ' (*Vyāyāma*). They are proficient in Dhanurveda (archery) and Veda, in club-fights, in the wielding of swords and shields, in the driving of elephants, in Nītiśāstra (Polity), Itihāsa, and Purāṇa, and other subjects, in the truths of the Veda and Vedāṅgas, and of fixed determination in all their undertakings " [i, 109, 17–20]. Pāṇḍu excelled in archery and Dhṛitarāshṭra in personal strength [ib., 21].

He appoints Droṇa as their Teacher. Bhīshma, as the guardian of the Pāṇḍu and Kuru princes committed to his care, appoints as their preceptor Droṇa, " learned in all the Vedas." Droṇa specially taught his students Dhanurveda in all its branches. They became before long perfect experts in the use of all kinds of weapons [i, 131]. There is, it may be noted, no mention here of the study of the sacred texts by the princes. In another place [i, 134], the following injunction is expressly laid upon Droṇa by Bhīshma in giving him charge of the education of the princes : " Unstring your bow and teach these princes the science of arms." Droṇa was selected as a teacher because he was a specialist in that subject which was taught him by the great Ṛishi Agniveśa. " I was engaged there," says Droṇa, " in serving my preceptor, and lived with him for a long time as an humble-minded Brahmachārin with matted locks on my head." Droṇa was given for his residence by Bhīshma " a neat and tidy house, well-filled with paddy and every kind of goods ", and commenced his instruction of the princes. He " gave instructions to all the princes in the science of arms ".

Arjuna the best Pupil. " Though he gave equal instructions to all, yet Arjuna became the foremost of all in agility and skill." " Arjuna took a great deal of care in worshipping the preceptor ; had great devotion to his study of the science of arms. Therefore he became a great favourite of Droṇa." " He practised with his bow even in the night." Pleased with him, Droṇa then taught him " the art of fighting on horseback, on the elephant, on the car, and on foot ". He taught him "how to fight with clubs; the sword, the lance, the spear, and the dart. He taught him the use of many other weapons, and how to fight with superior numbers ". As regards his other pupils, Duryodhana and Bhīma specialized in the art of fighting with clubs, Nakula and Sahadeva in handling the sword, Yudhishṭhira as a " car-warrior ", while Aśvathāmā excelled in the use of all arms.

Arjuna as Teacher of his son Abhimanyu and other Princes. The same kind of military training was also the portion of the next generation of princes. " That powerful boy (Abhimanyu, son of Arjuna) became equal to his father in counteracting the weapons hurled on him in great lightness of hand, in fleetness of motion forward and backward, and in traversing and wheeling." He " learnt from Arjuna the science of arms with its four branches and ten divisions . . . and he also became learned in the Vedas." Again : " All their rites of infancy and childhood, according to the ordinances, such as Chūḍākaraṇa and Upanayana were duly performed by Dhaumya. After having studied the Vedas those princes (sons of Draupadī) of excellent behaviour and vows learnt from Arjuna the use of all the weapons " [i, 223].

Contents of Kshatriya's Education. The education prescribed elsewhere for the sons of kings included the following: "Knowledge, the family-laws, the Veda-of-the-bow, the Veda, elephant riding, horseback-riding, chariot-driving, rules of propriety, word-science, music and the fine arts, legends, and tales" [xiii, 104; cf. v, 189].

The kind of religious or Vedic knowledge which these princes were expected to acquire will be further evident from the fact that in the great war we find among the active combatants a good many very young knights. One of the foremost of these was Abhimanyu who is represented as only sixteen years old, already married and regarded as a full-fledged knight [i, 67]. Old Droṇa [vii, 192, 65; 193, 43] at eighty-five is spoken of as "acting in battle as if he were a vigorous youth of sixteen". The same kind of evidence is also given in the Rāmāyaṇa where, when Rāma is about to be taken away from home on his military mission, his father exclaims: "He is as yet but a boy (*bāla*); he is not yet sixteen and has not acquired the art of using arms." This passage thus further shows that the age of sixteen marked the end of boyhood before which the prince was normally expected to have acquired the military arts and qualified for the vocation or mission of his life [*Rāmā.*, i, 23, 2; iii, 42, 23].

The conclusion to which all this evidence points is very well put by Hopkins: "How are we to interpret this? The Science of Arms required years of patient study. Is it conceivable that a boy otherwise occupied in physical training should by the age of sixteen be master of the special skill that gave him power on the battlefield and at the same time have found time to commit to memory even one Vedic collection? It is clear that the Law is later than the Epic on this point; and even there such knowledge is only to be assumed as desirable for the warrior in general. The active young knight and busy trader must have performed their duties toward the Veda in a very perfunctory way, if at all. The more reasonable supposition seems to me to be that, while in the early age there was no let to the desire of a young warrior if he wished to be Veda-learned, the conventional practices of his caste nevertheless constrained most of his attention to arms, and in his eight months of schooling (if even this, the later term of yearly study, be allowed for so early a time) he probably did nothing more than 'go over' the text of the Veda. It is absurd to believe that the memorizing of even one Vedic collection could have been attempted by such young warriors as those the Epic depicts. The practice must have been peculiar to the man of leisure, the priest. Indeed, it is not to this caste as a whole that the Epic ascribes such knowledge;

but the king alone is, theoretically, acquainted with the three-fold Veda. A sort of commutation of learning seems to be implied in the Sūtra period; for we read that the student, instead of learning all, may even as an alternative to the *anuvāka* (itself a concession) recite only 'as much as the Guru thinks best'; or 'only the first and last hymn of each seer'; or 'at the beginning of each hymn just one verse'" [*Śāṁkh.*, ii, 7, 22 ff.].[1]

We may add to this the significant query of Nārada who, wishing to know what King Yudhishṭhira has studied, only asks him whether he has learnt the Sūtras on horses, elephants, and chariots together with the Veda-of-the-bow (being the only Veda mentioned in this connection). Among other assumed subjects of royal study are mentioned Sūtras on other subjects such as those treating of poison, city-life, and military machines which together with the knowledge of magical weapons and sorcery make up the contents of the royal learning [ii, 5, 110, 120 ff.].

In the *Rāmāyaṇa* [i, 80, 27 ff.], the list of subjects the king is expected to study includes Dhanurveda, Veda, Nītiśāstra and the art (śikshā) of elephants and cars, besides the arts of painting (Ālekhya), writing (Lekhya), jumping (laṅghana), and swimming (plavana). In another passage we have mention of Writing and Numbers [(*lekhya-saṁkhyā*), ib., 80, 4 (cf. ii, 2, 6)], of fine arts (Gandharvavidyā), logic (Nyāya), polity (Nītiśāstra), etc.

There are several similar lists in the Mahābhārata. Reference has already been made to two such lists [xiii, 104, 125; v, 189, 1 ff.], where we have mention of *Śabdaśāstram* and the sixty-four *Kalās* together with *Yuktiśāstram* (i.e. "grammar, fine arts, and etiquette"). Another list enumerates the following [ii, 11, 25]: Ashṭāṅga-āyurveda (Medicine with its eight branches), Ṛigveda, Sāmaveda, Yajurveda, Atharvaveda, Sarvaśāstrāṇi, Itihāsas, Upavedas, Vedāṅgas, Vāṇī of seven kinds, Sāmas, Stutiśāstras (treatises of hymns), various kinds of Gāthā literature, Bhāshyas (*bhāshyāni tarkayuktāni*), Nāṭakas, Kāvyas, Kathākhyā-yikās (Kārikāḥ). Hopkins holds the view that probably this list

[1] "The twenty-second verse alone would give any liberty of shortening (*yāvad vā gurur manyeta*). Oldenberg, translating this, notes the consequence, and calls the plan an 'abridged method, by which students who had not the intention of becoming Vedic scholars and probably chiefly students of the Kshatriya and Vaiśya caste, could fulfil their duty of learning the Veda'. In xii, 132, 20, 21 (= Manu, viii, 44) we are told that the *dharmavid*, or king erudite in rules of duty, must know the 'four-fold system of right'. This is best explained by another verse in the same book (xii, 59, 33), where the three-fold (Veda) is one; logic, two; agricultural occupations (including trading, etc.), three; and the system of punishment, four. The age of manhood is reached at sixteen."

is earlier than the previous one, but both show that " the line of education was away from the Veda and that what time the princes had was given to culture, not to religion ". He further holds that " as the old royal personal fighting days ended—that is, as the princes were more and more expected to be figure-heads in war, and drove into battle to watch it on an elephant's back rather than to lead it in a war-car—their older bow- and sword-training was given up ; but the time so gained was spent in more effeminate, certainly not more dryly intellectual occupations. Perhaps the rather late Virāṭa, with the cowardly little crown-prince, shows us the step between ".

Contents of Military Training. We may also give in this connection some details of the military training which the Kshatriya princes receive in the Epic. The art of warfare was made up of several arts connected with the traditional divisions of the ancient Hindu army, viz. the horse, the foot, the elephant, and the chariot. The entire military science and art of the age seem to have been comprehended by the generic term *Dhanurveda*, the dhanu or bow being regarded as the type or symbol of all weapons or methods of warfare. Thus the *Dhanurveda* or the general science of weapons and warfare is mentioned in different references as conveying different kinds of military knowledge or accomplishments. In one [vii, 45, 17] the heroes are " equipped with the strength born of the skill acquired " (*śikshābalopetāḥ*). In another [vi, 74, 10 ; also 82, 37 ; 90, 42, etc.], " lightness of hand " (*pāṇilāghava*) is acquired. Other references [ix, 22, 16 ; vii, 142, 38 ; 169, 3] mention " lightness and cleverness " (*lāghava* and *saushṭhava*). The *Dhanurveda* also imparts the " knowledge of seizing weapons " (*Śastragrahaṇavidyā*, vi, 76, 7 and vii, 114, 4). It also teaches the arts of mounting a car (āroha), leaping down (paryavaskanda), running (saraṇa), leaping easily (sāntarapluta), discharging weapons simultaneously (samyakpraharaṇa), and of advancing and retreating (yāna vyapayāna) [vi, 76, 8 ; cf. *Rāmāy*., vi, 69, 30 ff.]. All this shows that the *Dhanurveda* is the same as Astraśikshā or art of handling missiles [vi, 118, 21]. Another passage [vii, 23, 39] even speaks of a man as being a paragon (pāraga) of proficiency " in the Dhanurveda of missiles and Brahmaveda ". The *Rathaśikshā* or skill with the car became also a part of the Dhanurveda, wherefrom the knight learnt the art of " circling " with his war-car, of " doubling and returning ", and the negative skill of avoiding being made a *viratha* (deprived of one's war-car), and preventing it from being splintered into fragments by the enemy's blows. There was also taught the skill in the use of armour so as to make it invulnerable. The skill seems to have been imparted by oral instruction. Droṇa knew "how to instruct one to wear the breastplate so that it should be invulnerable" [vii, 48, 27; 103, 17 (varma bhāsvaram)]. One passage [i, 139, 6, 17] extends the scope of Dhanurveda so as to include the knowledge of fighting with all weapons of which the bow is a mere type, viz. fighting with club, sword, car, bow, arrow, and missiles. This extended scope leads to its four divisions [i, 130, 21; iii, 37, 4; v, 158, 3; ix, 44, 22], according to the weapons taught or methods of using them [iii, 115, 45]. Though it is called a Veda (or more properly Upaveda) to denote its literary existence it was not studied naturally in the manner of the study of the other Vedas, of memorizing the texts. The learner must study it in isolation and by practice with his arms; if necessary, he must seek the aid of a teacher to show him their use; and, in one case, he makes an earthen idol of the ideal teacher and worships him, so that he may imbibe his excellence by his self-absorption. Ekalavya left home for the sake of his practice, which thus included both physical exercise and spiritual, for the perfect marksman must not see anything but the target [i, 132, 33; 133, 5; 131, 42; 132, 13, 14, 34–5]. That the study of the Dhanurveda is to be principally by practice is also shown from the case of Arjuna who goes out and practises even at night and thus becomes an expert in the various military arts such as those connected with the management of horses, elephants, and the like [i, 132, 28].

According to Hopkins, "the ultimate expansion of the theory of weapons resulted in the theory of war, and this was expanded again into a theory of polity; and we thus have on the one side our modern Nītiśāstra or system of royal polity, and on the other the practical instruction in the use of arms or the science of weapons. Thus in a late book we read: 'he will comprehend the science of weapons, and the different weapons, and the system of polity.'[1] A system of war is implied when we read, for example, of the system of Uśanas, the system of Aṅgiras' son, etc."[2]

[1] "xiv, 66, 24. In the later books the system of polity was so familiar as to be used in proverbs, e.g. xiii, 164, 7—'not everyone that has perused the works of polity is wise in polity.'"

[2] i, 100, 36. The best treatment of Epic material is given by Professor E. W. Hopkins in *JAOS.*, Vol. 13, to which this chapter is indebted.

Women and Education. The *Rāmāyaṇa* contemplates women who were *Bhikshuṇīs*. The best example of these is 'Śramaṇī' Śabarī who is described as *Chīra-Krishṇājināmbarā, Jaṭilā, Siddhā, Tāpasī*, with her Āśrama on the Pampā, and Guru named Mataṅga. Śabarī was not a *śabara* by caste. It was only a name [*Araṇyakāṇḍa*, 74, 9–33]. In the *Mahābhārata*, Ashṭāvakra converses with an old woman who describes herself as a Brahmachāriṇī. The daughter of Śāṇḍilya was also a Brahmachāriṇī, as also that of Ṛishi Gārgya. Janaka has a philosophical discussion with Bhikshuṇī Sulobhā.

Ayodhyā as a Centre of Culture. The educational and cultural conditions of the country in that age are seen at their best at Ayodhyā, the capital of Kings Daśaratha and Rāma. The city was noted for its Vedic Schools of Taittirīyas, Kāṭhakas, and Mānavas. It is stated that among the Brāhmaṇas of the city there was neither illiteracy nor inadequacy of knowledge [*R.*, i, 5–7]. There were the Associations of Brahmachārīs called "Mekhalīnāṁ Mahā-Saṁgha". This Students' Federation is mentioned as approaching the King with statements of their views on public questions and grievances. Students are also mentioned as residents of *Āśramas* as well as of *Āvasathas* which were like the licensed lodging-houses of modern times. The Aśramas were suburban retreats whither flocked the citizens to listen to learned discourses and discussions held there. These were like modern University Extension Lectures [*R.*, ii, 67]. These debates were generally carried on by Lokāyatas notorious for their casuistry. Ayodhyā was also the seat of the Purāṇic Schools of Sūtas and Māgadhas and was crowded by these bards and chroniclers [*R.*, ii, 100 ; 38–9 ; i, 5], of whom the Chief in those days was Ārya (Reverend) Chitraratha [*R.*, ii, 32]. There were also at Ayodhyā Ladies' Clubs called *Vadhū-Saṁghas*, Dramatic Societies called *Nāṭaka-Saṁghas*, which organized festivities called *Utsavas* and *Samājas* at the suburban parks, of which the main programme was acting and dancing [*R.*, i, 5–7 ; ii, 67]. Lastly, we have a reference to educational institutions conducted by private citizens in the city (*paurān*) which offered Lectures and Lessons attended by various bodies of students (*Śishya-Gaṇas*). These citizens included the Sūtas and Māgadhas, king's officers, artists and craftsmen of all kinds, and merchants who had travelled widely [*R.*, ii, 1–2 ; i, 5–7 ; ii, 67].

Āśrama of Bharadvāja at Prayāga. Lastly, we may mention one of the biggest Āśramas of the times, that of Ṛishi

Bharadvāja at Prayāga, which accommodated Bharata and his royal retinue, including the ladies of the Palace. The Āśrama was equipped with "white *Chatuḥ-śālās*"; stalls which accommodated the royal elephants and horses; *harmyas* or mansions; *prāsādas* or palaces, and their *toraṇas* or gateways; a separate *rāja-veśma* or royal guest-house fitted with several *toraṇas*, and furnished with beds, seats, and vehicles, coverlets and carpets, stores of food. The Āśrama also entertained its royal guests with the performances of musicians and dancing girls. All this lavish hospitality was extemporized for the occasion, showing the resources which Ṛishi Bharadvāja could command in the locality by his personality [*R.*, vi, 126; ii, 90–2].[1]

[1] A highly intensive study of the educational material of *Rāmāyaṇa* is contained in Dr. S. C. Sarkar's Patna University Readership Lectures to which I am indebted.

PLATE XV

HERMITAGES IN BHARHUT SCULPTURES (*c.* second century B.C.).

No. 6.—Supposed by Cunningham to be the hermitage of Ṛishi Bharadvāja at Prayāga, or of Atri at Chitrakūṭa; showing Rama, Lakshmaṇa, and Sītā standing before the Ṛishi. A more elaborate and dramatic representation of *Rāmāyaṇa* scenes in their sequence is to be found in four parts of a story-telling panel in a sculpture at Nāgārjunikoṇḍa (*c.* second century A.D.) [See Plate XLV of *Memoir* No. 54 of Archæological Department, Government of India.].

[*Facing p. 344*

Chapter XI

INDUSTRIAL AND VOCATIONAL EDUCATION

Evidence. Ancient Indian Literature, whether Sanskrit, Pāli, or the Prākṛits, being mainly religious in character, it does not furnish much evidence on the subject of industrial and technical education, though it is upon the basis of such education that ancient India was able to build up her own economic life and prosperity and figured in the ancient world as the chief exporting country, supplying foreign countries from time immemorial and through the ages with luxuries and other articles turned out by her cottage industries and handicrafts. Bits of evidence on this important and interesting subject are found scattered throughout this literature, and these may be pieced together to produce a picture of ancient Indian Industrial Education as a whole, though it is not possible to trace its history and development by different periods and stages, as in the case of general education and culture.

Ceremony of Admission. The ideas and rituals which prevailed in the sphere of general education influenced that of practical education in arts, crafts, and the professions. The most important of these were the Medical and the Military.

Upanayana Ceremony for study of Āyurveda. According to *Śuśruta-Saṁhitā* [ch. ii], the study of Medical Science or Āyurveda requires the separate performance by its student of a special Upanayana ceremony, although such a student, as a *dvija*, as a Brāhmaṇa, Kshatriya, or Vaiśya, should have already performed such a ceremony according to the rules of his order. The Āyurvedic Upanayana lays stress on physical and moral qualifications, on properly formed bodily organs such as tongue, lips, and teeth, eyes, nose and mouth ; and on cleanliness, good manners and morals, courage, humility, capacity, intelligence, patience, retentiveness, and zeal, purity of body, mind, and speech and capacity for taking pains. A student lacking these qualifications will not be eligible for Upanayana and admission.

The ceremony, as usual, was to be performed on an auspicious day. An altar 18 inches square was prepared, on which worship was offered to the Deity, to Brāhmaṇa, and to the Physicians. Next, *Samidh* or wood from four trees, Khadira, Palāśa, Devadāru, and Bilva, was soaked in curd, honey, and ghee and offered as *homa* to Fire, by utterance of the Mahāvyāhṛiti Mantra—Om Bhūḥ svāhā Om Bhuvaḥ svāhā Om Svaḥ svāhā Om Bhurbhuvaḥ Svaḥ svāhā. Then the following Deities were invoked: Brahman, Prajāpati, the two Aśvins, and Indra; as also the following Ṛishis, as being associated with the development of Āyurvedic science: Dhanvantari, Bharadvāja, Ātreya, and the like.

A Brāhmaṇa could perform the Upanayana ceremony for a Brāhmaṇa, Kshatriya, and Vaiśya student; a Kshatriya for a Kshatriya and Vaiśya student; and a Vaiśya for a Vaiśya student. But, according to some authorities, a Śūdra also may be initiated and admitted to a study of Āyurveda, if he was qualified by purity of his lineage and possession of virtues. Thus the study of Āyurveda was open to all the castes.

At the conclusion of the ceremony, the preceptor, in the presence of Agni as witness, will ask the pupil to take an oath that he will follow the injunctions stated. 'The pupil must abjure lust, anger, greed, inertia, vanity, conceit, envy, harshness, lying, laziness, and disreputable deeds. He must duly cut off his nails and hairs; wear pure silken clothes (as preventing infection); and practise *brahmacharya* and truthfulness. He must perform his prescribed duties, as the preceptor must perform his. He was also asked to treat, without charging fee and cost of medicines, the following persons: the *dvija*, *guru*, pauper, friend, ascetic, protégé, saint, orphan, and guest. He must avoid treating as his patients the hunter, fowler, the degraded and sinful.' The principle of these rules is that the physician must himself be possessed of a sound healthy body, observe rules of hygiene and avoid all kinds of defilement, infection, and contamination, and be a man of strict morals as having to deal with patients of both sexes and of all sorts and conditions.

The medical authorities contemplate a period of probation for testing the fitness of a pupil for the study to which he is formally admitted by Upanayana. This period is fixed by Suśruta at six months [*Ashṭāṅga Hṛidaya*, Sūtrasthāna, ch. 2].

Medical Holidays. Holidays were prescribed. These were the eighth, fourteenth, and new- and full-moon days; morning and evening twilights; when there were thunder, rain, and roar of clouds out of season; time of danger to the country and its king. Study was not also permitted at a crematorium, on an elephant, in a place for execution of convicts, in a field of battle, at a national festival, or in sight of inauspicious omens.

Upanayana for Military Education. Military science was called Dhanurveda. According to a work called *Dhanurveda-Saṁhitā* attributed to Vasishṭha, an Upanayana ceremony had to be performed by a military student who was given a weapon, while a Vedic Mantra was uttered by the preceptor. In the case of a Brāhmaṇa student it was a bow, for a Kshatriya a sword, for a Vaiśya a lance, and for a Śūdra, a mace. The preceptor, the military master, was to have been accomplished in the use of seven weapons, viz. the bow, the disc, the sword, the spear, the mace, the arms, and the *Khārikārā*.

Graduation. There was also a ceremony to mark the completion of this military training. It was called *Chhurikā-bandhanam*, because it meant the tying up of a dagger to the dress of the pupil as a token of his graduation. It is mentioned by Nārada as cited in *Vīramitrodaya* [see Altekar's *Education in Ancient India*, pp. 44–6].

Rules of Medical Study. After admission, the student commences the study of medical texts. These are imparted to him by his teacher slowly and in parts, in *padas* (syllables), *pādas* (one-fourth of a śloka or verse), and *ślokas*. When the texts are thus learnt and committed to memory, their meanings must next be thoroughly grasped. The student who has mastered the mere words of the texts but not their import which they cannot expound (*prabhāshaṇa*) is likened to a beast of burden which only undergoes the pain of carrying a load of sandal-wood without enjoying the pleasure of its smell. Such a student only undergoes the pain of study without being able to enjoy its fruits.

It is also pointed out that Ayurveda has many branches of study which throw light on one another. A student of one subject should approach the master of another subject for interpretation of allied topics or points. In medical study, proficiency in one particular subject or branch is not sufficient. The complete knowledge of Medicine as a whole cannot be contained within only one subject or branch but is spread over many subjects and branches which thus help in the interpretation of each. The meaning of a particular science is not understood in its full implications like the contents of a seed (*vīja-bhuta*) and is rendered explicit by the light derived from allied subjects. Therefore, a medical man cannot achieve success unless he is a master of several sciences (*Bahu-śruta*) [*Sūtra-sthāna*, chs. iii and iv].

It is again emphasized that a medical student must acquire

a double proficiency in both Theory and Practice (*Śāstra* and *Karma*) which are likened to the two wings on which a bird is borne in its upward flight. The bird of one wing cannot fly at all. They are also likened to the two wheels of a chariot which enable it to perform its functions in the field of battle. Similarly, a physician who is merely a pundit and grounded in the texts of his Śāstras (*Śāstrajña*) and is totally unskilled in the practical application of his theoretical knowledge will break down and will be at his wits' ends, unable to decide what he should do, puzzled by the actual sight of a patient, like a coward losing his sense in a field of battle (*mugdha* and *kiṁkartavyavimūḍha*). On the other hand, the mere empiric or quack who practises his profession without a theoretical knowledge of the Science of Medicine deserves censure and is liable to extreme penalty at the hands of the State. The best of medicines, the elixir of life, will become a poison if wrongly applied by a physician through his ignorance, while a physician who, with all his theoretical knowledge, is ignorant of the art of surgical operation (*chhedana*) and application of ointments and disinfectants (*snehādi-kārya*), is equally unacceptable. Such undeserving medical men only murder people under the licence of the State [ib., iii, 16–21].

Qualifications of a Physician. He must be well-read in the texts of Medical Śāstras or treatises (*adhīta-śāstra*) ; well up in the import of the texts studied ; skilled in practical work or surgical operations (like *Chheda* and *Sneha*) ; full of resourcefulness and originality (*svayaṁkṛitī*) ; possessed of light touch and swift hand (*laghu-hasta*) ; clean ; of an optimistic temperament or cheerful spirits (*śūra* = *vishādarahita*) ; ready with all necessaries and materials for treatment (*sajjopaskara-bheshaja*) ; of a resourceful mind ; possessed of keen intellect ; possessed of professional experience (*vyavasāyī*) ; learned in theory ; and devoted to truth and morality.

Factors of Success in Treatment. The success of medical treatment depends on other factors, though the most important factor is the physician, who is compared to the Adhvaryu without whom the other three priests, the Udgātā, the Hotā, or the Brahmā cannot properly perform the sacrifice. He is also likened to the helmsman who can successfully handle a boat even if it lacks its rudders. But his work depends upon the efficiency of Nurses (*parichāraka*) and the quality of medicines together with the subject of treatment, viz. the patient. An efficient Nurse should be possessed of many virtues: he should be full of fellow-feeling (*snehayukta*), should not be hostile to anyone, should be physically strong, skilled in keeping up the suffering patient (*vyādhitarakshaṇam*), able to apply the prescriptions of the physician (Vaidyavākya-kṛit), and untiring in his work. As regards the quality of medicines to make them efficacious, their raw materials or sources (like the medicinal plants) should be grown properly, gathered in proper time, duly measured, should be palatable and mixed up with due degrees of smell, colour, and taste, capable of curing ailments, not repulsive, not producing any undesired effects, and should be given in proper condition. The patient also should be one who is patient under suffering, is suffering from a curable disease, possessed of materials for treatment, free from greed, full of faith in God and obedience to the directions of his Doctor [ib., ch. 34].

Admission to Industry : Rules of Apprenticeship. Admission to an industry or craft was also governed by regulations. These are best given in their standardized form in the law-book of Nārada, and are stated as follows :—

"If a young man wishes to be initiated into the art of his own craft (*svaśilpaṁ ichchhan āhartum*), he must first obtain the sanction of his relations (*bāndhāvanāṁ anujñayā*) and then proceed to live with his master (*āchāryasya vaset ante*), after previously fixing the period of his training or apprenticeship (*kālaṁ kṛitvā suniśchitam*).

"Then the master must impart to his pupil his training at his own house where he is to provide his board and lodging. He must not make the apprentice perform other work (*na cha anyat kārayet karma*) but must treat him like a son.

"If the apprentice deserts his master who duly instructs him and is not at fault in any way (*adushṭam*), he should be compelled by forcible means to stay with his master and will be liable to corporal punishment and confinement.

"In case the training of an apprentice is completed before the stipulated time, he should not leave, but continue at his master's place up to the limit of the stipulated time and all the fruits of his work done during this time will be his master's (Śikshitopi kṛitaṁ kālam antevāsī samāpayet | Tatra karma cha yat kuryāt āchāryasyaiva tat phalam ||).

"When the apprentice has mastered the art of his craft within the stipulated time (*samāye*), he should make gifts (kṛitvā pradakshiṇām) to his teacher according to his means and then take leave of him (*nivartate*).

"An apprentice after graduation may have his services retained by his master who will then have the right to employ him after settling his remuneration with reference to his qualifications (vetanaṁ vā yadi kṛitaṁ jñātvā śishyasya kauśalam). In such a case, the pupil should not seek service with others."

These rules show that industrial apprenticeship was treated as a contract based on several stipulations. First, there was the stipulation as to the limit of time within which the master must engage to complete the course of training for which he admits the apprentice. As stated in the *Vīramitrodaya*, the master craftsman is to make an agreement in this form: "Let this apprentice stay with me so and so long." Secondly, the arrangement fixed the respective obligations of both the master and his pupil during the time of training. The obligations of the master were: (*a*) that he should treat his pupil as if he were his son, which meant (i) that he should give him free board and lodging in his house, (ii) that he should not treat him like a hired labourer, (iii) that he should teach him honestly and wholeheartedly without keeping back from him any secrets of his knowledge and craft, and (iv) that he should not exploit his pupil's skill and labour by employing him on work not related to his training but only for his own gain. Kātyāyana fixes a penalty for employing an apprentice in work not connected with his training: "He who does not instruct his pupil in the art (to which he is admitted) and causes him to perform other work, shall incur the first amercement; and the pupil may forsake him and go to another teacher, released from this indenture" [Colebrooke's *Digest of Hindu Law*, ii, 7]. The law-books also contemplate cases of undutiful teachers putting off instruction of their pupils even after their admission, and condemn them severely if such neglect continues for a year [*Kūrma Purāṇa* cited in *Vīramitrodaya*]. On the pupil's side, there were appropriate obligations, viz. (1) that he should not desert his teacher before time where there is no justifiable ground for such desertion, such as neglect of duty or any moral lapse on the part of the teacher. A runaway apprentice might be flogged and confined if it is of his own motion; but if it is under instructions of his kinsmen who had been the consenting parties to his pupilage, the deserted master could sue these guardians of the pupil for a breach of contract [Colebrooke's *Digest*, p. 8; cf. *Manu*, iv, 164; viii, 299–300; *Gautama*, ii, 43–4]; (2) that the pupil could not leave his teacher even if he had completed his training before time. For this unexpired period, the pupil should work for his teacher and yield to him the fruits of his work, serving out his full term. The theory was that it was by way of reward or compensation for the pupil's gain in time achieved by his master's superior methods of training. Yājñavalkya [ii, 187] also states the same position: "Even if the apprentice has had his training completed before time, he must live on in his master's house up to the time fixed (*kṛita-śilpopi nivaset kṛita-kālaṁ guror gṛihe*), giving to him all that he earns by his work for the time as a return for what his master has spent on him by way of free board, lodging, and tuition (antevāsī guruprāptabhojanastat phalapradaḥ)."

On this point, the question is raised by the commentator, "Whether the teacher has ownership even in what the pupil acquires by voluntary *exertion* in traffic and the like, independent of his craft, and by agriculture or similar means, and by treasure-trove or other *accident*. There are two opinions held on the point" [Colebrooke's *Digest*, ib.].

This rule also intimates that if the art could not be learned by the apprentice in the time first stipulated, there should be a formal extension of the apprenticeship with all its liabilities to the teacher and the apprentice [ib.].

Advantages of the System. The system of the apprentice and his master living together has many advantages. The apprentice always lives and works under his master's eye and has opportunities of observing the special points of his skill, his trade secrets, and imbibing his true "inward" method and genius, as the ultimate factor of success of his craftsmanship, when he lives in his home which is also his workshop, the home where in its freedom his whole personality always remains revealed, unobscured by the restrictions and formalities of a factory. It is the constant and intimate relationship of the home which, apart from actual and direct teaching, helps the disciple to master his teacher's method and skill in the shortest time. There is also another advantage of the home and the workshop being one. Here the teaching is learnt from the very beginning in relation to real things, difficulties, and problems, and primarily by service, by personal attendance on the master. And it is not only technique that is thus learnt here, but something more valuable: in the home as workshop, there is something else, besides mere plant and tools: there is life with its problems, its human relationships, culture, and religion, relieving the mechanical monotony of a mere workshop, a thing which is as necessary to art as technique itself.

A School of Sculpture. Two old inscriptions mention interesting examples of these craftsmen and the schools they conducted in connection with their crafts which they plied and pursued as cottage industries in their own homes combined with their workshops. One of these inscriptions was found on the famous Yaksha image discovered at Parkham and refers to the construction of the image (*Katā* = kṛita) by the sculptor Gomitaka described as the *ante-vāsī*, resident pupil, of the master Kuṇika. The second inscription found on the image of what was locally worshipped as "Mansā Devī" states that "the image of Yakshī Lāyāvā was constructed (*katā*) by the sculptor Nāka, the *ante-vāsī* or pupil of the master Kuṇika". It will thus appear that the School of Sculpture established by the master-craftsman Kuṇika was very famous in its locality and produced accomplished sculptors like Nāka and Gomitaka to whom India owes her earliest statues of colossal figures, male and female.

Caste and Craft. The rules of industrial apprenticeship as given by Nārada indicate that admission to a craft was free, provided the guardian's consent was obtained. Normally, no doubt, the Hindu system did not favour the free choice of occupations under its fundamental philosophical position that economic ends are not ends in themselves but must subserve the higher religious and spiritual ends of life. Therefore, as a social regulation, to promote the self-fulfilment of the individual, different castes were to pursue different crafts in consonance with the ideals and values for which each caste stood. But while this was the ideal, it did not mean that it did not permit of deviations from it in practice and in the actual circumstances of life. The *Smṛitis* agree that, under necessity which has no law (*āpad-dharma*), "in times of distress or failure to obtain a living through lawful labour," persons could take to any occupations. The economic life of the times is better revealed in the Buddhist texts with their touch of realism and references to its concrete facts and details. Some of the typical ones may be cited. In *Vinaya*, i, 77 and iv, 128, we find parents freely discussing the various professions and callings of the day which their son might choose, such as Writing [*Lekham*] or occupation of the Scribe or Clerk, Accountancy [*Gaṇanam*], and Money-changing [*Rūpam* to be learnt from the treatises called *Rūpa-sutta*]. In *Chullavagga*, v, 28 even the Bhikshus or Monks, with all their preoccupations of religious life, are allowed "the use of looms and of shuttles, strings, tickets, and all the apparatus belonging to a loom", presumably because it was considered that a Monk should be able to produce the scanty clothing prescribed for him, "the triple clothing" comprising the upper and lower cloth and a towel, so as to make the whole brotherhood and Vihāra self-contained in regard to a primary requisite of life. The Jātakas even tell of Brāhmans as physicians [iv, 361], goat-herds [iii, 401], merchants, hunters, snake-charmers [iv, 457], archers, and even cartwrights [iv, 207].

Guilds as Industrial Schools. While the home of the artisan functioned as the school for imparting instruction in the particular craft plied by him, the collective interests of the craft as a whole in a particular area or region were administered by an organization like a guild which was called *Śreṇī*. Each guild laid down its own laws for the administration of the interests of the particular craft belonging to it. The guilds were of various kinds like the crafts and were like so many industrial schools. The Smṛitis [e.g. Gautama, xi, 21] mention the main guilds to be those of (1) Cultivators, (2) Herdsmen, (3) Traders, (4) Money-lenders, and (5) Artisans, to which Bṛihaspati [i, 26] adds (6) Artists (= *chitra-kāras*), and (7) Dancers. There are also references to Guilds of Musicians, Priests, and Military adventurers. Thus all these may be taken to function like Schools of Fine Arts and Crafts in those days. Every industry or craft was self-governing by its *Śreṇī*, while it was pursued by an individual craftsman as a home or cottage industry, throwing open his own home or cottage as a school for training of apprentices in his craft.

The Sixty-four Arts and Crafts (Kalās) in Literature.[1] Many works of Sanskrit Literature, as well as Buddhist and Jain, contain references to the ancient Indian Arts and Crafts making up a traditional number of 64. These references, for instance, are found in the Rāmāyaṇa [i, 9, 5], Bhāgavata-Purāṇa [x, 45, 36], Mahābhāshya [i, 1, 57], Daśakumāracharita [ii, 21], Kādambarī, Vātsyāyana's Kāmasūtra, and also in the works of Vāmana, Māgha, Bhavabhūti, and others. Among Buddhist and Jain works containing these references may be mentioned Lalitavistara, Jātakamālā (p. 105), Kalpasūtra, Aupapātika-

[1] In treating this topic, I am much indebted to the Dissertation on *The Kalās* presented by Dr. A. Venkatasubbiah to the University of Berne for the Degree of Doctor of Philosophy.

Sūtra, or Praśnavyākaraṇa-Sūtra. Some works mention more than 64 *Kalās*, Jain works mentioning 72, while Lalitavistara gives 86. But the most ancient and established number is 64.

While the mere mention of 64 *Kalās* is contained in many works, some contain their actual lists. The principal works giving such lists are (1) Kāmasūtra, (2) Kādambarī, (3) Śukranītisāra, (4) Kalpāntaravāchyāni (a commentary on Kalpasūtra), (5) Rāmachandra's Commentary on the first verse of Lakshmaṇa Kavi's continuation of the Champūrāmāyaṇa by Vidarbharāja, (6) Yashodhara's commentary called Jayamaṅgala on the Kāmasūtra, (7) the Jain work Samavāyasūtra, (8) the Buddhist work Lalitavistara, and (9) the Buddhist work Sūtrālaṁkāra by Aśvaghosha. The list of *Śukranītisāra* as one of the latest of these works is given below and may be considered as the basis of a comparative study of the lists contained in other works. The list comprises the following items :—

1. *Nartanam*, Dancing, accompanied by suitable and allied expressions through features of the face, movements of the arm and hand, and the like (hāva-bhāvādisaṁyukta).

The *Rājataraṅginī* mentions thirty-two modes of dancing.

One text [*Lalita.*] calls it *Vādya-nṛityam*, dancing to the accompaniment of instrumental music.

Kādambarī describes this item not as a practical art but theoretical knowledge of the literature on dancing compiled by Bharata and other writers (Bharatādipraṇītāni Nṛitya-Śāstrāni).

Vātsyāyana mentions forms of dramatic art such as (1) *Nepathya-yoga*, " stage-play," and (2) *Nāṭakākhyāyikā-darśanam*, " histrionic and scenic representation."

2. Proficiency at playing on many instruments together in a concert, skill in playing in an orchestra (Aneka-vādya-vikṛitau tadvādane jñānam).

Kādambarī mentions these instruments as " *Vīnā*, *Muraja*, *Kāṁsyatāla*, *Darduraputa*, and the like ".

Vātsyāyana mentions " *Vīnā*, *Damaru*, and the like ".

The *Samavāyasūtra* mentions the following Arts of Music : (1) *Svaragatam*, knowledge of the seven *svaras* ; (2) *Vādyam*, playing on musical instruments ; (3) *Pushkara-gatam*, special skill at playing on the particular instrument called *pushkara*, a kind of drum ; and (4) *Samatālam*, knowledge of " beating time to music ".

Rāmachandra calls the Science of Music *Svara-śāstra*.

3. Skill at toilette, " assisting men and women in decorating themselves with dress and ornaments " (Strī-puṁsoh vastrālaṁkārasandhānaṁ).

The *Samavāyasūtra* calls it *Ābharaṇa-vihim*, " rules relating to ornaments," and *Taruṇī-paḍikamma*, " the art of decorating a maiden."

Vātsyāyana calls it *Nepathyaprayoga*, and Yaśodhara *Sarīra-saṁskāra*, " decoration of body."

4. *Anekarūpāvirbhāva-kriti-jñānam*, the art of producing various forms or figures out of stone, wood, and other materials, the art of the Sculptor.

The *Samavāyasūtra* calls it *Rūpam*, which is explained as " sculpture, painting, producing forms in cloth, gold, wood, etc."

5. *Śayyāstaraṇa-saṁyoga-pushpādigrathanam*, " the art of making beds and garlands with flowers."

The *Samavāya*. calls it " *sayaṇa-vihim* ". The *Lalita*. mentions *Mālya-granthanam*.

Among these domestic Arts of menial service, Vātsyāyana adds those of *Utsādana* (oiling and perfuming the body), *Saṁvāhana* (Massage), and *Keśamardana* (dressing the hair).

The *Samavāyasūtra* mentions the chemical art of Perfumery called *Gandha-yukti*.

6. *Dyūtādi-aneka-krīḍābhīrañjanam*, " the art of entertaining by gambling and other pastimes."

Yaśodhara enumerates fifteen kinds of gambling with dice, cowries, etc., and also with live creatures.

The *Samavāya*. calls gambling *Jūyam* and mentions a new game, *Aṭṭāvayam*, " a game played on a board of sixty-four squares."

7. *Anekāsanasandhānairraterjñānam*.

8. *Makarandāsavādīnāṁ madyādīnām kṛitiḥ*, " the art of preparing flower-juices and other intoxicating liquors."

9. *Śalyagūḍhāhṛitau śirāvraṇavyadhe jñānam*, " the art of extracting buried arrows, spears, etc., and of incision of open wounds and blood-vessels."

10. *Hīnādirasasaṁyogānnādisampāchanam*, " the art of cooking various dishes with the various *rasas* combined in different proportions."

Vātsyāyana calls it " *Vichitra-śākayūsha-bhakshya-vikāra-kriyā* ", " preparation of various vegetables, soups, and condiments " ; and also " *Pānaka-rasa-rāga-āsava-yojanam* ", " the art of preparing different kinds of drinks."

Yaśodhara calls it *Āsvādya-vidhānam*, "the art of preparing savoury foods."

The *Samavāyasūtra* describes the culinary art as *Anna-vidhi* and *Pāna-vidhi*, the art of preparing foods and drinks. Rāmachandra calls the culinary art *Sūda-Karma*.

11. *Vṛikshādi-prasava-āropa-pālanādi kṛitiḥ*, "the art of grafting and planting and culture of plants."

Vātsyāyana calls it *Vṛikshāyurvedayogāh*, "knowledge of the processes by which plants may be made to grow strong and healthy, abnormally small or big, etc."

Rāmachandra calls it *Bhūruhāṇāṁ dohanam*, "the art of grafting trees, making trees produce all sorts of abnormal fruits, etc."

12. *Pāshāṇadhātvādidṛitibhashmakaraṇam*, "the art of melting and reducing to ashes stones, minerals, and the like."

The *Samavāyasūtra* calls it "Dhaupāgam" = Dhātupākam, "melting and combination of minerals." It also mentions the following metallurgical arts, viz. (1) *Hiraṇya-pāka*, (2) *Suvarṇa-pāka*, and (3) *Maṇi-pāka*, treating respectively of silver, gold, and precious stones.

Vātsyāyana calls it simply *Dhātu-vāda*.

13. *Yāvadikshuvikārāṇām Kṛiti-jñanam*, "knowledge of the preparation of all things that can be prepared from the juice of sugar-cane."

14. *Dhātvaushadhīnāṁ saṁyoga-kriyā-jñānam*, "knowledge of the combination of minerals and herbs."

15. *Dhātu-sāṅkarya-pārthakya-karaṇam*, "the art of combining and isolating minerals."

16. *Dhātvādīnām saṁyoga-apūrva-vijñānam*, "the science of producing new compounds of minerals."

17. *Kshāranishkāsana-jñānam*, "the art of extracting the *Kshārarasa* out of minerals."

18. *Padādinyāsataḥ śastrasandhāna nikshepaḥ*, "the art of adjusting the bow with the foot, fitting the arrow and then shooting it."

19. *Sandhyāghātā-kṛishṭibhedaiḥ mallayuddham*, "the art of wrestling in different ways, utilizing grips and falls of diverse kinds."

The *Lalita*. mentions fights of four kinds, with *Vāhu* (arms), *Daṇḍa* (lathis), *Mushṭi* (fists), and *Asthi* (bones).

The *Kādambarī* mentions physical science as *Vyāyāma-Vidyā*.

20. *Abhilakshite deśe yantrādi-astra-nipātanam*, "the art of hurling weapons and missiles at observed marks."

The *Lalita.* mentions the three forms of marksmanship, viz. (1) *Akkshuṇṇa-vedhitvam*, "the art of hitting the mark accurately"; (2) *Marma-vedhitvam*, "hitting the heart of the mark"; (3) *Śabda-vedhitvam*, "hitting the mark or game by its sound."

The *Kādambarī* mentions military proficiency in the art of wielding the different weapons of those days such as *Chāpa* (bow and arrow), *Chakra* (discus), *Varma* (armour), *Kripāṇa* (sword), *Śakti* (spear), *Tomara* (javelin), *Paraśu* (axe), *Gadā* (club), and the like.

21. *Vādyasaṅketato vyūharachanādi*, "the knowledge of forming an army into *Vyūhas* in accordance with the directions conveyed by instrumental music."

22. *Gajāśvarathagatyā tu yuddhasaṁyojanam*, "taking part in battle on elephant, horse, or chariot."

23. *Vividhāsana-mudrābhiḥ devatā-toshaṇam*, "propitiating deities by worship in different postures and by different *mudrās* or dispositions of fingers."

24. *Sārathyam*, "the science of charioteering."

Kādambarī calls it *Rathacharyā*.

25. *Gajāśvādeḥ gatiśikshā*, "the art of training elephants and horses in movements."

26. *Mṛittikā-kāshṭha-pāshāṇa-dhātu-bhāṇḍādi-satkriyā*, "the art of producing vessels and the like out of such materials as clay, wood, stone, or metals.

Rāmachandra uses the terms *Vṛitra-kriyā*, "work in vṛitra, a kind of stone; *Loha-kriyā*, work in metals; *Aśma-kriyā*, work in stones; *Mṛit-kriyā*, "work in clay"; *Dāru-kriyā*, "work in wood"; *Venu-kriyā*, "work in bamboos"; *Varma-kriyā*, "armour-making"; *Añjana-kriyā*, "manufacture of collyrium"; *Charma-kriyā*, "manufacture of leather-goods"; and *Ambara-kriyā*, manufacture of textiles.

Vātsyāyana uses the following terms for some of these crafts: *Paṭṭikā-Vetra-vāna-vikalpaḥ*, "making of different things like cots and seats from canes and reed"; *Takshakarmāṇi*, explained as "the manufacture of *apadravyas* out of materials like gold, steel, or wood".

27. *Chitrādi-ālekhanam*, "painting of pictures."

Yasodhara calls it *Chitravidhi*. He also mentions the art of painting on cloth, which he calls *Pustakarma*.

Vātsyāyana calls it *Ālekhyam*.

28. *Taṭāka-Vāpi-Prasāda-Samabhūmi-Kriyā*, "the art of excavating tanks and wells and levelling the ground."

29. *Ghaṭṭādi-anekayantrānām Vādyānām kṛitiḥ*, "construction of machines like the water-wheel and of musical instruments."

Yaśodhara calls it *Upakaraṇa-kriyā*, construction of machines, apparatus, engines, etc., as explained by Monier-Williams.

Kādambarī calls it *Yantraprayoga*, "use of machines."

Vātsyāyana calls it *yantramātṛikā* which is explained as "construction of machines for purposes of locomotion, supply of water, and war".

30. *Hīna-madhyādi-saṁyoga-varṇādyai rañjanam*, "the art of painting with colours mixed in different proportions or quantities, large, moderate, and the like."

31. *Jala-Vāyu-Agni-saṁyoga-nirodhaiḥ kriyā*, "working with water, fire, and air in two ways, by utilizing them or by controlling them."

32. *Naukā-rathādir yānānāṁ kṛiti-jñanam*, "the science and art of constructing ships, chariots, and other vehicles for locomotion."

33. *Sūtrādi-rajjukaraṇa-vijñānam*, "the art of making yarns, ropes, etc."

34. *Anekatantu-saṁyogaiḥ Paṭabandhaḥ*, "weaving of cloth out of a variety of yarns."

35. *Ratnānāṁ Vedhādisadasat jñānam*, "the science of testing precious stones, and of the processes of cutting and boring them and similar processes."

Vātsyāyana calls it *Rūpyaratna-parīkshā*, "testing of precious stones and coins."

Rāmachandra calls it *Ratnaśāstram*.

36. *Svarṇādīnāṁ yāthārthya-vijñānam*, "the art of examining the properties of gold and testing its genuineness."

37. *Kṛitrima-svarṇa-ratnādi-kriyā-jñānam*, "the science and art of manufacturing artificial gold and imitation precious stones."

38. *Svarṇādi-alaṁkāra-kṛitiḥ*, "manufacture of ornaments from materials like gold."

Vātsyāyana calls it *Karṇa-patra-bhaṅga*, which means "the making of ear-ornaments".

39. *Lepādi-satkṛitiḥ*, "the art of enamelling, polishing, varnishing, etc."

40. *Charmāṇām mārdavādi-kriyā-jñānam*, "the science and art of tanning leather."

41. *Paśucharma-aṅga-nirhāra-jñānam*, "the science of separating the hide and the various limbs from the bodies of animals."

42. *Dugdhadohādi-ghṛitāntaṁ vijñānam*, "knowledge of the processes of milking and of making ghee from milk as its ultimate product."

43. *Kanchukādīnāṁ sīvane Vijñānam*, "the art of sewing bodices."

Vātsyāyana uses the general term *Suchivānakarmāṇi*, "the art of sewing, weaving, knitting, and plaiting, by the use of needle."

44. *Jale bāhvādibhiḥ taraṇam*, "the art of swimming in water with hands."

Rāmachandra uses a more significant expression, *Payasi plava-chāturyam*, which means "skill in diving in water".

45. *Gṛiha-bhāṇḍādeḥ mārjane vijñānam*, "the art of cleansing houses and household utensils and furniture."

46. *Vastra-saṁmārjanam*, "the art of cleaning clothes, laundry."

47. *Kshura-karma*, "the art of shaving."

48. *Tila-māṁsādi-snehānāṁ nishkāsane kṛitiḥ*, "the art of extracting the essence out of sesamum, meats, and fats."

49. *Sīrādyā-karshaṇe-jñānam*, "the art of ploughing, hoeing, etc."

50. *Vṛikshādi-ārohane jñānam*, "the art of climbing trees and the like."

51. *Manonukūlasevāyāḥ kṛiti-jñānam*, "the art of serving another to his heart's content."

52. *Venu-tṛiṇādi-pātrānāṁ kṛiti-jñānam*, "the art of making vessels out of bamboo, reeds, etc."

53. *Kācha-pātrādi-karaṇa-vijñānam*, "the science of manufacturing vessels and other articles out of glass."

54. *Jalānām saṁsechanaṁ saṁharaṇam*, "the science of irrigation by which water is distributed and collected."

55. *Lohādisāraśāstra-astra-kṛitijñānam*, "the art of manufacturing weapons out of metals."

56. *Gaja-aśva-vṛishava-ushṭrānāṁ Palyānādi-kriyā*, "the art of manufacture of saddles, etc., to be used for riding elephants, horses, bullocks, and camels."

57. *Śiśoḥ samrakshaṇe dhāraṇe krīḍane jñānam*, "the art of bringing up, handling, and playing with children."

58. *Aparādhijaneshu yuktatāḍana-jñānam*, " the art of handling offenders by suitable rebukes."

59. *Nānādeśīya-varṇānāṁ susamyak lekhane jñānam*, " proficiency in writing the alphabets of various countries."

The *Samavāya Sūtra* calls it *Leham* = Lekham, i.e. writing of various scripts. Eighteen such scripts are mentioned, such as Brāhmī, Yavanalipi, Kharoshṭhī, Pāhāri, Gandharvalipi, Maheśvarī, Drāviḍī.

Yaśodhara calls it *Lipijñānam.*

Rāmachandra uses the three terms *Deśabhāshāḥ, Lipijñānam*, and *Lipikarma*, which mean " knowledge of different languages and scripts ".

60. *Tāmbularakshādi kṛiti-vijñānam*, " the art of preparing tāmbula, i.e. betel-nuts, areca nuts, slaked lime, etc."

61. *Ādānam*, " power of comprehension of these *Kalās.*"

62. *Āśukāritvam*, " quickness of work."

63. *Pratidānam*, " imparting instruction in the *Kalās.*"

64. *Chirakriyā*, " slow or gradual work."

It will be seen that the lists of sixty-four *Kalās* as given in different texts do not agree in all particulars and also in the terms used for the *Kalās*. Some texts mention *Kalās* which are not known to other texts and are, therefore, important as showing the additional number of Arts and Crafts making up the economic and cultural life of the times and the diversity of occupations available in the country. Some of these have been indicated above and a few more are mentioned below.

The study of the Sciences and Humanities, the literary Art in general, are represented by the following subjects in the *Lalitavistara* :—

1. *Gaṇanā*. The *Samāvāya*. calls it *Gaṇitam*. It means Arithmetic.
2. *Saṁkhyā*, " the science of numbers."
3. *Veda*. *Kādambarī* uses the general term *Dharma-śāstra* for all these topics.
4. *Itihāsa*.
5. *Purāṇa*.
6. *Nirghanṭu*, Lexicon.
7. *Nirukta*, Etymology.
8. *Nigama*, Revealed Scripture.
9. *Śikshā*, Phonetics.
10. *Chhanda*, Metrics.
11. *Jyotisha*, Astronomy.

12. *Vyākaraṇa*, Grammar. *Kādambarī* calls it *Padam.*

13. *Yajña-Kalpa*, the Kalpa-Sūtras giving rules for conducting sacrifices.

14. *Sāṁkhya.*

15. *Yoga.*

16. *Vaiśeshika.*

17. *Veśika*, a system of philosophy.

18. *Bārhaspatya*, the philosophical system of Bṛihaspati, the Chārvāka or Lokāyata philosophy.

19. *Hetuvidyā*, Nyāya philosophy. *Kādambarī* uses the terms *Vākyam*, Logic, and *Pramāṇam, Pūrva-Mīmāṁsā.*

20. *Arthavidyā*, Economics. Yaśodhara calls it *Ājīva-jñānam.*

21. *Kāvya, Belles Lettres.*

22. *Grantha-rachitam*, the art of the writer or authorship.

23. *Ākhyātam*, the art of story-telling.

24. *Hāsyam*, the art of the Humorist.

To these Vātsyāyana adds the following subjects :—

25. *Abhidhāna-Kośa-Chhando-Vijñānam*, "knowledge of lexicons and metrics."

26. *Deśa-bhāshā-vijñānam*, "the science of language based on a study of the languages of different countries."

27. *Vainayikīnāṁ Vidyānāṁ Jñānam*, "the science of Education, Pedagogics."

28. *Mlechchhita-vikalpa*, the knowledge of languages other than Sanskrit. The *Samavāya-sūtra* uses the term *Jana-vācham* for a knowledge of the vernaculars; *Māgadhīyam*, proficiency in Māgadhi Prākṛit; and also *Paure-vācham*, urban, refined speech. This is equivalent to the term *Vachanaṁ Udāram* used by Yaśodhara, a sort of courtly speech. *Kādambarī* has the term *Sarva-deśa-bhāshāḥ*. All these terms show the specialized study in those days of Sanskrit and the Prākṛits, the literary and spoken tongues, and also non-Aryan (Mlechchha) languages.

29. *Āryā-prahelikā*, "proficiency in composition of verses in *āryā* metre and in the science of riddles."

30. *Śakunarūyam*, i.e. *Śakuna-vidyā*, "knowledge of the cries of birds." The *Lalitavistara* uses the wider term *Mṛiga-pakshī-rutam*, knowledge of cries of both birds and beasts. Rāmachandra uses the simple term *Śākunam* for this subject, the science of omens and portents.

Rāmachandra mentions the following additional subjects :—

31. *Sarvāni Apadānāni*, "all ancient chronicles."

32. *Sāmudrikam*, " palmistry."

33. *Vāksiddhi*, " the science of Yoga by which whatever is said will actually happen."

Kādambarī adds :—

34. *Graha-gaṇita*, " the science of Astronomy, Mathematics applied to the study of planets."

The *Samavāya-sūtra* describes Astronomy by the four terms *Chandra*-Lakshmaṇa, *Sūrya*-Lakshmaṇa, *Rāhu*-Lakshmaṇa, and *Graha*-Lakshmaṇa.

Yaśodhara mentions the Veterinary Sciences under the term :—

35. *Tiryakyoniḥ-chikitsā.*

Besides all these subjects representing the sciences and the literary art, culture, and religion, there are several additional technical arts and crafts mentioned in some of the texts.

The *Chemical* and *Pharmaceutical* Arts are mentioned by Rāmachandra as—

36. *Rasa-vāda*, treatment of mercury.

37. *Gandha-vāda*, treatment of sulphur.

38. *Dhātu-vāda*, Metallurgy.

The *Lalitavistara* mentions some arts of Architecture and Engineering such as—

39. *Nagara-niveśa*, Town-planning.

40. *Vāstu-niveśa*, the art of the architect who plans a building.

41. *Nagara-māṇam*, survey and measurement of cities.

42. *Skandhāvāra-māṇam*, measurement of camps.

Kādambarī adds :—

43. *Suraṅga-upabheda*, the construction of tunnels.

The *Lalita-vistara* mentions the art of dyeing as—

44. *Vastra-rāga* and

45. *Maṇi-rāga*, colouring of precious stones.

It also mentions :—

46. *Madhuchchhishṭakṛitam*, the craft of wax-modelling.

Vātsyāyana mentions the general military science as—

47. *Vaijayikīnāṁ vidyānāṁ jñānam*, the knowledge of the military arts by which victory is achieved.

It describes the athletic art as—

48. *Vyāyāmikīnāṁ vidyānām jñānam.*

To all these Rāmachandra adds some occult arts such as *Agni*-stambha, *Kharga*-stambha, *Jala*-stambha, *Vācha*-stambha, *Asi*-stambha, *Vāyu*-stambha, by which the innate properties of these substances are controlled or suspended. To these is also added the interesting art of *Vayastambha* by which ageing is arrested. There are also mentioned certain other arts or *siddhis* such as *Mantra-siddhi*, *Oushadha-siddhi*, *Maṇi-siddhi*, *Pādukā-siddhi*, *Mṛit-siddhi*, *Ghaṭikā-siddhi*, and *Vāk-siddhi*.

Arts and Crafts according to Pāli Texts. While these Sanskrit texts thus know of sixty-four and some additional *Kalās*, early Pāli texts, as will be seen below, mention the stock number of eighteen *Sippas* or Arts. But they do not state what the individual Arts were. The *Majjhima Nikāya* [i, p. 85; iv, pp. 281, 382] mentions some of these as Conveyancing or Law, Mathematics, Accountancy, Agriculture, Commerce, Cattle-breeding, and Administrative training. The *Milinda Pañha* [i, 6], gives a different list as follows: Holy Tradition and Secular Law; Sāṁkhya, Nyāya, Vaiśeshika; Arithmetic, Music, Medicine; four Vedas, Purāṇas, Itihāsas; Astronomy, Spells, Hetuvidyā, Magic; Military Art; Poetry; and Conveyancing, making up in all nineteen *Sippas*. The *Milinda* list was perhaps inspired by the Brahmanical list of eighteen Śāstras comprising four *Vedas*, six *Vedāṅgas*, four *Upāṅgas* consisting of Purāṇa, Nyāya, Mīmāṁsā, and Dharmaśāstra, and four *Upavedas* consisting of Āyurveda, Dhanurveda, Gāndharva-Veda, and Sthāpatya (architecture) or, according to some, Arthaśāstra [see *Vishṇu Purāṇa*, iii, 6, 28; and *Bhāgavata Puraṇa*]. The *Jātakas* differentiate, and that rightly, between religious and literary subjects like the *Vedas* or humanities, and the Śilpas proper indicating a craft or vocation based on practical skill. One Jātaka [vi, 427] mentions eighteen Crafts organized into guilds and mentions those of "masons, blacksmiths, carpenters, painters, men skilled in all arts and crafts".

Arts and Crafts in the time of Kauṭilya. In conclusion, it may be noted that considerable information regarding the arts and crafts of ancient India is furnished by a work of admitted antiquity, the *Arthaśastra* of Kauṭilya, which is undoubtedly based upon the material and data of the time of the Maurya emperor, Chandragupta (*c.* 323–299 B.C.). The *Arthaśāstra* gives an account of the work of the Heads (*Adhyakshas*) of various Departments of Industry, each of which was in charge of a particular industry, craft, or trade. The organization of so many Departments of Administration proves the progress of the many Arts and Crafts calling for a centralized control.

First, there was the Superintendent of Treasury (*Kośādhyaksha*) who dealt with the *Kalā* called *Ratna-parīkshā*. He controlled the business in pearls of all kinds, derived from oyster-shells, conch-shells, and the like, and the different kinds of gems and diamonds whose sources in those days are also indicated.

There are descriptions of trade in sandal-wood and other scented woods; of business in hides, skins, and leather; of woollen industry producing blankets of different kinds from the wool derived from different animals, sheep as well as wild animals; of different kinds of manufacture of textiles and other fabrics such as *dukūla* (fine) or *kshauma* (coarse), *kauśeya* (silk), or Chīnapaṭṭa (Chinese).

Weaving was a national industry controlled by the Officer called *Sūtrādhyaksha* who employed qualified labourers to manufacture yarns (*sūtra*), shirting (*varma*), clothing (*vastra*), and ropes. Women labour, the labour of widows, crippled women, ascetic women, and *Devadāsīs* who were no longer employed in temples, was specially employed to cut wool, fibre, cotton, hemp, and flax. Wages were paid according to quantity and quality of output.

Metallurgical industries were controlled by the Department of Mines under its Chief called *Ākarādhyaksha*. He must be proficient in *Śulbadhātuśāstra*, the science dealing with copper and other minerals; in the art of distillation and condensation of mercury and of testing gems (*Rasapāka-maṇirāgajña*). He should be assisted by a staff of experts in mineralogy, mining labourers, and equipped with necessary apparatus (*upakaraṇa-sampanna*). Mining operations are described, including chemical processes for extracting the metal out of ores by removing their impurities. Mining was a monopoly of the State, as also trade in metallic goods. No one could engage in Mining without a licence. Theft of mineral products was severely punished. Mines which produced minerals used in making utensils of general use, as also mines which required a large capital for their working were leased out to private parties who paid a fixed rent and a share in the profits (*bhāgena prakrayeṇa vā*). But Government reserved to itself the working of Mines which did not require much outlay.

There was also the Superintendent of Metals (*Lohādhyaksha*) who dealt with the manufacture of copper, lead, tin, mercury, brass, bronze or bell-metal, sulphurate of arsenic, and the like.

There was the Superintendent of Ocean-mines whose duty

was to collect revenue from pearls, corals, shells, diamonds, precious stones, and salts.

A special Salt Department dealt with the lessees of Salt-fields who had to pay, besides rent, a sixth of the salt manufactured by them. This portion was again sold to profit by the Salt Superintendent by realizing 8 per cent and 5 per cent as super-tax. Government, however, allowed students, ascetics, and labourers free salt for their food.

The *Arthaśāstra* also speaks of the Superintendent of Gold and Silver, the description of whose duties shows the extent to which the industries connected with the precious metals were developed in those days.

There was also a Director of Agriculture (*Sītādhyaksha*) to deal with the different branches of that industry.

Texts giving lists of *Kalās* make much of gambling. The practice of gambling called for State-control and, accordingly, we find Kauṭilya speaking of a Superintendent (*Dyutādhyaksha*) who supervised the gambling-halls which had to be licensed and hired.

There was a Director of Navigation (*Nāvadhyaksha*) whose Department controlled all traffic and transport by water, policed the rivers and sea-shore, supplied government boats, and collected all tolls levied at ferries, customs, and other charges at harbours, cess on river-side and sea-side villages, and one-sixth of the proceeds from all fisheries.

Thus, on the whole, the picture of economic life and progress given in the lists of sixty-four and more *Kalās* is seen in its proper setting in the important early work of Kauṭilya, showing how the control of the State was called for and had to be exercised through so many Departments of Administration, each of which was to deal with the interests of a particular industry separately. Thus Kauṭilya figures as an early authority on the subject of *Kalās*, or Arts and Crafts.

Chapter XII

SOME TYPICAL EDUCATIONAL INSTITUTIONS AND CENTRES

Ancient Indian Education Individual and not Collective. We have seen that the vital principle of Ancient Indian Education was that of individual and intimate relationship between pupils and their teachers as members of the same family, living in a common home, the home of the teacher functioning as the school in those days. Such a principle did not favour the growth of large educational institutions which, ignoring the vital differences between individuals, teach them collectively by "classes", and aim at mass-production in education. But education is a delicate biological process, a process of mental and moral growth which cannot be achieved by mechanical processes, the external apparatus and machinery of an organization. As in education, so in a more marked degree in the sphere of religion and spiritual life, India did not believe in the external and mechanical methods of organization and did not develop any ecclesiastical institutions like the churches. The interests of religious life and spiritual growth were not handed over to any institutions and their regimented life of routine, but were left to be dealt with between the guru and his pupil in their personal relationship from which the whole world was excluded. A man's inner religious life was thus treated as his supremely individual concern in which the collective life of the community should have no part. Spiritual growth, as we have seen, depends on one fundamental factor described as *Chitta-vṛitti-nirodha* and, therefore, all avenues of influences from the external world which might disturb or distract the mind should be closed, so that spiritual life may grow freely in the atmosphere of inner peace and quiet.

It was not Mechanized, as in large Educational Organizations. And yet Ancient India was not lacking in religious institutions like temples and *Maṭhas* and *Tīrthas*, or places of pilgrimage where crowds gather in the interests of religious life. That is because the external aspect or element of these organizations does not supersede or interfere with the inner religious life of the individuals they bring together. Hinduism does not believe in congregational worship. There is solitude in a crowd. The press of pilgrims in a crowded temple on a sacred day of festival leaves every individual pilgrim to himself, to say his personal prayers by himself, in his own way, and in secret and private. There is an inspiring tradition that at the temple of Jagannath at Puri, which is notorious for its daily crowds of worshipping pilgrims, Lord Chaitanya was free to take to a solitary corner of the temple, at some distance from the image of the deity Jagannath, where he was always seen in the trance of meditation on the deity.

It will thus appear that the emergence of temples and *Maṭhas* in Ancient India was not inconsistent with its religious principles and ideas which banned organization, in the Western sense, in the sphere of learning and religion, for fear lest even they, too, be " mechanized ". Mechanization is fatal to learning and spirituality where the mind and soul should be left free to grow in the natural way like living organisms.

Examples of Organization in Education : Vedic Saṁghas, Parishads, Charakas, Maṭhas. The beginnings of collectivism or of organization in education may be traced to the earliest Vedic times. As we have seen, even the Rigveda has several significant references to the *Saṁghas* or Assemblies of learned men meeting for those fateful and formative discussions which hammered into shape both the language and philosophy of the Vedas. The Upanishads tell of regular learned Conferences meeting at the courts of Kings by royal invitation and companies of *Chārakas* or wandering scholars touring the country in quest of higher knowledge, its centres and exponents. Then there were also stabilized institutions, the Academies of Science, like the Pāñchāla Parishat, which produced some of India's highest philosophy. Later came Jainism and Buddhism with their emphasis upon the system of organized brotherhoods accommodated in the rock-cut halls, *vihāras* and monasteries. The Brahminical system followed suit with similar institutions like *Maṭhas* and regular colleges, as we know them now.

Colleges endowed by Temple Charities in the South. Of these latter-day institutions, we shall give an account on the basis of their most important and typical examples. The records of these are to be found more in the south and in inscriptions from the tenth century onwards.

Salotgi. Nārāyaṇa, a minister of the Rāshṭrakūṭa emperor

Krishṇa III, founded a temple of the Trayī-Purusha, the hall of which accommodated a Sanskrit College. In course of time, the College had to build as many as twenty-seven Hostels for residence of its students who hailed from different provinces (*nānājanapadodbhavāḥ*). The expense of lights for the hostels was met from a special endowment of twelve Nivartanas (probably = 60 acres of land), while another endowment of 500 Nivartanas paid for the expenses of boarding for at least 200 students. The Principal of the College was maintained by the income of another endowment of fifty Nivartanas. The village where the College was situated, Salotgi, in Bijapur District, also supported the College by an arrangement that each villager should contribute to its funds 5 coins at each marriage, 2½ coins at each Upanayana, and 1¼ coin at each Chūḍākaraṇa ceremony to be performed by him, while at every social feast he was to invite its students and teachers [*Epi. Indica*, iv, 60].

Ennāyiram : Its 340 Students, 10 Teachers, and 300 Acres of Land. An inscription of the time of emperor Rajendra Chola I (of *c.* 1023 A.D.) [No. 333 of 1917] records the endowment made by a village of certain charities which included the establishment of a Vedic College at Ennāyiram in South Arcot District, providing for the free board and tuition of 340 students, distributed as follows among the different subjects of study: 75 for Rigveda, 75 for Yajur-Veda, 20 for Chhāndoga-Sāman, 20 for Talavakāra-sāman, 20 for Vājasaneya, 10 for Atharva-Veda, 10 for the Baudhāyanīya Gṛihya, Kalpa, and Gaṇa, 40 for Rūpavatāra, 25 for Vyākaraṇa, 35 for Prābhākara Mīmāṁsā, and 10 for Vedānta. The College was manned by ten Teachers, three for each of the two Vedas taught, two for Mīmāṁsā, and one for each of the other subjects.

Cost of Student's Boarding. The College was maintained by an endowment of 45 *Velis* (= about 300 acres) of land. Each student of Veda cost 6 Nālis (= ¾ Karuṇi) of paddy per day and ½ kalanju of gold (= 25 grains = Rs. 2/-) per year, to meet probably the cost of his clothing. A student of the more advanced subjects like Mīmāṁsā, Vedānta, and Vyākaraṇa, was given 66 per cent additional allowance.

Salaries of Teachers. A teacher got the daily allowance of 1 kalam (= 12 karuṇi) of paddy, while the cost of a daily meal was ¾ karuṇi. Thus he was given the cost of food for sixteen persons per day. He was also given a bonus of ½ kalanju of gold per year.

The Vedānta teacher got an additional allowance of 25 per cent.

The teacher of *Vyākaraṇa* was paid at 1 kalanju of gold per *adhyāya* of the *Ashṭādhyāyī* taught.

Another College of 340 Students. Inscription No. 343 of 1917 refers to the hostel attached to the temple where were daily fed 506 learned Brahmans, including the 340 College students, and also to provision made by the village for the daily supply of firewood for the hostel, while all surpluses of ghee, milk, and curds left after worship were made over to the hostel by the Temple authorities.

A College owning three Villages. Five inscriptions on copper plates of the Pallava king, Vijayanṛipatuṅga-varman [*Epi. Ind.*, iv] record the gift of three villages to support a College, " like the Gaṅgā, supported by Śiva on his matted locks." The College taught fourteen *Gaṇas*, comprising 4 Vedas, 6 Vedāṅgas, 1 Mīmāṁsā, 1 Nyāya, 1 Purāṇa, and 1 Dharmaśāstra.

A College with 190 Students and 12 Teachers for its Veda and 7 for Śāstra Departments. Inscription No. 176 of 1919 (of *c.* 1048 A.D.) records the endowment of another residential Sanskrit College which had a staff of 12 Teachers, 3 for Rigveda, 3 for Yajurveda, and 1 for other subjects each, such as Chhāndogya-Sāman, Talavakāra-Sāman, Apūrva, Vājasaneya, Bodhāyanīya, and Satyāshṭa (āḍha)-Sūtra. The College had a separate Department of Śāstra with a staff of seven Teachers to teach the seven subjects, Vedānta, Vyākaraṇa, Rupāvatāra, Śrī-Bhārata, Rāmāyaṇa, Manu-Śāstra, and Vaikhānasa-Śāstra.

As regards students, 60 studied Rigveda, 60 Yajurveda, 20 Chhāndogya-Sāman, and 50 other Sāstras together, totalling 190 students.

A School of Grammar at Tiruvorraiyūr. Inscription No. 202 of 1912 records the endowment of 60 Velis of land (= about 410 acres) for the construction of a separate Hall called *Vyākaraṇa-dānavyākhyāna-maṇḍapa* for the teaching of Pāṇini's grammar and worship of God Vyākaraṇadāna-Perumāl (Śiva) in the Temple at Tiruvorraiyūr. This School of Grammar was supported by further gifts recorded in Inscriptions Nos. 110 of 1912, 201 of 1912, 120 of 1912.

A College with a Hostel and Hospital. Inscription No. 182 of 1915 of A.D. 1062 records the gift of a Vaiśya establishing (1) a college for teaching the Vedas, Śāstras, Rūpāvatāra (perhaps a grammatical work), (2) a Hostel for its students, and (3) a

Hospital. The students were given free food and lights. The Hospital called *Vīra-śolan* (= Vīra-Chola) had fifteen beds and a staff of one physician, one surgeon, two servants for fetching drugs, fuel, and for other work for the Hospital, two maidservants to serve as nurses, and one general servant for the whole establishment. The Hospital was also equipped with a store of medicines, such as *Harītaki* of different kinds, *Bilvādighṛita*, *Vajra-kalpa*, *Kalyāṇalavaṇa*, and varieties of *taila* or oils.

A few other similar Institutions, and Teachers' Salaries. Inscription No. 259 of 1905 (of c. A.D. 1122) records the munificent gift of forty-four villages to a Temple for the purpose of giving food and clothing to Vedic students, religious teachers, and ascetics.

The Inscription on a Pillar at Malkāpuram in the Guntur taluk records an endowment establishing a number of institutions, a temple, a monastery, a feeding-house, colonies of Brahmins, schools of students of Śaiva Purāṇas, and a Maternity Home and a Hospital. The Staff of all these institutions included (*a*) three teachers for teaching the three Vedas, (*b*) five for teaching Logic, Literature, and the Āgamas, (*c*) one Doctor, (*d*) one Accountant (Kāyastha), (*e*) six Brāhmaṇa servants for the *Maṭha* and feeding-house, (*f*) Village-guards, called *Vīra-bhadras*, (*g*) Village Craftsmen called *Vīra-mushṭis*, to work as goldsmith, coppersmith, mason, bamboo-worker, blacksmith, potter, architect, carpenter, barber, and artisan. In the feeding-house were fed at all hours men of all castes from Brāhmaṇa to Chaṇḍāla—a remarkable instance of Śaiva catholicity.

Each teacher was granted for his maintenance two *puṭṭis*, while a carpenter or a drummer in the service of the Temple got as his wages one *puṭṭi* of land. The Principal was paid a salary of 100 *nishkas*, of which the value is not known.

A similar triple institution comprising a college, a hostel, and a hospital, is also recorded in an Inscription of A.D. 1068 [*Epi. Ind.*, xxi ; No. 185 of South Indian Epigraphy Report for 1915]. The College had an arrangement for free board and lodging for sixty students, of whom ten were admitted to Rigveda class, ten to Yajurveda, twenty to Grammar, ten to Pañcharātra philosophy class, three to Śivāgama class, while seven seats of the Hostel were reserved for Vānaprasthas and Sannyāsins.

Vedic teachers were paid sixty *kalams* of paddy and four *kāsus* of gold in the year (about a sixth of the salary paid at the Ennāyiram college, as stated above). The teacher of Grammar was paid double that salary, 120 ***kalams*** of paddy and 10 ***kāsus*** of gold (equal in value to 35 ***kalams*** of paddy). But even this salary was only half of that paid at the other college to the teacher of Grammar. A menial in Temple service got a salary of sixty ***kalams*** of paddy with two ***kāsus*** of gold in the year. Thus teachers' salaries were not the same in all institutions.

Learned Settlements. The cause of learning and culture was not confined, however, to these Schools or Colleges. It was recognized that learning should be a life-long pursuit and could not be confined within the limits of study which a College could undertake within the time fixed for it. Accordingly, we find public benefactions establishing not merely the purely educational institutions where the foundations of learning are laid but institutions of a wider scope, serving as centres of post-graduate, advanced study under savants devoting themselves completely to the pursuit of knowledge for its own sake. These endowments of higher learning and research sought to establish entire learned settlements or cultured colonies, made up of households of pious and scholarly Brahmans, in select areas. Inscription No. 99 of vol. ii, part v of *South Indian Inscriptions* records the gift of a whole village for supporting 308 learned Brahmans in their sacred avocation of research and teaching, who were chosen as masters of the Vedas and Smṛitis and known as "Chaturvedin, Trivedin, Somayājin, Shaḍaṅgavid, Bhaṭṭa, Kramavid (proficient in the *Krama-pāṭha* of Rigveda), Sarvakratuyājin, Vājapeyin, etc". They were thus masters of both the texts or tenets and practices of Dharma and could promote learning and religion together. Inscription No. 7 of 1912 records another similar gift establishing a colony of 308 Brahmans. Inscription No. 277 of 1913 records an endowment establishing a group of 108 learned Brahman families with provision for all the necessaries of life, including a library called *Sarasvatī Bhāṇḍāra.* These learned settlements were centres of light and life, showing how theory and practice should go together, how precept should be supported by example, ethics by conduct, learning was to be lived, and truth or religion was to be realized in the activities of daily life. The cause of learning was thus very well served by these endowments supporting advanced scholars in a life of research and religion and pursuit of Truth for its own sake, to the exclusion of all other pursuits.

Sometimes, advantage was taken of these learned settlements or *Sabhās* to judge of literary works of authors, as stated in Inscription No. 198 of 1919. The Sabhā met under a royal order and heard the work of a poet recited. On its verdict, the poet was granted land as reward of his merits. It was a relic of the old and famous *Saṅgams* which judged of the works of Tamil poets and upheld the standard of Tamil Literature.

Noted centres of Education in Mysore. Some of the Mysore Inscriptions show how the Province was abounding in such wider cultural institutions which were known in three distinct varieties called *Ghatikā*, *Agrahāra*, and *Brahmapurī*. Sk. 176 (of *Epigraphica Carnatica*, vol. vii) tells of a pupil who, wishing to be a master of *Pravachana*, went to Kāñchī, visited each of its *Ghaṭikās* for instruction, and became a quick and accomplished debater. Thus a *Ghaṭikā* was a centre of learning and religion and small in size.

An *Agrahāra* was a wider institution, a whole settlement of learned Brahmans, with its own powers of government and means of maintenance granted by generous donors founding them. The Agrahāra was governed by its *Sabha*, some of whose proceedings are recorded in inscriptions [ib., vol. ix, pp. 127–132].

Belgame. An important centre of education in Ancient Mysore was Belgame, the capital of the Banavase 12,000 province (the figure indicating the revenue fixed for it), which contained three *Puras*, five original *Maṭhas*, seven *Brahmapurīs*, scores of *Agrahāras*, Temples, Jain and Buddhist *Bastis* and *Vihāras*. The evolution of this place as a centre of culture is recorded in inscriptions. An early Sātavāhana grant of the first or second century A.D. laid its beginnings in a Brahman settlement [Sk. 263]. A Kadamba king of the third century imported from the north thirty-two Brahman families and settled them in the Agrahāra of Talgunda, near Belgame. Sk. 177, 178, 185 tell of the growth of the Agrahāra, owning as many as 144 villages, the gift of the Kadama King Mayūravarman. Sk. 14–18 refer to grants made to 1,300 Brahmans of Begur in northern Edenad 70 of Banavase 12,000.

The Inscriptions describe the subjects of study to comprise "the four Vedas with their Aṅgas and Upāṅgas; Mīmāṁsā, Lokāyata, Bauddha, Sāṁkhya, Vaiśeshika, and other Śāstras and Āgamas; eighteen Smṛitis, Purāṇas, Kāvyas, and Nāṭakas. Sk. 92 and 96 describe how learned was the Head of the Kodiya Maṭha at Belgami, named Vāmāśakti. He was a Pāṇini in Grammar, Bharata in Drama and Music, Subandhu or Māgha in Poetry, and Nakulīśvara in Siddhānta.

DHĀRĀ (MALWA): Stone Image of *Vāgdevī*, "Goddess of Learning"

[*Facing p. 373*

Sl. 277 of A.D. 1158 testifies to the existence of three Medical Dispensaries at Belgame. Sk. 102 describes how the Kodiya Maṭha of the same place was resorted to by destitute and diseased persons for medical treatment.

Maṭhas. Without multiplying further evidence, what is adduced is sufficient to show how the interests of education and learning were served by a variety of institutions supported by religious endowments The Colleges proper sprang up as annexes of the Temples, while their work received a wider scope in a more extended sphere in institutions like the Maṭhas and settlements of learned men functioning like the Academies of science of modern times. The *Maṭhas* specially are indigenous Indian examples of educational organization by which different and distant centres of culture and religious life, religious brotherhoods of different localities, are affiliated to a central and common seat of authority at headquarters and regulated and controlled by it. The best example of this federal type of educational and religious organization is furnished by the Golaki Maṭha, of which accounts are given in a series of inscriptions of the Kurnool district of the thirteenth century A.D., showing how this particular Maṭha grew up and exercised its spiritual influence and direction over as many as 3 lacs of villages under a succession of its famous chiefs and teachers. The religious life and culture of the Tamil country were very largely influenced by numerous Śaiva Maṭhas which acquired great power and popularity under the Chola kings. The Maṭhas of Śivayogins or Māheśvaras were also great cultural influences in those days [Nos. 164, 177, 402, and 583 of 1908], while No. 465 of 1909 testifies to a similar Vaishṇava Maṭha constituted by learned Brahmans from eighteen Vaishṇava countries.

A College at Dhārā. King Bhoja of Malwa (A.D. 1018–60), a patron of learning, founded at his capital, Dhārā, a college appropriately located in a Temple of '*Vāgdevī*', 'Goddess of Learning', whose image in stone is a masterpiece of Brahmanical sculpture [Plate XVI]. The inscription on its pedestal mentions the king called 'Bhoja-Narendra-Chandra', the sculptor 'Manthala, son of Sūtradhara (craftsman), Sahira', 'the writer, Śivadeva', and the date, 'Saṁvat 1091' = A.D. 1034. The Image shows to its right the figures of a bearded Ṛishi, his disciple, the donor, and, to the left, the Mother of Vāgdevī, Durgā on lion [*Rūpam*, January, 1924].

PART II

BUDDHIST EDUCATION

CHAPTER XIII

THE BACKGROUND

Buddhism as a phase of Hinduism. We shall now trace the history and describe the essential features of what may be called Buddhist Education which, rightly regarded, is, however, but a phase of the ancient Hindu or Brahminical system of education as described in the previous chapters. Buddhism itself, especially in its original and ancient form, is, as has been admitted on all hands, rooted deeply in the pre-existing Hindu systems of thought and life. " To my mind," said Max Müller [*Chips from a German Workshop*, i, 434], "having approached Buddhism after a study of the ancient religion of India, the religion of the Veda, Buddhism has always seemed to be, not a new religion, but a natural development of the Indian mind in its various manifestations, religious, philosophical, social, and political." Barth [*The Religions of India*, p. 101] calls Buddhism " a Hindu phenomenon, a natural product, so to speak, of the age and social circle that witnessed its birth ", and " when we attempt to reconstruct its primitive doctrine and early history we come upon something so akin to what we meet in the most ancient Upanishads and in the legends of Brahminism that it is not always easy to determine what features belong peculiarly to it ". Rhys Davids [*Buddhism*, p. 34] calls Gautama Buddha " the creature of his time ", of whose philosophy it must not be supposed that " it was entirely of his own creation ". Hopkins goes so far as to assert [*Religions of India*, p. 298] that " the founder of Buddhism did not strike out a new system of morals ; he was not a democrat ; he did not originate a plot to overthrow the Brahmanic priesthood ; he did not invent the order of monks ".

Doctrines common to both : those of Ātman, Sorrow, Deliverance, Desire, Karma, Rebirth. Oldenberg [*Buddha*, Introduction] has well shown how " for hundreds of years before

Buddha's time movements were in progress in Indian thought which prepared the way for Buddhism" (p. 6). Hindu thought, turning aside from the very outset from life and its realities, addressed itself to the world of spirit which it peopled with divinities symbolizing the different forces or phenomena of nature to be worshipped through sacrifice. There thus grows up a religion of sacrifice with an elaborate symbolism and literature, but the irresistible quest of the substance soon leads to a search for Unity in all diversity, outgrowing the oldest Vedic thought. Thus arose gradually the conceptions of the Prajāpati, of the Ātman and Brahma, wherein "the yearning spirit, wearied of wandering in a world of gloomy, formless phantasms, finds its rest" (p. 30). But "the glorification of the Ātman becomes involuntarily an ever increasingly bitter criticism of this world" (p. 42). "When thought, liberal to itself, had laden the idea of the Ātman with all attributes of every perfection, of absolute unity, of unlimited fulness, the world of plurality, measured by the standard of the everlasting One, must have necessarily appeared a state of disruption, restriction, and pain" (ib.). Yājñavalkya declares in the Upanishads: "Whatever is beside Him is full of sorrow"; "as the sun, the eye of the Universe, remains far off and unaffected by all sickness that meets the (human) eye, so also the One, the Ātman, who dwells in all creatures, dwells afar and untouched by the sorrows of the world" (p. 43). Here, for the first time, is delivered that message of sorrow or pessimism which forms the common and abiding note in the manifold expressions and systems of Indian thought through the ages. A natural transition from this philosophy of Pessimism leads to the conceptions of Metempsychosis and to their concomitants and antidotes, the doctrines of Deliverance, a message of Hope against the other message of Despair, the formulation of the ways of escape from the appalling fatality of "the endless migration from world to world, from existence to existence, the endlessness of the struggle against the pallid power of that ever-recurring destruction" (p. 45). The older Vedic conceptions of Deliverance comprised "the use of the right words and the right offerings" (p. 44), and, later, with the rise of the Upanishadic speculations regarding the Ātman, the attainment of "the unity of the soul with its true mode of being, the Brahma", while, as a natural counterpart of this doctrine, "the wandering of the soul through the domains of death" was regarded as "the fruit of its non-union with the Brahma"

(p. 47) caused by Desire or attachment to the world of plurality. Thus by a natural process is evolved the great doctrine of Karma "as the power which predetermines the course of the migration of the soul from one state of being to another". Deliverance accordingly comes to mean cessation of Karma through extinction of *Kāma* or through extinction of that Ignorance which is the root of all *Kāma* or Desire, and hence through the attainment of the saving knowledge accomplishing the return from plurality to the One. The different schools of Indian thought arise from the different definitions they give of this highest knowledge or Truth, the different solutions they propose of the problem of existence which is held in common to be an unmixed evil. There is thus a common *Indian* view of life to which all sects or systems of thought including Buddhism subscribe.

Buddhist Scheme of Life as influenced by Brahmanical. We are not, however, concerned with the doctrines of Buddhism, the answer that Buddhism has sought to give to the question which all other schools of Indian thought try to answer in their own several ways, the question, How is release to be achieved from the endless course of births and rebirths to which life is liable? We are concerned rather with those external practices of Buddhism by means of which it developed its social and educational organization for the advancement and diffusion of its particular truths, the ideals of thought and life for which it stood. Philosophy or Religion, especially in India, has been always lived, and not merely contemplated, and so it has always developed its outer side in strict accordance with the inner. The two developments must always run parallel to each other in vital harmony. Thus it is that as in the old Brahminical speculations we see the sources of the dogmatics of Buddhism, so in the Brahminical scheme and ordering of life or social organization was largely laid the foundation of the Buddhist Community and Church. Far from discarding and denouncing the Brahmanic ideal of life, "Buddhism achieved, in one sense, the full realization of this Brahmanic ideal" [Max Müller, ib., i, 438]. "Buddhist society, as we know it from the sacred writings of the Buddhists, is far more the fulfilment than the denial of the ancient schemes and dreams of the Brahmanic lawgivers" [ib., p. 437].

Indeed, the entire organization of the Buddhist Church or Community may be deemed to have been based upon the following re-statements or modifications of the older Vedic or Brahminical religion, as pointed out by Max Müller (ib., p. 440):

"If sacrifices, particularly those which involve the killing of animals and extravagant expenditure, are not only useless but mischievous, Buddha said, 'Let them be forbidden.'

"If the Vedas have no claim to a revealed character, let them be treated like any other book, but do nót waste your whole youth in learning them by heart.

"If the Vedic gods are mere figures and names, let us look for something which is more than figure and name.

"If penances, particularly those excessive penances of the dwellers in the forest, benefit neither the spirit nor the flesh but produce only bodily decrepitude and spiritual pride, let them be abolished, or at all events rendered less severe.

"Lastly, if he who leaves home, and wife, and children, or who never knew what a home was, is nearer to heaven than the best of householders, let all who can, leave their homes as soon as possible and become 'homeless', the very name which Buddha gave to the members of his fraternity."

We have already indicated how some of these doubts and questionings raised by Buddhism have been anticipated in the later Vedic or Upanishadic speculations, but what was in a sense implicit or not fully expressed in them has been rendered more explicit and given full utterance to by Buddhism which has thus selected and emphasized some special points in the older religion and ignored others.

Monachism not a monopoly of Buddhism. Thus Monachism was not the exclusive characteristic of Buddhism or its special contribution to Indian religious life. Different forms of religious, ascetic and monastic life had already grown up in close conformity to the speculations regarding the Universal One and deliverance referred to above. The Doctrine of the Ātman dominating the entire range of Indian thought produced a scheme of life under which "män must live as though he lived not", divesting himself of all earthly ties in a thoroughgoing spirit of a world-disclaiming abstraction. The great Upanishadic utterance rang through the country as a summons to self-sacrifice at the altar of Truth: "The intelligent and wise desire not posterity: what are descendants to us, whose home is the Ātman? They relinquish the desire for children, the struggle for wealth, the pursuit of worldly weal, and go forth as mendicants."

Its Brahminical Forms. The Brahmanical order of life provided for a progressive realization of this idea of renunciation through the discipline of the four Āśramas, of which only the last two directly lead up to it. Even the *Vānaprastha*, the man in the third Āśrama of life, does not wander about absolutely homeless but would have a fixed place of abode in the forest where his wife would follow him as well as their sacred fire, and a part of their old household duties in connection with sacrifice would still be performed. It is, however, to be noted that exceptions to these general rules were also quite common, though these exceptions became the rule with the Buddhist Order or Community. Thus we read of householders at once passing on to the life of hermits, dissolving all earthly ties without undergoing the penances of the third Āśrama. Similarly, a *Brahmachārī* electing perpetual pupilage without marrying and entering upon the householder's state was a very usual phenomenon and a regular institution was made of it with special rules for its governance. This institution was adopted, as we shall see, as the starting-point of the Buddhist religious organization. There are other features in the old Vedic monasticism which are borrowed by Buddhist though it is not so apparent. In the first place, the right to renunciation did not belong exclusively to the Brahman caste alone. We have already seen how the observance of the rule regarding the division of life into four Āśramas or stages was binding upon all the three twice-born classes which made up a large proportion of the total Indian population. We may also recall scenes depicted in the Upanishads of learned disputations at the courts of kings in which scholars of different classes and castes participate equally—the Brahmans equally with the princes and Kshatriyas and even women. Nay, the kings are represented as the enthusiastic and active organizers of these philosophical Congresses and Conferences. And, indeed, if the right to listen to the discourses on deliverance be conceded to all, why should the right to seek the means of that deliverance in a life of renunciation be denied to them ? No one, by reason of his caste or social position, was debarred from the citizenship of the kingdom of the spirit, from the sacred, inviolable right or birthright to renounce home, wife, and child, goods and chattels and embrace, as a mendicant monk, a life of poverty and purity in pursuit of the highest end of existence. Princes and peasants equally with Brahmans had the right " to those spiritual treasures to obtain which men parted with all earthly treasure ".

The second feature of this Vedic monasticism seems to have been that these seekers after truth organized themselves as close corporations and treated the knowledge and the doctrines they developed as something fit for the few and the elect, or the specially qualified, and not meant for the masses or to penetrate the national life. " The father might impart the secret to his son, and the teacher to his pupil, but, in the circle of the believers in the Ātman, there was wholly wanting that warm-hearted enthusiasm which holds that it then, and then only, properly enjoys the possession of its own goods, when it has summoned all the world to participate in their possession " [Oldenberg, op. cit., p. 63]. The Upanishads, in the literal sense of the term, signify a body of select and secret doctrines and their esoteric character marks them out sharply from Buddhism. The strongly democratic spirit of the Buddha and his teachings and his overmastering solicitude for the amelioration of the masses receive their culminating expression in the following saying attributed to him : " I shall not enter Nirvāṇa until the life of holiness [1] which I point out has been successful, grown in favour, and entended among all mankind, and is in vogue and thoroughly made known to all men." In the story, this declaration or decision has not been reached by the Buddha without a struggle. For a time he is possessed by the Upanishadic spirit of treating truth he had attained as a select and secret doctrine too high for others and thus to be confined only to himself. The *Mahāvagga* thus recounts the story [i, 5, 2, etc.] : " Into the mind of the Exalted One, while he tarried, retired in solitude, came this thought : ' I have penetrated this deep truth, which is difficult to perceive, and difficult to understand, peace-giving, sublime, which transcends all thought, deeply-significant, which only the wise can grasp. Man moves in an earthly sphere, in an earthly sphere he has his place and finds his enjoyment. For him it will

[1] It should be observed that it is " the life of holiness " which Buddhism emphasizes much more than the philosophy of life, speculations concerning the mysteries of life and death and such ultimate truths. It is no wonder that on account of its eminently popular character impressed upon Buddhist thought the whole world could be summoned to participate in its truths, while Brahmanism as represented in the Upanishads and Āraṇyakas leads to levels and reaches of thought where only the select few under special training in abstraction can follow. The intellectual strength of Brahmanical speculation which accounts for its exclusive and esoteric character should not be the ground for ascribing to it a moral weakness, a deficiency in sympathy. The Buddha himself is said to have declared as his last words [*Dīgh. Nik.*, ii, 100] : " What, then, Ānanda ? Does the Order expect that of me ? I have preached the Truth without making any distinction between exoteric and esoteric doctrine ; for in respect of the truths, Ānanda, the Tathāgata has no such thing as the closed fist of a teacher who keeps something back." Against this is to be considered the fact that the doctrines of the Upanishads were investigated by select circles of inquirers in the solitude of the woods (as Āraṇyakas) where no distraction was likely to intervene between Truth and its seeker.

be difficult to grasp this matter, the law of causality, the chain of causes and effects, the extinction of all conformations; the withdrawal from all that is earthly, the extinction of desire, the cessation of longing, the end, the Nirvāṇa. And so—

> "'Why reveal to the world what I have won by a severe struggle?
>
> "'The truth remains hidden from him who desire and hate absorb.
>
> "'It is difficult, mysterious, deep, hidden from the coarse mind;
>
> "'He cannot apprehend it, whose mind earthly vocations surround with night.

"'When the Exalted One thought thus, his heart was inclined to abide in quietude and not to proclaim the Doctrine,' whereupon Mahābrahmā, exclaiming, 'Alas! the world is lost and undone,' hastens to the Buddha and besought Him to preach the Doctrine. The prayer was granted by the Buddha in the following words:

> "'Let opened be to all the door of eternity;
>
> "'He who hath ears, let him hear the word and believe.
>
> "'I thought of affliction for myself, therefore have I, O Brahmā,
>
> Not yet proclaimed the noble word to the world.'"

It may be noted in this connection that this spirit of the Buddha suggested one of the essential doctrines of *Mahāyāna* Buddhism as embodied in the ideal of the Bodhisattva who, in contrast with the Śrāvaka (Arahat) and Pachcheka-Buddha (or private Buddha), following the Buddha for the sake of their own complete Nirvāṇa, is distinguished by his determination not to accept the final release "for the sake of the complete *Nirvāṇa* of all beings".

The third noticeable feature in these pre-Buddhistic religious conditions was that not merely was there a constant stream of recruits swelling the ranks of ascetics, monks, and hermits in the country under the operation of the laws of Āśramas throwing people out of home into homelessness, but these were also being organized into fraternities developing their own systems of doctrine and discipline in different degrees of independence of the authority of Vedic ritualism. Long before the age of the Buddha there arose these monastic orders with the external forms and technique of their religious life fully developed and fixed, for to the religious consciousness of the times the monastic life appeared to offer the best and surest means of attaining their ends to those associated in a common quest of salvation. The most luxuriant growth of these religious fraternities was in the congenial and fruitful soil offered by the eastern parts of the Gangetic valley at a distance from the home and headquarters of conservative Brahmanism. The seat of the Vedic cult was, as has been already pointed out, towards the western parts where the Vedic Aryans first settled themselves in the 'holy land' proper, from which Manu [ix, 225] would expel all heretics. From that centre Vedism in its progress towards the east lost much of its pristine purity, rigid orthodoxy, and formalism, in its assimilation of the foreign elements in a new environment. Parts of the *Śatapatha Brāhmaṇa* and some of the Upanishads belonging to these eastern tracts introduce us (as we have already seen) to the moving scenes of lively learned debates at the courts of kings of Kāśī, Kosala, and Videha, where Brahmans contend on equal terms for intellectual supremacy with Kshatriyas and even women to whom orthodoxy would assign the status of the Sūdra in respect of admission to sacred science. But they also show us that the Brahmans themselves permitted, encouraged, and participated in these philosophical controversies which are the true forerunners of the later heresies. From a philosophical standpoint, Jainism or Buddhism has hardly any ground for a break with the previous thought. It is also patent at the same time that in these eastern parts, far away from the base of its supplies, the leadership in religious thought passed considerably and conspicuously to the Kshatriyas, of whom came both the Buddha and Mahāvīra, the two most distinguished heretics.

Pre-Buddhist Brahmanical Ascetic Orders. Thus Hindu society, especially in Eastern India, was possessed of a multitude of religious sects before the rise of Buddhism. The two largest and most prominent of them were distinguished by the names of the Brahmans and Samaṇas. These are mentioned together in various early works, e.g. Megasthenes (who gives a long account of these orders), the edicts of Asoka, Vinaya [ed. Oldenberg, ii, p. 295], Dhammapada (v. 388), Suttanipāta (vv. 99, 129, 189, 440, 529, 859, 1078), Lalita Vistara (pp. 309, 318, and 320), Mahābhāshya [ii, 4, 9], etc.

The chief characteristics of these orders are best given in the *Sutta-Nipāta*. The Brahmans are called *Vādaśīla* or disputatious (v. 381, etc.), *Lokāyatas* and *Vitaṇḍas*, i.e. casuists and sophists [*Mil. Pan.*, i, 10; also *Chullav.*, v, 3, 2, etc.]. Contrasted with the Samaṇas, they are called *Tevijjas*, i.e. versed in three sciences (vv. 594, 1019) or Vedas, *Padakas* (versed in metre), *Veyyākaraṇas* (versed in grammar) and proficient in *Jappa* (recitation or jalpa), *Nighaṇḍu* (vocabulary), *Keṭubha* (etymology ?), *Itihāsa* as the fifth Veda, etc. Three different sects of these Brahmans are also mentioned, viz. the Titthiyas (Sans. Tīrthikas), Ājīvikas, and Nigaṇṭhas (vv. 380, 891–2). These sects were constituted by disciples gathering round famous teachers. Among these, six are mentioned as living in the Buddha's time, viz. Purāṇa Kassapa, Makkhali-Gosāla, Ajita-Kesakambali, Pakudha-Kachchāyana, Sañjaya-Belaṭṭhiputta, and Nigaṇṭha-Nātaputta. These are described as having " an assembly of Bhikkhus, a crowd of followers ", and as " well-known teachers, famous leaders, considered excellent by the multitude " (*Sabhiyasutta*). Each of these great teachers was known for his own particular philosophical system. [See also *Milinda-pañha*, i, 11.] Besides these, we have also the famous teacher, the Brahman Bāvarī, living on the banks of the Godāvarī in Assaka's territory who had sixteen other disciples, all Brahmans, each having a 'host of pupils' and 'widely renowned throughout the world'. They are represented as itinerant scholars, visiting by turns the chief centres of culture and civilization, viz. Patiṭṭhāna, Māhissati, Ujjeni, Gonaddha, Vedisā, Vanasāvhaya, Kosāmbī, Sāketa, Sāvatthi, Setavya, Kapilavatthu, Kusinārā, Pāvā, Vesāli, and the city of Magadha, " all with matted hair and bearing hides " [*Sutta-Nipāta-Pārāyaṇavagga*]. We have also another teacher, the Brahman Sela, " versed in the three Vedas, Nighaṇḍu, Keṭubha, Sākkharappabheda (i.e. sa + *akshara* + *prabheda*, and hence akin to the Vedāṅga, *Śikshā*), Itihāsa the fifth Veda, Pada, Veyyākaraṇa, Lokāyata (casuistry or materialism)," and " the teacher of hymns of 300 pupils " [ib. *Sellasutta*]. There are also mentioned five other distinguished Brahman teachers, viz. Chankin, Tārukkha, Pokkharasāti, Jāṇussoṇī, Todeyya, with Vāseṭṭha and Bhāradvāja as pupils of Pokkharasāti and Tarukkha respectively, themselves " acknowledged masters of the three Vedas " and other allied subjects [ib., v, 594].

Non-Buddhist Orders of Śramaṇas. As regards the Samaṇas, they are distinguished as of four kinds, viz. Maggajinas (victorious by the way), Maggadesins (teaching the way), Maggajīvins (living in the way), and Maggadūsins (defiling the way) [*Suttanipāta*,

vv. 85–8]. There are disputes among these Samaṇas [ib., vv. 828, 883–4], as a result of which different schools of philosophy arise, of which there were as many as sixty-three at the time of the Buddha [ib., v, 538], designated as *Diṭṭhi* (Dṛishṭi) or heresies.[1]

While the orders of *Brahmans* depended on birth and were recruited exclusively from one caste, those of Samaṇas laboured under no such restrictions and were thrown open to all, high born or low born, who would adopt the ascetic life, renouncing worldly careers. These orders were further characterized by different degrees of independence of Vedic orthodoxy achieved by their founders and leaders, and, under the absolute freedom of thought and protection of the liberty of conscience that have always prevailed in India, sects were being added to sects according to the different paths of deliverance by which the masters discovering them led their followers in quest of salvation. These numerous ascetic and philosophizing circles were always wandering through the country in search of opportunities to fight out their differences in public disputations before their adherents, opponents, and the general people in the manner of the Greek sophistic. The country also liberally provided for such opportunities as quickening the intellectual life of the people. We read, for instance, of 'The Hall' specially erected in Queen Mallikā's park for the purposes of such discussions of the different systems of opinion prevailing in the country and of the wandering teacher Poṭṭhapāda initiating there a discussion with his large following of 300 mendicants. "The very fact of the erection of such a place is another proof of the freedom of thought prevalent in the eastern valley of the Ganges in the sixth century B.C. Buddhaghosa tells us that after 'The Hall' had been established, others near it had been built in honour of various famous teachers; but the group of buildings continued to be known as 'The Hall'.

[1] The subject of "Indian Sects or Schools in the time of the Buddha" is discussed in the *JRAS* by Rhys Davids (1898, p. 197) and Bendall (1901, pp. 122 f.). The former mentions that the *Aṅguttara-Nikāya* [part iii, p. 276], refers to ten such sects named as follows: (1) Ājīvako, (2) Nigaṇṭho, (3) Muṇḍasāvako ("a Nigaṇṭha disciple, a Jain"), (4) Jaṭilako, (5) Paribbājako, (6) Māgaṇḍiko (?), (7) Tedaṇḍiko ("school of Brahman beggars who carried three staves bound up as one"), (8) Aviruddhako (?), (9) Gotamako ("a school founded by another Gotama"), (10) Devadhammiko (deva-worshippers ?). The latter quotes from another ancient work called *Ratnolkā-dhāraṇī* a list which mentions the Charakas, Parivrājakas, followers of Gotama (No. 9 in the previous list) who observe the vow of silence, the Achelakas (naked ascetics), the Ājīvikas, ascetics having the *dīrghajaṭā* or taking the vow of celibacy (*kumāravrata*), or practising the penance of *pañchatapa*. He also cites a passage from the Mahāvastu (iii, 412, 7–10) which mentions a *Traidaṇḍika* (No. 7 above) and a disciple of a different Gautama.

There Brahmans, Nigaṇṭhas, Achelakas, Paribbājakas, and other teachers met and expounded, or discussed, their views" [Rhys Davids in *Dialogues of the Buddha*, i, 224, n.].

Thus the Buddhists were only one among other Samaṇa sects of the country; the Buddha was only one, though the most illustrious one, among many other religious reformers like Mahavīra, Gosāla, at first a pupil and later a rival of the former, and his nephew Jamāli leading an independent sect; nay, even the Buddha was not the first to be honoured by that title of 'the enlightened one' or the other title of Jina, the Conqueror. Thus the Buddha himself was frequently styled 'the Samaṇa Gotama', and his disciples 'the Samaṇas who follow the son of the Śākya house'.

The Controversies and Conversions of the Buddha. Thus Buddhism had to fight its way to supremacy with other Brahman and Samaṇa sects. The texts record numerous instances of such fights, the intellectual tournaments in which the Buddha was proving his mettle. They also record their invariable results, the triumph of Buddha, the accession of converts deserting their old masters who are silenced when the Buddha "raises his lion voice in the assemblies" or "roared like a lion in the forest" [*Suttanipāta*, v. 1015], and the impetus given to the spread of the new faith. But, besides these public discussions of the Buddha in assemblies, the texts record his private discussions with individuals and householders whom he might come across in the daily course of his begging rounds. Such would mostly come to scoff, but remained to pray. A Brahman householder of Sāvatthi, seeing the Buddha approach him for alms, accosts him in the following words of contempt: "Stay there, O Shaveling; stay there, O Samaṇaka (i.e. wretched Samaṇa); stay there, O Vasalaka (i.e. outcast)!", but presently becomes converted by Buddha on listening to his discourse on the question put to him [*Suttanipāta-Vasalasutta*]. Sometimes, again, the Buddha would be approached in his place of rest by circles of wandering scholars for the solution of their doubts followed by their conversion [ib.].

Some of the most important of the Buddha's converts came naturally from the Brahmans. The legends tell us that the Buddha was anxious to impart his gospel first to his two old Brahman teachers who were unfortunately dead by that time. His first sermon at Benares was heard by the group of five Brahman ascetics headed by Kondañña, the quondam partners of his earlier spiritual struggles, whom he himself seeks out to make his first converts and the original members of his church. Next follow the thousand Brahman hermits of Uruvela under their leaders, the three Kassapa brothers, all devoted to the Vedic cult and performance of sacrifices, till the Buddha converts them. Soon after, at Rājagaha, the Buddha gained as his disciples the two young Brahmans, Sāriputta and Moggallāna, who ranked next to their master in the circles of the church. They were among the 250 disciples of a renowned teacher, Sañjaya, and their conversion led to the dissolution of the entire sect and following of Sañjaya who in vain tried to keep them together under him. This event is stated to have produced a great sensation in the city of Rājagaha where the populace became temporarily agitated over the success of the Buddha's cult as causing 'childlessness', 'widowhood', and 'subversion of families' in the country through its youths 'betaking themselves to the ascetic Gotama to lead a religious life'.

But the Buddha found in the rival Samaṇa sects and their leaders harder material to deal with than in the adherents of the ancient faith. Of one of these heretics, Makkhali Gosāla already referred to, the Buddha declared: "Of all doctrines of other ascetics and Brahmans, the doctrine of Makkhali is deemed the worst." Another heretic, named Sachchaka, declares: "I know no Samaṇa, and no Brahman, no teacher, no master, no head of a school, even though he calls himself the holy supreme Buddha, who, if he face me in debate, would not totter, tremble, quake; how much more a human being!" Thus some of his worst and most dangerous opponents did the Buddha find in these circles of professional dialecticians and controversialists whose regard for truth and moral life was subdued by their taste for casuistry and an overweening materialism, cynicism, and scepticism which it is always difficult to convince.

It is also evident from the history of these conversions that the Buddha's disciples were all drawn from the already existing ascetic orders of the country, whether Brāhmaṇa or Samaṇa, and trained beforehand in the discipline of monastic life. Their entry into the Buddhist brotherhood did not therefore imply any revolution in their ways of life; it meant only a change in their religious opinions, and also in the object of their heart-felt homage. It is thus that we find that the formula with which the Buddha admitted his first disciples into his order ran in the following words: "Come hither, O monk; well preached is the doctrine, walk in purity, to make an end of all suffering." It was thus the monks well versed in the doctrines and technique of monastic life, and not the untutored lay men, that constituted the early Buddhist congregation and are called 'ascetics who adhere to the Samaṇa who is the son of the Śākya house', who already bore on their persons all the visible marks, such as the yellow garment and tonsure which signify separation from the home and the world, from all earthly ties.

We thus see how largely did Buddhism, in the spheres of both thinking and living, work with the materials derived from the previous cultures.

The Buddha a product of the Brahmanical System. This thesis also receives a most conclusive confirmation from the details of the Buddha's own career as preserved in the traditional texts. The details will show how largely was he himself the product of the then prevailing Brahmanical educational systems. We have already seen how in the very first step that he takes towards the Buddhahood, the renunciation of the home [1] and the world, the world of riches to which he was born, he was not at all singular but following the path trodden by all seekers after truth in all ages and all ranks of society. Our ancient literature is full of examples of the spirit of acute, *utkaṭa*, *vairāgya* under which the rich, the fortunate, and the noble not less than the poor, the destitute and the lowly, the young with a distaste for life before tasting it as much as the old who have had enough of it, even women and maidens, as eagerly leave their homes and adopt the ascetic life as a positive good as their dear ones entreat them to desist from such a step. The Buddha's next step was to give himself such training for the new life he chose as was available in the country. He placed himself under the guidance of two successive gurus. The first was the Brahman, Ālāra Kālāma, at Vesāli, having a following of 300 disciples who taught him the successive stages of meditation and the doctrine of the Ātman, from which the Buddha turns back dissatisfied [2] on the ground

[1] "Buddha, on leaving the palace, made perhaps the most noteworthy journey ever made by mortal. Every step almost has since beeen marked by costly marble carvings and shrines and statues under canopy-mounds, which successive generations of pilgrims have smothered in flowers."—Lillie, *Life of Buddha*, p. 67.

[2] Regarding this episode, Dr. A. K. Coomaraswamy justly remarks [*Buddha and the Gospel of Buddhism*, pp. 29, 199]: "We recognize here the critical moment where Buddhist and Brahman thought part company on the question of the Ātman. Whether Ālāra failed to emphasize the negative aspect of the doctrine of the Brahman, or Gautama (who is represented as so far entirely innocent of Brahmanical philosophy) failed to distinguish the neuter Brahman from the

GAUTAMA AT SCHOOL [Ajanta Painting, Cave No. XVI, *c.* sixth century A.D.].

The School is " in a verandah in his father's palace ; Gautama being instructed, with three other boys, by a Brāhmaṇa teacher. On their laps are tablets . . . Caged birds, musical instruments, a battle-axe, bows, a water-pot (probably of silver) hang against the walls ; while pigeons are cooing under the eaves above, where their cot is formed of perforated woodwork with small arched openings ". Gautama, as a prince, was given, along with literary education, education in music and military arts like archery.

[*Facing p. 386*

that it " does not lead to aversion, absence of passion, cessation, quiescence, knowledge, supreme wisdom, and Nirvāṇa, but only as far as the realm of nothingness " [Warren, *Buddhism in Translations*, p. 336]. Next, he attaches himself to the sage of Rājagaha with 700 pupils, Uddaka, the disciple of Rama, but " he gained no clear understanding from his treatment of the soul " [Aśvaghosha, *Buddha-charita*, xii, 82, in *S.B.E.*, xlix]. It is, however, evident that, as Rhys Davids points out [*American Lectures*, p. 102], " Gotama, either during this period or before, must have gone through a very systematic and continued course of study in all the deepest philosophy of the time." It is also represented that the Buddha, qualified as he was both mentally and spiritually, mastered the doctrines of these early teachers so quickly that each treated him " every whit the equal of himself " and offered to make him a co-teacher of his disciples [Warren, op. cit., pp. 336, 338]. Gotama, however, did not " honour these doctrines with his adhesion " (ib.), and " craving the summum bonum, the incomparable peaceful state, came in the course of his journeying among the Magadhans to Uruvela ", near Gayā, where perceiving " a delightful spot with an enchanting grove of trees and a silvery flowing river (the Nairañjanā River, according to the *Buddha-charita*), easy of approach and delightful, with a village near by in which to beg, he settled down as everything was suitable for struggling ". He settled down to a life of austere penance and engaged himself in a veritable life-and-death struggle for the attainment of the Truth he wanted for a period of six years. The solitude of his struggle was relieved by the fellowship of a group of " five mendicants, desiring deliverance ", who

god Brahmā, we cannot tell." He also says : " The parting of Gautama and Ālāra represents, perhaps, the greatest tragedy recorded in religious history. It has been remarked with perfect justice by A. Worsley : ' It is possible that had Gautama chanced to meet, in his earliest wanderings, two teachers of the highest truth, the whole history of the Old World might have been changed [*Concepts of Monism*, p. 197].' " He further points out that from a study of the Buddha's dialogues it would appear that he never encountered a capable exponent of the highest Vedāntic idealism like a Janaka or Yājñavalkya, he meets no foeman worthy of his steel ; that either he was acquainted only with popular Brahmanism against which Buddhist polemic is chiefly directed, or he chose to ignore its higher aspects. Cf. Oldenberg's remark : " God and the Universe trouble not the Buddhist ; he knows only one question : how shall I in this world of suffering be delivered from suffering ? " [*Buddha*, p. 130]. Thus Buddhism became a popular religion with none of the esoteric doctrines and discussions which confine higher Brahmanism or the Vedic, Upanishadic, philosophy and religion to the " fit audience though few ".

Ālāra Kālama is mentioned as the teacher of the young Mallian Pukkusa who spoke to the Buddha about his great power of abstraction shown once when he was not conscious of the passage of a caravan of 500 carts by him sitting on the roadside [*Maha. Par. Suttas.*, iv, 35].

attached themselves to him as his disciples. "For six years, vainly trying to attain merit, he practised self-mortification, performing many rules of abstinence, hard for a man to carry out." Then concluding that "truth cannot be attained by one who has lost his strength, he resumed his care for the body", and, on the bank of the River Nairañjanā, persuaded himself to take some milk offered by Nandabālā, the daughter of the leader of the herdsmen of the neighbourhood. "Thinking that he had returned to the world, the five mendicants left him, as the five elements leave the wise soul when it is liberated" [adapted from the *Buddha-charita*]. They left him at a time when he needed most the strength of human sympathy in his solitary and desperate struggle towards truth,[1] a struggle which is soon ended by his attainment of enlightenment and the doctrine of Nirvāṇa. These details in the history of his education and spiritual development show how largely they were directed by the prevailing Brahmanical theories of self-culture and training. Even where the Buddha's originality in his system of training is most generally asserted, when he gives up penances as mere weariness of the flesh, it cannot be maintained when we consider that Brahmanical thought even in earlier times was quite conscious of their limitations. Yājñavalkya, as a hermit, declares to his wife: "Of a truth, O Gārgi, he who does not know this imperishable One, though in this world he should distribute alms and practise penance for many a thousand years, thereby wins but finite good" [*Bri. Up.*, iii, 8, 10]. This line of criticism culminated later in a different theory of *tapas* as defined by Manu: "The *tapas* of the Brāhman is concentrated study; of the Kshatriya, protection of the weak; of the Vaiśya, trade and agriculture; of the Śūdra, service of others." It may be noted in this connection that the Buddha's first teacher Ālāra proposed to him 'a rigorous course of sacred study, discoursing on the supreme Brahman' and 'a rule of conduct' whereby

[1] In the *Mil. Pañh.*, iv, 6, 3 are mentioned as the Buddha's teachers those eight Brahmans who took note of the marks on his body and made known his future glory, viz. Rāma and Dhaja, and Lakkhaṇa and Manti, and Yañña, and Suyāma, and Subhoja, and Sudatta; as also 'the Brahman Sabbamitta of high lineage in the land of Udichcha (north-west), a philologist and grammarian, well read in the six Vedāṅgas whom Suddhodana the king, the Bodhisat's father, sent for and handed over the boy to his charge, to be taught'; besides his later teachers, Ālāra and Uddaka the son of Rāma. According to the tradition of the *Lalita Vistara* (ch. x) the Buddha was sent early to a 'writing school' under its master Viśvāmitra. There he inquires about what he is to be taught among the sixty-four kinds of writing he himself knows of beforehand.

the devotee 'cultivating absolute content with any alms from any person, carries out his lonely life, indifferent to all feelings, and satisfied in himself' [*Buddha-charita*]. It would thus appear that, after he had left the life of penance or extreme self-mortification, he practically reverted to this earlier system of life on the eve of his Buddhahood.

General Attitude of Buddhism towards Brahmanism. In conclusion, we may note the attitude that the Buddha and his system take towards Brahmans and Brahmanical systems. That attitude can be inferred from several typical pieces of evidence. The Buddhist dogmatic [cf. *Lalita Vistara*, ch. iii] asserts that a Buddha can be born only as a Brahman or as a Kshatriya and not 'in a low family such as that of a Chaṇḍāla or of a basket-maker or of a chariot-maker or of a Pukkasa'. This shows that Buddhist thought does not make light of the Brahmanical distinctions of caste. In the *Ambaṭṭha-sutta* more than usual consideration is shown to the young 'pupil of a respected Brahman', for "truly not undesired by the Exalted One is such an interview with such noble youths". Similarly, a scion of the house of the Mallas is welcomed by Ānanda as "a very distinguished and well-known person" whose "adherence" to the new religion is declared to be of "great efficacy" and the Buddha grants him an interview in that view [*Mahāvagga*, vi, 36]. In the texts it is frequently to be found that free access to the Buddha is always accorded to a person if he is "a certain Brahman". Even where persons of lower castes are entertained, it is on the ground of their true and highest Brahmanhood which comes of "holy zeal and chaste living, restraint, and self-repression". Sunīta was such a person born of a humble family whose work was to "sweep the withered flowers out of temples and palaces" [Oldenberg's *Buddha*, pp. 156, 157 nn., giving these references]. The case of Sunīta may be compared with that of Satyakāma Jābāla of the Upanishads whose genuine Brahmanhood is recognized behind his doubtful parentage. Oldenberg [ib., p. 155], very forcibly points out that, in spite of its theory of equality, a marked leaning to aristocracy (of all the three varieties, birth, brain, and bullion) lingered in ancient Buddhism as an inheritance from the past, and proves it by a reference to the composition of the inner circle of the Buddha's disciples which counted "Brahmans like Sāriputta, Moggallāna, Kachchāna, nobles like Ānanda, Rāhula, Anuruddha, sons of the greatest merchants and highest municipal dignitaries, like Yasa, invariably men and youths of the most respectable classes of society, and with an education in keeping with their social status ", while there is hardly " any instance in which a Chaṇḍāla—the Pariah of that age—is mentioned in the sacred writings as a member of the order ". It may be further pointed out that the compound *Samaṇa-Brāhmaṇa* which constantly appears in the Buddhist texts only indicates the equality of position given to the two classes. In the words of Childers [*Dictionary*, p. 427], " nothing shows more strongly the universal veneration in which the Brāhmans were held in Gautama's time, a veneration due to their birth and intellectual endowments, than the fact that Gautama, whose mission it was to break down the Brahmanical system, nevertheless held up the Brāhmans themselves to the respect of his followers, placed them on a level with his own monks, and even adapted their name into his own system, applying it figuratively to the Arhat or Buddhist monk who has attained the highest sanctification. Hence we have the word *Samaṇa-Brāhmaṇā* (pl.) in which *Brāhmaṇa* sometimes has its ordinary meaning and sometimes its secondary meaning of Arhat." Besides the linguistic evidence, Childers brings forward other evidence in support of his correct contention. In *Vasalasutta* (vv. 129, 129), the Buddha condemns as an outcast the man who " by falsehood deceives either a Brāhman or a Samaṇa or any other mendicant " or " by words annoys " such " when meal-time has come and does not give him anything ". A passage in the *Dhammapada* (v. 389) enjoins kind treatment of Brāhmans and another (v. 142) declares that a man in fine apparel may yet be a Brāhman, Śramaṇa, and a Bhikshu if he is virtuous. It is man's character, and not his clothes, that counts in religion. Childers cites the interesting story of King Praśenajit's minister Santati hearing Buddha's words and instantly attaining Arhatship and Nirvāṇa while the priests cannot settle whether in his courtly attire he is to be considered as a Samaṇa or a Brahman. The Buddha settles their doubt by declaring: " It is right to call a son of mine (i.e. a convert) both a Samaṇa and a Brāhman." The Buddha paid an honour to Brahmanism by exempting the Brāhman ascetics called Jaṭilas, on the ground of their spiritual progress, from the probation necessary to their ordination (*Mahāv.*, i, 38, 3], while a similar honour was shown by his acceptance of invitations from Brāhmans without any idea of converting them. One such host was Keniya whom he praised for his devotion to

Brāhmans (ib., vi, 35], and he also applauded the Sāvitrī hymn and fire-sacrifice to confirm him in his faith [ib., vi, 35, 8]. Lastly, it is necessary to note that this attitude of Buddhism towards Brāhmans, thus fixed by its founder, and sanctioned by his high religious authority, persists through later times till it is strengthened by a sort of legislative sanction in the imperial decrees of Asoka who in his Edicts is never tired of repeating his injunction that due reverence must be shown to Brāhmans and followers of other sects as much as to followers of his own faith. We may conclude this thesis with the following findings of Rhys Davids: "The fact we should never forget that Gotama was born and brought up and lived and died a Hindu. . . On the whole, he was regarded by the Hindus of that time as a Hindu. . . Without the intellectual work of his predecessors his own work, however original, would have been impossible. . . He was the greatest and wisest and best of the Hindus and, throughout his career, a characteristic Indian" [adapted from his *American Lectures*, pp. 116, 117].

Buddhism did not seek Hindu Social Reform. A word may also be said about the Buddhist principles of social organization as distinguished from the Brahmanical ones. It has been very generally held that Buddhism rose as a revolt against the caste system of Brahmanism. To hold this view is to completely misunderstand the very mission of Buddhism. Although the Buddha was fond of attacking the mere Brahmanhood of birth and insisting on the Brahmanhood of virtue, yet the idea of being a social reformer never entered his mind or into his schemes. Nothing was farther from or more foreign to his nature and temperament than this supposed enthusiasm of the Buddha for the work of social uplift of the masses or asserting the claims of the depressed and oppressed classes, their birthrights as human beings, against those privileged merely on the ground of birth under the Brahmanical system. In the first place, it must be understood that the institution of caste was not known in the Buddha's time as a system of grave and glaring injustice loudly calling for its mending or ending ; it did not yet develop the rigidity and inelasticity of the rules of its arbitrary classification in which its critics find its most objectionable and obnoxious features ; we have authoritative precedents like that of Satyakāma Jābāla which point to the law then operative that Brahmanhood was conferred on the strength of spiritual qualification where the physical qualification was lacking ; and, what is more, the pride of birth with its inevitable inequalities was checked by the law relating to the four Āśramas of life which emphasized the spiritual objective of the institution and made all the castes equal in a common obedience to it. In the second place, it is to be recalled that the Buddha renounced the world to set up and live in an ideal world of his own to be peopled only by persons of the same persuasion. It was not an attempt to reform or abolish castes, it was an attempt to reform entire society out of its existence, to abolish it completely so to speak. He did not believe in the economic, social, or political life of man but only in the religious or spiritual life, the life dedicated to its highest end as conceived by him. Thus caste has no significance for him; the problems of social reform do not trouble him; they have no place in his scheme of life. Buddhist society was thus a society of simplified human beings, of ascetics and monks who divested themselves of the complex and complicated earthly relationships. It was thus itself a kind of a special caste constituted by those who under the Brahmanical system of life would belong to its third and, especially, the fourth Āśrama of life. No doubt, the Buddhist fraternity was open without distinctions of caste to all who would don the garb of monks and embark upon a religious pilgrimage; but so was the Brahmanical fourth Āśrama of life, the life of a Yati or Sannyāsī who is beyond the pale of society and its conventions. Thus, far from there being any real or fundamental conflict of ideals between Brahmanism and Buddhism, the latter only sets before itself a more limited scope and ideal and covers only a part of the ground trodden by the former. While Brahmanism is a religion of both Time and Eternity, Buddhism addresses itself to Eternity alone.

General Indebtedness of Buddhism to Brahmanism. The characteristic of Buddhism is its organization of Monks into *Saṁgha*. This central idea of Asceticism has its source in Brahmanism. The Brahmanical scheme of life divided it into four *Āśramas*, of which three are based on asceticism. The *Brahmachārī* is of two classes: (1) *Upakurvāṇa*, student for a period; (2) *Naishṭhika*, a life-long student. The Brahmachārī of the second class is a *Sannyāsī* like a Buddhist Bhikshu [*Chhāndogya Upa.*, ii, 23, 1]. The *Vānaprastha* and *Sannyāsī* are regular ascetics like Buddhist monks. Buddhism has adopted for its monks most of the rules of *Brahmacharya*. The first duty of the Brahmachārī is begging and the Buddhist term *Bhikshu* implies one who begs for livelihood. The third *Āśrama* is also called that of a Bhikshu by legal authorities like Gautama or Āpastamba. The rules of *brahmacharya* as to alms-bowl, manner of begging, eating, sitting, sleeping, cutting of hair, clothing, abstention from luxuries like garlands, scents, oils, sporting in water, etc., are all adopted by Buddhism for its Bhikshus. Even the Buddhist doctrine of *Ahiṁsā* is Brahmanical. The texts forbid Brahmachārī tread on land that is ploughed, or grows crops, lest life is destroyed. For the same reason, the *Parivrājaka* is forbidden travelling in rains, but should keep to a rain-retreat, an institution specifically Buddhist. Again, in the Brahmanical system, the Sannyāsī who renounces home is called *Aniketa*, should live under a tree as a *Vṛiksha-mūlika* [*Bau.*, ii, 10, 63, 67]. Later texts allow him better residence such as *Śūnyāgāra*, *Devāgāra* (temple), *Maṭha*, *Kuṭī*, *Araṇya*, *Giriguhā*, and the like [*Vaikhānasa*, vi, 3, 6; *Vaśishṭha*, x, 8–10]. Buddhism also shows the same evolution in the housing of the Bhikshu. He starts as an *Anāgārika*, living under a *Vṛiksha-mūla* [*Mahāvagga*, i, 30, 4], and in *Araṇya* (forest), *Kandara*, *Giriguhā*, etc. [*Chullavagga*, vi, 1, 1–2]. A merchant prince of Rājagṛiha offered to provide for improved housing, whereupon the Buddha allowed the following: (1) *Vihāra*; (2) *Ardhayoga* (= *Suparṇa Vaṁkagṛiha*); (3) *Prāsāda*; (4) *Harmya*; and (5) *Guhā* of "bricks, stone, wood, or earth". Normally, however, the Bhikshu lived in a leafy hut (*tinakuṭī*) [*Bhikshu-Prātimoksha*, ii, 1, 1–2]. Again, Buddhism runs after physical purity (*śauchāchāra*) as much as Brahmanism. Brahmanism treats religion as something to be lived, as more a matter of conduct than philosophy. *Brahmacharya* itself means "the practice (*charyā*) of Brahma (= Veda)". The teacher is called *Āchārya*, "he who *practises* the precepts of religion." Thus Brahminical education emphasizes right habits more than mere study of books. These have been already described. Buddhism is full of such practices (*āchāra*). The *Vinaya* gives regulations regarding such trivial details of life as the size of tooth-brush, of clothing, seat, needle-case, manner of eating, as will be seen below. The dominance of ceremonies in Buddhist life has come in for censure in an Edict of Asoka [Rock Edict, ix]. Lastly, the Brahmanical system of fasting on select days has also been adopted by both Jainism and Buddhism. It is also to be noted that the *Parivrājikā* is the precursor of the Buddhist *Bhikshuṇī*. There were non-Buddhist ascetic Orders before the rise of Buddhism. Thus the Order of Nuns is not an innovation of Buddhism [cf. *Bhikshu-Prātimoksha*, 41].

Chapter XIV

THE SYSTEM
(according to *Vinaya*)

Buddhist Education purely Monastic. The history of the Buddhist system of education is practically that of the Buddhist Order or Saṁgha. Buddhist education and learning centred round monasteries as Vedic culture centred round the sacrifice. The Buddhist world did not offer any educational opportunities apart from or independently of its monasteries. All education, sacred as well as secular, was in the hands of the monks. They had the monopoly of learning and of the leisure to impart it. They were the only custodians and bearers of the Buddhist culture.

Its Rules. Thus the rules of Buddhist education are those of the Buddhist Order. As has been already pointed out, these rules are not the invention of the Buddha but modelled upon those of numerous other monastic orders professing other faiths and also of Brahmanism itself, the common source from which all such sects arose.

Initiation. The ceremony of initiation into the Buddhist Order and the Church follows closely the lines of the Brahmanical initiation of studentship as described above. Under the Brahmanical system the youth has to find his teacher to whom he has to formally apply for admission to studentship in the following words: " I am come for the *Brahmacharya.* I desire to be a Brahmachārin." Then the teacher " ties the girdle round him, gives him the staff into his hand, and explains to him the Brahmacharya (the rules of conduct of a religious student), by saying: ' Thou art a Brahmachārin ; drink water ; perform service ; sleep not by day ; study the Veda obediently to thy teacher ' " [*Āśvalāyana Gr. Su.*, i, 22 ; *Pāraskara*, ii, 2, 3 ; *Śat. Br.*, xi, 5, 4 seq.]. The Bodhisattva himself is represented in tradition to say to Uddaka, the Brahman teacher, whom he approached for instruction in saving knowledge : " I desire, O friend, according to thy teaching and thy direction, to walk in the Brahmacharya." And, as the Buddha, he inaugurates his Order by admitting his first disciples in the following words : " Come hither, O monk, the doctrine is duly preached ; walk in the Brahmacharya, to put an end to all sorrow." Thus the Buddhist monastic order began as a union of the master and his disciples after the Brahmanical model. The finding of a teacher was a condition of ordination as laid down in the text: "Let no one, O Bhikkhus, who has no *Upājjhāya*, receive the *Upasampadā* ordination." The teacher must be an individual person and not a fictitious one like the Saṁgha as a corporate body. The text does not permit such a fraud on the system: "Let no one receive the *Upasampadā* ordination with the Saṃgha as *Upājjhyāya*" [*Mahāvagga*, i, 69]. The idea of the individual responsibility of the teacher for his pupil's training and conduct was thus rightly emphasized.

Pravrajyā. The first step in Buddhist initiation is called *Pabbajjā* or "going forth". It means that a person presents himself for admission into the Order by "going out" of his previous state, whether it be that of a layman and householder or of a wandering ascetic or monk belonging to a different sect. The admission to the Order was thrown open to all the castes. The candidate for admission must take leave of all the visible marks of the life he has left, the marks of caste as of clothes. He casts himself out into the Order which has made a short work of all distinctions of caste on the principle which is deliberately and diametrically its very opposite, the principle of equality and fraternity. In the words of the Buddha himself: "As the great streams, O disciples, however many they may be, the Gaṅgā, Yamunā, Achiravatī, Sarabhū, Mahī, when they reach the great ocean, lose their old name and their old descent, and bear only one name, 'the great ocean,' so also, my disciples, these four castes, Nobles, Brahmans, Vaiśya, and Śūdra, when they, in accordance with the law and doctrine which the Perfect One has preached, forsake their home and go into homelessness, lose their old name and old paternity, and bear only the one designation, 'Ascetics, who follow the son of the Śākya house'" [*Chullav.*, ix, 1, 4]. As instances of persons of low castes being admitted as monks, we may mention Upāli the barber and 'a vulture-tormentor' [*Chullav.*, i, 32].

But, though in theory the Order might be recruited from all castes, in practice the admission to it was sought by a few, that small and select class of persons who were spiritually advanced enough to adopt the life of asceticism, renouncing the life of pleasures and 'out-going' activities.

Resemblance with Brahmanical System. It may also be

noted that the *Pabbajjā*, this "going out" of home into the Order, is akin to the Brahmanical system of studentship under which the young disciple has to go out of his own home, the care and company of his parents and relations, to live with his chosen preceptor as an *antevāsī* in his hermitage or Āśrama in a new home and environment under rigorous conditions of discipline and training. Under the Buddhist system, too, the layman admitted to the Order is placed under the discipline of a preceptor who is to control his conduct. As in the Brahmanical system, a minimum age limit was fixed for initiation, viz. eight years, and children below that age were not accepted by the Order. Again, the minimum period of studentship in the Brahmanical system was twelve years ; the same is the period of the Buddhist novitiate. Corresponding to the epithet *Brahmachārī* conferred upon a youth after his Upanayana is the Buddhist epithet *Sāmaṇera* applied to the youth who is a *pabbajita*, i.e. has become a homeless one on his performing the ceremony of initial or preliminary ordination (*pabbajjā*).

Rules of First Ordination (Pabbajjā). We shall now describe the other particulars of this preparatory ordination of *Pabbajjā*. In the case of a layman under twenty years of age seeking admission to the Order, he approaches, tonsured, the Vihāra or monastery of his choice with a suit of the yellow robes of the monk in his hands and presents himself before an elder of the monastery for initiation. The elder then invests him with the yellow robe and calls upon him to take the following oath of Three Refuges (*Saraṇattaya*) three times: "I take refuge with the Buddha. I take refuge with the Religion. I take refuge with the Order" [*Mahāvagga*, i, 12, 3–4]. Next, the following Ten Commandments are administered to him (the *dasasikkhāpadāni*), viz. abstinence from (1) taking life, (2) taking what is not given, (3) impure practices, (4) telling a lie, (5) intoxicating drinks, "arrack," etc., (6) eating out of time, (9) dancing, singing, and seeing shows, (8) using garlands, scents, unguents, ornaments, and finery, (9) use of a high or large couch or seat, and (10) receiving gold and silver. It will be noted how most of these interdicts figure in the code of regulations governing the life of a Brahmachārī too. Then the ceremony is over, and the novice is committed to the care of his elder or preceptor who brings him up till he is fit for the higher ordination.

Restrictions to Admission. With regard to adults or persons above the minimum age limit seeking admission to the Order, there were imposed certain conditions of eligibility which must have restricted recruitment for the Order to some extent and demonstrate the practical good sense and expediency of the Buddhist legislators in spite of their uncompromising spiritual idealism. Thus admission to the Order was not permitted to youths seeking it without the consent of their parents, thus showing the laudable concern of an Order of homeless ascetics for the integrity of the home, for the discipline of family life, and the respect due to its obligations without which family as well as society would be disintegrated and disorganized. This restriction was first introduced by the Buddha at the request of his father who grieved over the loss of all his male heirs by the adoption of the Order by all of them including his grandson Rāhula. The next restriction upon admission was on the ground of gross and glaring physical defects such as serious sicknesses or bodily deformities of which contagious diseases, consumption, leprosy, boils, itches, and fits are given as examples.[1] Serious moral defect was also a bar to admission ; confirmed criminals [e.g. a matricide (*Mahāvagga*, i, 64)] were kept out. A due discharge of one's legal obligations was also insisted upon, the obligations due to the State or resulting from economic transactions under the ordinary circumstances of life under Society and State which the applicant for orders proposed to leave. This rule had the effect of barring out government servants, and especially soldiers, the right to whose services belonged inviolably to the State ; and debtors upon the fruits of whose labour their creditors had the first charge ; and slaves who must procure their release from their owners. Thus these regulations show how the Order in its concern for the spiritual health and well-being of its members felt a due concern for their physical health, too,

[1] A complete list of persons disqualified on the ground of bodily defects and deformities is given in the Mahāvagga, i, 71. The principle of this disqualification does not seem to be a very commendable one. It was simply a concession to the tastes and susceptibilities of the lay public, to a doubtful sense of decency that would not look with a kindly eye upon the dwarf or the hump-back, upon the lame, the deaf and the dumb, or even the man afflicted with elephantiasis. A sound body was no doubt to be desired, but it was easy to desire it too much. At least the persons afflicted from birth by Nature deserve better treatment than those punished by man. In the list a cripple is on a par with a " proclaimed robber ". The weakness of Buddhism, and, indeed, of all proselytizing religions in the early stages of their career is this undue panting after popularity, and even pandering to low and vulgar tastes instead of ignoring and educating them. There might be much native moral excellence behind physical disabilities that would repay proper treatment. The eagerness of early Buddhism to secure aristocratic and opulent adherents has been already noticed as another weakness.

and the need of their coming to it with a clean and unblemished record as regards their previous career and life. The *Pabbajjā* did not permit the "going out of", or a self-willed, cowardly, fraudulent, or dishonest escape from, one's obligations to the family, the State, and the Society. The sacredness and inviolability of these moral, political, social, and economic obligations were thus very properly emphasized and recognized by the Order, which did not countenance the violent and revolutionary methods of accomplishing spiritual evolution. Man's inner growth must correspond to the silent and peaceful processes of growth visible in external nature or the objective world.

In addition to the foregoing chief limitations of admission to the Order the texts lay down a few minor ones. Persons who were found to be "shameless" and not duly "modest" were not to be admitted. This was to be ascertained by the regulation of keeping the proposed pupils under observation for the first four or five days until it was seen how they behaved to the other Bhikkhus of the Order [*Mahāv.*, i, 72]. Again, persons who "furtively" attached themselves to the Order were also to be kept out [ib., i, 62].

Final Ordination of Upasampadā. The preliminary ordination of the *Pabbajjā* inaugurates the period of novitiate which is ended by the final ordination of the *Upasampadā*, the arrival at the full status of monkhood or a Bhikshu, a full-fledged member of the Order. The period between the two ordinations was twelve years at its maximum and was not continued beyond the twentieth year of the postulant. The period of novitiate was, however, reduced to four months in the case of the postulant being previously a member of another monastic order [*Mahāvagga*, i, 38, 3]. The Brahmanical Vānaprasthas, called the Jaṭilas, fire-worshippers with matted hair, were, however, exempted from all probation (*parivāsa*) on the ground of their advanced doctrines, as also the Śākyas, the Buddha's kinsmen [ib.]. Sometimes, again, the two ordinations were gone through simultaneously [1] when the grounds for separating them in time did not exist, as in the case of Koṇḍañña and other ascetics with him [*Mahāvagga*, i, 6, 32].

[1] It would seem from the texts [*Mahāv.*, i, 6, 7] that the original disciples of the Buddha such as the Five Mendicants, Yasa, and his companions numbering sixty, received the two ordinations together, but an interval between them was prescribed for the later adherents of the church converted by these original disciples, though even in these cases exceptions were allowed. There was an exception even in Asoka's time in the case of the lay devotee Bhaṇḍuka (*Dīpav.*, xii, 62 f.).

The higher ordination of the Upsampadā by which a Samaṇera completes his course of probation and enters upon the full membership of the Saṁgha for which he is destined and has been prepared since his Pabbajjā ordination, marks an important point of distinction between the Brahmanical and Buddhist systems of education. Under the former system, the Brahmachārin, on completion of his studentship, and coming of age, returns to his home and family as a *Snātaka* and presently marries and becomes a *Gṛihastha* or householder. His "going out of home" or *pravrajyā* was for a temporary period. In the case of the Buddhist, the "outgoing from home into homelessness" (agārasmā anagāriyaṁ pabbajjā) is final. The Brahmanical system, however, provided for exceptions. Brahmachārīs were given the option to remain as such through life at his teacher's, and, after his death, with his family according to his choice [*Āpast.*, ii, 9, 21, 6; 8; *Gautama*, iii, 3, 7; *Manu*, ii, 247], the special designation of *Naishṭhika* being applied to them as a mark of distinction. But the exceptions became the rule in the Buddhist system. In the Brahmanical scheme, the final renunciation of the home and the world belongs to the third and fourth stage or Āśrama of life when the man, after passing the successive stages of the Brahmachārin, the Snātaka, and the Gṛihastha, becomes a *Parivrājaka*, a Bhikshu or a *Yati* or a *Sannyāsī*, a hermit and a wandering mendicant. The entry upon these stages of life is thus described by Manu: "When the Brahman who is living in the state of a householder sees his skin becoming wrinkled and his hair becoming grey, if he sees his son's son, then let him go forth into the forest. Let him leave all food, such as one enjoys in the village, and all household furniture behind him; to his sons let him commit his wife, and let him go to the forest, or let him go forth with his wife. Let the Brahman make the Prajāpati-offering and give all his possessions as remuneration of sacrifice; his holy fire let him take up in his own body, and thus let him go forth from his house." As Kern well points out, these Brahmacārins for life and the Bhikshus or Sannyāsīs formed the nucleus of different sects, each following the doctrines of its masters [*Manual of Ind. Buddhism*, p. 74].

The particulars of the Upasampadā ordination may now be described. While the Pabbajjā is, as has been already seen, a one-sided transaction with which the Order as a whole has nothing to do, the Upasampadā consisted of a ceremony which has to be completed before the Order and by their participation.

Democratic Procedure in its performance. Every step in the ordination has to be passed by the Order in a meeting specially convened for the purpose. The quorum for such a meeting was laid down. It required the presence of at least ten members who must be fully qualified elders [Mahāvagga, i, 31, 2]. In border countries, however, where "there were but few Bhikkhus" and hence "difficulty and trouble in getting together a meeting of the Order in which ten Bhikkhus were present", the quorum was reduced by the Buddha to five members including the chairman [ib., v, 13, 11].[1] An ecclesiastical vote of the Chapter of elders was termed *Kammavāchā* (which means "the proceedings at a *Kamma* or ecclesiastical Act, by which some question is decided by vote"). The sense of the meeting was obtained by a vote or Resolution arrived at in either of the two following ways, viz. (1) by a summary decision at which the Resolution before the house (*ñatti*) would be given only one reading (*ñattidutiya-kamma*) ; (2) a decision by the third reading (*ñattichatutthakamma*). The decision by three readings was applied to all the stages in the ceremony of the Upasampadā ordination. The method of voting was very simple. The assenting members kept silence and the dissenters spoke out. In the case of divided opinions in the Chapter, the question was referred to arbitration by a small sub-committee elected on the spot and possessed of special qualifications laid down. If the question was not settled thus, it was put to the vote. A taker of votes was then elected. He distributed voting slips (*salākā*) of different colours to indicate different opinions [*Chullavagga*, iv, 14, 26], and thus ascertained the vote of the majority. There was a rule that no member should leave the meeting without declaring his vote [*Pāt.*, p. 52].

The proceedings of the Ordination may now be described. As has been already stated, the ordination can be conferred only by a Chapter of at least ten elders who should all be learned, competent, and of not less than ten years' standing (*Mahāvagga*, i, 31]. One of them must introduce the novice to the President of the Chapter in a formal resolution, *ñatti*. Then he, or any other member, is appointed by the Chapter to give the candidate preliminary instructions. The instructions are to be given aside. They comprise a series of questions to the candidate to

[1] It may be noted that the texts allow the quorum to vary with the purposes of the Saṁgha meetings. "The lowest number which can constitute a Saṁgha is four" [*Mahāv.*, viii, 24, 1], but such a Saṁgha is not entitled to perform the Upasampadā ordination. Saṁghas of five, ten, twenty persons and more are referred to with their different powers [ib., ix, 4].

ascertain his eligibility under the specified conditions already stated (regarding his being free from certain diseases, debts, obligations of royal service, his age, the consent of his parents). He was also asked his name, the name of the *Upājjhāya* he had chosen, and whether he had his alms-bowl and robes in due state. He was also instructed as to the manner of answering these questions before the Chapter when they would formally put them to him. On completion of these instructions, the instructor takes permission of the Chapter to present the candidate. The candidate is to present himself in a proper, respectful manner specified. He should "adjust his upper robe so as to cover one shoulder, salute the feet of the Bhikkhus with his head, sit down squatting, raise his joined hands" and entreat the Order three times to confer initiation on him "out of compassion" [*Mahāvagga*, i, 29, 2]. Then a member of the Chapter other than the instructor formally moves the Resolution for initiation of the candidate and, with the permission of the Assembly, "asks him about the Disqualifications" and other requirements, and, on the answers being satisfactory, the Resolution is repeated three times and then declared as carried, the members expressing their assent by silence. At the conclusion of the ceremonies, the hour, date, and season of the ordination, together with the details of the assembly (*Saṅgīti*) are recorded and communicated to the newly ordained monk so that he may also know his spiritual age. Then he is carefully taught the four *Requisites* (*nissayā*) and the four *Interdicts* (*akaraṇīyāni*) of the monastic life. The four Requisites are: (1) eating of the food collected in the alms-bowl only (*piṇḍiyālopabhojana*); (2) wearing robes made of rags collected (*paṁsukūlachīvara*); (3) lodging at the foot of a tree (*rukkhamūlasenāsana*); and (4) using cow's urine as medicine (*pūtimuttabhesajja*). The monk was, however, permitted to accept better things as gifts from laymen.[1] The four Interdicts comprised (1) sexual intercourse, (2) theft, (3) taking life, (4) boasting of superhuman powers (a piece of interesting evidence pointing to the practice of religious swindling among the monastic orders of the times) [cf. *Chullav.*, v, 8].

Rules for Renunciation of Monkhood. Thus the ordination

[1] Once Devadatta tried to utilize this concession to discredit the Saṁgha by urging that the genuine Bhikkhus should be dwellers of woods and must not go to villages; should beg for alms and not accept invitations; should clothe themselves in cast-off rags and not accept gifts of robes from laymen; should dwell under the trees and not under a roof; and should abstain from fish. But the Buddha left the exceptions to the free choice of the monks themselves [*Chullav.*, vii, 3, 14, 15].

of the Upasampadā was performed in a most rational and business-like way without the use of any mystical symbols and methods indicative of the special solemnity and significance of the occasion to the person taking orders or of his spiritual transformation and re-birth. But if the admission to the Order was so simple in its process, the withdrawal from it was also not more difficult. Infringement of any of the prohibitions is punished by expulsion from the Order, while an ordained monk might seek separation from the Order if he feels the promptings of the flesh, "if his father, mother, wife, or the laughter and the jest, the pleasantry of old days, are in his thoughts." Only he has to declare his weakness before a witness (who need not be a monk), who must hear and understand him to say that he renounces the Buddha, the Doctrine, and the Order. Thus the Order did not try artificial methods to keep themselves together in the interests of their real spiritual growth, which was not a matter to be forced.

Upādhyāya and Āchārya as Teachers. We shall now discuss the arrangements for educating the monks. Even the higher ordination of Upasampadā does not give the ordained monk liberty of conduct or independent status. As has been already indicated, he was placed in charge of two superiors qualified by learning, character, and standing, who were called the *Āchārya* and *Upādhyāya*. It is difficult to distinguish their functions from the texts. They are described in *Mahāvagga* [i, 25–33]. The distinction seems to be that the *Upādhāya* was the higher authority entrusted with the duty of instructing the young Bhikkhu in the sacred texts and doctrines, while the *Āchārya* assumed responsibility for his conduct and was thus called also *Karmāchārya* in reference, probably, not merely to his part in the ecclesiastical Act but also to his tutorial responsibility as regards discipline. [See I-tsing, tr. Takakusu, pp. 106, 198.] According to Buddhaghosha [commenting on *Mahāv.*, v, 4, 2], the *Upādhāya* is to be of ten years' and the *Āchārya* of six years' seniority. But, of course, mere seniority is no qualification unless the monk was also learned and competent [ib., i, 35]. In Brahmanical education, however, the *Āchārya* ranks higher than the *Upādhyāya* [Manu, ii, 145; Yājñavalkya, i, 35; and *S.B.E.*, xiii, p. 179 n.]. Thus an *upasampanna bhikshu* has to live under the control of two teachers for his mental and moral training. This period of training or dependence (*nissaya*) is for at least ten years [*Mahāvagga*, i, 32, 1; but in i, 54, 4 the period is reduced to five years for "a learned and competent Bhikkhu" and extended to "all his life" for an "unlearned one"], after which he was allowed to give a *nissaya* to others, i.e. receive pupils as an *Āchārya*. For it is the *Āchārya* who is called the *nissaya-da* (giver of protection), while his protégé was called *nissaya-antevāsika* (pupil in dependence). The relations between the two are also indicated: "The *Āchāriya*, O Bhikkhus, ought to consider the *Āntevāsika* (i.e. disciple living with his teacher) as a son; the *Antevāsika* ought to consider the *Āchāriya* as a father. Thus these two, united by mutual reverence, confidence, and communion of life, will progress, advance, and reach a high stage in this doctrine and discipline" [*Mahāvagga*, i, 32, 1]. Corresponding to the *Āchāriya* and his *Antevāsika* are the *Upājjhāya* and his *saddhivihārika* with similar relations (nissaya) between them [ib., 36, 1]. The higher rank of the *Upājjhāya* is evident from the fact that a *nissaya* or the relationship between the *Āchārya* and *Antevāsika* will be in abeyance in the presence of the *Upājjhāya* [ib.] whom the pupil will be bound to follow for the time being.

Application to Upādhyāya for Admission to Study. The Bhikkhu has to make a formal application to his proposed preceptor, Upājjhāya, for accepting him as his pupil in the following manner: "Let him who is going to choose an Upājjhāya adjust his upper robe so as to cover one shoulder, salute his feet, sit down squatting, raise his joined hands and say, 'Venerable Sir, be my Upājjhāya,' three times." The Upājjhāya will then indicate by nodding or words his acceptance of the applicant as his pupil (*Mahāv.*, i, 25, 7].

Pupil's Daily Duties. The Buddhist system, like the Brahmanical, enjoins upon the pupil the duty of serving his preceptor as a part of education. The pupil is to rise early from bed and give his teacher teeth-cleanser and water to rinse his mouth with; then, preparing a seat for him, serve him rice-milk in rinsed jug, and, after his drinking it, wash the vessel and sweep the place. Afterwards he is to equip him for his begging round by giving him fresh undergarment, girdle, his two upper garments, and his alms-bowl rinsed and filled with water and then is to dress and equip himself similarly if he wants to accompany his teacher but must not walk too far from or near him. He is not to interrupt his teacher in speaking, even if he makes a mistake. In returning, the pupil must get back ahead of the teacher to be ready with necessary things and help him to change his clothes. Then, after serving him with some food, if required, he is to help him in bath by getting him cold or hot water as may be desired, and, in case of bath in the *Jantāghara* (Sans. *yantragṛiha*, i.e. a bathing place for hot sitting baths), to provide him with kneaded powder for rubbing the body with, moistened clay for besmearing the face with, as a protection against the heat of the fire, and a chair belonging to the bathroom. He is to attend to his teacher there without disturbing his seniors or dislodging his juniors from their seats. If the pupil has to bathe himself, he must finish it quickly so as to be in time with his body dried and dress changed to receive his teacher out of the bathroom with water for washing his feet, a footstool, and a towel [ib.].

After bath comes an interval of teaching if the teacher is so inclined. The teaching would be in the form of answering questions or delivering a discourse [ib., 14].

Another line of menial work for the pupil was to sweep clean the Vihāra where his teacher dwells by removing all furniture in the room for the purpose, including the bedding and bedstead, carpet and mattress, which were to be sunned and dusted. Then he has to put all the things in their proper place again. He had also to clean out other apartments of the Vihāra such as store-room, refectory, fire-room, etc. [ib., 15, 16]. Elsewhere there is a detailed description as to how the junior Bhikkhu must clean the Vihāra [*Chullav.*, viii, 1, 3].

Thus has the pupil to serve his teacher, and him alone, for he is not to render such service to, or accept it from, anybody else. Nor is he to give or receive anything without his teacher's permission. He is not to enter the village or go to a cemetery or go abroad on journeys without his teacher's permission [ib., i, 25, 24]. The permission might be granted if he would travel with a learned Bhikkhu in his company to control him [ib., ii, 21, 1].

Lastly, if his teacher is sick, he must nurse him as long as his life lasts and wait until he has recovered [ib.].

Teacher's Duties. This whole-hearted devotion of the pupil to his teacher had its counterpart in the corresponding attitude and conduct of the teacher towards his pupil. If the duties of the pupil are exacting, those of the teacher also are planned on a similar scale. First, he must give the Bhikkhu under his charge all possible intellectual and spiritual help and guidance "by teaching, by putting questions to him, by exhortation, and by instruction". Second, where the pupil lacked his necessary articles such as an alms-bowl or a robe, the teacher was expected to supply them out of his own belongings. Third, if the pupil falls ill, the teacher must nurse him as long as his life lasts, and wait until he has recovered. During this period of his illness, the teacher is to minister to his pupil in the same way as the pupil serves him in health, down to even rising from bed early to give his pupil " the teeth cleanser and water to rinse his mouth with ", getting water for the washing of his feet, etc. [*Mahāv.*, i, 26].

Pupil Helping Teacher. The relations between the teacher and pupil were expected to be so intimate that the latter even tried to minister to his teacher's mental troubles. To remove his teacher's " discontent " or " indecision ", the pupil would first try his own means and beguile him by religious conversation or get the help of others. The pupil was also to combat by discussion any false doctrines which the teacher might take to or to get others to do it [ib., i, 25, 20–2].

The relations of the pupil toward his teacher did not, however, transcend those toward the Order as a whole to which they both owed a common allegiance as members. Where the teacher offended gravely against the Order, the pupil was to get him duly punished by the Order, and, when the penal discipline is duly undergone, to get the Order to rehabilitate his teacher. In the case of the Order passing any unduly severe sentence, the pupil is to do what he can to get it modified, mitigated, or nullified by arguing with the Order on the one hand, and seeing that the teacher " may behave himself properly, live modestly, and aspire to get clear of his penance that the Order may revoke its sentence ".

Expulsion. There were also rules for the expulsion of a pupil by his teacher. " In five cases a Saddhivihārika ought to be turned away: when he does not feel great affection for his Upājjhāya, nor great inclination towards him, nor much shame, nor great reverence, nor great devotion " [ib., i, 27, 6].

Termination of Studentship. There are again enumerated five cases of cessation of a *nissaya* between the Upajjhāya and Saddhivihārika or the Āchāriya and Antevāsika, viz. when the teacher " is gone away, or has returned to the world, or has died or is gone over to a schismatic faction or when he gives order to the pupil to separate " under rules of expulsion stated above [ib., i, 36].

Qualifications of a Teacher. The duties of the teacher point to the qualifications required of him. Without these a monk was not entitled " to give a *nissaya* " or " ordain a novice ". These are exhaustively enumerated [*Mahāvagga*, i, 36]. He must be well up " in what belongs to moral practices, self-concentration, wisdom, emancipation, and the knowledge and insight thereto " ; must be " able to help others to full perfection " in these ; must be " believing (' not guilty of heresy '), modest, fearful of sinning, strenuous, of ready memory, not guilty of transgressions in morals or conduct, not uneducated or foolish " ; and must be " able to train a pupil in the precepts of proper conduct, to educate him in the elements of morality, to instruct him in what pertains to the Dhamma, to instruct him in what pertains to the Vinaya, to discuss or to make another discuss according to the Dhamma a false doctrine that might arise " ; and so forth [ib.].

Number of Pupils. Regarding the number of pupils a teacher could entertain, we have the following direction : " I allow, O Bhikkhus, a learned, competent Bhikkhu to ordain two novices or to ordain as many novices as he is able to administer exhortation and instruction to " [ib., i, 55].

Residential Schools or Vihāras. The unit of the Buddhist educational system was thus this group of young Bhikkhus or monks living under the guardianship of a common teacher, the Upājjhāya or Āchāriya, who was individually responsible for their health and studies, manners and morals, their spiritual progress. We have already discussed the methods by which each such individual group or knot of a teacher and his pupils was organized, and the relations and regulations which obtained within the limits of each group. But these groups or schools were not always existing as isolated and independent units or institutions in the Buddhist world, as they did so largely in the Brahmanical world of culture. They federated themselves into a larger unit called the Vihāra or monastery. Thus we have to view them as parts of that larger organization and in their relations to its general, collective life which developed its own code of discipline and regulations binding upon all. While Brahmanical culture depended upon the system of individual schools and ideal successions of teachers and disciples, the Buddhist culture was the product of confederations of such schools in larger monastic institutions comprising numbers of teachers and students (sometimes as many as 10,000, as at Nālandā) promoting and partaking of a wider, collective, academic life with its own advantages as an educational and educative agency and factor. We shall now describe the rules and regulations governing this larger academic life of the monastery as a seat of education and a centre of culture of the times, that collective life in which the individual life of each educational group was merged.

A Vihāra as a Federation of different individual groups of Students and Teachers. Since the Monastery was a federation of individual educational groups or schools, the efficiency of its organization depended upon the 'federal' principles of administration which aimed at three distinct objects, viz. (*a*) the independence and efficiency of each constituent group of pupils bound to an individual teacher, (*b*) the adjustment of relations between the different constituent groups, and (*c*) the framing of laws governing the establishment as a whole and binding upon all its members, the teachers and the taught alike. We have already dealt with the disciplines and regulations by which the first of these objects was realized, the system of relations existing between an individual teacher and his pupils united in a common pursuit of culture. We shall now deal with the methods connected with the other two objects of the federal educational institution or a religious guild.

Regulation of Relations between these Groups in a Vihāra. Special rules were called for to maintain the harmony of relations between different groups. Disciplinary steps against the novices of a group had to be taken through the head of the group, the Upājjhāya of the novices concerned. Once the Chhabbaggiya Bhikkhus[1] laid a ban upon novices without the consent of their Upājjhāyas, who, searching after and not finding them, complained, "How is it that our novices have disappeared ?" and on being told the cause of their disappearance protested, "How can the Chhabbaggiya Bhikkhus lay a ban upon our novices without having obtained our consent ?" On this, the Blessed One prescribed the rule: "Let no one, O Bhikkhus, lay a ban upon novices without consent of the Upājjhāyas" [*Mahāvagga*, i, 58]. The next mischief of the Chhabbaggiya Bhikkhus was to draw the novices of senior Bhikkhus over to themselves. This dissolution of their following put their teachers, the Theras, to serious personal inconvenience and on their complaint the

[1] The company of the "six Bhikkhus" with their attendants, among whom were included Paṇḍuka, Lohitaka, Assaji, and Punabbasu. They are represented throughout the Vinaya-Piṭaka as constantly and consistently violating the regulations or finding loopholes and exceptions not covered by them for mischief-making.

Blessed One ruled: "Let no one, O Bhikkhus, draw the followers of another Bhikkhu over to himself" [ib., i, 59]. Thus this rule was required to stop intrigues of the Professors of a Vihāra with students and preserve a proper standard of academic etiquette and decorum governing the delicate relations among the staff. There were, however, certain cases agreed to, on which disciplinary action against the offending novices would be in operation directly and automatically without any reference to their Upājjhāyas. The most serious of them were ten in number, comprising the following: destroying life, stealing, committing impurity, lying, drinking intoxicating liquors, defaming the Buddha, the Dhamma, and the Saṁgha, holding false doctrines, and misconduct with Bhikkhuṇīs. These offences were to be punished by immediate expulsion of the offenders from the Order. There are enumerated five other less serious cases when a novice was directly punishable, viz. "when he is intent on the Bhikkhus receiving no alms, meeting with misfortunes, and finding no residence, when he abuses and reviles the Bhikkhus and when he causes divisions between Bhikkhus and Bhikkhus" [*Mahāv.*, i, 57, 1]. At first the novices committing these offences were punished by being forbidden entrance to the Saṁghārāma or monastery, and they retaliated by "going away, or returning to the world or going over to Titthiya schools" whereupon it was prescribed that they should be forbidden only the places "where they live or which they used to frequent" [ib., i, 57, 2].

Common Regulations binding on all Groups in a Vihāra. We shall now proceed to consider the general rules and regulations governing the common life of a monastery to which all members were subject irrespective of their status and standing. These were naturally determined by the ends of monastic life and discipline, those supreme ends for which all other ends of life were sacrificed as being unworthy, for which the enjoyments and obligations of worldly life were renounced by persons associating themselves in a common struggle. All that was even remotely likely to affect the whole-hearted pursuit of those ends was to be rigorously and ruthlessly abjured. The gulf between the ascetic life and the worldly life was always to be kept sufficiently wide so as not to be crossed. It is, however, to be recalled that the Buddhist Order of ascetics was only one among others flourishing in its times. These Orders all agree as to the ends and the general character of the means, the ascetic practices to be pursued towards the ends, but they must naturally differ as to the exact forms and details of those practices. Buddhist asceticism developed its own system of rules and regulations according to its particular view and definition of the ascetic life. It followed the Middle Path, avoiding the one extreme of self-indulgence and the other of self-mortification. Taking the evil of the world and life to be *dukkha*, pain or sorrow, in the ultimate analysis, Buddhism could not approve of any positive and artificial additions to the sum of life's sufferings by the infliction of pain or disease on one's own self or on others. The Buddhist canonical classification of mankind divided it into (1) self-tormentors or self-burners (*attantapo*), i.e. those who practise penance or *tapas*, (2) tormentors of others, such as butchers, fowlers, hunters, fishermen, thieves, executioners, gaolers, and all perpetrators of cruelties, (3) tormentors of both self and others such as "the great functionaries who, when holding sacrificial ceremonies, perform rites involving some personal discomfort, and also have herds of animals slaughtered and keep their slaves in fear of punishment", and (4) tormentors neither of self nor of others, such as those who have left the home and the world for the life of recluse, renouncing the cares and connections that torment the world, owning no property in animals or human beings and are thus filled with charity and compassion for all living beings and hence "become cool" (*sītabhūta*) and not in a state of burning [*Majjhima*, i, 341, 411; ii, 159; *Aṅguttara*, ii, 205; *Puggala*, 55, cited in the article on Buddhist *Asceticism* of Mrs. Rhys Davids in the *Encycl. of Religion and Ethics*]. The ascetics of Buddhism belonged to the fourth class of humanity. We have already referred to the turning-point in the Buddha's life when he lost faith in the prevailing systems of uncompromising self-mortification as aid to spirituality which he condemned as a merely "bitter course of painful hardship" and was eager to find out "another path to Enlightenment".

This particular ascetic ideal of the mean or "middle path" between the extremes of self-indulgence and self-suppression is systematically and consistently worked out in all the details of Buddhist monastic life and discipline which may be conveniently considered in relation to the three primary requisites of human existence, viz. food, clothing, and shelter.

Two Bases of Monasticism: Chastity. But before going into these details of monastic life we should have a clear idea of the two fundamental principles which mark out monastic life, apart from its details, from the ordinary layman's life of the world. The structure of worldly life has its basis in marriage and property; that of the life monastic rests on their very opposites, viz. celibacy and poverty. One of earliest expressions of the ascetic ideal describes those following it thus: "They cease from seeking for children, and seeking for possessions, and seeking the worldly, and they itinerate as beggars. For what seeking for children is, that is also seeking for possessions; what seeking for possessions is, that is also seeking for the worldly; the one is seeking as much as the other" [*Śatap. Br.*, xiv, 7, 2, 26]. To become a monk meant the dissolution of the marriage tie. "As a man whose head is cut off cannot live any longer with his trunk alone, thus a Bhikkhu who practises sexual intercourse is no Samaṇa" [*Mahāv.*, i, 78, 2]. The texts make a monk address his forsaken wife as his quondam partner and as sister [ib., i, 78, 1; Oldenberg's *Buddha*, p. 355 n.]. Monkhood meant, indeed, a dissolution of all blood-relationships. The Buddha, after his monkhood, is addressed by his son Rāhula not as father but as Samaṇa, while his wife is hardly even recognized [*Mahāv.*, i, 54, 1–2]. The relations of the monk do not, however, necessarily disown him. From their standpoint the relationship continues and is open to the monk for resumption whenever he wants it. As has been already stated, Buddhism is indifferent to such backslidings of monks. In the *Suttavibhaṅga* [*Pār.*, i, 8, 2], a monk's longing for worldly life thus expresses itself: "I have a wife for whom I must provide; I have a village on the income of which I desire to live; I have gold, on it I shall live," thereby showing that his old connections, personal and material, may be resumed. A monk was also allowed, even when he has entered upon *Vassa* or residence during the rainy season, to visit his sick relations such as his parents, brother, or sister, if they desired it [*Mahāv.*, iii, 7]. He was also allowed to give robes to his father and mother if he so desired [ib., viii, 22].

Poverty: Possessions or Property not permissible to an individual Monk. Next to the vow of chastity is that of poverty as an essential mark of monastic life. A monk must live by mendicancy and not by his property, the fetter which binds man to the world. Hence he is called a Bhikshu, Bhikkhu, beggar. The Bhikshu is known even to the *Rigveda* [x, 117]. The poor are always with us. The Rigveda enjoins the rich to support the poor as a duty. Going from home into homelessness meant the surrender of all property and embracing poverty, the superior sanctity and glories of which are very often proclaimed in the texts. " It is difficult for the man who dwells at home to live the higher life in all its fulness, in all its purity, in all its bright perfection. I wish therefore to cut off my hair and beard, to clothe myself in the orange-coloured robes, and to go forth from the household life into the houseless state." Thus declares an intending *bhikkhu* [*Mahāv.*, v, 13, 1], and the declaration was the most usual one in such cases. The following passage expresses the standing attitude towards family life and property regarded as fetters holding in bondage the spirit struggling for freedom: " Wise people do not call that a strong fetter which is made of iron, wood, or hemp; passionately strong is the care for precious stones and rings, for sons and a wife " [*Dhammapada*, v, 345]. We have already noticed the Interdict administered to a *Sāmaṇera* on his ordination that he must on no account receive gold and silver as presents. Violation of this Interdict was regarded as a serious offence. " Whatsoever Bhikkhu shall receive gold or silver, or get someone to receive it for him or allow it to be kept in deposit for him—that is a Pāchittiya offence involving forfeiture " [*SBE.*, xiii, p. 26]. The method of procedure laid down for dealing with this offence was that the offending Bhikkhu must first surrender the treasure to the Saṁgha who would then transfer it to some *Ārāmika* or *Upāsaka* for getting in exchange honey, ghee, or oil to be the common property of the Saṁgha save the guilty Bhikkhu who would be deprived of its enjoyment. If, however, the layman does not agree to the proposed utilization of the gold and silver, he will be asked to throw them away. If he is not agreeable to either of the two proposals for disposing of the untouchable treasure, then, as a last way out of the difficulty, a Bhikkhu was to be formally appointed by the Saṁgha, distinguished for his moral pre-eminence, to be the " Bullion-remover " (*Rūpiyachhaḍḍaka*) with instructions to cast it away so as to leave no sign to indicate where it might be (*animittam katvā*) [ib.]. The Saṁgha, or any member thereof, was not allowed on any pretext whatsoever to accept or seek for gold or gifts in cash. Gifts in kind alone were acceptable, but not their money values [*Mahāv.*, vi, 34, 21]. Thus, if a layman tendered to a Bhikkhu " the value in barter of a set of robes ", it was ordained that the Bhikkhu must humbly say he could not accept " the robe-fund ", but only the robes, which further must be bought only by his agent and not by himself, so that he might not have any direct contact with cash [*Pāt.*, p. 23]. The regulations for Re during the rainy season prescribe that the Bhikkhu must remove from a place where he stumbles upon "ownerless treasure", the very sight of which was thus to be avoided! [*Mahāv.*, iii, 11, 4]. The rule regarding gold and silver was applied to some extent to a jewel. A Bhikkhu picking up a jewel or anything deemed a jewel must lay it aside "that he to whom it may belong may take it away" [*Pāt.*, p. 53]. It is this uncompromising attitude towards the encroachments of greed that kept the Saṁgha for centuries in its pristine purity, free from all earthly contamination. But the operation of the ordinance further shows that the forms or kinds of property which the individual Bhikkhu could not hold, the Saṁgha in its corporate capacity could not also hold. The contrary view is very often taken, but erroneously. The forms of property which were legitimate for the individual were alone legitimate for the Order too.

Possessions permitted to the Saṁgha. In one place, indeed, we find an inventory of the various classes of goods and property which are declared to be "untransferable" to the individual monks but are always to be treated as the indivisible common property of the entire Saṁgha and "not to be disposed of either by the Saṁgha or by a company of two or three Bhikkhus (a Gaṇa) or by a single individual". The list includes the following "five things", viz. (1) A park (*Ārāma*) or the site for a park, (2) A Vihāra or the site for it, (3) A bed or a chair or a bolster or a pillow, (4) A brass vessel, jar, pot, or vase; implements like a razor, axe, hatchet, hoe, or spade, (5) Creepers, bamboos, muñja, babbaja, or common grass or clay; and (6) things made of wood or crockery [*Chullav.*, vi, 15, 2]. It is, however, clear from another passage [*Mahāv.*, viii, 27, 2] that some of these things might form part of the possessions of an individual monk on whose death they would be disposed of according to the general principle indicating the line of division between the collective property of the Saṁgha and the individual property of its members. It is, nevertheless, undeniable that the vow of poverty so rigorously enjoined upon the individual monk was not at all meant for the Saṁgha which the Buddha himself permitted to grow rich by permitting it to receive the benefactions of its lay well-wishers which flowed in an abundant stream under the Buddha's direct encouragement. The Buddha, however, dictated the forms in which alone these gifts of property would be acceptable to the Saṁgha. Even these forms are found to cover a wide range including parks, pavilions, and lotus-ponds and buildings of various descriptions from the cave and the cell and the attic to storied houses and vihāras equipped with all appurtenances for healthful life [iii, 5, 6, ib.], and sometimes even materials for buildings [ib., iii, 8]. The Saṁgha also received property by bequests of the dead [*Chullav.*, x, ii, and *Mahāv.*, viii, 27, 5, already cited]. The Saṁgha in receipt of things too valuable for their use were permitted to barter them "in order to increase their stock of legally permissible furniture" [*Chullav.*, vi, 19, 1]. The Buddha freely permitted the dedication of all such gifts to the Saṁgha and encouraged it by pronouncing it to be very meritorious and prescribed the duty of his disciples to offer all facilities required by donors for the transfer or execution of their gifts [cf. *Mahāv.*, iii, 5]. There is, however, no evidence to show that the Order held property in the forms of slaves, horses, or live stock, or even lands for agricultural pursuits which were forbidden the Bhikkhu in the following injunction: "A monk who digs the earth or causes it to be dug is liable to punishment" [*Pāt.*, *SBE.*, xiii, p. 33], but the *Mahāvagga*[1] [vi, 39] has a passage alluding to cultivation or sowing of the land belonging to the Ārāma of the Order. While the Saṁgha was thus allowed to receive property of various kinds and grow steadily rich, there was no relaxation permitted in the vow of poverty imposed upon the individual monk who could not count as his exclusive possessions more than the following eight articles, viz. the three robes (to be described later), a girdle for the loins, an alms-bowl, a razor, a needle, and a water-strainer not only to remove the impurities of his drinks but also to intercept destruction of life. These are all objects for individual and exclusive and not for collective and common possession and enjoyment. This self-imposed poverty of the monk was proclaimed daily by his begging rounds.

[1] "Of seedlings belonging to the Saṁgha grown upon private ground, half the produce, O Bhikkhus, you may have, when you have given a part to the private owner. Of seedlings belonging to a private person, grown upon ground the property of the Saṁgha, you may have the use, when you have given a part to the private owner." This probably means that the Order did not *directly* undertake the planting of trees or sowing of crops, though they supplied the seeds, and the land on which they would be sown by agriculturists or cultivators proper. The "plantations" of the Ārāmas are referred to as needing protection against goats and cattle [*Chullav.*, vi, 3, 10]. The grounds of the Ārāma were in charge of an *Ārāmika* or park-keeper who was one of the officials on the staff of the Saṁgha [ib., vi, 21, 3]. King Bimbisāra made a gift of the services of 500 park-keepers to the venerable Pilindavachchha, which gave rise to a distinct village called Ārāmikagāma [*Mahāv.*, vi, 15]. It is clear that the park-keeper was not a Bhikkhu or member of the Order. Besides keeping the grounds in order, his duty was to protect the monks from disturbance of visitors by guarding the entrance to the Ārāma [ib., x, 4, 2].

Chapter XV

DISCIPLINE

Regulations as to Food and Begging. We shall now study the regulations of the Order regarding the primary wants of life. These wants had to be supplied from the proceeds of begging and the gifts of the laity. We may recall the ruling in regard to food for the newly ordained monk: "The religious life has morsels of food given in alms for its resource. Thus you must endeavour to live all your life. Meals given to the Saṁgha, to certain persons, invitations, food distributed by ticket, meals given each fortnight, each Uposatha day (i.e. the last day of each fortnight) or the first day of each fortnight are extra allowances" [*Mahāv.*, i, 30, 4]. The mode of the daily begging is prescribed. "When the time has been called in the Ārāma, a Bhikkhu should put on his waist cloth so as to cover himself all round from above the navel to below his knees, tie his belt round his waist, fold his upper robes and put them on, fasten the block on, wash his hands, take his alms-bowl, and then slowly and carefully proceed to the village. He is not to turn aside from the direct route and push on in front of senior Bhikkhus. He is to go amidst the houses properly clad, with his limbs under control, with downcast eye, with his robes not tucked up, not laughing, or speaking loudly, not swaying his body or his arms or his head about, not with his arms akimbo, or his robe pulled over his head, and without walking on his heels" [*Chullav.*, viii, 4, 3]. When he enters a dwelling, he should note carefully beforehand its entrance and exit. "He should not go in nor come out roughly. He should not stand too far off, nor too near, nor too long, and should not turn back too easily. When food is being given to him he should lift up his robe (Saṁghāṭī) with his left hand so as to disclose his bowl, take the bowl in both his hands and receive the food into it without looking at the face of the giver if it is a woman. After the food has been given he should cover up the bowl with his robe and turn back slowly and carefully" [ib., viii, 5, 2].

Begging for food was thus an institution common to both the Brahmanical and Buddhist systems of training. There is, however, seen a difference in the manner prescribed for the begging. While the Brahmachārin was allowed to ask for alms by words specially specified, as we have seen, the Buddhist Bhikkhu must beg in silence [cf. *Mil. P.*, iv, 5, 31], so as to give the laity an opportunity of giving him food and doing a meritorious act. It can hardly be called "begging" in the modern sense of the term.

Alms-bowl. The begging bowl was to be made of only iron or clay and not other materials [ib., v, 9, 1]. It was usually put in a bag (*thavikā*) carried by a shoulder strap [ib., v, 9, 4].

Other Outfit for Begging. As further equipment for his journeys on begging, the monk carried needles, scissors, drugs, a strainer for filtering water, and might also use sandals if the journey was along rough paths [ib., v, 13, 1].

The Monk's Dietary. We shall now consider the articles that make up the monk's diet [*Pāt.*, pp. 37–42]. Two kinds of food are distinguished, *hard*, such as biscuits, cakes, meats, fruits, and *soft*, such as boiled rice and curries. The Buddha on the eve of his enlightenment took milk-rice from Sujātā at Uruvelā. Immediately after his enlightenment the two merchants, Tapussa and Bhallika, offered him rice-cakes and lumps of honey [*Mahāv.*, i, 4, 3], and, according to Aśvaghosha [*Buddha-charita*, xv, 61], "three sweet substances (sugar, honey, and ghee) and milk." Evidently, these must have been regarded as the ideal food of a Bhikkhu. The following delicacies are mentioned, viz. ghee, butter, oil, honey, molasses, fish, flesh, milk, and curds, but none but a sick Bhikkhu "should request them for his own use and partake of them" [*Pāt.*, 40]. The language of this restriction does not seem to bar these delicacies out of dinners voluntarily offered to the monks by their lay well-wishers. Accordingly, it does not conflict with the account of the Buddha himself taking meat, and pronouncing fish to be "pure" food when "the eater has not seen, or heard, or suspected that it has been caught for that purpose" [*Chullav.*, vii, 3, 15; cf. *Mahāv.*, vi, 31, 14]. Kern points out [*Indian Buddhism*, p. 84, where he differently understands the above prohibition] that the use of non-vegetarian diet by Buddhist monks was in imitation of Brahmanical practices which allowed it under certain restrictions [cf. *Gautama*, xviii, 27–38; *Āpast.*, i, 5, 17, 29 ff.; *Manu*, v, 27]. The Brahman ascetic was, however, forbidden meat and honey [*Āpast.*, ii, 9, 22, 2; *Manu*, vi, 14; but there is an exception in *Gautama*, iii, 31]. The Buddhists, in spite of their decrying the Brahmans, were always anxious to pass for Āryas and fond of frequently repeating that very word. The Saṁgha in one passage [*Mahāv.*, vi, 33] permits a meat dinner by outsiders in its own premises where they were given shelter in storm and rain. "They boiled congey and boiled rice and mixed curries and cut up meat and split firewood." As regards other foods, we have mention of sweet-meats (*Pūva*) and rice cakes (*Mantha*) which seem to have been given usually and in large quantities in alms, as they were prepared in the houses of the laity on all festive occasions. Five food products derived from the cow are mentioned, viz. milk, curds, ghee, butter milk, and butter. Bhikkhus on journeys were permitted to provide themselves with supply of rice, salt, molasses, beans, oil, and ghee [*Mahāv.*, vi, 34, 21]. Eight kinds of drinkables are mentioned, fruit juices, and drinks prepared from leaves, flowers, and roots [ib., 35]. Beans were specially recommended among vegetables [ib., vi, 16, 2]. Soup and boiled rice sometimes figure as the Bhikkhus' ordinary diet [ib., i, 25, 1]. Salt and oil, rice and meal were collected "in quart pots from house to house" by the two sons of an old barber monk for the entertainment of the Buddha with 250 disciples [ib., vi, 37, 2]. "All solid food in the shape of fruits" was always allowed [ib., vi, 38]. The taking of tender fruits was not permitted but only those having no life in them or injured by fire, sword, or nails [*Chullav.*, v, 5]. Fermented liquors and strong drinks were forbidden [*Pat.*, op. cit.]. The Interdict on this point has been already referred to.

The most religiously disposed Bhikkhu would observe as regards his meals the rule of *Paiṇḍapātika*, i.e. of living on food obtained by begging from door to door and carried in the bowl itself. He who would come back first from his round for alms in the village was to make the preliminary arrangements for the dining of the whole fraternity, such as getting ready the seats, water for washing and drinking, towels, etc. He who comes last will, after taking his own meals if he has not taken them elsewhere, clean out the dining-room (*Chullav.*, viii, 5, 3]. Sometimes, an individual Bhikkhu would be given food more than sufficient for himself. In that case, he must not accept more than two or three bowlfuls as the maximum quantity for purposes of distribution among the Saṁgha [*Pāt.*, op. cit.].

Begging of Food confined to approved Households. As regards taking meals out of their Vihāras, the Bhikkhus must as individuals or in companies so conduct themselves as not to bring any discredit to the Order. A novice must be acquainted beforehand with the official declaration of the Order as regards lawful and unlawful resorts for alms and families in want. Seeking food uninvited at an approved household was forbidden [*Pāt.*, p. 57]. The approved household is defined as that which is rich in faith but poor in goods, whose liberality towards the Order lands it in want. A householder was officially declared as disapproved and disqualified by the Order formally passing as a body the Resolution of " turning the bowl down " in respect of him, after which he will be deprived of the privilege of having any intercourse with the Order by way of offering it food or lodging. The Saṁgha was to boycott him completely. This Resolution of boycott was applied against a layman found guilty of the following eight acts of hostility against the Order, viz. when he brings loss of gifts on the Bhikkhus, or harm to them, or causes them want of residence, or reviles and slanders them as also the Buddha, the Dhamma, and the Saṁgha [*Chullav.*, v, 20, 3]. A boycott was declared against Vaḍḍha the Lichchhavi for having brought a groundless charge of a breach of morality against the Venerable Dabba the Mallian, and the Saṁgha turned the bowl down in respect of him by adopting a Resolution to that effect. The boycott was raised when the offender conducted himself aright, expressed penitence, and asked for the restoration of his former status. The Saṁgha then turned up the bowl as respects him by a special Resolution to that effect.

Manner of Begging. Dealings with the approved households were carefully regulated. A Bhikkhu must not force his way into a house when a meal is going on, and take his seat there. Nor must he take the meals procured by the intervention of a Bhikkhuṇī unless they were previously and independently promised. The Bhikkhus, invited to laymen's houses, must not, while eating, allow a Bhikkhuṇī to stay there and give directions, saying: " Here give curry, give rice here." They must rebuke her for such officiousness, saying: " Stand aside, sister, as long as the Bhikkhus are eating " [*Pāt.*, p. 56]. The Bhikkhus must not go in a body to the same householder and ask for meals and thus be a burden upon him. Not more than three were permitted to seek alms at a common place together [*Chullav.*, vii, 3, 13]. Exception to this rule was allowed in the case of sickness, distribution of robes, or on a journey by foot, or on board a boat, or when, after *Vassa*, the monks travelled in great numbers to visit the Buddha, or when a general invitation is issued to all Samaṇas as a class including non-Buddhists [*Pāl.*, pp. 37–42, *SBE.*, xiii].

The monks are not to exercise any choice as to invitations but to accept them as they come. They should, however, prefer those which are invitations to take not merely meals but also robes [ib.].

Manner of Eating. When taking meals on invitation they must eat straight on whatever was given and not pick or choose in regard to the food served [ib.]. There is an interesting description of the Saṁgha or a band of monks taking their meals together on invitation, which shows the rules of etiquette at eating [*Chullav.*, viii, 3–6]. The senior monks sit apart from the juniors. Drinking water is to be received carefully in the bowl held with both hands so as not to splash anybody. Boiled rice should be similarly received in the bowl with a room left for the curry. If there be ghee, oil, or delicacies, the senior monk should say: "Get an equal quantity for all." The alms given are to be "accepted with mind alert, paying attention to the bowl, with equal curry and equally heaped up". The food is to be received carefully and any fragments of it falling must be picked up and eaten, for "each single ball of rice, for example, is the result of hundredfold labour" (*Chullav.*, v, 26]. The senior monk is not to start eating until the boiled rice has been served to all. The monk must not cover up the curry or the condiment with the rice, desiring to make it nicer, nor should ask for any rice or curry, unless he is sick. "Others' bowls are not to be looked at with envious thoughts. The food should be rolled up into round mouthfuls." The process of eating is to be marked by dignity and decorum as regards the movement of the mouth, tongue, and hand. The jar containing drinking water is not to be taken hold of with hands soiled with food. The senior monk is not to accept water for washing until all the monks have finished eating. In returning home, the junior monks should go first and the seniors after them. Before parting, the senior monk was to return thanks to the host on behalf of his party, of whom four or five who were seniors, or next to him in seniority, must wait for him while he was thus engaged [ib., viii, 4, 1].

It was further laid down that a Bhikkhu who has finished his meals must not accept a second course on invitation lest it should "stir up longing" [*Pāt.*, op. cit.]. This is the rule of *Khalupaśchādbhattika.* There is also another rule of "eating at one sitting", *Aikāsanika* [*Majjhi. N.*, i, 437]. The rule of eating out of prescribed times has been already referred to. The wrong time of eating was after sun-turn [*Pāt.*, op. cit.]. There was again another rule of " eating from one vessel only " (*pattapiṇḍika*).

Standing Invitations. Sometimes a Bhikkhu might secure a permanent host and patron to give him the necessaries of life. Lest this should render his begging and its exertions unnecessary and thereby deprive him of a healthy educative and moral influence, it was laid down that he must not accept for a period exceeding four months such a standing invitation for food, clothing, shelter, and medicine [*Pāt.*, op. cit.]. Such standing invitations would sometimes be extended to the entire fraternity. We read of " an arrangement made at Rājagaha that the Bhikkhus were to receive excellent meals successively in the houses of different rich Upāsakas " and the sight of their felicity tempts a Brahman to join the Order " for his belly's sake " [*Mahāv.*, i, 30, 1]. We are also told how " at Vesāli a regular service of sweet food had been established, the laity taking the duty in turns " [*Chullav.*, v, 14, 1]. We also read of a householder possessed of good food giving " a perpetual alms to the Saṁgha, a meal for four Bhikkhus ". " He with his wife and children used to stand at the place of alms and serve ; and offer to some Bhikkhus boiled rice, and to some congey, and to some oil, and to some dainty bits " [ib., iv, 4, 6].

Invitations of Corporations. Monks were entertained as guests by both individuals and collective bodies or corporations. We read of " the turn to provide the Saṁgha with a meal " coming to a certain *Pūga*. The senior monk Sāriputta presided at this dinner given by the corporation and moved the usual vote of thanks at the conclusion of the dinner [*Chullav.*, viii, 4, 1].

Meals at Rest-houses. Failing kindly hosts, the monks would resort to the public rest-houses (*Āvasatha*) for meals, but they were not to take more than one meal there [*Pāt.*, op. cit.]. These rest-houses formed one of the amenities of life among the travelling public of ancient India. Some of them were even equipped with all the necessaries of life to be freely given to travellers. Asoka's concern for them shows itself in some of his Edicts. The institution was a most distinguishing feature of the later Gupta empire, too, as is shown by Fa-hien's first-hand observations in connection with the organization of public charities in Middle Kingdom and Central India. Pāṭaligāma had one such village rest-house where the Buddha with "a great company of brethren" was invited by the villagers to take his meals. "They made the rest-house fit in every way for occupation, placed seats in it, set up a water-pot and fixed an oil lamp" and announced to the Buddha that all things were ready. Then "the Blessed One robed himself, took his bowl and other things, went with the brethren to the rest-house, washed his feet, entered the hall, and took his seat against the centre pillar, with his face towards the east" surrounded by his disciples [*Mahā-parinibbāna-Sutta*, i, 20–2].

A Monk as Host. If the Bhikkhu had himself to play the host, he was not to entertain as his guest and feed with his own hand an Achelaka (a naked ascetic), a Paribbājaka and Paribbājikā [*Pāt.*, op. cit.].

The Buddha's notable Hosts. As has been already stated, the Buddha was always receiving and accepting invitations to dine out with his disciples. The Buddha, staying in a grove near the hermitage of the Jaṭila Uruvela Kassapa, was offered daily food by him at his place [*Mahāv.*, i, 16]. The next important invitation in his career came from the Magadha King Seniya Bimbisāra who "ordered excellent food, both hard and soft, to be prepared" for the Buddha and the fraternity of Bhikkhus numbering 1,000, "who all had been Jaṭilas before." The king "with his own hands" served the food [*Mahāv.*, i, 22]. King Śuddhodana of Kapilavastu, the father of the Buddha, entertained at his palace at Kapilavastu the Buddha and his Order with a "savoury meal". The Seṭṭhi of Rājagaha similarly invited the Buddha and his fraternity to a dinner for which he gave the following "command to his slaves and work-people: 'So get up at early morn, my men, and cook congey, and cook rice, and prepare curries and prepare delicacies'" [*Chullav.*, vi, 4, 1]. This invitation was followed by that of his brother-in-law, the merchant prince, Anāthapiṇḍika, the invitation which was so big with consequences both to the host and the Order. The meals comprised the usual "sweet food both hard and soft" [ib.]. The same meals were also served by Visākhā, the mother of Migāra, at her "mansion", to the Buddha [*Mahāv.*, viii, 15]. Sunidha and Vassakāra, the chief ministers of Magadha, treated him and his company to "sweet dishes of boiled rice and cakes" [*Mahā-parinibbāna-Sutta*, i, 30]. The courtesan Ambapālī of Vesāli vied with the Licchchhavi youths of the nobility of that free city for the honour of entertaining at her house the Buddha and his disciples who were then staying at her mango-grove. When the young noblemen said to her: "Ambapālī, give up this meal to us for a hundred thousand," she proudly answered: "My lords, were you to offer all Vesāli with its subject territory, I would not give up so honourable a feast." She then "made ready in her mansion sweet rice and cakes, set the sweet rice and cakes before the Order with the Buddha at their head and waited upon them till they refused any more" [ib., ii]. At Andhakavinda the Buddha and his 1,250 disciples with him were entertained by a Brahman who treated them to just the food which he found wanting in the provision-room of the Order, viz. rice-milk and honey lump [*Mahāv.*, vi, 24]. Once the people of a place entertained the Order with the Buddha at its head with solid rice-milk and honey lumps to such satiety that the Bhikkhus had no appetite that day when they had to assemble for meals in the dining-hall. The next day the entire body of the Bhikkhus, 1,250 in number, with the Buddha at their head, accepted the invitation of a certain minister, newly converted, who made elaborate arrangements for the dinner, preparing for each individual a dish of meat, besides other excellent food hard and soft. When dinner was being served, the Bhikkhus said: "Give us little, friend; give us little." The host said: "Do not take little, reverend sirs, because you think: 'This minister is but newly converted.' Much food, both hard and soft, has been prepared by me, and 1,250 dishes of meat; I will offer to each Bhikkhu one dish of meat. Take, reverend sirs, as much as you want." The Bhikkhus said: "This is not the reason, friend, for which we take little. But we have satiated ourselves in the morning with solid rice-milk and with honey-lumps; therefore we take little." The minister at this explanation lost his temper and said: "How can their Reverences, when I have invited them, partake of solid rice-milk with other people, as if I were unable to give them as much as they want?" Then he went round angry, filling the bowls of the Bhikkhus, and saying, "Eat or take it away!" On the matter reaching the ears of the Buddha, he rebuked the Bhikkhus, saying: "How can these foolish persons, having been invited to one place, partake of solid rice-milk with other persons?" [ib., 25]. Sīha, the Commander-in-Chief of the Lichchhavi republic, entertained the Buddha and his Order to a meat dinner for which he gave instructions beforehand to one of his subalterns [ib., 31, 12]. Quite a remarkable example of hospitality towards the Order is shown by Meṇḍaka, the householder, who fed the Order daily during their stay in his city, the Bhaddiya-nagara, in the kingdom of the Māgadha King Seniya Bimbisāra. When the Order left that place, Meṇḍaka followed them with his hospitality, with cartloads of salt, oil, rice, and hard food, and 1,250 cowkeepers, each with a cow, to wait upon every individual Bhikkhu with fresh milk, and other sweet food, hard and soft, to boot [ib., 34, 17]. The Buddha with 250 disciples was the guest of the Mallas of Kusinārā who " established a compact to the effect that whosoever went not forth to welcome the Blessed One should pay a fine of 500 hundred pieces (the square *kahāpaṇas* of copper or bronze as figured in the Bharhut bas reliefs and mentioned in the *Dhammapada*) ". A certain succession was also fixed in which the inhabitants of Kusinārā should each in succession provide food for the Saṁgha. When the turn came to Roja the Malla, he inspected the Saṁgha's store-house and finding its deficiency in potherbs and meal fed the Bhikkhus with them with his own hand [ib., 36]. Finally, we may mention the last invitation of the Buddha given to him by Chunda, " the worker in metals," at Pāvā, who " made ready in his house sweet rice and cakes and a quantity (*pahūtam*) of dried pork (? *Śūkara-maddava* [1]) ? The Buddha at once perceived that the latter food was not to be assimilated by anyone in earth or heaven among gods and men but a Tathāgata. Thus he alone made his meal upon it and had what was left over buried in a hole, while " the other food, the sweet rice and cakes " was served to the members of the Order. Then " there fell upon him a dire sickness, the disease of dysentery, and sharp pain came upon him, even unto death ". Later, at the point of death, lest remorse be roused in Chunda for his meals causing it, the Buddha was considerate enough to send him through Ānanda the consolation that he acquired special merit as the giver of the Buddha's last meal like the giver of his first food [*Mahā-par.-sutta*, iv, 14–21, 57].

Gifts of Provisions. Besides these invitations to dine out, the Bhikkhus also received supplies of provisions for their meals

[1] Rhys Davids holds that " there is great doubt as to the exact meaning of this name of the last dish the Buddha partook of ", and that " the fact is that the exact sense is not known ". He cites Dhammapāla who says that the word means " not pork or meat at all but the tender top sprout of the bamboo plant after it has been trampled upon by swine ", and, according to others, " a kind of mushroom that grows in ground trodden under foot by swine ", or " a particular kind of flavouring or sauce ". It may even mean " tender flowers ", *mārdava* in Sanskrit meaning " tender, pitiful, etc." [*SBE.*, xxxv, p. 244 n.].

from the lay devotees. We read of a Vihāra receiving such a large quantity of ghee, butter, oil, honey, and molasses that they had to be stored up in vessels till they were being damaged by rats, while the Bhikkhus suffered in reputation as "being storers up of goods". While deeming the articles to be useful as medicines, the Buddha ordered that "when such are received they must be used within a period of seven days during which they may be stored up" [*Mahāv.*, vi, 15, 10; cf. *Pāt.*, p. 27]. During the period of a famine in Rājagaha the Bhikkhus were supported by the people by gifts of salt, oil, rice, and hard food brought to the Ārāma [ib., 17, 7]. We read of Suppiyā of Benares, the tender-hearted benefactress of the Order, flowing with the milk of motherly affection, visiting the Ārāma, going around from Vihāra to Vihāra and from cell to cell, asking the Bhikkhus: "Who is sick, venerable Sirs? For whom, and what shall I procure?" One sick Bhikkhu said: "I have taken a purgative, sister, and I want some broth." Promising it, Suppiyā, on returning home, gave order to a pupil (evidently of her husband): "Go, my good Sir, and see if there is any meat to be had." Unfortunately on that day the killing of cattle being interdicted, the youth searching through the whole of Benares could not find any meat on hand, whereupon, as the texts tell us, the believing and pious Suppiyā, to keep her word, cut off her own flesh and gave it to her maid-servant, saying: "Go, my girl, get the strength out of this meat and give it to a sick Bhikkhu in such and such a Vihāra. And should anybody call for me tell him that I am sick." When the news of her sickness reached the Buddha, he had her brought to him, "and in the moment the Blessed One saw her, that great wound was healed; and there was good skin there, with the tiny hairs thereon" [ib., 23]. We read again of the merchant Belaṭṭha Kachchāna who, while "travelling on the road from Rājagaha to Andhakavinda with five hundred carts all full of pots of sugar", approached the Buddha and his company and with his permission gave to each Bhikkhu one pot of sugar [ib., 26].

The Buddha's non-Buddhist Hosts. But the circle of the Buddha's hosts included not merely his own lay devotees but also the devotees of other faiths. The homage paid by the latter to the Buddha was the greatest compliment to his spiritual pre-eminence which thus won a universal recognition. Thus we read of the Brahman ascetic, Keniya the Jaṭila, living at Āpaṇa, hearing of the Buddha's reputation, was anxious to pay his respects to him, and thought: "What now should I have taken (as a present) to the Samaṇa Gotama?" Considering that he was an abstainer from food at night and wrong time like the Ṛishis of old [viz. Aṭṭhaka (Ashṭaka, author of Rigveda, x, 104, or Atri), Vāmaka (?), Vāmadeva, Vessāmitta, Yamataggi (Jāmadagni), Āṅgirasa Bhāradvāja, Vāseṭṭha, and Bhagu (Bhṛigu)], he saw the Buddha with "a quantity of drinkables carried on pingoes" with which he had permission to satisfy the Buddha and his disciples with his own hand. Moved by the Buddha's discourse, he asked for "the privilege of providing the to-morrow's meal" for him and his Bhikkhus. But the Buddha said: "Great, O Keniya, is the company of the Bhikkhus. Two hundred and fifty are the Bhikkhus in number. And thou art greatly devoted to the Brahmans." But Keniya's zeal had its own way at the end, and he offered with his own hand at his house plenty of "sweet" and "nice" food, both hard and soft, to the Buddha and his company [ib., 35]. The arrangements for the dinner were made on a generous scale with the co-operation of all his "venerable friends and servants, relatives and kinsmen" whom the Brahman requested to render him "bodily service" and "complying with his request, some of them dug fire-places, some chopped fire-wood, some washed the vessels, some placed water pots, some prepared seats", while the host himself provided a circular pavilion for the reception of his honoured guests [*Sutta Nipāta*, iii, 7, 21, 22]. The dinner was followed as usual by a discourse of the Buddha in which he praised the Rigvedic hymn of the Sāvitrī as the chief of the sacred verses, but the discourse was not followed on this occasion by its usual result of the conversion of the guest.[1] Another example of a dinner given by a non-

[1] Somewhat allied to this example of the entertainment of the Buddha by non-Buddhists and of the Buddha's toleration towards them is that related in the story of the Lichchhvi Commander-in-Chief Sīha already referred to. In the story, when Sīha deserts his own sect of the Niganṭhas and becomes converted to Buddhism by the Buddha's religious discourse delivered after dinner, the Buddha generously asks him not to transfer all his liberality to him at once but to continue it towards his quondam religious brethren so that they may not turn away disappointed from a house which by its long established charities became the refuge of the helpless [*Mahāv.*, vi, 31, 11]. Similarly, when Uruvela Kassapa decides to be ordained, the Buddha asks him not to decide it in a hurry but, as the leader, guide, and highest of his 500 Jaṭila followers, "to go first and inform them of his intentions" [ib., i, 20, 18]. Before his conversion, the Buddha showed a fine consideration towards his feelings by withdrawing from the scene of his great sacrifice to which would come "all the people of Aṅga and Magadha", bringing with them as offering "abundant food, both hard and soft", so that the Buddha's superior merits might not spoil his reputation with his followers as he secretly feared.

Buddhist to the Order is that of " a certain high official at court " (of the Magadhan king) who was a follower of the Ājīvakas. The dinner was disturbed by Upananda the Śākyan coming late, and ousting from his seat the Bhikkhu next to him in rank, even when he was eating, whereupon the minister, annoyed, complained to the Buddha who gave the ruling that " a Bhikkhu is not to be made to get up out of his seat before the meal is over " (*Chullav.*, vi, 10, 1].

A Monk's Meals. A review of the evidence as set forth above will show that the daily meal of the Bhikkhu would commence with a slight repast of fruit and cakes with milk or water as the beverage in the early morning, to be followed by the principal meal of the day usually made up of rice and curry which was taken between eleven and twelve. This is evident from the regulation that the meal was not to be prolonged beyond the time when the sun cast a shadow [*Chullav.*, xii, 2–8, and *Pāt.*, p. 40], but must be taken " before and up to noon " [*Mahāv.*, vi, 40, 3]. Sometimes, rice-milk would be served for the early morning meal or breakfast before the Bhikkhus would start on their begging rounds [*Mahāv.*, i, 25, 8]. We read of some Bhikkhus of tender age whom their guardians admitted to the Order under a false idea of the comforts of its life setting up a clamour for rice-milk, for soft food and hard food, as soon as they rose from bed in the early morning. The elderly brethren answered their clamour coolly by saying: " Wait, friends, till day-time ; you shall get what is here or must go out for alms." But the boys were not to be silenced ; they threw their bedding about, made it wet, and kept on crying for food [ib., i, 49, 4]. After the principal meal no more solid and substantial food was permitted. Only slight repasts were allowed in the afternoon after sun-turn.

Medicine. In connection with food we have to consider the various articles which were recommended to be taken only as medicaments. The detailed information given by the texts [*Mahāv.*, vi] on this subject afford us incidentally " a very fair insight into a good deal of the medical lore current at that early period, that is about 400 B.C., in the valley of the Ganges. It is a pity that the current authorities on the history of law and medicine have entirely ignored the details obtainable from these ancient books of Buddhist Canon Law " [Rhys Davids, *American Lectures*, pp. 57–8]. Rules for preparing various kinds of medicines together with medical and surgical operations are given in the Vinaya, from which we may have some idea of the condition of medical science and practice in India in that early age.

The orthodox ruling on the medicines to be used by the monks was as follows: "The religious life has decomposing urine as medicine for its resource. Thus you must endeavour to live all your life. Ghee, butter, oil, honey, and molasses are extra allowances" [*Mahāv.*, i, 30, 4]. In practice, the "extra allowances" were freely used and often added to according to the necessities of the cases of sickness. Among the ailments of the monks figures frequently the sickness of the hot season for which the five extra allowances were prescribed as medicaments. On account of their constant need, the Saṁgha was glad to get them as gifts from its supporters and would often lay by a store of them. Every Vihāra was permitted to have a store-house in a special detached building. The texts trace the origin of this permission to the sickness of the Venerable Yasoja for whom drugs were brought, but they were put out of doors by the Bhikkhus for want of a proper store-house (*Kappiya-bhūmi*), till "vermins ate them and thieves carried them away" [*Mahāv.*, vi, 33, 5]. We may now refer to the more important of the numerous other articles prescribed as medicines. The uses for medicinal purposes were known of certain roots, leaves, fruits, gums (e.g. Hiṅgu) and salts, as also some astringent decoctions prepared from some of these. Chunam was used for itches or boils, while as preventive against skin diseases was prescribed the use of dry cow dung, and some kinds of clay and colouring matter. We have references to eye ointments of various kinds; to oil to be rubbed and to aroma to be sniffed up in cases of headache; to certain herbs, hemp-water, steam-bath, and bath in medicated water as antidotes to rheumatism. Medicinal oils are prescribed for disorders of the stomach, and for wind in the stomach the use of salt, of sour gruel, of a particular kind of gruel made of ginger and two varieties of pepper, and of Tila seeds, rice, and beans. As regards beans, one could take with profit as much quantity as he liked. The use of dung and urine of the cow and of some kinds of ashes and clay is prescribed in cases of snake-bite. Varieties of artificial and natural juices and meat broth were known. We have an interesting report of Sāriputta suffering from fever at Sāvatthi which abates on his eating the edible stalks of some lotuses procured by Moggallāna, his inseparable friend. Lastly, we have evidence regarding surgical treatment. We read of a lancet operation to cut off proud flesh ; of compresses, bandages, and oils for the treatment of wounds ; of a fistula cured by lancing and treated by ointment [*Chullav.*, v, 27, 4] ; and of the use of a clyster.

The best diet for health is stated to be rice-milk with its " ten-fold merit in giving life, colour, joy, strength, readiness of mind, removing hunger and thirst, setting right the humours of the body, purifying the bladder, and promoting digestion " [*Mahāvagga*, vi, 24]. It was for these " ten advantages " that Visākhā decided, with the Buddha's permission, to provide the Saṁgha for life " with a constant supply of congey " [ib., viii, 15, 10]. With rice-milk is also coupled honey-lump. It may be recalled that these two foods were divinely suggested to the two merchants Tapussa and Bhallika as being the most proper meal to be given to the Buddha " who had just become Sambuddha " in his condition of prolonged fasting [*Mahāv.*, i, 4, 2].

Jīvaka the Physician of the Buddha. The medical treatment of the Buddha and his fraternity was entrusted by the generosity of the Magadha King Seniya Bimbisāra to Jīvaka Komārabhachcha, " the royal physician, an excellent young doctor " who had orders to wait upon the king, his " seraglio and the fraternity of Bhikkhus with the Buddha at its head " [*Mahāv.*, viii, 1, 15–16]. He was a most distinguished medical authority of his times, well versed in both medicine and surgery, and had calls from distant places like Sāketa, Benares, and Ujjenī, always to treat diseases which baffled the skill of other medical practitioners. The free provision of such expert medical aid for the Order was one of its other temptations to the lay public to join it. There is a story that on the outbreak in Magadha of the five diseases of leprosy, boils, dry leprosy, consumption, and fits, the people suffering from them approached Jīvaka and said : " Pray, Doctor, cure us and all that we possess shall be yours and we will be your slaves." But the Doctor said : " I have too many duties, Sirs, and am too occupied. I have to treat the Magadha King Seniya Bimbisāra, and the royal seraglio, and the fraternity of Bhikkhus with the Buddha at their head. I cannot cure you." Now those people thought : " Indeed the precepts which these Śākyaputtiya Samaṇas keep and the life they live are commodious ; they have good meals and lie down on beds protected from the wind. What if we were to embrace the religious life among the Śākyaputtiya Samaṇas : then the

Bhikkhus will nurse us and Jīvaka Komārabhachcha will cure us." Thus these persons got themselves ordained by the unsuspecting Bhikkhus and then secured the Bhikkhus to nurse and the physician Jīvaka to treat them. The demands of the sick made the Bhikkhus constantly beg for food for the sick and for the tenders of the sick as also medicine for the sick, while Jīvaka, having to treat so many sick Bhikkhus, neglected some of his duties to the king. This stratagem worked so well that persons similarly afflicted with one or other of those diseases began to offer themselves for monkhood not for the sake of the religious life but simply to exploit the Order, to get themselves nursed and cured and then " to return to the world ", for the entry into the Order was as easy as exit therefrom. The entire corrupt practice was, however, one day completely exposed when Jīvaka in the course of one of his medical rounds noticed a runaway renegade tramping the public roads and subjected him to a cross-examination which revealed the whole truth. On Jīvaka reporting the matter to the Buddha he ruled that no person seeking the Order in sickness should be admitted [*Mahāv.*, i, 39].

Monk's duty of nursing the Sick Brethren. The duty of nursing the sick among them was laid upon all the Bhikkhus. The texts relate an interesting story regarding the origin of this rule. Once a certain Bhikkhu having a disturbance in his bowels lay fallen in his own evacuations, unattended by any one because he was of no service to the Bhikkhus. The Buddha, going round the sleeping-places of the Bhikkhus with Ānanda, noticed the sick Bhikkhu in that condition and asked Ānanda to fetch some water. He himself poured the water over that Bhikkhu while Ānanda wiped him down. Then " the Blessed One taking hold of him at the head and the venerable Ānanda at the feet, they lifted him up and laid him down upon his bed ". Afterwards, the Buddha convened a meeting of the Saṁgha at which he rebuked the Bhikkhus thus : " Ye, O Bhikkhus, have no mothers and fathers who might wait upon you ! If ye, O Bhikkhus, wait not one upon the other, who is there indeed who will wait upon you ? Whosoever, O Bhikkhus, would wait upon me, he should wait upon the sick." He then prescribed detailed regulations on the whole question of nursing the sick. The duty of nursing the sick Bhikkhu lay primarily upon his immediate associates, his Upājjhāya, Āchāriya, Saddhivihārika, Antevāsika, a fellow-Saddhivihārika or a fellow-Antevāsika as the case might be.

That is to say, the teacher and his pupil must first nurse each other in case of illness. A Bhikkhu who is neither a teacher nor a pupil should be waited upon by the Saṁgha itself. The patient is advised to conform to the following requirements to facilitate his nursing: he must do what is good for him, must know the limit of the quantity of food that is good for him, must take his medicine, must take his nurse who desires his good into his complete confidence and let him know all about his disease and his condition, whether he is getting better or worse or continues in the same condition or when his bodily pains are too much. Similarly, the nurse is required to have the following qualifications: he must be able to prescribe medicines, must know what diet is good and what is not good for his patient and serve it accordingly, must wait upon the sick out of a feeling of love and not a desire for gain, must not revolt from removing evacuations, saliva, or vomit and must be capable, lastly, from time to time, " of teaching, inciting, arousing, and gladdening the patient with religious discourse " [*Mahāv.*, viii, 26].

Nursing was encouraged by a special reward. A sick Bhikkhu dying, his bowl and robes were to be given to his nurse by a special Resolution passed in a meeting of the Saṁgha. In the event of two nurses waiting upon him, the gift would be divided between them equally, even if one of them were a mere Sāmaṇera and the other a fully ordained Bhikkhu. If the dead Bhikkhu leaves property in excess of the requisites which his attending Bhikkhus can legitimately claim, it is to be first appropriated by the Saṁgha then present there, and, if there is still an excess, it is to be reserved for " the Saṁgha of the four directions, those who have come in, and those who have not " [*Mahāv.*, viii, 27].

The summons of a sick Bhikkhu living at a distance for aid must be obeyed by the fraternity even if they are then confined to their retreat in the rainy season when peregrinations are otherwise prohibited. Such aid must be given on the mere report of the illness, even if no summons are received [ib., iii, 6, 1–2].

Besides nursing and provision for treatment and medicines, the necessities of the sick were attended to in other respects. Sick Bhikkhus taking their meals were not to be ousted from their seats. They were also allotted suitable sleeping-places of which they had, for the time being, exclusive possession [*Chullav.*, vi, 10].

Clothing. We shall now discuss the regulations regarding the clothing of the Bhikkhus. As in the case of Food, there is a minimum prescribed for the Clothing too. "The religious life has the robe made of rags taken from a dust heap for its resource. Thus you must endeavour to live all your life. Linen, cotton, silk, woollen garments, coarse cloth, hempen cloth are extra allowances." But even the injunction regarding the minimum of clothing which the Buddhist Bhikkhu must use refers only to its material or quality, but is quite generous as regards its quantity. Indeed, the doctrine of the Middle Path has been very well exemplified in the regulations of the Order in this regard. They will appear to be designed under very advanced and correct conceptions of decency and decorum which a community of monks can ill afford to ignore when it is meant to have such an intimate and constant contact with the lay public as the Buddhists cultivated. These regulations must have been also deliberately designed to distinguish as definitely and easily as possible the Buddhist Order of Ascetics from those other Orders of Ascetics of the day like the Nigaṇṭhas, the Achelakas, and the Ājīvakas, who professed and practised the principle of a return to nature in the matter of clothing. The Buddha was therefore the more determined to have his own band of brethren dissociated from these extremists in asceticism by external marks and practices no less than by their internal doctrines. This is clear from a passage in the *Mahāvagga* [viii, 28] which tells of a certain Bhikkhu who, interpreting the Buddhist doctrine of moderation as applied to clothing to mean nakedness, comes up to the Buddha in that natural condition and insists upon his interpretation being adopted, saying: "It were well, Lord, if the Blessed One would enjoin nakedness upon the Bhikkhus." This had only the effect of drawing out of the Blessed One the following stern rebuke and ruling: "This would be improper, O foolish one, unsuitable, unworthy of a Samaṇa, unbecoming. How can you adopt nakedness as the Titthiyas do?" And lest there be any ambiguity as to what shall constitute nakedness in the Buddhist view, he proceeded to proscribe the following varieties of garment as being each "the symbol the Titthiyas use": viz. garments of grass, bark, phalaka cloth ("perhaps made of leaves"), hair, skin of a wild animal, feathers of an owl, and antelope skins (with the hoofs left on). In the rains when the full dress of the Bhikkhu would be drenched and heavy and a wearisome encumbrance [cf. *Mahāv.*, vii, 1, 1], special garments were prescribed of the size of six spans by two and a half which would be just enough to go round the loins from the waist half down to the knee [see *Pāt.*, p. 54], and give an appearance of decency. Visākhā, that great benefactress of the Order, had once to complain to the Buddha that his Bhikkhus behaved as naked ascetics to let the rain fall on them with their robes thrown off, and since "impure was nakedness and revolting", she begged the Buddha's permission "to provide the Saṁgha life long with special garments for use in the rainy season" [*Mahāv.*, viii, 15]. But apart from their appearance in public, the Buddha would not also tolerate nakedness of the monks when they have to deal with one another in the Vihāra on occasions of mutual salutations, bath, or meals when mutual services are needed [*Chullav.*, v, 15].

The full complement of the Bhikkhu's dress comprised three parts and hence was called *Ticīvara.* The three parts were known as Antaravāsaka, Uttarāsaṅga, and Saṁghāṭī [see *Mahāv.*, i, 76 ; viii, 13, 15, 20, 23 ; *Chullav.*, x, 17]. The Saṁghāṭī was "the waist-cloth wrapped round the waist and back, and secured with a girdle". The Antaravāsaka was "the under-garment wrapped round the loins and fastened by an end of the cloth being tucked in there or by a girdle" called *Kāya-bandhana.* It reached below the knee. The Uttarāsaṅga was the upper robe which was wrapped round the legs from the loins to the ankles with its end drawn, at the back, from the right hip, over the left shoulder and allowed to fall down on the back. "In the Mahāvagga we have constant references to the practice of adjusting the robe over one shoulder as a mark of special respect. The earliest statues of the Buddha which represent the robe as falling over only one shoulder are probably later than the texts" [*SBE.*, xvii, p. 212 n.].

The origin of the rule determining the dress of the Bhikkhu is traced in the texts to the need that the Buddha himself felt of using no less than four robes to protect him against the cold of one winter night he spent at Vesāli. But lest there might be "persons giving themselves up to superfluity" in the matter of clothing, he wanted to fix its limits. The maximum quantity of clothing allowed was fixed on the basis of the needs of the physically weaker brethren, "those men of good birth in this doctrine and discipline who are affected by cold and are afraid of cold." Hence the ruling: "I allow, O Bhikkhus, the use of three robes (to wit), a double waist cloth, and a single upper robe, and a single under-garment" [*Mahāv.*, viii, 13].

But this dress was prescribed not merely for health but also for decency. The Bhikkhu had normally to beg every day and had thus to adjust himself to social opinion as regards his dress and bearing which must be attractive and winning so as to inspire respect and provoke generosity in response to the begging. "Properly clad," says the text, "will I go amidst the houses, putting on my under-garment and robe all around me and properly clad will I take my seat amidst the houses with my body under proper control (i.e. 'not with dirty hands or feet'). With downcast eye will I go amidst the houses and take my seat with robes not pulled up, and with my head uncovered" [*Pāt.*, pp. 59–61]. We have already referred to the prescribed behaviour of Bhikkhus going on their begging rounds and to the houses of the laity on invitation to meals as pictures of dignity and sobriety, not showing the slightest sign in their carriage of any levity or lightness [*Chullav.*, viii, 4, 3]. Another text declares: "You are not, O Bhikkhus, to enter the village in your waist cloth and nether garment" [*Mahāv.*, viii, 23].

The robes, as we have seen, might be of different stuffs or materials like cotton, silk, wool, and the like, but they should not be of untorn (*achchhinnaka*) cloth [ib., viii, 11]. They should be *paṁsukūlika*, i.e. made up of "rags taken from the dust heap or of bits picked up in the bazaar" [ib., viii, 14]. The rags were also collected from cemeteries [ib., viii, 4, 1]. The robes thus made were on the model of the rice-fields of Magadha "divided into short pieces and in rows and by outside boundaries and by cross boundaries", a model which the Buddha asked Ānanda to follow [ib., viii, 12]. The robes were also to be of a standard size, viz. less than 8 inches in length according to the accepted inch [ib., viii, 21].

The Bhikkhus were allowed to accept presents of robes. "Lay robes" are distinguished from *paṁsukūla* robes [ib., viii, 1, 35]. The former might be made of new cloth [ib., viii, 1, 6]. "But a set of robes made entirely from untorn pieces is not to be worn." Half at least of each of the three robes must be from torn pieces [ib., viii, 21]. We read of people going to the Ārāma with presents of robes which were to be received by a Bhikkhu, specially appointed for the purpose, who had to keep within doors. Then these were to be laid by another special Bhikkhu, not in an open hall, where they might be damaged by rats and white ants, but in a separately appointed store-room, varying in size and build according to necessities, in charge of a Bhikkhu appointed as store-keeper [ib., viii, 5–8]. But such storage must not exceed the period of ten days after which they must be distributed among the Saṁgha [ib., viii, 13]. There should also be distribution, if the store-room be " overfull of clothes ", by a Bhikkhu specially appointed for the purpose who was to make the distribution equitably among the members present, giving half to the Samaṇeras [ib., viii, 9]. Sometimes, lay men would give ready-made robes to individual Bhikkhus, but those seeking more merit would give *Kaṭhina* or cotton cloth to the whole Saṁgha assembling in a formal meeting for the performance of the *Kaṭhina* ceremony requiring all the members of the parish from different Saṁghas to be present and join in the work of making robes out of the cloth before the day is over, even the senior monks lending a helping hand if necessary [ib., vii]. The robes must be dyed always. Six kinds of dye are allowed together with the necessary arrangements for boiling and receiving them in suitable vessels [ib., viii, 10].

Use of Mat, Rug, and other Clothing. Besides the suit of robes, the Bhikkhu was allowed the use of mat " for protecting the body and the robes ", use of " itch-cloth " if he were suffering from " the itch, or boils, or a discharge or scabs ", of cloth to wipe faces with, and of cloth required for the water-strainer and the bag in which the bowl and other things were carried [ib., viii, 16–20]. To these were also added the bed covering [ib., viii, 20] and the rug which must last for at least six years [*Pāt.*, p. 25].

Foot-wear. The use of shoes or foot-wear was permitted when rough paths had to be trodden, as has been already stated. Shoes " with only one lining to them " were permitted [*Mahāv.*, v, 1, 30] but even these must not be worn " in the open Ārāma " [ib., 4, 2], or " in going into the villages " [ib., 12], except in cases of sickness. The texts give various descriptions of possible and impossible shoes and the materials for their manufacture only to forbid their use. An incoming Bhikkhu, when about to enter an Ārāma, must " take off his sandals, turn them upside down, beat them to get the dust off, and take them up again in his hand " and, on entering the premises, must " ask for the cloths with which sandals are cleaned and clean his sandals " first with a dry, and afterwards with a wet, cloth and then lay the cloths duly washed on one side [*Chullav.*, viii, 1, 2].

CHAPTER XVI

RESIDENCE

Residence. From food, medicine, and dress we now come to the dwelling of the monk, on which the texts give us much interesting and apparently trustworthy information. Originally the monks were devoid of any dwelling-house properly so called. They " dwelt now here, now there—in the woods, at the foot of trees, on hill-sides, in grottoes, in mountain caves, in cemeteries, in forests, in open plains, and in heaps of straw ". Then the Seṭṭhi of Rājagaha seeing them coming from all such places offered to erect fixed dwellings for them. The offer was accepted by the Buddha who ruled: " I allow you, O Bhikkhus, abodes of five kinds (*pañcha lenāni*)—Vihāras, Aḍḍhayogas [*Suvaṇṇa-vaṅgagehā* (Buddhaghosha),[1] i.e. a gold-coloured Bengal house, or a house shaped like a garuḍa bird (Childers)], Pāsādas or Prāsādas (i.e. storied dwellings or towers), *Hammiyas* or Harmyas (i.e. stone houses with a flat roof), and *Guhās* or caves " (defined by Buddhaghosha as a hut made of bricks, or in a rock, or of wood) [*Mahāv.*, i, 30, 4, and *Chullav.*, vi, 1, 2]. Then the merchant " had sixty dwelling-places put up in one day " which, under the Buddha's directions, he dedicated " to the use of the Saṁgha of the four directions whether present or to come ". The Buddha gave him thanks in the following words which admirably explain the need of dwelling-places:

" Cold he wards off and heat, so also beasts of prey,
And creeping things and gnats, and rains in the wet season.
And when the dreaded, heated winds arise, they are kept off.
To give Vihāras to the Saṁgha, wherein in safety and in peace
To meditate and think at ease, the Buddha calls the best of gifts.
Let then the able man, regarding his own weal,
Have pleasant monasteries built and lodge there learned men.
Let him with cheerful mind give food to them and drink,
Raiment, and dwelling-places, to the upright in heart."

[*Chullav.*, vi, 1, 2.]

Varshāvāsa (Rain-retreat). The need of a shelter was imperative in the rainy season when the monks were enjoined

[1] The reading is more correctly *supaṇṇa vankageha*, 'like a Garuḷa bird's crooked wing,' where the roof is bent on one side [Pali Text Society's Dictionary]

to take to a retreat (*vassāvāsa*, lit. retreat of the year), suspending itinerancy. This injunction is stated to have been the consequence of another concession of Buddhism to popular feeling which was outraged by the monks travelling about in the rains and destroying the life they call into being in the green herbs, vegetables, and animalculae. "Even the Titthiyas," so murmured the people, "whose doctrine is supposed to be ill preached, even they try to avoid this injury to life by making themselves retreats; even birds make themselves nests at that season of the year, while the Śākyaputtiya Samaṇas alone are out for destroying life!" [*Mahāv.*, iii, 1].

'Vassa.' Buddhaghosha [quoted in *SBE.*, xiii, p. 299 n.] thus describes how the monks were to begin the retreat: "They are to look after their Vihāra (if it is in a proper state), to provide food and water for themselves, to fulfil all due ceremonies, such as paying reverence to sacred shrines, etc., and to say loudly once, or twice, or thrice: 'I enter upon Vassa in this Vihāra for these three months.' Thus they are to enter upon Vassa." This statement of Buddhaghosha shows that by his time the place of retreat might be the very Vihāra in which the monk usually lived, and, also, that while the retreat during the rains at some fixed abode was compulsory to every monk, it was optional in other times. The *Vinaya*, as we shall presently see, points to the more usual earlier custom of the monks taking up their places of abode in new dwellings rather than in their old ones. "There are two periods for entering upon Vassa, the earlier and the later. The earlier is the day after the full moon of Āshāḍha (June–July); the later, a month after this" [*Mahāv.*, iii, 2, 2].

There are regulations for determining the legitimate location for the retreat. It might be in a cattle pen, in a ship on a voyage, or even in a cart on a journey with a caravan. But one must not live in a hollow tree like a goblin or on the branch of a tree like a huntsman, and not in the open air, nor in a house for keeping corpses, nor under a sun-shade like a cowherd, nor an earthenware vessel like the Titthiyas [ib., iii, 12].

Change of Retreat. The retreat was chosen on the principle that it must not be liable to interruption from any cause. The texts give us an idea of the possible interruptions of the times. Monks were permitted to change their retreat if they were troubled by beasts of prey, by snakes, by robbers or "demons", or if they are cut off from the source of their supply of food, medicine, and other services of laymen in the neighbouring village, where they begged, being destroyed by fire or flood or broken up by robbers or if their own residence is similarly destroyed. The monks must also remove from the neighbourhood of temptations offered by women, relations, kings, robbers, and rascals, or of other monks who cause divisions in the Saṁgha or from the place where they stumble upon "an ownerless treasure" [*Mahāv.*, iii, 9–11].

Travelling in rains when permitted. For urgent reasons, mostly connected with religion or other imperative duties, the monks were allowed to travel out of their retreat, but the absence must not exceed a period of seven days. Thus they could respond to the call of a Bhikkhu in sickness needing their nursing, or one asking for help in his inward struggles, doubts of conscience, or tendency towards false doctrines, or one who, having committed a grave offence, has to be dealt with by a duly constituted Saṁgha with its quorum made up. Monks were also allowed to respond to the call of sick parents, brothers, sisters, relations, and co-disciples (*Bhikkhu-gatika*) [ib., 6–7].

Another imperative call was that from a lay-devotee (Upāsaka) who wanted the monks to hear him recite "a celebrated Suttanta" lest it "fall into oblivion" [ib., 5, 9].

Lastly, the monks were of course "to go out on the Saṁgha's business" [ib., 8]. Such business was mostly connected with the execution of gifts offered by the laity. Such gifts were largely forthcoming during the *Vassa* when the lay donors could more easily get into touch with the monks with their movements suspended, and thus opportunities of serving the Order by their support.

Different kinds of Dwelling provided for a Saṁgha. The texts speak of the variety of the gifts. We read of an Upāsaka offering a quantity of wood cut in the forest for a Vihāra in ruins and sending word to the monks in retreat that they might "fetch that wood" [ib.]. We read how Udena, a Kosalan devotee, having a Vihāra built for the Saṁgha, sent a messenger to the Buddha and his monks, then spending the rains at the Jetavana park at Sāvatthi, with the following words: "Might their Reverences come hither! I desire to bestow gifts on them and to hear the Dhamma and to see the Bhikkhus" [ib., 5, 1–5]. In this connection, we are also told that these gifts to the Order from their Upāsakas comprised the following, viz. the five types of dwelling already mentioned, and their various adjuncts, of

PLATE XVIII

KARLA : INTERIOR OF CAVE-MONASTERY
[*c.* second century A.D.]

[*Facing p.* 437

which we have an interesting list including "a store-room, a refectory, a fire-room, a warehouse, a privy, a place to walk in, a house to walk in, a well, a well house, a *jantāghara*, a *jantāghara* room, a lotus-pond, a pavilion, a park or the site for a park" [ib., 6].

We thus find that the dwellings of the monks covered a wide range both as regards their build and their structure. From the mere hut made of sticks collected in the forest, and grass, and the solitary cell or cave, we come to higher and higher forms of building in the Vihāras, either as detached houses or as complex wholes, Prāsādas, storied houses, and Ārāmas, elaborately equipped with all kinds of dwelling, assembly-halls, dining-halls, structures for warm baths and ablutions, and council-chambers, and equipped also with furniture of diverse kinds satisfying every need of health and life and securing a fair level of comforts.

Hut. At the bottom of the scale was the hut for the use of the solitary Bhikkhu, which was of the standard size measuring 12 spans (of the Buddha's span) in length and 7 spans in breadth [*Pāt.*, p. 9]. It must also have an open space around it so as to allow a bullock cart to pass round it. Its site must also be approved by the Saṁgha as free from danger ("either to living creatures by clearing the site or to the future resident after it is built"). We read of a Bhikkhu collecting by begging the materials for the construction of such a hut [ib.].

Cave. Next we have the *Guhā*, the crypt or cave, of which we have already referred to the various forms as explained by Buddhaghosha, according to whom it might be an artificial structure made of brick or wood, or an excavation out of a rock. The earliest historical examples of the latter form are the caves excavated by Asoka, and his grandson Daśaratha, in the Barabar and Nagarjuni hills of Gaya and presented as free gifts to the rivals and opponents of the Buddhists, the Ājīvikas.

Vihāra. Lastly come the storied house, the Vihāra, and the Ārāma. We read of a rule that no monk "shall hurriedly sit down or lie down in the upper storey of a dwelling common to a Saṁgha" (lest he might unwittingly upset the furniture) [*Pāt.*, p. 34]. The private chambers of monks were sometimes "on an upper storey" [*Chullav.*, vi, 3, 3]. There is a reference to King Bimbisāra wishing "to build a *pāsāda*, covered with cement and clay, for the use of the Saṁgha" and in that connection five kinds of roofing are mentioned, viz. those of brick, stone, cement, straw, and leaves [ib., vi, 3, 11]. We also read of Visākhā, the mother of Migāra, being "anxious to have a storied building (*pāsāda*) with a verandah (*ālinda*) to it, supported on pillars with capitals of elephant heads, built for the use of the Saṁgha" [ib., vi, 14, 1].

The *Vihāra* was originally the private apartment of a single Bhikkhu [*Chullav.*, ii, 1, 2]. Such Vihāras lay near one another in numbers. Later, the term came to denote a larger building with apartments for many monks. Thus we read of Suppiyā, the self-sacrificing sister of the brotherhood, "going around from Vihāra to Vihāra and from cell to cell," asking of each individual occupant thereof what he required as food or medicine [*Mahāv.*, vi, 23]. We are again told of a Vihāra taken up for their Retreat by seventeen monks who are subsequently joined by six others for whom also accommodation is found there [*Chullav.*, vi, 11]. We also read of Vihāras being "crowded with people" [ib., 3, 3]. We may also compare the expression: "Go, therefore, O Bhikkhus, *each one to his Vihāra*" [ib., vii, 3, 10]. Elaborate details are given regarding the construction of a Vihāra in the extended sense and of its equipment, which show that it must have been a very complex structure fitted with all arrangements necessary for the life of a numerous community of monks residing together in the same building.

It is to be noted that the impulse to the construction of Vihāras for monks came from the words of the Buddha himself, such as the following: "To give *Vihāras* to the Saṁgha where, in safety and in peace, to meditate and think at ease, the Buddha calls the best of gifts. Let then the able man, regarding his own weal, have pleasant monasteries built and lodge their learned men" [*Chullavagga*, vi, 1, 5]. Incidentally we may again note that this growth of collective life and organization in education is a fundamental point of distinction between the Buddhist and the Brahmanical system, which depended more upon the solitude of hermitages in the woods as an aid to spiritual life than the social atmosphere of a Saṁgha humming with the activities of several thousands of monks in residence in the neighbourhood of busy haunts of men where they could go for begging.

Details of Construction. Vihāras were fitted with doors, doorposts, and lintel, with arrangements for bolts, lock, and key; with windows made with railings, network, or slips of wood, and window-blinds and shutters; solid benches against the wall of a room or under the verandah against the outside wall of the house [*Chullavagga*, vi, 2]; "verandahs, covered terraces, inner verandahs and overhanging eaves" together with "movable screens" "lest the verandahs might be too public" [ib., 3, 5]; halls or sheds for the *Kaṭhina* ceremony with a high basement, against inundation, with facing of brick, stone, or wood and flight of steps protected by balustrade [ib., v, 11, 6]; "service-hall" [ib., vi, 3, 6]; cloisters on high basement with solid facing, steps with protecting balustrade, and railing, and a separate waiting hall; bath-house similarly constructed and fitted with door, bolt, lock, and key, arrangements for hot baths, necessary furniture, solid flooring, and facing of the walls as antidote to damp, drains to carry off the water, antechamber [ib., v, 14], and sometimes a separate hot bathroom, Jantāghara, furnished with clay (which might be scented) for protection against heat, and chairs where hot or steam baths were taken, with an attached cell or cooling room [ib., viii, 8, 2; v, 14, 3, and *Mahāv.*, i, 25, 12]; wells (to provide against want of water in the bathroom) lined with solid facing with a lid to it, a shed over it properly built and furnished with troughs and basins, and water vessels of brass, wood, or skin, while the water was raised "by the use of a long pole balanced as a lever, of a bullock-machine, or of a wheel and axle" [*Chullav.*, v, 16]; and, lastly, the store-house built as a separate house with necessary fittings for securing the stores [ib., vi, 3, 8], where sometimes shelter was given to outsiders overtaken by rain and storm on their promising to provide the Saṁgha with a meal [*Mahāv.*, vi, 33], while sometimes the stores of the Saṁgha were kept on laymen's premises [ib., 33, 5].

Its Outhouses. It will thus appear that there were several outhouses or detached buildings, each serving an independent purpose, in connection with the Vihāra, viz. the privies or cloisters, the bath-house, the hall for the *Kaṭhina* ceremony or robe-distribution, the bathing house in connection with the well, and the store-house, and the conference Hall of the Saṁgha [*Chullav.*, viii, 2], all of which were built on a common design and solidly.

Its Ramparts. The Vihāras were enclosed within "ramparts (*prākāra*) of three kinds—brick walls, stone walls, and wooden fences" [*Chullav.*, vi, 3, 8].

Its Inner Chambers. We shall now go into the interior of these Vihāras. The privacy of the inmates was maintained by the provision of "inner chambers" for sleeping purposes which were to be of three kinds—"chambers in shape like a palankeen, or like a quart measure, or chambers on an upper storey." They would be "at one side of the small Vihāras and in the middle of large ones". In imitation of the arrangements in the Vihāras of the Titthiya sects, the sleeping rooms were whitewashed, the floors were coloured black, and the walls coloured with red chalk [*Chullav.*, vi, 3]. Some Vihāras were thatched and thus cold in winter and hot in summer whence it was arranged "to cover them with skins and plaster them within and without" [ib., vi, 2, 2]. To prevent rain leaking through, recourse was had to "a protecting arrangement and cement" [ib., vi,-3, 4], while a ceiling-cloth was used as a protection against snakes falling from the roof [ib.].

Its Furniture. Within the rooms we find the furniture of the Bhikkhu to include bedsteads "made of laths of split bamboo" [ib., vi, 2, 3], with a texture of string woven across through the pierced sides [ib., vi, 2, 6], with legs of standard height equal to 8 inches of accepted inch [*Pāt.*, p. 53]; varieties of chairs except the long-armed ones [*Chullav.*, v, 37, 1; vi, 2, 4]; pillows of cotton of the size of a man's head [ib., vi, 2, 6]; pins in the wall and bone-hooks to hang the bags on [ib., vi, 3, 5]; cupboards, bamboos, and strings to hang robes on [ib., v, 11, 7]. The Bhikkhus were further allowed the use of mosquito curtains [ib., v, 13, 3], mosquito-fans, or fly-whisks, sunshades [ib., v, 23], nail-cutters, and all the apparatus of a barber [ib., v, 27, 2–3], needles, thimbles, and scissors to be kept in a drawer or a box in the workshop [ib., v, 11, 5], and, lastly, to decorate their rooms with representations of wreaths and creepers and not of men and women [ib., v, 11, 6; vi, 3, 2]. On account of its valuable furniture, fittings, and stores, it was ordained that the Bhikkhus must not leave a Vihāra without placing someone in charge of it, whether a Bhikkhu or a Sāmaṇera, and, failing either, the Ārāmiko, the gardener of the Saṁgha [*Chullav.*, viii, 3, 2].

Ārāma. Some of the larger Vihāras were set in the midst of a large compound with extensive grounds technically called the Ārāma or park. We have already seen that the grounds were sown with crops [*Mahāv.*, vi, 39], under a system by which the harvest was divided equally between the Saṁgha and the agriculturists to whom the cultivation would be committed. We also read of the plantations of the Ārāmas being protected against the inroads of "goats and cattle" by means of fencing of bamboo, or thorn, or of ditches, and of gateways, "with gates made of stakes interlaced with thorny brakes, with fences (across the gateway) made of the akka plant, with ornamental screen-work over the gateway ('of which such excellent examples in stone have been found at the Sānchi and Bharhut Topes'), and with bars" [*Chullav.*, vi, 3, 10].

Its Baths. The Ārāmas afforded the pleasures of bathing. Pools were constructed at the entrance to the Ārāma and the privacy of both was secured by enclosing them with "brick walls, stone walls, and wooden fences". Lest the pool be muddy, it was usual to flag it with three kinds of flooring of brick, stone, or wood, and provide it with a drain so that the water might not settle. Sometimes an Ārāma might have a tank. We read of the gift of such a tank by an Upāsaka to the Saṁgha. Lest the sides of the tank should fall in, it was usual to line the tank with facing of brick, stone, or wood, and to provide flights of stairs of those materials for easy access to the water, flanked by a balustrade for protection. Lest the water should become "stale", pipes were used "to lay on the water, and to drain the water off" [ib., v, 17].

Rules of Bath. It may be noted in this connection that certain rules were to be observed by the Bhikkhus in making use of the public, as well as private, bathing places. "Sporting in the water" (i.e. "throwing water over one another and chasing one another") was forbidden [*Pāt.*, p. 44], as also rubbing their bodies against wood, or up against each other, or with any wooden instrument or a string of beads [*Chullav.*, v, 1, 1–3]. "The ordinary mode of shampooing, with the hand, was allowed" [ib., v, 1, 5]. A Bhikkhu suffering from scab was allowed the use of a *mallaka* ("a kind of back-scratcher made up of hooks of split crocodiles' teeth") [ib., v, 1, 4]. No Bhikkhu was allowed to bathe at intervals of less than half a month, except during the last one month and a half of the heats and the first month of the rains, or during the time of sickness or of travelling [ib.].

Hot Bath. There was also "a rule of conduct for the Bhikkhus in respect of the hot bathroom (*jantāghara*), according to which they ought to behave themselves therein" [*Chullav.*, viii, 8, 2]. The Bhikkhu who first enters the bathroom is to clean the fire-place of ashes, if any, and sweep the bathroom, its flooring, the cell, the ante-chamber of the bath, the cooling room, and the hall. He must also get ready the necessaries of bath by pounding the chunam, moistening the clay (to be used against heat) with water, and filling the jar with water. "A seat is not to be taken so as to hustle the senior Bhikkhus and junior

Bhikkhus are not to be ousted from their seats. If possible, shampooing is to be performed for the senior Bhikkhus in the hot bathroom." "A bath is not to be taken in front of the senior Bhikkhus, nor above them. One who has bathed and is getting up out (of the water) is to make way for one who is getting down into the water." "Whoso comes last out of the hot bathroom is to wash it, if it be dirty; to wash the vessel in which the clay is kept, to put the chairs used in the hot bathroom in order, to extinguish the fire, to close up the doorway, and then come out" [ib.]. No Bhikkhu was allowed to comb his hairs or to use a looking-glass [ib., v, 2].

It may be noted in passing that these regulations were suggested, according to the texts, by the various sanitary difficulties which arose from the living together of many Bhikkhus. "Each such difficulty is quite solemnly said to have been reported to the Blessed One, and he is said to have found a way out of it." A fixed bathing place was given when it was found that "the Bhikkhus used to bathe anywhere all over the Ārāma and the Ārāma became muddy" [*Chullav.*, v, 17, 1], and the privies were constructed when it was found that "the Bhikkhus made water here and there in the Ārāma, and the Ārāma was defiled" [ib., v, 35].

The Jetavana Vihāra as an ideal Vihāra. The best example of a Vihāra was that constructed for the Saṁgha by the merchant prince Anāthapiṇḍika in the Ārāma made in the garden of Prince Jeta. The ideal site for such an Ārāma as indicated by the Buddha was that it must be "not too far from the town and not too near, convenient for going and for coming, easily accessible for all who wish to visit him, by day not too crowded, by night not exposed to too much noise and alarm, protected from the wind, hidden from men, well fitted for a retired life". The Jetavana being such a site, the merchant was anxious to acquire it for his Master but was told by the owner: "It is not, Sir, for sale even for a sum so great that the pieces of money would be sufficient to cover it if they were laid side by side." The merchant took advantage of this supposed offer by saying: "I take, sir, the garden at the price." The Prince, puzzled at this unexpected reply, tried to back out, saying: "No, O householder, there was no bargain meant." But the merchant insisted on this unusual bargain being closed, though he had everything to lose by it: he was serving his religion in the manner of a Shylock. He took the matter to law, demanding the specific performance of the contract, and "asked the Lords of Justice whether a bargain of sale had been made or not. And the Lords decided thus: 'The Ārāma is taken, Sir, at the price which you fixed.'" In pursuance of the Court's judgment and decree, the merchant "had gold brought down in carts" and covered the entire space of the extensive garden with the gold pieces laid side by side (the pieces being not round but square ones according to their representation on a bas-relief at the Bharhut Stūpa). But there was left one small space close by the gateway which could not be covered by the gold brought. The donor was sending for a fresh supply when he was stopped by the Prince, now moved by this charity which, he declared, "was no ordinary matter": "It is enough, O householder. You need not have that space covered. Let me have that space, and it shall be my gift." Anāthapiṇḍika, considering the Prince to be a valuable acquisition to the Order, yielded to his wishes. "And Jeta, the Kumāra, erected thereon a gateway with a room over it." "And Anāthapiṇḍika, the householder, built dwelling rooms, retiring rooms, storerooms over the gateways, service halls, halls with fire-places in them, storehouses outside the Vihāra, closets, cloisters, halls for exercise, wells and sheds for the wells, bath-rooms and halls attached to the bath-rooms, ponds and open-roofed sheds or arbours (*maṇḍapas*)" [*Chullav.*, vi, 4].

Other famous Vihāras. There were several other Vihāras and Ārāmas placed at the disposal of the Saṁgha in the time of the Buddha. The specifically Buddhist India was noted for its four chief centres or cities at each of which the Saṁgha owned a number of monasteries serving as the seats of Buddhist learning. Thus we read of Yashṭivana, Venuvana, and Sītavana at Rājagṛiha [1]; Jetavana and Pūrbārāma at Śrāvastī; Mahāvana, Kūṭāgāra Hall, and Mango-grove at Vaiśālī; and Nigrodhārāma at Kapilavastu. We also read of Ghoshitārāma at Kauśāmbī and the Mango-grove of Chunda the Smith at Pāvā.

Vihāra Staff. The management of these elaborately equipped establishments where so many monks lived together naturally called for a numerous and varied staff of officials with a well worked-out differentiation of functions. The Saṁgha staff included the following officers: (1) the Apportioner or Distributor of lodging-places. The usual method was first to count the Bhikkhus, then to count the sleeping places available, and then to apportion accordingly [*Chullav.*, vi, 11, 3]. When the supply was greater

[1] A list of the several dwelling-places used by the Buddha at Rājagṛiha is given in Mahā-parinibbāna-Sutta, ch. iii, 57.

than the demand, the distribution was to be on the basis of the apartments (*Vihāras*) available and even of buildings (*Pariveṇas*) [ib.]. Resident Bhikkhus were often "worried by having constantly to provide sleeping accommodation for travelling Bhikkhus who came in from country-places" [ib., vi, 15, 1]. Bhikkhus belonging to the same division or having common subjects of study were usually given lodging places in the same quarter [ib., iv, 4, 4]. Novices wanting in merit were of course given inferior lodging-places [ib., iv, 4, 5]. The office of the regulator of lodging-places was coupled with that of (2) the regulator or apportioner of rations. The two offices were combined by the Venerable Dabba the Mallian who, having attained to Arahatship when he was only seven years old, and thus "gained everything that a learner can reach to", and finding nothing further left for him to do, thought of what service it was possible for him to render to the Saṁgha and in a true spirit of positivism, came to the conclusion that "it would be a good thing for me to regulate the lodging-places for the Saṁgha and to apportion the rations of food". The appointments were then formally offered to him by a Resolution of the Saṁgha [ib.]. Novices got inferior rations. We read of gifts to senior Bhikkhus by lay-devotees of ghee, oil, and dainty bits and to novices of only scraps of food and sour gruel [ib.]. Other members of the Saṁgha staff included (3) the overseer of stores, (4) receiver of robes, (5) distributor of robes, congey, or fruits, (6) distributor of dry foods, (7) disposer of trifles (e.g. needle, pairs of scissors, sandals and braces, girdle, filtering cloth, regulation strainer, etc.), (8) receiver of under-garments, (9) receiver of bowls, (10) Ārāmikas or those who kept the grounds of the Ārāmas in order, (11) Superintendents of Ārāmikas to look after their work, and (12) Superintendents of Sāmaṇeras to keep them to their duties [*Chullav.*, vi, 21].

Vihāra as a School of Arts and Crafts. These offices show that the monks had to engage in various kinds of practical, secular work instead of being constantly or exclusively occupied in purely religious or spiritual exercises. In fact, the monasteries opened up ample opportunities for business training or education in the practical arts and crafts for their inmates. Thus we frequently read of instances when the Bhikkhus are deputed to serve as "building overseers" to take charge of building operations on behalf of a lay donor constructing a Vihāra for the purposes of the Saṁgha [ib., vi, 17], so that the buildings might be in accordance with " the rules of the Order as to size, form, and object of the various apartments ". Such an overseer was called *Navakammika*. The appointment was formally made by a Resolution of the Order [ib., vi, 5, 3]. The Bhikkhus who superintended building works were of course provided with requisite clothes, food, lodging, and medicines at the cost of the donor of the building [ib.]. We read of a Bhikkhu taking advantage of such hospitality by demanding a special dish at a particular meal—tila seed cake—and, on his conduct being reported to the Buddha, he was rebuked [ib., i, 18]. Bhikkhus had to superintend not merely new constructions but also repair works [ib., vi, 5, 2]. Sometimes what with superintending new works or repairs to old works the Bhikkhus managed to assign these offices to one another for terms of twenty or thirty years or even for life. This abuse called for a rule whereby the period of *Navakamma* was fixed according to the character of the construction concerned. Thus " with reference to the work on a small *Vihāra* it may be given in charge as a *Navakamma* for a period of five or six years, that on an *Aḍḍhayoga* for a period of seven or eight years, that on a large *Vihāra* or a *Pāsāda* for ten or twelve years " [ib., vi, 17].

Along with the supervision of building operations, we may notice that the Bhikkhus are allowed " the use of a loom and of shuttles, strings, tickets, and all the apparatus belonging to a loom " [*Chullav.*, v, 28]. The Bhikkhus are also represented as being ill at ease without the practice of some handicraft [ib.]. They are also expected to prepare their own robes and keep them in fit condition with the help of all necessary weaving appliances [ib., v, 11].

Chapter XVII

INSTRUCTION

Training of Monks. It was, however, chiefly for purposes of their religious education and spiritual culture that the monks were brought together in the monasteries. We have already seen how the monastery was a kind of federation of groups of teachers and pupils, of junior monks living in dependence upon the seniors. Every Bhikkhu is expected to accept a pupil, " to provide himself with a Sāmaṇera, to give a Nissaya, and to confer the Upasampadā ordination " [*Chullav.*, i, 27]. We have also already discussed the relations that must obtain between these junior monks or pupils and their seniors or teachers, whether *upādhyāyas* or *āchāryas*. We shall now adduce further evidence on the subject as furnished by the earliest Buddhist works.

Parivāsa or Probation. The Vinaya texts distinguish four principal kinds of probation for the Bhikkhus. The first of these applied when the follower of another of the reforming sects was received into the Buddhist Order. Upon such a person was imposed a Parivāsa (a probation-time) of four months. The probationer is required to submit to a strict course of discipline. He must not enter the village too early nor come back to the Vihāra too late. He must not frequent the society of objectionable persons such as harlots, widows, adult girls, eunuchs, or Bhikkhuṇīs. The probationer is to be condemned when he does not show himself " skilled in the various things his fellow Bhikkhus have to do, is not diligent, not able to consider how things are to be done, not able to do things himself, and not able to give directions to others ". He is also to be condemned when he does not show keen zeal when the doctrine is preached to him, or when questions are put on the same. He is also expected to be pleased when the Buddha is praised, and not to be displeased when the sect he has deserted is criticized [*Mahāv.*, i, 38.]

A probationary Bhikkhu, further, is not entitled to the full privileges belonging to a regular Bhikkhu. His shall be the worst seat, the worst sleeping-place, and the worst room in the hostel. He must not live on alms personally received. He is not fit for a forest life (for he always needs control and guidance). " He must always live with a regular Bhikkhu." But he must not live with Bhikkhus of communities different from his own. And while living with a regular Bhikkhu he is to observe various forms of showing honour to him [*Chullav.*, ii, 1, 2].

Its Restrictions. The other three kinds of probation are of the nature of penal discipline for a certain period to be submitted to by Bhikkhus who fall under an ecclesiastical censure. We read of a stupid Bhikkhu who violated rules by living in lay society in unlawful association with the world, for which he was placed on probation under an Act of Subordination passed against him. Later on, he rehabilitated himself by correct conduct. The Act of Subordination would also be passed to punish the offences of staying too long in a public rest-house and frequenting a village on more than ordinary occasions [*Chullav.*, i, 9, 1]. Numerous, indeed, are the forbidden practices of the monks under training. They resemble those forbidden to the Brahmachārins under the Brahmanical system. They are detailed in several texts [e.g. *Chullav.*, i, 13 ; *Tevijja Suttanta* (Majjhima Śīlam)]. The following practices among others are forbidden: injuring plants or vegetables (whence agriculture is tabooed as an occupation of the Bhikkhu), storing up property, witnessing public spectacles (like theatrical representations, recitations, concerts, musters and reviews of troops [cf. *Pāt.*, p. 43]), engaging in games detrimental to progress in virtue, adorning bodies, indulging in mean talk (including fortune-telling), wrangling and acting as a go-between (between kings, ministers, etc.). [For agreement as to these injunctions between Brahmanical and Buddhist texts, see my *Local Government in Ancient India*, 2nd ed., Clarendon Press, pp. 65–75.]

Disciplinary Measures. Sometimes, disciplinary measures have to be taken against monks offending not as individuals but as a body. Thus we are told of a Saṁgha that forfeits public support by its ill behaviour and is replaced by another Saṁgha or body of monks. An Act of Banishment is passed against the offending Saṁgha whereby they are turned out of the particular place where they had misbehaved and caused scandal but not out of the Order or Church [*Chullav.*, i, 13, 6].

Games and Sports. All this discipline and restriction of monastic life left some room for its lighter side, for games and sports which have their own appeal in human nature. A list of such permissible games and sports is given in the *Chullavagga* [i, 13, 2], which mentions even dancing with ladies, besides the following: " Games with eight or ten pieces; with tossing up; hopping over diagrams formed on the ground; removing substances from a heap without shaking the remainder; games of dice and trap ball; sketching rude figures; tossing balls; blowing trumpets; having matches at ploughing with mimic ploughs; tumbling, forming mimic wind-mills; guessing at measures; chariot races; archery matches; shooting marbles with fingers; guessing other people's thoughts; mimicking other people's acts; riding elephants, horses; driving carriages; swordsmanship; wrestling; boxing with fists; and spreading robes out as a stage on which girls were invited to dance." Perhaps the most significant items in this list are those relating to dancing and acting, suggestive of the Art of the Stage. As regards the admissibility of Gambling, we must recall its Vedic origins, showing that it has figured in all ages as a national indoor game of India. It found its way even into the severe and serious atmosphere of Nālandā. Archæological excavation has found there a gaming-die, and gaming dice in Monasteries Nos. 1 and 1*a* and at other Buddhist sites, proving that the austere monks gave in to such innocent recreations [*Arch. S. R.*, 1923–4, p. 74].

Studies of Monks of different grades. From the discipline of the monks under training we now pass on to their studies. The ordinary instruction of a pupil-monk seems to have comprised the " giving of recitation, holding examination, making exhortation, and explaining Dhamma " [*Chullav.*, viii, 7, 4]. We read of some Bhikkhus specializing in reciting the Dhamma, of some in propounding the Suttantas, some in the Vinaya, and of some specializing as preachers of the Dhamma [*Mahāv.*, iv, 15, 4]. The Bhikkhus as students were assigned to different classes according to their progress in studies. The lowest class seems to have been made up of students " who were repeaters of the Suttantas ". The method recommended for this rote-learning was " to chant over the Suttantas to one another ". The next higher class was of those students " who were in charge of the Vinaya " which they would master by discussing it with one another. To a yet higher class belonged those Bhikkhus who were training themselves up as teachers of the Dhamma. And, as part of this training, they were required to talk over the Dhamma one with another before they should preach it to others. There were, lastly, Bhikkhus of the highest classes who were given to meditation, i.e. the practice of the four *Jhānas* or meditations [for the definition of which see Rhys Davids'

Buddhism, p. 176, and Mrs. Rhys Davids' *Buddhism*, pp. 199, 200]. Besides these classes of students, some Bhikkhus were distinguished and classed as Epicurians, being " wise in worldly lore and abounding in bodily vigour ". All these different classes of students were separately lodged in the hostel lest their mixing up should cause disturbance to their different studies [*Chullav.*, iv, 4].

Cultivation of Vernacular. Thus a community of Bhikkhus was like a school made up of different forms or classes representing different grades of talent, maturity, and progress in studies. But the Bhikkhus also differed from one another in other respects. Hailing from different parts of the country, they differed in their dialects, besides " differing in name, lineage, birth, and family ". We are told of two Bhikkhu brothers who were " Brahmans by birth, excelling in speech, excelling in pronunciation " trying to reduce this confusion of tongues among Bhikkhus by a proposal to adopt Sanskrit as their common language. Said they: " The Bhikkhus corrupt the word of the Buddhas by repeating it in their own dialect. Let us, Lord, put the word of the Buddhas into Sanskrit verse (*chhandas*)." But the Buddha did not approve of the proposal, because it would not conduce to conversions but rather hinder them. Sanskrit would repel the ordinary people or masses who were to be reached through their own vernaculars. The religion of the Buddha meant for the classes as well as masses thus cultivated, and was preached through, the popular speech as distinguished from the difficult and refined language, Sanskrit, especially in its earlier form, *Chhandas* or Veda-dialect, for which the two Brāhman brothers pleaded. The Buddha with perfect wisdom ruled: " I allow you, O Bhikkhus, to learn the word of the Buddhas each in his own dialect " [*Chullav.*, v, 33, 1]. Thus Buddhism gave an impulse and impetus to the study of the vernacular dialects of the country which so much facilitated its spread to distant and different countries by means of missionaries as organized under the great emperor Asoka for instance.

The above story indicates that Sanskrit was supplanted and superseded as a medium of instruction in the Buddhist schools by the vernacular dialects.

Subjects tabooed. Along with Sanskrit were tabooed several subjects of study, viz. the Lokāyata system together with the " low arts " of divination, spells, omens, astrology, sacrifices to gods, witchcraft, and quackery [ib.].

Subjects Taught. Thus from the evidence just cited, it is clear that the curriculum of the monks included what are termed Suttanta, Dhamma, and Vinaya, together with Suttas and Sutta-Vibhaṅga. The meanings of these terms as used in the earlier texts are different from their accepted and later meanings. Thus there is a passage in the *Pātimokkha* (p. 50) which refers to the Dhammas as being included in the Suttas, the former comprising the scheme of offences given in the *Pātimokkha*, and the latter standing for the separate clauses of that Formulary [cf. also *Chullav.*, iv, 14, 22, 23 ; iv, 14, 19 ; ix, 5, 1 ; *Mahāv.*, i, 36, 14 ; i, 37, 14]. The use of the word *Sutta* is not yet confined to the texts of what is afterwards known as the Sutta-Piṭaka. " In the oldest tradition the discourses or conversations now called *Suttas* seem not to have been called by that name, but are referred to as *Suttantas* " [*SBE.*, Vol. 13, pp. xxviii–xxx]. We read of some devout men or women well versed in reciting some well-known Suttantas [*Mahāv.*, iii, 5, 9, 12]. We also read of brethren " reciting the Dhamma, those versed in the Suttantas intoning some Suttantas together, the custodians of the Vinaya discussing the Vinaya, and the preachers of the Dhamma discoursing about the Dhamma " [ib., iv, 15, 4 ; *Cullav.*, iv, 4, 4 ; vi, 6, 2]. Lastly, as regards the term Sutta-vibhaṅga, it is used to indicate " some part of the Vinaya literature apparently distinct from the Suttas of the *Pātimokkha*. ' The Suttas have been handed down to him, but not the Suttavibhaṅga ' " [*SBE.*, op. cit.].

Teaching mainly oral. Education in the age of these earlier Buddhist texts was not yet depending upon written literature. This, however, does not mean that the art of writing was not developed then. It is referred to as a source of livelihood or an occupation in the *Mahāvagga* [i, 49, 1]. The *Vibhaṅga* recommends to the Bhikkhuṇīs the art of writing [*SBE.*, vol. 13, p. xxxiii], while the Sutta-Vibhaṅga in explaining another passage from the same refers to the possibility of causing the death of a person by mischievous and misleading representations in writing [*SBE.*, op. cit.]. But the evidence available does not point to the use of writing for the purpose of preserving and transmitting an extensive sacred literature. As Doctors Rhys Davids and Oldenberg point out [ib.], there is not the least trace of any reference to manuscripts in the detailed accounts which the Vinaya texts give of the whole of the personal property of the Buddhist Ārāmas and Vihāras, of which all possible items from the bigger furniture to the smallest needle are enumerated or referred to. Along with manuscripts there are no references to such accessories of writing as ink, pen, style, leaves, or other materials for writing, nor to the operations connected with the copying out of manuscripts which must have occupied a large part of the activities of the monks should they have had to do with written literature for their education. But besides this negative evidence, there is positive evidence proving the very limited use of writing in those days for purposes of education. The Bhikkhus of a certain place not knowing the *Pātimokkha*, one of them is commissioned to learn it from a neighbouring fraternity and import the knowledge [*Mahāv.*, ii, 17, 5, 6]. Similarly, we read of a lay-devotee or a Upāsaka inviting a fraternity of Bhikkhus to hear him recite an important Suttanta so that they might learn it and preserve it from oblivion [ib., iii, 5, 9]. These passages show that the system of oral tradition was as much the characteristic of Buddhist as of Brahmanical education, though the causes of its adoption might be different in the two cases. It cannot consistently be supposed of Buddhists that they considered the writing of their sacred texts as an irreverent treatment of them or a sacrilege when they were so advanced in their views or so heterodox as to prefer the popular speech to the refined and sacred Sanskrit and abolish all distinctions of caste within the pale of their fraternity. The disuse of writing was more probably due to the scarcity of any convenient practical material on which the known characters might be inscribed, as pointed out by Rhys Davids and Oldenberg [*SBE.*, op. cit.].

Regular and Special Teachers. Besides the regular teachers, the Upādhyāyas and Āchāryas, arrangements were also made for the imparting of instruction by distinguished teachers who were acknowledged as authorities and specialists in their subjects. Thus Upāli was such a specialist in the Vinaya, the *Vinayadhara*: " and so many Bhikkhus, old and middle-aged and young, learnt the Vinaya from the Venerable Upāli " [*Chullav.*, vi, 13, 1]. Thus the Vinaya classes that Upāli taught were very popular and largely attended. Upāli delivered his discourses standing, out of respect for the senior monks. And the seniors heard him standing, out of respect for the subject of his discourse. The rule in such cases was for the teacher or lecturer to sit on a seat of equal height or higher, while his audience, if his seniors, might sit on seats of equal height or lower [ib.]. Listening to religious discourses as a means of instruction is also instanced in another passage which describes how Devadatta "instructed and incited and aroused and gladdened the Bhikkhus far into the night with religious discourse" and yet the Assembly was still alert and sleepless, whereupon he said to Sāriputta: "Will you, friend Sāriputta, be so good as to think of some religious discourse to address to the Bhikkhus? My back is tired and I would stretch myself a little." Then Sāriputta discoursed on the marvels of preaching, followed by Moggallāna, who discoursed on the marvels of Iddhi [*Chullav.*, 4, 2–3]. One of the ideal Saṁghas whose seat was at the Eastern Bamboo Park made it a rule that every five days they should "spend a whole night, sitting together, in religious discourse" [*Mahāv.*, x, 4, 5].

Some Special Teachers. The texts tell us of the names of some of these distinguished teachers who were known as the *Thera* (senior) Bhikkhus. They are: Sāriputta, Mahā-Moggallāna, Mahā-Kachchāna, Mahā-Koṭṭhita, Mahā-Kappina, Mahā-Chunda, Anuruddha, Revata, Upāli, Ānanda, and Rāhula. These Thera Bhikkhus are described as travelling together through the country of Kaśī [*Chullav.*, i, 18, 1]. Another passage in Vinaya [*Mahāv.*, viii, 24, 5–6] mentions the Theras, the brothers Isidāsa, and Isibhatta (at Sāvatthī), Nilavāsī, Sāṇavāsī, Gopaka, Bhagu, and Phalika-sandāna at Pāṭaliputta. The pupils of these Theras are sometimes mentioned, e.g., Kakudha, a Koliyan, the pupil of Moggallāna [*Chullav.*, vii, 2, 2].

Spurious Teachers. The Vinaya mentions five kinds of false teachers who falsely give out that their "conduct, mode of livelihood, preaching of the Dhamma, system of exposition and insight arising from knowledge", are above all reproach. Their disciples, knowing the falsity of these pretensions, are spoken of as protecting them against exposure, lest the public stop honouring them with gifts of the requisite clothing, food, lodging, and medicine for the sick, though they anticipate that "sooner or later they will become known by that which they themselves will do" [ib., vii, 2, 3].

Discussion as a Method of Education. The Buddhist system of education, like the Brahmanical, lays equal stress upon the efficacy of the method of debate and discussion in Education. In fact Buddhism, being more proselytizing than Vedism or Brahminism, was more interested in the cultivation by its leaders and votaries of the powers of debate by which it could spread and win converts from other religions. The Buddha's whole career of forty-five years of ministry was practically a continuous

A Muttra Sculpture (*c.* first century B.C.)

Showing an Assembly of monks seated in three rows and addressed by their leader standing, with a parasol in his left hand indicating his rank (pre-Gandhāra).

[*Facing p. 452*

round of debates and discussions with the exponents of other Schools of Thought or answering of questions put to him at the Assemblies of his own disciples. The canonical Buddhist Texts are full of references to the conversions of the Buddha, following his delivery of a discourse. Indian religion had already then, as we have seen, split up into any number of Schools and Sects whose followers, organized into ascetic brotherhoods like the Buddhists, were constantly meeting at Assemblies for discussions of their different doctrines. The *Sutta Nipāta* (382) characterizes these Brāhmaṇa ascetics, *Parivrājakas*, as *Vādaśīla*, disputatious, *Vitaṇḍas*, and *Lokāyatas*, sophists, casuists, and materialists. There are many instances recorded in Buddhist Texts of the leaders of Brahmanical ascetic sects meeting the Buddha at discussions. Similarly, Jainism also had to take its part in the religious disputations of the day. We read how the followers of Pārśva led by Keśī had a fateful discussion with those of Mahāvīra under Gautama in the Park called Tinduka at Śrāvastī, as a result of which Jainism divided into two sects. There were similar controversies between the followers of Mahāvīra and Gosāla, followed by a similar schism.

The places of such important discussions which marked cultural and religious life in those days were public halls which are called in Pāli texts *Santhāgāras* or *Samayappavādaka-śālās*. They also mention some places where such discussions actually took place: the Hall in Queen Mallikā's park at Srāvastī for "discussion of different systems of opinion"; the Gabled Pavilion erected by the Lichchhavis in the Mahāvana outside Vaiśālī; the sweet-smelling Champaka grove on the lake of Queen Gaggarā at Champā; or the Moranivāpa (where peacocks were fed) at Rājagṛiha, a Parivrājaka centre under Sakuladāyī [see my *Hindu Civilization*, pp. 218–224].

Buddhist literature throws considerable light on the rules for the conduct of such discussions and proceedings of the *Saṁgha*. The earliest work describing the methods of disputation is the *Kathāvatthu* [i, 1–69] of Asoka's time. The *Chullavagga* gives an elaborate account of the working of *Saṁghas* as democratic parliamentary assemblies [ib., pp. 209–216]. We may only refer here to a special treatise on the subject of debate, *Saptadaśa-bhūmi-śāstra-yogāchārya* of Maitreya of about A.D. 400, which was translated into Chinese in A.D. 646 and was known to the great Asaṅga at Ayodhyā [Watters' *Yuan Chwang*, I, 355–6]. The fifteenth volume of this important work is a treatise on the art of debate in seven chapters. The first chapter defines the *subject* of debate which must be a useful one. It rules out useless subjects. The second chapter defines the *place* of debate which should be an assembly of scholars, the palace of a King, or the office of a Minister, or the Parishad. The third chapter points out the *means* of Debate. The Thesis to be proved (*sādhya*) depends on eight kinds of proof, viz. (1) *Siddhānta*, conclusion, (2) *Hetu*, reason; (3) *Udāharaṇa*, example; (4) *Sādharmya*; affirmative example; (5) *Vaidharmya*, negative example; (6) *Pratyaksha*, perception; (7) *Anumāna* inference; and (8) *Āgama*, scripture. The fourth chapter lays down the qualification of the debaters. They must be acquainted with each other's scriptures; should be able to speak continuously without a break and intelligibly; and should speak in harmony, sometimes soft, and sometimes loud, to please their audience. The fifth chapter mentions the points of defeat (*nigrahasthāna*), viz. (1) opposing a proposition and then speaking in agreement with it; (2) leaving the subject started and introducing another; (3) talking irrelevantly (*atīta-vākya*). The next chapter discusses the fitness of the debate by its subject, place, or audience. The seventh chapter recommends self-confidence in the debater.

It will thus appear that Buddhist Education made dialectic skill and ability in argumentation a most important part of intellectual equipment essential to leadership.

Learned Meetings. Another agency of education, especially moral education, furnished by monastic life, was the institution of the periodical gatherings of the monks from different monasteries in religious congregations for purposes of confessions of sins twice in the month, at full moon and at new moon. These meetings helped the monks to transcend the limitations of life in individual monasteries in a larger public life and brotherhood. It was ordained that the monks of a district must assemble to celebrate the fast day of the Vedic cultus by a confessional meeting. The meeting was to be convened by the seniors among the monks. The complete fraternity must be present at the meeting. The completeness was in relation to the diocese, which was defined as extending as far as one residence, the landmarks of which were determined by mountain, tree, rock, wood, path, anthill, a sheet of water and a river, but not up to its opposite bank, unless there was provision for regular communication by a ferry boat or a dyke. The place or the hall of the confessional gathering had also to be fixed and proclaimed beforehand. It might be one or other of the five types of building legitimate for monks, as explained above. The Saṁgha as a body by a Resolution must fix the place of the meeting, which must be duly announced, so that members might be cognizant of it. In the meeting, the Theras must assemble first. They must get the young Bhikkhus who are residents of that place to sweep it beforehand, prepare seats, light lamps, and provide for drink and food. The meeting must be attended by every member of the fraternity. If a member is sick, he must send a declaration of his innocence before the assembled Chapter through another Bhikkhu. Otherwise he must be carried on his bed or chair to the Assembly, or, if he is too ill, the Assembly must go to him and hold their meeting so as to secure his attendance. The exemption from attendance was granted only to a member who had turned mad. The confession was not common or collective, but individual. The common offence of the whole Saṁgha was to be confessed before the guiltless Bhikkhu of another diocese [*Mahāv.*, ii].

Next to these half-monthly confessional meetings was the yearly recurring ceremony of Pavāraṇa or Invitation to be initiated with the following words: "I invite the Saṁgha to charge me with any offence they think me guilty of, which they have seen or heard of, or which they suspect during the period of Vassa" [*Mahāv.*, iv, 2, 1].

The Buddha's Daily Life as the Standard for Monks. The Buddha's daily life, which may be taken as setting the standard to which that of all Bhikkhus must approximate, has been described in Buddhaghosa's commentary on the first of the Dialogues of Gotama. "He rose early in the morning (i.e. about 5 a.m.) and, out of consideration for his personal attendant, was wont to wash and dress himself, without calling for any assistance. Then, till it was time to go on his round for alms, he would retire to a solitary place and meditate. When that time arrived, he would dress himself completely in the three robes, take his bowl in his hand and, sometimes alone, and sometimes attended by his followers, would enter the neighbouring village or town for alms. Then the people understanding that 'to-day it is the Blessed One has come for alms' would vie with one another, saying: 'To-day, Sir, take your meal with us; we will make provision for ten, and we for twenty, and we for a hundred of your followers.' So saying, they would take his bowl, and, spreading mats for him, and his attendant followers, would await the moment when the meal was over. Then would the Blessed One, when the meal was done, discourse to them, with due regard to their capacity for spiritual things, in such a way that some would take the layman's vow, and some would enter on the paths, and some would reach the highest fruit thereof. This done, he would arise from his seat and depart to the place where he had lodged. And when he had come there, he would sit in the open verandah, awaiting the time when the rest of his followers should also have finished their meal. And when his attendant announced that they had done so, he would enter his private apartment. Thus was he occupied up to the midday meal. Then afterwards, standing at the door of his chamber, he would exhort the congregation of brethren into strenuous efforts after the higher life. Then would some of them ask him to suggest a subject for meditation suitable to the spiritual capacity of each, and when he had done so, they would retire each to the solitary place he was wont to frequent, and meditate on the subject set. Then would the Blessed One retire within the private chamber for short rest during the heat of the day. Then, when his body was rested, he would arise from the couch, and for a space consider the circumstances of the people near, that he might do them good. And, at the fall of the day, the folk from the neighbouring villages or town would gather together at the place where he was lodging, and to them, seated in the lecture hall, would he, in a manner suitable to the occasion and to their beliefs, discourse on the Truth. Then, seeing that the proper time had come, he would dismiss the folk. Thus was he occupied in the afternoon. Then, at close of the day, should he feel to need the refreshment of a bath, he would bathe, the while some brother of the Order, attendant on him, would prepare the divan in the chamber perfumed with flowers. And in the evening, he would sit awhile alone, still in all his robes, till the brethren returned from their meditations began to assemble. Then some would ask him questions on things that puzzle them, some would speak of their meditations, some would ask for an exposition of the Truth. Thus would the first watch of the night pass, as the Blessed One satisfied the desire of each and then they would take their leave. And part of the rest of the night would he spend in meditation, walking up and down outside his chamber; and part he would rest, lying down, calm, and self-possessed, within" [Adapted from translation of Rhys Davids, *Buddhism* (American Lectures), pp. 108–112].

Monks seeking solitude of forests for meditation. Up to now we have been considering the system under which the monks live together in a state of mutual dependence and relationship for purposes of their self-culture. But the Quest of the Ideal which leads these monks out of home into homelessness would not make some of them accept the half-way house of a monastery, but seek the solitude of the forest for a life of meditation. " Many of the Order, unfitted for taking part, even as teachers, in the battle of life, spent all their days in seclusion, being known as forester Bhikkhus. Others sought the silence of the upland woods and caves to complete the utter mastery of detachment, requisite to usher in the cool and peace of Nibbāna, or to recruit from wearing mission work " [Mrs. Rhys Davids, *Buddhism*, p. 204]. It was, however, the elderly and maturer Bhikkhus who were eligible for the forester's life, as has been already stated. The Buddha himself would sometimes seek in solitude a respite from the worries caused by " litigious, contentious, quarrelsome, and disputatious Bhikkhus " and like the tusker would " take delight in dwelling alone in the forest " [*Mahāv.*, x, 4, 7]. We read of the Venerable Bhaddiya living " in the forest, at the foot of a tree, in solitude, but without fear or anxiety, with mind as peaceful as an antelope's " [*Chullav.*, vii, 1, 6]. Another monk, Kassapagotta, lived alone at Vāsabha-gāma in Kāśī, where he was visited by some Bhikkhus whom he entertained as guests on proceeds of his begging for several days till their travel-weariness was over [*Mahāv.*, ix, 1]. We are also told of another monk keeping Vassa alone, receiving robes and dividing them among incoming monks not exceeding four in number [ib., viii, 24]. Life in solitude was sustained by a love of it for its own sake which utters itself significantly in Buddhist literature. This point has been well brought out by Mrs. Rhys Davids [*Buddhism*, pp. 205 f.]. " It is pleasant to see how largely the joy of life in the wild (generally supposed to be a phase of modern consciousness only) gets blended with the spiritual aspirations. We see the solitary as a lover of the heights—were they not ' clean and pure ', ' lonely and free from crowds ', ' a hiding place ' and type of the lofty thoughts of great minds ? [*Mil. Pan.*, ii, p. 353 : ' On the Alpine qualities of a Bhikkhu ']. We see him ' become in heart a wild creature ', filled with the forest sense of things (***arañña-saññin***), bathing in mountain tarn, listening in his cave to the music of the rains and to the crash of the storm, joying in the beauty of crag and cloud, of verdure and blossom, of bird-life and the cries of forest-creatures." We may sample this early Wordsworthian note in some typical passages cited by Mrs. Rhys Davids from the *Psalms of the Brothers and Sisters*. "To him for whom nothing is left, exceeding good it is that he do live in woods alone . . . to lead the forest-life the Buddha praised . . . I'll seek the jungle that I love, the haunt of elephants . . . lone and unmated in the lovely woods." Again : under the lowering sky and thundering clouds "the brother sits within the hollow of the hills alone, rapt in thought's ecstasy—no higher bliss is given to men than this". Dhammapāla's commentary on these poems gives biographical details of each Brother's life. One Thera who loved the woods was, we learn, known as Woodland (Vana)-Vachchha. Of another Thera, Usabha, we read : "Finishing his novitiate he went to study in the forests of Kosala at the foot of the mountains. Noticing the loveliness of the woods and the mountains, he said : 'These trees and creepers are unconscious, yet by the season's fulfilment have they won growth. Why should not I, who have also obtained a suitable season, win growth in the things that are good ?' "

As Oldenberg points out [*Buddha*, p. 367*n*], "the comparative estimation of solitude and of life with others could naturally be only a purely personal matter, and so it appears in the sacred texts. Sometimes we read expressions like these : 'Let him seek out remote places, therein to dwell ; there let him walk that he may become free from all bands. If he does not find peace there, let him live in the Order, guarding his soul from sins with wakeful spirit' [*Saṁy. N.*, quoted in the *Mil. Pañ.*, p. 402]. And then it is said again : 'If he finds a wise associate, a noble comrade of upright walk, then let him live with him, overcoming all temptation. If he does not find one, then let him go forth alone, as a king who abandons his conquered kingdom, like the elephant into the forest' " [*Dhammapada*, 328, seq.]

Buddhist limitations to solitary life. The fact of the matter is that even among Bhikkhus who live in the solitude of the woods, it is very unusual for them to live absolutely alone without having other Bhikkhus in the neighbourhood. "The provisions of the laws of the Order are wholly based on the supposition that small knots of brethren living near each other come together, who depend on each other to unite for confession, to instruct one another, to strengthen one another in doubt and temptation, to care for one another in sickness, and to keep up spiritual discipline among themselves. 'For,' says the old confessional formula, 'the band of the disciples of the Exalted One is so bound together that one exhorts the other and one stabilishes the other' " [ib., p. 364]. But besides the need of attending confessional meetings, the solitude of the Bhikkhus living in forests was further limited by the needs of life itself. They had to live sufficiently close to a village to be ableto reach it on their daily begging rounds [*Chullav.*, viii, 6]. We have already noticed the case of a Bhikkhu living in the forest being visited by guests whom he fed by begging for alms. We have also referred to the size of the standard hut for the dwelling of the solitary Bhikkhu and the need of its site being free from the dangers of forest life, although it must be "in solitude and quiet where the wild beasts have their dwelling and the gazelles" (quoted in Oldenberg's *Buddha*, p. 360 n.).

Thus the Buddhists, as in other matters, followed the middle path even in regard to the solitary life. The limitations upon the seclusion of the solitary Bhikkhus are clearly indicated in the very rule of conduct prescribed for them [*Chullav.*, viii, 6]. A Bhikkhu "dwelling in the woods" "should rise betimes, place his *bowl* in the *bag*, hang it over his shoulder, arrange his upper *robe* (over both shoulders), get on his *sandals*, put the *utensils* of wood and earthenware in order, close the *doorway* and *lattice*, and then leave his lodging-place". This shows how he must be tied to the neighbourhood of the haunts of humanity and to other material articles (indicated by the italicized words) for the support of his life. Nay, it is not unoften that he has to expect and entertain visitors, and so it is ordained that "a Bhikkhu living in the woods should keep drinking-water, and water for washing, and fire, and drill sticks and tinder, and walking staves ready" [ib.].

Features of difference between Buddhist and Brahmanical Education. We have now considered the chief features of the Buddhist Saṁgha regarded as an educational organization and shall now comment upon those which distinguish it from the Brahmanical system of educational organization. We have already remarked that the Brahmanical system was predominantly what may be called the domestic system of education under which the individual teacher's home was the school of the young admitted to it as pupils. The influence of the home was installed as an indispensable educational factor, though it was the home not of the natural but the spiritual parents of the pupil. Under the Buddhist system the home was superseded by the monastery. In fact Buddhist education begins with the destruction of domestic ties as the starting-point. The necessity of a domestic environment under the Brahmanical scheme did not thus favour the expansion of the small school under an individual teacher into a larger educational federation controlled by a collective body of teachers, as was the characteristic of the Buddhist system. The Brahmanical ideal did not permit the 'home industry' to be supplanted by the 'factory', so to speak. Smaller and larger organizations have their characteristic merits and defects in industry as well as in education. It has been well said that it was his Society rather than his Doctrine, his Saṁgha rather than his Dhamma, which, while it helped in the spread of the Buddha's religion, also helped in its decline in India. We have already seen that while private property was abolished within the Buddhist brotherhood, the brotherhood itself came to possess vast properties and became rich enough to support larger numbers of monks. Then the brotherhood was very liberal as regards admissions to it. As observed by Rhys Davids [*Buddhism*, p. 153], "when successive kings and chiefs were allowed to endow the Society, not indeed with gold or silver, but with the 'necessaries' of the monkish life (including lands and houses), it gradually ceased in great measure to be the school of virtue and the most favourable sphere of intellectual progress, and became thronged with the worthless and the idle." The Order was an admirable solution of the problem of poverty, as Max Müller has forcibly pointed out [*Chips from a German Workshop*, vol. i, p. 442], but did not solve very well the problems for which it was brought into being. Even at the time of the very rise of the Order, we have seen how one rule after another was laid down to guard it against unworthy applicants. The Vinaya texts amply indicate how the level of physical life in the monasteries was higher than the level of average life outside them. There was no struggle for existence within the Order. The Buddhist brother lived on the charity of his brotherhood, while the brotherhood lived on the charity of the laity or the Upāsakas who supported the brotherhood as a religious duty. The Buddha himself, when once complimented for his ascetic life and love of solitude, did not accept the compliment by frankly acknowledging: "While some of my disciples affect ascetic practices, I some days eat more, or wear robes made for laymen, or accept invitations to dine, or dwell indoors, or among my fellows"

[*Majjhima-Nikāya*, ii, 5, quoted by Mrs. Rhys Davids in her *Buddhism*, p. 203]. We have already seen how the rules of the Order were not noted for any excesses of ascetic praxis: under them "the body is to be decently draped, cleansed and massaged, regularly fed, sheltered in the rainy season, rested during the noonday heat, and medically treated when ailing" by the best physician of the country [Mrs. Rhys Davids, op. cit., p. 203]. It was no wonder that the Order which ensured such healthful physical existence should attract many undesirables. The Vinaya texts are full of interesting stories on the subject, some of which have been already referred to. When a rebellion has to be suppressed in his border provinces, the emperor Bimbisāra finds that his generals have deserted to the Order. His Officers of Justice consider that the Upādhāya of the deserters should be beheaded, the monk proposing their ordination should have his tongue torn out, and the Chapter should have half of their ribs broken [*Mahāv.*, i, 40]. The king's decree that monks should not be harmed invites robbers to seek that protection [ib., i, 41–5]. Even parents find it difficult to maintain discipline among their sons lest they fly to the Order [ib., i, 48]. The parents of Upāli, one among seventeen youths of Rajāgriha, anxious for his life of ease after their death, decide upon his monkhood as the best occupation for that purpose in preference to all other usual occupations of the times such as Writing (*Lekha*) (at which "his fingers will become sore"), Accountancy or Arithmetic (*Gaṇanā*) (at which "his breast will become diseased by too much thinking"), or Drawing (*Rūpaṁ*) (at which "his eyes will suffer") [ib., i, 49].

Apart from the risk of the Order being swamped by the unworthy or those who seek it for motives other than religious, there were certain other features in its organization which were not very helpful educationally, and were not also conducive to the permanence of the institution. Thus, in the first place, the relationship between teacher and pupil or the control exercised by the former upon the latter under the Brahmanical system is not so deep or intimate in the Buddhist. In the monastery, among the full-fledged monks especially, all differences of rank were abolished except the respect or privilege that is naturally commanded by seniority or length of spiritual standing. The Resolutions of the Saṁgha had to be passed by the entire body in a meeting in which all members, seniors and juniors, had equal voting power. In a word, while the Brahmanical system was based on the monarchical principle, the Buddhist corresponded to the republican or democratic type. No doubt the Saṁgha was equipped with a staff of numerous office-bearers, but they did not bear any hierarchical character, and, entrusted as they were with the management of the external affairs in the life of the community, they could not claim any position of authority. The republican principle was no doubt not fully operative while the Buddha was alive and moved among his fraternities as their visible head, but even during his life-time the Saṁgha developed numerous and scattered centres controlled by the common invisible head in the Doctrine and Law declared by the Buddha. The conditions were completely changed after his death when the numerous local Saṁghas (or communities of monks sojourning in the same diocese) ceased to own the central authority of a united Saṁgha to which they would all be affiliated and subordinated. The looseness of the organization was further increased by the constant changes in the composition of the local Saṁghas themselves. The result of all this was that there was no common authority to reconcile the differences that inevitably arose among the synods, or, within the same synod, regarding doubtful points of monastic life and discipline. The Vinaya Texts are full of admonitions for the promotion of concord among the brethren and prevention of schisms, and sometimes refer actually to seditious Saṁghas, but more effective than these admonitions and references would have been some institutions which might regulate the relations between different communities and members thereof. No church can exist without Church-government and this explains, too, the future the Buddhist Church had in India [see Oldenberg's *Buddha*, pp. 337–345].

Women in Buddhist Education. In concluding this account of the system of Buddhist education as organized and imparted by the monasteries or Saṁghas, we have to refer to the position accorded in it to the women. The Bhikkhus could not help coming into contact with women in their begging rounds. In Hindu households, the women had the management in their own hands and would dole out alms to beggars. We have already referred to a passage [*Chullav.*, iv, 4, 6] describing how a householder with his wife and children would receive and serve the Bhikkhus with food. Another passage [ib., viii, 5, 2] lays down the correct behaviour of the Bhikkhu towards "the woman who is giving the food". And yet the very scheme and philosophy of life proposed by Buddhism would only regard women as objects to be shunned by the religeux. It was only after the double pressure of his foster-mother, Mahāpajāpatī, and his favourite disciple, Ānanda, that the Buddha, with considerable reluctance and misgivings, consented to admit women as his disciples on their renouncing the world and householder's state [*Chullav.*, x, 1]. But the rules laid down for regulating their life betray at every step the mental and moral inferiority attributed to the other sex. They keep the nuns in a condition of complete subordination to the monks. The first of the Eight Chief Rules for them ordains that "a Bhikkhuṇī even of a hundred years' standing" must look up to a Bhikkhu "if only just initiated" [ib.]. Under other rules, the Order of nuns could not complete any transaction unless it was confirmed by the Chapter of the monks, while, as regards the ordination of a nun, the probationary period is made as long as two years, after which the Ordination has to be sanctioned by both the Saṁghas of Nuns and Monks. Other rules enjoined strict separation between monks and nuns. A monk specially selected by the brotherhood was to impart instruction and admonition to the nuns twice every month in the presence of another monk. The discipline and duties of daily life were the same for nuns as for monks except that the solitary life was practically forbidden them.

With all these restrictions based on the estimate of woman's worth, the Order of Nuns opened up avenues of culture and social service to the women of Buddhist India for which some of them became very distinguished. The young Church was also able to engage to a remarkable extent the sympathy and generosity of many a lay lady. The munificence of the matron Viśākhā is equalled only by that of the merchant prince Anāthapiṇḍika. Viśākhā was the head of an illustrious roll which included many other names, like Ambapālī of Vaiśalī or Suppiyā of Benares. Whatever might be his opinion on the womanhood, the Buddha was always generously responsive to the offers of hospitality and financial support proceeding from individual women of religious zeal.

But besides producing some remarkable characters among the laity of the other sex, Buddhism produced numerous remarkable women within its own fold, who played a prominent part as leaders of thought in that religious reformation. The Order of Nuns was the training-ground of these women. We have unfortunately hardly any information in the sacred works, giving details of the actual training they had in the nunneries.

That some of the nuns qualified themselves in the knowledge of the sacred texts so far as to be accepted as the teachers of other junior nuns is evident from a passage in the *Chullavagga* [x, 8], which mentions that a Bhikkhuṇī was the pupil of the Bhikkhuṇī Uppalavaṇṇā. Regarding their studies, the same passage informs us that the Bhikkhuṇī "followed the Blessed One for seven years, learning the Vinaya, but she, being forgetful, lost it as fast as she received it". It was then ordained that Bhikkhus should teach the Vinaya to Bhikkhuṇīs.

Some Women Leaders of Buddhism. We shall now proceed to give a notice of some of the most distinguished nuns who took a prominent part in the work of the early Buddhist Reformation and Church. In the commentary called *Manorathapūrāṇī* of Buddhaghosha in *Aṅguttara Nikāya* there is an interesting chapter concerning those ladies whom the Buddha regarded as his chief disciples. Among them are to be noticed several who entered the Order and were known as *Therīs*. Thirteen such *Therīs* are specially mentioned by the Buddha for their merit. The most distinguished of them was Dhammadinnā. Her husband, resolving to renounce the world in the interests of his spiritual life, offered her as much treasure as she desired in taking her leave. The offer was proudly rejected by her. She herself took to the religious life and in due time became fit to be a teacher of the Doctrine. The commentator then describes how the tables were turned when her husband sought spiritual wisdom from his wife who solved all difficult metaphysical questions with the ease of 'one who severs the stalk of a lotus with the sword'. Further information regarding these women leaders of the Buddhist Reformation is given in the commentary of Dharmapāla on the *Therī-Gāthā* which is believed to be the collection of verses of the women who were the first to join the Buddha's Order in his very life-time. We have already seen how it was the piety and persistence of Mahāpajāpatī, the sister of the Buddha's mother, that overcame his opposition and secured for deserving women the right of entry into the Order and religious life. She entered the Order with a following of 500 other Śākya ladies and constituted with them the Order of Nuns that was hardly inferior to that of Monks in piety and learning. This nucleus of the Order was formed of members representing different classes and ranks of society. Thus one such member was Somā, daughter of King Bimbisāra's chaplain, converted by the Buddha at the gate of Rājagṛiha. She embraced the Order not as a means of escape from the ills of life, but out of deliberate preference for its inherent ideals. Anupamā, peerless, so named for her unrivalled beauty, daughter of wealthy parents, with no want of suitors courting her, " cutting off the glory of her hair, entered on the lonely paths of life and wandered forth to lose the sense of home," is another example of self-sacrifice among the aristocratic womanhood. Low life also made its contributions to the Order. The wives of a poor straw-plaiter and basket-maker and of a crook-backed Brāhman took orders to escape from their hard lot ; " from three crooked things, from pestle and mortar and my crook-backed lord," as one *Gāthā* puts it. Such members of the Order as Queen Khemā, and Sujātā, the wife of a wealthy citizen, are examples of the quest of the ideal for its own sake, renouncing happy conditions of life. A curious example is that of Chāpā who, by her conduct, drove her husband to be a monk, till she herself, chastened by the separation, followed her husband and joined the Order. The Order counted among its members some bereaved mothers, the loss of whose sons made them renounce the world and seek peace in religion. The most distinguished of such is Kisā Gotamī. The story goes how she approached the Blessed One for medicine that would restore life to the dead child she carried in her arms. The Buddha bade her fetch a little white mustard from a family of which no member had ever died. Thus she was consoled by the realization that what afflicted her afflicted all. She was subsequently known for her progress in virtue and philosophical learning which made the Buddha appoint her as the superintendent of the Convent at Jetavana. The beautiful Sundarī, a rich heiress, lost all interest in life and the world on her brother's death and joined the Order, renouncing " her great inheritance of Benares ".

Some of these *Therīs*, when they advanced in spirituality, did not give themselves wholly to the subjective, meditative life in cloistered seclusion, but took an honourable share in social service and missionary work for their faith. The most renowned of such women leaders was Paṭāchārā, the bereaved mother, who was sought for solace by other 500 bereaved mothers. As these 500 nuns under their head were taking their daily meal, a wretched woman approached them for alms, a homeless, childless widow disowned by her people for her infectious disease. Immediately, the Sisters of Mercy, " the saviours and good shepherds of the heedless and the lost," adopted her as one of their own. Some of them are mentioned as being successful speakers and preachers. There was Sukkā, to hear whom speak the people would flock out of the city and not feel tired of listening to her. It will thus be apparent from these examples that the Buddhist Convents opened out to the women opportunities for education and self-culture and varied spheres of social service in which they made themselves the equals of men, supplementing their work in the spread of their faith [C. A. Foley's article in the *Ninth Oriental Congress Report*, Vol. i, pp. 340 f.].

Education outside the Monasteries. The Buddhist monasteries could not absorb the entire population nor could they minister to the educational needs of the entire country. There were thus other centres and systems of education than those developed in connection with the monasteries.

Education of the Laity. We have already seen how intimately was the Buddhist Church or Saṁgha concerned and connected with a laity upon whom it depended for its very support and maintenance. The laity were those who believed in Buddhism but did not choose to belong to the Order and be ruled by its discipline. Now the Order or the monastery educated those who were its members living under a common roof and did not admit day scholars to its education. Thus the laity had to seek other centres and means of education. Nevertheless the young Church was very vitally interested in the growth of a believing and pious laity for the regulation of whose life rules are accordingly laid down. The laity are sought to be marked out from the general public by applying to them the terms *Upāsaka* (for the males) and *Upāsikā* (for the females) when they formally declare that they take refuge with the Buddha, the Dhamma, and the Saṁgha. But this declaration was not insisted upon as a rule. We find ordinary people, honouring and entertaining the monks, being called Upāsakas, and also Buddhist Upāsakas being Upāsakas of another church [Oldenberg's *Buddha*, pp. 162 n., 383; *Chullav.*, v, 20, 3]. There were also laid down certain duties of temperance and rectitude, but the Church had no part in securing their fulfilment. The only step that the Church took to keep the laity in order was by a declaration of boycott whereby " the bowl was turned down " in respect of the offenders, but this step affected the Church not less than the offenders, for it meant only the prohibition of giving and receiving material gifts and spiritual instruction as between the two parties [Oldenberg, op. cit., pp. 383, 384]. Certain business pursuits were also forbidden the laity, e.g. dealing in arms, in intoxicating liquors, in poison, etc. [ib.]. A comprehensive list of the duties of the laity is given in the *Sigālavāda Sutta* [cited by Rhys Davids, *Buddhism*, pp. 143 f.], which classifies them according to the several capacities or relationships householders have. The duties, for instance, of Parents and Children, of Pupils and Teachers, of Laymen and Monks are laid down. It is the duty of parents to have their children taught arts or sciences. "The pupil should honour his teachers by (1) rising in their presence; (2) ministering to them; (3) obeying them; (4) supplying their wants; (5) attention to instruction. The teacher should show his affection for his pupils by (1) training them in all that is good; (2) teaching them to hold knowledge fast; (3) instruction in science and lore; (4) speaking well of them to their friends and companions; (5) guarding them from danger." Among the duties of the monk towards the layman are to instruct him in religion, to solve his doubts, etc. A specimen of the instruction of the laity by monks is given in the Vinaya [*Mahāv.*, v, 1, 9], where the Emperor Bimbisāra, holding his rule and sovereignty over 80,000 townships, asks the Overseers of those townships to wait upon the Buddha for "instruction in the things of eternity". The Buddha "held to them a discourse in due order", speaking of "giving, righteousness, heaven, the danger, worthlessness and depravity of lusts, and of the advantage of renunciation".

It is thus clear that the laity depended for their religious education upon the monasteries which were the exclusive centres of such education because the monks alone had the monopoly as specialists and experts in the knowledge of the sacred lore. It is also clear that for their general, non-religious or secular education the laity and the public at large had to depend upon the systems and centres of education that existed in the country outside the Buddhist monasteries. We shall now proceed to give an account of these on the basis of the evidence available in Buddhist literature of which the literature of the Jātakas forms the principal part and will thus claim our chief attention.

CHAPTER XVIII

INDUSTRIAL EDUCATION

Industrial Education. The Vinaya texts are not without some evidence upon this subject. There is a passage [*Mahāv.*, v, 4, 2] in which some erring Bhikkhus are reprimanded as behaving towards their teachers worse than even laymen. " For even the laymen, O Bhikkhus, who are clad in white, for the sake of some handicraft that may procure them a living, will be respectful, affectionate, hospitable to their teachers." This passage refers to technical education and the relationship existing between the laymen, as apprentices, and the master craftsman whom they followed for their training in the handicraft selected. In this connection we may recall the evidence cited above regarding the Bhikkhus being allowed facilities in their very monasteries for training and practice in the handicrafts such as spinning and weaving, tailoring, etc. The Vinaya texts refer to a few other occupations pursued by the laity and the general public as sources of livelihood, e.g. Writing or the occupation of the clerk or scribe (*Lekham*), Accountancy (*Gaṇanā*), and Drawing (*Rūpam*) [see *ante*].

Education in Medicine and Surgery : Career of Jīvaka. Buddhist literature from the Vinaya texts downwards conveys a continuous volume of striking evidence regarding the progress achieved in ancient India in medicine and surgery. We have already cited the interesting evidence of the Vinaya on the subject of the medicines, drugs, and the surgical operations and treatment then in vogue. The most distinguished medical expert of the age was Jīvaka Komārabhachcha, of whose life and career the Vinaya gives several concrete and interesting details [*Mahāv.*, viii, 1]. He was the son of the courtesan, Sālavatī of Rājagṛiha, who was thrown away on a dust heap from which Prince Abhaya rescued him alive. He also brought him up till Jīvaka thought: " In these royal families it is not easy to find one's livelihood without knowing an art. What if I were to learn an art ! " Thus thinking he went to Takkasilā to study medicine under a " world-renowned physician " who lived there. He " learnt much and learnt easily, understood well, and did not forget what he had learnt ". After studying thus for seven years, he asked his teacher when his studies might be regarded as completed, whereupon his teacher prescribed to him the following test: " Take this spade and seek round about Takkasilā a yojana on every side, and whatever plant you see which is not medicinal, bring it to me." Jīvaka examined all the plants of the area specified and reported that he had not come across any plant that had no medicinal properties. The teacher, satisfied with his answer, said: " You have done your learning, my good Jīvaka," and gave him a little money for his passage home. The money was sufficient for his journey only up to Sāketa where he was therefore forced to earn by his art. At that time fortunately a Seṭṭhi's wife had been suffering for seven years from a disease in the head whom many great and world-renowned physicians had failed to cure, though much gold was spent on them as their fees. But young Jīvaka would not either be given a call until he proposed that his fees might be paid only if the patient were cured. Jīvaka had one *pasata* (handful) of ghee boiled up with various drugs and administered the medicine to the patient through her nose. By one dose she was cured and gave the doctor in all 16,000 *Kāhāpaṇas* together with a coach, horses, and two servants. These fees and presents Jīvaka tendered on his return to Rājagaha to the prince who brought him up for the expenses incurred for it. Next, Jīvaka cured the Emperor Bimbisāra of his fistula by one anointing and was then appointed as the royal physician and the physician of the Buddha and his Saṁgha. The next important case he treated was that of a Seṭṭhi at Rājagaha who had been suffering for seven years from a head disease. Jīvaka performed a surgical operation to cure him: he " tied him fast to his bed, cut through the skin of the head, drew apart the flesh on each side of the incision, pulled two worms out of the wound, then closed up the sides of the wound, stitched up the skin on the head, and anointed it with salve ". The next important call came from Benares to cure a Seṭṭhi's son who, by a gymnastic feat, got an entanglement of his intestines, for which " he could not digest anything, nor could he ease himself in the regular way, and looked discoloured with the veins standing out upon his skin ". Jīvaka performed another of his successful and difficult surgical operations. He " cut through the skin of the belly, drew the twisted intestines out, and showed them to his wife ". He then " disentangled the twisted intestines, put them back into their right position, stitched the skin together, and anointed it with salve". Before long the patient was cured and his father gave the surgeon 16,000 *Kāhāpaṇas*. The next call came from distant Ujjenī whose King Pajjota, suffering from jaundice, asked the Emperor Bimbisāra for the services of his physician. Jīvaka wanted to boil up ghee for his medicine, but as he understood that the patient had a great aversion to ghee, he resorted to an artifice of "so boiling up the ghee with various other drugs that it take the colour, smell, and taste of an astringent decoction". Then anticipating that the king would vomit the medicine and detect it to be ghee, he craftily arranged for his escape by getting from the king his orders that he should be free to move about and ride on any animal he chose "on the pretext of drawing out roots and gathering medical drugs". He thus effected his escape on the fastest she-elephant. Eventually the King of Ujjenī recovered from his illness and sent on to Jīvaka a present of a suit of Siveyyaka cloth [explained by Buddhaghosha to be (1) cloth used in the Uttarakuru country for veiling dead bodies when they are brought to the burying ground (*sīvathikā*), or (2) cloth woven from yarn which skilful women in the Śivi country spin]. Lastly, there are several instances recorded of Jīvaka's treatment of the Buddha and his brethren. Once, when the humours of the Buddha's body were disturbed, Jīvaka asked Ānanda to rub his body with fat for a few days but found that a purgative was necessary for him. Not considering it becoming to give him a strong purgative, he had three handfuls of three lotuses imbued with various drugs to be smelt by the patient. Each handful then produced ten motions. After that, the Buddha bathed in warm water and was asked to abstain from liquid food for some time till he was completely restored to health. Once the Bhikkhus, at Vesāli, eating sweet food, of which a regular service was established by the laity co-operating among themselves, became very sick with superfluity of humours in their body when fortunately Jīvaka went to that city on some business or other and attended on them [*Chullav.*, v, 14, 1].

Features of Medical Education. The story of Jīvaka, as related above, brings to light the following points: (1) Taxila must have been the most renowned seat of medical education in the country when it attracted students from such a distant part of the country as Rājagṛiha; (2) the course of medical studies there extended to a period of seven years, after which a practical examination was held, putting to the test the student's knowledge of medical botany, or his first-hand acquaintance with the medicinal plants and their properties; (3) the principal cities of India like Sāketa, Benares, or Rājagṛiha were in no want of renowned physicians whose fees for treating dangerous diseases and serious cases amounted to figures which would put to shame the earnings of modern physicians; (4) considerable progress was achieved in surgery when such difficult operations were successfully carried out as those upon the skull, or the belly to set right twisted intestines; (5) the range of practice of successful physicians covered an extensive area, embracing several provinces. Jīvaka of Rājagṛiha had calls from Sāketa, Benares, Vesāli, and Ujjenī, bringing him phenomenal earnings; (6) the success of the surgical operations must have depended upon the use of antiseptic medicines. Jīvaka's ointments must have been of this character.

Evidence of Milinda-Pañha. The progress of Medical Science is further testified to by the *Milinda Pañha.* The old teachers of medical science are named, viz. Nārada, Dhammantarī, Aṅgirasa, Kapila, Kaṇḍaraggisāma, Atula, and Pubba Kachchāyana. Each of these is known for a treatise of his own. The divisions of the subject are given, viz. the rise of disease; its cause, nature, and progress; its cure, treatment, and management [iv, 7, 20]. The course of medical training is described: a medical student must first apprentice himself to a teacher whom he has to procure by the payment of a fee or by the performance of service. Then he is given a training "in holding the lancet, in cutting, marking, or piercing with it, in extracting darts, in cleansing wounds, in causing them to dry up, in the application of ointments" as subjects under surgery, and "in the administration of emetics, purges, and oily enemas" as subjects under Medicine [vi, 11]. The successful surgeon is defined as one who is able the most quickly to perform his operation [iv, 8, 28]. The successful physician is defined as one who is "a true follower of the sages of old, one who carries in his memory the ancient traditions and verses, a practical man [*atakkiko*, 'without the theories (*vitarka*) resorted to by those ignorant of the practice of medicine'], skilled in diagnosis and master of an efficacious and lasting system of treatment, who had collected (from medicinal herbs) a medicine able to cure every disease" [iv, 6, 28]. A treatment is described of "a wound full of matter and blood, stinking of putrid flesh, in whose grievous hollow the weapon which caused it remains".

The doctor anoints it with "a rough, sharp, bitter, stinging ointment to the end that the inflammation should be allayed". When the inflammation goes down and the wound becomes "sweet", he cuts into it with a lancet and burns it with caustic. When he has thus cauterized it, he is to prescribe "an alkaline wash and anoint it with some drug to the end that the wound might heal up" [iv, 1, 33]. A treatment of a boil is also described: the surgeon is "to have a lancet sharpened, or to have sticks put into the fire to be used as cauterizers or to have something ground on a grindstone to be mixed in a salt lotion", i.e. to apply "a stinging lotion" [iv, 2, 13]. Lastly, there is a reference to doctors administering "medicines by way of draughts or outward applications" [iv, 2, 17].

Evidence of the Jātakas. The *Jātakas* also furnish interesting evidence on the condition of Medicine and Surgery. There is a reference to a family of doctors in Benares who were specialists in the cure of snake-bites. The method of cure was to extract the venom with special antidotes or; catching the snake, to make it suck its own poison out of the wound [i, 311]. There is a reference to a skilled Brahman physician who cured the King of Benares of dysentery when all the great physicians of his court could not cure him. Before treating the patient, he said: "Tell me the symptoms of your disease and how it came about—what you have eaten or drunken to bring it on, or what you have heard or seen" [ii, 213]. There is a reference to Bodhisatta returning to Benares, his home, after mastering all branches of learning including medicine at Takkasilā [iv, 171]. We may, lastly, refer to a skilled surgeon named Sīvaka who was called to root out the eyes of King Śivi. In the story, instead of piercing the king's eyes with the lancet and taking recourse to a surgical operation, he "pounded a number of simples, rubbed a blue lotus with the powder, and brushed it over the eyes till they came out" [iv, 408].

We have now considered the concurrent testimony of the Vinaya Texts, the Milinda Pañha, and the Jātakas upon the subject of ancient Indian Medicine and Surgery. We shall now consider the evidence of these works on the system of education as it obtained outside the Buddhist Monastic Schools.

CHAPTER XIX

THE MILINDA PAÑHA ON EDUCATION

Story of Nāgasena. The account of the education of the Brahman Nāgasena given in the *Milinda Pañha* [i, 22–6] illustrates the principal features of the systems of both Brahmanical and Buddhist education as they prevailed in its times (second century B.C.). When Nāgasena was seven years old his father sent him on for his education befitting a Brahman to a Brahman teacher. The teaching fee was paid in advance instead of being paid at the conclusion of the studentship under the usual rules. The amount of the fee was a thousand pieces. The subjects of study are classified into (*a*) *Sikkhā* or the three Vedas, and (*b*) *Arts* by which the subjects other than the Vedas are meant. Nāgasena under his teacher's instruction achieved the mastery of the Vedas which meant that he " had learnt the three Vedas by heart, could intone them correctly, had understood their meaning, could fix the right place of each particular verse, and had grasped the mysteries they contained ", so that " there arose in him an intuitive insight into the Vedas, with a knowledge of their lexicography, of their prosody, of their grammar, and of the legends attaching to the characters in them " and he became a skilled philologist, grammarian, and casuist. Considering the range of his learning his father had to admit that there was nothing more which a Brahman had to learn. Nāgasena's thirst for knowledge was not, however, allayed by Vedic learning. It drove him to Buddhist studies for which he approached the Venerable Rohaṇa who lived at his hermitage at Vattaniya. But Rohaṇa would not admit the boy to his instruction unless he entered the Order. His parents permitted him to enter the Order for the study of Buddhist Literature because " they thought that when he had learned it he would come back again ". Then Rohaṇa, considering in what he should first instruct him, whether " in the Discourses (Suttanta) or in the deeper things of the faith (Abhidhamma), decided upon teaching him the Abhidhamma first. Nāgasena soon mastered and knew by heart the whole of the Abhidhamma, i.e. the Dhammasaṅgaṇi, the Vibhaṅga with its eighteen chapters, the Dhātukathā with its fourteen books, the Puggala Paññatti with its six divisions, the Kathā Vatthu, the Yamaka with its ten divisions, and the Paṭṭhāna with its twenty-four chapters.

After thus finishing his studies, Nāgasena is sent on an educational tour for preaching by his teacher, on a career of intellectual conquest, in the course of which he is brought into touch with some of the noted literary men and centres of learning. Assagutta was such a noted man of letters dwelling at the Vattaniya hermitage. Another was Dhammarakkhita, who dwelt in the Asoka Park at Pāṭaliputta From his mouth he learnt by heart the whole of the three baskets [1] (Piṭakas) of the Buddha's word in three months and in three months more he mastered their meanings. Another was Āyupāla of the Saṅkheyya hermitage in the northern city of Sāgala where ruled the learned King Milinda with his 500 Yonakas. He was always "in the habit of harassing the brethren by knotty questions and by argumentations this way and that," and boasted thus: "All India is an empty thing, it is verily like chaff! There is no one, either Samaṇa or Brahman, capable of discussing things with me and dispelling my doubts." His boast was successfully challenged by Nāgasena who had by that time in due course of his wanderings arrived at Sāgala as the head of a numerous body of disciples attracted to him by his phenomenal learning, for he was master equally of the three Brahmanical Vedas and the Buddhist (the three Piṭakas).

The history of Nāgasena calls up and indeed transports us to the old world atmosphere of education and learning which we breathe in the Brāhmaṇas, and Upanishads, with its myriads of wandering scholars diffusing culture through the country, its intellectual tournaments, its learned debates at the courts of its learned kings, its hermitages and sylvan seats of education and the like. The spread of culture, whether Brahmanical or Buddhist, was proceeding on common lines.

A few other minor points brought to light in this story may be noted. We find the somewhat unusual practice of a teacher accepting a pupil on receipt of fees, a practice which is contrary to the rules of the Smṛitis of the earlier age, as explained above. Next, we notice that with the growth of Buddhist Philosophy and Learning, Brahman scholars, after completing the study of their traditional Vedic learning, would seek to add to their

[1] The expression means not "the three collections" but "the three bodies of oral tradition as handed down from teacher to teacher" [*SBE.*, xxxv, p. 28 n.].

intellectual equipment by a study of Buddhist Literature. The two cultures were thus co-existing without any hostility between them. Thirdly, we have a confirmation of the somewhat scanty evidence of the Vinaya that Buddhist learning had its centres not merely and exclusively in the monasteries, as is commonly supposed, but also in the forests, in the hermitages of solitary and spiritually advanced monks after the Brahmanical model. Fourthly, that Buddhist Learning was not confined to a mere class, the monks, but spread through all the ranks of the people is proved by the instance of a rich merchant of Pāṭaliputta (with 500 waggons travelling) introducing himself as a student of the Abhidhamma and anxious to hear some passages from it [i, 33].

Subjects of Study. The *Milinda* also indicates the range of Brahmanical learning, sacred and secular, of the times. It included the following: the four Vedas, Itihāsas, Purāṇas, lexicography, prosody, phonology, verses, grammar, etymology, astrology, astronomy, the six Vedāṅgas, interpretation of omens, dreams, and signs, prognostications to be drawn from the flight of comets, thunder, junction of planets, fall of meteors, earthquakes, conflagrations, and signs in the heaven and earth, study of eclipses of the sun and moon, of arithmetic, casuistry, of the interpretation of omens to be drawn from dogs, deer, and rats, mixtures of liquids, sounds, and cries of birds [iv, 3, 26]. Another passage in describing the learning of King Milinda mentions the following additional subjects: the Sāṁkhya, Yoga, Nyāya, and Vaiśeshika systems of philosophy, music, medicine, magic, causation, spells, the art of war, poetry, conveyancing, and states the number of the known arts and sciences (*sippas*) to be nineteen [i, 9]. The special knowledge of the Kshatriyas was to include a knowledge of all about elephants, horses, chariots, bows, rapiers, documents, and the law of property [iv, 3, 26]. Another passage mentions the arts of calculating, by using the joints of the fingers as signs or marks, of arithmetic (*gaṇanā*) pure and simple, of estimating the probable yield of growing crops, and of writing [ii, 3, 7]. The writing of a letter is referred to [ii, 2, 3], as well as a writing-master exhibiting his skill in writing [vi, 3].

The *Milinda* also indicates the studies of the Bhikkhus. They must " concern themselves with recitation of, with asking questions about, the discourses, and the pieces in mixed prose and verse, and the expositions, and the poems, and the outbursts of emotion, and the passages beginning ' Thus he said ', and the birth-stories, and the tales of wonder, and the extended treatises ". These make up the nine sections into which the Buddhist scriptures are divided [iv, 7, 1]. Besides these studies, the brethren must "trouble themselves about new buildings, about gifts and offerings to the Order" [ib.]. Hearing the Scriptures, recitation of them, asking questions about them, superintending building work, and seeing to gifts and offerings—all these comprise the duties of Bhikkhus as being conducive to their spiritual progress [v, 7, 6].

CHAPTER XX

EDUCATION AS DESCRIBED IN THE JĀTAKAS

The Jātakas. We shall now discuss the ampler evidence of the *Jātakas* on the system of education, the centres and conditions of learning to which they refer. The *Jātakas* are, it may be noted, sources of historical information not in the contents or substance of their stories, but in the social background or "setting" of those stories, their inevitable reflection of the contemporary conditions of life.

A significant story. The atmosphere of learning and culture which the *Jātakas* breathe, and the educational system they testify to are very well indicated in one of them [No. 252]: "Once on a time, Brahmadatta, the King of Benares, had a son named Prince Brahmadatta. Now kings of former times, though there might be a famous teacher living in their own city, often used to send their sons to foreign countries afar off to complete their education, that by this means they might learn to quell their pride and high-mindedness, and endure heat or cold, and be made acquainted with the ways of the world. So did this king. Calling his boy to him—now the lad was sixteen years old—he gave him one-soled sandals, a sunshade of leaves, and a thousand pieces of money, with these words: 'My son, get you to Takkasilā, and study there.'

"The boy obeyed. He bade his parents farewell, and in due course arrived at Takkasilā. There he inquired for the teacher's dwelling, and reached it at the time when the teacher had finished his lecture and was walking up and down at the door of the house. When the lad set eyes upon the teacher, he loosed his shoes, closed his sunshade, and with a respectful greeting stood still where he was. The teacher saw that he was weary, and welcomed the new-comer. The lad ate, and rested a little. Then he returned to the teacher, and stood respectfully by him.

"'Where have you come from?' he asked.

"'From Benares.'

"'Whose son are you?'

"'I am the son of the King of Benares.'

" 'What brings you here?'

" 'I come to learn,' replied the lad.

" 'Well, have you brought a teacher's fee? or do you wish to attend on me in return for teaching you?'

" 'I have brought a fee with me': and with this he laid at the teacher's feet his purse of a thousand pieces.'

"The resident pupils attend on their teacher by day and at night they learn of him: but they who bring a fee are treated like the eldest sons in his house, and thus they learn. And this teacher, like the rest, gave schooling to the prince on every light and lucky day. Thus the young prince was taught."

This passage introduces us practically to all the principal features of the educational system of the times. We shall now explain them and cite the additional or supplementary information which the other Jātakas convey.

Taxila as a Centre of Learning. Takkasilā was the most famous seat of learning. It attracted scholars from different and distant parts of India. Numerous references in the Jātakas show how thither flocked students from far-off Benares [i, 272, 285, 409; ii, 85, 87; iv, 50, 224; v, 127, 263, etc.], Rājagaha [iii, 238; v, 177, 247], Mithilā [iv, 316; vi, 347], Ujjenī [iv, 392], and Kosala [iii, 115], from the "Central Region" [ib.], and from the Sivi [v, 210], and Kuru [iii, 399; v, 457] kingdoms in the "North Country" [i, 356]. The fame of Takkasilā as a seat of learning was of course due to that of its teachers. They are always spoken of as being "world-renowned", being authorities, specialists, and experts in the subjects they professed. Of one such teacher we read: "Youths of the warrior and brahmin castes came from all India to be taught the arts by him" [iii, 158]. It is the presence of scholars of such acknowledged authority and widespread reputation that made Taxila the intellectual capital of the Indian continent from the different and distant parts of which there was a steady movement of qualified students drawn from all classes and ranks of society towards Taxila to complete the education they had in the schools of their native places. Thus the various centres of learning in the different parts of the country became affiliated, as it were, to the educational centre, or the central university, of Taxila which exercised a kind of intellectual suzerainty over the wide world of letters in India.

Sacrifice of Parents for their Sons' Education. Sending their sons a thousand miles away from home bespeaks the great concern felt by their parents in their proper education. It is like Indian parents sending their sons abroad for highest education. But in those pre-mechanical ages, when travelling was not easy or quick, the parents considered themselves fortunate if they could live to see their sons back home after completing their education. As shown in the case of the medical student, Jīvaka, the course of study at Taxila extended to as many as seven years. Jātaka No. 252 records how parents felt if they could see their sons return home after graduation at Taxila (*diṭṭhyā me jīvamānena putto diṭṭho*).

Taxila a Centre of Higher Education. The students are always spoken of as going to Taxila to "complete" their education and not to begin it. They are invariably sent at the age of sixteen or when they "come of age" [e.g. v, 162, 210]. This shows that Taxila was a seat not of elementary, but higher, education, of colleges or a university as distinguished from schools. Thus the age-limit for admission there was curiously enough the same as is prescribed by modern universities. It was also only the students of a maturer age that could be sent so far away from their homes for the furtherance of their studies.

Tuition Fees. The students were usually admitted to instruction by their teachers on payment in advance of their entire tuition fees. A fixed sum seems to have been specified for the purpose at Taxila, amounting to 1,000 pieces of money [i, 272, 285; iv, 50, 224, etc.]. In lieu of paying the fees in cash, a student was allowed to pay them in the shape of services to his teacher [cf. *Mil.*, vi, 11]. To this class apparently belonged the majority of the students who "attended on their teacher by day" and received instruction at night. We read of a school of 500 Brahman pupils whose duties were, among others, to gather firewood from the forests for their master [i, 317–18]. Sometimes, a student would prefer to devote his whole time to studies without sparing any time for such services or menial work, while at the same time he was too poor to be able to pay the teacher's fees in cash in advance. In such a case the student was trusted to pay the fees after the completion of his education. We read of one such student, a Brahman boy of Benares, who, after completing his education at Taxila, paid his teacher's fees by begging for them in distant countries beyond the Ganges. The fees are described to be "seven nikkhas" or a few ounces of gold, which may indicate that the teacher's fees were paid in gold in that time [iv, 224]. It may be recalled in this connection that, under the Brahmanical system, it was the more usual practice for the *brahmachārin* to pay fees to his teacher only when he becomes a *snātaka* and ends his studentship.

Public contributions to Education. Where students were too poor to be able to pay the teachers' fees in any of the several ways aforesaid, a charitable community often came forward to provide for them a free education. We read of a teacher of "world-wide fame" at Benares, who had in his school 500 young Brahman pupils to teach. The difficulty of maintaining such a school was removed by the generosity of the "Benares folk" who "used to give day by day commons of food to the poor lads and had them taught free" [i, 239].

Invitations to Meals. The cost of education was also to some extent taken over from the teachers and the taught by the occasional invitations to dinner extended to them by philanthropic householders. We read of a school of 500 students being invited to take meals by "a country family" at Takkasilā [i, 317], and of a similar entertainment given by an entire village [iii, 171]. These invitations would very often come by turns in such a way that they would work like a permanent provision of meals for the teachers and the taught.

State Scholarships. There was again another class of students who paid the teacher's fees from the scholarships awarded to them by the States to which they belonged. Generally such students would be sent as companions of the princes of their respective countries who were deputed to Takkasilā for education. We read of the sons of the royal chaplains of the courts of Benares [v, 263], and Rājagaha [iii, 238, and v, 247], accompanying their respective princes to Takkasilā for their education. Cases, however, are not wanting of students being sent on their own account for higher studies to Takkasilā at State expense. Thus we read of a Brahman boy of Benares being sent by the king at his expense to Takkasilā for the purpose of specializing in the science of archery [v, 127].

Fees paid not adequate to cost of Education. It is to be noted that the fees of tuition as fixed here can hardly be considered as adequate to its expenses. The teacher was not like the proprietor of a school conducted as a commercial concern. Probably no part of the fee of 1,000 pieces he could claim as the wages of his own labour. The fees were necessary to cover the cost of the maintenance of those who paid them, of free board, lodging, and other necessaries of the students who went into residence with their teachers under a common roof.

Day Scholars. But residence with the teacher was not a compulsory condition of studentship. Day scholars were also admitted to instruction. We read of Prince Juṇha of Benares running an independent house for himself, from which he attended his college at Taxila: "One night, after lessons he left the teacher's house in the dark and set out for home" [iv, 96].

Householders as Students. The admission of day scholars as students implied that of householders or married students. We read of "a country Brahman" who, finishing his studies in the three Vedas and the eighteen Sciences under a famous teacher in Benares, stopped on there to look after his estate, married, and became a regular householder. And yet he was allowed to continue his studies as an external student. He could, however, come but "two or three times every day to listen to his master's teachings" owing to the obstruction of his mischievous wife who always feigned sickness whenever he wanted to get away to the school [i, 463]. A similar case is that of "a young Brahman from a foreign land" who, while studying as one of 500 pupils of a famous teacher at Benares, "fell in love with a woman and made her his wife. Though he continued to live on in Benares, he failed two or three times in his attendance on the master." Sometimes he was so worried and harassed by his unmanageable wife that he absented himself altogether from waiting on the master. "Some seven or eight days later he renewed his attendances" [i, 300], when his master gave him necessary instructions after which he "paid no heed to his wife's caprices", while his wife also "ceased from that time forward from her naughtiness". There is another instance of a student being handicapped in his studies by the wicked ways of his wife [ib., 301–2]. Lastly, we may also refer to the instance of a teacher of 500 students at Benares who selects by a special test one of them for the hand of his grown-up daughter [iii, 18].[1]

Number and Composition of a School: Admission of all Castes except Chaṇḍālas. The maximum or standard number of pupils which an individual teacher admitted was 500 [i, 239, 317, 402; iii, 18, 235, 143, 171, etc.]. The number gave scope to great variety in the composition of the school. The students

[1] With some teachers "there was a custom that if there should be a daughter ripe for marriage she should be given to the eldest pupil" [vi, 347].

were quite a heterogeneous lot, drawn from all ranks and classes of society and representing diverse social conditions. Youths of Brahman and Kshatriya castes were of course in large numbers among them [cf. iii, 158]; there were also princes from distant kingdoms [i, 272; ii, 87; iii, 238; v, 162; v, 177, 210, 247; 262, 426, 457; iv, 96, 316; iii, 115, 415], and sons of magnates or magnificos, some of whom were Brahmans [ii, 99; v, 227; iv, 237, etc.]; there were, again, sons of merchants and tailors [iv, 38], and even fishermen [iii, 171], for we read of a teacher who was, on principle, against all restrictions on admission of students and would "preach the moral law to anyone he might see though he did not want it, to fishermen and the like" [ib.]. Chaṇḍālas were not, however, admitted as students. We read of two Chaṇḍāla boys from Ujjenī who, considering the misery of their lot due to their birth, thought: "We shall never be able to play the part of Chaṇḍālas; let us conceal our birth and go to Takkasilā in the disguise of young Brahmans, and study there." Thus introducing themselves they "followed their studies in the law under a far-famed master". One of the students was even successful in his studies. Their disguise was, however, detected at a dinner offered to the school by a villager by their use of the Chaṇḍāla dialect in an unguarded moment and they were at once expelled [No. 498].

Freedom of Choice of Studies. While all castes except the Chaṇḍālas were admitted to instruction, it seems that the castes so admitted did not always confine themselves to their traditional subjects of study. We read of a Brahman boy of Takkasilā who learnt divination under his teacher and later settled down as a hunter in the woods of Benares [ii, 200]. Another Brahman boy, son of a magnifico, preferred the study of magic charms to the exclusion of other subjects [ii, 99] Another is spoken of as having gone in for "the liberal arts" and ultimately specialized in Archery [iii, 219]. There is another reference to the same effect [i, 356]. It is again a Brahman boy that studies "the charm which commands all things of sense" [iv, 456]. There is a reference to a Brahman boy choosing "science" for his study [iii, 18], and to another mastering "the three Vedas and the Eighteen Accomplishments" [ii, 87; iii, 115, 122].

Democracy of Learning. We thus see that youths of all sorts and conditions of life, of different classes and castes, had all their divisions and distinctions merged in the democracy of learning. Princes and nobles, merchants, tailors, the poor students who were maintained by charity and could not pay their tuition fees—all rubbed shoulders with one another as fellow-disciples of a common school and teacher. The poor students had to undergo daily a course of exacting and low kind of menial service for the school, but the recognition of the dignity of all honest labour secured to them a status of equality with its aristocratic section. What further levelled all distinctions within the school was the insistence upon certain standards of simplicity and discipline in life to which all its members had to submit. The Prince of Benares is sent on to Takkasilā for his studies with the modest equipment given him by his own royal father of "a pair of one-soled sandals, a sunshade of leaves, and a thousand pieces of money" as his teacher's fees, of which not a single piece he could retain for his private use [No. 252 cited above]. Thus the prince enters his school as a poor man, divested of all riches. The same fact is pointed to by the story of Prince Juṇha of Benares who, accidentally breaking the alms-bowl of a Brahman by colliding with him in nocturnal darkness, was asked to pay him the price of a meal as a compensation. The Prince then said to the Brahman: "I cannot now give you the price of a meal, Brāhman; but I am Prince Juṇha, son of the King of Kāśī, and when I come to my kingdom, you may come to me and ask for the money" [iv, 96]. This shows that there was no money left with a prince which he might spend as he liked. Nor did the offences of princes escape their usual punishment. On the offence of a prince being reported to the teacher (the offence being taking some sweets from a vendor's basket without paying for them) "he caused two lads to take the young fellow by his two hands, and smote him thrice upon the back with a bamboo stick, bidding him take care not to do it again" [No. 252].

It speaks very well of these ancient kings that they deliberately, and as a matter of policy, proposed for their sons such a course of discipline and education as their best training in manners and morals, and as a powerful democratizing influence, "so that by this means they might learn to quell their pride and high-mindedness" [ib.].

Food. The food allowed to the students was of the simplest kind. We have mention of rice-gruel being prepared as breakfast by a maid of the teacher's house [i, 318]. At invitation they were given sugar-cane, molasses, curd, and milk [i, 448].

Discipline. The life of the students was also hard in other ways. Their standing duty was to gather firewood in the forests [ib.]. Their conduct was so much controlled that they were not allowed to go to a river for a bath except in the company of a teacher [No. 252].

Communal Colleges. Side by side with these colleges of a heterogenous or cosmopolitan composition, we also find references to colleges of particular communities only. Teachers with 500, and only Brahman, pupils are frequently mentioned [i, 317, 402, etc.]. Sometimes teachers would have only Brahman and Kshatriya pupils [iii, 158]. We also read of a teacher at Taxila whose school had on its rolls only princes as pupils—all " princes who were at that time in India to the number of 101 ", besides two other princes newly admitted from the kingdoms of Kuru and Benares [v, 457].

Senior Students as Assistant Masters. To manage a school of 500 pupils and undertake their education were no easy tasks for an individual teacher. He was, however, helped by a staff of Assistant Masters (*piṭṭhiāchāriya*). It was only the most advanced or senior pupils that were appointed as Assistant Masters [ii, 100 ; v, 457]. Assistance in teaching was also rendered by the senior pupils as such. We are told of a teacher appointing his oldest disciple to act as his substitute [i, 141]. Another teacher of Taxila, while going to Benares on some mission, appointed his chief pupil to take charge of his school during his absence, saying : " My son, I am going away from home ; while I am away, you are to instruct these my pupils " (numbering 500) [iv, 51]. These senior pupils, by being associated in the work of teaching, soon became fit to be teachers. We read of Prince Sutasoma of the Kuru country who " being the senior pupil soon attained to proficiency in teaching " and, " becoming the private teacher " of his comrade in the school, " soon educated him, while the others only gradually acquired their learning " [v, 457–8].

Teaching by shifts both in the day and at night. The college seems to have had a number of sittings every day. Instruction was imparted at times convenient to the students. The poorer scholars who paid for the expenses of their educational life by the performance of services or menial work for the school during the daytime could find time for study only in the nights when accordingly the teacher imparted instruction to them [ii, 278]. It was probably convenient for the day scholars to

PLATE XX

No. 1.—Gautama at School: practising writing.

No. 2.—Gautama at School: learning music.

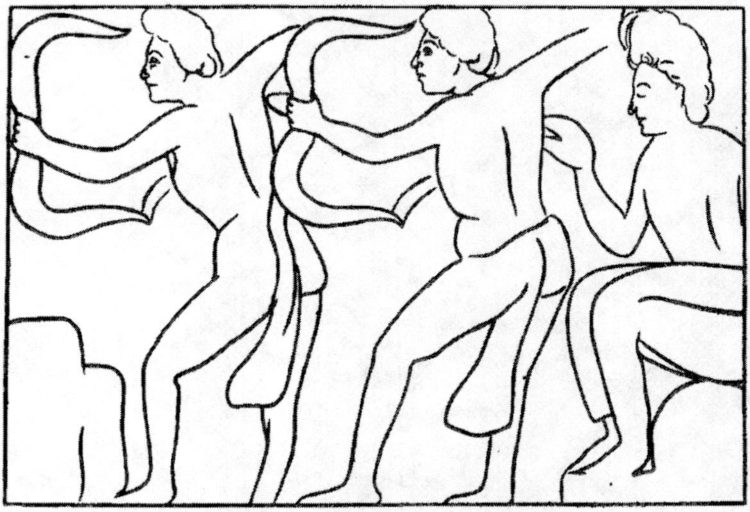

No. 3.—Gautama at School: being instructed in Archery.

GANDHARA SCULPTURES (*c.* second century A.D.).

[*Facing p. 485*

attend the night classes: we read of Prince Juṇha who "one night, after he had been listening carefully to his teacher's instruction, left the house of his teacher in the dark and set out for home" [iv, 96]. Another student of Benares who went to Takkasilā for a particular instruction implored his teacher thus: "Give me your time for this one night only. . . I will learn the whole after one lesson" [ii, 47]. As regards the students who paid their teacher's fees, "they are treated like the eldest sons in his house, and thus they learn." They were given "schooling on every light and lucky day" [ii, 278].

Crowing of Cock as Call to Study. Students seem to have commenced their studies very early in the morning, with the crowing of the cock. We read of a school of 500 Brahman students at Benares who "had a cock that crowed betimes and roused them to their studies". Probably a cock was domesticated in every school to serve as a clock! When the trained cock died, a second cock was secured which "had been bred in a cemetery and had thus no knowledge of times and seasons, and used to crow casually—at midnight as well as at daybreak. Roused by his crowing at midnight, the young Brahmans fell to their studies; by dawn they were tired out and could not for sleepiness keep their attention on the subject [already learnt (*gahitaṭṭhānampi*)]; and when he fell a-crowing in broad day they did not get a chance of quiet for repeating their lesson. And as it was the cock's crowing both at midnight and by day which had brought their studies to a standstill, they took the bird and wrung his neck" [i, 436]. It will appear from this passage that there was time for the private study of the students which they spent on repeating *new* lessons and revising *old* ones.

Birds as Aids to Study. As the crowing cock was utilized to rouse students from sleep to study in the early hours of morning, the Tittiri birds, according to the Tittiri Jātaka, were trained to recite Vedic Mantras and help students by such recitations.

Use of Writing in Education. In this passage, again, the reference to drowsiness preventing the students from understanding (lit. "seeing", *passanti*) the subject already learnt may be taken to indicate the use of books for their studies. The Jātakas frequently use the expression *sippaṁ vācheti*, i.e. "getting the sciences read". More definite is the following reference to the existence of written books at the time: "the Bodhisatta . . . caused a book of judgments to be written and said, 'By observing this book ye should settle suits'" [iii, 292].

We have again references to the various and widespread uses of writing in the Jātakas ; to the writing of epistles [i, 377 (mentioning a correspondent), ii, 95, 174 (sealing a letter), iv, 145 (contents of a message given), vi, 370, 385, 403], to the forging of letters [i, 451 ; iv, 124], to inscription on gold plate [ii, 36, 372, 376 ; iv, 7, 257, 335, 488 ; v, 59, 67, 125 ; vi, 29], to inscription over a hermitage [vi, 520 ; iv, 489 (inscription in letters of vermilion upon a wall)], to letters of the alphabet engraved on gold necklets [vi, 390], to inscriptions upon garments and accoutrements [vi, 408], to the scratching of a message on an arrow [ii, 90], to writing on a leaf [ii, 174 ; iv, 55 ; vi, 369, 400 (writing on a leaf fastened on an arrow)]. Lastly, there is another passage [i, 451], which indicates how the art of writing was being regularly taught to the young in the elementary or primary schools. It tells how when a rich man's son " was being taught to write ", his " young slave used to go with his young master's tablets and so learned at the same time to write himself ". The three R's were evidently taught in these schools. We may recall in this connection the passage in the *Kauṭilīya* [i, 5], showing how after the ceremony of *chūḍākaraṇa* a boy was to be taught *lipi* or writing and *saṁkhyānam* or counting and arithmetic.

Different Courses of Study. We shall now consider the courses of study that were offered by the Colleges of Takkasilā. The Jātakas constantly refer to students coming to Takkasilā to complete their education in the three Vedas and the eighteen Sippas or Arts [i, 259, 356, 402, 464 ; ii, 87 ; iii, 115, 122, etc.]. Sometimes the students are referred to as selecting the study of the Vedas alone [i, 402 ; iii, 235 ; iv, 293, etc.], or the Arts alone [iii, 18, 238 ; v, 127, 162, 177, 247, 426 ; iv, 456 ; iii, 143, 219, etc.]. We may conveniently distinguish education in the Vedas as Literary Education from Education in the Arts as Scientific and Technical Education.

Religion and Humanities. The invariable mention of the three Vedas shows that the study of the Atharva Veda was not included in the curriculum for general education at the time of the Jātakas. The Vedas were of course to be learnt by heart. We are told of a teacher at Takkasilā from whose lips 500 Brahman pupils learnt the Vedas [i, 402]. The Bodhisatta is frequently referred to as having learned the three Vedas by heart [cf. i, 259]. Instead of the three Vedas, we sometimes find mention of " sacred texts " [iii, 235], " holy books " [iv, 293], or " the law " [iv, 392]. Some of these terms may indicate the sacred literature

MUTTRA

Image in stone of Piṅgala, attendant of Sūrya, holding Pen in his right hand and an Ink-pot in his left [Gupta Period].

[*Facing p. 486*

of the Buddhists. We find even the direct mention of a Vinaya scholar and a Sūtra scholar [iii, 486].

Sciences, Arts, and Crafts. The subjects under the Sciences and Arts are not individually mentioned. Their number alone is frequently mentioned. We may refer in this connection to the passage already cited from the *Milinda Pañha* which gives the individual names of the nineteen Sippas then current. Some passages in the Jātakas, however, make individual mention of some subjects under scientific and technical education, but it is not certain whether they would come under the eighteen Sippas. We have mention of the following arts being taught in some of the colleges of Takkasilā, viz. (1) Elephant Lore (*Hatthi Sutta*) [ii, 47], (2) Magic Charms [ii, 100], (3) Spell for bringing back the dead to life [i, 510], (4) Hunting [ii, 200], (5) Spell for understanding all animals' cries [iii, 415], (6) Archery (*Issatthasippa*) [iii, 219; i, 356; v, 127, ii, 87], (7) The Art of Prognostication [iii, 122], (8) Charm for commanding all things of sense [iv, 456], (9) Divining from signs of the body [ii, 200], and (10) Medicine [iv, 171].

Specialization. It is to be noted that students are mentioned as taking up for their study only one of these subjects in which they wanted to specialize and make themselves experts.

Courses of Study in Theory and Practice. The study of these Sciences and Arts seems to have had a theoretical and a practical course. Knowledge of the literature of a subject had to be followed by its practical applications. In regard to some subjects like Medicine, for instance, the practical course had to be gone through under the direction of the teacher. The practical course in Medicine at Takkasilā included a first-hand study of the plants to find out the medicinal ones, as shown in the story of Jīvaka's education. In other subjects, the practical course was left to be completed by the students themselves when they left their colleges after finishing their instruction. Thus we read of a Brahman student "of a market town in the north country" who specialized in the science of Archery at Takkasilā and, after finishing his studies, went as far as the Andhra country in prosecution of the practical application of his art [i, 356]. There is mention of the Prince of Magadha who, having mastered all the arts of Takkasilā, "wandered through towns, villages, and all the land to acquire all practical usages and understand country observances" [iii, 238]. We have mention of another student, Setaketu, of Takkasilā who similarly "wandered, learning all practical arts" [iii, 235]. There is mentioned another prince of Magadha who, being trained in all sciences at Takkasilā, "left that place with the intention of learning the practical uses of arts and local observances" [v, 247]. We have an interesting reference to the Pāṇḍu brothers who, after receiving instruction in arts at Takkasilā, "travelled about with the idea of mastering local customs" [v, 426]. We read again of two sons of merchants and a tailor's son travelling together to learn the customs of the country folk after finishing their education in Takkasilā [iv, 38]. There is a similar reference to a student from Benares undertaking a travel after his education at Takkasilā [iv, 208]. A prince of Kosala is mentioned who after studying the three Vedas and eighteen liberal arts at Takkasilā left the place to study the practical uses of the sciences learned [iii, 115]. Lastly, there is an instance in which a student, on completion of his education in the Arts at Takkasilā and returning home to Benares, had to exhibit before his parents a practical demonstration of the technical knowledge he had acquired. In this connection, we may also recall the successful surgical operations executed by Jīvaka as soon as he had left Takkasilā on finishing his education, for they show that he must have had a previous practical training and experimentation in such difficult operations.

Education made practical. A practical turn was indeed given to all instruction as a pedagogic principle. We have already referred to the first-hand observation of plant-life as a compulsory part of medical education. We have again one Jātaka [No. 123] which shows how Nature-study was always insisted upon as the best means of awakening a healthy curiosity, a spirit of observation and inquiry which are indispensable aids to intellectual culture. In the story, a "world-renowned Professor" of Benares "had 500 young Brahmans to instruct", one of whom "had always foolish notions in his head and always said the wrong thing; he was engaged with the rest in learning the scriptures as a pupil, but because of his folly could not master them". The teacher was at pains to consider what method of instruction would be suitable for that "veriest dullard" of all his pupils. "And the thought came to him that the best way was to question him on his return from gathering firewood and leaves, as to something he had seen or done that day, and then to ask what it was like. 'For,' thought the master, 'this will lead him on to making comparisons and giving reasons, and the continuous practice of comparing and reasoning on his part will enable me to impart learning to him.' "

Foreign Travel as completing Education. The point of some of the examples cited above which should not be missed in this connection is that they demonstrate how the students of those days after their graduation undertook an extensive foreign travel to give a practical turn to their theoretical studies at the colleges, and qualify themselves for the life in the world by broadening the range of their experience and deepening their insight into human affairs by a first-hand study of the diverse manners and customs prevailing in the different parts of the country. Besides its direct educational value, this post-graduate travelling as giving a finishing touch to a student's training was encouraged and even insisted upon for another very substantial reason, especially in the cases of the students of the well-to-do classes who were brought up in luxury. This was to build up the physique or the physical constitution of the student by inuring him to the hardships of travelling, to make him " endure heat or cold " and stand all weathers and climates. And we have already referred to the recognition of the utility of the institution as a means of moral education especially of the students of the royal and aristocratic houses, who were sent to distant centres for their education, so that by their necessary travelling and living under strange conditions in foreign parts, they might be more humanized, with their native pride of position and spirit of exclusiveness crushed out of them under the spirit of a thorough-going democracy and fraternity which a seat of learning would always breathe [No. 252].

Special Schools of Taxila : Schools of Medicine, Law, and Military Science. Takkasilā was also famous for some of its special Schools. One of such Schools was the Medical School which must have been the best of its kind in India, if we may believe in the story of Jīvaka. It was also noted for its School of Law which attracted students from distant Ujjenī [iv, 392 ; also iii, 171]. Its Military Schools were not less famous. One such School could boast of counting all the then princes throughout India numbering 103 as its students [v, 457]. We have already seen how keen and widespread was the demand in the country for the courses and training offered by its Schools of Archery.

Thus the teachers of Takkasilā were as famous for their knowledge of the arts of peace as for that of war. In this connection, we may refer to the story of the Brahman boy of Benares of the name of Jotipāla who was sent at the king's expense for education in archery at Takkasilā. When he had finished his training and was returning home, the teacher presented him with his own sword, a bow and arrow, a coat of mail, and a diamond, and asked him to take his place as the head of 500 pupils to be trained up by him in the military arts, as he was himself old and wanted to retire [v, 127]. The Veda-of-the-bow claimed almost as many students as the sacred triple Veda in those days.

It is also evident that the demand for the knowledge of the *Sippas* or for technical and scientific education was not less keen than that for general education or religious studies.

Benares as a Centre of Education : Its School of Music. Next to Takkasilā ranks Benares as a seat of learning. It was, however, largely the creation of the ex-students of Takkasilā who set up as teachers at Benares [Nos. 130, 185, etc.], and carried thither the culture of that cosmopolitan educational centre which was moulding the intellectual life of the whole of India. Subjects in the instruction of which Takkasilā held the monopoly were being gradually introduced into Benares. We find established there schools for the teaching of spells and magic charms by students trained from Takkasilā [ii, 99]. For the study of the ordinary subjects there were of course established many schools [i, 464]. Benares, however, was not without its own alumni as educationists. There are several references to teachers of world-wide fame with the usual number of 500 pupils to teach [i, 239 ; iii, 18 and 233]. The son of a Brahman magnate worth eighty crores is educated in Benares [iv, 237]. There were again certain subjects in the teaching of which Benares seems to have specialized. There is a reference, for instance, to a School of Music presided over by an expert who was " the chief of his kind in all India " [No. 243]. With all this, the inferiority of Benares to Takkasilā as a seat of learning is apparent from the fact that there are hardly to be found many references in the Jātakas to the movement of foreign scholars towards that city for education in different subjects, as we find in such abundance in respect of the other city.

Hermitages as Centres of Highest Learning. Lastly, it is to be noted that the educational system of the times produced men of affairs as well as men who renounced the world in the pursuit of Truth. The life of renunciation indeed claimed many an ex-student of both Takkasilā and Benares. In the sylvan and solitary retreats away from the haunts of men, the hermitages served as schools of higher philosophical speculation and religious training where the culture previously acquired would attain its fruitage or a further development in a particular direction. These special schools of spiritual culture are also referred to as being composed of the standard number of 500 ascetics gathering round the personality of an individual hermit of established reputation to seek instruction as his disciples [i, 141, etc.]. We have, however, references to schools of larger sizes. We read of one which was so overcrowded with zealous pupils that the chief had to get other hermitages established by his seven senior pupils to relieve the congestion but to no purpose, for the original or parent hermitage continued to be crowded as before with aspirants after the religious life [v, 128].

The hermitages were generally established in the Himalayas [i, 406, 431 ; iii, 143 ; iv, 74]. Sometimes, however, the bands of ascetics would establish themselves near the centres of population and would have facilities for attracting recruits [iii, 115 ; iv, 293]. These imparted to their disciples a knowledge of their " arts, texts, and practices ". We read of Setaketu, originally the senior pupil of a school of 500 pupils at Benares, going to Takkasilā for education in the " arts ", on completion of which he wandered through the country learning all practical arts, when in a village he comes across a group of 500 ascetics who, after ordaining him, taught him all their " arts, texts, and practices " [iii, 235].

CHAPTER XXI

EDUCATION IN THE FIFTH CENTURY A.D.

(Account of Fa-Hien)

Value of the Account of a Foreigner and an Eye-witness. From the account of education as built up on the basis of the materials and indirect allusions scattered through the Buddhist sacred texts, we now turn to that given by an eye-witness himself from his first-hand observation of the working of the educational institutions then flourishing at the chief centres of Buddhist learning in India. Such an account would be doubly interesting and trustworthy when it proceeds from an eye-witness who is a foreigner. We have no means of positively ascertaining how far the educational conditions referred to in the sacred texts, were in actual existence, for the sacred texts are naturally more concerned with the exposition of the *ideal* conditions, precepts, and maxims, with what *ought* to be than with what *is*. The evidence of Fa-Hien is, therefore, all the more valuable, because, as picturing the existing conditions and realities, it helps us to obtain a confirmation of the sacred evidence which, by itself, cannot lead to definite and positive conclusions.

India drawing Pilgrims from China as its Holy Land. We must, however, consider the evidence of Fa-Hien in its proper setting. The very fact of the pilgrimage of Chinese scholars like Fa-Hien or Hiuen Tsang to India testifies to the tribute paid by China to the sovereignty of Indian thought and culture which made its influence felt beyond the bounds of India itself in distant countries which might be well regarded as then constituting a sort of a Greater India. India was in those days the holy land of China and other countries, teeming with centres of Buddhist faith and learning, to which the devout youth of the foreign countries were flocking for their instruction, to return home later as fully equipped and trained missionaries. Fa-Hien, or, for the matter of that, Hiuen Tsang, or I-Tsing, were but individual members of noble bands of missionaries who during the period of wellnigh ten centuries (from Kanishka to Dharmapāla) came to India on religious and literary pilgrimage to drink at the very fountains of the culture they professed.

The precise Object of their Mission. Fa-Hien himself was only one of a company of pilgrims who embarked upon a common holy mission. We read in his *Travels* [Legge's ed., p. 9]: "Deploring the mutilated and imperfect state of the collection of the Books of Discipline . . . he entered into an engagement with Hwuy-king, Tao-ching, Hwuy-ying, and Hwuy-wei, that they should go to India and seek for the Disciplinary Rules." [1] This passage also defines the objects of the mission. They were to collect in India the Vinaya texts for the purposes of the Buddhist Saṁghas of China. We are also to understand from this the limitations of the evidence of Fa-Hien who confines his observations only to that aspect of Indian thought and life which are associated with Buddhism. But within this limited range of inquiry, the information given by Fa-Hien is refreshingly realistic, positive, and concrete, being drawn from his first-hand observation and personal experience of actually existing conditions. What is thus lost in the scope of his evidence is amply compensated by its greater objectivity and trustworthiness.

Fa-Hien's Account limited to Buddhist India. Fa-Hien's evidence thus brings us into touch with Buddhist India, the chief centres of its learning, the actual working of its institutions, their internal conditions, rules, and regulations.

Its Extent. Buddhist India in Fa-Hien's time embraced a large area, extending from Udyāna on the north-western frontiers to Tāmalipti on the east, and was noted for the abundance of its monasteries, those strongholds and distributing centres of Buddhist culture which enabled it to maintain its hold upon the country, and helped to spread it evenly among the different parts thereof. In Udyāna (modern Swat) alone, where Buddhism was "very flourishing", Fa-Hien noticed no less than 500 Saṁghārāmas or monasteries peopled by monks of the Hīnayāna school (p. 28). In Pe-too or the Panjab, also, he found Buddhism very flourishing and represented by both its schools, Mahāyāna and Hīnayāna (p. 41). From this place, as he travelled south-east, he passed "by a succession of very many monasteries, with a multitude of monks who might be counted by myriads" (p. 42), until he came to Mathurā. Thence, following the course of the Yamunā river, he found, on both banks of the river, "twenty

[1] Even on his way Fa-Hien came across another fellow-pilgrim to India, "a Tartar who was an earnest follower of the Law" and another band of five pilgrims who had preceded him on the same journey [pp. 21 and 11].

monasteries which might contain 3,000 monks"; for there "the Law of Buddha was very flourishing". Indeed "everywhere, from the Sandy Desert, in all the countries of India, the kings had been firm believers in that Law" (p. 42). But Buddhism in Fa-Hien's time had not merely an extensive but also an intensive growth. He mentions the eighteen Schools of Buddhism, of which "each one has the views and decisions of its own masters" (p. 98), while he names only three of them, viz. the Mahāsaṁghika, the Sabbatthivāda (ib.), and the Mahiṁsāsaka (p. 111).

Account of Monasteries as seen by Fa-Hien. We shall now give Fa-Hien's accounts of the individual monasteries he himself visited in the course of his travels.

Fa-Hien does not mention any monasteries in Takshaśilā which figures so largely in the Buddhist Literature as a centre of learning (p. 32).

Purushapura (Peshawar) had a monastery where "there may be more than 700 monks" (p. 35).

In the city of He-lo (Hidda, west of Peshawar) was a Vihāra where the flat-bone of Buddha's skull is said to have been deposited, which is regularly worshipped with offerings by the kings of the country, his attendants, and the chiefs of the Vaiśyas. Near the city of Nagara was the Buddha's pewter staff in a Vihāra, and Saṅghāṭī or his robe in another, while at the place where the Buddha shaved off his hair and clipped his nails was another Vihāra with more than 700 monks (pp. 36–40).

The next individual monasteries mentioned are those of Saṅkāśya. One of these had 1,000 monks and nuns "who all receive their food from the common store and pursue their studies, some of the Mahāyāna, and some of the Hīnayāna" (p. 52). Another was called "The Great Heap". There was a third monastery "containing perhaps 600 or 700 monks" (p. 53).

"The city of Kānyakubja lying along the Ganges" had two monasteries "the inmates of which are students of the Hīnayāna" (p. 54).

The city of Śrāvastī was famous for the Jetavana Vihāra, originally of seven storeys, which the kings and people of the countries around vied with one another in decorating, and built in the centre of a large park. "Here Buddha lived for a longer time than at any other place," "for twenty-five years," "preaching his Law and converting men." Fa-Hien saw the monastery in a flourishing condition with a crowd of monks coming out to greet him and expressing their surprise[1] that "men of a border country should be able to come here in search of the Law" and saying to one another: "During all the time that we, preceptors and monks, have succeeded to one another, we have never seen men of Han, followers of our system, arrive here." Indeed, this ideal succession of preceptors and monks in the Jetavana monastery carried on its history for nearly 1,000 years up to the time of this visit of Fa-Hien!

Śrāvastī in earlier days seems to have been a university town. Round the Jetavana Vihāra as the centre there were originally no less than ninety-eight monasteries. Of these, Fa-Hien found only a few existing. One was the Vihāra originally built by mother Viśākhā (pp. 55–63).

Kuśanagara where the Buddha died was the seat of several monasteries seen by Fa-Hien.

In the city of Vaiśālī, Fa-Hien saw the Vihāra which the courtesan Ambapālī built in honour of Buddha "now standing as it was at first" (p. 72).

One of the most prominent centres of Buddhist learning in Fa-Hien's time was Pāṭaliputra where he saw the Mauryan "royal palace and halls" "exist now as of old" (p. 77). There were in the city one Mahāyāna monastery "very grand and beautiful", and another Hīnayāna one, the two together containing six or seven hundred monks. "The rules of demeanour and the scholastic arrangements in them are worthy of observation. Shamans of the highest virtue from all quarters, and students, inquirers wishing to find out truth and the grounds of it, all resort to these monasteries." This shows that besides offering elementary instruction to the younger monks and novices, these monasteries served as centres of advanced instruction for the maturer monks. This was due to their having as their residents several far-famed teachers. One of these was "a great Brahman, named Rādhāsāmi, a Professor of the Mahāyāna, of clear discernment, and much wisdom, who understood everything, living by himself in spotless purity. . . He might be more than fifty years old, and all the kingdom looked up to him", including the king who "served him as his teacher". "By means of this one man, the Law of Buddha was widely made

[1] A similar surprise was expressed earlier by the monks of some of the Panjab monasteries who said: "How is it that these men from a border-land should have learned to become monks, and come for the sake of our doctrines from such a distance in search of the Law of Buddha?" (p. 42).

known " (p. 78). The other distinguished teacher seen by Fa-Hien was also a Brahman Buddhist named Mañjuśrī " whom the Shamans of greatest virtue in the kingdom, and the Mahāyāna Bhikshus honour and look up to " (p. 79).

At Rājagṛiha, Fa-Hien found still existing as of old the Vihāra originally built for the Buddha and his 1,250 disciples by Jīvaka (p. 82). Outside the city, the traveller " found the Karaṇḍa Bamboo garden where the old Vihāra (the gift of Bimbisāra to the Buddha) is still in existence with a company of monks who keep (it) swept and (its grounds) watered " (p. 84).

At Gayā, " at the place where Buddha attained to perfect wisdom," Fa-Hien found " three monasteries, in all of which there are monks residing " (p. 89). Fa-Hien praised the efficiency of these institutions. " The disciplinary rules are strictly observed by them. The laws regulating their demeanour in sitting, rising, and entering when the others are assembled, are those which have been practised by all the saints since Buddha was in the world down to the present day " (p. 89).

From Gayā, retracing his steps towards Pāṭaliputra along the course of the Ganges, " he found a Vihāra named the Wilderness—a place where Buddha had dwelt, and where there are monks now " (p. 94).

Pursuing the same course, he came to Benares and " found the Vihāra in the park of ' The Rishis Deer-Wild ' " (p. 94), where there were two other monasteries in both of which he found monks residing (p. 96).

Proceeding onwards, he found at Kauśāmbī the Ghochiravana Vihāra where Buddha formerly resided, still existing as of old, with " a company of monks there, most of whom are students of the Hīnayāna " (ib.), and, at a distance from it, another monastery " which may contain more than 100 monks " (ib.).

At Champā, the Vihāras of olden times had still monk residing in them (p. 100).

Tāmaliptī, the last place visited by Fa-Hien, was a flourishing seat of Buddhism with twenty-two monasteries, at all of which there are monks residing " (ib.).

Maintenance of Monasteries. Life in these monasteries was governed by regulations which followed the lines laid down in the Vinaya.

The monasteries were maintained by the endowments of the laity, including kings and merchant-princes, " the heads of the Vaiśyas." They " built Vihāras for the priests and endowed them with fields, houses, gardens, and orchards, along with the resident populations and their cattle". These grants were "engraved on plates of metal" and were "handed down from king to king without anyone daring to annul them" (p. 43). The gifts of the laity also included other necessaries such as food, for instance. "When the kings make their offerings to a community of monks, they take off their royal caps, and along with their relatives and ministers, supply them with food with their own hands" (p. 42). This reminds us of the several Vinaya instances, cited above, of kings serving the Buddha and his Order with food with their own hands. With reference to another monastery we read thus of the gifts of the laity: "The families of their people around supply the societies of these monks with an abundant sufficiency of what they require, so that there is no lack or stint" (p. 89). The usual season for the making of these gifts was "a month after the annual season of rest" (i.e. Vassa) when "the families which are looking out for blessing stimulate one another to make offerings to the monks and send round to them the liquid food which may be taken out of the ordinary hours" (p. 45). In another place (p. 47) Fa-Hien refers to "the annual tribute (from the harvests)" paid to the monks and the gifts of "clothes and such other articles as the monks require for use" which they afterwards share among themselves. The donors of these gifts included not merely "the heads of the Vaiśyas" but also Brahmans (ib.).

Duties of Monks. "The regular business of the monks is to perform acts of meritorious virtue, to recite their Sūtras, and sit wrapt in meditation" (p. 44).

Oral teaching still the rule. Even in Fa-Hien's time, the time-honoured Brahmanical system of oral tradition was still obtaining as the method of instruction even among Buddhists. The subjects of study were not yet reduced to writing. "In the various kingdoms of North India he had found one master transmitting orally the rules to another, but no written copies which he could transcribe" (p. 98). This was a great disappointment to the traveller who had set out on his travel with the object of finding copies of the Vinayas, as we have already seen. Out of the numerous monasteries he had visited, it was only in two that his object was realized. Manuscripts of sacred texts which he could copy were found in the Mahāyāna monastery at Pāṭaliputra and in the monasteries in Tāmaliptī. Thus oral instruction was the only educational method followed in the north, while the rule was relaxed in the east where the aid of written literature to education was recognized.

MSS. copied by Fa-Hien. The MSS. copied out by Fa-Hien give us some idea of the works of Buddhist literature which were in request in China and also of the usual subjects of study of the monks in India, who do not seem to have any connection with secular subjects. The sacred texts copied out by Fa-Hien comprised the following: (1) The Vinaya, containing the Mahā-Saṁghika rules promulgated at the time of the Buddha. "This copy of the rules is the most complete with the fullest explanations" (p. 99); (2) The Sarvāstivāda rules in six or seven thousand *Gāthās*; (3) The Saṁyuktābhidharma-hṛidaya-śāstra in about six or seven thousand *Gāthās*; (4) A Sūtra of 2,500 *Gāthās*; (5) One chapter of the Parinirvāṇa-vaipulya Sūtra of about 5,000 *Gāthās*; and (6) The Māhāsaṁghika Abhidharma. In the monastery at Tāmaliptī Fa-Hien "wrote out his Sūtras" (p. 100).

Popularity of Sanskrit. It is interesting to note that the study of Sanskrit was continued in these Buddhist monasteries. At the Pāṭaliputra monastery Fa-Hien stayed for three years, "learning Sanskrit books and the Sanskrit speech and writing out the Vinaya rules" (p. 99).

Stūpas erected at Monasteries in honour of Teachers and Texts. We may now turn to the other features of monastic life as observed by Fa-Hien. Monasteries had topes erected in honour of the sacred characters in the history of Buddhism, such as Sāriputra, Mahā-maudgalyāyana, and Ānanda, to whom the full-fledged monks usually made offerings, the Śrāmaṇeras making their offerings to Rāhula. The Bhikshuṇīs usually made their offerings at the tope of Ānanda, "because it was he who requested the world-honoured one to allow females to quit their families and become nuns" (p. 45). Topes were also erected to sacred texts like the Abhidharma, the Vinaya, and the Sūtras, the Professors of each of these subjects making offerings to the tope connected with it (p. 46). The students of Mahāyāna "present offerings to the Prajñā-pāramitā, to Mañjuśrī, and to Kwan-she-yin (= Avalokiteśvara)". Thus every monastery, whether Hīnayāna or Mahāyāna, was equipped with a sort of a chapel where the inmates offered their worship.

Guests allowed at Monasteries for three days. These hostels of the monks were authorized to receive guests. The manner of their reception is thus described: "When stranger monks arrive, the old residents meet and receive them, carry for them their clothes and alms-bowl, give them water to wash their feet, oil with which to anoint them, and the liquid food permitted out of the regular hours (cf. Vinaya regulations cited above). When the stranger has enjoyed a very brief rest, they further ask the number of years that he has been a monk, after which he receives a sleeping apartment with its appurtenances, according to his regular orders, and everything is done for him which the rules prescribe" (p. 44). The guests were to be entertained ordinarily for three days only. This was the rule noticed by Fa-Hien in the Udyāna monasteries. "When stranger bhikshus arrive at one of them, their wants are supplied for three days, after which they are told to find a resting-place for themselves" (p. 29).

Assemblies held in the Hall of the Monastery. Besides individual study and meditation, the monks had always to meet together in the common room or hall of the monastery for purposes of religious discussions. "All the monks come together in a great assembly and preach the law," observed Fa-Hien (p. 45).

Non-Buddhist Sects and Charitable Institutions. Lastly, it is to be observed from Fa-Hien's evidence that the Buddhists alone had not the monopoly of leading the people. There were many other sects and systems of thought hardly less influential in the country than the Buddhists. In the Middle Kingdom alone, Fa-Hien noticed no less than "ninety-six sorts of views, erroneous and different from Buddhism, all of which recognize this world and the future world (and the connection between them). Each has its multitude of followers, and they all beg their food: only they do not carry the alms-bowl". These non-Buddhistic monkish communities and their followers were well-known for their charity and philanthropy, "setting up on the road-side houses of charity, where rooms, couches, beds, and food and drink are supplied to travellers, and also to monks, coming and going as guests, the only difference being in the time for which those parties remain" (p. 62). Besides these Brahmanical sects of ascetics, Fa-Hien observed "companies of the followers of Devadatta" as "still existing". It may be noted that the Middle Kingdom where these numerous non-Buddhistic communities flourished was, in Fa-Hien's time, a part of the Gupta Empire which, being officially orthodox Hindu, gave a great impetus to the revival of the Brahmanical religion and culture.

The revival was most marked in Magadha, the metropolitan province of the Gupta empire, where, according to Fa-Hien, "the inhabitants are rich and prosperous and vie with one another in the practice of benevolence and righteousness. The Heads of the Vaiśya families establish in the cities ('in all the other kingdoms as well'), houses of dispensing charity and medicines. All the poor and destitute in the country, orphans, widowers, and childless men, maimed people and cripples, and all who are diseased, go to those houses, and are provided with every kind of help, and doctors examine their diseases. They get the food and medicines which their cases require, and are made to feel at ease; and when they are better, they go away of themselves" (p. 79). This statement demonstrates that Brahmanism was as much known for its secular charities as Buddhism: it founded temples for the direct worship of God equally with the institutions for the relief of human suffering. Positivism was not foreign to the creed of Brahmanism which could thus recognize the duty of serving man as a mode of serving God!

Chinese Pilgrims visiting India at risk of life in search of her Wisdom. A few other points of interest may be noted in conclusion in connection with Fa-Hien's evidence. The duration of his travels in India was for fifteen years, from A.D. 399–414. "After Fa-Hien set out from Ch'ang-gan it took him six years to reach Central India; stoppages there extended over (other) six years; and on his return it took him three years to reach Ts'ing-chow" (p. 116). This shows that the educational conditions of India as observed and recorded by Fa-Hien in the fifth century A.D. had been prevailing in the country in still earlier times. There is, unfortunately, no positive evidence available like Fa-Hien's, which may enable us to trace the origin and growth of these historical monasteries of Buddhism which, already in Fa-Hien's time, and in the times anterior to him, had become such important and flourishing centres of Buddhist education and learning where was conserved all that was best and typical in Buddhist thought and life. The reputation of these schools, due undoubtedly to their real worth, travelled far beyond the limits of India and caused a large movement of foreign scholars towards them for their instruction, which continued steadily for nearly ten centuries. A profound and abiding regard for the learning and culture of India was needed to feed and sustain such a long-continued movement. Indeed, the enthusiasm for Indian wisdom was so intense, the passion for a direct contact with its seats was so strong, that it defied the physical dangers and difficulties which lay so amply in the way of its realization. An account of these dangers and difficulties is best given in the words of Fa-Hien himself: "When I look back on what I have gone through, my heart is involuntarily moved, and the perspiration flows forth. That I encountered danger and trod the most perilous places without thinking of or sparing myself, was because I had a definite aim, and thought of nothing but to do my best in my simplicity and straightforwardness. Thus it was that I exposed my life where death seemed inevitable if I might accomplish but a ten-thousandth part of what I hoped" (p. 117). Fa-Hien speaks here as the representative and spokesman of bands of scholars in whom the spirit triumphed over matter, the soul over sense, whose religious zeal and thirst for knowledge no earthly difficulty or physical risk could conquer. Truly remarked the old Chinese editor of Fa-Hien's *Travels*: "Henceforth I know that the influence of sincerity finds no obstacle, however great, which it does not overcome, and that force of will does not fail to accomplish whatever service it undertakes" (p. 118). It is again to be noted that actual experience, the facts of Indian life and learning, did not run short of the ideal expectations or disappoint the most extravagant hopes that prompted the pilgrimage of these foreign scholars. Fa-Hien's own impressions and appreciation on the subject at the conclusion of his tour are thus expressed by the compiler of his narrative: "The countries through which he passed were a few under thirty. From the sandy desert westwards on to India, the beauty of the dignified demeanour of the monkhood and of the transforming influence of the Law was beyond the power of language fully to describe; and reflecting how our masters had not heard any complete account of them, he therefore went on without regarding his own poor life, or the dangers to be encountered on the sea upon his return, thus incurring hardships and difficulties in a double form. He was fortunate enough to receive help and protection in his perils; and therefore he wrote out an account of his experiences that worthy readers might share with him in what he had heard and said" (p. 116). Such a first-hand report on Indian education would only add to the number of pilgrims anxious to visit its seats. No wonder that Fa-Hien was the pioneer of a growing and glorious band of Chinese pilgrims immortalized by the other two names of Hiuen-Tsang and I-Tsing, whose visits to India in search of her learning in defiance of the dangers and privations besetting the paths of travel in those days across deserts, and over snowy heights, through inhospitable, and sometimes hostile, natural and human conditions, constitute the most convincing testimony to the supremacy of India in the ancient world of culture.

CHAPTER XXII

EDUCATION IN THE SEVENTH CENTURY A.D.

[*Account of Hiuen Tsang* (*Yuan Chwang*)]

Period of Hiuen Tsang's Travel in India. We now turn to the evidence of Hiuen Tsang who followed Fa-Hien after an interval of nearly two centuries. Although during that interval there had been steady intercourse and exchange of visits between China and India, there have not been, unfortunately, preserved any records of the travellers concerned.

Hiuen Tsang travelled for sixteen years (A.D. 629–645) through Central Asia and India (excluding the South and Ceylon, of which he gives only a hearsay account).

The object of his travel and its success. The object of his travels was " to visit the holy land of his religion, to see its far-famed shrines, and all visible evidences of the Buddha's ministrations, to procure the sacred books of his religion in their original language and to learn the true meaning of their doctrines from orthodox pundits in India " (p. 11, ed. Watters, to be referred to throughout). The traveller brought with him to his native land no less than 657 sacred books of Buddhism, " images of the Buddha and his saints in gold, and silver, and crystal, and sandalwood," together with " many curious pictures, and, above all, 150 relics, true relics of the Buddha ", which had to be " borne on twenty horses " (p. 12).

Its Difficulties. The Chinese regard for India and her culture expresses itself in the Chinese designation, *Yin-tu*, given to the country. According to Hiuen Tsang, the term means " moon ", and is applied to India because, like the moon, India is the only country which, through a regular succession of great sages, illumined the spiritual darkness in which humanity was merged at the setting of the sun of the Buddha (p. 138). It was the intense yearning after Indian wisdom that fortified the heart of Hiuen Tsang against the dangers and difficulties of his extensive travel which were even greater in his case than in that of his predecessor, Fa-Hien. " He had been where no other had been, he had seen and heard what no other had ever seen and heard. Alone he had crossed trackless wastes tenanted only by fierce ghost-demons.

Bravely he had climbed fabled mountains high beyond conjecture, rugged and barren, ever chilled by icy wind and cold with eternal snow" (p. 12). The difficulties due to man were not less. An imperial edict forbade foreign travel. The expected companions of his travel gave up the project. Once a chief, for his truthfulness, revoked the order for his arrest! Once he had to go without a drop of water to drink for four nights and five days! At another time a royal host became too fond of him to part with him till he had to resort to hunger-strike as a means of release! Within India, while Fa-Hien travelled in perfect safety, Hiuen Tsang was once robbed of everything but his life and, on another occasion, while sailing down the Ganges from Kanouj with eighty country-folk, he was seized by a party of pirates as the most suitable human sacrifice for their deity till a storm arose to remind them of the wrath of Heaven and they set free the pilgrim and became his disciples! Even on his return journey Hiuen Tsang had to be conducted to the frontier by a mounted escort under a chief named Udhita (p. 297).

His Account of Brahmanical Education. The facts and conditions of Indian education and culture had considerably changed since Fa-Hien's time. Hiuen Tsang testifies to the ascendancy of Brahmanism as a result of the impetus given to it by the official support of the Gupta emperors. He also noticed the growth and extension of the Mahāyāna schools of Buddhism, though the Hīnayāna school still claimed superiority as regards the number of its followers. Thus at every centre of Buddhism which the traveller chose to visit, he observed not merely the Mahāyāna and Hīnayāna monks living either in the same or independent monasteries, but also numerous Deva-temples and Brahmanical sects and devotees "living pell-mell".

In spite of his chief interest being in Buddhist life and thought, Hiuen Tsang has recorded certain observations on Brahmanical education and culture which are all the more valuable on that score. Hiuen Tsang speaks on them from his personal experience and first-hand study, uninfluenced by any prejudice in their favour. We propose to deal with his notices of Brahmanical education first.

Ascendancy of Brahmanism and Sanskrit: Its many Sects. The ascendancy of Brahmanism in his time is demonstrated by the fact that the general name for India was "Country of the Brahmans". Says the traveller: "Among the various castes and clans of the country, the Brahmins were purest and in most esteem. So from their excellent reputation the name 'Brāhmaṇa-country' had come to be a popular one for India" (p. 140). The predominance of Brahmanism is further evident from the fact that Sanskrit became at that time the language of the cultured classes in which even wrote all the most famous Buddhist teachers. Hiuen Tsang regards the spoken and written language of "Mid-India" as at once the parent and the standard of all the dialects of "North India": "The people of mid-India are pre-eminently explicit and correct in speech, their expressions being harmonious and elegant, like those of the Devas, and their intonation clear and distinct, serving as rule and pattern for others. The people of neighbouring territories and foreign countries repeating errors until these became the norm, and emulous for vulgarities, have lost the pure style" (p. 153). The vitality of Brahmanism was further manifested in the growth of numerous ascetic orders or sects, each distinguished by its own special garb: "Some wear peacocks' tails; some adorn themselves with a necklace of skulls; some are quite naked; some cover the body with grass or boards; some pull out their hair and clip their moustaches; some mat their side-hair and make a top-knot coil. Their clothing is not fixed and the colour varies" (p. 148). Elsewhere Hiuen Tsang describes some of them as "professed Sectarians, Digambaras, and Pāṃśupatas, and those who wear wreaths of skulls as head ornaments" (p. 123). In another place (vol. ii, p. 47) he records: "Some of these cut off their hair, others made it into a top-knot; some went about naked and some smeared themselves with ashes."

Study of Vedas. As regards Brahmanical education, the students had to "learn the four Veda treatises", viz. the Āyurveda, the Yajūr-Veda, the Sāmaveda, and the Atharva-Veda. Hiuen Tsang's account of the contents of these works shows that he had very little direct knowledge of them. His omission to mention the Rigveda is probably due to the fact that he "had in view those Vedic works which were then in writing and known to or owned by the Brethren in North India. Some of these Buddhists were converted Brahmins, and it was perhaps by some of them, as has been suggested, that the Vedas were reduced to writing" (Watters' note, p. 160).

Oral Method of Teaching. Instruction was imparted orally and characterized by much earnestness and painstaking labour on the part of the teacher. The pedagogic method followed was that of trying to quicken and rouse the latent powers of thinking in the student and lead him on to conclusions. The methods of teaching are thus described: "These teachers explain the general meaning and teach them the minutiae; they rouse them to activity and skilfully win them to progress; they instruct the inert and sharpen the dull. When disciples, intelligent and acute, are addicted to idle shirking, the teachers doggedly persevere, repeating instruction until their training is finished."

Period of Studentship. The period of studentship was fairly long. It was ended when the pupil was thirty years old, when "their minds being settled and their education finished, they go into office". Hiuen Tsang refers to the practice referred to in the earlier Smṛitis of the retiring students paying the preceptor his fees for educating them. "The first thing they do then is to reward the kindness of their teachers."

Ascetics consecrating their lives to Learning. But the race of Naishṭhika Brahmachārīs, who chose to consecrate themselves to lifelong studentship and celibacy in quest of learning and truth, was not extinct in India in Hiuen Tsang's time. The description given of these noble bands of seekers after truth by the Chinese traveller is well worth quoting: "There are men who, far seen in antique lore and fond of the refinements of learning, are content in seclusion, leading lives of continence. These come and go (lit. sink and float) outside of the world, and promenade through life away from human affairs. Though they are not moved by honours or reproach, their fame is far spread. The rulers treating them with ceremony and respect cannot make them come to court. Now as the State holds men of learning and genius in esteem, and the people respect those who have high intelligence, the honours and praises of such men are conspicuously abundant, and the attentions private and official paid to them are very considerable. Hence men can force themselves to a thorough acquisition of knowledge. Forgetting fatigue, they expatiate in the arts and sciences; seeking for wisdom while relying on perfect virtue they count not 1,000 *li* a long journey. Though their family be in affluent circumstances, such men make up their minds to be like vagrants, and get their food by begging as they go about. With them there is honour in knowing truth (in having wisdom), and there is no disgrace in being destitute."

Such Asceticism proves success of Indian Education. Here is one of the best presentations of the essentials of that system of culture which is the unique achievement of the Hindu genius.

Brahmanical education, indeed, stands justified by its results. The highest aim of a school of learning is to produce in its alumni an absorbing love of learning for its own sake. The ancient Hindu schools of learning poured out streams of scholars in whom the love of learning grew up to be the overmastering passion subduing all other passions of the human heart and compelling the consecration of their entire life to its satisfaction. The pedagogic methods pursued in these schools were not the mechanical, soulless, and oppressive ones which crush out the very taste for learning in the students when they leave them, as is so often the case with most modern schools. They were living and natural methods that, under the congenial conditions of education they created, helped the seeds of thought in the tender minds committed to it to germinate and fructify, to generate in the young learners a spirit of inquiry, of the quest of truth which is the highest gift a teacher can bestow upon them. Thus it was that Knowledge or Truth could claim so many votaries in ancient India, as was noticed by the foreign traveller. A special value attaches to his statements because, as has been already pointed out, they come from a foreigner free from any pro-Indian bias and also from an eye-witness who speaks from his personal observation and experience and not from the evidence of antiquated records or idealizing texts of religion.

The second feature noticed by Hiuen Tsang in Brahmanical culture-system is the universal honour paid to learning by the kings and public at large. The honour was paid because it was not sought. This means that the learned men combined intellectual superiority with moral. In their sincere and earnest quest of Learning they renounced everything that might interfere with it, not merely goods and chattels, but even the tender ties of domestic love. They sought pleasure in learning alone and " honour in only knowing truth ". With their life thus simplified and their wants reduced, they preferred poverty to affluence and beggary to an assured maintenance, as least disturbing to their Quest of the Ideal.

Thirdly, as observed by Hiuen Tsang, these votaries of Learning " left the world to give the law unto the world ". They left society only to qualify themselves for serving it better as teachers and preachers, lecturing and travelling through the country without knowing any fatigue and thus aiding in the spread of learning and public instruction. A system that can ensure a permanent supply of qualified men giving themselves up to the service of the country by a life of complete self-denial, of continence and celibacy, of poverty, beggary, and wandering homelessness, can stand comparison with any other system in the world.

Account of Buddhist Education. We shall now deal with the conditions and circumstances of Buddhist education as observed by our traveller. Many were the centres of that education and the monks availing themselves of it. In the time of Hiuen Tsang Buddhist thought was represented by a good number of schools, each of which claimed and counted many monasteries specializing in the study of its doctrines and practices. We shall now refer to these institutions [1] in the order in which they are mentioned by our traveller.

Monasteries seen by Hiuen Tsang : Gaz. In the country of Gaz he noticed more than ten monasteries with 300 monks of the Sarvāstivādin school (p. 114).

Bamian. In Bamian "were some tens of Buddhist monasteries with several thousands of Brethren" of the Lokottaravādin school (p. 116).

Kapis. In Kapis "were above 1,000 monasteries with more than 6,000 brethren who were chiefly Mahāyānists" (p. 123). Here was the Chinese hostage's monastery where our pilgrim was lodged and entertained during the rainy season of A.D. 630. It had then 300 brethren, all Hīnayānists. The Kapis, a monastery, along with two other monasteries in Gandhāra and Chīnabhukti, in eastern Panjab, was built by Kanishka for the residence of hostages surrendered to him by a tributary state of the Chinese empire. A pit in the monastery contained a buried treasure given to it by the hostages whose representations in painting adorned its walls. Religious services on their behalf were also annually offered at the beginning and end of the Rain-season Retreat by the grateful monastery. The monastery had some caves at a distance where the hostages practised *samādhi*, Part of the buried treasure was unearthed by Hiuen Tsang for the purpose of some urgent repairs to the building (p. 125). There was another monastery in the neighbourhood built by a statesman named Rāhula (p. 126).

Lampa (Laghman). In the country of Lampa (Laghman) there were above ten Buddhist monasteries with only a few Brethren, mostly Mahāyānists, the non-Buddhists being very

[1] In the notice of these institutions we shall include only such as were seen to be actually working by our traveller and not those which were in ruins.

numerous (p. 181). The country is known for at least one distinguished Buddhist scholar, a Brahman, who visited China and translated in A.D. 700 from Sanskrit into Chinese a work of magical invocations (p. 182).

Nagarkot. Nagara-kot had many Buddhist establishments but few Brethren in them (p. 183).

Gandhāra. In Gandhāra, once a flourishing seat of Buddhism, "the majority adhered to other systems of religion" (p. 199). "There were above 1,000 Buddhist monasteries in the country, but they were utterly dilapidated and untenanted" (p. 202). These monasteries produced some of the greatest Buddhist scholars, such as "Nārāyana-deva (unidentified), Asaṅga, Vasubandhu, Dharmatāra Manoratha (unidentified), and Pārśva" (ib.). The capital of the country was Purusha-pura, famous for the great Vihāra built by Kanishka, where there were still "a few Brethren, all Hīnayānists" (p. 208). Prior to Nālanda, it was perhaps the most celebrated Buddhist College of ancient India. "From the time it was built it had yielded occasionally extraordinary men, and the Arhats and Śāstra-makers by their pure conduct and perfect virtue were still an active influence" (ib.). Here lived Pārśva, with his chamber still marked off, who converted the celebrated Brahman teacher of Mid-India named Aśvaghosha. Here was also marked out the chamber where Vasubandhu composed the *Abhidharma-kośa-śāstra*, as well as that where Vasubandhu's teacher, Manoratha, composed his *Vibhāshā-lun* (p. 211).

Pushkarāvatī. From the Kanishka monastery, the pilgrim came to the city of Pushkarāvatī (modern Hashṭanagar) where lived many Buddhist sages from Mid-India. It was here that Vasumitra composed his *Abhidharma-prakaraṇa-pada-śāstra* (p. 214). Close by was an old monastery where there were still a few Hīnayāna monks. "In it Dharmatrāta composed his *Tsa-abhidharma-lun* (unidentified)."

Palusha. The city of Palusha had a monastery with above fifty Hīnayāna brethren, where "the Master of Śāstras, Īśvara, composed *Abhidharma-ming-cheng-lun* (not traced)" (p. 217). In the neighbourhood were two Mahāyāna monasteries (p. 218) with few Brethren.

Hiuen Tsang, by the way, visited the city of Śalātura, famous as "the birthplace of the Ṛishi Pāṇini" (p. 221).

Udyāna. Udyāna was once a flourishing seat of Mahāyāna Buddhism with 1,400 monasteries inhabited by 18,000 Brethren, lining the two banks of its river, most of which were now in ruins. The few monks that lived there "occupied themselves with silent meditation; they were clever at reciting their books without penetrating their deep meaning; they lived strictly according to their rules and were specially expert in magical exorcisms". Their course of studies included the five redactions of the Vinaya of the Hīnayānists, although they were themselves Mahāyānists, viz. Dharmagupta, Mahīśāsika, Kāśyapīya, Sarvāstivādin, and Mahāsaṁghika (p. 226).

Bolor. The next centre of Buddhist learning visited by Hiuen Tsang was Bolor, where he found "some hundreds of Buddhist Monasteries and some thousands of Brethren who were without definite learning, and were very defective in their observance of the rules of their Order" (p. 240).

Taxila. From Bolor the pilgrim comes to Taksha-śilā, where the numerous old monasteries were now in ruins and the Brethren, who were all Mahāyānists, very few (ib.). At some distance from the city was "an old ruinous Monastery occupied by a few Brethren", where the great Sautrāntika Doctor of Buddhism, by name Kumāralabdha (recognized as one of the "four Suns illuminating the world" with Aśvaghosha, Deva, and Nāgārjuna), once composed his expository treatises (p. 245).

Towards the northern confines of Taksha-śilā, near the great Mānikyāla Tope, was a monastery with above 100 Mahāyāna monks (p. 255), which was seen about the beginning of the fifth century A.D. to be a large establishment with about 5,000 Brethren by another Chinese pilgrim monk (note of Watters, p. 256). There were also in that locality two other monasteries of Mahāyāna school, one with few and another with 200 Brethren (ib.).

Kashmir. Hiuen Tsang next visits Kashmir, where Buddhism was very flourishing. From the *Life* we gather that he entered the country by its western approach, passing on the way several Buddhist monasteries in which he performed worship and at one of which, the Hushkapura-Vihāra, he spent a night. On his arrival, he was lodged for the first night in the Jayendra Monastery and was transferred next day to the palace where the king appointed some score of Brethren headed by the illustrious Bhadanta (or ? Yasa) to wait on him. He also had the Scriptures read and expounded by Hiuen Tsang and appointed as his assistants twenty clerks to copy out MSS., besides five other men as his attendants. The pilgrim spent here two years, studying certain Sūtras and Śāstras and visiting Buddhist sacred places. He gives 100 as the number of monasteries then existing and 5,000 as the number of the Brethren living therein (pp. 258–261). Regarding the history of Buddhism in Kashmir, Hiuen Tsang relates the legend of its introduction by the Arhat Madhyāntika, the disciple of Ānanda, and of the settlement of 500 Arhats from Pāṭaliputra during the reign of Asoka in 500 monasteries built by that emperor (pp. 265, 267). These Arhats founded the Sthavira school in Kashmir as distinguished from the Mahāsaṁghika school formed by the Brethren from whom they separated (p. 269). Among the existing monasteries of Kashmir, Hiuen Tsang mentions one containing above 300 Brethren with "a tope built for a Tooth-relic of the Buddha", another with a standing image of him, and another fine large old monastery on a mountain, of which only a two-storeyed building in one corner was inhabited by thirty Mahāyāna Brethren, which was famous as the dwelling-place of the Śāstra-master, Saṁghabhadra (p. 280). In the neighbourhood was another small monastery famous for its 'old boy', the great Śāstra-master, Skandhila (ib.). At a distance from the capital, the pilgrim noticed two other monasteries, one called the Merchant's-wood Monastery, where wrote the Śāstra-master Pūrṇa, and the other a Mahāsaṁghika Monastery with above 100 inmates, where wrote the Śāstra-master Bodhila (p. 282).

From Kashmir the pilgrim passed through Punach and Rajaori, with five monasteries in ruins in the former and ten in the latter, with few Brethren (p. 284).

Cheh-ka. Next he comes to the Cheh-ka country between the Beas and the Indus, where there were only ten Buddhist monasteries. The capital of the country was Śākala, with a monastery containing about 100 Brethren, all Hīnayānists, where Vasubandhu composed a work (p. 291).

Chīnabhukti. The next place visited is Chīnabhukti with ten monasteries, in one of which, named "Pleasure-giving" monastery, was a monk named Vinītaprabha, distinguished for his learning and piety and the son of an Indian prince, under whom Hiuen Tsang studied various Abhidharma treatises for a period of fourteen months (p. 292).

Tamasāvana. The pilgrim next comes to the famous Tamasāvana Monastery, the Brethren from which were invited by Asoka to his Council. Hiuen Tsang found there above 300 Brethren of the Sarvāstivādin School who were thorough students of the Hīnayāna (p. 294). The Monastery was also famous as having had as its pupil the Śāstramaster Kātyāyanīputra (ib.), who wrote here one of his works.

Jālandhara. Jālandhara had more than fifty monasteries with over 2,000 Brethren of both Mahāyāna and Hīnayāna schools (p. 296). In one of these monasteries, the Nagaradhana Vihāra, Hiuen Tsang found the learned brother named Chandravarma with whom he spent four months, studying an Abhidharma work, as related in the *Life* (p. 297).

Kuluto. In Kuluto there were twenty monasteries with more than 1,000 Mahāyāna monks (p. 298).

Mathurā. The next centre of Buddhism was Mathurā, with more than twenty monasteries and 2,000 Brethren of both Vehicles (p. 301). The same number of monasteries is mentioned by Fa-Hien.

Sthāneśvara. At Sthāneśvara Hiuen Tsang found three Buddhist monasteries with more than 700 Hīnayāna monks (p. 314). In the neighbourhood was the Govinda Monastery " with high chambers in close succession and detached terraces " where the Brethren " led pure strict lives " (p. 316).

Śrughna. In Śrughna, " there were five Buddhist monasteries and above 1,000 Buddhist ecclesiastics, the majority of whom were Hīnayānists, a few adhering to other schools. The Brethren were expert and lucid expounders of abstract doctrines and distinguished Brethren from other lands came to them to reason out their doubts " (p. 318). It is also stated that these five monasteries were built at the places where these Śāstra-masters from other lands defeated in discussions the Tīrthikas and Brahmans to commemorate their victories (p. 319). One of these learned Doctors of Buddhism was Jayagupta by name, as we learn from the *Life*, with whom Hiuen Tsang stayed one winter and half of the spring following and " when he had heard all the *Vibhāshā* of the Sautrāntika School " he continued his journey (p. 322).

Matipura. At Matipura, " there were above ten Buddhist monasteries with above 800 Brethren, mostly adherents of the Sarvāstivādin school of the Hīnayāna " (ib.). In the neighbourhood was a small monastery famous as the place where " the Śāstra-master Guṇaprabha composed above 100 treatises " (ib.). At a distance from it was another monastery with above 200 Brethren, all Hīnayānists, where the Śāstra-master, Saṁghabhadra, who was " a profound scholar in the Vaibhāsha śāstras of the Sarvāstivādin school" ended his life (p. 325). He was the contemporary of Vasubandhu, the great Buddhist Doctor far-famed as peerless in dialectics, the author of Abhidharmakośa-śāstra, to refute whose doctrines Saṁghabhadra had left a treatise (ib.). From the *Life*, we learn that Hiuen Tsang remained for several months in this district, studying the work of Guṇaprabha named *Tattvasandeśa-śāstra* and that he met here a ninety-year old disciple of his, Mitrasena by name, who was a profound scholar in Buddhist learning (p. 328).

Brahmapura. At Brahmapura "there were five Buddhist monasteries with very few Brethren" (p. 329).

Goviśana. At Goviśana, a centre of Hinduism, "there were two monasteries with above 100 Brethren, all Hīnayānists" (p. 331).

Ahichchhatra. At Ahichchhatra "there were above ten Buddhist monasteries, and more than 1,000 Brethren, students of the Sammitiya School of the Hīnayāna" (ib.).

Vilaśāna. At Vilaśāna, a Hindu centre, "there were two Buddhist monasteries with 300 Brethren, all Mahāyāna students" (p. 332).

Saṁkāśya. At Saṁkāśya, or Kapitha, "there were four Buddhist monasteries with above 1,000 Brethren, all of the Sammatiya School" (p. 333). Near the capital was a large monastery containing "representations of Buddhist worthies in the highest style of ornament" (ib.), and peopled by "some hundreds of Brethren of the Sammatiya school" with myriads of lay dependents living outside it.

Kanyākubja. At Kanyākubja, Hiuen Tsang noticed 100 monasteries with more than 10,000 Brethren of both the Vehicles (p. 340), showing a great increase of Buddhism from the time of Fa-Hien who found here only two monasteries. Kanyākubja was then under the rule of the great king Harshavardhana of the Vaiśya caste, with his headquarters at Kanouj. He gave a great impetus to Buddhism by prohibiting the use of animal food, erecting thousands of topes on the banks of the Ganges and Buddhist monasteries at the sacred places of the Buddhists. "Once a year he summoned all the Buddhist monks together, and for twenty-one days supplied them with the regulation requisites. He furnished the chapels and liberally adorned the common halls of the monasteries. He brought the Brethren together for examination and discussion, giving rewards and punishments according to merit and demerit. Those Brethren who kept the rules of their Order and were thoroughly sound in theory and practice he 'advanced to the Lion's Throne' (that is, promoted to the highest place), and from these he received religious instruction ; those who, though perfect in the observance of the ceremonial code were not learned in the past, he merely honoured with formal reverence ; those who neglected the ceremonial observances of the Order, and whose immoral conduct was notorious, were banished from his presence and from the country" (p. 344).

In Kanyākubja the pilgrim remained for three months in the Bhadravihāra, studying with the learned Buddhist monk, Vīryasena, the *Vibhāshā* by Buddhadāsa (p. 353).

Navadevakula. From Kanyākubja he goes to Navadevakula with three monasteries containing 500 Sarvāstivādin monks (p. 352).

Ayodhyā. In the Ayodhyā country "were above 100 monasteries and more than 3,000 Brethren" of both Vehicles. The pilgrim noticed some old monasteries associated with the great Buddhist scholars, Vasubandhu, Śrīlabdha (the Sautrāntika), and Asaṅga (p. 355).

Hayamukha. Then comes the Hayamukha country "with five monasteries with above 1,000 Brethren" of the Sammatiya school and in the neighbourhood another with above 200 Brethren, which was once the abode of Buddhadāsa (p. 359).

Prayāga. Prayāga was a centre of Brahmanism with only two Buddhist establishments and very few Brethren, all Hīnayānists (p. 361).

Kosambī. In Kosambī there were more than ten monasteries, all in ruins, with only 300 Hīnayāna Brethren (p. 366). In the neighbourhood were the old Ghositārāma and sundry old buildings associated with Vasubandhu and Asaṅga, who wrote there (p. 370).

Viśoka. The country of Viśoka had above twenty monasteries with 3,000 Sammatiya Brethren and another large monastery where wrote the great Buddhist scholars, Devaśarman and Gopa, and where Dharmapāla "held a discussion for seven days with 100 Hīnayāna Śāstra-masters and utterly defeated them" (p. 374).

Śrāvastī. In Śrāvastī, Buddhism was in decline, with hundreds of its old monasteries mostly in ruins, with but few Brethren, all Sammatiyas, inhabiting them (p. 377), where Fa-Hien had noticed ninety-eight (in some texts eighteen) monasteries, all, except one, peopled (p. 380). Hiuen Tsang finds the Jetavana Vihāra in desolate ruin (p. 382).

Jetavana Vihāra. We may notice in this connection the past history of the Jetavana Vihāra and university as recovered from the Chinese texts by Watters (p. 386): "The original Jetavana monastery, which was probably neither very large nor substantial and was not well protected, was destroyed by fire in the Buddha's lifetime. After the death of Sudatta, the place was neglected as there was no one to look after the grounds and buildings. A new Vihāra was afterwards built on a greater scale, but this also was burnt to the ground. At one time, we read, the place was utterly abandoned by the Buddhist Brethren and was used as the king's stables, but the buildings were again rebuilt and reoccupied by Buddhist monks. In its palmy days, before its final destruction and abandonment, the Jetavana monastery must have been a very large and magnificent establishment," with the extent of its Park given as 130 square acres and with 120 buildings of various kinds. "There were chapels for preaching and halls for meditation, messrooms and chambers for the monks, bath houses, a hospital, libraries, and reading rooms, with pleasant shady tanks and a great wall encompassing all. The libraries were richly furnished not only with orthodox literature but also with Vedic and other non-Buddhistic works, and with treatises on the arts and sciences taught in India at the time."

Kapilavastu. In the Kapilavastu country were remains of above 1,000 monasteries and only one existing monastery with above thirty Sammatiya monks in it (p. 1, vol. ii).

Rāmagrāma. In Rāmagrāma "was the Śrāmaṇera monastery so called because its temporal affairs were always managed by a śrāmaṇera or unordained Brother". In Fa-Hien's time it "was a recent institution; Hiuen Tsang found in it only a small number of brethren who were very civil and hospitable" (p. 21).

Vārāṇasī. In the Vārāṇasī country where the people were known for their devotion to learning and were mainly followers of "the other systems", there "were above thirty Buddhist monasteries with more than 3,000 Sammatiya Brethren" (p. 47).

Sarnath. At Sarnath was still existing the famous Deer-park Monastery dating from the time of the Buddha. It was in eight divisions, all enclosed within one wall; the tiers of balconies and the rows of halls were extremely artistic; there were 1,500 Buddhist Brethren, "all of the Sammatiya school" (p. 48).

Ghazipur. In the district of Ghazipur "were above ten monasteries with nearly 1,000 Brethren" of the Little Vehicle (p. 59). Near the capital was the Abiddhakarṇa Saṁghārāma, "built for the use of Buddhist pilgrims from Tokhāra" (p. 60), and a few Mahāyāna monasteries in ruins.

Vaiśālī. In the Vaiśālī country there were some hundreds of Buddhist establishments, all of which, except three or four, were in ruins and deserted. In the neighbourhood of the capital was a monastery with a few monks of the Sammatiya school (p. 63). "It must have been distressing for our pilgrim to go over the waste jungle-covered ruins of a district which he had known from the Buddhist scriptures to have been once very flourishing" (p. 77). He comes to the Śvetapura Monastery in the neighbourhood, "having sunny terraces and bright-coloured halls of two storeys," where the brethren "were strict in their lives" and Mahāyānists (p. 79). The *Life* tells us that here the pilgrim obtained a copy of the Mahāyāna treatise, Bodhisattva-piṭaka (p. 80).

Vṛiji. In the Vṛiji country, the pilgrim saw monasteries above ten in number, with less than 1,000 Brethren, followers of both Vehicles (p. 81). In the neighbourhood was another monastery with "a few Brethren good and learned".

Nepal. The pilgrim next visited the Nepal country where he found monasteries counting "above 2,000 Buddhist ecclesiastics" (p. 83).

Magadha. In the country of Magadha he found "above fifty monasteries and more than 10,000 ecclesiastics" of the Mahāyāna school (p. 86). He refers to the old monastery of Kukkuṭārāma, now in ruins, where the Buddhists once lived along with the Tīrthikas, calling meetings by gong-beating. Once at a public discussion appointed by the king, the Buddhists were defeated by the Tīrthikas and had borne their humiliation for twelve years until the great Buddhist scholar, Deva, a disciple of Nāgārjuna in South India, obtained his master's permission to go to Pāṭaliputra city and meet the Tīrthikas in discussion who were utterly defeated in a twelve days' discourse by him (p. 100).

Tiloshika Vihāra. Between 40 and 50 miles in a south-west direction from the Kukkuṭārāma, and about 20 miles to the west of Nālanda was the large and famous establishment of the Ti-lo-shi-ka monastery, originally "erected by the last descendant of King Bimbisāra", having "four courts with three-storeyed halls, lofty terraces, and a succession of open passages. It was the rendezvous of eminent scholars who flocked to it from all regions". Hiuen Tsang found in it above 1,000 Brethren, all Mahāyānists (p. 105). From the *Life*, we learn that at the time of our pilgrim's visit, there lived in the monastery the learned Buddhist doctor, by name Prajñābhadra (p. 106).

Guṇamati Vihāra. Another famous monastery in the neighbourhood was one on the slope of a mountain with its high bases backed by the ridge and chambers hewn out of the cliff, which "was built in honour of Guṇamati Bodhisattva who here vanquished in discussion the great Sāṁkhya doctor, Mādhava" (p. 108). This Guṇamati, associated with Sthiramati and distinguished with him at Nālanda for the elegance of composition, was from Valabhī in Western India (p. 109).

Śīlabhadra Vihāra. Not far from the Guṇamati Monastery, on his way from Pāṭaliputra to Gayā, was another famous monastery built by the Śāstra-master Śīlabhadra, originally a scion of the Brahmanical royal family of Samataṭa, who, travelling through India in search of the wise, came to Nālandā and received instruction under Dharmapāla, of whose disciples he became the most eminent. A brahman of South India having come to Magadha to challenge the learning of his guru, Śīlabhadra utterly defeated him, and was rewarded by the king with the gift of a city which, however, he did not accept for himself as a monk but devoted to the endowment of a monastery (p. 110).

Mahābodhi Vihāra. We next come to the pilgrim's account of the Great Monastery known as the Mahābodhi Saṁghārāma in Gayā built by a former king of Ceylon. "Its buildings formed six courts with terraces and halls of three storeys enclosed by walls between 30 and 40 feet high; the sculpture and pointing were perfect." "There were nearly 1,000 ecclesiastics, all Mahāyānists of the Sthavira school, and all perfect in the Vinaya observances" (p. 136).

Nālandā. Hiuen Tsang next gives a detailed account of the famous Nālandā Monastery which is reserved for a separate treatment for the many important and interesting facts it gives regarding the working of that university.

In the neighbourhood of the Nālandā Monastery were two other monasteries, one with the Haṁsa tope (where, according to a legend, Hīnayāna Brethren adopted Mahāyāna, changing their creed), and the other called the Pigeon Monastery (p. 175), with over 200 Sarvāstivādin Brethren. There was another small monastery in the locality which had above 50 Brethren all Hīnayānists (p. 176).

Monghyr. Next the pilgrim comes to the district of Mount Īraṇa identified with modern Monghyr where were above ten monasteries and more than 4,000 Brethren, most of whom were Hīnayānists of the Sammatiya school. To these monasteries were added recently by a Buddhist neighbouring king, who had conquered the capital, two monasteries, each of which had 1,000 Brethren of the Sarvāstivādin school (p. 178). From the *Life* we learn that the pilgrim remained at the capital for a year studying the Vibhāshā-lun and another Abhidharma work under the teachers, Tathāgatagupta and Kshāntisiṁha (p. 180).

Champā. In the Champā country were some tens of monasteries mostly in ruins, with above 200 Brethren, all Hīnayānists (p. 181).

Kajangala. In the country of Kajangala, modern Rājmahal, were six or seven monasteries with above 300 Brethren (p. 183).

Puṇyavardhana. In Puṇyavardhana there were twenty monasteries and above 3,000 Brethren following both the Vehicles. In the neighbourhood was a magnificent monastery with "spacious halls and tall storeyed chambers, and 700 Brethren" of Mahāyāna school, among whom were many distinguished monks from "East India" (p. 184).

Kāmarūpa. Kāmarūpa was a centre of Brahminical religion and learning, of which the king, Bhāskaravarman or Kumāra, was a great patron who attracted for study there men of ability from distant lands. He treated accomplished Śramaṇas with great respect and invited our pilgrim to visit him (p. 186).

Samataṭa. Thence our pilgrim came to the country of Samataṭa on the sea-side where were more than thirty monasteries and above 2,000 Brethren, followers of the Sthavira school (p. 187).

Tāmralipti. The country of Tāmralipti had ten monasteries and more than 1,000 Brethren (p. 190).

Karṇasuvarṇa. In Karṇasuvarṇa (according to Fergusson to be identified with the districts of Burdwan, Birbhum, and Murshidabad) were more than ten monasteries and above 2,000 Brethren, all of the Sammatiya school (p. 191). There were also three other monasteries of the sect of Devadatta. Near the capital was the Raktāmṛita Monastery (modern *Rāṅgāmāṭi*), "a magnificent and famous establishment, the resort of illustrious Brethren" which "had been erected by a king of the country before the country was converted to Buddhism to honour a Buddhist Śramaṇa from South India who had defeated in public discussion a boasting disputant of another system also from South India " (p. 191).

Uḍra. In the country called Wu-Tu or Oṭa (i.e. Uḍra, Oḍra, modern Orissa) was Buddhism very flourishing with " above 100 monasteries and a myriad Brethren, all Mahāyānists ". Towards the south-west was the Pushpagiri mountain monastery with another hill-monastery in the locality (p. 193).

Kalinga. Kalinga was more Brahmanical than Buddhistic, with only above ten monasteries and 500 Brethren, " students of the Mahāyānist Sthavira school system " (p. 198).

Southern Kosala (Vidarbha). Southern Kosala (identified by Cunningham with Vidarbha or Berar) had " above 100 monasteries and about 10,000 Brethren, all Mahāyānists ", and was famous as the home of the great Nāgārjuna for whom the king of the country had quarried in a mountain a wonderful five-storeyed monastery, probably the Pigeon Monastery of Fa-Hien. " The monastery had cloisters and lofty halls ; these halls were in five tiers, each with four courts, with temples containing gold life-size images of the Buddha of perfect artistic beauty. It was well supplied with running water, and the chambers were lighted by windows cut in the rock. . . In the topmost hall was the library and in the lowest were the laymen attached to the monastery and the stores, and the three intermediate halls were the lodgings of the Brethren " (p. 201). Here the great scholar Deva who had come from ' Sengkala ' to have a discussion with Nāgārjuna became his disciple. The king, who was the patron and friend of Nāgārjuna, was a Sātavāhana (' Sha-to-po-ha ') and as the Sātavāhanas ruled from second century B.C. to the third century A.D. Nāgārjuna's date falls within that period. The mountain of his monastery is identified with that on which stands the famous Hindu temple of Śrī-Śailam by Burgess.

Andhra and Vengi. The Andhra country (Telingāna, according to Cunningham, and Vengi, according to Fergusson) had " twenty odd monasteries with more than 3,000 Brethren. Near the capital was a large monastery with a succession of high walls and storeyed terraces wrought with perfect art, and containing an exquisite image of the Buddha ". In the neighbourhood was an isolated hill on the ridge of which was a stone tope where was composed his treatise on Logic by Chen-na identified with the famous Buddhist scholar Diṅnāga, originally an orthodox

Brahman of Kāñchi who later joined the Vatsīputra sect of the Hīnayāna school, from which he was expelled by his teacher whom he had displeased and transferred himself to the school of Vasubandhu. He sojourned for some time in Nālandā where he was victorious in his discussions with several exponents of various schools (pp. 209, 212).

Dhanakaṭaka (Bezwada). In the country of Dhanakaṭaka (modern Bezwada) was a crowd of ruined monasteries, of which " about twenty were in use with 1,000 Brethren, mostly adherents of the Mahāsaṁghika system ". Near the capital were the Pūrvaśilā and Avaraśilā monasteries built on steep hills the sides of which were utilized in their construction curiously identified by Burgess with the great Amarāvatī Tope. According to the *Life*, the pilgrim spent here several months, studying " certain Abhidharma treatises of the Mahāsaṁghika school with two local brethren whom he in turn instructed in Mahāyāna scriptures " (p. 217). In the neighbourhood is a mountain-cliff [identified as " the isolated steep mountain to the south of Bezwada " (p. 221)], associated with the famous Buddhist scholar Bhā(va)viveka, author of two works in which he makes use of Sāṁkhya terminology in explaining the system of Nāgārjuna.

Chola Country. The Chola country was the country of Tīrthikas with the Buddhist monasteries in ruins, but Buddhism was more flourishing in the Dravida country with " more than 100 monasteries, with above 10,000 Brethren, all of the Sthavira school " with its capital Kāñchipura (but Negapatam according to Fergusson) famous as the birth-place of Dharmapāla. The capital had " a large monastery which was a rendezvous for the most eminent men of the country " (p. 226). From the *Life* we learn that at the time of Hiuen Tsang's visit the capital was visited by 300 Bhikshus of Ceylon who had left the island in consequence of famine and revolution there. On the pilgrim telling them of his intended visit to Ceylon for instruction, they told him that there were no Brethren there superior to them. Then the pilgrim discussed some Yoga texts with them and found that their explanations could not excel those given to him by Śīlabhadra of Nālandā (p. 227).

Koṅkana. The next seat of Buddhism was the Koṅkaṇa country with its " more than 100 monasteries and 10,000 Brethren who were students of both Vehicles. Close to the capital was a large monastery with above 300 Brethren all men of great distinction " (p. 237).

Mahārāshṭra. The pilgrim next came to the Mahārāshṭra country then under Pulakesin II where there were above 100 monasteries and 5,000 Brethren of both Vehicles. Near the capital were an old monastery and another on a mountain range with its lofty halls and deep chambers quarried in the cliff with a temple, of which the walls had depicted on them the incidents of the Buddha's career as Bodhisattva. The monastery was built by Āchāra of West India and is supposed by some to be no other than the famous Ajantā Caves (p. 240).

Bharoch. The next country visited is Bharoch where " were above ten monasteries with 300 Brethren, all students of the Mahāyānist Sthavira school " (p. 241).

Molapo (Mālwa). Mo-la-po (Mālava) was a flourishing Buddhistic centre with " some hundreds of monasteries and more than 20,000 Brethren belonging to the Sammatiya school of the Hīnayāna " under the patronage of its great king Śīlāditya who had reigned for sixty years before the pilgrim's arrival and had instituted the custom of holding every year a great religious assembly of Brethren called from all sides, each of whom was " presented with the three robes and religious requisites, or with precious valuables ". " This fine work had been continued for successive generations without interruption " (p. 242).

Kita (Kachchha). In the country of Kita (probably Kachchha), the pilgrim found more than ten monasteries and 1,000 Brethren who were adherents of both Vehicles (p. 245).

Valabhī. Valabhī " had above 100 monasteries with 6,000 Brethren, adherents of the Hīnayāna Sammatīya school " under its King Dhurvabhaṭa (son-in-law of Harsha and nephew of Śīlāditya of Mo-la-po) who was a sincere believer in Buddhism. " Not far from the capital was a large monastery erected by Āchāra (more probably Achala) in which the famous Buddhist scholars, Guṇamati and Sthiramati, had lodged and composed treatises which had great vogue " (p. 246).

Ānandapura. Ānandapura had " more than ten monasteries with nearly 1,000 Brethren belonging to the Hīnayānist Sammatīya school " (p. 247).

Surat. In Surat " were more than fifty monasteries with above 3,000 Brethren, the majority being students of the Mahāyānist Sthavira system " (p. 248).

Kuchelo. In the Ku-che-lo country with its capital Bhilmala " was only one Buddhist monastery with above 100 Brethren who were adherents of the Hīnayānist Sarvāstivādin school " (p. 249).

Ujjeni. In Ujjenī which was a Brahmanical centre "there were some tens of Buddhist monasteries of which the majority were in ruins, and only three or four were in a state of preservation; the Brethren, who were students of both Vehicles, were above 300 in number" (p. 250).

Chitor. In Chitor, another Brahmanical centre, were "some tens of monasteries with a few Brethren" (p. 251).

Sind. In Sind where the inhabitants were "thorough believers in Buddhism", "there were several hundreds of monasteries and above 10,000 Brethren, all of the Hīnayānist Sammatīya school. Most of these were indolent worthless persons" but there were some superior Brethren of whom many attained arhatship (p. 252).

Parvata. In the Po-fa-to (Parvata) country to the north-east of Multan (probably the region of Jummoo in Kashmir were "above ten monasteries and 1,000 Brethren, adherents of the two Vehicles". By the side of the capital was a large monastery with above 100 Mahāyānist Brethren where lived the great Buddhist scholars Jinaputra, Bhadraruchi, and Guṇaprabha. The monastery was now in ruins (p. 255). From the *Life* we learn that the pilgrim stayed two years in this place studying with a few learned Brethren he had found there (p. 256).

Kachchheśvara. South-west from Sind the pilgrim came to a country with its capital called Kachchheśvara where "there were above eighty monasteries with above 5,000 Brethren, the most of whom were of the Hīnayānist Sammatīya school" (ib.).

Lankala (Mekran). In the country called Lankala (probably the eastern part of Mekran) which was subject to Persia "there were above 100 monasteries and more than 6,000 Brethren of both Vehicles". This place was on the way to the "West-Woman-Country", probably the same as the Strīrājya in the north-west division of the *Bṛihat Saṁhitā* (p. 257).

Pitāśilā. In the Pitāśilā country were "above fifty monasteries and more than 3,000 Brethren, all of the Hīnayāna Sammatīya school". Here was another "old monastery built by the great Arhat Mahākātyāyana" (p. 258).

Afantu. In the A-fan-tu country which was under Sind, there were "above twenty monasteries with 2,000 Brethren, of whom the majority belonged to the Sammatīya school" (p. 259).

Falana (Gomal). In the country of Fa-la-na (identified with the valley of the Gomal River) were some tens of monasteries of which many were in ruins and above 300 Brethren, all Mahāyānists (p. 262).

Approximate number of Monks and Monasteries seen by the Chinese Pilgrim. Here ends Hiuen Tsang's account of Buddhist education in India. The account shows that though the period of Harsha and Hiuen Tsang was one of decline for Buddhism in India, yet the number of monks and monasteries was fairly large. The monasteries that were seen to be in working order and tenanted by monks numbered approximately 5,000 (excluding those which Hiuen Tsang describes as being dilapidated and deserted). The total number of the monkish population in the parts of India visited by Hiuen Tsang (including Ceylon) was as high as 212,130. This number was distributed as follows among the various sects or schools of Buddhism then flourishing :—

1. *Sthavira* :

In Gayā	1,000	(in a Vihāra founded by a Ceylon king).
,, Samataṭa	2,000	
,, Kalinga	500	
,, Dravida	10,000	
,, Ceylon	20,000	
,, Bhroach	300	
,, Surat	3,000	
	36,800	

2. *Sammatīya* :

In Ahichchhatra	1,000
,, Saṁkāśya	1,000
,, Hayamukha	1,000
,, Viśoka	3,000
,, Kapilavastu	30
,, Benares	3,000
,, Sarnath	1,500
,, Monghyr	4,000
,, Karṇasuvarṇa	2,000
,, Mālava	20,000
,, Valabhī	6,000
,, N. Sind	10,000
,, Karachi	5,000
,, Pitāśilā	3,000
,, Avanda (?)	2,000
,, Ānandapura	1,000
	63,530

3. *Sarvāstivādin* :

In Gaz	200
,, Tamasāvana Vihāra .	300
,, Matipur . . .	800
,, Pigeon Vihāra . .	200
,, Navadevakula . .	500
,, Gurjara . . .	100
,, Monghyr . . .	2,000
	4,100

4. *Lokottaravādin* :

In Bamian (several thousands).

5. *Hīnayāna*, without mention of any sects :

In Sākala . . .	100
,, Gandhāra . . .	50
,, Sthāneśvara . .	700
,, Śrughna . . .	1,000
,, Goviśāna . . .	100
,, Kosambī . . .	300
,, Ghazipur . . .	1,000
,, Magadha . . .	50
,, Champā . . .	200

6. *Mahāyāna* :

In Kapisa . . .	6,000
,, Udyāna . . .	18,000
,, Takshaśilā . . .	300
,, Kuluto (on the Upper Beas) . . .	1,000
,, Vitasana . . .	300
,, Magadha . . .	10,000
,, Puṇyavardhana . .	700
,, Orissa	myriads
,, S. Kosala . . .	10,000
,, Tiloshika vihāra . .	1,000
,, Dhanakaṭaka . .	1,000
,, Fa-la-na (Gomal Valley)	300
	48,600

7. *Bhikshus* who study both Hīna- and Mahāyāna:

In Mathurā . . .	2,000
,, Jālandhara . . .	2,000
,, Kanyākubja . .	10,000
,, Ayodhyā . . .	3,000
,, Vṛiji	1,000
,, Puṇyavardhana . .	3,000
,, Koṅkana . . .	10,000
,, Mahārāshṭra . .	5,000
,, Cutch	1,000
,, Ujjenī	300
,, Parvata . . .	1,000
,, Mekran . . .	6,000
	46,300

8. *Bhikshus* whose sects are not mentioned:

In Kashmir . . .	5,000
,, Rājmahal . . .	300
,, Tāmralipti . . .	1,000
,, Andhra . . .	3,000
	9,300

Totals of above:

Hīnayāna		107,930
Sthavira . .	36,800	
Sammatīya .	63,530	
Sarvāstivādin .	4,100	
(No name) .	3,500	
Mahāyāna . . .		48,600
Both Hīna- and Mahā-yāna		46,300
Bhikshus of unnamed sects		9,300
Total number of members of the Order . . .		212,130

These numbers of both monks and monasteries are exclusive of those which are not indicated definitely but only vaguely by the words "few", "some tens", "several thousands", or "myriads".[1]

These Monasteries produced some of the greatest Leaders of Buddhism. It will be seen from Hiuen Tsang's notice of these monasteries how largely they justified themselves as educational institutions by producing some of the greatest men in the history of Buddhist learning and religion. It is to Hiuen Tsang that we owe the information by which we are enabled to trace the schools traditionally associated with the following Buddhist celebrities, viz. Asaṅga, Vasubandhu, Pārśva, Aśvaghosha, Nārāyana-deva, Dharmatāra, Manoratha, Vasumitra, Dharmatrāta, Īśvara, Kumāralabdha, Deva, Nāgārjuna, Madhyāntika, Saṁghabhadra, Skandhila, Pūrṇa, Bodhila, Vinītaprabha, Kātyāyanīputra, Guṇaprabha, Śrīlabdha, Buddhadāsa, Devaśarman, Gopa, Dharmapāla, Guṇamati, Sthiramati, Diṅnāga, Bhāvaviveka, Āchāra, Jinaputra, Bhadraruchi, Mahā-Kātyāyana, besides the distinguished scholars associated with the Nālandā Monastery to be described later.

Those noted for their Teachers or Libraries. But the record of these monasteries in producing great scholars was also continuing even at the time of Hiuen Tsang's travels. Hiuen Tsang broke his journey at several monasteries which were renowned as seats of learning either for their teachers or for their libraries and rare books. Thus in Kashmir the king appointed Bhadanta with his disciples to minister to the needs of the pilgrim and twenty clerks to copy out the MSS. he wanted from the Palace Library, and under these satisfactory arrangements Hiuen Tsang spent two years studying certain Sūtras and Śāstras. In the Nagaradhana Vihāra, in Jālandhara country, Hiuen Tsang found a distinguished scholar named Chandravarma under whom he studied for four months. In one of the monasteries of the Śrughna country he spent one whole winter and half of the spring following in receiving lessons from the learned scholar Jayagupta. In a monastery in Matipur he came across a profound scholar, Mitrasena by name, then 90 years of age, who was a disciple of Guṇaprabha, one of whose works was found in the library there by Hiuen Tsang who remained for several months in studying it. The Bhadravihāra was a noted college in Kanyākubja, where Hiuen Tsang stayed for three months in studying

[1] The above computation follows the lines of that worked out by Rhys Davids in *JRAS.*, 1891, pp. 418–420, but it differs from the latter in regard to several figures drawn from the account of Beal which are not countenanced in the account of Watters followed here.

under Vīryasena. In the Śvetapura Monastery, in the Vaiśālī country, the pilgrim obtained a copy of a Mahāyāna treatise. In the Tiloshika Monastery near Nālandā was then living a distinguished scholar, Prajñābhadra by name. In Monghyr the pilgrim stayed for a year, receiving instruction from the teachers, Tathāgatagupta and Kshāntisiṁha. The monks of the Pūrvaśilā and Avaraśilā monasteries were noted for their proficiency in Abhidharma works, for the study of which the pilgrim spent there several months. In the Kāñchipura Monastery the pilgrim discussed Yoga texts with many Bhikshus who had just arrived there from Ceylon. Lastly, on his way back the pilgrim stayed for two years in a monastery in Jummoo (Po-fa-to) studying with a few learned monks he had found there.

Other Monasteries noted as Centres of Learning. In addition to the monasteries singled out by Hiuen Tsang for their teachers or books, there were a few others for which he has a general word of commendation. The Kanishka Vihāra at Purushapura was full of " Arhats and Śāstra-makers who by their pure conduct and perfect virtue were still an active influence ". The monastery of Pushkarāvati was the resort of " many Buddhist sages from Mid-India ". The few monks in the extant monasteries of Udyāna, once a flourishing centre of Buddhism, were noted for their strict intellectual and moral life. The monasteries in the Śrughna country were so famous for the erudition of their monks that distinguished monks from other lands came to them to have their doubts solved. The Tiloshika monastery of Magadha is described as " the rendezvous of eminent scholars who flocked to it from all regions ". The Mahābodhi Monastery at Gayā was distinguished for the perfection in the Vinaya observances on the part of all its 1,000 ecclesiastics. One of the monasteries in Puṇyavardhana attracted by its reputation many distinguished monks from " East India ". The Raktāmṛita Monastery in Karṇasuvarṇa was the resort of illustrious brethren. The Kāñchipura Monastery is also described " as a rendezvous for the most eminent men of the country ", whither flocked 300 monks from Ceylon at the time of Hiuen Tsang's visit, as we have already seen. Thus all these monasteries were then enjoying almost an all-Indian reputation as seats of Buddhist learning and culture.

Monasteries not noted for efficiency. Not all the numerous monasteries noticed by Hiuen Tsang were, however, efficient ones. Thus, though there were some hundreds of monasteries at Bolor with some thousands of Brethren, the Brethren were without definite learning and were very defective in their observance of the rules of the Order.

Contents of Primary Education : The Five Sciences. It now remains for us to dwell upon the kind and methods of education imparted at these monasteries as indicated by our traveller. It should, however, be noted at the outset that these monasteries were in charge of the higher education of the country, which was led up to by a well-developed system of elementary education. The monasteries were like colleges to which students were admitted on completion of their preliminary education, of which a separate account is given by Hiuen Tsang. A child is first introduced to a *Siddham* (which is from the expression *Siddhir-astu*, May there be success!), or a primer of twelve chapters giving the Sanskrit alphabet and the combinations between vowels and consonants. After his mastery of the Siddham, he was introduced at the age of seven to the "great Śāstras of the Five Sciences", viz. Vyākaraṇa (grammar), Śilpasthānavidyā (the science of Arts and Crafts), Chikitsāvidyā (Science of Medicine), Hetu-vidyā (Nyāya, logic, Science of Reasoning), and Adhyātmavidyā (Inner Science), which, according to Watters, included "the metaphysical and argumentative treatises of the great Doctors of Abhidharma". It is thus clear that the elements of both secular and religious knowledge, of philosophical and practical subjects, entered into the composition of this elementary course of education meant for the sons of Buddhist parents, so that it provided that necessary basis of a good general culture upon which specialization could be successfully attempted in the monasteries. Thus the Buddhist qualification for the religious teacher or leader demanded a knowledge of the practical arts and crafts necessary in serving humanity, such as a knowledge of medicine. We read, for instance, of the great Buddhist leader Kumārajīva that he studied the Śāstras of the Five Sciences mentioned above, and of the famous scholar Guṇabhadra that he, too, had learnt in his youth the Śāstras of those Five Sciences together with Astronomy, Arithmetic, Medicine, and exorcisms (p. 158, vol. i).

Contents of Higher Education at the Monasteries determined by the particular Buddhist Schools to which they belonged. As regards the higher education as imparted by the monasteries, the best details are given by our pilgrim in connection with the working of the Nālandā University to be noticed later. The education of the monasteries may be best considered under two aspects, theoretical (concerning curricula and studies) and practical (concerning conduct and discipline). The studies and curricula adopted by a monastery would depend upon the particular sect of Buddhism with which it was connected. As many as eighteen sects of Buddhism are mentioned by Hiuen Tsang, besides the grand division into the Great and Little Vehicles. Each sect had its own special literature bearing upon its characteristic tenets and practices and claimed a number of monasteries for their study and propagation. We have already seen how the monks and monasteries were distributed among the various schools of Buddhist thought at the time of Hiuen Tsang's visit. Thus in one monastery we find how the course of studies comprised the five redactions of the Vinaya of the Hīnayāna School under the names of Dharmagupta, Mahīśāsika, Kāśyapīya, Sarvāstivādin, and Mahāsaṁghika (i, p. 226). Another specialized in the teaching of Sautrantika Literature, the study of which detains the pilgrim there (p. 322), while there were others known for the study of Abhidharma works by which the pilgrim is attracted (e.g. see pp. 292, 297, etc.).

Monasteries admitting Monks of different Schools of Buddhism. Sometimes, as we have already seen, a monastery would accommodate monks of different schools, and sometimes even students so far apart in their tenets and practices as the Tīrthikas and Buddhists and Brahmans (i, 319; ii, 100, 108). These remarkable facts demonstrate that the so-called Buddhist monasteries were not run like denominational universities in the narrow spirit of a sectarian exclusiveness. Here taught or studied side by side adherents of opposed and incompatible theories. No creed or articles of faith barred the door of admission of a teacher or a student to the equivalents of the chair or the degree of such universities. Thus this ancient education, in a land noted for its many creeds, and for its sectarian divisions, stood boldly in practice for the abiding principle that the way to Truth lies through Liberty!

In general the monasteries confined their studies and teachings within the limits of the Buddhist Canon, whether Vinaya, Abhidharma, or Sūtra, but we find one or two instances where these usual limits seem to have been transgressed by the inclusion of some subjects of study not strictly connected with the traditional Buddhist Scriptures. We read of a monk in a monastery in Laghman producing a notable work on magical invocations, which was translated from Sanskrit into Chinese (i, 182), while in some of the monasteries in Udyāna the monks became distinguished as "experts in magical exorcisms" (p. 226). Some monasteries specialized in the study of Yoga texts (ii, 227). According to I-tsing, monasteries had provision for instruction in both sacred and secular literature.

Methods of Education : Test of Debating Capacity : Gradation of Scholars. As regards the methods of study, the old Brahmanical division between reciting the texts and understanding their meaning seems to have been still in force. We read of the monks of Udyāna as being "clever at reciting their books without penetrating their deep meaning" (i, 226). But undoubtedly much greater stress was laid upon the ability to expound the texts in public meetings at a time when much of the intellectual life of the country was occupied with the controversies and discussions between the exponents of the different schools of thought. As observed by Hiuen Tsang, "the tenets of these schools keep these isolated, and controversy runs high" (i, 162). Accordingly, monastic education devoted special attention to the development in the alumni of their powers of public debate and exposition, which were highly prized and rewarded. The cultivation of such intellectual capacities was systematically stimulated by recognition awarded on the basis of examinations. "The Brethren are often assembled for discussion to test intellectual capacity—to reject the worthless and advance the intelligent. Those who bring forward (or according to some texts, estimate aright) fine points in philosophy, and give subtle principles their proper place, who are ornate in diction and acute in refined distinctions, ride richly caparisoned elephants preceded and followed by a host of attendants. But as for those to whom religious teaching has been offered in vain, who have been defeated in discussion, who are deficient in doctrine and redundant in speech, perverting the sense while keeping the language, the faces of such are promptly daubed with red and white clay, their bodies are covered with dirt, and they are driven out to the wilds or thrown into the ditches" (ib). But besides the periodical examinations, the ordinary classification of the inmates of the monasteries was meant to promote the same end. Each community of Brethren had its own hierarchy promoted according to a recognized system which is thus described by Hiuen Tsang: "The Brother who expounds orally one treatise (or class of scripture) in the Buddhist Canon, whether Vinaya, Abhidharma, or Sūtra, is exempted from serving under the Prior; he who expounds two is invested with the outfit of a Superior; he who expounds three has Brethren deputed to assist him; he who expounds four has lay servants assigned to him; he who expounds five rides an elephant; he who expounds six rides an elephant and has a surrounding retinue."

Manual or menial work of Monks controlled by an officer called 'Karmadāna'. As regards the practical or moral side of monastic education, the discipline and conduct of the monks were regulated according to a system. In the first place, like the Brahmachārin in the Brahmanical system of education, much menial work was expected of the Buddhist monks too. As indicated in the passage just cited, the prevailing system was to place the control of the secular affairs of a monastery under an officer selected from the monks, called the *Karmadāna*, whose orders were to be obeyed by all the common monks for all kinds of menial work required. Exemption from this work had to be earned, as we have seen, by a monk proving himself proficient in one subject or section of the Canon and skilled in its eloquent exposition. We read of the Śrāmaṇera monastery of Rāmagrāma which was so called because its temporal affairs were controlled by a Śrāmaṇera or an unordained novice (ii, 21).

Spiritual Exercises. Secondly, above the stage of manual work, there were other practices binding upon the monks for their moral growth which varied with the sects to which they belonged. Thus while the Hīnayānists inculcated the practices of "sitting in silent reverie, the walking to and fro, and the standing still", the Mahāyānists enjoined "Samādhi and Prajñā".

Influence of Assemblies. Thirdly, assemblies of Brethren are held to "bring moral character into prominence". "As the moral are marked off from the immoral, so the eminent (the wise) and the stupid have outward signs of distinction." Again: "When the spiritual attainments are high, the distinctions conferred are extraordinary." Thus there was the system of public examination and recognition of moral, as of intellectual, merit.

Penalties. Fourthly, the discipline within the monastery was secured by a system of punishments graded according to the offences committed. "For offences against the Vinaya, the Community of Brethren has a gradation of penalties. If the offence is slight, a reprimand is ordered. For an offence next above this in gravity there is added a cessation of oral intercourse with the Brethren. When the offence is serious, the punishment is that they will not live with the offender, and this involves expulsion and excommunication. Expelled from a community, the monk has no home ; he then becomes a miserable vagrant or he returns to his first estate " (i, 163).

Worship of Images of Saints Installed in the Monasteries. Lastly, Hiuen Tsang refers to another feature in the religious education of the monks in the practice of their offering worship to the images or pictures of their respective patron saints set up in connection with the monasteries. Thus in connection with the Mathurā monks he says: " The Abhidharma Brethren offer worship to Sāriputra, the Samādhists to Mudgalaputra, the Sūtraists to Pūrṇamaitriyāniputra, the Vinayists to Upāli, the Bhikshuṇīs to Ānanda, and the Śrāmaṇeras to Rāhula ; and the Mahāyānists to the various P'usas " (i, 302). It may be noted in this connection that Fa-Hien refers to the slightly different practice of the monks offering worship not to the images, but to the topes attached to their monasteries such as those to Śāriputra, Maudgalyāyana, and Ānanda, as well as to the sacred texts, either the Sūtras or the Vinaya or the Abhidharma (i, 303).

Spread of Education. We have now considered the kind and type of intellectual and moral training provided for in these Buddhist monasteries. The total number of such monasteries (about 5,000 in our pilgrim's computation), each of which was a centre of higher education, shows how largely and evenly was such education diffused in the country. The education spread both intensively and extensively. Hiuen Tsang very often gives us notices of large monasteries flourishing in the vicinity of one another in the same local area. Within only 20 miles of Nālandā, for instance, there was the large and famous Tiloshika Monastery peopled with 1,000 Brethren and hardly less renowned than Nālandā as a seat of learning. According to our pilgrim, " it was a rendezvous of eminent scholars who flocked to it from all regions." Magadha, of all the provinces of India, shows the most intensive spread of education in our pilgrim's account.

Scholars from different parts of India meeting at Assemblies for Discussion. In conclusion, we may note that academic debates and tournaments which, as we have seen, formed so large a part of the intellectual life of the country under the Brahmanical system of education from the days of the Upanishads,

PLATE XXII

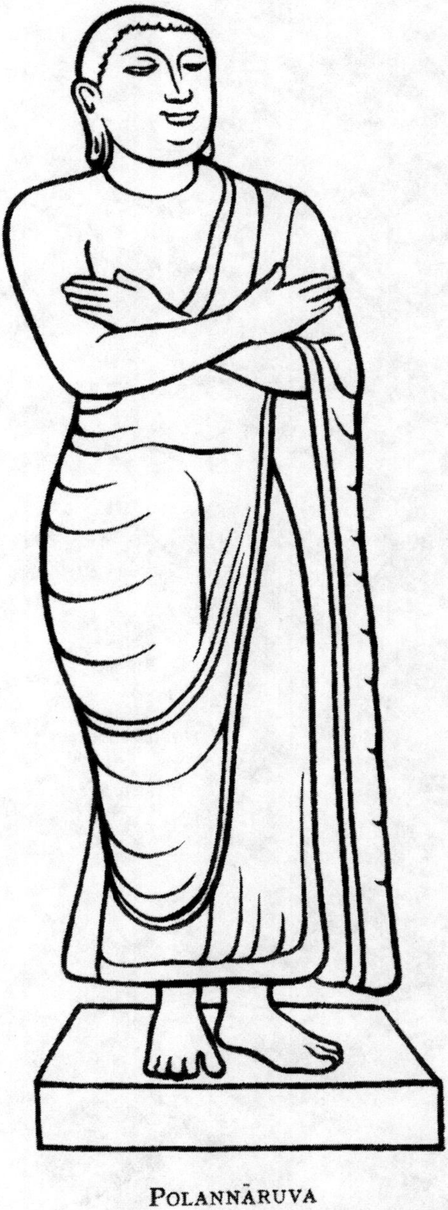

POLANNĀRUVA

Image of Ānanda, disciple of the Buddha [Plate 73 of Coomāraswamy's *Viśvakarmā*].

[*Facing p. 532*

were also a marked characteristic of the Buddhist literary world. Hiuen Tsang has collected the more important traditions and facts on the subject from which we realize how these intellectual tournaments, by no means rare in their occurrence, brought together scholars from distant and different parts of India, promoted active intercourse between different monasteries representing different schools of thought, and created a broad brotherhood of letters in which were united the intellectuals of different provinces. We find that even the distant South, overcoming the many physical factors of isolation, won for itself an honoured place in the Indian intellectual system as centred in the northern parts of India like Nālandā in the Magadha country. For instance, we read of the South Indian Buddhist scholar, Deva, going with the permission of his master, the great Nāgārjuna, to a monastery called Kukkuṭārāma in distant Pāṭaliputra where in a twelve days' discussion he defeated the Tīrthikas of that place (ii, 100). Another academic victory achieved by one South Indian Buddhist scholar over another was commemorated in the Raktāmṛita Monastery in the country of Karṇasuvarṇa. The great Buddhist scholar of the south, Diṅnāga, a Brahman of Kañchi by birth, made the buildings of the Nālandā monastery in Magadha resound with his victorious discussions with the exponents of various schools of thought of the times (ii, 209–212). A different Magadhan monastery commemorated the victory in debate of Śīlabhadra, a Brahman, and a prince by birth, who had renounced the world for the sake of Truth, over a South Indian Brahman scholar who came all the way to Magadha to challenge the learning of his Guru (ii, 110). Nor were these literary gatherings confined to the north. We read of the monks from Ceylon sojourning in Kāñchi, with whom our pilgrim has discussions on Yoga philosophy (p. 227). Among northern scholars again there are several notable discussions mentioned. A Magadhan monastery commemorated the victory achieved by Guṇamati, the Buddhist, over Mādhava, the Sāṁkhist (p. 108). We are told how Dharmapāla carried on a discussion for seven days with 100 Hīnayāna Śāstra-masters whom he utterly defeated in the end in a monastery in Viśoka (i, 374). We read of five monasteries in the Śrughna country built to commemorate the victories achieved by their Brethren who were experts in debate over the Tīrthikas and Brahmans (i, 319). The Brethren of these monasteries became so famous as " expert and lucid expounders of abstract doctrines " that " distinguished Brethren from other lands came to them to reason out their doubts" (p. 318). Lastly, we may note how this phase of intellectual life was encouraged by the paramount Indian sovereign at the time of the pilgrim's visit, viz. Harsha, who used to bring the Brethren together for examination and discussion and rewarded the meritorious (p. 344).

Chapter XXIII

I-TSING'S ACCOUNT OF EDUCATION IN THE SEVENTH CENTURY A.D.

I-tsing visited India soon after Hiuen Tsang. Seventh-century India has been described by another Chinese traveller who set foot on Indian soil in A.D. 672 within a few years after Hiuen Tsang had left it (A.D. 645). It was this fact which probably determined the lines and scope of I-tsing's account of India so as not to render it superfluous after Hiuen Tsang's copious account immediately preceding it. Accordingly, we miss in it the wealth of details, the range and variety of information, which make of Hiuen Tsang's record a sort of a Gazetteer for India of those spacious times. And yet, in covering the ground not trod in Hiuen Tsang's account, the account of I-tsing necessarily forms a valuable addition and supplement to Hiuen Tsang's.

His reverence for Hiuen Tsang. But apart from this, Hiuen Tsang exercised a considerable personal influence upon I-tsing. According to his biographer, he was an eye-witness of the noble enthusiasm of Hiuen Tsang and the ceremony of his funeral which was celebrated with special pomp under the Emperor's orders. Hiuen Tsang died during the time of I-tsing's stay in the capital. His references to Hiuen Tsang are always full of reverence. He calls him " the Tripiṭaka Teacher of China " (p. 74) and " the Bhadanta Hiuen Tsang who followed out his professional career in his own country " (p. 184), and places him on a footing of equality with renowned Buddhist scholars from India like Paramārtha and Kumārajīva. According to his biographer, I-tsing was a great admirer of both Hiuen Tsang and Fa-Hien, in whose footsteps he followed in seeking to slake his thirst for knowledge at its very fountains in India.

Object of his Mission: its difficulties. Like Fa-Hien, I-tsing's object was to study and gather the genuine texts of the Vinaya rules, to correct their misrepresentations in China, and to combat the erroneous views held by the *Vinayadharas* there in those days (Takakusu's ed., pp. 15, 18). At first I-tsing organized a band of scholars to undertake that mission and a joint travel to India, the home of Buddhist literature, but eventually he had to travel almost alone, his only companion being a youthful priest. Not at all depressed by this discouraging circumstance, he had the inspiring words of his teacher to lead him on to that arduous enterprise from which others had shrunk: "Go without hesitation; do not look back upon things left behind. I certainly approve of your pilgrimage to the holy places. Moreover, it is a most important duty to strive for the prosperity of Religion. Rest clear from doubt! This is a great opportunity for you, which will not occur twice" (p. xxviii).

Places visited by I-tsing and periods of his stay. The places actually visited by I-tsing in India were much fewer than those visited by Hiuen Tsang. These were: Kapilavastu, Buddhagayā, Vārāṇasī, Śrāvastī, Kānyakubja, Rājagṛiha (Nālanda), Vaiśālī, Kuśinagara, and Tāmralipti. He refers to several other places in India, viz. Lāṭa, Sindhu, Valabhī, Udyāna, Kāśmīra, and Nepāla, but his descriptions of these places do not appear to be those of an eye-witness. He was, however, careful to check the accuracy of hearsay accounts received by him. He himself states: "Although I myself did not see all these parts of India, I could nevertheless ascertain everything by careful inquiry" (p. 43).

At some of the places he spent more time for his studies than Hiuen Tsang. He stayed at Tāmralipti for four months. At Nālanda he stayed for as many as ten years.

His collection of Texts in India. His literary collections from India amounted to a considerable quantity. They comprised some 400 different texts of Buddhist works with the slokas numbering 500,000.

His acquisition of knowledge of Sanskrit and its Grammar. His internal acquisitions in India included a knowledge of Sanskrit and of Śabdavidyā (grammar and lexicography) (p. xxxi). He was thus able to translate on his return home no less than 56 works in 230 volumes. By the literature that he thus introduced into China in which were represented practically the whole texts of the Vinaya belonging to his own Nikāya (the Mūlasarvāstivādin school), he became the founder of a new school in China for the study of that particular branch of Buddhist literature.

Strength of Brahmanism. The predominance of Brahmanism over Buddhism continued in I-tsing's time. India was known by the name of *Brahma-rāshṭra* (pp. 118, 156). Sanskrit, called the *Brahma-language*, became the language of even the Buddhist works and a subject of study of the Buddhist monks. As stated by I-tsing, "a thorough study of Sanskrit Grammar may clear up many difficulties we encounter while engaged in translation" (p. 168). I-tsing refers to the ninety-six heretical schools of thought and mentions the Sāṁkhya and Vaiśeshika systems of philosophy (p. 2). Some of the existing sects of the times are described as follows: "Some think it necessary, in order to get rid of re-birth, to have their body naked (Digambara) and the hair plucked out; others insist, as the means of securing heaven, on anointing their body with ashes or tying up their locks of hair (probably Śaivas called Bhūtas by Hiuen Tsang). Some say life is self-existent, while others believe that the soul becomes extinct on death. There are many who think that existence is a perfect mystery, dark and obscure, and its reality is not to be explored, and it is too minute and complicated for us to know whence we have come into being" (ib.). I-tsing also refers to the Brahmans as being "regarded throughout the five parts of India as the most honourable caste" who do not associate with other castes (p. 182). "The scriptures they revere are the four Vedas, containing about 100,000 verses." "The Vedas have been handed down from mouth to mouth, not transcribed on paper or leaves. In every generation there exist some intelligent Brahmans who can recite the 100,000 verses" (ib.). There is a reference to Brahmanical methods of study, the meaning of which is not clear: "In India there are two traditional ways by which one can attain to great intellectual power. Firstly, by repeatedly committing to memory, the intellect is developed; secondly, the alphabet fixes one's ideas. By this way, after a practice of ten days or a month, a student feels his thoughts rise like a fountain, and can commit to memory whatever he has once heard (not requiring to be told twice). This is far from being a myth, for I myself have met such men" (p. 183).

Elementary Education: its Textbooks and Subjects: (1) Alphabets, (2) Grammar (Pāṇini and Kāśikā). Like Hiuen Tsang, I-tsing gives an account of the general and elementary education of the times prior to specialization and higher education in the monasteries. Education is begun at the age of six years. The first book of reading is called *Siddhirastu*, which gives 49 letters of the alphabet and 10,000 syllables arranged in 300 slokas. This Primer is finished in six months (pp. 170-2).

The second book of reading is the *Sūtra* of Pāṇini, containing 1,000 slokas which the " children begin to learn when they are eight years old and can repeat in eight months' time " (p. 172). Next follow the book on *Dhātu*, and that on the three *Khilas* which the boys would begin when they are ten years old and master after three years' diligent study (p. 175). The book to be read next is the famous *Kāśikāvṛitti*, " the best " of all the commentaries on Pāṇini's Sūtra, comprising 18,000 slokas, and composed by the learned Jayāditya, " a man of great ability with very striking literary power," who died nearly thirty years before I-tsing's notice of him in his account (i.e. A.D. 661–2). " Boys of fifteen years begin to study this commentary and understand it after years. If men of China go to India for study, they have first of all to learn this grammatical work, then other subjects ; if not, their labour will be thrown away."

(3) Composition, (4) Logic and Philosophy. " After having studied this commentary, students begin to learn *Composition* in prose and verse and devote themselves to Logic (Hetuvidyā) and Metaphysics (Abhidharmakosha)." Under Logic, they study the introductory work composed by Nāgārjuna, called Nyāya-dvāra-tāraka-śāstra, which teaches how to " rightly draw inferences (Anumāna) " and which was translated into Chinese by I-tsing in A.D. 711, while " by studying the *Jātakamāla* their powers of comprehension increase ". Besides the *Jātaka-māla* which was compiled under the patronage of the emperor Harsha (p. 163), there was another work which was equally popular and " regarded as standard literature ", viz. the *Suhṛillekha*, an epistle in verse, addressed by Nāgārjuna to his patron, king Jetaka Sātavāhana (p. 159), known for the beauty of its style and for its earnest exhortations as to the right way. I-tsing sent in advance to China a Chinese translation of this Epistle of Nāgārjuna (p. 166).

The Five Vidyās. Here ends the course of elementary and general education. Properly speaking, it comprised the study of the five subjects or Vidyâs, viz. (1) Śabdavidyā (grammar and lexicography), (2) Śilpasthānavidyā, " arts " ; (3) Chikitsā-vidyā, " medicine " ; (4) Hetuvidyā, " logic " ; and (5) Adhyāt-mavidyā, " science of the universal soul," philosophy. I-tsing gives us the details of study as regards (1), (4), and (5) in the foregoing extracts. Elsewhere he gives details regarding (3) or medical science (p. 127).

Medical Science. Of Medical Science, he mentions eight

sections treating respectively of (1) sores, inward and outward, (2) diseases above the neck, and (3) below it, or bodily diseases, (4) demoniac diseases due to attack of evil spirits, (5) the Agada medicine, i.e. antidote or medicine for counteracting poisons, (6) diseases of the children from the embryo stage to the sixteenth year, (7) the means of lengthening life, and (8) the methods of invigorating the legs and body. "These eight arts formerly existed in eight books, but lately a man epitomized them and made them into one bundle. All physicians in the five parts of India practise according to *this book*, and any physician who is well versed in it never fails to live by the official pay." I-tsing himself claims to have made "a successful study in medical science", but finally gave it up as it was not his proper vocation. But he explains why this subject was a part of the compulsory course of elementary studies for all, including those intended for monkhood. "Is it not a sad thing," he asks, "that *sickness* prevents the pursuit of one's duty and vocation? Is it not beneficial if people can benefit others as well as themselves *by the study of medicine*?" (p. 130). I-tsing mentions the principal medical herbs in India (p. 128) and the "rules on giving medicine" (ch. xxviii), which insisted on fasting as an effective cure (p. 133), by practice of which "each man is himself the king of physicians, and anyone can be Jīvaka" (ib.). There is a reference to the use of Tea (p. 135) and the *universal* disuse of any kind of onions in India (p. 137) which, because they "have a foul smell and are impure", are not to be eaten "except in case of illness" (p. 138). The surgical processes of cauterizing with fire or applying a puncture are also referred to (p. 129).

I-tsing does not give us any details of the studies or curriculum under that part of compulsory elementary education which went by the name of Śilpasthānavidyā, "arts," the second of the five Vidyās as stated above.

The completion of the study of the five Vidyās completes the course of elementary and general education. Then follows bifurcation of studies or specialization.

Higher and Specialized Study : (1) Of Grammar : Its Textbooks. There is a course of specialized and advanced studies in *Vyākaraṇa* which was "the name for the general secular literature" (p. 169). The following textbooks were prescribed : (1) The *Chūrṇi*, which is the name of Patañjali's famous commentary on Pāṇini's Sūtras, usually called the *Mahābhāshya*, containing 24,000 ślokas (p. 178). It cites the *Sūtras*, explains the obscure points, analyses the principles involved, and clears up many difficulties. "*Advanced* scholars learn this in three years." (2) The *Bhartṛihari-Śāstra*, which was a commentary in 25,000 slokas on the former work by the great scholar Bhartṛihari, who "was very famous throughout the five parts of India" and who "became seven times a priest and seven times returned to the laity". He died in A.D. 651–2 (p. 180). (3) The *Vākya-padīya*, another work of Bhartṛihari, with 700 slokas and a commentary portion in 7,000 slokas. It is a "treatise on the Inference, supported by the authority of the sacred teaching and on Inductive arguments" (ib.). (4) The *Pei-na* (probably Sanskrit Beḍa or Veḍa), a grammatical work of 3,000 slokas composed by Bhartṛihari, with a commentary portion in 14,000 slokas attributed to his contemporary, Dharmapāla. It treats of "the secrets of heaven and earth and of the philosophy of man".

Students completing this advanced study were regarded as masters of grammatical science and earned the title of *Bahuśruta* ("much heard" or "knowing much of the Śruti"). This course of specialization in Grammar was open to both priests and laymen (p. 180).

(2) Of Religion. There were again courses of specialization in religious or priestly studies which were organized and offered by the monasteries. The most famous of such seats of higher learning in the time of I-tsing's visit to India were "the Nālanda monastery in Central India" and that "in the country of Valabhī in Western India" (p. 177).

Rules of Admission to Monkhood. We shall now consider the rules governing the education and organization of the monasteries as given by our pilgrim. It would appear that the rules laid down in the Vinaya texts regarding admission to monasteries, to priesthood or ordination, were substantially followed in the days of I-tsing, whose evidence based upon first-hand observation is thus another welcome confirmation of that of the sacred texts whose precepts are otherwise liable to be supposed as merely *ideal* in their character. The student who wants to become a priest (i.e. homeless) first finds a teacher to whom he relates his wish. The teacher through some means or other inquires whether he has any moral disqualification, such as patricide, matricide, and the like. If he is eligible, the proposed teacher accepts him as a candidate for orders and leaves him at leisure ten days or a month and then imparts to him the five precepts (prohibiting murder, theft, lying, adultery, and intoxication). The candidate is now called an *Upāsaka*, which is his *first step* into the Law of the Buddha. Then the teacher, getting for him a triple clothing, a bowl, and a filter, addresses himself to the Saṁgha and relates that the candidate has a desire to be a priest (i.e. homeless). When the Saṁgha has admitted him, the teacher on his behalf asks the *Āchāryas* to conduct the ceremony. After this the candidate has his hair and beard shaven, bathes, and, putting on the priestly cloak, receives the bowl and becomes a *Pravrajita*. Next, in the presence of his teacher (*Upādhyāya*), the *Āchārya* imparts to him the ten precepts by reciting or reading them. After the priest has been instructed in these precepts, he is called *Śramaṇera*. The Śramaṇera is eligible for full ordination on his attaining the required age of twenty years. Then his *Upādhyāya*, arranging for him the six requisites [viz. the triple clothing or *tichīvara*, the bowl, the *nishīdana*, and a water-strainer (but the Pāli texts mention some different requisites, eight in number)], gets up a meeting of the Saṁgha of at least nine other members before whom he presents the candidate who pays respects three times to each member. After this ceremony, the candidate is instructed three times to learn the Mahāśīlas. Then the *Upādhyāya* invests him before the assembly with the garments, and the bowl which has to be approved by them and then accepted by the candidate. After this the Āchārya imparts to him the Mahāśīlas and he then becomes an *Upasampanna* Bhikshu. The exact hour, date, month, and season of the ordination are then written down so that his seniority might be determined. The last act of the ceremony is the gift by the candidate of some such thing as a girdle or a filter to the teachers or members of the Saṁgha ordaining him as a token of his gratitude to them (adapted from ch. xix).

Studies of Monks. Then begins the regular course of monastic education and discipline. The Upādhyāya imparts to his pupil the contents of the *Prātimoksha* as the first lesson, explaining to him the character of the offences and how to recite the precepts. "These having been learnt, the candidate begins to read the larger Vinaya-piṭaka ; he reads it day after day, and is examined every morning, for if he does not keep to it constantly he will lose intellectual power. When he has read the Vinaya-Piṭaka, he begins to learn the Sūtras and Śāstras. Such is the way in which a teacher instructs in India" (p. 104). I-tsing also refers to the Vinaya practice of requiring for each priest under training two teachers called the *Upādhyāya* and the *Karmāchārya* (ib.), the former being "the teacher of personal instruction" (adhyāya = lit. "teaching to read" and upa = "near"), and the latter "the teacher of discipline" who "teaches pupils rules and ceremonies" (p. 118).

To the ordinary and traditional curriculum of specialized priestly studies in the monasteries which included the Vinaya works, the Sūtras and the Śāstras (p. 181), some new works seem to have been added in course of time. Among these, I-tsing mentions the two hymns of 150 and 400 verses attributed to Mātṛicheta (the former of which was translated by I-tsing during his stay at Nālanda). "Throughout India," says our pilgrim, "everyone who becomes a monk is taught Mātṛicheta's two hymns as soon as he can recite the five and ten precepts (śīla). This course is adopted by both the Mahāyāna and Hīnayāna schools" (p. 157). "After one is able to recite them, one proceeds to learn other Sūtras" (p. 158). These two hymns were valued not merely for their contents but also for their language showing "how to compose verses". Next to them I-tsing mentions the *Buddhacharitakāvya* of Aśvaghosha which "is widely read or sung throughout the five divisions of India, and the countries of the Southern Sea" (p. 166), as well as the two other works already mentioned, viz. Nāgārjuna's *Suhṛillekha* and the *Jātakamālā*.[1] Advanced studies and specialization were also carried on in a few other subjects on which considerable literature had been developed, as described by I-tsing. Thus some Bhikshus might elect to study the *Yoga* system for which the curriculum included, as the first book of study, the *Yogācharya-Śāstra*, to be followed by Asaṅga's Eight Śāstras, which are named. If a priest wanted to distinguish himself in the study of *Logic* he was to master Jina's Eight Śāstras, which are also named. Similarly, six Pādas or treatises are mentioned in connection with the study of the Abhidharma or Metaphysics and four Nikāyas or classes of works in connection with the Āgamas. The mastery of the Abhidharma and Āgama works was regarded as essential for any Bhikshu who wanted to successfully combat heretics and disputants (pp. 186–7).

Daily Duties. As education in the monasteries aimed at

[1] I-tsing also mentions two other recently composed works which were also widely used. The first was the story of the Bodhisattva Jīmūtavāhana versified by King Śīlāditya, who popularized it by having it sung with dancing and acting, and the second was a poetical song about the Viśvāntara-Jātaka composed by a learned man in Eastern India, Chandradāsa by name (p. 164).

both intellectual and moral growth, the rules regulating the daily life of the inmates were framed with a reference to both the aims. What I-tsing observed of the relations between teacher and pupil is on the lines of the Vinaya rules on the subject already discussed. The day begins with the pupil supplying his teacher with tooth-wood, basin with water, and towel. He then walks round the temple and, worshipping the image, returns and makes inquiries of his teacher about his health. " Next, the pupil goes to salute his seniors who are in neighbouring apartments. Afterwards he reads a portion of the scripture and reflects on what he has learnt. He acquires new knowledge day by day and searches into old subjects month after month without losing a minute " (p. 117). The new knowledge is, of course, acquired with the help of the teacher who, " selecting some passages from the Tripiṭakas, gives a lesson in a way that suits circumstances, and does not pass any fact or theory unexplained " (p. 120).

The entire daily conduct of the pupil is inspected by the teacher who " warns him of defects and transgressions. Whenever he finds his pupil faulty he makes him seek remedies and repent " (ib.). The pupil serves his teacher as best as he may, such as rubbing his body, folding his clothes, and sweeping the apartment and the yard. " Thus, if there be anything to be done, he does all on behalf of his teacher. This is the manner in which one pays respect to one's superior." But the spirit of this loving and devoted service was met by its due response : for instance, " in case of a pupil's illness, his teacher himself nurses him, supplies all the medicines needed, and pays attention to him as if he were his child " (ib.). Thus the entire system of Indian education, whether Brahmanical or Buddhist, was based upon the principle of a personal touch or relationship between the teacher and the taught, whether the sphere of its working lay in the individual household of the teacher or in the collective establishment of a monastery. Both the domestic and monastic systems of education worked upon the basis of a common pedagogic principle, though they differed as regards the manner of its application as determined by their respective backgrounds or environments.

Grading of Monks. The monks of the monasteries, like the students of colleges, were suitably graded according to their capacities and the level of advance they attained. Within the community of monks, the lowest grade is that of the *Śramaṇera* who is promoted, after his Upasampadā ordination, to the grade of the *Dahara*-(small)*Bhikshu*. Higher than him is the *Sthavira* (elder), the Bhikshu, who has seen ten summers or passed ten summer retreats in that capacity, and who, for his standing, "can live by himself without having to live under a teacher's care" (p. 104). In another place (p. 119) I-tsing tells of a preliminary stage of Sthavirahood and of the mastery of the Vinaya, and not mere seniority, as the standard of such gradings. Thus he states: "After the lapse of five summers from the time that the pupil masters the Vinaya, he is allowed to live apart from his Upādhyāya. He can then go about among the people and proceed to pursue some other aim. Yet he must put himself under the care of *some teacher* wherever he goes. This will cease after the lapse of ten summers, i.e. after he is able to understand the Vinaya." Thus, according to this statement, it is the independence of the teacher, the cessation of *nissaya* (to use the Vinaya word), attained by a ten years' standing after graduation in Vinaya, which entitles a Bhikshu to the degree or rank of a *Sthavira*. A *Sthavira* necessarily attains the position of an *Upādhyāya* and an *Upādhyāya* must be a *Sthavira*. A higher rank probably belonged to the other classes of teachers, like the Karmāchāryas and others who could officiate in the ordinations, but the basis of the distinction is not defined. "The age of a Karmāchārya and private instructor, and of other teachers who are witnesses, is not limited; they must be fully acquainted with the Vinaya, being themselves pure" (p. 105). The highest grade for a Bhikshu was that of the *Bahuśruta*. This high title was conferred only on one who was "learned both in the sacred and secular literatures and famed as virtuous" (p. 104). We have already noticed what was the course of study in secular literature that was prescribed for this coveted degree and distinction of the *Bahuśruta*.

Privileges according to Grades. But the gradations of the monks in a monastery were indicated not merely by titles, but also by privileges. To venerable monks, if very learned, or those who had thoroughly studied at least *one* of the three Piṭakas were assigned some of the best rooms of the monastery and servants. "When such men gave daily lectures, they were freed from the business imposed on the (ordinary) monastics." They were given the further privilege of being permitted, when they went out, "to ride in sedan-chairs but not on horseback" (p. 64). These facts were observed by I-tsing at the Varāha monastery in Tāmralipti.

Admission of non-Buddhist Students : Provision of Secular Education. We have now considered the classification of the monks in a monastery in accordance with their educational needs and capacities. But it should be noted that these monks were students belonging to the religious section of the monastery, i.e. that section which imparted instruction in sacred literature only. But a Buddhist monastery had also a secular section. To this section were admitted students who were called *Brahmachārins*, and had no intention of renouncing the world and becoming Buddhist monks. That this section was highly popular in I-tsing's time is apparent from his following statement : " In the monasteries of India there are many ' students ' (Brahmachārins) who are entrusted to the Bhikshus and instructed by them in secular literature " (p. 106). That the Bhikshus in those days made themselves masters of both religious and secular literature has been already shown. As we have already noticed, proficiency in both was, indeed, insisted upon as the distinguishing distinction of a *Bahuśruta*, while we even read of monks who sought the king's service in practical administration by proving their talents at the intellectual contests organized for the purpose at the king's House of Debate. In fact, as we have already seen, monks under the Buddhist system were free to return to secular life. We read, for instance, of the famous scholar Bhartṛihari, who " became seven times a priest, and seven times returned to the laity " and wrote in self-reproach :

" Through the enticement of the world I returned to the laity.
Being free from secular pleasures again I wear the priestly cloak.
How do these two impulses
Play with me as if a child ? " (p. 179).

Indeed, after finishing their education, monks " can follow whatever occupation they like " (p. 178).

Admission of unordained Students. Besides organizing secular courses of study and throwing them open to non-Buddhist students or students from the Buddhist lay public, the monasteries still further widened their scope and sphere of usefulness by admitting to their religious sections even unordained students. These were called *Māṇavas* who might be potential, but not actual, monks with whom they only agreed in seeking instruction in the Buddhist scriptures. They come in the white robes of laymen but they cherish " the intention that they may one day become tonsured and black-robed ", i.e. become ordained (p. 105).

This interesting institution of not confining the monasteries only to monks was recommended on several grounds. On the one hand, the secular students served under the priests as pages, "bringing them the tooth-woods or serving them at the meals," and, on the other hand, their instruction might kindle in them pious aspirations, so that both parties are benefited in this way.

Breadth of Culture in these Monasteries. Both these classes of secular students, the *Māṇavas* and the *Brahmachārīs*, were also permitted to be in residence in the monasteries instead of being compelled to attend them as day-scholars. But they had, of course, to bring their own boarding expenses, for they could not under rules be fed from the property of the Saṁgha unless they had done some laborious work for the Saṁgha, who might then pay for it in the shape of feeding them according to their merit (p. 106). It was, of course, open for the monasteries to receive special grants of food for these classes of students (ib.).

Thus the Buddhist monasteries of the times became the seats and centres of both sacred and secular learning, and, being freely resorted to by both Buddhist monks and laymen, and even by non-Buddhists, materially aided in the diffusion of learning and culture in the country. The Buddhist monks also who came practically to have the monopoly in this learning and culture were catholic and generous enough to impart them to persons not belonging to their way of life. Not confining their sympathies and valued services within the limited boundaries of their own church and faith, they thus became the Directors of Public Instruction in the country. They recognized in a noble spirit of toleration that the country was above creed, and culture above church ! In disowning the divisions and distinctions of caste in the external organization of their brotherhood, the Buddhist monks could not consistently apply the same principle in another and more important sphere of their activities.

Unsuccessful Teachers and Pupils. Not all the teachers and the taught in the monasteries were always successful. We read of monks unable to understand the Vinaya and thus compelled "to live under another's care during the whole of their life-time". Sometimes the failure may be due to the want of a really able teacher. "If there be no great teacher, he must live under the care of a sub-teacher." From such a sub-teacher he may arrange to receive instruction twice a day in the morning and evening but with all this it may so happen that the meaning of the Vinaya text is not understood as it ought to be. The incapacity of a teacher is condemned by the Vinaya thus: "Rather be a butcher than be a priest who gives others full ordination and leaves them untaught" (p. 120).

Unsuccessful Monasteries. There were also not only individual failures among the monks, whether teachers or students, but also collective failures among them as brotherhoods, among the monasteries regarded as educational institutions. I-tsing speaks of some monasteries giving themselves up wholly to "unlawful life", violating the principal injunctions of the Vinaya (p. 194).

Successful Monasteries and their best products. As regards their successes, the monasteries produced some of the highest types of intellect and character. One of their principal aims was to produce successful preachers and dialecticians. Such persons were needed for the purposes of a proselytizing religion which had, moreover, to maintain its position against the numerous sects that were ready to challenge its supremacy in India in those days. Accordingly, the highest honour in the Buddhist world of scholarship was accorded to those who would "oppose the heretics as they would drive beasts (deer) in the middle of the plain and explain away disputations as boiling water melts frost" (p. 181). The successful disputants "become famous throughout Jambudvīpa (India) and receive respect above gods and men". Men of such international reputation are, of course, rare, "only one or two appearing in every generation." I-tsing mentions some of them belonging to the different periods of Buddhist history. "Such were Nāgārjuna, Deva, Aśvaghosha, of an early age; Vasubandhu, Asaṅga, Saṁghabhadra, Bhāvaviveka, in the Middle Ages; and Jina, Dharmapāla, Dharmakīrti, Śīlabhadra, Siṁhachandra, Sthiramati, Guṇamati, Prajñāgupta, Guṇaprabha, Jinaprabha of late years" (ib.). To these names he elsewhere (p. 183) adds those of Kāśyapa-mātaṅga and Dharmaraksha (who were the first Indian Buddhists in China, which they visited in A.D. 67); of Paramārtha (who came to China in A.D. 548 and translated thirty-one works), whose fame "reached even to the Southern Ocean (i.e. Nanking)"; of Kumārajīva (who came to China about A.D. 401 and translated fifty Sanskrit books into Chinese), who "supplied a virtuous pattern to the foreign land".

The institutions most successful in producing this kind of intellectual eminence in I-tsing's time were the monasteries at Nālanda and Valabhī. "There eminent and accomplished men gathered in crowds, discussed possible and impossible doctrines, and after having been assured of the excellence of their opinions by wise men became far-famed for their wisdom" (p. 177). The friction of the best minds that collected at those two famous centres of Buddhist learning was the best possible means of developing and sharpening the wits and powers of debate.

Learned Assemblies at the Courts of Kings who rewarded merit. But these learned disputations which thus formed the characteristic feature of Indian intellectual life were held not merely in the monasteries but also at the courts of kings under the encouragement of the State. The kings even in I-tsing's time, as in the days of old, were fond of organizing intellectual tournaments at which superior knowledge might be tested, rewarded, recognized, and proclaimed. "To try the sharpness of their wit they proceed to the king's court to lay down before it the sharp weapon (of their abilities); there they present their schemes and show their talent, seeking to be appointed in the practical government" (p. 177). I-tsing also tells us of the House of Debate in the royal palace where the literary tournaments were held. Those who emerge victorious there will at once achieve an international reputation: "the sound of their fame makes the five mountains of India vibrate, and their renown flows, as it were, over the four borders" (p. 178). The king rewards their talent by grants of land and advancing them to a high rank and also by having their famous names written down in white on the lofty gates of his palace [1] (ib.).

Literary Celebrities of the Times. I-tsing also mentions the literary celebrities of India in his time. He refers to them either as his contemporaries or personal acquaintances who were all alive between A.D. 670–700. He says: "The following are the most distinguished teachers who now live in the West. Jñānachandra, a Master of the Law, lives in the monastery Tilaḍha (in Magadha); in the Nālanda monastery Ratnasiṁha (who was teacher of Hiuen Chao when he was at Nālanda about A.D. 649); in Eastern India Divākaramitra (of whom Bāṇa's *Harsha-charita* gives an interesting account too); and in the southernmost district, Tathāgatagarbha. In Śrībhoga of the

[1] The Chinese passage is differently interpreted by Mr. K. P. Jayaswal [*JASB.*, June, 1911, p. 312]. According to him, it means that those who are victorious in debate are called upon to discourse upon the great systems of philosophy and not that their names are inscribed "on the lofty gates".

Southern Sea resides Śākyakīrti who travelled all through the five countries of India in order to learn, and is at present in Śrībhoja (in Sumatra)" (p. 184). To these names are to be added Rāhulamitra (p. 63) and Chandra (pp. 164, 183). The former belonged to the Tāmralipti monastery when I-tsing visited it. He was then about thirty years old; of "excellent" conduct and "exceedingly great" fame; thoroughly conversant not only with the three Piṭakas, but also with "the secular literature on the four sciences"; who "was honoured as the head of the priests in Eastern Ārya-deśa"; who had never spoken with women face to face except his mother and sister, and when questioned on this puritanism by I-tsing, answered in all humility: "I am naturally full of worldly attachment and without doing thus I cannot stop its source. Although we are not prohibited (to speak with women) by the Holy One, it may be right (to keep them off), if it is meant to prevent our evil desires." Every day he used to "read over the Ratnakūṭa-sūtra, which contains 700 verses" (p. 64). Mahāsattva Chandra lived in Eastern India and "was still alive when I-tsing visited that country". He was "like a Bodhisattva endowed with great talent" (p. 183). We have already referred to his authorship of the poem about Viśvāntara-Jātaka.

All these men, says I-tsing, were renowned as much for their character as for their learning, in both of which they aspired after the highest ideal. In character they were "anxious to follow in the footsteps of the Sages"; in learning, if it was Logic (Hetuvidyā) they studied, "they aspired to be like Jina," and if it was Yoga, they had Asaṅga as their model. In discourse, they followed Nāgārjuna, and, in philosophical exposition, Saṁghabhadra. With these distinguished scholars, our pilgrim had the benefit of a personal contact. Says he: "I, I-tsing, used to converse with these teachers so intimately that I was able to receive invaluable instruction personally from them. I have always been very glad that I had the opportunity of acquiring knowledge from them personally which I should otherwise never have possessed, and that I could refresh my memory of past study by comparing old *notes* with new ones" (p. 185).

Worship of Images, Chaityas, and Stūpas. Direct worship of images, chaityas, and stūpas set up in connection with the monasteries was a part of the religious training they provided. We read of the installation of the holy image of the Buddha, of which the ablution was celebrated daily with great pomp by all the monastics, who were summoned for the ceremony by the Managing Priest, Karmadāna, striking a *ghaṇṭā* or bell (p. 149). I-tsing also refers to images being installed even "in individual apartments of a monastery" (ib.). Besides the image of the Buddha, there were installed "in great monasteries in India" (p. 38) the images of Mahākāla, of the Nāga Mahāmuchilinda (seen by I-tsing in the Mahābodhi monastery at Gayā), and of Mother Hāritī in the dining-hall (p. 37). Besides worship of images, there was also the worship of Chaityas (the sacred buildings containing the relics of the Buddha or saints) and Stūpas (p. 152). Every afternoon the monks were to come out of the gate of their monastery and walk three times round a stūpa, offering incense and flower, and then kneeling down, while one of them chanted hymns. Then the assembly returned to the monastery to hear a Sūtra being read by a Sūtra-reciter. The Sūtra usually selected was the "service in three parts", compiled by Aśvaghosha. When this is ended, all the assembled priests exclaim "Subhāshita" or "Sādhu". Then the priests, in the order of their rank, salute the Siṁhāsanam as well as the seats of the saints (p. 154). The performance of these rites was observed by I-tsing at Tāmralipti. In the Nālanda monastery, where it was difficult to assemble its numerous monks in one place for congregational worship, the worship could only take place separately as most convenient to each member (ib.).

Change of Monasteries by Monks. Monks could change their monasteries. A stranger monk on arrival at a monastery would be first treated as a guest for five days and given the best of food so that he might recover from his fatigue, after which he was treated as a common monastic if he was not learned. If he *was*, and bore a good character, he was assigned his proper rank and treatment with his name "written down on the register of the names of the resident priests" (p. 64). All visitors were cordially welcomed by the word *svāgata* and by the word *susvāgata* if they were strangers (p. 124). The ceremonies of receiving them varied according as they were teachers, pupils, strangers, or friends (p. 125).

Physical Exercise. Along with the needs of mental and moral training, the monasteries, strange as it might appear, were not unmindful of the needs of physical health for which regular exercises were prescribed. I-tsing tells us that "in India both priests and laymen are generally in the habit of taking walks, going backwards and forwards along a path, at suitable hours, and at their pleasures. . . The walking hours are in the forenoon and late in the afternoon. They either go away (for a walk) from their monasteries, or stroll quietly along the corridors". This physical exercise was expressly undergone "for the sake of taking air" so as "to keep oneself in good health or to cure diseases". The Buddha himself took this exercise: "there are cloisters where he used to walk, on the Vulture-Peak, under the Bo-tree, in the Deer Park, at Rājāgṛiha, and in other holy places" which were two cubits in width and fifteen in length (p. 114). The Vinaya often speaks of monks preferring to walk up and down as an aid to meditation itself!

Self-government in Monasteries. Apart from their studies and discipline, which were controlled by their teachers, the monks had other matters in their own collective control. If we may generalize on the basis of what I-tsing says of a particular but a typical monastery (viz. that at Tāmralipti), the monasteries in his time were democratically governed and not governed by a bureaucracy of the kind described in the Vinaya. The bureaucratic element in their management was represented by the solitary official called *Karmadāna*, the managing monk, but his powers seem to have been very limited, being only to announce the commencement of any ceremonies or service, etc., by striking a bell and to superintend the preparation of food (p. 148). At the Tāmralipti monastery, "no principal office was appointed; when any business happened, it was settled by the assembly; and if any priest decided anything by himself alone, or treated the priests favourably or unfavourably at his own pleasure without regarding the will of the assembly he was expelled from the monastery" and dubbed a *kulapati* (householder). In the case of any improper and immoral act done by any monk, a special investigation was instituted by the monks meeting in an assembly where the culprit, his accomplices, and the witnesses were subjected to a cross-examination, and the due punishment was pronounced. "Thus all the priests submitted to their own laws without giving any trouble to the public court" (p. 63).

Names of Monks admitted or expelled entered in a Register. The expulsion from the monastery of the offending monk was recorded by his name being struck off its roll. For every monastery had, as we have seen, its own register-book. When a layman was admitted as a monk to a monastery, his name was written down on the register-book of the monastery and "thenceforth his name had no concern with the register of the State" (p. 65).

Self-government at Nālandā. The monastery of Nālanda was also democratically governed. I-tsing observed there that it was the great assembly of priests who assigned rooms every year (p. 86) there, for instance.

Menial and Administrative Staff. Among the staff appointed to manage the affairs of the monasteries, there are mentioned, besides the Karmadāna, officers called Vihāra-pālas, such as the keeper, the warder of the gate, and he who announces the affairs of the Saṁgha (p. 148), as also "the lay servants" who do not belong to the order of the monks, but might be professed Upāsakas. Their functions are indicated in the accounts of the Chinese travellers. Fa-Hien refers to them as attending at meals; Hiuen Tsang refers to them as attending on a venerable monk, while I-tsing gives us more details about their work. The "monastic lay servant" carries a chair and utensils when a monk goes to a reception (p. 36); he carries away the remnant of food eaten by the monk (p. 47); he carries incense and flowers in accompanying the precentor going round from one apartment of the monastery to another, chanting hymns (p. 154); the time-drum of the monastery is beaten by him, but he is not entitled to strike the gong announcing the beginning of the Service (p. 145); he had also to watch the clepsydra (p. 144); he is also employed to cultivate the fields belonging to the monasteries which the monks themselves could not directly cultivate under rules (p. 61); while lastly, as we have seen, he had to render menial service to a very learned priest or one who has mastered one of the Piṭakas, who was given the privilege of being attended by such servants.

Diet. The diet of the monks in I-tsing's time corresponded to the rules of the Vinaya and comprised the *Pañchabhojanīyas*, viz. rice, a boiled mixture of barley and peas, baked corn-flour, meat and cakes, and the *Pañchakhādanīyas* consisting of roots, stalks, leaves, flowers, and fruits (p. 43). There are mentioned also gruel made of dried rice and bean soup which "is served with hot butter sauce as flavouring", melted butter and cream to be "partaken of to any extent" (p. 40), and ghee, oil, milk which were abundant everywhere (p. 44). These articles of diet varied with the countries. "In the north wheat-flour is abundant; in the western district baked flour (rice or barley) is used above all; in Magadha wheat-flour is scarce but rice is plentiful; and the southern frontier and the eastern borderland have similar products to those of Magadha" (p. 43). None of the people of all the five parts of India ate any kind of onions (pp. 45, 138).

We gather from I-tsing that the monk's breakfast consisted of rice-water, his lunch, rice, butter, milk, fruits, and sweet melons, ending in light evening meal or supper [Takakusu, pp. 117, 26, 44].

Its excess at Invitations. At invitations to monks for meals it was usual to have the supply of food very much in excess of the requirements. I-tsing was duly warned of this practice when he gave a feast to the priests on a small scale one fast day at Tāmralipti (p. 40).

Measurement of time for regulating the day's duties. As a large part of the daily life of the monks was regulated according to time, the monasteries had to provide themselves with the means of measuring time. This was done by means of sun-dials called *Velāchakras*, time-wheels. Since the rule fixing the time for meals could not be violated, monks were expected to take such a dial with them even when they were travelling, whether on land or by sea. Besides, clepsydræ were also installed in the larger monasteries. These were usually gifts from kings together with the boys who watched them. The regulation of the clepsydra was somewhat different in the monasteries of Mahābodhi and Kuśinagara, where it was arranged that the smaller bowl should be immersed in the larger water-vessel sixteen times between morn and midday, while at Nālanda there were to be only four such immersions during the same interval (p. 145).

Monks helped to spiritual life. It was the duty of the monasteries to supply their inmates with all their necessaries of life as prescribed by the Vinaya, so that "one can be much freer, if one lives in the monastery engaged simply in meditation and worship, without needing to take thought about procuring clothes and food" (p. 194). This is the reason why monasteries were permitted to own large properties, while individual monks were denied that right.

Monasteries owning too much wealth. But "it is unseemly", as observed by I-tsing, "for a monastery to have great wealth, granaries full of rotten corn, many servants, male and female, money and treasures hoarded in the treasury, without using any of these things, while all the members are suffering from poverty" (ib.).

Monasteries following unlawful practices. I-tsing also refers to " some monasteries which do not supply food for the residents, but divide everything among them, and make them provide their own food ", and which " do not admit a stranger to reside there " (p. 195).

No doubt such monasteries are to be condemned and avoided as following unlawful practices (ib.).

Problem of cultivating the lands owned by Monasteries. As has been already stated, though the monks individually were not allowed to own property (except a few personal articles of daily use), they could own it collectively. Monasteries thus became owners of large properties by gifts and were able to maintain the monks from their own resources. The usual form of these properties was land. The lands in the possession of the Nālanda monastery gifted by " kings of many generations ", " contained more than 200 villages " (p. 65).

But though the monasteries owned lands, it was not for the monks to cultivate them directly. A monk might sow or plant but could not till, as that involved injuring life. Thus the utilization of its lands had to be arranged by the Saṁgha either with its own staff of servants or with other labourers. Under such arrangements, the Saṁgha could claim only a sixth of the produce, though " providing the bulls and the ground for cultivation ". In the Tāmralipti Monastery, however, as stated to I-tsing by its chief, Mahāyānapradīpa, the share of the produce was one-third. Some monasteries again violated this practice by themselves supervising the farming as carried on by their own servants, male or female, so as to appropriate the whole produce instead of sharing it with others.

As observed by I-tsing, though a monk could not till land for himself, he could do so for the Saṁgha. But the ideal monk " hates the cumbersome work of a farmer and permanently keeps away from it ". Such a one would prefer to sit " still in a place in a quiet forest and takes pleasure in company with birds and deer ; being free from the noisy pursuit of fame and profit, he practises with a view to the perfect quietude of Nirvāṇa " (p. 61). In the Tāmralipta monastery, for instance, the monks did not engage in farming themselves. " Thus they live their just life, avoiding worldly affairs and free from the faults of destroying lives by ploughing and watering fields " (p. 62).

It was allowable for monasteries to supply their monks with clothing from the produce of their lands, though the lands might be earmarked by their donors as gifts for food (p. 193). "Thus the church can make use of the benefaction as it likes, without any fault, as long as it carries out the original intention of the giver" (p. 194).

What Monasteries can lawfully own. I-tsing describes the properties which the monasteries could or could not lawfully possess. The gifts of "quadrupeds, elephants, horses, mules, asses for riding are to be offered to the royal household". So also helmets, coats of arms, etc. But bulls and sheep are lawful property. Gifts of precious stones, gems, etc., are acceptable for meeting the cost of copying the scriptures and of building or decorating the Siṁhāsana. Chairs inlaid with jewels are to be sold and their proceeds utilized by the monasteries (p. 191). The monks, even in I-tsing's time, did not handle gold or silver or any money according to the Vinaya prohibition, because we find it stated that they were provided with extra cloth as means of procuring medicines (p. 56).

Libraries to exclude non-Buddhistic works. Another kind of property held by the monasteries was their libraries. They were stocked only with Buddhist scriptures and their commentaries. If there were gifts of non-Buddhistic works, they were sold and the proceeds utilized by the monasteries for other purposes (p. 192).

Cultural Intercourse between China and India. In conclusion, we may note that, at the time of I-tsing's visit to India, there was noticed no interruption of the movement of Chinese scholars to India as the home of their holy learning and of Indian scholars to China to spread the holy learning. Since the time that Buddhism was introduced into China ("nearly 700 years ago"), "Indian Bhikshus," says I-tsing, "came to China one after another, and the Chinese priests, of the time being, crowded together before them, and received instruction from them. There were some who went to India themselves and witnessed the proper practice there" (p. 23). Among the Chinese scholars sojourning in India in his time, I-tsing mentions the names of three. At Tāmralīpti, I-tsing met a pupil of Hiuen Tsang, Mahāyānapradīpa by name, who stayed there for twelve years and acquired a thorough mastery of Sanskrit. With him as guide and companion I-tsing visited Nālanda, Vaiśālī, and Kuśinagara (p. xxxi). Previous to him was another zealous Chinese student named Hiuen Chao who stayed at Nālanda about A.D. 649 and studied under the teachers Jinaprabha and Ratnasiṁha (lviii). The third Chinese scholar mentioned by I-tsing was Wuhing, the Dhyāna master, with his Sanskrit name Prajñadeva, who, landing in Southern India at Negapatam, had visited the monasteries of Mahābodhi, Nālanda, and Tilaḍha, before I-tsing saw him. " Near Tilaḍha lived a teacher of logic from whom Wu-hing learned the logical systems of Jina and Dharmakīrti, etc. ". (xlvi). I-tsing bade him good-bye after seeing him off " six yojanas east of Nālanda ". Besides Chinese scholars, I-tsing refers to " the Mongolians of the North " sending students to India (p. 26).

CHAPTER XXIV

UNIVERSITIES

I. NĀLANDĀ [1]

Early History. Nālandā was the name of an ancient village which Cunningham [*Ancient Geography of India*, p. 468] identified with modern Baragaon, 7 miles north of Rajgir in Bihar. The earliest mention of the place is that in the Buddhist scriptures which refer to a Nālandā village near Rājagṛiha with a Pāvārika (or Pāva) Mango Park in Buddha's time [*Sum. Vil.*, p. 35; *Maj. Nik.*, vol. i, p. 377; cf. *Dīgha*, i, 221, 212; ii, 81–4]. The Jain texts carry the history earlier than the Buddhist. It was the place where Mahāvīra had met Gosāla and was counted as a *bāhira* or suburb of Rājagṛiha where Mahāvīra had spent as many as fourteen rainy seasons [*Bhagavatī Sūtra*]. A later Jain work, *Sametasikhara Tīrthamālā*, even mentions Burgaon as the then name of Nālandā. According to *Sūtrakṛitāṅga* [*SBE.*, xlv, 420], Nālandā had hundreds of houses and counted a rich citizen, Lepa, possessed of many " slaves, cows, buffaloes, sheep, horses, beds, seats, vehicles, chariots, gold and silver wares ", who offered his hospitality to the Buddha and became his disciple. Next, Tārānāth, in his *History of Buddhism* (of c. A.D. 1500), records the tradition that Nālandā was the birthplace of Śāriputta whose *Chaitya* was seen by Asoka who added a temple to it. And " in this way the first founder of the Nālandā *vihāra* was Asoka " (p. 72). But the place did not become educationally important before the rise of Mahāyāna Buddhism at the beginning of the Christian era. Tārānāth makes Nāgārjuna spend a large part of his life at Nālandā, with which he also associates his pupil, Ārya Deva. As these two Buddhist literary celebrities are generally assigned to the fourth century A.D., we may conclude that the institution had by that time become sufficiently known to have attracted

[1] *References.*—(1) H. D. Sankalia's *University of Nālandā* [Indian Historical Research Institute Series]; (2) Dr. S. C. Vidyābhushaṇa's *Mediaeval School of Indian Logic*, and (3) *History of Indian Logic*; (4) P. Basu's *Indian Teachers of Buddhist Universities*, and (5) *Indian Teachers in China*; and the Source-books: (6) Buniyo Nanjio's *Catalogue of Buddhist Tripiṭaka*, and (7) Dr. P. C. Bagchi's *Le Canon Bouddhique En Chine*.

scholars from the South from which both of them hailed. The importance of the place may be traced to the further interesting fact testified to by Tāranath that a Brahman contemporary of Nāgārjuna, Suvishṇu by name, erected there as many as 108 temples for the conservation of the Abhidharma of the Mahāyāna. It is also said [cf. *JASB.*, vol. i, N.S., p. 227] that the celebrated Buddhist Logician, Diṅnāga, came on invitation to Nālandā where he defeated in argument the Brahman Sudurjaya and other Tīrtha dialecticians. Since Diṅnāga was a disciple of Vasubandhu, he must have lived about A.D. 400. This story shows that Nālandā even in the fifth century was still the seat of Brahmanical learning and the chosen home of the Tīrthikas. This fact may explain why it has not received any notice in the hands of Fa-Hien in whose evidence we come, however, upon solid historical ground.

Nālandā as known to Fa-Hien. Nālandā, when Fa-Hien visited it, was called Nāla and was known as the place " where Śāriputta was born, and to which also he returned, and attained here his *pari-nirvāṇa*. Over the spot (where his body was burned) there was built a tope " which Fa-Hien found " still in existence " (p. 81, Legge's ed.). This is all that Fa-Hien could record about the condition of the institution in the fourth century which within the next three centuries grew up to be the greatest centre of Buddhist learning, as observed and described by Hiuen Tsang who stayed there for the total period of about five years. There is, however, a view that Fa-Hien did not at all visit Nālandā, and that the village, Nāla, which he had visited as the birth-place of Sāriputta, is called Nālaka or Nalagrāma in the Sudarśana Jātaka.

Account of Hiuen Tsang : Its Name. Hiuen Tsang mentions two traditions regarding the origin of the name of Nālandā given to the monastery. It was called after a dragon living in a tank in a Mango Park existing to the south of the monastery. This tradition is rejected by Hiuen Tsang but accepted by I-tsing (Watters, ii, 166). Hiuen Tsang prefers the Jātaka story referring the name to the epithet " Insatiable in giving " (*na-alam-dā*), which was won by the Buddha for his liberality in a former birth as king of this country.

Its Original Endowment. He further informs us regarding the *origin* of the monastery that its grounds were the gift to the Buddha by 500 merchants who bought them up for the purpose for as many as " ten koṭi of gold coins " (ib., 164).

Later Endowments : Construction of six storied Monasteries. This original endowment was the precursor of a continuous series of endowments through the centuries by a succession of sovereigns. The endowments took the form of buildings as well as lands from which came the wherewithal for the maintenance of the University. Hiuen Tsang thus mentions six monasteries as having been built by as many kings and these constituted the Nālandā establishment in his time. These six kings[1] were Śakrāditya, his son and successor Buddhagupta, Tathāgatagupta, Bālāditya, his son and successor Vajra, and an unnamed king of Mid-India. The King of Mid-India may be taken to be Harsha. He built a *vihāra* of brass at Nālandā [*Life*, p. 159], a high wall round the buildings, and a *saṁghārāma*, besides making provision for feeding forty monks daily [Watters' *Yuan Chwang*, i, 216, 218 ; ii, 170]. He was free for all this benefaction after disposing of that great enemy of himself and Buddhism, Śaśāṅka, King of Gauḍa [as suggested by H. Heras in *JBORS.*, xiv, 15]. At the formal opening of the monastery built by Bālāditya, " Brethren from all quarters were present by invitation of the king " (ib.). Of these six monasteries, the oldest, the Śakrāditya monastery, was probably not in a fit condition to be used as residence for monks at the time of Hiuen Tsang's visit, because he refers to the custom of forty Brethren being daily sent from another monastery to take their food there so as to keep up the memory of the establishment and of its generous founder. The University area was marked off by a lofty enclosing wall being built with one gate.[2] The gate opened into the great college, from which were separated eight other halls, standing in the middle of the Saṁghārāma [*Life*, p. 111]. The buildings, all storied ones, were majestic in their size and height, with richly adorned towers,

[1] It is difficult to establish the historicity or chronology of these six kings. Śakrāditya may be taken to be Kumāragupta I (A.D. 414–454) on the ground that Kumāragupta assumed the title of Mahendrāditya and Mahendra is the name of Śakra or Indra. Buddhagupta is the Gupta Emperor Budhagupta (*c.* A.D. 475–500). Bālāditya perhaps corresponds to Narasiṁhagupta Bālāditya of imperial Gupta dynasty or the last Gupta emperor of that name who had fought the Hūṇas about A.D. 525. He may also be identified with " Parameśvara " Bālādityadeva, King of Magadha, of Gupta Inscription No. 46 of Fleet. The other two names, Tathāgatagupta, and Vajra, are not identified. There is also a view that Buddhagupta = Skandagupta ; Tathāgatagupta = Puragupta (who showed his faith in Buddhism by placing the Crown Prince under Vasubandhu as tutor when he was known as King *Vikramāditya* and took the title of " *Śrī Vikramaḥ* " on his coins) ; and Vajra = Kumāragupta II.

[2] Dr. Spooner rejects this particular interpretation of the original passage which, in his view, does not refer to " the main enclosing wall of the entire precinct but rather the wall of the Tārā temple on the north " [*A.S. Report*, 1916–17, Eastern Circle, p. 45].

fairy-like turrets appearing like pointed hill-tops, and observatories lost in the mists of the morning. Even the upper rooms towered above the clouds, and from their windows one could see the winds and clouds producing ever new forms, and from the soaring eaves the sunset splendours and the moonlit glories. This observation of Hiuen Tsang is corroborated by the Nālandā Stone Inscription of Yaśovarman of the eighth century A.D., stating how the row of monasteries (*vihārāvalī*) had their series of summits (*śikhara-śreṇī*) licking (*avalehi*) the clouds (*ambudhara*). Down below, the grounds were variegated by deep, translucent ponds bearing on their bosom the blue lotus intermingled with Kanaka flower of deep red colour, while at intervals the Āmra groves spread over all their shade. The massive external grandeur of the buildings contrasted with the delicate artistic beauty of their interior. "All the outside courts, in which are the priests' chambers, are of four stages. The stages have dragon-projections, and coloured eaves, pearl-red pillars, carved and ornamented, richly adorned balustrades, while the roofs are covered with tiles that reflect the light in a thousand shades. These things add to the beauty of the scene. The Saṁghārāmas of India are counted by myriads, but this is the most remarkable for grandeur and height" (ib.). Hiuen Tsang also remarks: "In this establishment, the work of a succession of sovereigns, the sculpture was perfect and really beautiful" [Watters, ii, 165]. He also saw an image of Buddha in the Śakrāditya monastery [ib.]. I-tsing saw eight halls and 300 apartments in the whole monastery (p. 154).

Their remains as unearthed. It may be noted that the truth of these remarks regarding the artistic wealth of the Nālandā buildings is being amply borne out by the archæological explorations carried out at their site. Cunningham declared that the sculptures found here were the finest in all India. Of the entire monastic complex, up to now have been unearthed (1) one monastery to the south, (2) the north-west corner of another, the northern monastery, (3) the remains of a temple building farther to the north-east, and (4) another monastery to the west of (1).

As regards (1), the most southerly of the big monastic complexes, the main dimensions have been traced out. The north wall has a length of 203 ft. and a thickness of 6 ft. 6 in., while the side walls measure 168 ft. in length and 7 ft. 6 in. in thickness. The walls are "composed of most superior bricks,

PLATE XXIII

NĀLANDA.

No. 1.—Bird's-eye view of Monasteries, showing cells with verandah, courtyard, well, and shrine.

[*Facing p. 560*

of a light yellowish tint, and admirable texture, fitted together so perfectly that in some places the joints between the bricks are altogether inconspicuous. As brickwork, the construction is remarkable, far superior to any modern work that I have seen in recent years" [D. B. Spooner in A.S. Report, 1915–16, Eastern Circle, p. 35]. The rectangle formed by the main walls was lined with cells measuring severally 9 ft. 6 in., 10 ft. 11 in., and 12 ft. Some of these were single-seated and some double-seated with one or two benches of stone provided for sleeping. Each room also shows a niche to hold a lamp and another to hold books. Ovens of large sizes have also been unearthed, showing the common kitchen and messing of the monks in the monastery.

It has been found that this monastery had been repeatedly built over through successive ages and that at least five distinct monasteries have stood at different periods upon this spot. The lowest and oldest structure has yielded numerous antiquities comprising large sculptures and statuettes in stone and metal, attesting the high quality of the art. The finds at this site include multiple examples of the official seal of the Nālandā establishment, of the Śrī-Nālandā-Mahāvihara-Ārya-Bhikshu-Saṁghasya or "Venerable Community of Monks in the Great Vīhāra of Śrī-Nālandā". The Nālandā official seal curiously shows the same insignia as that of the monastery at Sārnāth, viz. the Wheel of Dharma flanked by two gazelles.

No. (3) shows its plinth covered with an extensive series of sculptured plaques in stone comprising as many as 211 sculptured panels, all different; and thus important for the history of design in Ancient India.

No. (2) shows a two-storeyed structure of which the few cells cleared yielded "one of the most perfect seated Buddhas", "quite a little gem" (ib.).

No. (4) shows repeated occupation by successive structures being constructed not one above another but rather as outer integuments enveloping the older monument. At least three such successive envelopes are traceable with valuable stucco decoration on their innermost core. Among the finds of the site may be mentioned one colossal black-stone Bodhisattva still *in situ*, and a large and "very fine" figure of Avalokiteśvara.

Further Benefactions. But besides gifts of buildings the University received gifts of lands. In Hiuen Tsang's time, "the king of the country remitted the revenues of about 100 villages for the endowment of the convent" (*Life*, p. 112). In I-tsing's time, " the lands in its possession bestowed upon the monastery by kings of many generations contained more than 200 villages " (p. 65). From these villages came to the monastery a daily supply of a large quantity of rice, weighing several hundred piculs (1 picul = 133⅓ lb.), and also of butter and milk, weighing several hundred catties (1 catty = 160 lb.) (*Life*, ib.). These provisions were contributed day by day by 200 householders in these villages (ib.).

We may note here the history of royal benefactions which built up Nālandā and endowed its work for several centuries. After Harsha, Hiuen Tsang mentions King Pūrṇavarmā who " presented to Nālandā a figure of Buddha standing upright, and made of copper, 80 ft. high ", to cover which he also had a pavilion erected of six stages [Watters, ii, 174]. This Pūrṇavarmā might have been a Maukhari (as suggested by H. Heras in *JBORS*., xiv, p. 18). Again, one of the Seals found at Nālandā mentions a king named Sureśvaravarman and gives his genealogy [*Arch. S. Annual Report*, for 1917–18]. Further, an Inscription states that Mālāda, a minister of King Yaśovarmmadeva, made various gifts to the monks of Nālandā, provided for their daily food, and paid money which could buy up the whole Vihāra [*Epi. Ind.*, xx, 37]. Dr. Hirananda Sastri thinks this Yaśovarmmadeva is Yaśodharma of Mandasor Inscription and King of Malwa [*Modern Review*, September, p. 307 ; *Ep. Ind.*, ib., p. 41]. But it is more likely that he was King Yaśovarmmadeva of Kanouj (*c.* A.D. 728–745).

Next followed the benefactions of the Pāla kings of Bengal. The name Dharmapāladeva occurs on a copper plate found at Nālandā bearing a defaced inscription [*Arch. S. R.*, 1926–7]. A number of metallic figures refers to King Devapāla [ib.]. Then there are two Inscriptions, one of which, as related below, refers to the construction at Nālandā of a Vihāra by Bālaputradeva, King of Suvarṇadvīpa (Sumātra), and the grant by King Devapāladeva of Bengal of five villages for the maintenance of this monastery at his request conveyed to the Pāla king by his ambassador named Balavarmman [*Ep. Ind.*, xvii, 310–327]. The other Inscription, called the Ghosrawa Inscription, relates how Devapāla favoured a Nālandā scholar named Vīradeva who was afterwards elected by the Assembly of Monks as the Head of the Vihāra [*Ind. Ant.*, xvii, 311]. Again, a figure of Goddess Vāgīśvarī bears an inscription which mentions King Gopāla II [*JASB., NS.*, iv, 105]. A Nālandā scholar named

PLATE XXIV

NĀLĀNDA.

No. 2.—A Stone Temple showing decorative stone plinth.

[Facing p. 562

Kalyāṇamitra Chintāmani copied the valuable work *Ashṭasāhasrikā Prajñāpāramitā* in the sixth year of the reign of King Mahīpāla, son of Vigrahapāla, as a token of respect for the King. The same work was also copied in the reigns of Rāmapāla and Govindapāladeva who is not identified. Lastly, a votive Stūpa unearthed at Nālandā refers to the Gurjara-Pratihāra King Māhendrapāladeva who had conquered Magadha about the tenth century A.D. [*Arch. S. R.*, 1924–5, p. 86].

Free Education. Out of the income of these estates the University provided for all its alumni free of cost their four requisites of clothes, food, bedding, and medicine. The number of the alumni in Hiuen Tsang's time "always" reached the figure of 10,000, counting "the priests belonging to the convent or strangers residing therein" (*Life*, ib.). The standard of living seems to have varied with the standing of the monks. Hiuen Tsang during his residence at Nālandā received each day 120 Jambiras (a fruit), twenty areca nuts, twenty nutmegs, an ounce of camphor, and a peck of the finest variety of rice called Mahāśāli rice which grew only in Magadha and nowhere else and was offered only to the king or to religious persons of great distinction. It was "as large as the black bean", and, "when cooked, was aromatic and shining, like no other rice at all". Besides the supply of these provisions, "every month he was presented with three measures of oil, and, daily, a supply of butter and other things according to his need" (ib., p. 109). In I-tsing's time, the number of students supported at the monastery exceeded 3,000 (p. 65).

Concentration on Study. The students "being so abundantly supplied", and having not had to worry about their material needs of life, "the four requisites," they could give themselves wholeheartedly to their studies and self-culture. "This is the source of the perfection of their studies to which they have arrived" (*Life*, p. 113). We have already noticed I-tsing's appreciation of this remarkable and necessary provision in Ancient Indian education.

Admission. The conditions of admission to Nālandā show that it was run as an institution of higher learning or post-graduate studies. The institution was noted for its specialization in the last stages of a University education, for aiding in the solution of doubts, and training in the arts of disputation and public speaking. "Hence," says Hiuen Tsang (Watters, ii, 165), "foreign students came to the establishment to put an end to their doubts and then became celebrated." Some of these, according to I-tsing [ed. Takakusu, p. 26], came even from Mongolia. From the *Life* of Hiuen Tsang [pp. xxvii–xxxvi], we learn that several foreign scholars from distant countries like China, Korea, Tibet, and Tokhara came to India for study at Nālandā, and securing valuable MSS. of Buddhism, during the short interval of forty years between the visits of Hiuen Tsang and I-tsing. They also came to achieve fame as scholars. I-tsing, like Hiuen Tsang, also testifies to this fact : "There eminent and accomplished men assemble in crowds, discuss possible and impossible doctrines, and after having been assured of the excellence of their opinions by wise men, become far famed for their wisdom" (p. 177). Thus Nālandā was practically a Research Institute for advanced students and was the highest court of judges of intellectual worth. The stamp of its approval was necessary for any opinion to gain currency in the country. The highest academic degree or distinction of the times was a Fellowship of Nālandā. As noted by Hiuen Tsang, "those who stole the name of Nālandā brother were all treated with respect wherever they went" (Watters, ib.). No wonder that this highly coveted and valued degree was liable to be "*stolen*". Hence it was by no means an easy matter to obtain admission to Nālandā. The entrance examination of Nālandā was very strict, so that its standard might be in keeping with that of its studies. The percentage of failures at the Matriculation Examination was necessarily very large. According to Hiuen Tsang, only about 20 per cent could succeed in obtaining admission to the University by passing its entrance test, and yet the University was never in want of students whose strength was 10,000 at that time! The doors of the University, comprising mainly "schools of discussion", were jealously guarded by the specialists in discussion, expert religious controversialists, who were always ready with difficult problems to try the competence of the claimants for admission. "Of those from abroad who wished to enter the Schools of Discussion, the majority, beaten by the difficulties of the problems, withdrew ; and those who were deeply versed in old and modern learning were admitted, only two or three out of ten succeeding" [Watters, ii, 165].

Considering the character of the Entrance Examination, the age of the students at admission must have been very high. It was as high as 20, considering their previous studies. According to I-tsing, a student at 15 had to study *Vṛitti-sūtra* which he finished at 20, after which he studied Philosophy for two or three years at advanced institutions like Nālandā or Valabhī [Takakusu, ed. I-tsing, pp. 175, 177, 181]. At the same time, it must be noted that this high age of admission applied only to the post-graduate section of Nālandā, and for advanced and external students. Nālandā also had its Department of Secondary Education for regular internal students for whom the above tests of admission did not apply. It admitted youngsters, the Brahmachārīs and Māṇavakas, freely, as already stated.

Standard of Scholarship. When the Entrance Examination was such a hard, and thoroughly sifting, process, the quality of the material to be handled and fashioned by the University was assured. The academic life was lived there at a very high level, both on its intellectual and moral side. The students of Nālandā "were looked up to as models by all India", as observed by Hiuen Tsang (ib.). They were all ideal Buddhists "in the strictness with which they observed the precepts and regulations of their Order" (ib.). According to the *Life* (p. 112) "the priests dwelling here are, as a body, naturally or spontaneously dignified and grave, so that during the 700 years since the foundation of the establishment, there has been no single case of guilty rebellion against the rules". Their intellectual life corresponded to an equally strict standard and attained an equally high level of efficiency and success. A picture of that life is thus drawn by Hiuen Tsang: "In the establishment were some thousands of Brethren, all men of great ability and learning, several hundreds being highly esteemed and famous; learning and discussing they found the day too short; day and night they admonished each other, juniors and seniors mutually helping to perfection." The average standard of intellectual equipment and learning of the Nālandā students is thus indicated by our pilgrim: "If among them were any who did not talk of the mysteries of the Tripiṭaka, such persons, being ashamed, lived aloof" (ib.).

1,500 Teachers in Charge of 8,500 Students. Out of the total number of 10,000 resident monks at Nālandā, as many as 1,510 belonged to the ranks of teachers. Of these, "there are 1,000 men who can explain twenty collections of Sūtras and Śāstras; 500 who can explain thirty collections and perhaps 10 (including Hiuen Tsang) who can explain fifty collections." Over them all, and over the entire establishment, presided Śīlabhadra, unique in learning and character. He "alone has studied and understood the whole number (of the collections of the Sūtras and Śāstras). His eminent virtue and advanced age have caused him to be regarded as the chief member of the community" (*Life*, p. 112).

One hundred Lectures per day. As many as one hundred chairs or pulpits were arranged every day for the lectures or discourses by so many teachers living there, "and the students attend these discourses without any fail, even for a minute" (ib.). This means that a hundred different subjects were daily taught to as many different classes of students, and that work was going on at the colleges at all hours, except those prescribed for sleep.

Range of Studies, both Brahmanical and Buddhist. Accordingly, the courses of study offered by the Nālandā University covered a wide range, almost the entire circle of knowledge then available. They were drawn from the different fields of learning, Brahmanical and Buddhist, sacred and secular, philosophical and practical, sciences and arts. The students at Nālandā, as stated in the *Life* (ib.), "all study the Great Vehicle, and also the works belonging to the eighteen sects, and not only so, but even ordinary works, such as the Vedas and other books, the Hetuvidyā, Śabdavidyā, the Chikitsāvidyā, the works on Magic or Atharvaveda, the Sāṁkhya; besides these, they thoroughly investigate the 'miscellaneous' works" (ib.). Hiuen Tsang himself became a student of Nālandā for the study of the Yoga-śāstra, in which the Nālandā Chancellor, Śīlabhadra, was the highest living authority (ib., p. 107). His study of the Yoga-śāstra was followed by his study of other subjects like Nyāya, Hetuvidyā, Śabdavidyā, and the like, as also of the books of the Brahmans with the wide area of knowledge covered by them including philological, legal, philosophical, astronomical subjects, and the Sanskrit Grammar of Pāṇini (*Life*, p. 121). "Thus he penetrated, and examined completely, all the collections of Buddhist books and also studied the sacred books of the Brahmans during *five* years"[1] (ib., p. 125). Thus Nālandā was the centre of all higher learning in all its branches. And so while it attracted a keen student of Mahāyāna like Hiuen Tsang who, though already a "Master of the Law", and honoured as such in India, yet found it profitable to stay there for some time for further intellectual progress, it equally attracted keen students of Hīnayāna like I-tsing who took advantage of its education for fully a decade. Verily,

[1] This is probably the source of the statement of Legge (*Fa-Hien*, p. 81 n.), that Hiuen Tsang lived at Nālandā for five years!

Nālandā had the merit of collecting at one centre the available authorities on every subject of learning.

Famous Teachers mentioned by Hiuen Tsang. Thus the fame of Nālandā as a centre of learning was principally due to the fame of its teachers among whom Hiuen Tsang mentions (with his penetrating characterizations) " Dharmapāla (the predecessor of Śīlabhadra as Chancellor of the Nālandā University) and Chandrapāla, who gave a fragrance to Buddha's teachings, Guṇamati and Sthiramati of excellent reputation among contemporaries, Prabhāmitra of clear argument, and Jinamitra of elevated conversation, Jñānachandra of model character and perspicacious intellect, and Śīlabhadra, whose perfect excellence was buried in obscurity ".

It may also be noted that Hiuen Tsang himself soon counted as one of the best products of Nālandā by his mastery of Mahāyāna Buddhism. For instance, when the emperor Harsha, while touring through Orissa, found there the dominance of Hīnayāna, whose priests ridiculed him for his misplaced gifts to Nālandā, he at once answered them by sending for four accomplished teachers of Mahāyāna from Nālandā. The four teachers selected for this deputation to Orissa included Hiuen Tsang himself, besides three others named Sāgaramati, Prajñāraśmi, and Siṁharaśmi [*Life*, p. 160]. Assam also was another kingdom which asked for Hiuen Tsang's spiritual ministration. Its king, Kumāra (Bhāskaravarman) sent for him with a letter carried by a special messenger to Śīlabhadra, the Abbot of Nālandā, whose delay in sending him caused the dispatch by the king of two more messengers and a threat of a military invasion of Nālandā and its destruction ! [ib., pp. 170, 171, 187]. The King of Assam was in his turn given a similar rebuff by his more powerful chief, Harsha, asking him to send back the Chinese Pilgrim, then his guest, on pain of " losing his head ". Thus Hiuen Tsang was very much in request for his learning which he had acquired as a student of Nālandā University.

It is interesting to note that the late Dr. D. B. Spooner actually discovered a seal of Bhāskaravarman at Nālandā, probably the very seal accompanying his letter of demand to Śīlabhadra for Hiuen Tsang's deputation to his kingdom of Kāmarūpa, as guessed by K. N. Dikshit [*JBORS.*, 1920, p. 131].

Ranking of Monks. It has been already seen that the resident monks, according to Hiuen Tsang's account, took precedence on the basis of their extensive rather than intensive knowledge.

Their rank depended upon the range of their studies rather than upon the depth of their knowledge of a particular subject. It was on this basis that Śīlabhadra was elected to the Chancellor's position in the University. The different grades of the monks carried with them different privileges. The University was duly jealous and mindful of the dignity that should belong to the position of its official head. Access to the Chancellor was not made cheap or easy. Interviews with him were of the nature of formal and ceremonial functions. This is shown by the account given of Hiuen Tsang's reception at Nālandā and of his presentation before the Chancellor. As his reputation as a scholar had already preceded him, the University sent a deputation of four of its most distinguished Professors to escort him. At a farm-house on the way, he halted for short refreshment where a great crowd gathered to greet him, consisting of 200 priests and some thousand lay patrons. They formed an imposing procession, carrying standards, umbrellas, flowers, and perfumes, and thus led the pilgrim to the gates of Nālandā. Then a formal meeting was held with the Sthavira in the chair by which a special seat was given to the distinguished visitor. Next, the Karmadāna was directed to sound the Ghaṇṭā and proclaim: "Whilst the Master of the Law (Hiuen Tsang) dwells in the Convent, all the commodities used by the priests and all the appliances of religion are for his convenience, in common with the rest." The meeting then selected twenty persons, noted for their learning and dignified bearing, to conduct Hiuen Tsang to the august presence of the Chancellor. When the party arrived, the chief almoner presented the Chancellor "with all things necessary without stint, paying his respects according to the proper ceremonial, approaching him on his knees and kissing his foot, and bowing his head to the ground. The usual greetings and compliments being finished, the Chancellor ordered seats to be brought and spread out, and desired Hiuen Tsang and the rest to be seated. When seated, he asked the visitor from what part he came. In reply he said: 'I am come from the country of China, desiring to learn from your instruction the principles of the Yoga Śāstra'" (*Life*, p. 107). After this formal introduction, Hiuen Tsang was assigned to the Bālāditya College with his residence fixed for a week at the house of the learned and aged scholar, Buddhabhadra, and, later, in an independent dwelling in accordance with his learning and status, together with an ample supply of provisions already described.

PLATE XXV

NALÂNDA.

No. 3.—A Monastery showing cells with verandah, courtyard, furnace, and well.

[*Facing p. 569*

Special Provision for Hiuen Tsang. Among the privileges pertaining to the status attained by Hiuen Tsang are mentioned the supply of menial servants and of a riding elephant (ib., p. 110). Two attendants were allowed to Hiuen Tsang, one of whom was a Māṇava and another a Brahmachārī. I-tsing saw the "venerable and learned priests at Nālandā ride in sedan-chairs but never on horse-back, while their necessary baggage is carried by other persons or taken by boys" (probably the Māṇavas and Brahmachārīs) (p. 30). The menial staff of the monastery included "porters" (p. 145).

Academic Titles. The ranking of monks led to the institution of titles indicative of the different degrees of status, standing, and grade to which they belonged. The highest title was *Kulapati* for the head of an institution numbering 10,000 students, as stated in a Smṛiti Text: "*Munīnāṁ daśasāhasraṁ* yonnadānena poshaṇāt | adhyāpayati viprarshiḥ asau kulapatiḥ smṛitaḥ." The next title of distinction was *Paṇḍita*. At the University of Vikramaśilā (*c*. A.D. 800), it indicated a degree conferred on a successful graduate. But at Nālandā it was reserved only for the Head of the whole Vihāra [Tārānāth, p. 161; Vidyābhūshaṇa, *Medieval Indian Logic*, p. 79].

Distribution of Rooms. Besides these privileges, the rooms of the monks were distributed according to their rank. Before the Varshā season or the rains set in, "rooms are assigned to each member; to the Sthaviras better rooms are given and thus gradually to the lowest. In Nālandā such rules are practised at present" (p. 86).

This annual assignment of rooms was made at Nālandā not by any individual authority or official, but by "the great assembly of priests". This democratic method had a double advantage, as pointed out by I-tsing: "for it removes one's selfish intention, and the rooms for priests are properly protected" (ib.).

Time-table. The daily duties of the monks at Nālandā were regulated strictly according to time, which was measured by means of the clepsydra. The day was one of eight hours, each of which was indicated by four immersions of the smaller bowl in the larger vessel of water. Each such immersion was indicated by one stroke of a drum, while the completion of one hour as defined above was announced by four strokes of a drum, two blasts of a conch-shell, and an additional beat of the drum.

The second hour ends at noon when eating is not allowed. The afternoon, like the forenoon, comprises two hours. The expiry of the first hour at night is announced by beat of the drum by the sub-director or Karmadāna himself. Sunrise and sunset are announced by beat of drum at the outside of the gate of the monastery by "the servants and porters" stationed there (p. 145).

Bath. Just as there was a time for meals, there was also one for baths. We have already seen the mention in Hiuen Tsang's account of the ponds existing in the grounds of Nālandā. The same observation occurs in the account of I-tsing, who thus describes a bathing scene there: "There are more than ten great pools near the Nālandā monastery and there every morning a ghaṇṭī (gong) is sounded to remind the priests of the bathing hour. Everyone brings a bathing sheet with him. Sometimes a hundred, sometimes a thousand priests leave the monastery together and proceed in all directions towards these pools, where all of them take a bath." The Vinaya rules were followed on the subject. There were also arrangements for baths in the monastery, if one did not like to go to the pond [p. 109].

Democratic Management. According to I-tsing, the rules and regulations governing life in the monasteries were more strict at Nālandā than elsewhere (p. 65). We have already given I-tsing's account of them. We may only here repeat that, in spite of its size and numbers, the affairs of the University, from the annual assignment of rooms to the trial and punishment of offences against the fraternity and expulsion of recalcitrants, were administered on democratic principles by the entire body of the students. The recognition of the principle that the cause of discipline among students is best promoted by boldly leaving it in their hands is in accordance with up-to-date pedagogic ideals, while as regards the other important matter of the assignment of rooms according to seniority, the same method, as observed by I-tsing, was the most efficacious in the prevention of heart-burnings and petty-mindedness, and it was so graceful for seniors to place themselves in the hands of the juniors as regards the details of their physical life and comforts. Thus the harmony of the establishment was secured by the due combination of the principles of autocracy and democracy in its management, the former principle applying only to the spheres of the intellectual and moral training of the alumni where guidance and direction were indispensable. The harmony of relations among the vast numbers of the teachers and the taught at Nālandā became an established tradition marking the entire course of its history, so that Hiuen Tsang could observe that during seven centuries there was not on record a single instance of that harmony being marred by a guilty rebellion.

Harmony of Life in the midst of utmost diversity of Studies and Beliefs. That harmony will be regarded as a still more surprising achievement when it is considered how it was established in the midst of wide and acute differences among the monks in their opinions and beliefs. The monks at Nālandā were not a homogeneous community. They were drawn from the different denominations of the Buddhist Church and carried into the University all the strife and discord of its different sects and schisms. But what still further added to the heterogeneous composition of the University was its admission of students of even non-Buddhistic systems of learning and courses of study. Indeed, Nālandā flung its gates wide open to all systems and schools of thought and belief in the country and became the arena where they might fight out their supremacy in debates and discussions. As we have already seen, Nālandā was known both in India and abroad for its " schools of discussion " which foreign students were so anxious to enter, that they might return with the best credentials for their capacity as preachers. It is difficult to say on the basis of our available evidence how far Nālandā offered any regular courses of instruction for beginners. We are told that students there, learning and discussing, found the day too short, while every student was expected to be well up in the mysteries of the Tripiṭaka as the minimum qualification. Thus it is that Nālandā had the signal merit of bringing together Schools, whose " tenets would keep them isolated ", at an age when " controversy runs high, and heresies on special doctrines lead many ways to the same end ", as observed by Hiuen Tsang [Watters, i, 162]. Nālandā became the common meeting-ground, in the India of the times, of the warring sects and creeds, with their " possible and impossible doctrines " [I-tsing, p. 177], and an opinion approved and recognized there would at once obtain a universal currency. The victors in these All-India Tournaments of Debate at Nālandā would be victorious over every opposition. But while its intellectual life was thus a round of animated controversies and acrimonious debates between contradictory and incompatible opinions and beliefs, that did not mar the academic repose and peace of Nālandā as a seat of culture. She faced boldly the intellectual differences of the times, the profound and earnest disagreements in opinions and cherished beliefs, in the very fundamentals of life, and presented a larger ideal which would evolve a common life and concord out of the divisions. That ideal was Freedom, Freedom of Thought, Opinion, and Belief, Toleration that would not constrain conscience, the first principle of a sound and scientific education. A writer in the *Hibbert Journal* [vol. xiii, p. 165] characterizes the Nālandā education as " an experiment in liberty of teaching ". That ideal was nothing new to Buddhism. It was derived from Brahmanism with its remarkable absence of any official creed and its readiness to accommodate within its pale a wide variety of deities and beliefs. Buddhism thus imbibed " the flexibility which marked the methods of the older faith ". The founder of Buddhism was well known for his consideration towards followers of other creeds whom he did not like to convert in haste, while this large and catholic ideal utters itself in no uncertain and feeble tones in some of the edicts of Asoka who stood for " the growth of the essence of the matter in all sects ". The ideal of Liberty leads to that of social service. The inspiration of this ideal is responsible for the administration of the University on a democratic basis as far as possible. Under this inspiration the Saṁgha counts more than the individual monks, the whole is always greater than the part. Thus sectarian differences are merged in a common life and service, in the service to a common ideal. Nālandā stood for this larger synthesis to be realized in and through life, in which the theoretical and conventional differences were reconciled. But the position is best explained in the eloquent words of the writer in the *Hibbert Journal* above referred to : " The secret of union lies in a common life, a common moral ideal, the conception of the service of man as realized in the person of Gotama, who, in the oft-repeated formula of the early texts, chose the homeless life for the welfare of gods and men, that he might become a Buddha, and lift off from the world the veils of ignorance and sin. That was the secret of the extraordinary missionary enthusiasm which carried the noble and the sage amid incredible hardships all through Middle Asia in the centuries preceding Hiuen Tsang, 'moved by the desire to convert the world'; for as the Chronicler of Ceylon remarks in relating the triumphs of an earlier date, 'when the world's welfare is concerned, who would be slothful or indifferent?' To this principle Buddhism has been always faithful. It has never made theological tests the basis of religious communion. Wide as have been its internal variations, it has always asked the disciple, 'Have you the right disposition?' rather than, 'Have you the true belief?' Neither among its different Schools, nor towards the rival establishments of Brahmans and Jains, or the philosophical sects that lay outside all three, the Agnostics and Materialists, did it ever raise the cry that the faith was in danger or kindle the fires of persecution. Such was Buddhist teaching in India in the seventh century A.D." The same writer refers to another confirmatory picture in the well-known contemporary record, Bāṇa's *Harsha-charita*, of similar educational conditions of Liberty and Toleration obtaining at a centre of learning of a different, though common, type. That was the hermitage of a Buddhist recluse in the forest of the Vindhya, Divākaramitra by name, who was a Brahman by birth and education. The reputation of his learning drew to his out-of-the-way and remote retreat crowds of students of all possible Schools of thought and belief: there were Buddhists of different varieties, "perched on pillars, dwelling in bowers of creepers, lying in thickets or in the shadow of branches, or squatting on the roots of trees"; there were Jains in white robes and worshippers of Krishṇa; there were ascetics of various orders, Sāṁkhists, Lokāyatikas, Vedāntins, followers of Nyāya and Vaiśeshika, of the Institutes of Law and of the Purāṇas, adepts in sacrifices and even Grammarians and others beside, "all diligently following their own tenets, pondering, urging objections, raising doubts and resolving them, discussing and explaining moot points of doctrine, in perfect harmony." The harmony is depicted as extending to the brute creation. True to the promises of the Yoga doctrines, the *Ahiṁsā* of the sage pervades the entire environment. We read of lions lying like lambs near the sage's seat, nay, of tigers turning vegetarians under his Buddhist teaching! "Doubtless this is in large part a satire; but the satire would have been unmeaning, had there been no basis for it in fact. These forest instructions were really many centuries old. Here was a University of another type, more flexible still, because unembarrassed by establishments needing great revenues for maintenance." "Some day, perhaps," continues the writer, "the great Universities of the West may deem these voices of the dim and distant past yet worth attention. They are more than mere curiosities of literature. They are the witness of the East to the abiding principle that the first condition of the quest for Truth is Liberty."

Library. We have already seen that I-tsing stayed for his studies at Nālandā for the long period of ten years (A.D. 675–685), during which he collected there some 400 Sanskrit texts amounting to 500,000 slokas (p. xvii). This shows that Nālandā possessed a well-equipped library. Information on the Nālandā University Library is given in the Tibetan accounts, from which we know that the Library, situated in a special area known by the poetical name of Dharmagañja (Mart of Religion), comprised three huge buildings, called Ratnasāgara, Ratnodadhi, and Ratnarañjaka, of which Ratnasāgara, which was a nine-storeyed building, specialized in the collection of rare sacred works like *Prajñapāramitā-sūtra* and Tāṅtrika books like *Samājaguhya* and the like. " After the Turushka raiders had made incursions in Nālandā, the temples and chaityas there were repaired by a sage named Mudita Bhadra. Soon after this, Kukuṭasiddha, Minister of the King of Magadha, erected a temple at Nālandā, and while a religious sermon was being delivered there, two very indigent Tīrthika mendicants appeared. Some naughty young novice-monks in disdain threw washing-water on them. This made them very angry. After propitiating the sun for twelve years, they performed a yajña, fire-sacrifice, and threw living embers and ashes from the sacrificial pit into the Buddhist temples, etc. This produced a great conflagration which consumed Ratnodadhi" [Dr. S. C. Vidyābhushaṇa's *Mediaeval School of Indian Logic*, p. 146].

History after I-tsing. Tibetan sources give some further interesting evidence on the history of Nālandā after I-tsing. It appears that the Tibetan king, Srong-tsan-Gampo (acc. A.D. 630), anxious to introduce to his country Indian writing and learning, sent to India his minister, Thon-mi, with a large quantity of gold to be given away as presents to the Indian scholars.

Thon-mi first approached the famous Brahman Sanskritist, Lipidatta by name, and, having learnt Sanskrit and the scripts under him, repaired to the Nālandā University, and there placed himself under the tuition of the teacher named Āchārya Devavid Siṁha, who imparted to him instruction in both Brahmanic and Buddhist sacred literature. It is said that Hiuen Tsang came to Nālandā just at the time when the Tibetan student was staying there. The next notice of Nālandā that we get is in connexion with the Tibetan King Thi-srong-den-stan (A.D. 743–789), who invited to Tibet the two Indian sages Padma Sambhava, a native of Udyāna, and Śānta Rakshita, a native of Gaur, who was then the Chancellor of the Nālandā University. In Tibet the two Indian scholars became involved in a religious controversy with a great Chinese scholar and, being unable to defeat him, induced the king to send for the famous Professor of Tantras at Nālandā named Kamalaśīla in A.D. 750. Kamalaśīla, in the presence of the assembled court, vanquished his opponent who was then asked by the king to leave Tibet.

That the fame of Nālandā continued unabated and even travelled beyond the borders of India is evident from the Inscription of Yaśovarman of the eighth century A.D., already cited, extolling the learning of its scholars and also from another Inscription recording how a king of Java and Sumatra, Bālaputradeva by name, had a monastery built at Nālandā, and also induced his friend, King Devapāla of Bengal, to make a grant of five villages towards the maintenance of this new monastery and expenses of adding to its Library MSS. copied for the purpose [*Epi. Ind.*, xvii, 310].

Nālandā Scholars in Foreign Countries. The success of Nālandā as a seat of learning is singularly demonstrated by the demand of foreign countries for the services of its trained scholars in introducing to them the saving knowledge and wisdom of India, which they were so keenly seeking.

We have already seen how the Far Eastern countries paid homage to India as their holy land and sent out pilgrims to gather the harvest of her learning and return home to sow its seeds in a new soil. The outstanding characters in this fruitful cultural intercourse were Fa-Hien, Hiuen Tsang, and I-tsing, but there were hosts of other pilgrims to India whose names and achievements are not known to us. We have already referred to several such pilgrims who had followed Hiuen Tsang and preceded I-tsing during the short interval of only forty years. They were Thonmi, Hiuen Chiu, Taouhi, Hwui Lu, Tang, Taou-sing, Āryavarman, Buddhadharma, all of whom sought Indian Wisdom as students of Nālandā as its chief centre and repository. In the same (seventh) century, we have also to record the visits of the Chinese monks, Ou-Kong and Ki-ye, to Nālandā.

Nālandā Literature and Scholars in Tibet. It is, however, to be understood that this cultural intercourse between these Asiatic countries and India was not one-sided. India was equally zealous in spreading abroad the message of her Truths. In this extension of her culture to foreign countries, the students of Nālandā took the lead. Nālandā deputed her own students to propagate Buddhism in Tibet and China. Nālandā had already equipped herself for this task by organizing at the University a School of Tibetan studies. Its scholars, learning Tibetan, employed themselves upon the task of translating into Tibetan select Buddhist works from Sanskrit. They created the Literature which converted Tibet to a new religion. These books have survived their mortal authors and are immortal creations carrying on their beneficent work to this day as the source of spiritual nourishment of an entire people.

We shall now briefly refer to some of these works which had effected a religious revolution in Tibet only to demonstrate and properly appraise the magnitude and value of Nālandā's achievements as a seat of learning.

Works of Ārya Deva. We have already seen that Ārya Deva was one of the earliest scholars of Nālandā, who had lived in about the fourth century A.D. He was the author of three works, all of which are introduced to Tibet in its own language. His last work, known as *Madhyamaka-bhramaghāta-nāma*, was actually written by him at Nālandā, it is said, at the request of Hdsambuhi-glin-gi-rgyal-po (Jambudvīpa Raja) Sukhāchārya (*alias* Udayi, Sadvaha), and was translated into Tibetan by Upādhyāya Dīpaṁkara Śrī Jñāna (who was born in A.D. 980).

Śīlabhadra. The next Nālandā scholar was Śīlabhadra, who was the President of Nālandā at the time of Hiuen Tsang's visit and the teacher of Hiuen Tsang, as we have seen. Śīlabhadra was a logician and one of his works is included in the Tibetan Tripiṭaka in its Tibetan translation. It is called " Ārya-Buddha-bhūmi-vyākhyāna ".

Dharmapāla. The next scholar was Dharmapāla who, by the time of Hiuen Tsang's visit, had retired from the President-ship of Nālandā in favour of Śīlabhadra. He wrote in Sanskrit a grammatical commentary called " Varṇa-Sūtra-Vṛitti-nāma " on the original grammar of Mahāchārya Chandragomin. He wrote four Buddhistic works in Sanskrit which are all translated into Tibetan. They are called (1) Ālambana-pratyaya-dhyāna-śāstravyākhyā, (2) Vidyāmātra-siddhi-śāstra-vyākhyā, (3) Śata-śāstra-vaipulya-vyākhyā, (4) Vali-tattva-saṁgraha.

Chandragomin. The great scholar, Chandragomin, was also one of the best products of Nālandā who had made an important contribution to its reputation. He is the author of as many as sixty books in Sanskrit on Buddhism, which have been translated into Tibetan. He was a Bengali, born in Varendra, and studied first under Buddhist teachers, Sthiramati, and Asoka. He travelled to the South when he wrote a commentary on Pāṇini. Chandrakīrti of Nālandā also wrote a commentary on Pāṇini. It was Chandrakīrti who introduced Chandragomin to Nālandā, for whom he organized a great reception by a procession of three chariots. According to Tārānāth, Chandragomin lived in the eighth century, being the contemporary of Harsha's son Śīla.

Śāntarakshita as a Missionary in Tibet. A reference has been already made to the great Nālandā Professor Śāntarakshita, who was the pioneer in the propagation of Buddhism to Tibet in the eighth century. When he visited Tibet at the invitation of its King, his Ministers escorted him with an army to his Palace. At his instance, the King constructed the first Buddhist Monastery in Tibet in A.D. 749 on the model of the famous Odantapurī Vihāra of Magadha, and appointed him as its first Abbot. He worked in this office for thirteen years and died in A.D. 762. He is the author of two works: (1) Vāda-Nyāyavṛitti-vipañchitārtha and (2) Tattva-Saṁgraha.

Padmasambhava. We have already mentioned the other Professor of Nālandā, Padmasambhava, who was also requisitioned by the King of Tibet for preaching Buddhism. He came from Nālandā to Tibet in A.D. 747 and introduced the Tantrika element in Tibetan Buddhism. He was one of the prominent exponents of the Yogāchāra school of Tantrika cult. He is the author of " Samaya Pañchaśikā ", which was translated into Tibetan.

Kamalaśīla. Kamalaśīla was another Professor of Nālandā who was brought to Tibet by its king to work with Śāntarakshita and Padmasambhava. We have already seen how these three Buddhist scholars were able to expel from Tibet a Chinese monk by defeating him in argument and leave the way open for a complete Indianization of Tibet.

Sthiramati. Sthiramati is the next scholar of Nālandā who is known for his work in Tibet, for which he was specially fitted by his mastery of the Tibetan language, along with Sanskrit. He straightway translated many Sanskrit works and select Buddhist doctrines into Tibetan. He also introduced into Tibet many works on Sanskrit Grammar in which he was a specialist. He particularly studied the Kalāpa system of Sanskrit Grammar.

At Nālandā his place of residence was the temple of Tārābhaṭṭārikā, a school of scientific study of those days.

Buddhakīrti. Nālandā supplied Tibet with another scholar named Buddhakīrti, who was proficient in Tibetan and Tantrika Buddhism. He was originally a colleague of Mahāpaṇḍita Abhayakaragupta of Vikramaśilā Vihāra.

Five Minor Scholars. Five other scholars of Nālandā are mentioned as working in Tibet in the Catalogue of Tibetan Tripiṭaka. Their names are Kumāra Śrī, who composed a Buddhistic work in Sanskrit; another namesake of Kumāra Śrī; Karṇapati, who translated into Tibetan at Nālandā the important work called "Mahāyāna-Lakshaṇa-samuchchaya"; Karṇa Śrī and Sūryadhvaja, who worked together and translated two important Sanskrit works into Tibetan at Nālandā; and Sumati Sena, who lived long at Nālandā and wrote in Sanskrit a book called "Karma-siddhaṭīkā".

Nālandā Scholars working as Missionaries in China. The pioneers among Indian Scholars working as missionaries in foreign countries were Kumārajīva, Guṇavarman, or Paramārtha, the translator of the life of Vasubandhu, all belonging to the fifth century A.D. They were followed by many scholars who proceeded to China from Central India, many of whom were scholars of Nālandā. We read of a Pandit of Nālandā named Śubhakara Siṁha settling down in China in the beginning of eighth century A.D. Four of his works were translated from Sanskrit to Chinese. Cultural intercourse between China and India was interrupted for some time by political conditions. But it revived in the tenth century when we find the Nālandā scholar Dharmadeva taking up work in China as a member of the Imperial Bureau of Translators of Buddhist texts into Chinese under the Song Dynasty (A.D. 960–1127). Up to A.D. 981 Dharmadeva translated forty-six works into Chinese, which were mostly *Tantras* and *Dhāraṇīs* (e.g. *Vasudharā-Dhāraṇī*, *Buddha-hṛidaya-Dhāraṇī*, etc.). In the period of nineteen years, from A.D. 981, he translated another seventy-two works. He also translated into Chinese the popular Mahāyāna work, *Sukhāvatīvyūha*.

Lastly, we have to record the name of Pou-to-ki-to, who is described in China as "Śramaṇa of the Temple of Nālandā of Central India". He gave the Emperor a present of some relics of the Buddha and Sanskrit Texts.

Of the many Indian scholars who had gone to China from Central India, it may be assumed that many had their education completed at Nālandā as the only centre of highest learning in India in those days.

Foreign Scholars at Nālandā. We may now refer briefly to the movement of scholars of foreign countries to Nālandā in search of the learning of which it was then known as the only and most important centre in Asia. We have already related how this movement began with Fa-Hien and went on expanding under the stimulating successes attending the Missions of Hiuen Tsang and I-tsing. We have also seen that Fa-Hien did not visit India alone but with a company of scholars whom he names as Hwuy-king, Tao-ching, Hwuy-ying, and Hwuy-wei, while, on his travels in India, he met " a Tartar who was an earnest follower of the Law ", and out on the same mission as his, and then another band of five pilgrims in pursuit of the same religious purpose (see *ante*). Again, we learn from I-tsing that, after Hiuen Tsang's visit, and before his, in the interval of about forty years, as many as fifty-six scholars visited India from such foreign countries as China, Japan, and Korea [*JRAS.*, xiii, *N.S.*, p. 556], most of whom came to Nālandā for study. Some of them also came by the sea-route *via* Tāmralipti and the others by land *via* Khoten, Tibet, and Nepal, undaunted by the difficulties of that route. A brief account may be given of these earnest foreign seekers after India's learning.

Hiuan Chao. The Shaman Hiuan Chao came to India through Tibet. He first stayed at Jalandhara where he studied Sanskrit, the Buddhist *Sūtras*, and the *Vinaya*, and then proceeded for higher study to Nālandā, where he stayed for three years. Here he also saw another fellow-Chinese student named Shin-Kwong and a scholar from Ceylon who gave him a copy of the *Yoga* and other sacred works. In A.D. 664 he again came to India and was seen by I-tsing at Nālandā [ib., pp. 563-4].

Tao Hi. Tao Hi was another scholar who came to Nālandā and studied Mahāyāna. He had a Sanskrit name, Śrīdeva. He made a gift to his Alma Mater of 400 Chinese *Sūtras* and *Śāstras*. I-tsing could not meet him but was shown the chamber in which he was living there [ib.].

Āryavarma from Korea. In A.D. 638 a Korean scholar, Āryavarma by name, left Changan and came to Nālandā where he studied the *Vinaya* and *Abhidhamma* and copied many Sūtras. Unfortunately, he died at Nālandā at the age of 70 [ib.].

Korean Hwui Yieh. The same year saw the visit to Nālandā of another Korean, Hwui Yieh, a Doctor of Law, who stayed here for a long time and died at 60, like the other Korean. I-tsing, while handling some Chinese books at Nālandā, came across the following line: "The Korean priest Hwui Yieh wrote this record." Yieh wrote some Sanskrit works which were preserved at Nālandā [ib., p. 565].

A Tukhāra Student. I-tsing also saw at Nālandā a scholar from the Tukhāra Country, known for his bodily size and strength and called Bodhidharma [ib., 566].

Tao-shing. Tao-shing, with his Sanskrit name Chandradeva, came to India in A.D. 649, and to Nālandā, where his youth was admired by the king [ib.].

Tang. Tang, a Mahāyāna monk, came to India by way of the sea, stayed at Tāmralipti to master Sanskrit, and then admitted himself to Nālandā [ib., 558–9].

Tao-Lin. Similarly, Tao-Lin (Śīlaprabha), travelling by the same route, came to Nālandā where he studied *Kosha* [ib.].

Hwui-Ta. Hwui-Ta, a monk of Kungchow, took the sea-route to India and stayed at Nālandā for ten years [ib., p. 561].

Wou King. Another monk, Wou King, studied *Yoga*, *Kosha*, and other works at Nālandā and died there [ib., p. 562].

These names are known to us only because they are mentioned by I-tsing. We can imagine how many unnamed scholars, unknown to fame, were studying as silent students of Buddhist scriptures at Nālandā.

Scholars from different parts of India at Nālandā. We have already referred to the tradition connecting the great scholars, Nāgārjuna and Āryadeva, with Nālandā. Rāhulabhadra was another scholar who "held office as a teacher in Śrī Nālandā when King Chandra erected fourteen fragrant Halls and fourteen incomparable religious Schools" [*Vidyābhūshaṇa, Medieval Indian Logic*, p. 146]. It may also be assumed that the Great Masters, Asaṅga and Vasubandhu, were also associated with Nālandā, as they lived in the latter part of the fifth century A.D. when Nālandā was already growing up as a centre of education [*JRAS.*, 1905, p. 35]. Tārānāth says that "Asaṅga lived in the period of his later life for twelve years at Nālandā" [p. 118]. The early part of his life was spent at Peshawar and Ayodhyā [Takakusu, *JRAS.*, ib., pp. 35–44]. Diṅnāga was the next famous scholar of Nālandā, who hailed from the South, as a native of Kāñchī. According to a legend, he was living in a cave when he was sent for by the Pandits of Nālandā to defeat in argument the invincible Brahman, Sudurjaya.

The scholars, Guṇamati and Sthiramati, from Valabhī, the founders of its monastery, are connected with Nālandā as its teachers by Hiuen Tsang [Watters, ii, 268]. Their date is uncertain. But it may be sixth century A.D. The *Valabhī Grant* of Dharasena I [*Ind. Anti.*, vi, 12] refers to Sthiramati as builder of a Vihāra at Valabhī and is dated *Saṁvat* 269 = A.D. 558, if it is Gupta Saṁvat. The grant is in honour of "the Vihāra built by Sthiramati", showing that it was somewhat later than the building. He should also come after the date of Vasubandhu as his disciple. So he should have lived about the sixth century.

Dharmapāla also hailed from the South and was a native of Kāñchīpura. Padmasambhava was a native of the north-western frontiers, the country about Ghazni [Waddell, *Lamaism*, p. 26].

Even Śīlabhadra was not a native of Nālandā or Magadha but of Samataṭa, the son of its king, and a Brahman by caste. He renounced the world and became a student at Nālandā where his powers of debate were so much appreciated by the King of Magadha that he offered to present him with a village. This gift he did not accept in the true spirit of a monk [Watters, ii, 109–110].

We may lastly mention Vīradeva who was a native of Nagarahāra near Jalalabad.

Thus most of these scholars who were natives of different and distant parts of India flocked to Nālandā to complete their studies and build up its reputation as a seat of learning by their own contributions to knowledge.

Nālandā Rituals and Art : Later Phases of Mahāyāna : Tantrayāna and Vajrayāna. As Education at Nālandā was predominantly religious in character, a large part of that Education comprised the practices and rituals of religion. That religion was Mahāyāna Buddhism, including its later developments which claimed their due attention at Nālandā as they emerged in the course of its history. Some of these were later than the times of Hiuen Tsang and I-tsing, who are accordingly silent about them. These developments are known as Tantrayāna, and, in their later forms, as Vajrayāna and Kālachakrayāna,[1] which established themselves about the tenth century A.D.

[1] The central conception of this Tāntrika or Vajrayāna phase of Mahāyāna Buddhism is that of Dhyānī Buddhas, each with his own Śakti, and of various yogic practices and other means of *sādhanā* whereby Buddhahood can be

Evidence of Images. Evidence, however, of these later phases of Mahāyāna Buddhism is found in full measure at Nālandā, where have been unearthed numerous images of various deities, both male and female, in bronze, copper, black or white sandstone. We have, therefore, to explain what business the University had with these images by relating these to its studies and religious practices.

Earlier Rituals. Some of the beginnings of these practices are testified to by both Hiuen Tsang and I-tsing. Hiuen Tsang, for instance, mentions the worship at Nālandā of the deities Tārā [Watters, ii, 103, 174], Avalokiteśvara, Hāritī [ib., i, 110], Buddha, and Bodhisattva. I-tsing refers only to the images of Buddha and Hāritī [Takakusu, p. 37], but mentions the observance by the monks at Nālandā of several compulsory rituals which foreshadow the later developments of Mahāyāna. These, as we have already seen, comprised (1) the morning Bath, which was taken in the many tanks of Nālandā by " a hundred or a thousand priests leaving the monastery together " [ib., 108–9]; (2) Ablution of the Holy Image of the Buddha in the open court of the Monastery in scented water to the accompaniment of music by girls, followed by setting up the image in the Temple. The whole ceremony was performed by the resident monks under the direction of the *Karmadāna* (ib., 147–9]. The Ablution of the Image was, however, regarded as so obligatory that it was carried out every day " by the priests in individual apartments of a monastery " [ib., p. 149], but perhaps at Nālandā it was conducted as a common public ceremony. (3) *Chaityavandana*, which was going round a Stūpa three times every afternoon to the accompaniment of chanting of hymns and select *slokas*,

attained. Its theory and Tāntrika practices are fully given in the work *Guhyasamāja-Tantra* of about the third century A.D. An earlier work on the subject is *Mañjuśrīmūlakalpa*.

According to the *Guhyasamāja-Tantra*, the Buddha, asked by the Assembly, of Bodhisattvas and others to reveal the *Guhyasamāja* (secret or spiritual society), sat in different meditations, uttered different kinds of Mantras, and created five Dhyānī Buddhas with their five different Śaktis.

The five Dhyānī Buddhas are : (1) Akshobhaya, (2) Vairochana, (3) Ratna-Ketu, (4) Amitābha, and (5) Amoghavajra.

Their five Śaktis are : (1) Devasarati, (2) Moharati, (3) Īrshārati, (4) Rāgarati, and (5) Vajrarati.

He also created four guardians of four gates (or quarters), viz. (1) Yamāntaka, (2) Prajñāntaka, (3) Padmāntaka, and (4) Vighnāntaka.

The *Guhyasamāja* also mentions a few minor deities ; Mañjuśrī, Aparājitā, Jambhala, and the like.

It also indicates the different practices or *Siddhis* making up the worship or Sādhanā proper for each particular deity [Bhaṭṭāchārya, *Guhyasamāja*, Introduction].

followed by the recitation of a short Sūtra, and reading of a Selection from Scriptures made by Aśvaghosha, known as "Service in Three Parts". I-tsing saw the ceremony performed in this manner at the Tāmralipti Monastery, but it was differently performed at Nālandā on account of the difficulty of bringing together in one place the large number, thousands, of its monks. So the Nālandā practice was for "one precentor to go round from place to place, from one Hall to another, chanting hymns, slokas, and the 'Service', accompanied by monastic lay-servants and children carrying incense and flowers" [ib., 152–5].

Some of the Monks would perform this ceremony by themselves, "sitting alone, facing the shrine (Gandhakuṭī), praising the Buddha in their hearts; or going to the temple in small parties, kneeling side by side in worship" [ib.].

Emergence of new Deities and their Worship. This simple ritualism was undergoing changes in accordance with changes in Mahāyāna worship. Many new deities were being added to its pantheon so as practically to transform the old faith into a new religion. The collective and congregational worship of a few deities was now being replaced by the individual worship of each, in accordance with the particular system of worship or *sādhanā* proper for each such Tāntrika deity. Nālandā, therefore, had naturally to move with the times and assimilate and make the best of these later religious developments. Even in the sphere of these new developments, Nālandā took the lead by the creative genius of its teachers and became the founder of what may be considered in certain respects a new style and school of Indian Art, which extended beyond the bounds of India and influenced the Art of Java, by the numerous examples of images of various deities executed by its craftsmen and artists in response to the religious requirements of the thousands of its students.

Yet, in the field of rituals, as in that of theoretical studies, Nālandā was as catholic and cosmopolitan as ever. The images of the deities which were requisitioned were not confined only to Mahāyāna or Vajrayāna, but were representative of all prevailing faiths. They may broadly be grouped under three classes: (1) Early Mahāyāna, (2) Tāntrika Mahāyāna, and (3) Purely Brahmanical.

First, there are the images of Buddha, of which the best sample is the standing figure of Buddha in bronze with a high *ushṇīsha*. Another good example is a seated figure of Buddha of stone.

Secondly, we have images of Maitreya, Mañjuśrī, Avalokiteśvara, and other Bodhisattvas.

Next, we have images of female deities, Hāritī and Tārā. The best example is the bronze Tārā of eighteen arms, ornamented, and encircled by *prabhā*. There are also images of Prajñāpāramitā and Vasudhārā.

Later Mahāyāna is represented by the image of *Vajrapāṇi*, an emanation of Dhyānī Buddha, Akshobhaya.

Tantrayāna brings in figures of new deities: *Trailokyavijaya*, who is shown as trampling over Maheśvara and Gaurī; *Heruka*, with his garland of skulls and dancing on a lotus; *Jambhala*, the Buddhist god of wealth; *Mārīchī* with three faces and eight arms, and companions called Varttālī, Vadālī, Varālī, and Varāhamukhī.

There are also found other Tāntrika images, those of Yamāntaka, Vajrasattva, Aparājitā, Mañjuvara, and Vajrapāṇi. Of these, Vajrapāṇi is a Divine Bodhisattva who carries in his tiara the image of his spiritual father, Akshobhaya. *Mañjuvara* is a manifestation of the popular Mañjuśri. *Yamāntaka* is a regular Kālachakrayāna deity with its three faces, protruding tongue, canine teeth, big belly, garland of severed human heads, and riding a buffalo. *Aparājitā* is represented as trampling upon Ganeśa and being served by Indra and Brahmā. There is also another female figure found, identified as that of Koṭiśrī, but it may be that of *Vajraśāradā*, seated on lotus.

Lastly, Brahmanical religion is represented by the figures of Vishṇu, Śiva, Balarāma, Vāsudeva, Ganeśa, Sūrya, Pārvatī, Gaṅgā, and Sarasvatī.

Nālandā Art : Its supposed Founders, Dhimān and Bitpālo. A word may now be said on the possible origin and affiliations of the Art of which these images are the outcome and examples. Some light is thrown on the point by the following words of Tārānāth : " In the time of King Dharmapāla, there lived in Varendra an exceedingly skilful artist named Dhīmān, whose son was Bitpālo ; both of these produced many works in cast-metal, as well as sculptures and paintings, which resembled the works of the Nāgas. The father and son gave rise to distinct schools. In painting, the followers of the father were called the Eastern School ; those of the Magadha were called followers of the Madhyadeśa School of Painting. So in Nepal, the earlier schools of art resembled the Western School ; but, in the course of time, a peculiar Nepalese School was formed, which, in

PLATE XXVI

NALANDA.

A Bronze Image of standing Buddha.

Facing p. 585

painting and casting, resembled the Eastern types" [p. 180 of his book].

It may be surmised with some justification that Dhīmān and Bitpālo were associated as teachers of Arts and Crafts with Nālandā, where has been discovered the largest number and variety of the cast models for which they were known.

Bronzes of Nālandā influencing Javanese Art. It is generally assumed that the Art of Nālandā is to be considered as belonging to the Pāla School of Art and not an independent school, because the majority of the images found at Nālandā bear the names of Pāla kings. But the case whether Nālandā Art is to be treated as an independent School or a branch of the Pāla School of Art has been recently presented with great ability by Kempers in his Treatise called "The Bronzes of Nālandā and Hindu-Javanese Art". He points out that Nālandā exercised its cultural influence over the Archipelago for the simple reason that "among the constituent parts of Hindu-Javanese culture, one of its essential features, Mahāyāna Buddhism, originates from Nālandā. . . In the Malay Inscription of Śrīvijaya found at Talang Toewo and dated in the year A.D. 684, there occur some terms which are of a distinctly Mahāyānist character. M. G. Coedes has proved that they belong to the sphere of Vajrayāna or Tantrayāna which arose at Nālandā from the Yogāchāra School at a time not long anterior to that of the Inscription of Talang Toewo. So we may take it for established that Nālandā has exercised a great influence on the religious life in Malay Archipelago", and, further, that the relation between Nālandā Monastery and the Archipelago must have been long continued (in view of the close epigraphical similarities between Pāla and Javanese Inscriptions).

Pāla School of Art. Kempers, by a critical study of a mass of examples of the art of both Nālandā and Java, records his conclusion that "the Hindu-Javanese bronzes in general have not developed from Pāla art, but the Pāla images have enriched the art of Java with a number of motifs and types; that the bronzes of Nālandā, while partly exhibiting a distinct resemblance to some bronzes from Java, belong to Pāla Art".

II. Valabhī

Royal Grants. Nālandā had its rival in a University on the other side of India at Valabhī which was the capital of the Maitraka kings for the period A.D. 475–775. Valabhī University, like Nālandā, was the outcome of royal benefactions. Its first Vihāra was founded by Princess Duḍḍā, the daughter of the sister of Dhruva I [*Grant of King Guhasena of Valabhī*, in the *IA*., iv, 174]. Again, in A.D. 580, King Dharasena I made a grant in favour of another Vihāra called Śrī Bappapāda which was founded by Āchārya Bhadanta Sthiramati [ib., vi, 9].

Description by Hiuen Tsang and I-tsing. Hiuen Tsang saw at Valabhī "some hundred Saṁghārāmas with about 6,000 priests" [Watters, ii, 266]. According to I-tsing, Nālandā and Valabhī were the two places in India where scholars used to reside for two or three years to complete their education. Valabhī, like Nālandā, also attracted students from all parts of India to hold discussions of "all possible and impossible doctrines", and achieve fame when their opinions were approved by the Masters of Valabhī [Takakusu, p. 177]. We have already referred to the statement of Hiuen Tsang that Sthiramati and Guṇamati were once in charge of the Monastery at Valabhī. This Monastery was equipped with a Library which was considered deserving of a royal grant for the express provision for purchase of books [*Saddharmasya pustakopachayārtham*, in the Grant of Guhasena I of A.D. 559 (*IA*., vii, 67 f.)]. Students of Valabhī, like those of Nālandā, after graduation, used to present themselves at the Courts of Kings to prove their capacity, present their theories, and even demonstrate their administrative talent to be employed in government service as related by I-tsing [ib.]. This shows that Valabhī provided for other studies than the purely religious, secular Vidyās like Dharma, Nīti, Vārttā, or Chikitsā Śāstras.

Valabhī was the rival of Nālandā in another respect. Hiuen Tsang states that "most of its priests study the Little Vehicle". It thus specialized in Hīnayāna, as Nālandā in Mahāyāna.

Reference in 'Kathāsaritsāgara'. Lastly, a reference may be made to the interesting fact related in the *Kathāsaritsāgara* [xxxii, 42–3], which tells of a Brahman, Vasudatta, sending his son, Vishṇudatta, as soon as he completed his sixteenth year (*pūrṇashoḍaśavatsaraḥ*) to "Valabhīpuram" for his education (*Vidyāprāptaye*) from his native place in Antarvedi in the Gangetic valley. This shows that the dutiful Brahman father did not consider Benares or Nālandā as suitable for his son's education and took the risk of sending him on to a distant place like Valabhī for the purpose. Unfortunately, we do not possess enough information in proportion to the admitted pre-eminence of Valabhī as a seat of learning in India of those days.

III. Vikramaśilā

Site. Like Nālandā and Valabhī, the University of Vikramaśilā was also the result of royal benefactions. We owe its history to Tārānāth's well-known work which states that King Dharmapāla founded Śrī Vikramaśilā Vihāra on a suitable site, a hillock on the bank of the Ganges in Northern Magadha. Cunningham identified it with the village Silāo near Baragaon [*ASR.*, viii, 75], Dr. S. C. Vidyābhushaṇa with Sultanganj in Bhagalpur District, N. L. De with Pātharaghāṭā hill, near Colgong in Bhagalpur District [*JASB.*, vi, 7], while Dr. A. R. Banerji-Sastri of Patna College takes it to be Keur, near Hulsaganj " in direct line with Nālandā (within a distance of 15 miles) and Odantapuri " [*JBORS.*, xv, 276].

Buildings and Staff. King Dharmapala had the Vihāra constructed after a good design. It was surrounded by a strong wall. At the centre was erected the Temple adorned with Mahābodhi images. There were also erected within the enclosure fifty-three smaller temples of private character and fifty-four ordinary temples, totalling 108 temples. Then he made provision for teaching by the appointment of 108 teachers and other staff comprising " an Āchārya for Wood-offering, an Āchārya for Ordination, another for Fire-offering, a Superintendent of Works, a guard of pigeons, and a supplier of Temple servants ". It is stated that the cost of maintaining each of these 114 members of the staff was equal to that of four men.

Administration. The teaching was controlled by a Board of eminent teachers and it is stated that this Board of Vikramaśilā also administered the affairs of Nālandā. This kind of co-ordination of work and management between the two Universities was perhaps due to King Dharmapāla being their common head. Accordingly, we find teachers like Dīpaṁkara and Abhayakara Gupta working at both the Universities or exchanges of teachers between them, as has been already mentioned.

Six Colleges and a Central Hall. We further learn that the University came to have six Colleges, each with a staff of the standard strength of 108 teachers, and a Central Hall called the House of Science with its six gates opening on the six Colleges. It is also stated that the outer wall surrounding the whole Monastery was decorated with artistic work, a portrait in painting of Nāgarjuna adorning the right of the principal entrance and that of Atiśa on the left [S. C. Das, ***Indian Pandits in Tibet***, in *JBTS.*, i, 1–11]. On the walls of the University were also painted portraits of Pandits eminent for their learning and character.

Six 'Dvāra-Paṇḍitas'. The gates of the University were guarded by the most erudite of its scholars called *Dvāra-Paṇḍitas*, so that admission to it might not be cheap and its standard of scholarship lowered. There were six such redoubtable 'gate-keepers'. During the reign of Chanaka (A.D. 955–983), we come across the names of the following eminent Logicians acting as 'Gate-keepers', 'Custodians of its Scholarship':

1. Ratnākaraśānti, East Gate.
2. Vāgīśvarakīrti of Benares, West Gate.
3. Naropa, North Gate.
4. Prajñākaramati, South Gate.
5. Ratnavajra of Kāśmīra, First Central Gate.
6. Jñānaśrīmitra of Gauḍa, Second Gate.

President. The President of the University was always the most learned and religious sage. At the time of its founder, Dharmapāla, it was Buddha-jñāna-pāda. During A.D. 1034–8 Dīpaṁkara or Śrījñāna Atiśa was the Head under whom Sthavira Ratnākara acted as the superior of the monastery [S. C. Vidyābhūshaṇa, *History of Indian Logic*, pp. 519–520].

Its History as written in the phenomenal achievements of its Scholars. We do not know much of the working of this University, its rules and regulations governing the daily life and studies of its resident students, as we know in the case of Nālandā, thanks to the comprehensive account left to us by a foreign pilgrim of the eminence of Hiuen Tsang on the basis of his first-hand knowledge as its student for several years, which has been further supplemented by an equally full account of another foreigner, I-tsing, who had even a greater advantage in observing its working as a student for a much longer period. And the accounts of these Chinese pilgrims have a further value for the spirit of detachment, criticism, and objectivity in which they are written. Unfortunately, Vikramaśilā is not as fortunate as Nālandā in the matter of the conservation of its history. But its history is written large in the biography of the great men it has produced, the scholars who were invited by foreign countries, chiefly Tibet, to spread its learning, culture, and religion. From the foreign accounts of some of these scholars, we glean something of the history of their Alma Mater. Indeed, the success of the work of Vikramaśilā as a seat of learning is amply demonstrated by the quality and quantity of its output, the prodigies of piety and learning it produced, and the profound contributions they made to knowledge and religion by their numerous writings which practically built up the culture and civilization of another country, Tibet. Tibet has gratefully treasured up the memories of some of these graduates of Vikramaśilā, a few of whom it has canonized as its patron-saints. We shall now trace the history of Vikramaśilā in the Tibetan accounts of some of its famous scholars and teachers.

Vikramaśilā Scholars working in Tibet and writing in Tibetan : 1. **Jñānapāda.** Āchārya Buddha Jñānapāda had his guru named Siṁhabhadra, after whom he was appointed as the royal priest of King Dharmapāla who later appointed him as the Āchārya for Ordination at Vikramaśilā. There he developed his study of *Mantra-Vajrāchārya* and became the founder of a new cult of which Vikramaśilā was the only centre in those days. About nine of his Sanskrit works on Tantra which are lost are preserved in Tibetan.

2. **Vairochana.** Vairochana Rakshita was a pupil of Padmasambhava, on whose departure to Tibet he came to Vikramaśila, where he wrote several works in Sanskrit, such as *Bodhisattva*-charyāvatāra-pañjikā, *Ratna-vāda-chakra*, and the like and translated into Tibetan several Tantrika works like *Vinaya-Saṁgraha*, Śukla-*vajra-yoginī-sādhana*, or *Prajña-pāramitā-hṛidaya-sādhana*. He followed his guru later to Tibet in the time of its King Khri-Sron-Ide-Btsan, about A.D. 750. He won the titles of *Mahāpaṇḍita* and *Mahāchārya*.

3. **Jetāri.** Jetāri was a native of Varendra, the son of Brahman Garbhapāda, the chaplain of King Sanātana, a feudatory of the Pāla Kings of Bengal. King Mahīpāla [A.D. 899–940] conferred upon him the title of *Paṇḍita* on his completion of study at Vikramaśilā where he worked as a Professor. He was the teacher of the distinguished scholars, Ratnākaraśānti who learnt from him Sūtra and Tantra and became 'a gate-keeper' of the Vihāra in about A.D. 983, and also of the more distinguished Dīpaṁkara Atiśa.

4. **Prajñākaramati.** Prajñākaramati was one of the 'gate-keepers' of the Vihāra, who wrote several works, two of which are in Tibetan.

5. **Ratnākara.** Ratnākaraśānti, another 'gate-keeper', as we have seen, was first at Odantapura University where he received Ordination in the Sarvāstivāda School. Later, he

joined Vikramaśilā as a pupil of Jetāri. He went to Ceylon to preach Buddhism at the invitation of its king. He wrote about thirteen works in Sanskrit, among which may be mentioned "Vajra-bhairava-gaṇa-chakra-nāma" and "Śrī-sarva-rahasya-nibandha-rahasya-pradīpa-nāma".

6. **Jñāna Śrī.** Jñāna Śrī Mitra, a 'gate-keeper', and a native of Gauḍa, first belonged to the Śrāvaka School and later changed to Mahāyāna. He wrote several works in Sanskrit, such as "Pramāṇa-viniśchaya-ṭīkā" and "Tarka-bhāshā", and learnt Tibetan into which he translated the first of these works.

7. **Ratnavajra.** Ratnavajra, another 'gate-keeper', was a native of Kāśmīra, where he studied the texts of Buddhist "Sūtras and Mantras" and also "Sciences" up to his 36th year, when he came to Magadha, visited Vajrāsana (Bodh-Gaya), and joined Vikramaśilā, to further his studies, winning the title of "Paṇḍita" and the position of a "gate-keeper". He came back to Kāśmīra after some time, where he convinced in debate and converted to his faith some renowned *Tīrthajas* and then travelled to Udyāna, whence finally he came to Tibet where he learnt Tibetan, into which he translated many Buddhist works, of which fourteen are mentioned, such as "Mahāmāyā-sādhana", "Śrī-Heruka-sādhana-nāma", "Śrī-Akshobhya-Vajra-sādhana", and other Tantrika works.

8. **Vāgīśvara.** Vāgīśvara Kīrti, another 'gate-keeper', was a native of Benares, a worshipper of "Tārā Devī", and author of a Sanskrit work "Mṛityubañchanopadeśa", which was introduced to Tibet by Dīpaṁkara.

9. **Dīpaṁkara.** Dīpaṁkara Śrī Jñāna, also known as Āchārya Atiśa, was the greatest of Indian scholars who worked as missionaries in foreign countries. Born of a royal family in Gauḍa in A.D. 980, he renounced his riches and became a monk at the monastery of Krishṇagiri under a teacher named Rāhula Gupta. At 19 he took the sacred vows from Śīla Rakshita, the Mahāsāṁghika Āchārya of Odantapurī Vihāra, who gave him the new name of Dīpaṁkara Śrī Jñāna, by which he is known. At 31 he received the highest ordination from Āchārya Dharma Rakshita. He was a master of both Hīnayāna and Mahāyāna, of Vaiśeshika, and Tantras. After thus completing his education, he sailed off to Suvarṇadvīpa (identified with Thaton in Pegu), where he was initiated further into the mysteries of Buddhism by Āchārya Chandrakīrti, the High Priest of that place. There he studied for twelve years and then returned to

India, visiting Ceylon on the way. He defeated in a discussion at Vajrāsana (Bodh-Gaya) many Tīrthikas assembled there and was soon elected as the Head of the Community of Buddhist Monks of Magadha and Gauḍa. King Naya Pāla, in recognition of his learning and reputation, fittingly appointed him to the Headship of Vikramśilā. At this time the Tibetan king, Chan Chub, anxious to purge Tibetan Buddhism of its many corruptions, sent his envoy to secure the services of a great Indian Paṇḍita for the purpose. The envoy selected had already been to India and studied Sanskrit there. He came to India after overcoming unusual dangers and difficulties on the way and delivered his king's invitation to Dīpaṁkara who answered: " I have now grown advanced in age and have the keys of many monasteries in my charge and many works still remain unfinished. So I cannot shortly set out for Tibet."

Afterwards, under divine inspiration from Goddess Tārā, he decided to leave for Tibet against the strongest wishes of his esteemed colleagues, Ratnakīrti, Vairochana, Kanakaśrī of Nepal, and many others, and was accompanied on his journey up to Mitra Vihāra by Paṇḍitas Bhūmigarbha, Nagtcho, Gya-tson, Bhūmi Saṁgha, Vīrya Chandra, and others. On reaching Tibet, he was received by " a song of welcome sung by all the people " and conducted to the king by an escort of 300 horsemen. By his work he purged Tibetan Buddhism of its many and gross corruptions which had crept into it in time and founded the new religion of Lamaism, though it was left to his disciple, Brom-ton, to become the founder of the first great hierarchy of Tibet. He worked in Tibet for thirteen years (A.D. 1040–1053) and died at Nethan near Lhāsa at 73. But he is a permanent influence in Tibet mainly through his works showing him as the greatest writer on Tibetan Buddhism on which about 200 works are ascribed to him, mostly on Vajrayāna. He was also a profound scholar in Tibetan, into which he translated twenty-two Sanskrit works.

10. **Vīryasiṁha.** Vīryasiṁha is principally known as an associate of Atiśa whom he helped in translating into Tibetan at Vikramaśilā the important Sanskrit works " Saṁsāra-manonirṇayāṇīkāra-nāma-saṁgīti " and " Kāya-Vākya-Chitta-supratishṭhā-nāma ".

A Tibetan Account. Some interesting details regarding the Vikrama-śilā Monastery are given in a Tibetan account of the visit of the Tibetan monk Nag-tsho who was deputed by the Tibetan king to Vikramaśilā for the purpose of inducing its great scholar, Atiśa, to come to Tibet and take charge of Buddhist propaganda in that country.

Gate. Nag-tsho arrived at the gate of the Monastery in the evening when the gate could not be opened under its rules. He found shelter for the night at a Dharmaśālā at the gate. The gate was opened in the early morning when Nag-tsho was asked by a Tibetan monk to proceed to the Tibetan House of the Monastery meant for the residence of its Tibetan students.

Tibetan House. At the Tibetan House, Nag-tsho saw its senior monk, Gya-tson, who advised him to be a resident pupil of Sthavira Ratnākara, who was also the chief of Atiśa himself, although Atiśa had the highest reputation for learning and character. Gya-tson also said: " We Tibetans have no influence here, but still I am well known to Atiśa."

An Assembly. For next day was fixed a congregation of all classes of monks at Vikramaśilā. There was an Assembly of 8,000 Bhikshus. First entered Vidyā Kokila who was to preside over it. The more distinguished monks were given reserved seats. The Raja of Vikramaśilā (King of Magadha) was given an exalted seat. " But none of the monks, old or young, rose from their seats to mark his arrival." But all the monks, including the king, rose from their seats when the learned monk, Vīra Vajra, entered. Last came Atiśa " from whose waist hung down a bundle of keys ". He held the keys as the warden of several hostels or monasteries at Vikramaśilā.

Atiśa's Liberality. In the following morning, the Tibetan messenger saw Atiśa at his Vihāra. Next day, he saw Atiśa distributing alms and food to the poor, and how a beggar boy, failing to get his share, ran after Atiśa, exclaiming : " Bhālā ho O, Nāth Atiśa, Bhāt-ona, Bhāt-ona," " Blest be thou, O patron Atiśa, give me rice ! "

The Tibetan was much impressed by his charity, while Atiśa also was very much moved by the great trouble and expenses repeatedly borne by the Tibetan for his sake. Atiśa, now deciding to go to Tibet, told the Tibetan messengers that they would have to wait for eighteen months, which he would take to finish his work on hand before he could leave his charge of the monasteries for Tibet.

At the time of his departure for Tibet, Atiśa made over charge of the various offices he had held to the monastic authorities. His guide, Nag-tsho, packed the travelling appurtenances of the party in sixty loads which were carried by thirty bullocks. Atiśa on the way visited some holy places like Vajrāsana and Mitra Vihāra. He had Gya-tson, who was then laid up with fever at Śrī Nālandā, carried in a *dooly* to Vikramaśilā before leaving the place.

Before leaving, Atiśa, in his usual spirit of charity and self-sacrifice, distributed the Tibetan gold brought to him as a present for his deputation in four parts. The first part was given to his teachers and the Āchāryas of Vikramaśilā, the second given as a trust to President Ratnākara who was to use it for the benefit of the whole clergy of the monastery, the third was sent to Vajrāsana to endow religious service there, and " the fourth part he sent to the king for distribution among the general Buddhist *Saṁghas* of the country ".

Tea Drinking. It is interesting to note that on his first setting foot on Tibetan soil Atiśa was entertained with the national drink of Tibet which was *Tea.* The Tibetan monk, offering the drink which was unknown to the Indian guest, described it thus: " Venerable Sir, it is called *chā*. . . We do not know that the *chā* plant is eaten, but the leaves are churned (being mixed with soda, salt, and butter) in warm water and the soup is drunk. It has many properties." It will thus appear that the use of Tea spread from Tibet to India [Buddhist Texts Society Journal, Part I, 1893, p. 27].

11. **Abhayakaragupta.** Abhayakaragupta was a native of Gauḍa. After learning the five *Vidyās* of the day (already described), he became a monk and was appointed by King Rāma Pāla of Magadha to perform the religious ceremonies of the Palace. In the thirteenth year of the reign (*c.* A.D. 1114), he composed his great work " Muni-maṭālaṁkāra ".

Magadha was then a stronghold of Buddhism under the sustained patronage of its rulers. It was represented by 3,000 monks in residence at Vikramaśila Vihāra, 1,000 at Vajrāsana (Bodh-Gaya), and 1,000 more at Odantapuri. A religious festival would bring together 5,000 monks, including Mahāyānists, and Śrāvakas who then numbered over 10,000. It is stated that King Rāma Pāla gave free food daily to forty Mahāyānists and 200 Śrāvakas of Vajrāsana (Bodh-Gayā).

Though Abhayakaragupta was the head of Mahāyāna School, he was respected by the Śrāvakas. He remained at Vikramaśilā for a long time " under the protection of the son of King Śubhaśrī of Eastern India ", and was an eye-witness of the first Turuksha invasion of Magadha. He was a great writer in Sanskrit and translator in Tibetan. He is credited with the translation into Tibetan of seven works dealing with the *sādhana* of Mahākāla, Mahākālāntara, and the like, and with the authorship of twenty-six Sanskrit works, all of which mark him out as an authority on Tantra Cult. He was known by the high title of 'Ārya-Mahāpaṇḍita'.

12. **Tathāgata Rakshita.** Tathāgata Rakshita is supposed to have been a native of Orissa, a Kāyastha by caste, but of a family of physicians by profession. As a student at Vikramaśilā, he won its titles 'Mahapaṇḍita' and 'Upādhyāya'. He was a Professor of Tantra, on which he wrote extensively. He translated his own and others' works into Tibetan.

13. **Ratnakīrti.** Ratnakīrti won successively the titles of Upādhyāya, Paṇḍita, and Mahāpaṇḍita as a student at Vikramaśilā. His Tibetan translations have enriched Tibetan Literature and introduced to Tibet the true spirit of Indian Buddhism. Among his works may be mentioned "Dharmaviniśchaya-prakaraṇa-nāma".

14. **Mañjuśrī.** Mañjuśrī was a Paṇḍita of Vikramaśilā and known only by his translations carried out at that place. His works show him to be a devotee of Tārā.

15. **Dharmakīrti.** Dharmakīrti, a native of Tibet, came to study Sanskrit at Vikramaśilā, where he later translated from Sanskrit into Tibetan the work "Samaya Pañcha" of Padmasambhava. He subsequently translated many Sanskrit works into Tibetan.

16. **Śākya Śrī Bhadra.** Śākya Śrī Bhadra was a native of Kāśmīra, and known as a Logician. He was at Vikramaśilā and an eye-witness of its tragic destruction by Moslems.

Destruction of Vikramaśilā by Moslems. As related by the author of *Tabakāt-i-Nāsari* [Raverty, i, 552], "the greater number of the inhabitants of that place were Brahmans (Bhikshus ?), and the whole of these Brahmans had their heads shaven; and they were all slain. There were a great number of books on the religion of the Hindus (Buddhists) there; and when all these books came under the observation of the Musalmans, they summoned a number of Hindus that they might give them information respecting the import of those books; but the whole of the Hindus had been killed. On becoming acquainted (with the contents of those books), it was found that the whole of that fortress and city was a college, and, in the Hindu tongue, they call a college Bihār (Vihāra)."

After the destruction of the Vikramaśilā Vihāra, Śrī Bhadra repaired to the University of Jagaddala whence he proceeded to Tibet, accompanied by many other monks who settled down there as preachers of Buddhism.

IV. JAGADDALA

Its foundation by King Rāma Pāla. According to the historical Epic *Rāmacharita*, King Rāma Pāla of Bengal and Magadha, who reigned between A.D. 1084–1130, founded a new city which he called Rāmāvatī on the banks of the rivers Gaṅgā and Karatoyā in Varendra and equipped the city with a Vihāra called Jagaddala. The University could barely work for a hundred years, till the time of Moslem invasion sweeping it away in A.D. 1203. But in its short life it has made substantial contributions to learning through its scholars who made it famous by their writings. An account of these scholars is given below.

Its Noted Scholars. 1. **Vibhūtichandra.** It is stated that the famous work "Jñāna-Chakshuḥ-Sādhana-nāma" passed through several Masters till it was transmitted to Vibhūtichandra by Śākyaśrībhadra, with whom he is thus associated. Very probably he followed him to Tibet from Jagaddala where he took shelter after Vikramaśilā was destroyed by Moslems, as already related. He was a great Tibetan scholar and translated many Sanskrit works into Tibetan and bore the title of "Mahāpaṇḍita".

2. **Dānaśīla.** He won several titles Paṇḍita, Mahāpaṇḍita, Upādhyāya, and Āchārya for his profound knowledge of both Tibetan and Sanskrit. He is said to have translated into Tibetan as many as fifty-four works, all of which exercised a great influence on Tibetan Buddhism, in which he is given an equal place with the great Masters Dīpaṁkara or Abhayakaragupta.

3. **Śubhakara.** He is said to have been the *guru* of Śākya Śrī and composed a Sanskrit work "Siddhaika-vīra-tantraṭīkā" which was later translated into Tibetan.

4. **Mokshākaragupta.** He was a Master of Logic on which he wrote the Sanskrit work "*Tarka-bhāsha*" which was translated into Tibetan. He bore the titles of Bhikshu and Mahāpaṇḍita.

V. ODANTAPURĪ

Very little is known of this University, although at the time of Abhayakaragupta there were 1,000 monks in residence here, as has been already stated. Odantapurī is now known for its famous scholar named Prabhākara who hailed from Chatarpur in Bengal.

It appears that this University had existed long before the Pāla kings came into power in Magadha. These kings expanded the University by endowing it with a good Library of Brahmanical and Buddhist works. We have also seen how this Monastery was taken as the model on which the first Tibetan Buddhist Monastery was built in A.D. 749 under King Khri-sron-deu-tsan on the advice of his guru, Śāntarakshita.

VI. Mithilā

Mithilā, as we have seen, was a stronghold of Brahmanical culture at its best in the time of the Upanishads, under its famous Philosopher-king Janaka who used to send out periodical invitations to learned Brahmans of the Kuru-Pañchāla country to gather at his court for purposes of philosophical discussions. Under him Eastern India was vying with North-Western India in holding the palm of learning. In those days, the name of the country was not Mithilā but Videha. In the time of the Rāmāyaṇa, the Mahābhārata, and Buddhist literature, Mithilā retained the renown of its Vedic days.

Its subsequent political history is somewhat chequered. When Vijaya Sen was King of Bengal, Nānyadeva of the Karṇātaka dynasty was King of Mithilā in A.D. 1097 [Inscription on the ruined walls of the fort of Simrāon]. King Vijaya defeated him [Deopara Vijaya Sen Inscription], but was defeated by his son Gaṅgadeva who recovered Mithilā from him. This Karṇāta Dynasty ruled Mithilā for the period *c.* A.D. 1150–1395, followed by the Kāmeśvara Dynasty which ruled between *c.* A.D. 1350–1515. It was again followed by another dynasty of rulers founded by Maheśvara Thakkura in the time of Akbar, and this dynasty has continued up to the present time.

Mithilā as a seat of learning flourished remarkably under these later kings. The Kāmeśvara period was made famous in the literary world by the erudite and versatile scholar, Jagaddhara, who wrote commentaries on a variety of texts, the Gītā, Devī-māhātmya, Meghadūta, Gīta-Govinda, Mālatī-Mādhava, and the like, and original treatises on Erotics, such as *Rasika-Sarvasva-Saṅgīta-Sarvasva*.

The next scholar who shed lustre on Mithilā was the poet

Vidyāpati, the author of Maithilī songs or Padāvalī generally. He has inspired for generations the later Vaishṇava writers of Bengal.

Mithilā made conspicuous contributions in the realm of severe and scientific subjects. It developed a famous School of Nyāya which flourished from the twelfth to the fifteenth century A.D., under the great masters of Logic, Gaṅgeśa, Vardhamāna, Pakshadhara, and others.

This School of New Logic (Navya Nyāya) was founded by Gaṅgeśa Upādhyāya and his epoch-making work named " Tattva-Chintamani ", a work of about 300 pages whose commentaries make up over 1,000,000 pages in three centuries of its study. Gaṅgeśa is supposed to have lived after A.D. 1093–1150, the time of Ānanda Sūri and Amarachandra Sūri, whose opinions he has quoted.

Gaṅgeśa was followed by his son Vardhamāna (A.D. 1250), who wrote eight learned works on Nyāya, and by Pakshadhara Misra (A.D. 1275) who was so called because he was victorious in a debate of a fortnight (*paksha*). Pakshadhara's nephew and pupil was the great master Vāsudeva Misra. Another great name in this list of masters is Maheśa Thakkura. His pupil, Raghunandanadāsa Rāya, an accomplished logician, went out on an intellectual *dig-vijaya* (conquest of all quarters) at the instance of Emperor Akbar who, pleased with his performance, made a gift to him of the whole tract of Mithilā which, in turn, the loyal pupil transferred to his guru as his fee for teaching him (*guru-dakshiṇā*). Maheśa Thakkura thus became the founder of the Darbhanga Raj family.

Śaṅkara Misra wrote important works on Vaiśeshika, Nyāya, and Smṛiti.

Vāchaspati Misra flourished about A.D. 1450 as the Parishad or Court-officer of the Kāmeśvara kings, Bhairava and Rāmabhadra. He started writing on Smṛiti but soon drifted into Nyāya under the prevailing philosophical spirit of the age. He is known for his learned works " Nyāya-sūtrādhāra ", " Khaṇḍana-Khaṇḍādhāra ", " Anumāna-Khaṇḍa-ṭikā ", and " Nītichintamaṇi ", a work on Ethics.

Misaru Miśra (of *c.* A.D. 1475) wrote an original work named " Padārtha-Chandra " on Vaiśeshika. But it is interesting to note that the work is actually attributed to a learned lady as its author, Lachhimā Devī, the Chief Queen of Chandrasiṁha, step-brother of King Bhairavasiṁha.

A host of scholars kept up the literary history of Mithilā during the three centuries, thirteenth, fourteenth, and fifteenth, though the scholars named above represent its highest level and achieved an all-Indian reputation and a permanent place in the realm of scholarship. By its scholastic activities Mithilā in those days, like Nālandā of former times, used to draw students from different parts of India for advanced and specialized studies in Nyāya or Logic, of which it was then the chief centre.

It is interesting to note that, corresponding to the system of admission at Nālandā and Vikramaśilā by difficult examination by learned Dvāra-Paṇḍitas, Mithilā instituted a peculiar examination for graduation or completion of study. It was called *Śalākā-parīkshā*, by which the candidate for graduation had to explain that page of a MS. which was pierced last by a needle run through it. This was thus a test of the capacity of the candidate to explain unprepared any part of the texts he had studied so as to demonstrate his mastery of the subject in all its parts. The diploma of the Mithilā University was then conferred on the successful student [Monmohan Chakravarti, *History of Mithilā* and *History of Navya Nyāya*; Satis Chandra Vidyābhūshaṇa, *History of Indian Logic*].

VII. Nadia

Nadia is the popular name of Navadvīpa on the Bhāgīrathī at its confluence with Jalāṅgi. Once it was a centre of trade borne by the Bhāgīrathī between Saptagrāma (on the river Sarasvatī near Hoogly) and the United Provinces, and in the other direction by the Jalāṅgī between Saptagrāma and Eastern Bengal.

A relic of its old history is traced in some old buildings and fragments of pillars of stone found in a village called Suvarṇa-vihāra close to the modern town of Krishnagar, which are supposed to indicate that it received the attention of the Pāla kings.

Its rise to renown dates from c. A.D. 1063 or A.D. 1106, when King Lakshmaṇa Sena of Gauḍa made it his capital.

The Court of Lakshmaṇa Sena (A.D. 1106–1138) became a great centre of learning. His Prime Minister was the famous Halāyudha, well known for his works, "Brāhmaṇa Sarvasva," "Smṛiti-sarvasva," "Mīmāṁsā-sarvasva," and "Nāya-, sarvasva." Halāyudha's elder brother was also a learned man who wrote his "Paśupati-paddhati" on Hindu rituals.

There were several other renowned men of letters in different subjects, who built up the reputation of Nadia as a seat of learning. There was the poet, Jayadeva, the author of immortal " Gīta-govinda ", a masterpiece of literature of any age or clime. There was the poet, Dhoyī, the author of " Pavanadūta ". There was a third distinguished poet Umāpati, of whom it is stated that he made " language to sprout into luxuriant foliage ". The severe subject of Law found its exponent in Śūlapāṇi, author of the important work " Smṛiti-viveka ".

The dynasty of Lakshmaṇa Sena came to an end by the conquest of Bakhtiar Khilji and his flight to Vikramapura in Eastern Bengal about A.D. 1197.

It is, however, to the credit of the Moslem rulers of Bengal that Nadia rose to be a great centre of Hindu learning known throughout India during the period of their rule (A.D. 1198–1757). The destruction of the Buddhist Vihāras, Nālandā and Vikramaśīlā, gave Brahmanical learning some opportunity to renew its work on new foundations at Nadia under Moslem rule which did not interfere with the religion and culture of the people, and the indigenous social institutions. The need of a new centre of learning in Bengal was also created by the proud practice of Mithilā not to allow any of its students to take away from its schools any of its books or even notes of the lessons or lectures delivered there. Graduates were allowed only to leave with their diplomas but not with any MSS. This peculiar rule confined the learning of Mithilā within its own limits and prevented its extension beyond them. This challenge of Mithilā was answered by Raghunātha Śiromaṇī who first began by instituting a Chair of Logic in Nadia and broke the monopoly of Mithilā in the teaching of that subject.

The story of the foundation of the Nadia School of Nyāya is connected with the great scholar Vāsudeva Sārvabhauma (*c.* A.D. 1450–1525) who was born in Nadia and, after being educated by his father in Grammar, Literature, and Jurisprudence, went to Mithilā at 25 to specialize in Logic. There he was admitted by the *Śalākā-parīkshā* and explained one by one 100 pages as they were probed by the needle and was awarded by his guru the high title of *Sārvabhauma* in recognition of his supreme merit. Finding that the teachers of Mithilā rigidly guarded the treasures of its knowledge by not permitting copy of the texts taught, Vāsudeva committed to memory the whole of *Tattva-chintamaṇi* and the metrical part of *Kusumāñjalī*, and, fearing risk to his life on his way back to Nadia, changed his course and came to Benares where he studied Vedānta for some time. Then at Nadia he reduced to writing from memory the two works he had learnt at Mithilā, and founded his Academy of New Logic there.

Nadia soon outrivalled Mithilā by its first student, Raghunātha, defeating in argument his teacher of Mithilā where he was deputed by Vāsudeva to exact from Mithilā a charter for Nadia to confer degrees.

The Nadia University method of making an appointment to a Chair or Professorship was somewhat singular. What was required in the applicant was not merely original work to his credit, but the ability to teach, specially the possession of dialectical skill. A candidate who could hold his own against his opponents in open debate at an Assembly of Scholars acting as judges was considered competent for a Chair at this University.

Raghunātha Śiromaṇi was the founder of a School of Logicians adorned by many famous names up to recent times. Among these may be mentioned Mathurānatha (*c.* A.D. 1570) who wrote many valuable works on Logic which are known by the general name of *Māthurī*; Rāmabhadra (*c.* A.D. 1680), himself the founder of a school which produced scholars of the stamp of Jayarāma Nyāya-pañchānana and Jagadīśa Tarkālaṅkāra, author of the famous work "Śabda-śakti-prakāśikā"; and Gadādhara Bhaṭṭāchārya (*c.* A.D. 1650) of Lakshmipasa in Bogra district of Eastern Bengal, who joined the school of Harirāma Tarkavāgīśa at Nadia and became its head after his death. Gadādhara is described as "the prince of Indian Logicians", who carried to its highest stage of development the subject of New Logic by his numerous works forming a special literature called *Gādādharī*. Some of the later scholars who shed lustre on Nadia and continued its traditions are mentioned below :—

(1) Harirāma Tarka-siddhānta (about A.D. 1730).

(2) Ramanārāyaṇa Tarka-pañchānana (about A.D. 1760).

(3) "Buno" Rāmanātha (probably 1770) [so called because he had his school in a wood (*vana*)].

(4) Krishṇakānta Vidyāvāgīśa (probably A.D. 1780).

(5) Śaṅkara Tarkavāgīśa (about A.D. 1800).

(6) Śivanātha Vidyāvāchaspati (A.D. 1810).

(7) Kāśīnātha Chūḍāmaṇi (about A.D. 1820).

(8) Daṇḍī (about A.D. 1830).

(9) Śrīrāma-Śiromāṇi (author of "Padārtha-tattva").

It may be noted that No. 6, Śivanātha, exhibited his dialectical ability in a debate with the famous Jagannātha Tarka-pañchānana of Bansberia.

Along with the Chair of Logic, there was also at Nadia a Chair of Smṛiti which was inaugurated by Raghunandana, the most distinguished Jurist of his time in the sixteenth century A.D. He was followed by a succession of famous Smārtas, among whom may be mentioned Śrīkrishṇa Sārvabhauma, Srīkrishṇa Tarkālaṅkāra, Gopāla Nāyālaṅkāra, Rāmānanda Vāchaspati, Vīreśvara Nāya-pañchānana, Krishṇakānta Vidyāvāgīśa, and Mathurānatha Padaratna.

There was also a strong School of Tantrika studies inaugurated by Krishṇānanda Āgamavāgīśa.

Nadia also boasted of a Chair of Astronomy inaugurated by Rāmarudra Vidyānidhi in A.D. 1718. He was the author of "Jyotisha-sāra-saṁgraha". The duty of the School was to prepare Almanacs for the Nawab's court at Murshidabad and the East India Company's judicial and administrative authorities.

There are some interesting facts recorded about the University of Nadia in the January issue of the *Calcutta Monthly* for 1791. It states that the University possessed three chief centres of learning at Navadvīpa, Śāntipura, and Gopālpārā, patronized by the Mahārājā of Nadia. Navadvīpa alone counted 1,100 students and 150 teachers. In the time of Rājā Rudr aof A.D. 1680, the number of students was 4,000 and teachers 600. It appears that all these schools were for advanced post-graduate studies and that students seeking them spent even twenty years at these schools. They generally got by heart the texts they studied. These schools were conducted like seminars or colloquiums. Their method of work was for two teachers to start a debate on an abstruse topic, which the students had to follow and could supplement by their own questions. The advancement of knowledge by means of learned open debates has been India's indigenous traditional educational method through the ages.

Spread of Indian Learning to Foreign Countries. We have already seen how the products of these Universities, the scholars trained by them, distinguished themselves by their work in foreign countries like Tibet, China, and the islands of the Indian Archipelago, in a singular spirit of adventure in voyages of discovery to unknown lands, and of dedication to the cause of Learning for its own sake, as exiles from their own native place. The work of these self-sacrificing scholars in the extension of

Indian Learning and Culture to foreign countries so as to build up a Greater India beyond the boundaries of India proper is one of the greatest achievements in India's long history, and the best testimony to the value and vitality of Indian thought fostered in these Indian Schools and Universities. The Buddhist Civilization of China was the work of a succession of Indian scholars continued for several centuries. Some of these were, as we have seen, students of Nālandā, but many others hailed from other centres of learning in Northern India and made China their adopted home to carry on their missionary enterprise.

Indian Scholars working as Missionaries in China. According to Maspero, the Chinese emperor Ming-ti (A.D. 58–75) interested himself in Buddhism and sent to India an embassy of eighteen persons to study its doctrines. They returned with Buddhist holy books, statues, and two Hindu monks named Kāśyapa Mātaṅga and Dharmaratna. Kāśyapa was a Śramaṇa of Central India and a Brāhmaṇa by caste, but was in Gandhāra when he was invited by the Chinese envoy to come to China. He faced all the difficulties of the journey from Gandhāra to China through Chinese Turkistan over steep hills and across the desert of Gobi. He had also to face the difficulties of language. Sanskrit was then spoken up to Khotan. The Indian Pandit and his associate picked up only the local frontier dialect of China on their journey, and later regular Chinese, into which they translated a Buddhist sūtra and five other Sanskrit works.

These two Indian scholars were pioneers who opened up a vast field of work in China, attracting any number of scholars from India. The following were the most prominent Indian scholars who worked in China in the first three centuries A.D., viz. (1) Saṁghavarman, (2) Dharmasatya, (3) Dharmakala, (4) Mahābala, (5) Vighna, (6) Dharmaphala, (7) Kālaśivi (A.D. 255), (8) Kālaruchi (A.D. 281), (9) Lokaraksha, and others. These contended against heavy odds in building up the Chinese Buddhist Church on the basis of Indian texts translated into Chinese. Dharmaphala took with him a Sanskrit text from Kapilavastu and translated it in A.D. 207 with the help of another monk of Tibet who was from "Central India". Even in A.D. 222, Dharmakāla, who also came from "Central India", found the Chinese monks quite ignorant of the rules of Vinaya. He, therefore, at once undertook the translation of *Prātimoksha* of the Mahāsaṁghikas, which was finished in A.D. 250. Among these Indian monks working in China were some who were Tibetans but had settled in India, whence they came to China. One of these was Khansan-Hwui, the son of the Prime Minister of Khan-Ku (= Kambu = Kamboja = ulterior Tibet), who became a favourite of the Chinese emperor, had a monastery built, and translated into Chinese fourteen works including several Jātakas and a Mahāyāna Sūtra about A.D. 251.

The next generation of Indian Scholars imparted by their learning a great impetus to Chinese Buddhism and was represented by the following famous names, viz. (1) Dharma-Raksha, (2) Gautama Saṁgha-Deva, (3) Buddha Bhadra, (4) Saṁghabhūti, (5) Dharmapriya, (6) Kumārajīva, (7) Vimalāksha, (8) Puṇyatrata, and others. Dharma-Raksha (*c.* A.D. 381), mastering Chinese in a short time, and 36 languages, translated 111 works into Chinese (such as Śrāmaṇyaphala-Sūtra). Gautama was a Śramaṇa from Kipin or Kashmir who came to China about A.D. 383 and translated seven works, including Madhyamāgama Abhidharma-hṛidaya-Śāstra, and other works.

Kumārajīva was born in a family of hereditary ministers of an Indian State. His father turned a monk and went to Koutcha where he became the priest of the king whose daughter he married. Young Kumārajīva at the age of 7 was taken to a convent by his mother and at 9 came to Kashmir for education under Āchārya Bandhudatta from whom he learnt the Nikāyas. He then came to Kashgar where he studied the Abhidharma with six Pādas, and then to Koutcha where, in the royal convent, he studied Vinaya under the monk Vimalāksha. There was a regular battle for his services between the King of Koutcha and the Chinese emperor whose general took him away as a prisoner. Later in 401, he saw the emperor who invited him to propagate Buddhism in China. By working for twelve years he translated into Chinese more than one hundred Sanskrit works. His translations read like original Chinese works and count as masterpieces of Chinese literature. His works are exclusively on Meditation or Samādhi and do not include any Tāntrika works. They include biographies of Aśvaghosa and Nāgārjuna. Kumārajīva was associated in his work with his colleagues Vimalāksha (his guru), Buddha Bhadra, and Puṇyatrata. He is also known as the teacher of the famous Chinese pilgrim to India, Fa-Hien. Both Vimalāksha and Puṇyatrata hailed from Kashmir (Kipin).

Kashmir, in fact, in those days was the stronghold of Buddhist Learning and Religion and supplied China with many erudite

Indian scholars to work for the cause of Chinese Buddhism. Among these may be mentioned the following, viz. (1) Buddhayasas, (2) Dharmayasas, (3) Dharmakshema, (4) Buddhajīva, (5) Dharmamitra. Of these, the most renowned was Dharmakshema, who was a native of "Central India", and translated into Chinese many important works between A.D. 414–421, including the *Buddhacharita* of Aśvaghosa, the *Bodhisattva Prātimoksha*, *Mahāparinirvāṇa-sūtra*, and the like. His life was unfortunately cut short by an assassin as the result of two Chinese local kings contending for his services!

But the most distinguished of Kashmir scholars to work abroad was Guṇavarman who was of the royal family. At an early age he became known as the master of Tripiṭaka and became a monk at 20. At 30, on failure of royal issue, he was elected to kingship by the Ministers, but he declined the honour, left Kashmir, and proceeded to Ceylon and thence to Sho-po = Java, where Fa-Hien a little earlier had found Hinduism flourishing. It was left to Guṇavarman to spread Buddhism in Java. Reports of his work reached the Chinese emperor through Chinese monks from Java, who in A.D. 424 sent for him through a mission of monks. Before they arrived, Guṇavarman had sailed in the ship of an 'Indian' named *Nandi* (*Nan-Ti*) and, pushed by a favourable wind, was landed at Canton. The Chinese emperor at once ordered the local authorities to supply the Indian Pandit with provisions and send him to the capital. He arrived at Nanking in A.D. 431 and was received personally by the emperor who lodged him in a temple called Jetavana Vihāra and became his disciple. His work was less literary and lay more in the sphere of organization. He is known as the founder of the Saṁgha for Buddhist nuns. He died in China at 67.

Guṇabhadra was another great Indian scholar who came to China about the end of the fifth century to dedicate himself to the cause of Buddhism. He was a Brāhmaṇa of "Central India" and was nicknamed Mahāyāna for his mastery of its literature. In eight years (A.D. 435–443), he translated into Chinese as many as seventy-eight works. He died at 75 in A.D. 468.

The next century, A.D. 500–600, saw a continued influx into China of Indian scholars, among whom the more well-known are the following, viz. (1) Dharmaruchi, (2) Ratnamati, (3) Bodhiruchi, (4) Buddhaśānta, (5) Gautama Prajñāruchi, (6) Upaśūnya, (7) Vimokshasena, and others. Dharmaruchi was from Southern India and translated three works into Chinese. Ratnamati was from Central India. He rendered into Chinese "Mahāyāna-Tantra-Śāstra", showing that Tāntrika Mahāyāna had already spread to China. He also translated "Saddharma-Puṇḍarīka". Bodhiruchi became an accomplished Chinese scholar and translated more than thirty works in twenty-seven years (A.D. 508–535), such as "Laṅkāvatāra-Sūtra". Buddha-śānta, another master of Chinese, translated ten works in fifteen years (A.D. 524–539).

Even the sacred city of Benares contributed one monk for purposes of India's work in China. He was Gautama Prajñā Ruchi who translated eighteen works in three years (A.D. 538–541).

Upaśūnya was a prince, the son of a king of Ujjayinī, who renounced his position and became a monk. He came to China where he translated three works in A.D. 538–540 and two other works in A.D. 545 and 565, securing a Sanskrit Text from a Khotanese monk in A.D. 558.

Udyāna supplied China with another Indian Missionary, Vimokshasena, who translated about six works.

Another famous monk and scholar of Udyāna was Narendrayasas who, after touring the whole of India and Ceylon, started for China with five companions, crossing the Hindu Kush. Their progress was stopped for a time by local fighting between the Turks and the Chinese. He arrived in China in A.D. 556 at 40 and translated seven texts while residing in a temple. In A.D. 577 an anti-Buddhist dynasty came into power and sent into exile these Indian monks. It was supplanted in A.D. 581 by a pro-Buddhist Dynasty. By that time, a Chinese Mission, who had visited India during A.D. 575–581, and were stopped on their way back in the territory of the Turks, were free to return to their native land, bringing with them a large number of Sanskrit Texts. A Board of thirty translators was appointed by the new emperor and Narendrayasas was recalled from his exile in A.D. 582 and placed in charge of the Board. Within three years, he brought out eight works in Chinese. He died in A.D. 589.

Paramārtha was a famous scholar, a native of Ujjayinī, who arrived at Nanking in A.D. 548. He translated about fifty works and died in A.D. 569 at 71. His *Life of Vasubandhu* is a well-known work, as well as his *Tarka-Śāstra*.

In A.D. 557, China was visited by a learned mission of four

Indian monks, including the two Āchāryas, Jñānabhadra and Jinayaśas, with their two disciples, Yasogupta and Jinagupta. Jinagupta became the most famous of these, as the author of thirty-six Chinese works including a rendering of *Buddha-Charita* and *Saddharma-Puṇḍarika*. He was a native of Gandhāra, a citizen of Purushapura (Peshawar), and a Kshatriya. At 7 he became a monk and joined the Mahāvana Vihāra. Jinayasas was his Upādhyāya and Jñānabhadra his Ācharya. At 27 he joined his teachers to form a company of ten travellers to China, of whom only four named above survived the hardships of the journey and reached China in A.D. 557. The emperor had a new temple constructed for the residence of the Indian monks who translated there several Sanskrit works. After A.D. 577 there came to power a dynasty hostile to Buddhism, as already related, so that the Indian monks had to leave China. Jinagupta came to live among the Turks, and met in their country the Chinese Mission returning from India and held up there, as already narrated. Chinese politics took a favourable turn with the return to power of a pro-Buddhist dynasty in A.D. 581, as already stated, when the Chinese Mission from India found a safe passage to China, with their precious baggage of Sanskrit works for the translation of which the emperor appointed a Board of scholars under Narendrayasas and, later, under Jinagupta recalled from Turkish territory. He was assisted in his work by an Indian monk and two Chinese monks, while ten other Chinese monks were appointed to revise the translations and see that they preserved the original sense. Lastly, two more Chinese scholars were added to the Board for making the translations as perfect as possible. This combination of Sanskrit and Chinese scholars on the Board of Translators made its work very efficient. Jinagupta thus translated thirty-seven works, including a few astronomical texts. He died in A.D. 600 at 78.

Gautama Dharmajñāna, son of Gautama Prajñāruchi of Benares, won the distinction of being appointed as Governor of a District in A.D. 577. Later, he was called to the capital where he translated a work in A.D. 582.

Vinītaruchi, a native of Udyāna, reached China in A.D. 582 and translated two works.

Dharmagupta, following the same difficult route to China as Jinagupta, arrived in China in A.D. 590 and worked hard up to A.D. 619 in translating ten works such as Nidāna-sūtra and Śāstra. He died in China in A.D. 619.

The seventh century saw only six Indian monks coming to China, but three Chinese monks, Hiuen Tsang, Wang Hiuen-tse, and I-tsing, coming to India and returning to China laden with the treasures of its learning.

Prabhākaramitra, a native of Central India, arrived in China in A.D. 627 and died in A.D. 633 at 69 after translating three works such as "Prajñā-pradīpa-śāstraṭīkā", and "Sūtrālaṁkāra-ṭīkā".

Átigupta (*O-ti-khu-to*) of Central India came to China in A.D. 652 and wrote one work, "Dhāraṇī-Saṁgraha-Sūtra."

The next monk to come from India was Nandi. Travelling all over India and Ceylon and collecting 1,500 Hīnayāna and Mahāyāna Texts, he came to China in A.D. 655 and was sent by the emperor next year to a distant island to secure there some medicine for him. He returned after seven years and translated three works into Chinese.

Divākara was a monk of Central India who translated nineteen works (attributed to him in Nanjio's *Catalogue*) during twelve years (A.D. 676–688).

Ratnachinta was a monk from Kashmira and translated seven works during A.D. 693–706.

Dharmaruchi was a Kāśyapa Brāhmaṇa of South India, whose name was changed to Bodhiruchi by the Chinese emperor. For twenty years (A.D. 693–713), he worked in China, rendering into Chinese as many as fifty-three works.

Pramiti, a monk from Central India, came to China and translated in A.D. 705 one work with the assistance of another Indian monk, Meghaśikha, of Udyāna, and a Chinese monk.

He was followed by Vajrabodhi, a South India Brāhmaṇa of Malaya country, who arrived in China in A.D. 719 and translated four works by A.D. 730. He died in A.D. 732.

Śubhākara Siṁha was a monk from Nālandā who came to China in A.D. 716 and translated four works by A.D. 730. He died in A.D. 735 at the age of 99.

The greatest Indian scholar of the century to work in China was Amoghavajra. A Brāhmaṇa monk of Northern India, he accompanied to China his guru, Vajrabodhi, in A.D. 719. After his death in A.D. 732, Amoghavajra came to India in A.D. 741, travelled all over India and Ceylon, and returned to China in 746 with many MSS. Seeing his learning, the emperor conferred upon him the high title of "Prajñā-moksha", and, later, the higher title of "Tripiṭaka Bhadanta". He wanted to return to

India in A.D. 749 and reached the sea-shore on his journey, when the emperor thought he could ill spare him and at once recalled him. He thus narrated himself his career to the emperor in presenting him with his translations from Tripiṭaka : " From my boyhood I served my teacher (Vajrabodhi) for fourteen years (719–732) and received instructions in the doctrine of Yoga. Then I went to the five parts of India and collected several Sūtras and Śāstras, more than 500 different Texts, which had hitherto not been brought to China. In A.D. 746 I came back to the capital. From the same year till the present time (A.D. 771) I translated seventy-seven works." Amoghavajra translated many works on *Dhāraṇīs* (such as " Sarva-roga-praśamana-dhāraṇī ", treating of mysterious formulae for curing diseases) and *Tantras*, and is known in China as the promulgator of Tāntrika Buddhism. He died in A.D. 774 at the age of 70.

The movement of Indian scholars to China declined after Amoghavajra and the ninth century is almost a blank in this respect. The tenth century saw only three Indian monks in China, as recorded in Nanjio's *Catalogue*. From the year A.D. 973 the movement partially revived with the arrival of four Indian monks in China, followed by the arrival in 973 of the Master of Tripiṭaka named Dharmadeva of Nālandā University, under whom a Board was formed by the emperor for the translation of Indian Buddhist Texts. He was associated in the Board with another Indian scholar, Dānapāla, and other Chinese monks versed in Sanskrit to ensure the precision and literary standard of the translations in Chinese. In eight years (A.D. 973–981), he translated as many as forty-six works, mostly on Tantra and Dhāraṇī, on which the texts he had secured as a student of Nālandā. He died in A.D. 1001.

Two Indian scholars visited China in A.D. 980. Their Chinese names are (1) *Tien-si-tsai* and (2) Che-hou (= Dānapāla ?). The former is stated to have been a Kashmiri or a native of Jalandhara (*Jo-lan-to-lo*). In twenty years, he translated eighteen works, such as *Dharmapada* or *Daśanāma-sūtra*. He served with Dānapāla on the Board of Translators. Dānapāla hailed from Udyāna and is said to have translated as many as 111 works, mostly on *Dhāraṇīs*.

Chinese texts mention a few Indian monks visiting China after Dānapāla. They are named *A-jon-i-to* (with his wife named Mohinī) ; Kālaśānti from Central India, who presented the emperor with some Buddhist Texts and relics in A.D. 995 ;

Rāhula from Western India who also brought some texts for the emperor, and two other monks from Nālandā and Central India.

The visit of a few more Indian scholars to China in the eleventh century brings to a close a glorious chapter of Indian History recording how the cultural contact between India and China had continued for wellnigh 1,000 years and established Buddhism in China.

In 1004, Dharmaraksha (*Fa-hu*) of Magadha came to China with Buddhist Texts and Relics and translated twelve works, such as Ratna-megha-tantra, Vajra-tantra, and Prajñāpti-pāda-śāstra.

Sūrya-yasas was another Indian monk who came to China about the same time and translated two works into Chinese.

The Indian monk, Maitreya-Bhadra, was appointed the Rājaguru in China about A.D. 1110. He translated five works including one on " ceremonial rules for homa sacrifice ".

The Chinese texts next speak of a band of Indian scholars visiting China, and numbering thirteen. They hailed from different parts of India such as " Northern India ", Kashmir, " Western India ", " Central India ", Udyāna, and Varendra (*Fo-lin-nai*). The Indian names are known of only three of them, viz. Śīlabhadra, Śraddhāpāla, and Jñānaśrī. The last came to China in A.D. 1053 and translated two works such as " Tathāgata-jñāna-mudrā-sūtra ".

The political disturbances following the Moslem inroads into India interfered with these peaceful movements of scholars between China and India along the land-routes. When Kubla Khan looked for Indian monks for translating the Tripiṭaka into Mongolian, he could not find any !

It will be seen from the above account that, contrary to the prevailing opinion, Indian scholars played a far more active and prominent part than Chinese scholars (of the eminence of Fa-Hien, Hiuen Tsang, or I-tsing) in introducing Indian thought to China, and maintaining a fruitful cultural intercourse with that country, on the basis of the creation of a new Buddhist Literature in Chinese through so many centuries. This is a story of self-sacrifice in the cause of Learning and Religion which has hardly a parallel. The self-sacrifice involved not merely facing physical risks of life attending the pilgrim's progress from the Indian frontiers to China, along difficult and dangerous land-routes crossing steep hills, and inhospitable deserts, and through politically unsettled and hostile regions. It also meant a life of long or permanent exile where only a burning zeal for learning could keep up the drooping spirit. It again meant unusual linguistic capacity in mastering a difficult and strange language like Chinese into which abstruse Sanskrit works had to be translated in forms intelligible to the Chinese. It was the same self-sacrifice of Indian scholars that found for itself another vast field of work in Tibet whose religion and civilization it had built up by the continued work of centuries. It was a credit to the many centres of Indian Learning where such efficient linguistic schools of Tibetan and Chinese had been built up, and where scholars were so efficiently trained not merely in intellect and academic studies, but also in character, in enthusiasm for the truths taught, in capacity for the utmost self-sacrifice in the sacred cause of Learning, and carrying it to distant and unknown foreign countries. The gradual growth of a Greater India was the work of these Indian Schools. It is a romance of Indian History, and a unique achievement in the annals of mankind.

INDEX

Stephen Austin and Sons, Ltd., Printers, Hertford.